PRAISE FOR THIS BC

This book is a timely collection of thoughtful essays tl
Ethiopia and contributes to an understanding of the country s challenges. It covers
a wide range of issues by mostly Ethiopian authors. The excellent introduction
effectively summarizes the book for time-challenged readers.

DAVID SHINN, PH.D., author of *China and Africa: A Century of Engagement*
(University of Pennsylvania Press, 2012)

Since April 2018, Ethiopia has been undergoing a process of reform that has been
breathtaking in its speed and absorbing in its multi-faceted nature. Nor has the
process yet been consummated. Attempting to analyze this reform process might
thus be like attempting to hit a moving target. Yet, the editors of this volume have
succeeded beyond expectations in assembling an array of scholars representing
various disciplines to explore the political and economic dimensions of the reform
as well as its implications for the federal arrangement and the country's foreign
policy. The authors delineate the historical setting of the reforms, analyze their
various facets, and almost invariably conclude by indicating the way forward. The
interplay of agent and structure are analyzed and the inherent challenges of change
coming from within highlighted. The volume is thus a handy companion to anyone
who wants to gain a deeper understanding of the process of change that Ethiopia
has been undergoing in the past two years or so.

BAHRU ZEWDE, PH.D., Emeritus Professor of History,
Addis Ababa University

The editors of this volume have assembled an extraordinary set of essays that provide
the definitive account of the contentious processes of change in Ethiopia since 2018.
The scholarship demonstrates deeply informed insights based on primary research,
an understanding of the country's rich histories and cultures, and engagement in
the most important challenges Ethiopians face today. This volume will be valued by
specialists and all seeking to understand the potential for transformation and the
dangers that challenge this vitally important state. This book will be the touchstone
for scholarship on contemporary Ethiopia for years to come.

TERRENCE LYONS, PH.D., author of *The Puzzle of Ethiopian Politics*
(Lynne Rienner Publishers, 2019)

ETHIOPIA
IN THE
WAKE OF
POLITICAL
REFORMS

ETHIOPIA IN THE WAKE OF POLITICAL REFORMS

EDITED BY
Melaku Geboye Desta, Dereje Feyissa Dori
and Mamo Esmelealem Mihretu

TSEHAI
Publishers & Distributors

Ethiopia in the Wake of Political Reforms. Copyright © 2020 The authors

Apart from any fair dealing for the purpose of private study, research, criticism or review, as permitted under the Copyright Act, no part of this publication may be reproduced in any form, stored in a retrieval system or transmitted in any form by any means – electronic, mechanical, photocopy, recording or otherwise without the prior permission of the publisher. Enquiries should be sent to the address mentioned below.

Disclaimer: The opinions expressed in this book are those of the authors and do not necessarily reflect the views of the agencies that have sponsored or supported the research.

TSEHAI books may be purchased for educational, business, or sales promotional use. For more information, please contact our special sales department.

TSEHAI Publishers
Loyola Marymount University
1 LMU Drive, UH 3012, Los Angeles, CA 90045

www.tsehaipublishers.com
info@tsehaipublishers.com

Paperback ISBN: 978-1-59-907251-7
Hardcover ISBN: 978-1-59-907252-4
Electronic Book ISBN: 978-1-59-907253-1

First Edition: 2020

Publisher: Elias Wondimu
Book design and typesetting: Sara Martinez
Copy editor: Jeff Nazzaro
Cover photo: Aron Simeneh

A catalog record data for this book is available from:
Wemezekir Ethiopian National Library, Addis Ababa, Ethiopia
Library of Congress, Washington, DC, USA
British Library, London, UK

10 9 8 7 6 5 4 3 2 1

Printed in the United States of America

Los Angeles | Addis Ababa | Oxford

Contents

Acknowledgments i
Introduction 1
Melaku Geboye Desta, Dereje Feyissa Dori, and Mamo Esmelealem Mihretu

PART ONE | Political Reform

1.1 The Ethiopian State's Long Struggle for Reform 39
Christopher Clapham

1.2 Rethinking Transitology 55
Structural Influencers of Political Change in Ethiopia
Semir Yusuf

1.3 Republican Renewal and Democratic Transition in Ethiopia ... 85
Medemer, a Lofty Mantra or a Laïcité for Contemporary Ethiopia?
Kebadu Mekonnen Gebremariam

1.4 Ethiopia at the Juncture of Political Reform 123
A Gendered Analysis
Sehin Teferra

1.5 Civil Society in Ethiopia 141
Reversing the Securitization of Civic Activism?
Camille Louise Pellerin

1.6 Choosing the Road and Smoothing the Bumps 169
The Media and Politics
William Davison

1.7 Transitional Justice and Reconciliation in
     Ethiopia's Hybrid Transition 199
     The Case of the Reconciliation Commission
     Solomon Dersso

1.8 Restorative Justice Modalities 221
     *What Can Be Learned about Peace and Reconciliation
     from Imperial Ethiopia?*
     Charles Schaefer

PART TWO | Economic Reform

2.1 From Histopia to Futopia 249
     A Guide to a Successful Economic Transition in Ethiopia
     Lars Christian Moller

2.2 The Case for the State-Private Partnership Model
     of Development for Ethiopia 275
     Berhanu Abegaz

2.3 The Political Economy of Land Policy in Ethiopia 301
     Evolving Rationales and Challenges of State Ownership
     Tom Lavers

2.4 Ethiopia Beyond Middle Income 333
     Transforming the National Mindset
     Kenichi Ohno

PART THREE | Federalism and Nation Building

3.1 Ethiopia in Change 361
     Reinventing Narratives, Remaking a "Nation"
     Shimelis Bonsa Gulema

3.2 State of Ethiopian Federalism 2018–2019 403
     Taking Intergovernmental Relations Seriously?
     Yonatan T. Fessha

3.3 Conflict-Induced Internal Displacement in an Ethnolinguistic Federal State 423
Gedeo-Guji Displacement in West Guji and Gedeo Zones in Focus
Nigusie Angessa

3.4 Between Hope and Despair 445
Reflections on the Current Political Developments in Afar
Abubeker Yasin

PART FOUR | Foreign and Security Policy

4.1 Ethiopia's Defense Reform Agenda 463
Progress and Challenges
Ann M. Fitz-Gerald

4.2 Eritrea-Ethiopia Rapprochement 489
Benefits, Issues and Challenges
Senai Woldeab

4.3 Neither Old nor New 523
Ethio-Eritrean Relations through the Dawn of Change in Ethiopia
Awet T. Weldemichael

4.4 Ethiopia's Engagements with Its Fragile Neighbors 549
An Examination of the Concept and Application of Buffer Zones as a Security Strategy in Ethiopia's Relations with Somalia
Abdeta Dribssa Beyene

Contributors 579
Index 587

Acknowledgments

The book project was first conceived as part of a broader exercise to take stock of and appraise the performance of the current administration a year after it came to power and introduced comprehensive and sweeping reforms that surprised, inspired, and dazzled virtually the entire world. From the start, as editors, we sought to initiate a structured mechanism for productive discourse among experts and close observers with diverse perspectives. However, we quickly realized that a project of this scope and significance, involving nearly two dozen busy scholars and practitioners from around the world, would take much longer, imposing a huge demand on our time in coordinating the peer-review and quality-assurance processes and thereby also engaging our contributors with too much to-and-fro. Through all of this, we were fortunate to have the understanding, support, and encouragement of many people to whom we are immensely grateful; their support, encouragement, and inspiration was instrumental for us to see this project through to its completion.

To kick off the whole exercise, we identified potential contributors, secured their agreements in principle, and, in April 2019, organized a highly successful Authors' Roundtable at the Radisson Blu Hotel in Addis Ababa, which offered a platform for open, vigorous, and highly stimulating discussions on each of the themes covered in the book, allowing the contributors to get early feedback on their papers. The Roundtable also allowed the editors to engage with most of the authors and distill the key arguments, narratives, and counter-narratives, which helped us to make different parts of the book speak to each other to a significant extent and ensure the final output was a real book with a set of defined themes and shared narratives, rather than a mere collection of independent chapters. In this whole process, special thanks are due to the contributors who responded to our endless requests without fail and to our peer reviewers, who were generous with their time and expertise.

Also, the Authors' Roundtable would not have been possible without the generous financial support of two institutions: the Institute for Security Studies and the Life & Peace Institute (LPI). The LPI further supplemented its financial contribution with support by allowing Dr. Dereje Feyissa, one of the senior experts on its staff, to play a central role as a member of the editorial team on this project. We also extend our gratitude to Mr. Hallelujah Lulie, who managed the project ably in its initial phase by helping assemble an impressive list of contributors and playing a key role in organizing the Roundtable, and to Ms. Melat Tekalign, Ms. Nasren Adem, and Mr. Nathnael Seifu, who provided invaluable support at different stages of the project. Muaze Tibebat Daniel Kibret was always there, in the background, providing inspiration and constant encouragement to the conception, development, and completion of this project from day one; we are immensely grateful to him. Finally, Tsehai Publishers and its director, Mr. Elias Wondimu, were highly instrumental in the whole process of bringing this book to completion, for which we are tremendously grateful.

The Editors
May 27, 2020
Addis Ababa, Ethiopia

Introduction

Melaku Geboye Desta, Dereje Feyissa Dori, and Mamo Esmelealem Mihretu

Ethiopia is undergoing a political transformation unprecedented in its long history of statehood. When the Haile Selassie regime was deposed in 1974 by the military junta that called itself the Derg, the junior military officers who led the coup declared the purity of their intentions—to replace the monarchy with a government of the people, a republic, and in the process address the fundamental grievances of the oppressed masses, including the "land question." Seventeen difficult years later, the reality was different; the Derg indeed passed a law that nationalized all land and made it the property of the state. The Derg also took the first tentative steps towards religious equality as well as a certain degree of recognition of the "national question." However, any achievements accomplished by the Derg were overshadowed by the brutality it unleashed on its own people and the civil war by which it was consumed.

When the seventeen years of wanton human rights violations, civil war, and strife came to an end in 1991 with the coming to power of a rebel movement led by the Tigray People's Liberation Front (TPLF), which later joined three other predominantly ethnic-based political groupings to form the Ethiopian People's Revolutionary Democratic Front (EPRDF), the promise had three fundamental components: internal peace, democracy, and development. The quest for internal peace was understood to depend on the "national question," for which an ethno-federal political settlement was presented as the solution; the democratic project purported to rebuild the state based on the principles of freedom, equality, and the rule of law;

the development project aimed to bring about rapid, sustained, and broad-based economic growth to take millions out of poverty. Twenty-seven years later, the record was mixed. The ethnic-based federation has arguably gone some way towards redressing some of the grievances of ethnic minorities, albeit, as Christopher Clapham put it, at the cost of possibly "rigidifying ethnic identities and inhibiting social integration." The developmental state model also delivered rapid and sustained economic growth and a significant reduction in poverty, though, once again, at a cost of massive corruption, colossal failures in public investment managment, and considerable wastage. However, the democratic project was a complete failure; indeed, the twenty-seven years of life under the EPRDF only demonstrated the depths of depravity to which unchecked and highly ethnicized political power can descend in brutalizing fellow citizens, thereby only replacing a cruel military dictatorship for another one based on ethnic identity. In both cases, the violent struggles that ushered in the changes ended up perpetuating the same model, dictatorship. Only the dictators at the top changed.

The three-year period of political tension and crisis preceding the political transition in April 2018 in Ethiopia is usually compared with a boiling clay pot, its bubbles held down by a heavy metal lid. However, the level of anger bubbling inside that pot was such that, as time went by, the very stability of the state came under serious threat. Lack of political freedoms, dispossession of land and other resources used to reward ethno-political elites at the expense of ordinary law-abiding citizens, the widespread use of torture and state-sponsored violence as a tool to suppress dissent, and rampant corruption and mismanagement of public resources became the order of the day. Led by a seemingly unorganized youth movement, nationwide civil disobedience brought much of the economic activity in the country to a standstill, with the risk of ungovernability rising.

When Prime Minister Abiy Ahmed and his team came to power in April 2018 riding this wave of nationwide discontent, the rhetoric was once again similar to previous periods of transition. It is only natural for any movement or group that newly acquires political power to use its early days in office to overpromise and attempt to buy legitimacy in the eyes of its citizens, talking and acting broadly in line with what the majority are likely to approve of. Supporters of the new leadership and those disaffected by the previous regime inevitably got their hopes and expectations raised with a utopian vision of a united, inclusive, and prosperous future society in which citizens matter as citizens rather than as faceless and nameless members of an ethnic, religious, or other congregation; they argued that, instead of replacing one dictator with another, the current change promised to do away with dictatorship altogether and replace it with a system of accountable and democratic governance. For the first time in our long history, they argued, there was now the promise of transferring real power from a cabal of self-serving elites to the people.

Those opposed to the ongoing changes painted a dystopian future of ethnic and religious clashes pregnant with the possible fragmentation of the country into ethnically constituted enclaves à la Yugoslavia. To the extent the country might survive as a single political unit, they saw a return to dictatorship akin to that which prevailed during the Derg period, where all forms of atrocities would be justified in the name of Ethiopian unity and integrity. Some in this category would not stop at just painting a gloomy picture of Ethiopia's future; they also seemed determined to turn their prophesies into reality by all means at their disposal.

Such rare moments in history require constant and profound reflection. The first-year anniversary of these political changes provided an occasion to take stock of the achievements registered thus far, appreciate the gravity of outstanding challenges and gaps, identify and seize emerging opportunities, and propose ideas on how best to expand the horizon of possibilities for all Ethiopians.

As promising as this latest incarnation of Ethiopian reforms might be, it is early yet—too early to say whether it will end any differently from the previous two incarnations highlighted above. At the same time, there are marked differences between the current transition and the previous ones in two important areas. Firstly, unlike the changes that brought the Derg and the EPRDF to power, the 2018 reformers came to office by peaceful means, winning votes from within the highest decision-making organs of the then ruling party itself, the EPRDF. It is remarkable that, although seemingly unorganized and largely youth-led protests had been simmering for a while and erupting here and there over the preceding three years, the drivers of radical transformation came from within the ruling party. But it is not clear if these insider drivers came up with a new agenda of their own; instead, they seem to have adopted a vision for change that was taking shape at the same time and forcefully pursued by the youth-led protest movement.

Secondly, unlike the Derg, which announced its arrival onto the national political scene through the extrajudicial executions of the senior leadership of the imperial regime, or the triumphalism and vengeful rhetoric of fundamental transformation of the Ethiopian state by the EPRDF when it entered Addis Ababa, the 2018 reform group came to office preaching the republican virtues of liberty, equality, and fraternity, releasing thousands of political prisoners, unbanning scores of political groups and media outlets, and, importantly, advocating the doctrine of *Medemer*, the concept of synergy, togetherness, and unity in diversity. The reform leaders claimed to adopt an evolutionary approach that would build on the gains of the past, rather than a revolutionary path that would throw away everything from the previous twenty-seven years and start with a clean slate.

Determined to institutionalize and consolidate the democratic gains, the new government also embarked on a comprehensive reform of the legal system targeting repressive laws and associated institutions. Sweeping and radical changes were introduced in the way government would be run, including through the appointment of the first female head of state in recent Ethiopian history, the first-ever female head of the judiciary, and the first-ever gender-balanced cabinet. On the economic front, too, the new administration promised to chart a new direction through expanded space for robust and active participation of the private sector, enabling it to generate more and better jobs for Ethiopia's young and growing workforce. The new administration also recognized the diaspora as "integral to Ethiopia's identity and renewal," marking a clear departure from the antagonistic relations between the government and the diaspora for much of the previous decades. In foreign policy, too, the administration's signature achievements—the transformation of the security landscape in the Horn of Africa and the restoration of peace with Eritrea—promised to redraw the geopolitical map of the region and beyond.

There is much in this that is unprecedented in the history of Ethiopia. Like anything that can be described as unprecedented, it is hardly possible to tell where this change will lead. The past few years have shown that, in Ethiopia, serious threats of possible reversals are rarely far from the surface. It is with this appreciation that this book project was conceived with a trio of objectives: (i) to situate the changes taking place in the country in their historical and geopolitical context so as to understand and appreciate their magnitude and implications; (ii) to appraise the direction taken in the first year of the change process and what can be learned from it; and (iii) in recognition of the uncertainties and vulnerabilities involved, to encourage reflection and constructive discourse among scholars, practitioners, and commentators to generate ideas on how best to maximize the potential for the promises to flourish and for the threats to diminish. This volume is thus dedicated to understanding, conceptualizing, and explaining the nature, pace, and direction of the current transition and, in many cases, generating ideas related to policy directions for further reflection and/or consideration. In putting this book together, we were guided by the belief that there can be no substitute for a reasoned, objective, and nonpartisan assessment of the direction of the transition and its chances of success in transforming Ethiopia towards the oft-promised land of liberty, democracy, and prosperity internally and a force for peace and stability regionally and globally.

In doing this, the editors and contributors are all too well aware of the challenges such an undertaking entails such as too little time has passed since the transition started; too little information is available in the public domain to provide a sufficient basis for informed and objective analysis; views about the transition are so polarized in today's Ethiopian society that the contributing scholars, analysts, and editors cannot claim to be free themselves. This book attempts to reflect a diversity of views in a balanced and objective manner. In that spirit, a small team of academics and practitioners initiated the project to bring together researchers and scholars with acknowledged expertise in a variety of fields related to Ethiopia, including its history, politics, economy, and foreign policy, to share their assessments and reflections objectively, freely, and impartially, with the quality of arguments and analyses as the only yardsticks.

When we started the actual work, the fact that colleagues from the Office of the Prime Minister assumed a visible role in the exercise created some understandable unease from many of the participants, who needed clarity and reassurance that this was not a political-party agenda to varnish the image of the new prime minister and his team while masquerading as an independent academic exercise. Fortunately, our contributors gave us their trust and accepted our words of reassurance. We are confident that we have not disappointed them; what is contained here represents the views of our contributors and our contributors only. To the extent we had to engage them in some back-and-forth throughout the editorial process, we consciously limited ourselves exclusively to issues of substantive rigor and clarity of style. Each contribution has been subjected to a double-blind review for its relevance, rigor, and factual accuracy to the extent possible. In undertaking the review exercise, the editors ensured that no judgment would be passed as regards the views expressed in the contributions, which remained as submitted by each contributor. It follows that the views expressed in each contribution remain those of the author's and may not be attributed to the editors or to the publisher.

The final product of this exercise is a rich compendium of twenty chapters, grouped under four broad themes: political reform, economic reform, federalism and nation building, and foreign and security policy. This introduction aims to do two things: (i) to lay down the context within which the book project was conceived and (ii) to provide a snapshot of the different parts of the book focusing on shared themes explored, threads of thought pursued, and how all of them fit into the jigsaw puzzle that is Ethiopia today. To the extent possible, we also highlight, in each part of the book, the major issues raised and debated, approaches adopted, and conclusions reached.

PART I: POLITICAL REFORM

Although we have clustered the different contributions to this book in four broad areas, it is clear that virtually all of them are aspects of political reform or its manifestations and consequences. To that extent, our clustering is motivated more by a desire to improve the ease with which the book can be approached, read, and understood than any strict delineation of subject matter. Applying this utilitarian approach, we have eight chapters falling under political reform, which are highlighted here.

Part I of the book opens with a *tour d'horizon* of reform efforts throughout the modern history of Ethiopia. In a chapter titled "The Ethiopian State's Long Struggle for Reform," **Christopher Clapham** traces the idea of modernity in Ethiopia to the accession of Emperor Tewodros in 1855, by which time Ethiopians were "caught between the consciousness of their country's long history of statehood on the one hand and a deep awareness of its 'backwardness' on the other." Awareness of this paradox among Ethiopia's elites is perhaps the single most enduring factor behind all reform efforts to this day, an effort that Clapham describes as a series of attempts to make Ethiopia "a fully modern or developed state." While this "high modernist project" may have started as long ago as 1855, the same remains at the center of Ethiopia's political rhetoric and development plans in the twenty-first century. Clapham uses agency and structure as his analytical tools to examine the successive waves of reform since Tewodros, including those spearheaded by Menelik, Haile Selassie, the Derg, and the EPRDF, demonstrating the central role of the cultural and economic structures of society in effectively dictating the pace, if not the outcome, of all reform efforts. The impact of the physical terrain of the country in shaping the work habits and settlement patterns of its agrarian population, the history of powerful national security forces and related concentration of political power in the hands of rulers, and the entrenched inequalities between different segments of society, among other factors, proved too sticky for any wave of reform to fully succeed. According to Clapham, the top-down approach to reform launched by Tewodros continued with little success until the fall of the Derg, in the process demonstrating the limits of an approach in which reform ideas were imposed from above rather than building them up from a popular base. The new experiment launched by the EPRDF in 1991, which purportedly started from the opposite end, managed to rule for twenty-seven years, which "amounted to the second-longest period of stable government in modern Ethiopian history, surpassed only by the reign of Haile Selassie." However, the use of ethnic identity as the basis for the formation of the federal system under the 1994 constitution, a first in Africa, also contained the seeds of its undoing by "rigidifying ethnic identities and inhibiting social integration." This remains the defining challenge of current and future generations of leaders, who will personify the next waves of reforms sure to continue in this old nation. Clapham concludes by emphasizing that the key to success in today's reform efforts lies in "the construction of a political order within which all of the country's major actors can find a place." If and when the country gets this right, all other issues, including those related to economic policy, the security system, and Ethiopia's relations with its neighbors, will fall into place almost naturally. All Ethiopians, including those at various leadership levels in society, will do well to heed Clapham's considered advice that developing "habits of tolerance and compromise" is an existential imperative; in its absence, "any consensual political order must rapidly collapse."

Clapham's focus on structural issues and his wise counsel for sober reflection about the cultural determinants of success in the effort to establish a consensual political order are taken to the next level by **Semir Yusuf's** contribution, entitled "Rethinking Transitology: Structural Influencers of Political Change in Ethiopia." Following a systematic examination of the concept of transitology or the transition paradigm, terms coined to capture and analyze political transitions that have taken place especially since the 1970s, when autocracies around the world started falling away, Semir identifies the propositions underlying this paradigm, summarizes the corresponding critiques and precautions on each of them, tests them against the structural factors prevailing in today's Ethiopia, and concludes with his own set of aspirations and recommendations. Starting from a recognition that Ethiopia is undergoing a "textbook case of political liberalization," Semir warns against taking "transition for granted in any given country," including Ethiopia, for there are a number of structural factors that can easily work against such transitions. According to Semir, for a country like Ethiopia at this stage in its history, a look at the major components of the transition paradigm leave little room for optimism. For example, the transition paradigm assumes that political transition involves movement away from autocracy and towards democracy, going through the stages of political liberalization, democratization, and democratic consolidation. Almost inevitably, critics argue that this one-size-fits-all characterization of transition is supported neither by abstract theory nor empirical evidence. The same can be said about the other components of the transition paradigm, thereby leading Semir to focus on the structural factors, including the important question of the rule of law, that impede or expedite real transition in the direction of policies, institutions, and practices that conform to the major assumptions of the transition paradigm. Semir shares the same fears as Clapham in that, for both of them, Ethiopia's history of powerful security forces and authoritarian rule constitute important "structural" impediments to democracy. Semir adds that, historically, governments rarely recognize and protect citizens' rights willfully; they do so only under one or another form of organized pressure from citizens themselves. It follows from this that, for Semir, the fate of the current transition process and whether it will end in the democratization of the state is in the hands of the state itself, hardly a promising prospect. While this is a time of hope and expectation about the prospect of democratization in Ethiopia, such sober analysis of the structural and historical factors potentially impeding the realization of the goals of the current wave of reform is called for today more than ever.

The structure-focused analyses of the current transition process from Clapham and Semir are then aptly supplemented with **Kebadu Mekonnen's** theoretical investigations into the philosophical underpinnings of the current reform effort called *Medemer*. In a contribution entitled "Republican Renewal and Democratic Transition in Ethiopia," Kebadu asks whether *Medemer* is a "lofty mantra or a *laïcité* for contemporary Ethiopia." Inspired by the history and evolution of French republican ideas, Kebadu wonders whether Ethiopia's relatively recent encounter with republicanism, a post-1974 accidental phenomenon as it turned out, is real, and whether *Medemer* provides a viable philosophical basis to carry it through, nurture it, and sustain it until it is safely bequeathed to posterity. Noting how Ethiopia's version of republicanism faced competing claims to sovereignty emanating from multiple ethnic identities uniquely institutionalized in the country's constitution, a case of "multiple sovereignties operating within the Ethiopian state," Kebadu argues how Ethiopia during the EPRDF era became "a republic in name only." Kebadu then goes further and identifies the organizing norms of French republicanism—*liberté, égalité, fraternité*—but also situates them in their broader and contemporary context. For Kebadu, a number of institutional characteristics is shared across different variants of modern republics, most of which relate to the presence of constitutions, bills of rights, elections, independent judiciaries, and a commitment to safeguard the individual person and her private property. It is these traditional norms of French republicanism and the shared characteristics of modern republics that Kebadu later uses as a yardstick with which to measure Ethiopia's fledgling republic. This theoretical, comparative, and historical analysis, while rich and insightful in itself, is also alive to the challenges faced by Ethiopia today and attempts to draw lessons that our political leaders can learn from history. A good example here comes from Kebadu's description of the so-called Dreyfus affair in France at the end of the nineteenth and beginning of the twentieth centuries, which led to the adoption of a 1905 law that established strict separation between church and state, thereby laying the foundation for "*laïcité* as a core constitutional principle" in French law and jurisprudence. From this Kebadu draws two important inspirations of immense practical significance for today's Ethiopia: (i) the need for Ethiopia to "approach religious tolerance with great diligence and care" so as to ensure religious-identity-based politics does not serve as a pathway for "anti-republican sentiments" that "threaten social cohesion"; and (ii) the need to extend the same cautious approach to the handling of ethnic-identity-based politics through "a remodeled notion of *laïcité* as an antidote to tribalism." It is at this point that Kebadu quotes Kwame Anthony Appiah approvingly: "To set out to govern identities is to set out to govern the ungovernable." In the end, not only does Kebadu answer his question of whether *Medemer* is a "lofty mantra or a *laïcité* for contemporary Ethiopia" in favor of the latter, he is unequivocal in advocating that *Medemer* must crystallize into a constitutional principle of *laïcité* with an instrumental intent—as a tool "for de-ethnicizing affairs of the state" in Ethiopia. In the absence of such an instrumentalist ambition and a determination to use it as a guide in making necessary constitutional reforms to achieve such de-ethnicization of politics, Kebadu fears that "*Medemer* may eventually turn out to be an empty slogan." Kebadu is clear that if these lessons were to be heeded by Ethiopian political leaders and elites more generally, the takeaway on ethnicity might help get Ethiopia's fledgling republic out of its current predicament while that on religion could avert similar threats in the not-too-distant future.

Ethnicity and religion have been the two politically significant sources of identity and division in Ethiopia's politics of the day, and **Sehin Teferra** adds to the overall portraiture by bringing gender into the picture, surmising as to why it "has not been given due attention as compared to ethnicity or religious identity." In her contribution entitled "Ethiopia at the Juncture of Political Reform: A Gendered Analysis," Sehin interrogates Ethiopia's political reform processes with a gender lens. While Sehin praises these reforms for having left "a distinct imprint on the state of gender relations in Ethiopia," enabling women to enjoy a "radically altered representation at the highest echelons of government," she also worries that gender may have "quickly lost relevance within the politics of the reform process." Sehin then scrutinizes what she calls narratives about the place of women in the reform process, which she fears might have been motivated by the prime minister's own short-term political calculations rather than a genuine and sustained commitment to women's fair representation in senior leadership positions in the country. Sehin moves from these general fears and observations to specific and detailed issues relating to a host of socioeconomic challenges with a disproportionate impact on women, including gender-based violence in the context of what she sees as diminished accountability and rule of law, poor education and employment opportunities, trafficking in women and migration, health and family planning, marriage and family life, female genital mutilation, and child marriage. Sehin does not just describe these and several other persistent challenges facing women in Ethiopian society today; she also puts forward a number of policy prescriptions and approaches on how to address them progressively, systematically, and decisively. A major plank of her recommendations revolves around the concept of gender mainstreaming, including gender-sensitive budgeting across government, which she considers to be a critical precondition in order to address the systemic discrimination against women prevalent in the country. Sehin concludes by calling on the government to integrate gender analysis into the political-reform process, supplemented with revision of current policy on women into a policy on gender equality administered by a government ministry with that mandate, reexamination of existing laws from a gender perspective, and subjecting the education system to a "gender overhaul."

The interrogation of the reform process that Sehin conducts from a gender perspective is then taken to the next level by **Camille Louise Pellerin**, who examines the implications of the reform process for civil society and civil society organizations (CSOs) more broadly. In a contribution titled "Civil Society in Ethiopia: Reversing the Securitization of Civic Activism," a highly significant and long-controversial subject, Pellerin discusses how the ever-diminishing space for civil society during the repressive rule of the EPRDF "eventually contributed to the countrywide emergence of large-scale anti-government protests," thereby forcing it to implement political reforms. Using formal and informal interviews conducted over a span of four years, Pellerin provides the national and regional political-economy context within which the 2009 Charities and Societies Proclamation was born, the extent to which the administration of that law was effectively merged with the intelligence and security apparatus, and how it made the regulatory environment virtually impossible for CSOs to operate in the country, with the only exception being those that were either affiliated with or created by the ruling party, the EPRDF, itself. In a remarkable chain of events, if citizens deprived of opportunities to express their grievances and vent their frustrations in an organized fashion were forced to go on a series of unorganized and spontaneous-looking mass protests that forced the rulers to accept reform, one of the first concrete outcomes of that reform process was the repeal of the repressive Charities and Societies Proclamation of 2009 and its replacement with the new and highly liberal Civil Society Organizations Proclamation No. 1113/2019 that was adopted by parliament on February 5, 2019. Pellerin describes the history and repressive content of the 2009 law and its impact on Ethiopian citizens, carries out a comparison between that law and its 2019 replacement, and concludes with reflections on the larger picture of broadening the political space in the country. Pellerin highlights the major features of the 2009 law on the basis of how charities and societies were classified and regulated, such as foreign versus local (based on source of funding), membership-based versus non-membership-based (based on their organizational structure), charities versus societies (based on whether they were meant to serve the general public or just their own members), etc. Pellerin then shows how the way a particular CSO is classified determined what that CSO would be allowed to do. For example, only Ethiopian charities were allowed to work on political issues involving the rights of citizens, while foreign charities were limited to work on socioeconomic development issues only. To the extent any foreign charities managed to negotiate exemptions from those strict limitations and work on rights-related topics, they "had to renounce from publicly criticizing the EPRDF." Pellerin observes that the process by which the old law was revised, the content of the resulting proclamation, as well as the institutional choices made for its enforcement testify to the fact that the 2019 law was "inspired by an attempt to open the political space for civil society." While Pellerin acknowledges this as a commendable development, she is also clear that the real test lies in the practical application of the new law, the competence and mindset of the civil servants in charge of its administration, and the extent to which CSOs disaffected by their decisions can access speedy and impartial justice.

Civil society organizations provide citizens with platforms through which they can advance the causes they believe in and express their constitutionally guaranteed rights to freedom of assembly. An equally vital and powerful tool in the struggle for democracy and human rights relates to the freedom of the press. This is where **William Davison** comes in with his contribution titled "Choosing the Road and Smoothing the Bumps: The Media and Politics." Davison's contribution is in the nature of a commentary on the 2018 political reforms in Ethiopia, starting with the roots of the public resentment that precipitated the reforms, and the party-internal and -external conditions that forced, but also allowed, the EPRDF to reform itself and avert its own potential extinction. Importantly, Davison also uses this chapter to share his own ordeal while reporting for Bloomberg News from within Ethiopia during much of the relevant period, which culminated in his expulsion from the country. Informed by these personal travails, Davison's contribution exhibits a degree of richness that comes only from having been at the coalface, so to speak. According to Davison, Ethiopia's political challenges stem from "fundamentally different understandings" not just of its past and future but also of its present, thus emphasizing the acute need to reorient the political discourse from polarized ideological rhetoric towards a policy-focused debate that should have "the desired effect of de-escalating the degree of confrontation." Davison has timeless messages to his peers in the profession: "Rather than acting as proponents or opponents, more outlets, and more journalists, should focus on informing the policy debate and providing critical scrutiny, even if they are generally in favor of whatever it is that they are covering." Davison's contribution does not limit itself to the mainstream media; he also gives due attention to the role played by social media. According to Davison, social media played a central role during the mass protests that led to the 2018 reforms, mainly because no credible alternative channels of critical information existed "due to growing government intolerance." Davison's contribution underlines the indispensable role of an independent and free media for the establishment of a democratic political culture in Ethiopia: "To forge a path away from dangerous differences over identity and ideology, and towards managed disagreement over policy and practices, objective journalism must, somehow, eventually drown out its sensational, seductive, and inflammatory competitor." Davison also touches upon the critical issue of officeholders using their personal social media accounts to make sometimes potentially dangerous statements, thus calling attention to the need to develop a code of conduct governing the public expression of political opinions by civil servants and other officeholders. Davison praises the opening-up exercise launched by reform leaders since April 2018, but he also warns that the resulting political liberalization has "so far, arguably contributed to deepening polarization."

Like all major transitions from one system of governance to another, accountability for past atrocities has been an important issue for the new leadership in Ethiopia to contend with. In a contribution titled "Transitional Justice and Reconciliation in Ethiopia's Hybrid Transition: The Case of the Reconciliation Commission," **Solomon Dersso** provides a legal analysis of Ethiopia's current approach to transitional justice, in some cases providing an article-by-article commentary of the national law that established the new reconciliation commission in Ethiopia. According to Solomon, the transitional justice system adopted by the government of Ethiopia is unique to itself, which he characterizes as a hybrid system in the sense of pursuing broader goals of reconciliation simultaneously with criminal prosecution of alleged individual culprits. Solomon is critical of the process by which the commission was established, which he describes as neither transparent nor participatory and therefore lacking in "process legitimacy." Solomon puts all transitional justice processes as resulting fundamentally from one of two possible types of transition—termination of a state of conflict and its replacement with peace (either negotiated or imposed) and the overthrow of a dictatorship and its replacement with democracy. The current Ethiopian transition falls under neither of these categories, according to Solomon, who calls it instead a hybrid transition—one in which "parts of the old regime are on the driving seat of the transition." What concerns Solomon in particular is that the transitional justice process adopted by Ethiopia lacks any "identifiable political agreement" among competing political forces in the country "on the objectives, mandate, and expected role of the commission." For Solomon, the "conspicuous absence of process" in the establishment of the commission and the appointment of its officers is compounded by the "poor drafting of the proclamation" that established this important body. Solomon discusses the material and temporal jurisdiction of the reconciliation commission. In terms of the former, Solomon sees the commission's mandate as having two distinct but related pillars: social and political conflicts among different segments of the Ethiopian society and gross violations of human rights by the state. When it comes to the temporal dimension, the proclamation appears open-ended, referring only to "gross human rights violations in different time and historical occasions." Solomon calls for balance between compassion and empathy for the aggrieved on the one hand and rule of law, due process, and objectivity for perpetrators of past wrongs on the other and concludes his contribution with a moving poem by the Filipino poet J. Cabazeres titled "Discovering True Peace Through Sincere Reconciliation." Solomon submits that his preliminary analysis "on the process leading to the establishment of the commission and the nature of the composition of the commission leaves a lot to be desired." However, he is also clear that the commission must be supported and enabled "to pursue a transitional justice process that thoroughly, even-handedly, and independently probes the full extent of the violations perpetrated, the category of individuals or political, professional, or ethno-cultural groups that suffered the most from the violations perpetrated, the persons who presided over the institutions used for perpetrating state violence, and the various conditions that made such systematic violence possible, including the failure of the justice system."

Solomon's legal analysis of transitional justice is then followed by a historical approach to the same issue from **Charles Schaefer.** In a contribution titled "Restorative Justice Modalities: What Can Be Learned about Peace and Reconciliation from Imperial Ethiopia," Schaefer tackles this complex but important subject head on. In doing this, Schaefer urges Ethiopians to avoid a wholesale adoption of Western models of transitional justice; instead, he advises them to first look into their own historical past and draw on the wealth of Ethiopia's own long experience administering what he considers to be ingenious, flexible, and infinitely adaptable legal remedies, only updating and modernizing them as and when necessary. In developing his argument, Schaefer starts with a brief introduction to the methods of transitional justice with which the world typically accounts for past injustices and human rights violations, an often-binary choice between punishment and retribution on the one hand and forgiveness and restoration on the other. He then describes how these approaches have been used in the past both within Ethiopia (e.g., how the TPLF-led regime conducted the Red Terror trials after the fall of the Derg as a means of retribution) and beyond (including the Truth and Reconciliation Commission of South Africa based on an *ubuntu*-inspired concept of restorative justice and the *Gacaca* system of Rwanda that has elements of both retribution and restoration) and finishes by providing a detailed account of how imperial Ethiopia's leaders at different times since before the *Zemana Mesafint* dealt with conflicts that often centered around succession to or control of the throne. Indeed, Schaefer is not an advocate of either retributive or restorative justice; he sees problems with both. While the problems with retribution are too obvious to recount, those of restoration include the elusive nature of a "forgive and forget" approach that is often intended to lead to societal reconciliation—reconciliation among races, classes, etc. It is for that reason that Schaefer sees more promise in Ethiopia's imperial past, of which he writes, "Imperial Ethiopian history provides a deeper, historically based narrative about restorative justice, which rectifies many of the generally recognized shortcomings associated with restorative justice." Schaefer concludes by recommending an eclectic approach that builds on Ethiopia's historical tradition but also takes into account new developments from abroad that can make the old system work in today's Ethiopia. Finally, Schaefer identifies five lessons that Ethiopian decision makers involved in transitional justice matters today need to bear in mind:

> First, assume that the administration of justice must be done in public view using the most appropriate media to ensure transparency. Second, acknowledge that granting general amnesties often does not resolve conflict but rather defers them. Better to combine clemency with the potential for retribution that typified imperial Ethiopia's concept of "forgive but never forget." Third, always hold out that magnanimity can pay dividends. Fourth, recognize that justice is culturally defined and so consider appropriated Ethiopian understandings of justice like the concept of *irq*, or the ability to perceive contradictions and ambiguity within the articulation of truth and justice. And fifth, apply flexibility to meting out justice, for one-and-done sentencing restricts justice to a time and place that five or ten years down the road appear unjust and offensive.

PART II: ECONOMIC REFORM

The political reforms underway in Ethiopia inevitably have economic dimensions and manifestations. For nearly a decade and half, the Ethiopian economy has registered strong growth. For a low-income economy that had been mired in stagnation and, at times, decline for several decades, this is surely a major accomplishment. However, the achievement of high growth—even high levels of *sustained* growth—must ultimately be judged in terms of its impact on the lives and freedoms of the people. Precisely for that reason, this volume attempts to place the issue of economic reform in the larger context of demands for political freedom, democracy, and social justice. While this book has been under preparation, there has been a great deal of spirited discussion about Ethiopia's economic achievements, failures, and future directions. Several questions are being raised involving participants with a diversity of views. What should be the role of government in the economy? Was Ethiopia a developmental state? Is Ethiopia today a developmental state? Does the new administration have a clear economic strategy? Should economic growth be the main goal of economic strategy? Or is economic growth best seen in terms of the expansion of human freedoms and capabilities? What is the place for nonmarket institutions and nonprofit values? The four chapters in this section of the book make constructive, insightful, and essential contributions on these and related questions.

In a contribution titled "From Histopia to Futopia: A Guide to a Successful Economic Transition in Ethiopia," **Lars Moller** reviews the economic model behind Ethiopia's recent rapid economic performance, which he calls *histopia*, and offers a progressive vision with a unique blend of policy options to guide a successful economic transition, which he calls *futopia*. The progressive vision that Moller outlines is rooted in principled pragmatism and is to be contrasted with "Utopia"—as another contributor to this volume, Berhanu Abegaz, puts it—"a canonical modern capitalist economy that is private led, profit seeking, and competitively disciplined" and "an economy that is liberalized overnight." Moller's contribution is remarkable in that it anticipated the "homegrown economic reform strategy" that the government subsequently announced. Moller's analysis begins by summarizing the story and source of Ethiopia's stellar economic growth performance under *histopia*, where he duly acknowledges the substantial improvement in human capital and access to basic services that accompanied the growth, driven primarily by an ambitious public-investment agenda focused on economic development. Moller also describes how the public-investment agenda was supported by a variety of orthodox and heterodox financing mechanisms, including financial repression policies such as negative real interest rates, which helped direct savings to public investment by keeping the cost of financing low while a tightly managed exchange rate regime made imports artificially cheaper. Moller then makes a compelling case for the end of *histopia* because, in his view, the choice of the growth model behind it is both costly and unsustainable, and, out of necessity, a new model must be found which will offer a solid foundation for continuing economic growth. Key among the factors underlying the unsustainability of *histopia*, according to Moller, are: (i) external debt burden and the risk of external debt distress, wastage, inefficiency, corruption, and overall mismanagement of public-investment projects; (ii) weak capacity to generate foreign currency owing to poor competitiveness and low productivity in key sectors of the economy, and a tightly managed exchange rate regime that produced substantial and sustained real overvaluation of the local currency and attendant anti-export, pro-import bias; (iii) poor job creation capacity of the economy against a context of rapid demographic transition; and (iv) policy bias against private sector investment under which "the government starved the private sector for credit through the familiar 'crowding out' channel." To ameliorate these shortcomings of *histopia*, Moller proposes a *futopia*, in which Ethiopia revisits the heterodox policy instruments it deployed in the past and replaces them with a unique blend of policy choices that rest on three pillars: sound macroeconomic management, private-sector and productivity-driven growth, and additional structural reforms. In terms of macroeconomic management, Moller argues for a fiscal policy that creates space for sustainable capital spending over the medium term and a monetary policy under which a commercially oriented treasury bill market should be used to contain inflation. Moreover, Moller suggests that Ethiopia needs a more flexible exchange rate policy aimed at correcting overvaluation and reducing forex shortages, while a deeper domestic debt market would allow the public and private sectors to reduce reliance on foreign financing. *Futopia* would also need to place stronger emphasis on building human capital in addition to physical capital. At the level of structural reforms, Moller advocates reform of the telecommunications and energy sectors. At the same time, while such policy shifts might be desirable, it is not lost on Moller that implementation challenges, including lack of political capital, technical capacity, and vested interests, are likely to pose significant hurdles. It is at this stage that Moller proposes three external anchors that could contribute towards sustaining domestic reform efforts: a program with the IMF, accelerated WTO membership, and development policy financing arrangements with the World Bank.

While Moller's contribution readily acknowledges the rapid economic growth in the past decade and a half, **Berhanu Abegaz**, in a contribution titled "The Case for the State-Private Partnership Model of Development for Ethiopia," offers a reality check by focusing on the depth of poverty in Ethiopia and the absence of easy solutions to it. Berhanu begins his chapter by considering the basic conceptual framework for a long-term development strategy, which in many ways bears close resemblance to Moller's *futopia*. At its core, both Moller and Berhanu insist on an economic strategy that is not monolithic but draws on a variety of institutions chosen pragmatically. To that end, Berhanu outlines three broad approaches to development: (i) in what he calls a developmentalist state-party model, the economic system is essentially captive to the vanguard political party, thereby making sustained long-term growth doubtful; (ii) in the liberal private-ownership economy model, where a "competitive market mechanism is enforced with secure property rights," Berhanu sees little room for shared growth in an economy such as today's Ethiopia, where a strong bona fide private sector is missing; as a result Berhanu proposes (iii) a hybrid "state-private partnership" approach based on the East Asian model, whereby an "evolving division of labor" is forged between "a growth-friendly state" and a profit-seeking private sector, and operates within the framework of a market economy. In advocating for this third model of development, Berhanu starts from the structural poverty that exists in Ethiopia, where one in ten citizens sadly subsists on food aid in a typical year. In line with Tom Lavers's argument in a separate contribution in this volume, Berhanu makes repeated reference to the so-called "starvation plots"—the ever-diminishing farm plots that cannot support adequate livelihoods for a fast-growing population. In its most basic form, the informal rural economy of subsistence agriculture and petty trade provides livelihoods for 80 percent of Ethiopians. Berhanu sees economic development in a larger context of political and institutional arrangements and faults the economic model that has been pursued by the EPRDF, which he labels a rent-seeking, party-state model of development for failing to address the deep-rooted and endemic poverty in Ethiopia. For Berhanu, in its "futile search for political legitimacy through public sector driven growth," the EPRDF has brought "an unprecedented level of institutionalized venality." It is Berhanu's contention that, in the absence of a market-friendly state and a wealth-creating private sector, a direct transition from a state-stifled subsistence economy to a functioning open-market economy is unlikely to materialize. Berhanu thus concludes that to succeed the hybrid strategy requires an independent domestic private sector, private ownership of land, and a balanced, urban-rural industrial strategy.

Moving to the specific issue of land policy, in a contribution titled "The Political Economy of Land Policy in Ethiopia: Evolving Rationales and Challenges of State Ownership," **Tom Lavers** provides a detailed account of the central challenges facing land policy and administration in Ethiopia and underlines the political and economic trade-offs involved in this endeavor. According to Lavers, state ownership of land is one of two centerpieces of Ethiopia's "developmental state" model, the second being state dominance of the financial sector. In making his case, Lavers starts with the history of land reform in Ethiopia since the Derg days and reflects on the evolution of competing narratives invented to justify state ownership over the years. Lavers then discusses the role of land policy during the period of Agriculture Development Led Industrialization strategy, when state ownership was justified first and foremost on protection of smallholders from market forces, which former prime minister Meles Zenawi characterized as "the only social security available to small holders." State ownership of land also enabled the government to allocate land to support its strategic priority sectors and activities. The government also used state ownership of land to manage and indeed impede rural-urban migration and labor mobility. In reality, Lavers argues that land provided little by way of social security as "a generation of Ethiopians living in rural Ethiopia . . . have no access to land through redistribution." Lavers identifies four critical challenges facing land policy and administration in Ethiopia: (i) the problem of landlessness, under which many in rural Ethiopia either have no land or work on "starvation plots," which has led to recurring rural food insecurity; (ii) the system of land dispossession, which is highly resented by the farmers because of the nominal compensation scheme in place and the state's unashamed profiteering from their adversity by leasing the same plots out to wealthier individuals at considerably higher prices; (iii) complicated dynamics unleashed by urban expansion, which brings face to face the incompatible urban and rural land tenure regimes in the country, causing severe tensions each time a peri-urban area is reclassified as urban land and bringing with it an immediate escalation in the price of such land, a perfect recipe for abuse by the authorities; and

(iv) the politicization of ethnicity and territory as an explosive issue that has become a source of immense instability in different parts of the country. By equating territory with distinct ethnolinguistic groups, Lavers argues that the current institutional arrangement implies a clear hierarchy between "ethnic insiders," members of the ethnic group around which the region is defined, on the one hand, and "outsiders," those who belong to an ethnic group from a different region of the country, on the other. After highlighting the central challenges in land policy and administration, Lavers argues that the solution to the land problem will not come from land policy alone. While he acknowledges that agricultural intensification, land tenure security, and land certification could help, Lavers is of the view that privatization is not the answer; indeed, unless handled carefully, privatization may well make some of these problems worse. For Lavers, the only plausible long-term solution to rural landlessness lies in off-farm employment.

Following Tom Lavers's contribution on the critical resource endowment of land and its role in societal well-being, **Kenichi Ohno** addresses the question of mindset and policy capabilities as important factors that explain growth in national income. In a contribution titled, "Ethiopia beyond Middle Income: Transforming National Mindset," Ohno takes on the subject of Ethiopia's aspiration to join the middle-income group by 2025, which he believes is not unachievable given the current income level and growth momentum. Indeed, Ohno sets his gaze further down the road, highlighting the need for Ethiopia to enhance its mindset and build policy capabilities so as to avoid a future middle-income trap and climb onto the high-income trajectory. According to Ohno, the transition from the low-income to middle-income level as defined by the World Bank does not require particularly high policy competence or strong private-sector dynamism; these become critical mainly when a country attempts to push its development trajectory forward and confronts the middle-income trap, which occurs "when an economy is unable to create value beyond what is delivered by given advantages," such as natural resources endowments and large infrastructure projects that "superficially sustain growth." Development, understood to mean a constant and self-propelling process of domestic value creation, can be guaranteed only through the development of human capital and skills upgrading, technology, knowledge accumulation, and innovation. For Ohno there is nothing natural or inevitable about this process; rather, national leaders and technocrats, in other words capable governments, play a vital role in accelerating and sustaining the development process beyond the middle-income bracket. Ohno points to the intangible, subjective element of mindset as a key differentiator of capable governments that are driven towards these shared goals. He summarizes the essential attributes of vibrant and successful societies to be "pragmatism, willingness to learn, quick and effective action, risk taking through trial and error, absence of bureaucratic fuss and delay, diligence, teamwork, commitment to quality, pursuit of public good, and passion for national development." The *kaizen* cooperation between Ethiopia and Japan is one such initiative targeting mindset transformation towards efficiency and high quality. Ohno concludes by advising Ethiopia to work on improving the mindset of its workers, enabling and improving the capacity of mid-level government officials, and focus on policy quality rather than speed.

PART III: FEDERALISM AND NATION BUILDING

The political-economy reforms in Ethiopia are taking place against the backdrop of a nascent federal state structure in which the relationship between the center and its constituent parts is still in a state of flux. Part III thus discusses how the reform process has played out in the area of federalism and nation building. One of the most contentious political issues in post-1991 Ethiopia has been the federal restructuring of the historically entrenched unitary state, particularly its institutional design. Called an ethnic federalism by its detractors and a multinational federation by its proponents, today's Ethiopia has charted a unique path in instituting a federal political order based on ethnic identity. This is above all expressed in the location of sovereignty. Constitutionally, all sovereign power resides in the "Nations, Nationalities and Peoples of Ethiopia," which are regarded as the building blocks of the federation, with "an unconditional right to self-determination, including the right to secession." For supporters of this constitutional arrangement, the ethno-federal restructuring is a key political settlement that guarantees the survival of Ethiopia as a nation which was at the brink of disintegration by the early 1990s, evidenced in the proliferation of ethno-nationalist liberation movements, most of which had a secessionist political orientation. Critics, however, have highlighted the divisive nature of the new political order, severely undermining national cohesion as ethnic belonging, not national identification, took precedence. Although there is an emerging consensus about the federal structure, a debate has been raging on the specific institutional design of the Ethiopian federation for almost three decades. This debate has intensified further since 2018 in the context of the political liberalization and freedom of expression that have accompanied the reform process. Both the argument for maintaining the status quo and a complete overhaul of the ethno-federal structure are unlikely to be tenable, further complicating the daunting task of simultaneously building a nation while accommodating ethnic diversity. Four important contributions examine the various dimensions of these contentious issues, two of them focusing at the national level while the remaining two bring regional and local perspectives.

In a contribution titled "Ethiopia in Change: Reinventing Narratives, Remaking a Nation," **Shimelis Bonsa Gulema** offers a critique of the pan-Ethiopian and ethno-nationalist paradigms, both of which involve binary thinking that imposes coherence onto Ethiopia's inherent complexity. Through a historical perspective, Shimelis locates the genesis of the debate to the late nineteenth century, which saw the historic transformation of the more homogeneous Ethiopian polity into the modern state of Ethiopia, which is much more diverse. With its core in the northern and central highlands, Ethiopia was much more composite and constituted a nation in the cultural sense of the term, while Ethiopia at the turn of the nineteenth century was very heterogeneous, comprising a multitude of cultural communities. According to Shimelis, there are two radically different schemes to interpret the historical dynamics that shaped the identity of the Ethiopian state, based on the question of whether Ethiopia is an empire or a nation. Ethno-nationalists argue that empire better captures the political character of the Ethiopian state since the late nineteenth century. Opposed to this view are those who represent Ethiopia as a nation, which, despite the many differences among its constituent parts, enjoyed an essential unity. As noted by Shimelis, while it is understandable, even desirable, that pan-Ethiopian nationalism valorizes Ethiopia's achievements, it has also a darker side that "glosses over the agonies of the nation, which includes the atrocities its intensely patriarchal state committed against the poor, peasants, women, minorities, and members of different ethnic and religious communities." On the other hand, the ethno-nationalists' counterhegemonic narrative replicates the logic of the nationalist discourse it seeks to refute while at the same time it imposes homogeneity within the ethnic group they claim to represent. For Shimelis this is not mere academic debate but one that "constrains the political imagination." Moving forward, he recommends a more inclusive historiography tasked with inscribing "Ethiopia's profoundly intertwined history, a history that underscores that we are a multicultural pluralistic society unified by shared histories and destinies but also recognizes the specificities of our experiences."

Moving from the normative debate on the Ethiopian federation, **Yonatan T. Fessha**, in his contribution titled "State of Ethiopian Federalism 2018–2019: Taking Intergovernmental Relations Seriously," poses an empirical question, asking what has changed in the federal structure and the political practices related to it since the 2018 reforms started. He contends that one visible change relates to the rise, to the point of proliferation, of disputes in intergovernmental relations within the federation, which never occurred prior to 2018 because such issues were effectively resolved through political party channels. Intergovernmental relations have been weak in federal Ethiopia under the EPRDF because the party played a powerful role in deciding on such issues. However, with the EPRDF losing its coherence and direction in its later days, intergovernmental relations were severely constrained, posing serious threats to the integrity of the federation. Yonatan identifies three types of dysfunctional intergovernmental relations: increased tension between regions; unconstitutional intervention of the federal government in the affairs of regions; and encroachment by regions into federal competencies. Rising interregional tensions have been witnessed first in the form of territorial disputes between the Amhara and Tigray Regions, the Amhara and Benishangul Regions, and the tensions simmering between ODP/Oromia and ADP/Amhara Regional States over the distribution of political power at the federal level and over the thorny question of the political status of Addis Ababa. For the unwarranted federal intervention in regional states, Yonatan cites the example of federal military operations in the Somali Regional State in the summer of 2018, manifested above all in the ousting of regional president Abdi Mohamoud Omar (Abdi Illey) from power. Although political repression and human rights violations in the Somali Region under Abdi Illey might be cited as textbook examples of local tyranny, the manner in which the federal army was deployed raised constitutional issues. According to Yonatan, although the constitution envisages federal intervention in the context of a rapid deterioration in human rights in states, such intervention normally needs to be sanctioned by the regional governments and the House of Federation. To illustrate how regional states encroach into federal competencies, Yonatan cites an incident on the arrest of forty fully armed members of the Federal Police by the Tigray Regional State because the state government had not been made aware of the reason they were coming to the state. According to Yonatan, "Courtesy and effective criminal law enforcement strategy might require intergovernmental coordination and information exchange with relevant state officials. But that is not the same as requesting permission." While welcoming the increasing assertiveness of regional states vis-à-vis the federal government, Yonatan also suggests that this must not come at the expense of "constitutional federalism." Yonatan expresses concern about the regional state's defiance of the constitutional prerogatives of the federal government that could ultimately lead to a de facto confederation. Given the polarized debate over history and the identity of the Ethiopian state that Shimelis discusses, this loosening of the Ethiopian federation with emerging confederal features are worrisome signs that cast doubt on the country's future as a united and stable polity.

The two other contributions under Part III bring regional perspectives to the subject of federalism and nation building. In a contribution titled "Conflict-Induced Internally Displaced People (IDP): The Case of Ethnic Tensions between Gedeo and Guji Communities," **Nigusie Angessa** conducts a case study that offers an empirical critique of ethnic federalism without questioning its intentions. According to Nigusie, despite the benefits the federal system has brought for "the nations, nationalities and peoples" in the country, intergroup tensions among different ethnic communities have increased both in scope and intensity since 2018—more than any time before. Nigusie uses the Gedeo-Guji conflict as a case study to show how the system, which was introduced to defuse ethnic tensions, has in fact changed the sources, trends, and dynamics of intergroup conflicts in the country. What is most disturbing about the negative consequences of ethnic federalism is how it has severely undermined social cohesion among groups with a long-standing history of coexistence and robust socioeconomic exchanges across ethnic boundaries. While echoing a similar process of social fissures elsewhere in the country, such as the hardening of social boundaries among the fluid identities of pastoralist societies in southern Ethiopia, the widening rift between the Guji and Gedeo represents perhaps the most glaring problem caused by ethnic federalism and the politics of exclusion associated with it. One problematic area relates to the misalignment between settlement patterns and administrative boundaries. Before the placement of the Gedeo and the Guji, respectively, into the Southern Nations, Nationalities and Peoples Region (SNNPR) and Oromia regional states, they always occupied the same administrative area, which strengthened ties between the two groups, evident in the emergence of new settlements—the Gedeo in present-day West Guji and the Guji in present-day Gedeo zones. In the most contested areas, such as Guji-Gedeo, ethnic federalism has generated two conflicting sources of narratives of political entitlement: history versus demography. Migration patterns have significantly changed the demography of the Guji zone as more and more Gedeo community members migrated because of higher population densities in their areas. Feeling insecure as a minority and devoid of constitutional rights of self-rule, the Gedeo then resorted to a demographic strategy, one that provoked the Guji to invoke settlement history as a reason to present themselves as "natives," while characterizing the Gedeo as "outsiders." Far from resolving the issue, the 1995 and 1998 referenda exacerbated the conflict, as what was lost to either side was calculated not only in territorial terms but also in terms of sacred sites considered vital to social reproduction. Nigusie argues that the federal system by itself may not be a problem; rather, the way the political system is understood and interpreted locally might be to blame for the conflict. In the deadly confrontation between the two groups, which peaked in 2018–19, local political elites and business groups played the role of conflict entrepreneurs framing the conflict as an existential issue, possibly spreading rumors of impending attacks through anonymous mobile calls and SMS messages.

Following an approach similar to Nigusie's, **Abubeker Yasin** examines how the reform process at the federal level has played out in the Afar Region. In a contribution titled "Between Hope and Despair: Reflections on the Political Developments in Afar," Abubeker shows why understanding the reform process at the regional level is important, particularly in the so-called developing regional states, as the reform package includes a promise of reconfiguration of the historic center-periphery relations the EPRDF's political modus operandi seem to have reinforced. The EPRDF had a two-tier conception of the Ethiopian federation, consisting of so-called "developed" and "developing" regional states, respectively representing the highland and lowland regions of the country. This highland-lowland dichotomy is not merely topographical; rather, it signifies a political distance to the Ethiopian state, with the highlands, particularly the central and northern highlands, representing the political core, with the lowlands forming a political periphery, a political distance that is further reinforced by sociocultural differences. The ruling parties of the so-called developing regional states were not members of the EPRDF but rather allied to it as subordinates. The EPRDF's reason for this asymmetry had to do with the purportedly clan-based nature of these societies who lacked class differentiations, making them unsuitable for revolutionary democratic mobilization. The upshot of that, so the argument went, would be that these regions would first have to go through a profound socioeconomic transformation for them to be "fit" for EPRDF membership. Apparently as part of an affirmative action program to redress regional inequality, the federal government created a "twinning arrangement" according to which each "developing regional state" was attached to an adjacent developed regional state. In this particular case, for example, the Afar Regional State was attached to the Tigray Regional State, an arrangement that was deeply resented in the Afar Region as a modern-day iteration of the highlanders' hegemonic project in the lowlands. Within the Afar Region, this created political divisions, as regional politics was dominated by elites hailing from northern Afar with close geographical and political links to the TPLF and the Tigray Region in general. The regional political leadership in Afar—with the longest political tenure—was also criticized for sidelining the educated elite, failing to deliver economic development and basic social services, and unable to contain interethnic conflicts. It is thus no wonder that the Afar enthusiastically welcomed the 2018 reforms in the hope their democratic aspirations would be met, a sustainable peace would dawn, and regional economic development programs would be launched to address the vulnerability of the region to recurrent drought and resulting dependence on food aid. Abubeker suggests, however, that the hope for better times soon turned into despair as the old guard continued to exert influence in regional politics and the much-desired peace eluded them following the intensification of the Afar-Issa conflict. With the benefit of hindsight, now that the regional ruling party—the Afar National Democratic Party—has joined the ruling Prosperity Party, it remains to be seen how far the hopes the Afar have pinned on the reform process will translate into not only meaningful self-rule at the regional level but also a greater political voice at the federal level and improved interethnic relations with their neighbors.

PART IV: FOREIGN AND SECURITY POLICY

The political-economic reforms launched in 2018 manifested themselves not only on the political economy and internal structure of the federation but also on the country's foreign and security policy at regional and global levels. This section on foreign and security policy brings together four seminal contributions, addressing issues of defense and general security sector reform, normalization of relations between Ethiopia and Eritrea and its implications for Ethio-Eritrean relations now and in the future, and the likely implications of the reforms for Ethiopia's relations with Somalia.

In a contribution titled "Ethiopia's Defense Reform Agenda: Progress and Challenges," **Ann Fitz-Gerald** discusses the security-sector dimension of Ethiopia's ongoing reforms using a clear analytical framework centered around three key considerations—accountability, suitability, and sustainability. Fitz-Gerald makes clear from the outset that a fundamental objective of the reform process in the security sector revolves around the imperative to draw "a clear boundary between politics and the military." Starting with a conceptual and historical discussion of the two major "knowledge domains" pertaining to defense reform, civil-military relations and broader security sector reform, Fitz-Gerald addresses her subject using primary empirical data collected from field research in Ethiopia as well as the relevant policy and academic literature. Fitz-Gerald bases her evaluation of Ethiopia's defense reforms on a clear understanding of the role played by a strong military in the country's history, including in the effort to foil successive attempts at colonization in the nineteenth century, to secure its borders from contesting neighbors in the twentieth century, and to protect itself from extremist and terrorist forces in the twenty-first century. Fitz-Gerald then refers to the 2002 national security white paper known as the "Foreign Affairs and National Security Policy and Strategy," which constituted Ethiopia's first-ever and, to date, only attempt at an "integrated national security policy or mechanism." Fitz-Gerald also makes reference to a new law, Defense Forces Proclamation No. 1100/2019, which she contends was not based on any new national security framework, strategy, or policy. Fitz-Gerald observes that reviewing legislation without first developing a national security strategy or policy risks causing a "lack of policy coherence" that can be detrimental to the country. Fitz-Gerald adds that Ethiopia is "one of very few countries on the African continent to develop a defense doctrine based on its largely conventional warfare and counterinsurgency experience to date." At the same time, Fitz-Gerald also notes that international media and human rights organizations often ask questions about, for example, "accountability and oversight of the armed forces, the division of roles and responsibilities between the military and the police, corruption, and the role of the military in politics." Finally, Fitz-Gerald also devotes a section of her contribution to the role of the defense institutions in the economy, including the now infamous Metals and Engineering Corporation (METEC) and the military-industrial complex associated with it. Appraising the change of tone since the 2018 reforms started, Fitz-Gerald notes that the new prime minister's emphasis now is "on the armed forces being a force for the people and loyal to the 'government of the day,'" which, she argues, has strengthened the profile of the defense minister's office within government. Other manifestations of the ongoing reforms in the country that Fitz-Gerald addresses relate to the recent addition of a navy and a cyber and space command, the disbandment of the Central Command, and reintroduction of the regional brigade system in which "regional, battalion, company, and unit command structures will now only include one officer from each ethnic group." While the intention behind this new approach is clearly laudable, Fitz-Gerald is skeptical about the extent of civil society involvement in developing this new defense and security policy. Finally, Fitz-Gerald concludes by observing that "perhaps the greatest challenge facing the security forces of the country is to support the capacity and development of the federal and regional police forces and ensure the primacy of these internal security forces for addressing internal security issues."

Moving from security policy to a major regional issue, in his contribution titled "Eritrea-Ethiopia Rapprochement: Benefits, Issues and Challenges," **Senai Andemariam** takes us through the different phases of the peace initiative launched by Prime Minister Abiy Ahmed in the twilight of his premiership that culminated, in a matter of barely three months, in the conclusion of a landmark peace agreement signed in Asmara on July 9, 2018, which was later reaffirmed at a ceremony in Jeddah, Saudi Arabia, on September 16, 2018. Senai discusses the potential implications of the rapprochement and the hurdles that need to be overcome to realize the full benefits for the two countries and beyond. Starting with what he called the "near-dream-like waving of Ethiopian flags in the streets of Asmara and other Eritrean cities" in preparation to welcome Prime Minister Abiy Ahmed to Asmara on the first landing of an Ethiopian Airlines flight since the war, Senai lays down the scene surrounding the signing of the landmark Joint Declaration of Peace and Friendship by the two leaders in Asmara on July 9, 2018. Senai then recounts the chain of fast-paced events unleashed by this achievement—the historic visit to Addis Ababa by President Isaias Afwerki of Eritrea on July 14, 2018; Prime Minister Abiy's request to the United Nations for sanctions against Eritrea to be lifted; the opening of air and telecommunications links between the two countries, followed by the now short-lived opening of the land borders between them; the restoration of diplomatic relations between Eritrea and Somalia; the commencement of a rapprochement between Djibouti and Eritrea; and the signing of a seven-article "Agreement on Peace, Friendship, and Comprehensive Cooperation between Eritrea and Ethiopia" at the port city of Jeddah, Saudi Arabia, on September 16, 2018 in the presence of the host, King Salman bin Abdulaziz, and UN Secretary-General António Guterres. Senai then identifies and discusses what he calls objective and subjective internal factors that made it possible for Ethiopia and Eritrea to reach peace and the enabling external environment created within the Horn, the Red Sea region, the Arabian Gulf, and beyond. Senai identifies and discusses the multilevel benefits that can be reaped from the restoration of peace between the two countries—from national to bilateral, regional, and global. Senai concludes with a detailed exploration of three issues that he believes can help us to understand the rapprochement comprehensively and objectively: (i) the trigger of the rapprochement; (ii) the peace formula; and (iii) institutionalization and transparency. On the issue of the trigger, Senai suggests a host of domestic and external factors, including the economic, political, and reputational cost of UN sanctions to Eritrea, the popular uprisings in Ethiopia since 2015, the "serious depletion" of Eritrea's youth due to years of migration, and the policies of regional and global powers towards Eritrea more generally. On the so-called peace formula, Senai applies his legal skills to identify the core elements of that formula from two renditions of the peace accord between the two countries—the Asmara and Jeddah Agreements: the formal declaration of the end of the state of war between the two countries; the launch of a broad-based agenda of cooperation between them; the resumption of links in transport, trade, communications, and diplomacy; the pledge to implement prior decisions on the boundary between the two countries; and a commitment to work jointly towards regional and global peace, development, and cooperation. Finally, on the question of institutionalization and transparency, Senai underlines their crucial importance as we move from the exchange of commitments towards their implementation, which he rightly considers to pose the most serious challenge going forward. Senai is clear that, given the hostile relationships between the two countries since Eritrea's independence and the decades-old history of armed struggle preceding it, both sides need to tread carefully in trying to bring back a sense of normalcy to the bilateral relationship. To amplify his point, Senai quotes Bereketeab's cautionary note that, when Ethiopians and Eritreans say things like "'we are one people' or 'the border has no meaning' [or use] . . . phrases such as 'integration and unity' or 'reconciliation,'" they often mean different things. If Ethiopia and Eritrea are to overcome their history and ensure the future is better than the past for the sake of their citizens, such advice needs to be heeded and confidence built at all levels of society in both countries. For that, nothing is more critical than placing the current rapprochement on transparent and institutionalized foundations.

Senai's historical-legal analysis of the peace accord between Ethiopia and Eritrea is taken to the next level by **Awet T. Weldemichael**. In a contribution titled "Neither Old Nor New: Ethio-Eritrean Relations through the Dawn of Change in Ethiopia," Awet discusses, often in language and tone similar to Senai's, the evolution of the relationships between the two countries since the arrival of Prime Minister Abiy on the Ethiopian political scene. But Awet also sees "contradictions" represented by Abiy's ascent to power in Ethiopia—a contradiction between "dazzling changes that have since rescued Ethiopia and the region from the edge of the precipice," on the one hand and "the ominous continuity that contributed to bring the country to the verge of total chaos" over which he presides on the other. Awet starts from the premise that not only is this contradiction real, it is at its most apparent "in Ethiopia's thawing relations with Eritrea," which he explores in depth. Awet introduces his chapter with an overview of the history of Eritrea's relations with Ethiopia since the end of Italian colonialism in Eritrea; highlights the UN-sponsored deal of 1951 through which Eritrea became part of Ethiopia in a federal structure; describes how the annulment of the federation ten years later led to a thirty-year war of independence by Eritreans; provides an informative account of the form and depth of political and military cooperation between the TPLF and the Eritrean People's Liberation Front (EPLF) in their coordinated and successful struggle to topple the then government of Ethiopia; the close personal relationships between the leaders of the two rebel forces who later became heads of state for their respective countries and how the souring of that relationship led to the bitter two-year war between the two countries; the "no-peace, no-war" situation that prevailed for nearly two decades since the end of active hostilities in 2000; and the closure of that chapter following the successful peace initiative launched by Abiy in 2018. Awet is full of praise for the thawing relationship between Ethiopia and Eritrea, which he describes as "a cause for celebration"; but he is also wary of the fact that, once again, the peace between these two nations seems to hang on the personal relationships and dynamics between the two leaders rather than institutionalized processes. Awet goes further and describes Abiy's strategy as "Isaias-centered," where the method is to restore "the Eritrean president to statesmanship that he had long lost"; he then argues that its outcome is detrimental to "Eritreans' dignity in the intermediate term" and potentially undermines their "hard-won sovereignty in the long" term. Awet is particularly critical of what he sees as relations and deals shrouded in secrecy that can potentially undermine the legitimacy of whatever is worked out between the two leaders. According to Awet, the current rapprochement can easily suffer stagnation and even possible reversal in the relationships between these two countries, depending on how three key foreign powers choose to play their cards: the United States, Saudi Arabia, and the United Arab Emirates. Awet advises the two leaders, Prime Minister Abiy and President Isaias, "to be wary of overreliance on external support and influence—for they are the shifting sands of international diplomacy." Awet concludes by calling for a "change of both course and discourse in order to institutionalize the relations of these two sisterly countries and put them on a more promising, stable footing." Transparency in the relationships between the two countries, depersonalizing the relationships away from the two leaders, and ensuring ownership of the peace process by the peoples of the two countries and institutionalization are the keys to a sustainable peace, according to Awet.

The discussion on the security and foreign policy dimensions of Ethiopia's reforms, which has thus far been focused on reform of the security sector and the normalization of relations with Eritrea, then moves to an exploration of its implications for Ethiopia's relations with Somalia. In a contribution titled "Ethiopia's Engagements with its Fragile Neighbors: An Examination of the Concept and Application of Buffer Zones as a Security Strategy in Ethiopia's Relations with Somalia," **Abdeta Dribssa Beyene** investigates Ethiopia's multifaceted approach to fend off threats emanating from Somalia. Underlining the fragility of many of the countries in the Horn of Africa, Abdeta focuses particularly on security threats posed by these fragile neighboring states for a variety of reasons, including ungoverned spaces in those countries serving as safe havens for terrorist and extremist groups to operate in and, in some cases, the void being used to plan attacks on neighboring countries (e.g., the activities of Al-Itihaad Al-Islamiya and Al-Shabaab against Ethiopia and other neighboring countries), as well as the use of those countries by other powers, big and small, for proxy wars. It is from this perspective that Abdeta discusses Ethiopia's approaches to security threats emanating from the territory of Somalia, with particular reference to the use of buffer zones inside Somali territory to that effect. Abdeta understands a buffer zone to mean "a certain geographical area that is designated or created to serve certain political, security, or other purposes." Starting with a general discussion of the historical relations between the two countries since the establishment of the state of Somalia in 1960 and the Greater Somalia agenda championed by its leaders in the 1960s and 1970s that led to two major wars with Ethiopia, Abdeta describes how Ethiopia's approach towards Somalia has evolved over the past several decades, particularly since the collapse of the Somali government in the early 1990s. Abdeta then describes the various attempts at peacemaking, often undertaken with the help of third parties, including Ethiopia, Egypt, the US, IGAD, the OAU, and the UN, most of which were unsuccessful; signs of success had to wait until the establishment of the Transitional Federal Government (TFG), whose seeds were planted in the 2004 peace conference in Kenya. The establishment of the TFG did not, however, preclude Ethiopia from continuing its relations with regional governments in Somalia, particularly those of Puntland and Somaliland; on the contrary, Abdeta shows that it was in the mutual security interest of all parties to strengthen the relationship and fight their common adversaries that are always ready and able to exploit the governance void to launch attacks on Ethiopia as well as the regional and federal government institutions of Somalia itself. Abdeta reflects on what the ongoing transition in Ethiopia is likely to mean for Somalia and the Horn and what role the Gulf countries would play. He concludes his contribution on an optimistic note—that the changes in Ethiopia "have the potential to signify a gigantic historical transformation in the Horn of Africa, with immense positive implications for the region" and beyond. At the same time, Abdeta also cautions that the changes taking place in Ethiopia may have left the Federal Member States (FMS) of Somalia feeling irrelevant and abandoned, which is potentially damaging to Ethiopia's own long-term interests. According to Abdeta, the current Ethiopian administration, in its relations with Somalia, needs to engage in a delicate balancing act between supporting islands of peace, which have been trusted partners for a long time, and strengthening them as buffer zones, while simultaneously assisting the federal government's efforts at peacemaking at the national level.

CONCLUSION

As can be seen from the introduction thus far, this book interrogates the political reforms set in motion in Ethiopia in April 2018 systematically, independently, objectively, and honestly. The reforms are, first and foremost, political. A new team has assumed political power. New people have brought with them new thinking and unleashed new power dynamics. However, because the reforms came through a peaceful internal power struggle within the EPRDF, some of the "new" people in power are in fact "old," thereby representing change and continuity at the same time.

Yet there is no mistaking the fact that the change is radical in its orientation and comprehensive in its scope. Although the constitution of the country remains the same, the tone and image of the state, and its political and economic direction, have all changed. Not only were political prisoners freed, banned political parties and media outlets reinstated, and repressive laws and institutions amended and/or abolished, but the doctrine of revolutionary democracy also quickly gave way to *Medemer* as the guiding ideology of the ruling party and its government; the developmental state model of economic management has been replaced with a homegrown economic policy of opening up, privatization, and broader space for private-sector participation; and the no-peace, no-war situation that had characterized Ethiopia's relations with Eritrea for nearly two decades was brought to an end through a dramatic peace deal signed between the two parties. Two years after the onset of those reforms, and with the benefit of hindsight, perhaps nowhere is this change more dramatic than in relations between the different constituent parts of the state, horizontally between regional states *inter se* and vertically between the federation and the regional administrations.

Like all changes of this magnitude, the future is pregnant with risks and opportunities: anything is possible, and nothing is preordained. The choice is for all Ethiopians to make. While it is true that not everyone has an equal say in determining the future, it is incumbent upon each and every Ethiopian to contribute their share, however little, to inform and shape its direction and pace. This book is our modest contribution towards that worthy goal.

Our initial ambition was to complete this book within a couple of months from the first anniversary of the April 2018 reforms; indeed, the very project was conceived as part of an exercise to reflect on the first year of reforms. However, in a project that involves nearly two dozen busy scholars and practitioners from around the world, deadlines proved hard to meet, in some cases allowing some of the information and analysis contained in the book to be overtaken by events on the ground. Nevertheless, the core ideas and issues addressed in the book remain relevant today and are likely to remain so for some time to come.

In summary, while there are good reasons to celebrate the 2018 reforms as a new dawn of hope towards a peaceful, united, and prosperous nation enjoying multiparty democracy, free enterprise, and peaceful coexistence and cooperation with its neighbors, the analyses and insights contained in this book also teach us that we cannot take any particular outcome for granted. In the long history of Ethiopia, similar opportunities have presented themselves, raising our hopes on far too many occasions, only to have them dashed one after the other. To make today's opportunities different, we need to learn from our past mistakes, appreciate our current circumstances and opportunities, and work out a new and viable political settlement. In the final analysis, whatever new political settlement we reach, only strong institutions can guarantee a peaceful, prosperous, and sustainable future for our children and grandchildren. No individual person, group or political party, however nobly intentioned, is a substitute for the rule of law, independent institutions, and a collective will and determination to succeed.

PART ONE

Political Reform

1.1 The Ethiopian State's Long Struggle for Reform

1.2 Rethinking Transitology: Structural Influencers of Political Change in Ethiopia

1.3 Republican Renewal and Democratic Transition in Ethiopia: *Medemer*, a Lofty Mantra or a *Laïcité* for Contemporary Ethiopia?

1.4 Ethiopia at the Juncture of Political Reform: A Gendered Analysis

1.5 Civil Society in Ethiopia: Reversing the Securitization of Civic Activism?

1.6 Choosing the Road and Smoothing the Bumps: The Media and Politics

1.7 Transitional Justice and Reconciliation in Ethiopia's Hybrid Transition: The Case of the Reconciliation Commission

1.8 Restorative Justice Modalities: What Can Be Learned about Peace and Reconciliation from Imperial Ethiopia?

1.1 The Ethiopian State's Long Struggle for Reform

Christopher Clapham

INTRODUCTION

Ever since the idea of modernity started to impose itself on the peoples of the Horn of Africa—a moment that can best be encapsulated in the accession of Emperor Tewodros in 1855—Ethiopians have been caught between the consciousness of their country's long history of statehood, on the one hand, and a deep awareness of its "backwardness," on the other. Pride in the country's achievement as the sole African state to retain its independence through the colonial era has been counterpoised against a sense of its inability to match not only the more "developed" states of Europe and Asia but even many of the former colonial African territories to which Ethiopians had long considered themselves superior. As a research student in the mid-1960s, I was astonished to find that many of my Ethiopian contemporaries regretted that their own country had *not* been colonized, as they ascribed Ethiopia's poverty to an anachronistic and incompetent imperial or feudal regime, which they contrasted with neighboring countries that appeared (often naïvely, in retrospect) to be forging ahead as a result both of the level of development achieved under colonial rule and of the impetus and enthusiasm generated by the nationalist struggle for independence. Reform, in an Ethiopian context, has therefore come to refer to the attempt to incorporate into the existing state structure those elements that would enable the country to become a fully modern or developed state, capable of taking its place among its peers in the international system and, in the process, reconciling the varied and often conflicting elements that this project would need to incorporate. That this has proved to be such a long, difficult, and often violent process in part reflects the inherent problems of the high modernist project itself but also results from structural tensions within the Ethiopian state, many of which remain unresolved to this day. This contribution, therefore, seeks to provide a necessarily sketchy overview of how this struggle for modernity has worked (or indeed, very often and visibly failed to "work") during Ethiopia's relatively recent past and to outline the challenges that reform continues to face up to the present time.

THE DILEMMAS OF ETHIOPIAN REFORM

Looked at thematically, the reform process in Ethiopia provides a striking example of the familiar interlinkage of agency and structure. Given the very strong emphasis ascribed to leadership in Ethiopia's political culture, it is unsurprising that agency, or the capacity of individuals to reach and implement decisions that would change the lives of themselves and those around them, has enjoyed a particularly prominent role in accounts of reform in Ethiopia over the entire period from Tewodros to the present. As a result, reform has generally come in waves, as successive leaders have taken measures designed to promote the project of modernity in ways that would, inevitably, strengthen the government and the ruler himself. After Tewodros, the next great wave came with Menelik, justly regarded as the founder (for good or ill) of the modern Ethiopian state, to be followed eventually by the reforms instituted in the early years of Tafari/Haile Selassie, which were geared to impose a centralized state on a conglomeration of disparate provinces. Following the long stasis of the declining years of the imperial regime, the 1974 revolution represented not so much a wave as a tsunami, sweeping away an enormous amount of accumulated Ethiopian history and seeking (much less successfully) to erect a new and revolutionary order in its place. From a broader perspective, the Derg tested its predecessor's project of centralized state formation to the point of destruction. Its failure, in turn, confronted the Ethiopian People's Revolutionary Democratic Front (EPRDF) regime that took power in 1991 with the need to address the problems that the Derg regime had not only failed to resolve but had frequently exacerbated, and come up with its own diagnosis of the problems of Ethiopian governance.

Despite the successes achieved over the subsequent quarter century, this effort likewise revealed weaknesses that have prompted a further wave of reform at the present time.

Agency, however, can only be appreciated in the context of structure or those deep-seated features of culture, economy, and society that need to be effectively harnessed to achieve a lasting reform. Yet, at the same time, culture, economy, and society often form the barriers that reform has to overcome. The structural features affecting Ethiopian governance are often particularly intimidating. On the one hand, they encompass the legacies of societies formed by environments ranging from the country's mountainous north and the plough agriculture that sustains its relatively dense populations, through to areas of desert or lowland scrub that, at best, support little more than sparse nomadic pastoralism, with a great variety of other forms of livelihood in between, each of them generating social structures and values of their own. Any reforms applied across the whole of this vast and varied social landscape must inevitably differ, both in the ways in which they operate in practice and in the reaction they are likely to provoke from the indigenous populations. These underlying social factors must then be added to the peculiar structural problems created by the features of the Ethiopian state, which was historically responsible for the form that the country now takes and for the deep inequalities that have been entrenched within it. In addition to the straightforward power differential between peoples associated with this state over many centuries and those upon whom it has been imposed by conquest in relatively recent times, this has resulted in very different attitudes towards the state and indeed towards the acceptability of government itself.

At the core of the dilemmas of reform, therefore, lies the fact that while Ethiopia was able to construct and maintain a state unequaled in sub-Saharan Africa, the *way* in which that state was constructed ran counter in critical respects to requirements that the ultimate goal of modernity imposed, creating in the process a set of barriers deeply entrenched in the country's geography, history, and social structure that had to be confronted and overcome, often at considerable costs. That effectiveness was encapsulated, first and foremost, in the state's military capability and the habits of command essential to the maintenance of its independence. This was nowhere more strikingly expressed than in Emperor Menelik's ability to put in the field on a single day—March 1, 1896, a time of famine, assembled in the furthest northern frontier of his empire—an army generally reckoned to number over a hundred thousand men, many of them armed with modern rifles. No other precolonial African regime came remotely close to equaling this achievement, which in turn paved the way for Ethiopia's international recognition and its incorporation into a global order, represented first by the League of Nations and subsequently by the United Nations and other institutions, including the African Union. In the process, the quest for modernity came to be associated with the state and the removal of any obstacle opposing the power of its ruler. Those aspects of modernity that were most keenly sought after and effectively implemented all conformed to this objective. In addition to the maintenance of powerful security forces—always a key priority, directed to internal control quite as much as defense against external aggression—these aspects of modernity included the construction of a communications network centered in Addis Ababa, the establishment of an educational system to train the state bureaucracy, and the linkages to the global economy that were needed to generate the resources that the structure of rule required.

Many of these processes were shared with the postcolonial African states that gained their independence from the late 1950s onwards, an achievement that was almost invariably followed by the rapid concentration of power in the hands of their new rulers and the dismantling of whatever limitations to this power that had been instituted by the departing colonialists as part of the independence settlement. Elsewhere in Africa, as in Ethiopia, authoritarian rule was justified in terms of the twin objectives of nation building (or the attempt to diminish or remove the potential sources of conflict implicit in the diversity of ethnic groups, a trait most African states share with Ethiopia) and development, which was almost invariably associated with increased state power, usually under the mantra of some form of socialism. There were, nonetheless, very significant differences between Ethiopia and most of its African neighbors, which most basically derived from the ways in which these states had been created in the first place.

THE POLITICS OF EMULATION

One of these differences, particularly relevant in the context of reform, is that while formerly colonial states tended to look for models of modernity associated with their colonial rulers, in Ethiopia these models were to be found among that distinctive group of states, invariably monarchies, that had, like Ethiopia, successfully resisted direct colonialism and retained their independence into the modern era. The reform process essentially sought to identify states that were similar enough to Ethiopia to permit plausible comparison but that had, at the same time, managed to combine an essentially European quest for modernity with an inherited indigenous power structure, which in turn made them potential sources for emulation. One key requirement during the imperial period that lasted until 1974 was the leadership of a powerful king or emperor. The first such model, imperial Russia, was symbolized by the name of the remarkable homemade cannon, Sebastopol, forged by Emperor Tewodros in order (unavailingly) to protect his mountain stronghold of Magdala against the British in 1868. The cannon was named after the fortress defended by the Russians against the British and French during the Crimean War of 1854–56 (Clapham 2006). Even though Russia shared several characteristics with Ethiopia, notably Orthodox Christianity, it nonetheless made a poor advertisement for modernity, and the first generation of reforming Ethiopians looked instead to Japan, a non-European empire-state that announced its arrival on the international scene with its decisive defeat of Russia in the war of 1904–5. Led by Gebre-Heywat Baykedagn, this group of modernizing intellectuals may plausibly be regarded as Ethiopia's first real reformers (Bahru 2002). Their most visible achievement was the first Ethiopian constitution, promulgated in 1931 by Emperor Haile Selassie and closely based on the Japanese Meiji Constitution of 1889. Even though this formally subordinated the power of the emperor to a written legal order, including an unelected parliament, it served in practice more to enhance imperial control than to restrict it, and its practical impact was in any case negligible.

The quest for reform did not end with Haile Selassie's restoration in 1941 after the five-year interlude of Italian occupation. On the contrary, it became more frenetic than ever, with the introduction of one initiative after another: the revised constitution of 1955, the codification of the legal system, the issuing of five-year plans for economic development, the establishment of a Ministry of Land Reform, and a host of others. The problem lay not so much in the inadequacy of the reforms themselves but in the incapacity of the imperial system of government to create a structure within which they could be effectively implemented. The roots of this incapacity lay in turn in the absence of any political mechanism through which the mass of Ethiopia's peoples could be linked to the way in which they were governed. There was no equivalent in Ethiopia to the "nationalist" parties formed in colonial Africa to agitate for the end of colonial rule, which in the process required the would-be leaders of the projected independent postcolonial states to build up a basis of support throughout the territory and respond to demands emerging from below. The provision in the 1955 constitution for the lower house in the national parliament to be elected by universal adult suffrage (the Senate continued to be appointed directly by the emperor) was not accompanied by any political party structure, which would undoubtedly have been suppressed, given the threat that politicians with a popular base in the country would have presented to imperial rule.

I remain sceptical as to whether the imperial system of government was reformable along the lines envisaged by its proponents at the time, which would have involved its evolution according to a model derived from the United Kingdom or Japan, leaving the monarch as titular head of state within a structure in which effective power was exercised by elected politicians within a competitive party system. In any event, it never got the chance but was instead overthrown in the 1974 revolution by a coalition of opponents in which the physical force was supplied by the junior ranks of the armed forces and the ideological impetus by the generation of students and recent graduates who generated increasingly vocal opposition to the monarchy during the final decade of the imperial regime (Bahru 2014). No more than their imperial predecessors, however, did the revolutionaries of 1974 have viable political linkages to the countryside and its peoples, whom they continued to regard as mere backward peasants whose central role in the revolutionary process was to be modernized by an urban (albeit now Marxist) elite that enjoyed a monopoly over the physical and intellectual resources required for the process.

The revolution—which matched those in France after 1789, Russia after 1917, and China after 1949—resulted in deep-seated reforms that dramatically changed the character of the Ethiopian state. The most important of these was the great land reform of 1975, under which all land in the country became the property of the state, followed by the establishment through the *kebelle* system of a structure that gave the central government a vastly greater level of control than any previous regime had been able to exercise. Along with these went the imposition of another modernizing model, derived this time from the Soviet Union, complete with its associated institutional paraphernalia, notably including a vanguard Leninist party— the Workers' Party of Ethiopia— introduced to mark the tenth anniversary of the revolution in 1984.

From a broader perspective, however, these initiatives may be seen as carrying through to its logical conclusion the trajectory of the entire Ethiopian reform process since it had first been promoted by Tewodros over a century earlier: the creation of a powerful and centralized state, capable of imposing its control over the whole of the national territory and securing its independence from threats, both internal and external. Both the army and the student movement were basically centralizing participants in the Ethiopian political process, whose raison d'être lay in providing both the force in one case and the ideological expertise in the other that the modern Ethiopian state required. The ethos of the military, in particular, was intensely nationalistic and implacably opposed to any challenge to central government control—this was most obviously represented by demands for Eritrean independence in the north of the country (as then constituted) and Somali self-determination in the southeast. Though the student movement was considerably more diverse, it too was, to a large extent, nationalist in its orientation. While the language of "democracy" entered the Ethiopian political discourse for the first time, as represented by the People's Democratic Republic of Ethiopia formally instituted in 1984, this was very strictly subordinated to the vision of the dominating group led by Mengistu Hailemariam that had emerged victorious from the bloodletting of the mid-1970s. As in France under Napoleon, Russia under Stalin, or China under Mao Zedong, the effect of revolution was to create a state that was far more powerful, centralized, and personalized than the monarchical regime that it displaced.

Where Ethiopia differed most sharply from these predecessors was in the underlying construction of the state itself. While all three of them were multiethnic—with Russia, in particular, encompassing a large number of diverse nationalities—all of them rested on a dominant core nationality that was ultimately in a position to impose its control on its essentially peripheral minorities. This was simply not the case in Ethiopia, which did indeed have a core ethnic component, constituted in this case by the Amharic- and Tigrinya-speaking Orthodox Christians of the northern plateau regions, but in which the very success of Emperor Menelik's territorial expansion of the late nineteenth century reduced these to a minority within what they continued to regard as their own country. While limited numbers of formerly subject peoples were incorporated into the imperial regime, this occurred only in a form that did not threaten the existing power structure. Underlying any broader project of reform was, therefore, the need to expand participation in the political order beyond the tiny group associated with the imperial court that effectively constituted Ethiopia's government under the imperial regime—or even the rather larger constituency under the Derg—to the mass of Ethiopians, who in most cases had previously figured only as the subjects of an autocratic system of government with which they shared neither history, language, or religion. Almost invariably described (in language characteristically derived from the Soviet Union) as the national question, this was to become the critical challenge facing any project of reform in the Ethiopian context.

THE CHALLENGE OF PARTICIPATION

It is axiomatic that, sooner or later, any viable political order must provide a mechanism that not only enables its citizens to participate in governance but also, much more importantly, provides them with a sense of identity with the state, its structure of governance, and with their fellow citizens. In former colonial Africa, this sense of belonging came to be associated—to a vastly more successful degree than could ever have been expected at the time of independence nearly sixty years ago—with the often arbitrary territorial units created by colonial partition. It might plausibly have been supposed that territories such as Zambia or Congo, which were simply created on the map by British or Belgian colonialists, would cease to exist once the powers that had created them were withdrawn and displaced by indigenous governments. That this has not happened owes a great deal, certainly, to the support provided by the international system to the integrity of postcolonial states and to the vested interests of African governing elites in preserving a structure of order and power from which they themselves were the principal beneficiaries. But it would, nonetheless, never have been possible had not the great majority of ordinary citizens come to regard themselves as belonging to the territorial units that European colonialism had imposed on them. It never ceases to amaze me, for example, that the citizens of the former Belgian Congo identify themselves with some intensity as Congolese, regardless of the arrogant and arbitrary way in which their territory was created by Leopold II of Belgium in the late nineteenth century and the massive suffering (and negligible benefits) that they subsequently endured from their governments, both colonial and independent.

A key role in securing this remarkably positive outcome in colonial Africa has to be ascribed to the "nationalist" political parties formed in order to foment and organize the struggle against colonial rule. The "nationalism" that these promoted was effectively invented, since there was, at that time, no nation for these parties to represent. The need to form a viable opposition to colonialism remained and forced would-be elites into the countryside and created a party structure that, however adapted, continues to underlie the domestic politics of postcolonial states, whether this structure was dominated by a single nationwide party or whether (as in Nigeria and Kenya, for example) it involved the mobilization of rival parties, formed inevitably on largely ethnic lines. It has been absolutely critical to Ethiopian politics that no such process took place, with the result that the impetus for political modernization or reform continued to be driven—until very late in the day—by elites based in the urban areas and especially Addis Ababa. These elites incorporated essentially centralist conceptions of Ethiopian identity that rested on the country's "great tradition" of nationhood that looked back to Axum, Lalibela, and Gondar and incorporated elements such as Orthodox Christianity and the Amharic language that failed to acknowledge the very different religious and ethnic identities of many Ethiopians.

Insofar as the imperial regime had any project at all for the creation of an Ethiopian national identity, the assumption that people from outside the highland and Orthodox Christian core could "become" Ethiopian by adopting its religious and cultural characteristics remained. As a strategy for elite accommodation within the imperial system, this has worked fairly well over a long period of Ethiopian history, attested by the presence of leading Oromo notables in the government in Gondar in the eighteenth century, individuals like Dejazmach Balcha under Menelik in the late nineteenth and early twentieth centuries, or the long-serving Oromo finance minister

Yilma Deressa under Haile Selassie. There was even room in the imperial regime for some Muslim provincial leaders, such as Sheik Khojali in Benishangul or Sultan Abajifar in Jimma. As a mechanism for incorporating large communities into Ethiopian governance, it was, however, hopelessly inadequate, and any serious attempt to tackle the issue of "nationalities" (to use the Marxist vocabulary introduced by student activists in the 1960s) had to await the revolution. Even then, however, the uncompromising centralism of the Derg and its bitter opposition to any attempt to mobilize regional (let alone ethnic or religious) identities placed very severe restrictions on what it could do. The Derg's assumption was that by destroying the cultural symbols and the sources of economic exploitation that underlay the imperial system of government, notably including the monarchy, the privileged position of the Ethiopian Orthodox Church, and the private ownership of land, it would be possible to lay the foundations of a revolutionary nationalism in which all Ethiopians were equal. Mengistu Hailemariam himself, coming from southern Ethiopia and rising through the army to become the supreme leader of the country, demonstrated the equality of opportunity that the revolution had made possible. Even Mengistu, however, may best be regarded as a Balcha-like figure, rising on an individual basis within a system still associated with the highland core, rather than providing any mechanism open to hitherto excluded peoples as a whole.

In part, the failure of the Derg's nation-building project may be ascribed to the total failure of the revolutionary regime to provide its people with the benefits that they had been promised. The socialist economy established in the Soviet model demonstrated the incapacity of that model worldwide, while the revolutionary land reform, far from enabling peasants to benefit from control over their own means of production, subjected them instead to an agricultural marketing corporation whose first priority was to supply cheap food to the towns and the army. Initiatives supposedly devised to promote agricultural production, of which the most intrusive was villagization, actually had the opposite effect. The 1984 famine that brought Ethiopia global attention was by no means entirely the result of the regime's policies, but they were certainly a contributory element. Military conscription to fight the regime's endless wars in Eritrea and Tigray was another major factor in eroding its legitimacy. But much more basically, the legacies of resentment—created by the way in which some parts of the empire had been forcibly incorporated into it in the late nineteenth century and subsequently exploited by a class of alien landlords—were far too great to be bridged by a project that essentially sought to remold the subjected peoples in the image of their conquerors. Indeed, in its later years, the Derg regime (or People's Democratic Republic of Ethiopia, as it was officially titled by this time) came to acknowledge that some recognition of the diversity of Ethiopia's numerous peoples would be required and established the Institute for the Study of Ethiopian Nationalities to start, at least, the process of mapping what those nationalities actually were, albeit still within the highly restrictive structure of a state based on the model of the Soviet Union. Most fundamentally of all, therefore, the fall of the Derg demonstrated the collapse—at an appalling cost in human lives and misery—of the assumption built into every attempt at reform from the time of Tewodros onwards, that the creation of a "modern" Ethiopia depended first and foremost on the construction of a powerful and centralized state that could then push through, from the top downwards, the measures required to haul Ethiopia, by whatever measure of force was needed, into the modern era. It thus made clear that any viable project of reform would have to be built up from a popular base, not simply imposed from above.

THE CHALLENGE OF REFORM UNDER THE EPRDF

The EPRDF regime that came to power in May 1991 was therefore faced by the challenge of reform at several different levels. First, it needed to restructure an economy derived from a Soviet model, the inadequacy of which was very visibly demonstrated by the collapse of the Soviet Union itself just two years earlier and the apparent triumph of the market, or capitalist alternative, which, at that time, looked to be the only structure available. Second, it needed to create a political mechanism to replace the discredited party-state imposed by the Derg and, in the process, to rectify the massive democratic deficit that every Ethiopian regime up until that time had shared. And third and most basically of all, it had to restructure the Ethiopian state itself and turn it into a genuinely national institution rather than a means through which to impose the power of some of Ethiopia's diverse peoples over the others. It had to do all this, moreover, from the extremely narrow political base provided by a movement, the Tigray People's Liberation Front

(TPLF), whose leadership came from the same deeply Marxist-oriented student movement as the government it had just overthrown. It was imbued with the attitudes and experiences characteristic of Maoist liberation movements the world over and could claim to represent only the small region of the country, Tigray, to which it had been restricted until only a short time before achieving final victory.

As we are aware, at the present time, of the problems that the EPRDF's blueprint for restructuring Ethiopia has encountered, prompting the current agenda for reform, it is all the more necessary to recognize its considerable achievements over the twenty-seven-year period that ended in 2018. For a start, those twenty-seven years amounted to the second-longest period of stable government in modern Ethiopian history, surpassed only by the reign of Haile Selassie between 1941 and 1974. While simple longevity tells us nothing about the quality of governance, it does, at least, indicate an ability to manage some of the problems of ruling a complex and often violent political landscape. The contrast with the Derg, which depended on a very high level of repression and was at no point able to achieve any period of peace throughout its sixteen years or so in power, is particularly striking. This longevity rested, in turn, on the explicit recognition of Ethiopia's diversity and the need to dismantle a historical structure of rule that rested on the assumed hegemony of one part of the country over the others.

It also provided a prolonged period of economic growth without precedent in Ethiopia's previous history that extended well beyond Addis Ababa and its immediate environs to encompass—to an inevitably greater or lesser extent—the greater part of the national territory. Most remarkably of all, twice it was able to achieve one of the most difficult feats of political management: the peaceful succession of a new leader to the highest political office—first with the installation of Hailemariam Desalegn after the death of Meles Zenawi and second with that of Abiy Ahmed after Hailemariam's resignation. This double transition, nonetheless, exposed two significant weaknesses in the EPRDF formula, both of which derived from the underlying Marxist ideology that Meles and his colleagues shared with virtually the whole of the 1960s student generation, of which they formed a part.

The first of these weaknesses was Meles's unshakeable commitment to Joseph Stalin's conception of the national question, which was applied to the Soviet Union (where it made a very significant contribution to the subsequent breakup of the USSR into fifteen separate states) and was likewise embodied in the institutional structure of the Federal Democratic Republic of Ethiopia. This held, in keeping with Marxist doctrine, that ethnicity was no more than a superstructural manifestation of underlying issues of economic exploitation and that once these economic causes had been removed, the separate ethnic (or "national") identities that they had fostered would wither away. Ethiopia did indeed have very significant problems of economic exploitation, which in turn undoubtedly had an ethnic component, but the corollary did not follow. Particularly problematic was the *explicit* identification of nationality as the basis for the formation of the federal system, which correspondingly came to be identified with territoriality (and the creation of boundaries between federal units) and identity (and thus the privileged position implicitly conferred on "nationals" of the nominate ethnicity within each of the designated territories).

Virtually every African state has had to contend with the challenges presented by ethnic pluralism (which, in the great majority of cases, resulted from the arbitrary partitions imposed by colonial rule), and so an implicit element of ethnicity has been built into the political construction of large and ethnically diverse states such as Nigeria. In virtually every African state likewise—and certainly extending to Ethiopia—ethnicities have become blurred over time as the result of intermarriage, population movement, and the formation of new identities as the basis for political action, notably within large cities. The *formal* designation of ethnicity or nationality as the basis for political participation has, nonetheless, been confined in Africa to Ethiopia and has had a powerful impact in rigidifying ethnic identities and inhibiting social integration.

The second weakness was the commitment to the Leninist "vanguard" party as the sole permissible agency for political participation, which likewise formed part of the ideological package espoused by Ethiopia's student revolutionaries. This indeed proved to be an extremely powerful tool through which to combine ideological commitment with organizational effectiveness and also enabled, at the very least, a measure of co-optation of hitherto excluded social groups into the ruling structure. It has been especially critical for liberation movements seeking to build linkages across ethnic lines in the face of intense repression and hostility from established regimes. At the same time, its limitations have also become clear, most important of which has been its monopolizing character: it is simply impossible for two or more vanguard parties to coexist peacefully, and any contest between such parties rapidly turns into a fight to the death from which only one can emerge victorious. Although they are open to a measure of reform, through purges of supposedly corrupt elements on the one hand and the co-optation of reformist elements on the other, they very readily degenerate (like the Communist Party of the Soviet Union) into corrupt oligarchies that have lost touch with newly emerging social strata. In former liberation movements especially, with China and Cuba as classic examples, "liberation credentials" can retain a key status within the party long after these have lost all relevance to the society as a whole. When, as in Ethiopia, vanguard rule is combined with very rapid socioeconomic development, this in itself inevitably creates relative winners and losers, with a tendency for the winners to be found disproportionately among those who hold the most powerful positions within the party structure, and for the losers to become correspondingly alienated.

CONCLUSION

The central conclusion of this necessarily sketchy outline of the challenges of reform in Ethiopia is that the key to success lies in the construction of a *political order* within which all of the country's major actors can find a place. The other elements in the reform process discussed in this book, including the rectification of weaknesses in the developmental state model, the reform of the security apparatus, and Ethiopia's relations with its neighbors, though important, are nonetheless secondary and dependent on the achievement of the primary task. And though this task encompasses a substantial element of institution building, at the level both of the political party system needed to displace the now plainly inadequate vanguard party represented by the EPRDF and of the constitutional order, it is also clear that institution building on its own is not enough: it is necessary to develop habits of tolerance and compromise, without which any consensual political order must rapidly collapse.

REFERENCES

Bahru Zewde. 2002. *Pioneers of Change in Ethiopia: The Reformist Intellectuals of the Early Twentieth Century.* Oxford: James Currey.

———. 2014. *The Quest for Socialist Utopia: The Ethiopian Student Movement, c.1960–1974.* Oxford: James Currey.

Clapham, Christopher. 2006. "Ethiopian Development: The Politics of Emulation." *Commonwealth and Comparative Politics* 44, no. 1: 111–21.

———. 2017. *The Horn of Africa: State Formation and Decay.* London: Hurst.

1.2 Rethinking Transitology
Structural Influencers of Political Change in Ethiopia

Semir Yusuf

INTRODUCTION

The current political change in Ethiopia has grabbed the attention of the international community. Western governments, donor agencies, academics, and journalists have all talked about the political "transition" taking place in this country. Indeed, some important reforms are underway in the political and economic realms in Ethiopia. However, we should not take "transition" for granted in any given country, as there are various factors that affect the direction, speed, and evenness of political change. In this chapter, I emphasize the structural weight on the political dynamics in current-day Ethiopia by way of questioning some aspects of the traditional understanding of political transition. My major argument will be that a series of structural forces—anchored on the state and its relations with social forces[1]—appear to pose significant challenges to, and affect the nature and speed of, political change in Ethiopia. I will first briefly discuss the assumptions behind traditional transitology and its critiques. I will then examine a few of the structural challenges and opportunities surrounding the current political change in Ethiopia by way of demonstrating the complexity that transition, if and when it exists, involves.

TRADITIONAL TRANSITOLOGY: TENETS AND CRITIQUES

The debate on transitology is still alive and is even getting richer as we approach the paradigm's thirty-plus years of existence. With the fall of autocracies in southern Europe, Latin America, East and South Asia, eastern Europe, and finally parts of Africa between the 1970s and 1990s, there was a dire need among concerned Western governments, international organizations, and academics to grapple with the fast-changing political dynamics in the developing world. Since the 1980s, the political transition paradigm thus went on becoming a very important framework of analysis to study political change in these countries. Initiated by the pioneering works of Rustow (1970) and O'Donnell and Schmitter (1986) and then further developed by a host of other scholars from different parts of the world, transitology seized the attention of many democratic comparativists (see Cohen 2000; Jowitt 1998; Verdery 1996; Wiarda 2001).

By the turn of the twenty-first century, transitology met a severe setback. It was scathingly criticized and even declared dead (Carothers 2002). However, it refused to die. With the rise of such momentous world events as the Color Revolutions and the Arab Spring, it was revivified (Diamond et al. 2014; Mohamedou and Sisk 2013). Although debated and disputed, political transition is still widely in use, especially in some parts of East Asia and the Horn of Africa.

ASSUMPTIONS

It is difficult to summarize the generic ideas of political transition, not least because the term has meant different things for different scholars. Critics of the term have understood it in ways that have failed to satisfy its supporters or third parties. The most widely cited summary of the transition paradigm is to be found in Carothers's (2002) "The End of the Transition Paradigm." According to Carothers, the paradigm rests on following five major assumptions: (A) Movement away from autocracy is movement toward democracy. (B) Political transition is a staged process, usually beginning with political liberalization, followed by democratization, and finally ending in democratic consolidation. (C) There are certain key indicators that signify the "normality" of the transition process, elections being the major ones. (D)

There are no structural impediments to political transition. (E) There is a state capable of managing transition. Although heated debates have flared up as to whether these assumptions truly represent the ideas of all those charged of "transitologism" (see Gans-Morse 2004), it is difficult to deny that they feature prominently in several studies on Latin American, central Asian, eastern European, and African countries,[2] making them important points of departure to understand the pillars of the transition paradigm.

DEFICIENCIES OF TRANSITOLOGY IN THE CONTEXT OF THE HORN REGION

Critics have taken issues with these assumptions at the level of theory but more so at the level of empirics (Bunce 1995; Burawoy and Verdery 1999; Carothers 2002; Jowitt 1998; Saxonberg and Linde 2003; Verdery 1996; Wiarda 2001). These scholars submit that transitology's assumption—that lessons about political processes detected in one region in a given historical period can be readily employed in other regions and in different time periods—would pose certain problems for research. Such an assumption, among other things, "leads to an emphasis on inappropriate explanatory variables, the development of misguided research agendas, and the faulty interpretation of empirical evidence" (Gans-Morse 2004, 321). Critics also take issues with transitology's apparent teleological presumptions about the progression of political change, which assumes that it usually ends, more or less, with liberal democracy (Burawoy and Verdery 1999; Carothers 2002; Cohen 2000; Pickel 2002). Diverse evidences from across the world have brought to light the flaws of the transition paradigm. Below, I will reaffirm those flaws, using some countries in the Horn of Africa—a region less frequently cited in the transitology literature—as examples.

First, in contrast to the paradigm's first assumption, movement away from autocracy is not always movement toward democracy. Sometimes, countries transition from one form of autocracy to another form. Other times, they move from a full-blown autocracy to several variants of hybrid regimes. Still in other occasions, there is nothing significant that "moved" in the politics of a country, contrary to what regime leaders and their international backers try to advertise about a country being "in transition." The 1991 political transitions in many countries in the Horn and beyond—

including Ethiopia, Eritrea, Rwanda, and Sudan—was indeed movement away from some forms of autocratic regimes. The new leaders in some of these countries were hailed by the international community as a "new breed of leaders" with strong commitment to good governance and democracy (Musisi 2016). However, the movement away from autocracy has not led to the development of democratization as assumed. In countries such as Ethiopia and Rwanda, multiparty politics have been safely caged within the ambit of stable authoritarianism (Abbink and Hagmann 2013; Rafti 2008), while in others, Eritrea being a notable example, there has not even been a façade of constitutionalism and democratization (Tronvoll and Mekonnen 2014). Despite much progress—which is itself controversial—even Kenya, according to critical assessments (e.g., Levitsky and Way 2010), has long remained to be a competitive authoritarian state, one with visible democratic features but that is ultimately authoritarian to the core.

Secondly, there is nothing teleological about the paths of political transition. There is no regularity or determinism in political transitions. Political change is often messy and does not usually follow specified routes. Political development in Kenya, for instance, has gone through a process difficult to be captured by the stages of the democratization paradigm. Opening up of the political system occurred in 2007, which, however, led to severe political crisis; this led to another constitutional reform in 2010, followed by a limited opening up of the system until Kenya was hit by still another round of political crisis in 2017–18, again followed by an interelite pact and relative stability. It is indeed disputable to claim Kenya is in transition (Rana 2017; Wadekar 2018), but even if we suppose it is following the most sympathetic opinions (e.g., Harbeson 1998; Holmquist and Ford 1998), it is not clear what stage at which Kenya could be categorized (see Brown 2004).

Third, taking elections as a key indicator of democratic transition could be misleading. Critical studies (Gandhi 2008; Schedler 2006) on institutions under authoritarian rule have shown that apparently democratic institutions, such as elections, are neither useless shams nor precursors to democratization but are important tools used by autocratic leaders in their quest for international as well as local legitimization of their rules. For anyone who studies elections in Rwanda, Sudan, and Ethiopia (Abbink 2017; Kakuba 2015; Kim 2016; Rafti 2008; Stroh 2012), this should be clear.

Rather than indicators and precursors of democratization, elections in these countries are used to "obtain support from some segments of the society" and also "share privileges with regime opponents, thereby neutralizing the resisting power of the latter." Put otherwise, "As a forum through which dictators can make policy concessions, nominally democratic institutions are instruments of co-optation" (Gandhi 2008, xviii).

Finally, contrary to the paradigm's last two assumptions, there are important structural hurdles (including state fragility) to making a transition to democracy. This is not to dispute the role of elites in democratizing or autocratizing polities. The huge roles played by elites in destabilizing, restabilizing, and autocratizing states could be exemplified by the roles played by Kenyan and South Sudanese elites in destabilizing their respective countries and also in striking peace deals in recent times. However, the perspective that puts much focus on the interests and behaviors of elites leaves out the question about the sources of those interests and behaviors. In addition, it also falls short of explaining the derailment of democratic politics despite the goodwill of ruling elites. Finally, but most usually, such an overemphasis on elite decision neglects the structural and institutional factors that facilitate the coming into fruition or retrenchment of the authoritarian aspiration of elites. Agents work within the context of powerful underlying factors that shape their interests and impact their capacities. Important structural challenges to democracy in the Horn include a long tradition and structures of an absolutist state in Ethiopia, whose agents have consistently inherited institutions of domination and hegemony; a coherently organized rebel group that transferred its systems of domination to the state after it became *the state*, as in Eritrea; an extremely fragile set of institutions and barely functioning state structures that lack the capacity to manage political transition peacefully, as in South Sudan; enduring and extreme clan-based fractionalization that has made political stability a rarity, as in Somalia; and so on. In many cases, international support for autocratic regimes, imposition of Washington Consensus-based economic policies promoted by international financial institutions, severe economic crises, and other factors have also undermined state capacity in this region.

This last critique of transitology (that structural factors need to be taken seriously), in fact, is closely related in explanation to the other critiques of traditional transitology. The structural factors influence[3] the direction, pace, and nature of political transition. They can help us answer the questions as to why not all movements away from autocracy are also movements toward democracy and why the road toward democracy is sometimes bumpy and difficult and other times not so. That is exactly why we should investigate the challenges and opportunities surrounding any political transition. Below, I discuss these factors in the context of Ethiopia.

But before that, a few words about the current political dynamics are in order. Prime Minister Abiy Ahmed's coming to power in April 2018 was followed by accelerated political reforms. Media freedom has expanded with the unblocking of 264 news sites. Thousands of political prisoners were released, and all banned political parties were allowed to operate freely in the country. It has also broken new ground on gender parity by appointing its first female head of state and chief justice, as well as awarding half of its twenty cabinet slots to women. Repressive laws—such as the anti-terrorism law and the Charities and Societies Proclamation of 2009 (governing civil society organizations)—have been overturned and are in the process of being replaced by more liberal laws, too. Taken together, these are clear indications of political liberalization.

However, they are not signs of the inevitability of democratic transition, nor are they indications of the fulfillment of all conditions toward that transition. The rule of law has not yet prevailed in many parts of the country; the coercive apparatuses have not yet clearly charted and internalized new democratic visions and modes of operation, thereby guaranteeing that use of force by state agents will, from now on, be not only effective but also transparent and in line with universal standards of human rights;[4] democracy-friendly and widely agreed-upon constitutional design to effectively manage ethnic division has yet to be designed and put into practice in the entire country; there are no clear and credible indications that all major political organizations in the country have willfully endorsed the legal and democratic route to political contestation as the only acceptable political game in town; and of course, the more "visible" indicators of democratization, such as free, fair, competitive, and regular elections, have yet to be tested. If we go further, to a more substantive conception of democracy, then a lot more deficiencies could be added to the list, such as the redistribution of national wealth to achieve more social justice, thereby enabling citizens to effectively utilize their constitutionally guaranteed rights. Needless to say, many of these conditions cannot normally be expected to be achieved in a short span of time, pointing to the fact that democratization is a long and usually arduous process, especially in divided and economically challenged countries, as Ethiopia currently is.

Outlining the progresses and the deficiencies is important but is not enough. As I mentioned earlier, as an antidote to the rather voluntaristic and shallow explanations of political change among traditional transitologists, it is also important to lay out the diverse structural factors that affect the pace, evenness, and success of political transition in Ethiopia. Hence, there is a need for assessing the structural challenges and opportunities surrounding the current political liberalization in the country, to which I will now turn.

CHALLENGES TO DEMOCRATIC TRANSITION IN ETHIOPIA

The major challenges today about democratizing Ethiopia lie, paradoxically, in the legacy of strong state and current (perceived) state fragility. I will outline how some of these problems came about, what shape they have taken on the ground, and with what implications.

Tradition of Absolutism and Weak Contestation to State Hegemony

In Ethiopia, a major hurdle in transitioning to the rule of law and a political system that upholds the rights of citizens—core elements of any definition of democracy—has been the general lack of strong contenders[5] to the state's hegemonic aspirations (resulting in weak contestation); and when and where such contenders existed, the contestation has not been favorable to the emergence of such a system (i.e., bad contestation). Moreover, the power asymmetry between the state and other forces is a path-dependent structural factor to explain democratic deficit, whereby the successively inherited state structures of domination and control have come down to us more refined and enhanced from regime to regime. The presence of either of the conditions mentioned above (weak or bad contestation) has historically enervated the possibility of successful political transition, and it, or a combination of both conditions, seems to pose a serious challenge—along with a lack of state resilience and coherence[6]—to current-day attempts at democratizing Ethiopia.

Historically, the protected rights of citizens and the prevalence of the rule of law have rarely been conferred willfully by the state to its subjects. Rights of citizens have usually been taken away through robust and successive contentions and contestations between the state and (semi)-independent forces. The history of those countries in the West that are now widely seen as paragons of democratic governance is a witness to this assertion. These countries were under feudal and absolutist monarchies only a few centuries ago. The emergence of democratic governance was, by and large, a by-product of state making. As renowned historian and sociologist Charles Tilly (1990) notes, in those European countries where "capitalized coercion" prevailed, democracy developed out of the contentious and conciliatory relations among the state, the bourgeoisie, the aristocracy, and the peasantry, resulting from state expansion. As the state posited to push its frontiers, fighting off its neighbors, it was, at the same time, forced to negotiate with those forces already under its own suzerainty, intending to get concessions from them, including finance and man power. The state also acted as a "protection racket," selling to its subjects security from aggression by other states in a world where state expansion prevailed (Tilly 1985).

The process brought forth two unintended consequences: bureaucratization and political liberalization. The first process is exemplified by Tilly's oft-quoted aphorism: "The state made war and war made the state." The state went on building institutions, organizing its activities, and getting more and more formidable. But, on the other hand, the state also learned to reconstruct itself in a more inclusive manner, giving representation to and protecting the rights of at least some sections of the population hitherto unshielded from its unbridled power. State concession to give representation and recognize rights of citizens is a major outcome of the existence, in that context, of strong contenders to power—mainly the capitalist class, which was, in turn, an outcome of the enormous urbanization and commercialization of agriculture. As another preeminent sociologist notes, the bourgeoisie emerged as a robust independent class that was capable of forcing the concession of the state to share political privileges and be bound by some form of law (Moore 1966). The aristocracy in some cases allied with the bourgeoisie or were themselves transformed into one, thereby mustering more power to challenge state authority, with notable success. When neither of these options were a possibility, the landlords were swept away by the impending capitalist production, with the result that all vestiges of feudal political economy were abolished in the process of a bourgeois revolution that resulted in capitalist democracy. Hence, democratization in all these cases came in congruence with state making, in the context where capitalism reigned supreme and the bourgeoisie emerged as a powerful class.

The Ethiopian imperial expansion had both a degree of similarity with and a notable divergence from Europe's imperial past in terms of state making. On the one hand, as in Europe, the state made war and war went on making the state. The Ethiopian state has deep indigenous roots; it has existed for a long, almost uninterrupted period of time, and, most importantly, it has emerged through intense and continuous warfare. This state of affairs has rendered it more robust than the average postcolonial African state, which is, by and large, a colonial creation. However, this process did not engender any significant democratic move on the part of the state. The major reason arguably lies in the fact that the state was not confronted by strong contenders demanding either representation or limited government. In Ethiopia, the aristocracy was relatively weak vis-á-vis the Crown and the bourgeoisie was almost nonexistent. Contrary to European feudalism, where the aristocracy had a strong resource basis—landed and hereditary tribute-collecting prerogatives—and later on organized as well (e.g., the lords that formed the House of Commons in England), the aristocrats in Ethiopia, in general, were not guaranteed landholding rights (in core Abyssinia), but usually just tributary rights. In addition, the tributary rights themselves were not automatically hereditary; they had to be willed as such by the Crown, which then would become *riste-gult*. Peasants—with some limitations—were the owners of the land.[7] Under normal circumstances, the monarch had the upper hand in allocating resources and sources of livelihood for the aristocrats. True, the aristocracy and the nobility traditionally owned armies and contributed to the "national" war-making project, but this became less important with the acquisition of arms from outside during Kings Yohannes and Menelik, and even this power of the aristocracy was scrapped in the post-1941 period. The landlords were by no means helpless, though, and they at times flexed their muscles and rebelled against and obstructed important steps toward state centralization and bureaucratization; however, ultimately, the state usually got the better of them, leaving their status, in principle, precarious, as they depended on the state for their existence as a class. The four emperors from 1855 onwards—Tewodros, Yohannes, Menelik, and Haile Selassie—consistently worked on further cutting down the administrative powers of the landlords to the point of restricting the granting of titles. Over time, the Crown built its power, which safely overshadowed that of the nobility. After Menelik's conquest, aristocratic entrenchment became more intense in the south. But there the experiment was relatively short-lived, and there were internal divisions within the aristocracy, undercutting any potential to pose danger to the emperor's hegemony. In any case, even in the south, the state, represented by the emperor, was the ultimate owner of all lands, and the aristocrats had *gult* and *riste-gult* rights, at least officially.

On the other hand, conditions for the emergence of capitalism were unfavorable in the country. The aristocrats were uninterested in technological advancements (due to the nature of their relationship with the land) and depended on trade, not production, as their source of richness (Donham 1986). They were highly parasitic. Their European counterparts (mainly in England), in contrast, developed commercial interests and used their financially uplifted class benefits as a bulwark against the prerogatives of the royalty (Tilly 1990). Ethiopian peasants also shunned technological advancements in agriculture due to the disincentives associated with the tradition of tribute-taking in the country. In the absence of an equivalent to what was in Europe called the "custom of the manor," what was taken from the peasants in imperial Ethiopia was arbitrary and at times immense (Donham 1986). In the absence of any strong motivation for investment and technological advancement on the part of the landlords and the peasantry, the production process did not lend itself to capital accumulation. There were no remarkable moves toward commercialization and urbanization to help grow a strong bourgeoisie. Commercialization of agriculture began in the 1950s, and the aristocracy got actively engaged in it, but it was too brief to bring about a strong, independent bourgeois class. Urbanization was very weak, and when urban centers emerged in the eighteenth and nineteenth centuries, they simply served the purpose of becoming seats of local nobles that skimmed off production from the countryside. This was contrary to the European urban centers that emerged as self-governing communes, lords having no control over them in general (Moore 1966). In addition, international isolation until the twentieth century was a barrier to the growth of a strong middle class. When the country opened up in the post-1941 period, the manufacturing and international trade sectors were heavily controlled by foreigners. Hence, no indigenous bourgeoisie emerged (Markakis and Ayele 1978).

As the state expanded, it was not forced to make concessions in ways that could usher in a period of political liberalization. In the process, rather, the state—to be more specific, the Crown—amassed huge power unencumbered by contending forces and became robust. It deployed its power to further paralyze the powers of the aristocracy and the middle class and centralize its rule along the way, culminating in the establishment of an absolutist state. The foundations for a postimperial autocratic rule were strongly established.

The new incumbent, the Derg, thus inherited the structures of a centralized, absolutist state, reinvigorated them, and took state power to a whole new level. Its repressive, mobilizational, and controlling power was unprecedentedly enhanced and was given a new mission to accomplish. Ethiopia got, by then, its most penetrative state, with, again, impressive powers by the standards of African states of the time.

The state did not go unchallenged, though. Partly an outcome of the failure of nation building in the previous era, the most serious challenge appeared in the form of ethno-nationalism and mostly took a violent form. The long-standing and widespread armed struggle, however, did not in any way contribute toward the ushering in of a political opening in the country through state concession, echoing the earlier assertion that not every contestation gives birth to democracy. The war, in fact, dealt away with any remaining hope for such a transition when the burgeoning middle class was decimated by the incessant combat that did not even spare marketplaces (de Waal 1991). By the time the Derg was brought down, Ethiopia was again by no means a conducive environment for democratization.

Revolutionary warfare is associated with durable authoritarianism (Levitsky and Way 2013). Among other things, revolutionary warfare annihilates independent centers of power, rendering the political environment conducive for authoritarian (re)-entrenchment, and enables the victor in the war to transfer its organizational capacity to the state as it captures it, enhancing the new state's repressive capacity. By the time the EPRDF captured state power, organized opposition, independent civil society, and the middle class were awfully weak, an outcome of the war. An insurgent group with impressive organizational capacity—partly explaining its victory over its contenders, the Derg, and other enemy insurgents—the TPLF sought to re-create (with some success) a tightly controlled party and state structure that partially mirrors its own pre-1991 structures. But the underlying condition that facilitated such an enhancement of the power of the state remains, as the inherited structures of control already embedded within the state, including local governance structures, security systems, and state control over vital resources such as land. Such institutions and structures of control, along with a weak civil society, created conditions for an easy propping up of/retrenchment of an autocratic state.

Given such a political environment, the question is not if the EPRDF could become authoritarian post-1991 but why it resorted to establishing nominally democratic institutions from the start and remained committed to maintaining them ever since. While the local institutional conditions facilitated autocracy, colossal changes at the global level appeared to militate against that. The global pro-democracy rhetoric was important not just because it informed the foreign policies of Western states vis-à-vis countries in the developing world undergoing political change but also because it had a transformative effect on the subjectivities of local citizens and actors. Leaders in such states had to devise strategies to balance the need for political survival and that for gaining legitimacy, especially internationally, giving rise to the establishment of such institutions. However, as it turned out, these institutions have not merely been shams with no practical effect on the ground—at least not in Ethiopia. Rather, they were arsenals in the hands of the ruling party in its quest for legitimization of its rule. Elections, for instance, as mentioned elsewhere, were used not only to garner support for the regime locally, but also to temper political opposition through cooptation of regime opponents (Gandhi 2008). It is important to note, however, that the EPRDF established its hegemony over the state not just through soft measures but also, and mainly so, through coercive tactics.

Its hegemony was not uncontested, though; it was just that those contesting it were for long not strong enough to force fundamental change in ways that contributed toward democratic transition. The armed movements, if at all democratically relevant, were anyway too weak to influence change, due partly to the extensive power of the state but also to their own internal organizational weaknesses. Moreover, the sole refuge for Ethiopian rebels, Eritrea, counterintuitively helped diminish the power of the rebels to strongly challenge the EPRDF's rule (Teshale 2018). Legal political parties were also feeble and divided (again of their own making and external pressure). The general political environment, infused with central control and the securitization of independent public engagement, did not create a favorable climate for the emergence of strong civic, economic, or political contenders to state hegemony. The already largely asymmetric power balance between the state and its contestants led to the even more impairment by the state of any foundation for the emergence of an independent center of power post-2005.

The current liberalization, then, is underway at the backdrop of such a social power vacuum.[8] Precisely because relevant actors have long remained weak, the most important responsible body for transitioning Ethiopia toward a democratic state is the state itself. Such a scenario is problematic because it leaves the fate of Ethiopia's democratization in the hands of that very entity (i.e., the state) that the rule of law is supposed to protect citizens from. Sliding back to authoritarianism may not be quite smooth today (due to the higher level of political consciousness and liberationist sentiments across the country, especially among the youth), but the project of transitioning to democracy cannot be surely said to be in absolutely safe hands either, although there is definitely that possibility.[9] Ultimately, the project is largely dependent on the will of the ruling party.

Weakening of Order and the Challenge of Reconstructing State Power

But leaving the task of democratizing the state to the state itself is problematic for still another reason that is related to state capacity,[10] again a point neglected in traditional transitology. This is especially the case in authoritarian-led multinational federations as Ethiopia has been for over two decades. The dissolution or weakening of state authority in a centralized but ethnically federated state opens up a Pandora's box of unbridled ethno-nationalist sentiments and movements. Centralized rule undermines the very logic of self-rule, one of the two basic conditions for the existence of a federal form of government, implying that such countries do not have a genuine federal system in place. In Ethiopia, precisely due to the autocratic *and* ethnically engineered rule, ethnic dissatisfaction had remained widespread and had been simmering for as long as the central grip was firm. Ethnic grievance was undergirded by the ripening of ethnicized consciousness and politics, for which the overall ethnically charged national political atmosphere and the specific ethnic-based regional institutions operated as conduits.

When the central grip started to slacken—to which ethnic movements partly contributed—the ethnic genie burst out and political order waned suddenly. Ever since the coming to power of the current government, the Ethiopian political landscape has been rocked by several, at times mutually contending, ethnic nationalisms. Ethnic entrepreneurs from different corners have mobilized their constituencies and escalated demands for genuine self-determination and proportional political representation. More alarmingly, intense violent conflicts have erupted in different parts of the country and cost several lives. Massive displacements targeting ethnic minorities have put Ethiopia as one of the leading countries in terms of the number of internally displaced persons in the world today. The deterioration of order has become rampant in the country, and the government has so far failed to effectively "repack the Pandora's box" (Vaughan 2003, 248). Aligning with Leff's (1999) characterization of politics in post-centralized and ethno-federated countries, the contention then has not been between the state and citizens or the opposition, per se, but between the state and ethno-nationalist forces of all sorts and also among themselves, at times challenging the very legitimacy and existence of the overall political community.

The condition of domestic politics in the absence of a strong but liberalizing state coming out of a centralized *and* federal rule has *a degree*[11] of similarity with realist international politics, characterized essentially by interstate competition in the absence of a world government with regulative powers. Ethnic groups, tribes, and clans, and the groups claiming to represent them, immediately assume a central position in the looming political contestation, and they compete for security, power, and hegemony. It is not that they do not want order but that they want order under their dominion. The effort by some groups to enhance their security creates insecurity in other groups. Intense competition sometimes results in violent conflicts, and even those resolved peacefully have no guarantee of holding for long. Individuals are pulled to their co-ethnics and consider it essential to show the utmost solidarity and loyalty to their "brothers and sisters" in this time of uncertainty and volatility. The Ethiopian political landscape at present features some of these qualities, and they are a source of concern for various stakeholders.

Interethnic rivalry resulting from state incoherence also results in what we refer to in the social sciences as the "tragedy of the commons." As the tragedy of the commons dictates, actors that share a given collective goal at times not only fail to work toward the achievement of that long-term goal but also put in danger the fulfillment of that very goal in their individual pursuit of selfish interests in the short run. Even if the fulfillment of that collective goal is in the interest of all actors, each actor acts with the intention of reaping maximum benefits from a given opportune circumstance, frustrating its own and others' permanent interests in the process. In Ethiopia today, a successful transition to an inclusive democratic system is arguably in the interest of most political actors in the country. However, each actor would think that it could take maximum advantage of such an opportune time as we are in currently to reap self-centered interests (such as ensuring domination of the political process) and execute its plans unilaterally, endangering the whole transitional process and, by implication, the long-term benefits for all of a successful democratic transition. The tragedy of the commons would be acute as a problem when the state is (perceived as) weak, but the problem is also societal; it is also about actors' mutual perceptions and the nature of their horizontal relations.

At times the mutual perceptions of actors are defined by the nationalist paradigm to which they subscribe. The question of contending nationalisms in Ethiopia raises issues of ontology, of who Ethiopians are as a people. Such fundamental questions as what Ethiopia is, what its history is, and what the general way forward is are serious and long-standing bones of contention among different groups in the country. In this situation, agreeing on the need to establish democracy may not mean much since the very essence of democracy—justice, equality, and freedom—means very different things to different people/groups. Thus, the differences are huge and complex, and it takes a good deal of prudence, perseverance, and creativity to navigate through the concerns and dreams of each contestant to power and to create a system in which all visions are represented.

It is not easy for any state undergoing such a crisis to bring back to order, or put into a new order, the vigorous force of (contending) ethno-nationalisms and reconstruct state authority. In Ethiopia, reordering politics is rendered complicated, mainly due to three reasons (Yusuf 2019).[12] First, the state has for a considerable period since 2017 lost some of its autonomy, as the line between state/party structures and protest networks that previously pushed the government to liberalize its politics has blurred in some areas of unrest. The relative lack of state autonomy has complicated law enforcement and the proper regulation of interethnic relations. Moreover, there had persisted internal divisions along philosophical, methodological, and visionary lines within the ruling party, the EPRDF, composed mainly of ethnic parties. The parties were also pulled apart by different and contending ethnic constituencies, further eroding unity of purpose at a time when the country direly needed it. While the ruling party has, at the time of writing, just transformed itself into a monolithic national party, the extent to which it can effectively mend internal divisions is yet to be seen. Finally, as a government ostensibly wanting to make a clear break from the authoritarian past, the new line between upholding the rule of law and sliding back to authoritarianism has not yet been clearly drawn, causing ambiguity about the how and when of security enforcement.[13]

Hence, the state, having lost some of its internal cohesion and autonomy from social forces, is struggling to recuperate with its full force. It is also, at times, unwilling to duly take security measures to contain violence and restore order between warring groups due to fear of authoritarian relapse. Incidentally, it is also sometimes accused of taking undue action against opponents, *in part* reflecting the same problem of state ambiguity towards a legitimate and proportional use of force. State fragility in today's Ethiopia is thus partly perceived but partly actual, too.

As the forgoing discussion demonstrates, the deeper problems associated with democratization, then, paradoxically, are about state strength and state fragility at the same time. They are about the inherited structures (and culture) of state control and domination as much as they are about the crisis within that coercive apparatus upon which control and domination were founded. The first factor (hegemonic state) is problematic *now* primarily in terms of its legacy: in the way it has successively weakened potential contenders to state power. The second factor is an issue in terms of its present actuality: the state as it exists now is in crisis of some sort internally and has for some time in the last two years been perceived as such by different sections of the population. The two challenges have left the country's political landscape dominated by ethno-nationalist contestations both against the state and among themselves. This predicament puts at risk the discursive and institutional foundations of a political community as much as any notion of a smooth democratic transition.

OPPORTUNITIES

Although currently incoherent and relatively lacking resilience, the Ethiopian state, in general terms, is not an average African postcolonial state whose incessant attribute is fragility. Based on prior arguments made by some scholars (Clapham 2017; Kymlicka 2006), one can, as already mentioned, reasonably argue that state formation in this country could be usefully compared more with the European model of state formation rather than the African one, which has important implications for state resilience. As in Europe, the Ethiopian state has deep indigenous roots, has existed for a long period of time, and, most importantly, has emerged through intense and continuous warfare. This gave the Ethiopian state distinct robustness and coherence compared to many other African states.[14] Its mobilizational and repressive powers have especially been remarkable by African standards.

This same process of state formation, however, rendered it weaker in another sense. Abyssinians created a state that converted them into a minority, which in turn brought about a huge challenge in terms of creating a legitimate state—a fundamental problem that Clapham deals with in this volume. Tackling this problem head-on and effectively—which answers the very crisis of state illegitimacy—will leave us with the question of democratization as the other major (albeit closely intertwined with the former) political problem in the country. And in this regard, while, as I already mentioned, the state has to enter into effective negotiations with non-state actors, it should, at the same time, remain resilient enough to maintain the rule of law and order and protect the rights of citizens. Coercive and mobilizational power are key elements of the resilience that democratization requires; the use of such power just needs to be seen as legitimate. State strength is a nonproblem as long as that state is open to, and is a fair reflection of, the diverse and changing interests of its citizens and groups.

In addition to the historical existence of a robust state, the other opportunity about political transition in this country is the manner with which the current political change was achieved. The fact that the current political change is an outcome of a combination of social movement and in-party reform, not a result of armed insurgency, is an important source of hope as well. The previously mentioned research of Levitsky and Way (2013) shows that ruling cliques that come out of protracted insurgency or revolutionary warfare turn out to be not only authoritarian but also durable. Conversely, social-movement-led regime change has been associated with successful democratic transition (Teorell 2010). At the very least, in present-day Ethiopia, one can reasonably assume the presence of a wide-spread and heightened level of democratic enthusiasm among a large section of the population, an element that could have been badly hurt if change was brought through warfare. Moreover, opposition parties and civil society organizations are decidedly weak but are more easily revivable now than would have been the case if the country had to go through a protracted insurgency. Thus, in contrast to 1991, the 2018 political change in Ethiopia, partly due to its emergence out of a more or less peaceful social movement and internal division within the regime, could have a better chance of democratic success, if wisely capitalized on by all stakeholders[15].

The above list of challenges and opportunities is by no means exhaustive. It is just meant to indicate the existence of a diverse array of forces that affects political processes in present-day Ethiopia. As we analyze the ongoing political change in the country from the angles of the ideal type of both democracy and autocracy, we need, at the same time, to examine to what extent the structural forces outlined earlier (and many others not mentioned) would push the reforms toward either end of the ideal types. This is as far as it goes, since only time will tell which ones—the challenges or the opportunities—will take over the politics of the country and push it toward a more defined (or difficult-to-define) category.

CONCLUSION

Traditional transitology neglects some critical aspects of political change, including structural forces that work against successful, smooth, or fast-paced political transition to democracy. It is high time that analysts abandon simplistic or uncritical notions of political transition when they study political processes in Africa in general and Ethiopia in particular. Although

Ethiopia today is going through a textbook example of political liberalization, there are several foundational hurdles that need to be transcended to take the country further toward the path of (stable) democracy. Most of these hurdles have to do with the nature of the state as it has existed on a historical plane. The legacy of absolutism and the combination of that legacy with federal mode of rule have recently produced apparently contradictory trends, both of which have complicated transitional politics in the country.

The first important task left for the state to help achieve a smooth transition is, therefore, to reactivate state power and keep autonomy from contending ethno-political movements in the country. This involves, among other things, the reconstitution of the ruling party on new foundations that could help it forge internal unity and clarity of purpose. The process of reconstituting the EPRDF/the Prosperity Party on such foundations, whatever that amounts to, should be inclusive of diverse voices in the front and should involve a series of candid intraparty negotiations based on genuine efforts to incorporate reasonable concerns and interests of different groups. The utmost effort needs to be made to create large-enough zones of comfort for members to discuss freely issues of concern and help them join the bandwagon of democratic transition in Ethiopia. The new thinking and relative internal cohesion should then be used to bring back, after state autonomy, state capacity to enforce the rule of law and order.

The other very important task tends to balance the first one: the new administration, while reactivating its own power, should, at the same time, help the flourishing and consolidation of strong contenders to state hegemony, including the middle class, civic organizations, and political parties. The state's main role in this respect is to continuously and closely engage with these forces and make sure all impediments to their consolidation are effectively overcome all through the way. It should also opt for a consultative approach to governing the country as it navigates through the tumults of political liberalization. These measures do require a deep and unflinching commitment to democratic transition on the part of the ruling party.[16] They are a practical litmus test for its repeated promise of ensuring such a transition in this country.

The business class, civil society activists, and opposition politicians should, on the other hand, use all opportunities available to the maximum to build their institutional and mobilizational capacity while at the same time help construct a peaceful political environment overall. Civic organizations should especially work toward creating cross-ethnic platforms that defy the intense competition along ethnic lines for tempering tensions in the country. Political parties, alongside other influential societal actors, should enter into a series of forward-looking national dialogues where they candidly iron out and negotiate modalities of incorporating the visions and concerns of all into the process of jointly reconstructing the Ethiopian state. In order to succeed, such efforts require, among other things, a relentless focus on the big picture and long-term goal of transitioning the country into a stable and inclusive democracy. Powerful international actors should transfer finance and skills to professionalize statecraft (especially the security apparatus) and to alleviate poverty in the country. At the same time, they should refrain as much as possible from any intervention that vividly disfavors one group against another in the wider Ethiopian political spectrum.

NOTES

1. Needless to say, these are not the only structural factors affecting political change in Ethiopia. In the interest of space, only these two will be treated in this chapter.
2. See, for instance, Bova 1991; Korbonski 1999; Munck and Leff 1997; Schmitter and Karl 1994 and 1995; Tedin 1994; and Welsh 1994 for clearly transitologist studies on postcommunist societies.
3. As do agents. See footnote 9. The thrust of the arguments in this chapter is not to approve of structural determinism but to give due emphasis to structural forces affecting political processes. The aim is to balance the excessive fixation on agents in traditional transitology, which has, incidentally, influenced several analyses of post-2018 political reforms in Ethiopia.
4. A senior government official at the Ministry of Peace told this researcher that a certain package for revamping the security apparatus on a new ideological and programmatic basis is currently under preparation.
5. These are usually non-state forces such as the middle class, civil society organizations and opposition parties. But one set of classes closely

associated with state power, the aristocracy and the nobility, that historically played, in some Western countries, a critical role in the transition process by challenging the hegemony of the Crown, was generally weak in Ethiopia, too.

6. To which we will come in the following section.

7. The assertions about the landholding rights of the aristocracy in imperial Ethiopia are disputed by some scholars. See, for instance, Bekele (1995). His arguments, however, are deemed controversial. See Crummey (1997).

8. The "vacuum" should be qualified, however. Recently, various contending powers have emerged (some offshoots of the pre-political-change social movements), mostly in the form of ethno-nationalist forces, formal and informal. Their organizational capacity is questionable, however. But even if we assume that some have strong organizational capacity, the problem of bad contestation (mentioned earlier) remains. Competing nationalisms, some questioning the basic foundations of the Ethiopian state and usually on a collision course with one another, do not bode well for the aspiration of (smoothly) democratizing Ethiopia.

9. The analysis pursued in this chapter, although structure-centered, is not determinist, either. Its aim is to point out the diverse array of forces that facilitate, rather than determine, the continuation of autocratic rule. There is always some room for elites to make use of such structures for different ends or introduce some changes to the structures themselves in ways that facilitate democratic transition.

10. It would sound ironic to question the capacity of the state in Ethiopia after the foregoing and subsequent discussions about state strength in this country. It should be noted that—as will be mentioned again later—although the Ethiopian state has features of robustness by African standards, that robustness has varied over time, and the current state of relative fragility is an outcome of some specific factors, such as hitherto being an autocratic and ethno-federal state now undergoing liberalization.

11. The qualification here is very important. Realist notions of international relations resonate with the current Ethiopian political reality only to the

extent that state and party institutions that appear incoherent/fragile can trigger a sense of security dilemma among some ethnic groups in the country. The assumption here is not that anarchy has prevailed in the country, as Realists would understand it.

12. At the time of writing, the COVID-19 pandemic is ravaging human lives and economies across the globe. *If* it could make significant *and* prolonged inroads into Ethiopia, it may surely have significant implications not only for the economy but also for political order in the country. Will it diminish political tensions or complicate them even further? If it does help in placating tensions, will a more stable political environment give the state/the ruling party the respite it direly needs to resolve some of these internal problems and consolidate its power? Will the consolidation of state power unfold at the expense of the power of regime contenders? Will such a better consolidated state use its power to democratize or "autocratize" Ethiopia? If tensions, on the other hand, grow and degenerate into unrest, how will the concomitant bad contestation affect the country's prospect of democratic transition? Time will tell.

13. A senior government official disclosed to this researcher that confusion has remained within the coercive apparatus regarding the distinction between working toward the prevalence of the rule of law on the one hand and retrenching authoritarian practices on the other. That reflects on the actual efforts (or lack thereof) to enforce political order.

14. Although its mobilizational, controlling, administrative, and repressive power is indeed stronger, there are other areas that would make the Ethiopian state weaker than its African counterparts. Most importantly, its capacity to garner legitimacy, especially from the ethnic/religious subjects that did not historically form its core, is unimpressive. See immediately below.

15. One challenge here is that even though the current political change is not a result of rebel victory, it is still up for competition (although to a lesser degree than would be the case in the context of armed struggles) for entitlement from different sections of the society that have contributed (or believe they have done so) in different ways to the anti-regime struggles since the early 90s.

16. Based on the very analysis pursued in this chapter, it would be naïve to hold any assumption that a ruling party at whose disposal is a set of enabling structural conditions for authoritarian relapse can at the same time make efforts to democratize the state it governs. Without negating that argument, we should also not totally rule out the possibility of democratic transition in such a context, as indicated elsewhere. The challenge presented here to the ruling party is to stay true to its promises.

REFERENCES

Abbink, Jon. 2006a. "Discomfiture of Democracy? The 2005 Election Crisis in Ethiopia and Its Aftermath." *African Affairs* 105, no. 419 (April): 173–99.

———. 2006b. "Ethnicity and Conflict Generation in Ethiopia: Some Problems and Prospects of Ethno-Regional Federalism." *Journal of Contemporary African Studies* 24, no. 3: 389–413.

———. 2017. "Paradoxes of Electoral Authoritarianism: The 2015 Ethiopian Elections as Hegemonic Performance." *Journal of Contemporary African Studies* 35, no. 3: 303–23.

Abbink, Jon, and Tobias Hagmann, eds. 2013. *Reconfiguring Ethiopia: The Politics of Authoritarian Reform.* New York: Routledge.

Abebe, Semahagn Gashu. 2014. *The Last Post-Cold War Socialist Federation: Ethnicity, Ideology and Democracy in Ethiopia.* Federalism Studies. New York: Routledge.

Ambrosio, Thomas. 2014. "Beyond the Transition Paradigm: A Research Agenda for Authoritarian Consolidation." *Demokratizatsiya: The Journal of Post-Soviet Democratization* 22, no. 3: 471–94.

Bekele, Shiferaw, ed. 1995. *An Economic History of Ethiopia, Vol. I: The Imperial Era, 1941–74.* Dakar: CODESRIA.

Bellin, Eva. 2004. "The Robustness of Authoritarianism in the Middle East: Exceptionalism in Comparative Perspective." *Comparative Politics* 36, no. 2 (January): 139–57.

Bova, Russell. 1991. "Political Dynamics of the Post-Communist Transition: A Comparative Perspective." *World Politics* 44, no. 1 (October): 113–38.

Brown, Archie. 2000. "Transnational Influences in the Transition from Communism," *Post-Soviet Affairs* 16, no. 2: 177–200.

Brown, Stephen. 2004. "Theorizing Kenya's Protracted Transition to Democracy." *Journal of Contemporary African Studies* 22, no. 3 (September): 325–42.

Bunce, Valerie. 1995. "Should Transitologists Be Grounded?" *Slavic Review* 54, no. 1: 111–27.

———. 1998. "Regional Differences in Democratization: The East Versus the South." *Post-Soviet Affairs* 14, no. 3 (May): 187–211.

Burawoy, Michael. 2001. "Transition without Transformation: Russia's Involuntary Road to Capitalism." *East European Politics and Societies* 15, no. 2: 269–90.

Burawoy, Michael, and Katherine Verdery, eds. 1999. *Uncertain Transition: Ethnographies of Change in the Postsocialist World.* Lanham, MD: Rowman & Littlefield.

Carothers, Thomas. 2002. "The End of the Transition Paradigm." *Journal of Democracy* 13, no. 1 (January): 5–21.

Choudhry, Sujit, ed. 2008. *Constitutional Design for Divided Societies: Integration or Accommodation?* Oxford: Oxford University Press.

Clapham, Chistopher. 2017. *The Horn of Africa: State Formation and Decay.* London: Hurst.

Cohen, Stephen F. 2000. *Failed Crusade: America and the Tragedy of Post-Communist Russia.* New York: W. W. Norton.

Croissant, Aurel, and Stefan Wurster. 2013. "Performance and Persistence of Autocracies in Comparison: Introducing Issues and Perspectives." *Contemporary Politics* 19, no. 1: 1–18.

Crummey, Donald. 1997. "An Agrarian Economy." Review of *An Economic History of Ethiopia, Vol. I: The Imperial Era, 1941–74*, edited by Shiferaw Bekele. Dakar, 1995. *Journal of African History* 38, no. 1: 141–43.

de Waal, Alex. 1991. *Evil Days: Thirty Years of War and Famine in Ethiopia.* New York: Human Rights Watch.

Diamond, Larry. 2002. "Elections Without Democracy: Thinking About Hybrid Regimes." *Journal of Democracy* 13, no. 2 (April): 21–35.

Diamond, Larry, Francis Fukuyama, Donald L. Horowitz, and Marc F. Plattner. 2014. "Reconsidering the Transition Paradigm." *Journal of Democracy* 25, no. 1: 86–100.

Donham, Donald L. 1986. "Old Abyssinia and the New Ethiopian Empire: Themes in Social History." In *The Southern Marches of Imperial Ethiopia, Essays in History and Social Anthropology,* edited by Donald L. Donham and Wendy James. Eastern African Studies. Cambridge: Cambridge University Press, 3–48.

Easterly, William, and Laura Freschi. 2010. "Why Are We Supporting Repression in Ethiopia?" *New York Review of Books,* November 15, 2010. https://www.nybooks.com/daily/2010/11/15/why-are-we-supporting-repression-ethiopia/.

Fisseha, Assefa. 2006. "Theory Versus Practice in the Implementation of Ethiopia's Ethnic Federalism." In *Ethnic Federalism: The Ethiopian Experience in Comparative Perspective,* edited by David Turton, 131–64. Eastern African Studies. Oxford: James Currey.

Gandhi, Jennifer. 2008. *Political Institutions under Dictatorship.* New York: Cambridge University Press.

Gans-Morse, Jordan. 2004. "Searching for Transitologists: Contemporary Theories of Post-Communist Transitions and the Myth of a Dominant Paradigm." *Post-Soviet Affairs* 20, no. 4: 320–49.

Göbel, Christian. 2011. "Authoritarian Consolidation." *European Political Science* 10, no. 2: 176–90.

Göbel, Christian, and Magnus Andersson. 2011. "Authoritarian Institution Building and the Quality of Democracy in Taiwan and Thailand." Paper presented at the IPSA/ECPR Joint Conference, Sao Paulo, Brazil (February).

Gudina, Merera. 2006. "Contradictory Interpretations of Ethiopian History: The Need for a New Consensus." In *Ethnic Federalism: The Ethiopian Experience in Comparative Perspective,* edited by David Turton, 119–30. Eastern African Studies. Oxford: James Currey.

Harbeson, John W. 1998. "Guest Editor's Introduction: Political Crisis and Renewal in Kenya: Prospects for Democratic Consolidation." *Africa Today* 45, no. 2: 161–83.

———. 2005. "*Ethiopia's Extended Transition.*" *Journal of Democracy* 16, no. 4: 144–58.

Henze, Paul B. 1995. "Ethiopia: The Collapse of Communism and the Transition to Democracy; Adjustment to Eritrean Independence." Santa Monica: RAND.

Hinnebusch, Raymond. 2006. "Authoritarian Persistence, Democratization Theory and the Middle East: An Overview and Critique." *Democratization* 13, no. 3: 373–95.

Holmquist, Frank, and Michael Ford. 1998. "Kenyan Politics: Toward a Second Transition?" *Africa Today* 45, no. 2: 227–58.

Jowitt, Ken. 1997. "Challenging the 'Correct' Line: Reviewing Katherine Verdery's *What Was Socialism, and What Comes Next?*" *East European Politics and Societies* 12, no. 1 (December): 87–106.

Kakuba, Sultan Juma. 2015. "Elections and Legitimacy in Authoritarian Regimes: A Comparative Study of Egypt and Sudan." *International Journal of Politics and Good Governance* 6, no. 6.1: 1–23.

Kefale, Asnake. 2013. *Federalism and Ethnic Conflict in Ethiopia: A Comparative Regional Study*. Routledge Series in Federal Studies. London: Routledge.

Kim, Nam Kyu. 2016. "Anti-regime Uprisings and the Emergence of Electoral Authoritarianism." *Political Research Quarterly* 70, no. 1 (March): 111–26.

Korbonski, Andrzej. 1999. "East Central Europe on the Eve of the Changeover: The Case of Poland." *Communist and Post-Communist Studies* 32, no. 2 (June): 139–53.

Kymlicka, Will. 2006. "Emerging Western Models of Multinational Federalism: Are They Relevant for Africa?" In *Ethnic Federalism: The Ethiopian Experience in Comparative Perspective*, edited by David Turton, 32–64. Eastern African Studies. Oxford: James Currey.

Leff, Carol. 1999. "Democratization and Disintegration in Multinational States: The Breakup of the Communist Federations." *World Politics* 51, no. 2 (January): 205–35.

Levitsky, Steven, and Lucan A. Way. 2010. *Competitive Authoritarianism: Hybrid Regimes after the Cold War*. Cambridge: Cambridge University Press.

———. 2013. "The Durability of Revolutionary Regimes." *Journal of Democracy* 24, no. 3 (July): 5–17.

Linz, Juan J., and Alfred Stepan. 1996. *Problems of Democratic Transition and Consolidation: Southern Europe, South America, and Post-Communist Europe*. Baltimore: Johns Hopkins University Press.

Markakis, John, and Nega Ayele. 1978. *Class and Revolution in Ethiopia*. Nottingham: Spokesman.

Menaldo, Victor A. 2012. "The Middle East and North Africa's Resilient Monarchs." *Journal of Politics* 74, no. 3 (July): 707–22.

Metaferia, Getachew. 2009. *Ethiopia and the United States: History, Diplomacy, and Analysis*. New York: Algora.

Mohamedou, Mohammad-Mahmoud Ould, and Timothy D. Sisk. 2013. "Bringing Back Transitology: Democratisation in the 21st Century." GCSP Geneva Papers.

Moore, Barrington, Jr. 1966. *Social Origins of Dictatorship and Democracy: Lord and Peasant in the Making of the Modern World*. Boston: Beacon.

Munck, Gerardo L., and Carol Skalnik Leff. 1997. "Modes of Transition and Democratization: South America and Eastern Europe in Comparative Perspective." *Comparative Politics* 29, no. 3 (April): 343–62.

Musisi, Frederic. 2016. "What Has Become of the 'New Breed' of Leaders?" *Daily Monitor*, March 27, 2016. www.monitor.co.ug/Magazines/PeoplePower/What-has-become-of-the-new-breed-of-leaders/689844-3134638-hficv1z/index.html.

O'Donnell, Guillermo, and Philippe C. Schmitter. 1986. *Transitions from Authoritarian Rule: Tentative Conclusions about Uncertain Democracies*. Baltimore: Johns Hopkins University Press.

Ottaway, Marina. 1995. "The Ethiopian Transition: Democratization or New Authoritarianism?" *Northeast African Studies* 2, no. 3: 67–84.

Pickel, A. 2002. "Transformation Theory: Scientific or Political?" *Communist and Post-Communist Studies* 35, no. 1 (March): 105–14.

Rafti, Marina. 2008. "A Perilous Path to Democracy: Political Transition and Authoritarian Consolidation in Rwanda." Discussion Paper, Institute of Development Policy and Management, University of Antwerp.

Rana, Aziz. 2017. "Kenya's New Electoral Authoritarianism." *Boston Review*, August 17, 2017. http://bostonreview.net/politics/aziz-rana-kenyas-new-electoral-authoritarianism.

Rustow, Dankwart A. 1970. "Transitions to Democracy: Toward a Dynamic Model." *Comparative Politics* 2, no. 3: 337–63.

Sarbo, Dima N. 2009. "Contested Legitimacy: Coercion and the State in Ethiopia." PhD diss., University of Tennessee.

Saxonberg, Steven, and Jonas Linde. 2003. "Beyond the Transitology—Area Studies Debate." *Problems of Post-Communism* 50, no. 3: 3–16.

Schedler, Andreas, ed. 2006. *Electoral Authoritarianism: The Dynamics of Unfree Competition*. Boulder, CO: Lynne Rienner.

Schmitter, Philippe C., and Terry Lynn Karl. 1994. "The Conceptual Travels of Transitologists and Consolidologists: How Far to the East Should They Attempt to Go?" *Slavic Review* 53, no. 1 (Spring): 173–85.

———. 1995. "From an Iron Curtain to a Paper Curtain: Grounding Transitologists or Students of Postcommunism?" *Slavic Review* 54, no. 4 (Winter): 965–78.

Stroh, Alexander. 2012. "The Effects of Electoral Institutions in Rwanda: Why Proportional Representation Supports the Authoritarian Regime." GIGA Working Paper No. 105 (July).

Tedin, Kent L. 1994. "Popular Support for Competitive Elections in the Soviet Union." *Comparative Political Studies* 27, no. 2 (July): 241–71.

Teorell, Jan. 2010. *Determinants of Democratization: Explaining Regime Change in the World, 1972–2006*. Cambridge: Cambridge University Press.

Teshale, Semir. 2018. "Insurgency in Ethnically Divided Authoritarian-led Societies: A Comparative Study of Rebel Movements in Ethiopia, 1974–2014." PhD diss., University of Toronto.

Tilly, Charles. 1985. "War Making and State Making as Organized Crime." In *Bringing the State Back In*, edited by Peter B. Evans, Dietrich Rueschemeyer, and Theda Skocpol. Cambridge: Cambridge University Press, 169–91.

———. 1990. *Coercion, Capital, and European States, AD 990–1990*. Cambridge, MA: Blackwell.

Tronvoll, Kjetil, and Daniel R. Mekonnen. 2014. *The African Garrison State: Human Rights & Political Development in Eritrea*. Rochester, NY: James Currey.

Vaughan, Sarah. 2003. "Ethnicity and Power in Ethiopia," PhD diss., University of Edinburgh.

———. 2011. "Revolutionary Democratic State-Building: Party, State and People in the EPRDF's Ethiopia." *Journal of Eastern African Studies* 5, no. 4: 619–40.

Verdery, Katherine. 1996. *What Was Socialism, and What Comes Next?* Princeton, NJ: Princeton University Press.

Wadekar, Neha. 2018. "Kenya's Dangerous Path Toward Authoritarianism." *New Yorker*, February 9, 2018. https://www.newyorker.com/news/news-desk/kenyas-dangerous-path-toward-authoritarianism.

Waltz, Kenneth N. 1979. *Theory of International Politics*. Reading, MA: Addison-Wesley.

Welsh, Helga A. 1994. "Political Transition Processes in Central and Eastern Europe." *Comparative Politics* 26, no. 4 (July): 379–94.

Wiarda, Howard J. 2001. "Southern Europe, Eastern Europe, and Comparative Politics: 'Transitology' and the Need for New Theory." *Eastern European Politics and Societies* 15, no. 3: 485–501.

Yusuf, Semir. 2019. *Drivers of Ethnic Conflict in Contemporary Ethiopia*. ISS Monograph no. 202, Institute for Security Studies.

1.3 Republican Renewal and Democratic Transition in Ethiopia

Medemer, a Lofty Mantra or a Laïcité for Contemporary Ethiopia?

Kebadu Mekonnen Gebremariam

Nowadays, no political doctrine commands more currency than that of national sovereignty and its attendant recourse to a collective right to self-determination. In Ethiopia, the idea, familiarly tagged as the "national question," has inspired movements that toppled both the imperial monarchy and later the Derg regime, which presided over the first Ethiopian republic. Prior to Prime Minister Abiy's administration, one marked feature of the Ethiopian People's Revolutionary Democratic Front's (EPRDF) reign was sustained mobilization of state power in defense of the ethnic federalism enshrined in the 1995 constitution, a period characterized by the recognition of multiple sovereignties operating within the Ethiopian state. Such a model left the nation a republic in name only, bereft of the minimal sovereignty necessary to maintain the modicum of character worthy of a true republic. And yet, claims for national sovereignty are still pertinent today and are invoked with renewed urgency as the boundaries of peoplehood are increasingly drawn more and more narrowly.

With its signature formula—*Medemer,* an Amharic word roughly translated as "convergence" or "coming together," which rhetorically resembles the Latin motto *e pluribus unum*—the new administration introduced extensive reforms signifying a radical break from the EPRDF's past. The structure and depth of the proposed reforms appear to indicate that *Medemer* is hardly an empty slogan freshly minted for the occasion. Instead, *Medemer* figures as an organizing ethos that sets in motion a profound shift towards the renewal of the underlying structure of our republic and the principles that underpin it. At least at the level of rhetoric, the doctrine redefines fraternity as a civic virtue exalted above the natural fetters of kinship and ethnicity. As a consequence, this paradigm shift moralizes the notion of a citizen while casting new light on the idea of public reason. The moral idea prods us to ask ourselves whether we are worthy citizens of the nation, whereas the idea of public reason is redefined in ways that weaken, and in some cases systematically preclude, the dictates of citizens' discordant and comprehensive doctrines from carrying weight on decisions pertaining to constitutional essentials and basic questions of justice.

For *Medemer* to be of enduring national significance, it is imperative that the idea is anchored on concrete constitutional and structural reforms that have the power to renew our fundamental social contract and transform this fragile republic into a stable and democratic nation. That means nothing short of the birth of the third republic. If that isn't the original intent, it certainly should be.

INTRODUCTION

This chapter attempts to present a critical reflection on republican renewal and democratic transition in Ethiopia. It contrasts the historical evolution of Ethiopian republicanism with the rich tradition of French republicanism and reflects on what a young republic like Ethiopia can learn from the latter. After having put the historical lessons in perspective, this chapter examines the sweeping reforms towards democratization that the current prime minister has introduced. This chapter explores Prime Minister Abiy Ahmed's *Medemer* thought, and it closes with a plea for taking seriously the existential threat the republic faces due to the ethnically charged political climate.

The two perennial questions that fomented the Ethiopian Student Movement (ESM) of the 1960s and 1970s—namely the land question and the national question—invariably inspired revolutions that toppled both Haile Selassie and the Derg regimes. While the Derg regime suppressed the national question in favor of the other, the EPRDF reversed the course by adopting the national-question-comes-first view, presuming that the land question would resolve itself once national self-determination was granted to the nations, nationalities, and peoples of Ethiopia (NNPs). The institutionalization of ethnic federalism was a watershed moment purported to have settled the national question once and for all. Instead, the strategy essentializes and, as a consequence, turns to stone what it professes to recognize (a condition conveniently termed the Medusa syndrome). It therefore inflames rather than redresses historic fractures within the Ethiopian body politic, contrary to what the national-question-comes-first camp would have us believe. If one says that the national question is the power broker of recent party politics in Ethiopia, that won't be very far off the mark.

Let us now turn to elucidate the basic tenets and historical turns of French republicanism and explore what, if anything, we can learn from it.

REPUBLICANISM AS A POLITICAL IDEAL

The history of French republicanism provides an excellent blueprint for examining questions pertinent to the nature and value of republicanism both as a political ideal and as political practice. As a political ideal, it is rooted in the ideas that underpin the French Revolution and in the Enlightenment that precedes it. Republicanism is also characterized by a set of institutions that confer a formal and stable platform, albeit with a similar political temper, to the revolutionary tradition that helps mainstream the latter into public political life. The revolutionary strand sought, and still seeks, to restore the natural moral equality between all human beings, presumptively through the formal abolition of hierarchy in civic, social, and political life. Equality in civic status means that the aristocracy is no longer the sole custodian of superior regard and deference but that the revolution injects an upward equalization of rank. It conveys the idea that every citizen is now accorded the same standing and deference—an equal dignity—interpreted in terms of a bundle of rights and privileges that were invariably accorded to the nobility (Waldron 2012), hence the birth of a transcending form of citizenship—an equal status that supersedes an individual's circumstances of birth, class, and other markers of social standing. Not only has the revolutionary strand stipulated the organizing norms of the republic—*liberté, égalité*, and *fraternité*—but it also carved out for citizens civil and political rights that function within a corresponding sphere of freedoms, including freedom of thought and political expression and freedom of religion. The revolutionary spirit sought to interpret a moral conviction about the inherent equality between all human beings in political terms and hopes the institutions built in its wake shall correspond to this with great precision. In contrast to the egalitarian ethos that underpins modern republics, according to Hannah Arendt, Athenians adopted a legal precept of treating freeborn male citizens as equals merely for the pragmatic reason that it made possible the vibrant political community they wouldn't otherwise have (1977, 278), whereas the modern conception of equal citizenship is principally grounded on the moral conviction about the inherent equality of all human beings.

Certainly there were republics as far back as antiquity in the time of Greek city-states, whereas notions of religious toleration and freedom of political expression emerged in England within the monarchical system.[1] What characterizes modern republics would seem to be the set of institutions and the unity of normative direction between them; modern republics are constituted by constitutions, a bill of rights, elections, an independent judiciary, and safeguards to the person and private property. "These institutions, and many others, create a republican mentality, a recognisable political culture that informs the identity of the population and underpins its politics." (Livesey 2001, 49). One can say that the republican model of citizenship is deeply embedded in French public life, whose guidance extends beyond direct participation in public political life. The republican ethos that dictates the strict separation between the private and public domains was evident when, for instance, an overwhelming majority of the French public showed disinterest in holding President François Hollande culpable for a sexual liaison while married, when a similar affair would have ignited a political storm in the United States. Even the president of the republic, with all the powers vested in him, would not be regarded as having forfeited his rights as a private citizen, especially what the term private in private citizen entails: his right to privacy.

Both the revolutionary and institutional strands of French republicanism are best understood as mutually reinforcing, although historically they sometimes stood at odds with one another. There were moments of great strife during the early republican years, when the spirit of the revolution was under sustained attack from Robespierre and the Jacobin faction that he founded, during which Tocqueville observed, "Of all ideas and sentiments which prepared the Revolution, the notion and the taste of public liberty, strictly speaking, have been the first ones to disappear." However, it is not uncommon for citizens, in sync with the revolutionary tradition, to mobilize themselves for addressing particular problems of profound national significance. In time of crisis when, for instance, the institutions of the republic have failed to exact justice against rogue elements of the military and, as a consequence, proved to be impotent to safeguard the rights of citizens, or when the institutions are undermined by the insolence of power, then the revolutionary moment would be called upon to inspire citizens into political action. In those situations, institutional republicans seek to draw guidance from the revolutionary ideals of *liberté*, *égalité*, and *fraternité*. In the following section, I turn to a historical example where the revolutionary impulse served as the republic's saving grace.

THE DREYFUS AFFAIR AND *LAÏCITÉ*

French republicanism has evolved over time, undergoing four fundamental renewals to date (hence the talk of France's five republics), where each moment of transformation is usually preceded by pressing political concern or crisis of great national significance. No political scandal has had a more enduring effect to the republic than what has come to be known as the Dreyfus affair. It lived in infamy from 1894 until its initial resolution in 1906, yet the shockwaves vexed the nation for decades more. It began with the conviction for treason of Alfred Dreyfus, a French artillery captain of Jewish descent accused of passing French military secrets to the Germans via their embassy in Paris. It came to pass that his conviction was motivated by anti-Semitism. Two years after his banishment to Devil's Island—a penal colony in French Guiana—new evidence has surfaced indicating that the real traitor was Major Ferdinand Walsin Esterhazy. However, in an attempt to save face, higher military officials suppressed evidence, which led to the acquittal of Esterhazy by the military court. On top of that, the army responded with more charges against Dreyfus, based on fabricated documents. That did not, however, vanquish the affair from reaching the public; words about the conspiracy came out courtesy of the infamous editorial entitled "J'accuse...!" in which the writer Émile Zola vehemently denounced the injustice committed against Dreyfus. The affair revealed a profound rift in French society, as two opposing camps soon emerged: pro-republican Dreyfusards, consisting of intellectuals and students, and the promilitary anti-Dreyfusards, comprised of an amorphous ensemble of right-wing nationalists, Catholic traditionalists, and monarchists. It came to pass that the students confronted the right-wing nationalists and settled their differences with an embittered fight on the streets of Paris that ended in the defeat of the anti-Dreyfusards. "The Dreyfus affair showed that, when threatened, the institutional republicans could rely on the revolutionary tradition to rally even their left-wing political opponents" (Livesey 2001, 50).

Consequently, a law was passed in 1905 that declared a strict separation of church and state, prohibiting state recognition of any religion. That effectively banned state funding of any religion, religious teaching in public schools, and the display of religious apparel by individuals in the public space. The 1905 law laid the foundation for the establishment of *laïcité* as a core constitutional principle, although the term *laïcité* did not figure once in it. The word appears in the legal lexicon much later, courtesy of the constitution of 1946 (the Fourth Republic), which describes France as an indivisible, secular, democratic, and social republic (*"La France est une République indivisible, laïque, démocratique et sociale"*). Nowadays, *laïcité* is not only a fundamental legal concept and republican principle, it is also an organizing norm of French public life on which the civility, chivalry, and social faux pas of everyday life are predicated.

There are at least two takeaways from the Dreyfus affair from which a young republic like ours can draw lessons. One relates to the idea that republican states should approach religious tolerance with great diligence and care, that they must strike a balance between freedom of belief, including the mandatory respect in regard to that, and the uncritical diffusion of religious doctrines in public political discourse, regardless of how reasonable such doctrines might be. With *laïcité* regarded as a core constitutional concept, French republicanism stipulates the boundaries of public reason, framing the realm of the permissible in alignment with—and in the manner conducive to the entrenchment of—the foundational principles of republicanism. As a consequence of that, the French republic averts the perpetual danger posed by religious persuasion morphing into a recognizable political identity. Denying political salience to religious identity forecloses one potential pathway for anti-republican sentiments that could manifestly threaten social cohesion from gaining traction in the public sphere. This may be seen as a practical attempt at realizing Jean-Jacques Rousseau's vision of a free society as one that makes personal freedom compatible with citizenship of a nation. It is the vision of society as an entity holding a distinct moral status with a monopoly of force and a prerogative for self-preservation, although its existence is predicated upon the social compact of its members, "whose life and liberty are naturally independent of it" ([1762] 1998, 31). What seems to be in the best interest of the body politic does not necessarily align with the particular and competing interests of citizens. The question is, Rousseau interjects, "to distinguish clearly between the respective rights of the citizens and of the sovereign, as well as between the duties which the former have to fulfil in their capacity as subjects and the natural rights which they ought to enjoy in their character as men" ([1762] 1998, 31). I shall add that, amongst the republican values, *laïcité* appears to explicitly impose limitations on the sphere of religious expression to the extent it draws a strict separation between freedom of worship in the private sphere and judgments about what is important in the public sphere or constrains what counts as permissible use of public reason.

Secondly, not only does *laïcité* complement the revolutionary triad—liberty, equality, fraternity—it also provides the substantive thread by which they are sewn together. It proclaims that the social contract that underpins the legitimacy of the sovereign reflects no particular identity or comprehensive religious doctrine. And to the extent that the constraints *laïcité* brings to bear on the sphere of permissible discourse ostensibly clarifies the basis of the social pact, it underwrites fraternity. Rousseau is on point when emphasizing the deeper significance to the body politic of the citizens' uncritical regard of the public space as a platform or marketplace for competing interests (particular wills). Such regard of public reason where it is permissible for private parochial interests to pervade the public realm, Rousseau warned, "would bring about the ruin of the body politic." The more plausible alternative is to proclaim that a particular will has no purchase in the determination of the common good through public deliberation. Whenever a particular will conflicts with the common interest (general will), the latter gets lexical priority and at the same time becomes categorically binding on the individual members of society. Rousseau explains that,

> for such is the condition which, uniting every citizen to his native land, guarantees him from all personal dependence, a condition that ensures the control and working of the political machine, and alone renders legitimate civil engagements, which without it, would be absurd and tyrannical, and subject to enormous abuse. ([1762] 1998, 18)

The significance of *laïcité* extends all the way down to the fundamental intuition that a democratic republic is best conceived as a cooperative social arrangement predicated on the criterion of reciprocity. And one of the preconditions of reciprocity is for citizens to contend with—and act in recognition of—the fact that "they cannot reach agreement or even approach mutual understanding on the basis of their irreconcilable comprehensive [religious, philosophical, and moral] doctrines" (Rawls 2001, 132). This is, therefore, to say that a reasonable public political discourse must presume that these doctrines are reasonable, and must be accorded due recognition and respect, but cannot be deployed as the right kind of reasons that citizens may give one another on matters pertaining to constitutional essentials.

The question of whether other identity-conferring comprehensive doctrines or features of the human condition, such as familial, clan, and ethnic ties, should be immune to exclusion from substantive debates about fundamental political questions is just one of the many conundrums this chapter seeks to address. Of course, those who reject the form of republicanism that adopts constitutional democracy will of course have a different answer to the question. It seems fair to assume that essentialist communitarian views about political relations would basically populate the public political discourse with the various versions of one overarching question: What would be the right or true interest of society X (clan or ethnicity) and of individual Y simply by virtue of sharing that lineage? One who rejects the notion of a political community as a cooperative venture and justice as a fair arrangement of such a relation may find it disconcerting that this chapter does not engage with his/her view. Insofar as the political relation is conceived as congenital or lineal, the political arrangement favored by a society thus defined would be incompatible with the essentials of a constitutional and democratic polity. Although it is conceivable for essentialist communitarian doctrines to adopt a democratic system of governance, in such cases the latter would simply be incidental rather than an indispensable element of the former.

Whereas maintaining the background presumption that democratic constitutionalism is a sound political theory and republicanism is a legitimate doctrine for the state, whether clan interests count as "the kinds of reasons citizens can reasonably give one another when fundamental political questions are at stake" (Rawls 2001, 132) would remain a pertinent question to ask. In particular, the following questions suggest themselves: If we have valid grounds to separate state and religion, must we not similarly conceive of a separation between clan and state as equally justified? If republicanism denies political salience to the sanctity of religious beliefs, ought it not also reject the sanctity of tribal identity "when fundamental political questions are at stake"? Wouldn't a further step in the evolution of republicanism be a constitutional adoption of a remodeled notion of *laïcité* as an antidote to tribalism?

I shall address these questions in the penultimate section of this chapter when exploring the normative significance of the *Medemer* philosophy, which the current administration of the Federal Democratic Republic of Ethiopia (FDRE) espouses as its fundamental guiding principle for transforming the country into a profoundly democratic republic. Can *Medemer* help redefine the nation in terms that accommodate but at the same time transcend ethnicity, clan, and religious and regional differences? To be clear, in public political discourse of late any reference to a transcending national identity is often met with furor by people with an ethnocentric bent, where advocates for transcending petty tribalism consequently are branded as reactionary chauvinists, hell-bent on invoking the ghosts of imperial past. With respect to that, imperceptible progress has been made in contemporary discourse in Ethiopia from what it used to be during the revolutionary period (1961–91). It is pointless to beat the same drum in exactly the same way we used to and expect a different tune to suddenly play out. We must, therefore, disentangle the vision for a transcending idea of the Ethiopian nation—conceived as a political identity—from two closely allied notions. One is a quasi-metaphysical idea of transcendence, which confers some measure of a historical deterministic gloss over national identity, implying that one becomes an Ethiopian as such by fate, not by choice or historical happenstance. The other is homogeneity; to think of a nation as a transcending political entity, in this sense, is to think of it as a monolithic cultural behemoth that swallows many cultural minions then spits them out as its own incarnates. When asking whether the most important insights we can draw from the *Medemer* maxim includes a novel way of conceiving the Ethiopian nation as transcending differences, it should be clear that by transcending I do not intend to imply either transcendentalism or homogeneity.

A BRIEF ACCOUNT OF REPUBLICANISM IN ETHIOPIA: HISTORY, PATTERNS, AND FAULT LINE

Ethiopian republicanism is the offspring of the February 1974 revolution, which, owing to the radicalism that inspired it, drew comparisons with the French and Russian Revolutions. The revolution overthrew the imperial regime of Haile Selassie I; while it succeeded in dismantling the old sociopolitical structure, it failed to envision a new social order capable of resolving the underlying reasons that ostensibly triggered it—namely, the problem of land ownership and the question of nationalities. Both were the flagship slogans of the ESM, the main protagonist of the revolt against the monarchy. It was intuitive for different factions within the student movement to join forces against the medieval system of land ownership, which bled dry and rendered most of the peasantry subservient to the feudal class. Dismantling such an oppressive regime was justifiably the direct consequence of the moral impermissibility of having it in the first place. The radical student movement "translated the peasant lamentation, *daha tabadala, feteh taguadala* (the poor are mistreated, justice is trampled upon) into the call, *maret laarashu, tawagulat attesheshu* (land to the tiller, fight for it without retreat)" (Tibebu 2008, 347). However, their famous rallying cry, "land to the tiller," did not lend itself to a single concrete interpretation in terms of substantive land policy (up until the military regime had eventually nationalized all land, rural and urban alike). The radicals were not as good at replacing the ancien régime as they were at dismantling it. That partly explains the power vacuum created in the immediate aftermath of the February revolution and the relative ease with which the military junta rose to power.

With respect to the national question, two opposing views emerged, between nationalist movements on one side and the two prominent multinational Marxist organizations on the other. To be clear, all political movements of the time adopted Marxism as their ideological basecamp, to which they constantly return for guidance and propaganda. The first group espoused imperial Ethiopia as primarily characterized by Amhara hegemony over the nations and nationalities of Ethiopia. In this view, it was both morally imperative and politically necessary to solve the national question first; the normative primacy of the national question meant that all other questions, such as class, gender, and the plight of the peasantry, would find proper solutions once freedom was won for the nations and nationalities. The main adherents of this view included the Eritrean Liberation Front (ELF), Eritrean People's Liberation Front (EPLF), Tigrayan People's Liberation Front (TPLF), Oromo Liberation Front (OLF), and Western Somali Liberation Front (WSLF). Most within the "national-question-comes-first" view, with the exception of the TPLF ("despite some flirtation with the idea [of independence] in the early years of the movement" (Clapham 2002, 28)), believed in the colonial thesis, according to which Ethiopia is portrayed as a Semitic Christian colonial empire that lorded over other nations and nationalities with impunity, whose logical antidote is the right of nations and nationalities for self-determination up to secession.[2] Whereas the TPLF has in principle accepted Eritrea's right to self-determination, including secession, it did not openly identify its own national question as a colonial question, hence opening up the possibility of a solution to be found within Ethiopia.

The other group, however, advocated the class-solidarity-comes-first view. It is argued that such a view perfectly captures the basic tenet of Marxist ideology, according to which the class interests of workers override "superstructural manifestations of ethnicity" (Clapham 2002, 21), not to mention its strategic utility for transcending center/periphery divides within the Ethiopian state. Two prominent multinational Marxist parties—formed in 1975 and outwardly styling themselves as heir apparent to the ESM, with competing claims for impeccable revolutionary credentials—advocated that, although the national question is pertinent, the class question ought to be solved first. The parties were the Ethiopian People's Revolutionary Party (EPRP) and the All-Ethiopia Socialist Movement (AESM, often referred to by its Amharic acronym, MEISON). Each professed to be the true vanguard of the proletariat and its revolution, a claim that subsequently led to bloodshed that devoured a generation during the infamous period known as the Red Terror.[3] Like the French Revolution, the February revolution had given rise to a new brand of political actors on the scene: the professional revolutionist, homme de lettres, whose life is spent "in study and thought, in theory and debate, whose sole object was revolution" (Arendt 1977, 258–59). Although these intellectual radicals-turned-politicians initially forged a strategic alliance with the Eritrean rebels, in what Markakis can only describe as "a clever exercise in ideological sophistry" (2011, 163), they invoked the Marxist schema to reject the colonial thesis and, as a consequence, justify their refusal to recognize the existence of an Eritrean nation. There was never a historical correlation between feudalism and colonialism, hence the argument runs, and the idea of Ethiopia as a feudal colonialist empire would be preposterous. Furthermore, according to one of the leading intellectuals of the revolutionary generation, Andreas Eshete, "The transition from nationality to nation can be affected only through the abolition of feudal relations and the introduction of bourgeois relations. This did not take place in Eritrea" (1970, 15; see also Markakis 2011, 163). This is not to say that student radicals and the Marxist parties they established were unsympathetic to the national question; instead they naively thought that the ideology provided a plausible model for dealing with it.

This faction of the student radicals sought to reconcile their fervent defense of the territorial sovereignty of the state with, by the standards of the day, the irreverent claim that the assimilationist project had resulted in tyrannical oppression of the various nationalities of the state. The radicalism of the day swept away the possibility for reconciling their defense of the territorial integrity of the Ethiopian state (which the main factions within the ESM stood in passionate defense of) with the now-deconstructed concept of the nation. Initially, the perceived promises of the revolution and the high spirits that attended the birth of the new body politic conferred optimism and a sense of progress, but it was not accompanied by grave concern from those who engaged in revolutionary agitation with the justice, stability, and durability of the new structure of government. The failure can be partly explained by the Marxist intellectuals' obsession with the social question and partly by the fact that their decisions and behavior were dictated by considerations of party strife, which blindsided them from paying serious attention to questions of state and government.

In keeping up with the student radicals, the military junta (the Derg) officially adopted Marxism as the regime's ideological substratum. However, its embrace of Marxism was borne out of necessity, not so much on account of a profound understanding of its purported merits. As an act of self-preservation, it played one-up with the student radicals, sensing an ominous disaster should the radicals succeed in upstaging its authority. The soldiers perceived that center control was slipping and swiftly proceeded with a declaration of *Andinet* (unity) and *Ethiopia Tikdem* (Ethiopia First) as the nation's inviolable mottos. A clarification to *Ethiopia Tikdem* was subsequently printed in the *Ethiopian Herald* (December 23, 1975) that affirmed the "equality of all nationalities in Ethiopia," followed by a forbidding declaration that "Ethiopia shall remain a united country, without ethnic, religious, linguistic and cultural differences."

There are a few meaningful ways in which the Ethiopian Revolution (or the era of revolutions, to be precise) differs from the French Revolution. One significant difference is that during the period of upheaval (1961–91), Ethiopia went through three turbulent revolutions at the same time, each with its own raison d'être pressing upon the country a peculiar set of puzzles to solve. These are the revolutions in Eritrea, Tigray, and Ethiopia at large (Tibebu 2008). Historians have noted that the thirty-year-long Eritrean Revolution was set in motion on September 1, 1961, with a single shot fired by Hamid Idris Awate (a Muslim) at Mount Adal, Eritrea. A year prior to that momentous incident, the ELF was formed by Muslim Eritrean students living in Cairo. Subsequently, inspired by the Eritrean revolt, Somali Muslims in the Ogaden and Oromo Muslims in Bale joined the uprising against what they perceived as tyrannical subjugation by a Christian empire. What began as a Muslim rebellion was later joined by non-Muslims, not only in Eritrea but all across the country, which ironically sowed the seeds of its demise as a principally Muslim movement. With the radical ESM bursting onto the political scene, the EPLF emerged as the dominant driving force and continued to lead the revolution until their triumphant march, hand-in-arms with the TPLF, on the streets of Addis Ababa in May 1991. Victory over the Derg led to Eritrea's secession from Ethiopia, and the rest is history.

The Tigrayan Revolution began in earnest with the formation of the TPLF in 1975, shortly after the February 1974 Ethiopian Revolution.

Although historically Tigray has retained a measure of political autonomy since as far back as *Zemana Mesafint* (the Era of Princes), there was festering resentment against the economic dependence and loss of power against the distant center of power long before the TPLF's existence, which induced resistance testament to the first Woyane rebellion, in 1943. The rebellion was "later 'reinvoked' to serve as both precedent and call to arms for the TPLF's nationalist struggle in the late 1970s" (Vaughan 2003, 153).

The third, the all-Ethiopian revolution, has more affinity with the 1960 attempted coup led by the Neway brothers (General Mengistu Neway and his Western-educated brother, Germame Neway). The coup was a watershed moment that shook the foundations of Haile Selassie's government, and it was widely considered as "the spark that ignited the fire of student radicalism" (Tibebu 2008, 346).[4] Bahru Zewde eloquently described its ripple effects: "The torch of change that the rebels had kindled was not extinguished with their physical elimination. On the contrary, it sparked a more outspoken and radical opposition to the regime" (Zewde 2001, 214). The seeds of resistance thus planted came to fruition in the mid-1970s when the student movement, in alliance with mutinous elements of the military, deposed the emperor and effectively put an end to the centuries-old imperial order. The revolution itself was largely bloodless, but many of the events that followed in its wake proved otherwise, as violence spread like a raging fire in a forest that had accumulated too much deadwood.

Returning to the point of difference between the French and Ethiopian Revolutions—unlike the French Revolution, the trinity of revolutions Ethiopia went through are characterized by a lack of unity of purpose due to the broader range of problems that triggered them, not to mention the center/periphery divide reflected in each of the three distinct revolutions. The principal driving force for any of the three revolutions, if anything, was never in the first instance republican in intent. In 1974, Ethiopia became a republic not by design but stumbled upon it pretty much by accident as the chain of events had led to that. The age of revolutions was led by rebels and radicals who neither had the temperament for civility nor an appetite for civilian government. Two recurring Marxist-inspired agendas manifested throughout the trinity of revolutions: national self-determination (including and up to secession) on the one hand and the desire for establishing a proletariat dictatorship within the purview of the state inherited from the feudal empire on the other. In either case, the end either implies the disintegration of the state into multiple sovereignties or presupposes a future utopian (in reality, dystopian) ideal superseding any ties to the republic. According to the Marxist creed, the idea of a state is itself a product of a bourgeois society and must, eventually, be discarded.

For all intents and purposes, the 1960 attempted coup d'état comes close to what could be loosely described as a reformist coup, precisely an attempt at modernizing the state within the confines of the existing tradition of authority. The rebels remained loyal to the traditional system of power and authority, as they asked Crown Prince Asfaw Wossen to broadcast a proclamation, evidently under duress, announcing "the new Ethiopian Government formed by me" (Greenfield 1965, 377ff.). Yet there is no evidence to suggest that the underlying intent was transitioning the state to republicanism. With the exception of a vague reference to the new "government of the people," in the rebel broadcasts "there [was] very little appeal to 'liberal' themes, such as constitutional reform, human rights, elections, and the return to civilian rule, which one might expect in the overthrow of a dictatorial regime" (Clapham 1968, 503). Given the secrecy with which the plot was held and the fact that none of the major plotters lived to tell their truth, making an inference as to whether or not leaders of the coup had concealed motives for a more drastic change to be had *a posteriori* (in the event of success) would be speculative at best.

One significant disadvantage had by Ethiopian radicals, in contrast to their French counterparts, with whom they are separated by almost two centuries, was the dearth of indigenous intellectual tradition congenial to republican thought that they could draw guidance from. It would be fair to say that, in contrast, the French Revolution drew currency from the rich intellectual and cultural tradition provided by the European Enlightenment. Conversely, the Ethiopian radicals' enchantment with Marxism "was episodic and died in its infancy" and "it was event-driven, and event-impressed" (Tibebu 2008, 349). A mere five years transpired between the ESM's official adoption of Marxism (1969) and the outbreak of the revolution in 1974—perhaps enough time to wholesale regurgitate what they had taken in but clearly precious little time to digest, analyze, and properly appropriate the theory in ways that aligned with the Ethiopian context. It might be that Marxism-Leninism is inherently impervious to adaptation or that the radicals' understanding of Ethiopian culture, history, value systems, and conceptual and linguistic frameworks was skin deep. The truth may consist of an element of both. One common denominator of Marxism-Leninism, as it was tried and tested in diverse places across the world (from Stalinist USSR, DPRK, Maoist China, and Cambodia during the Khmer Rouge, to Ethiopia during the Derg) during the twentieth century, is that the doctrine invariably kindles a passion for violence and has hundreds of millions of corpses to show for it. That speaks a lot as to why some commentators labeled its Ethiopian variant as *Chingaf* (miscarriage) Marxism and correctly so, since Marxism had not taken root in Ethiopia when its dictates were dispatched as marching orders for sending young people to what turned out to be the gallows and slaughter houses of revolutionary action.

There is, however, a richer and sophisticated indigenous intellectual culture in Ethiopia that is rooted in the traditional scholasticism of the Ethiopian Orthodox Church (EOC):

> This intelligentsia produced a fine coterie of first-rate scholars including Mahetmeselassie Woldemaskal, Mekonnen Endalkachew, Taklatsadeq Mekuria, Saifu Mahtemeselassie, Kebede Mikael, and Haddis Alemayehu, to name but few. . . . This intelligentsia had a reformist bent; it advocated change in Ethiopia, but not in a revolutionary manner. It admired modern Western civilization (*me'erabawi seletane*). Its admiration had limits, though. It was mostly the material–technical know-how of the Western world that attracted this group of intellectuals. They opted to appropriate from Western modernity those aspects that were acceptable to Ethiopia's own needs. They called for an *appropriate appropriation* of Western modernity on Ethiopian grounds, rejecting anything that goes counter to Ethiopia's culture and honour. The so-called Japanizers fall into this category. (Tibebu 2008)[5]

The radical Marxists shunned these intelligentsia, branding them as "bourgeois," "feudal," "*adhari*" (reactionary), and so on, partly due to the radicals' manifest contempt of the EOC with which the latter are associated. They despised the EOC for its unflappable allegiance to the Crown. Consequently, the radicals decided to throw the baby out with the bathwater when, ironically, their own appropriation of Marxism often mistook the chaff for the grain. This is therefore to say that the intellectual foundation of the

1974 revolution was neither organic nor did it manage to appropriate the Marxist paradigm in ways tailor-made to the specific Ethiopian situation. For reasons of space, I leave further reflections on this topic for another occasion.

BEYOND THE AGE OF REVOLUTIONS: EPRDF ETHIOPIA AND STATE RECONSTRUCTION

The EPRDF was established by the TPLF and Ethiopian People's Democratic Movement (EPDM) two years before the total capitulation of the Derg army, which crystalized into the rebels' capturing of Addis Ababa in May 1991. The Oromo People's Democratic Organization (OPDO) and the (later disbanded) Ethiopian Democratic Officers' Revolutionary Movement (comprised of a small group of captured Derg soldiers) joined the coalition later. Currently, the EPRDF consists of four political parties: the TPLF, Amhara Democratic Party (ADP), Oromo Democratic Party (ODP), and Southern Ethiopian People's Democratic Movement (SEPDM).

Although the EPRDF appeared to have renounced (at least in rhetoric) Marxist-Leninist ideology upon entry into the Menelik palace, it clearly deploys the same ideological tools in its institutional approach to solving the national question. The project of ethnic federalism,[6] later given constitutional grounding with a clear legal recourse to self-determination including and up to secession, was widely viewed by the leaders as an instrument that would deter, defuse, and neutralize, rather than foster and radicalize ethnonationalist sentiments. This is like overfeeding a beast in the hope that it will get too big—thus docile and apparently tamed—to pursue and bite you. Not only is such a conviction practically proven wrong, it reveals an underlying tension between two elements in Marxist-Leninist-Stalinist (MLS) thinking about nationalities and self-determination. The first is the intuitive idea that effective social mobilization is an inside job, that it should be done by utilizing to that effect the modes of self-definition, including the cultural traditions, knowledge, and value systems of a given community. MLS framework permits that a vanguard party can even engineer the form and content such mobilization could take, which is clearly consistent with the social-constructivist view. The second element of MLS thought rather prescribes objective criteria for what counts as "nation," "nationality," or "people," identifiable from the outside regardless of how their members view themselves. This opens the door for a vanguard party—in our case, the EPRDF—to stipulate the boundaries between "nations, nationalities, and peoples" and demarcate regional boundaries and subregional administrative arrangements, then granting such demarcation the right to self-governance. The 1995 constitution established nine regional states and two municipal administrations within the federation, where state borders are delimited on the basis of "language, identity, settlement patterns, and consent of the people concerned" (as per Art. 46, Sec. 2 of the constitution). The EPRDF's policy regarding ethnic federalism embodies both incompatible modes of "primordialism (the notion of the intrinsic 'naturalness' of certain nations and nationalities, and [the] corresponding idea that a 'correct' map of their location can be drawn up) and of instrumentalism (suggestive of the political mobilisation and construction of a malleable ethnic identity)" (Vaughan 2003, 170).

In EPRDF Ethiopia, the land issue is juxtaposed with, and its moral appeal circumscribed by, the national question, lending itself to an endless cycle of territorial claims as a means for redressing historical injustices the peasantry has endured since the *Gebbar* system. Using this blunt instrument that is ethnic federalism, the EPRDF prides itself on having provided a workable formula for addressing the land question precisely by rendering the slogan "land to the tiller" superfluous. In contrast to the unionist wing of student radicals and the Derg regime, who invoked class solidarity to attenuate the secessionist group, by flipping the script the EPRDF invokes national self-determination to address the land question in one sweep. With the establishment of ethnically defined regions and the preference for political mobilization from the inside of the community comes a necessary designation of individuals as "native" and "settler" in places that are not ethnically homogeneous. Some regional constitutions explicitly grant ownership of the regional state to specified groups (notably the constitutions of the Oromia, Tigray, Benishangul, Afar, Somali, and Harari regional states), whereas the constitutions of the Amhara and Southern Nations, Nationalities and Peoples' made no explicit reference to designated custodians of the respective regions but made some generic allusions to the peoples residing there. In some parts of Amhara, for instance, 30–45 percent of the population is ethnic Oromo, whereas Amhara and Gurage constitute a large contingent of people who live in cities and settlements across the country (Joireman 1997, 405–6). Since territories are delineated as ethnic homelands and political representation is organized on the same grounds, some groups take that as an opportunity to claim exclusive "ethnic rights" over land, which resulted in ethnic tensions. These tensions are sometimes induced, nurtured, and inflamed by politicians from the presumably indigenous groups, which often crystallized into ethnic cleansing. Since the 1990s, a wave of conflicts over land has gripped the country, most notably the Anuak massacre of December 2003 in Gambella ("Targeting the Anuak" 2005), deadly clashes between Gumuz and Oromo in eastern Wollega in 2008 (Smith 2007, 6), and large-scale fighting between the Guji and Gedeo over the control of Hagere Mariam district in 1998 (Tronvoll 2000, 22). The country is still reeling from massacres and large-scale displacements of people between the Oromia and Somali regions, tensions between Qemant and Amhara over regional and administrative issues in north Gondar, forced evictions and attacks on "non-native" civilians around the outskirts of Addis Ababa, and the humanitarian crisis in Gedeo/West Guji, with over 620,000 internally displaced persons living in limbo amidst acute malnutrition. (Reliefweb 2019). Hannah Arendt posited that "corruption of the people themselves—as distinguished from corruption of their representatives or a ruling class—is possible only under a government that has granted them a share in public power and *has taught them how to manipulate it*" (1963, 252). Her remarks hit the right chord in explaining the social corruption and loss of moral compass in Ethiopia, which admittedly is not always accompanied by manifest intolerance of others (defined in ethnolinguistic terms) and the active desire to commit aggression towards them. On top of social corruption, there must be a sustained campaign to install a narrow conception of identity loaded with the vocabulary resentment and bitterness in the hearts and minds of people. Similarly, Amartya Sen asserted that "violence is fomented by the imposition of singular and belligerent identities on gullible people, championed by proficient artisans of terror" (2006, 2).

It has been argued that, at least as far as Ethiopia is concerned, the relation between ethnolinguistic federalism and conflicts is not merely incidental but can be essentially tied to the inherent contradictions within the Marxist ideology on which the EPRDF's policy is grounded.[7] The problem appears more complex and deeper than inherent tension within the constituent elements of the Marxist thought about nationalities and their right to self-determination (International Crisis Group 2009).

HOMOGENEITY, ESSENTIALISM, AND THE MEDUSA SYNDROME

Neither nationalism nor the idea of self-determination are objectionable concepts in and of themselves, as most people tend to agree that "we are entitled to rule ourselves." This idea of collectively sharing the public affair with citizens is precisely what the ancients called liberty (Constant 1819). What is contested is who precisely the "we" consists of. The boundaries of the "we" can either be expanded or narrowed down depending on the collective vision and aspirations of a given body politic. Although throughout history boundaries have been drawn to demarcate "we" from the others, the mistake is in thinking that those boundaries are natural. There are no natural boundaries. "Once you move beyond the village world of the face-to-face, a people is always going to be a community of strangers. That is a first quandary—one of scale," writes Kwame Appiah (2018, 74). The incest taboo forecloses the root to the homogenization of society through a direct line of shared ancestry. But that is not what people generally mean when they invoke the ancestral line of argument; it is mostly about communal, ethnic, or tribal ties, shared cultural heritage, origin myth, history, and language. Shared lineage, whether real or imagined, is in itself no guarantee for shared character; it requires the subjective condition that there is a strong and enduring sense in the hearts and minds of people that they belong to a nation. It does not, however, necessarily follow that every time both conditions are met it must be matched with political arrangements requiring the creation of a state. There are more nations than states in the world, and the term nation-state is routinely used to designate a fraction of the latter wherein a nation is coincident with a state. But this is not to say that nationhood is the exclusive domain of people with common ancestry; on the contrary, a sense of belonging to a nation is often cultivated as a result of a shared psychological makeup manifested in a common culture. Furthermore, given "the great diversity of ways in which we could carve out our ancestries" (Appiah 2018), we have to give up the notion of "the intrinsic naturalness of certain nations and nationalities," along with the desired homogenization, on the road to claiming nationhood. To be clear, my claim is not that Ethiopia is a natural entity and not a social construct. All nations are social constructs of one sort or another, whether the notion is construed in terms of tribal or civic terms, whereas one of the main objections of ethno-nationalists against the

Ethiopian state is that the latter lacks normative primacy because ethnocultural identities are intrinsically natural. Thus, my argument is simply that civic national identities are more in accord with the democratic aspirations of modern republics. They are open to value pluralism, while at the same time taking seriously the normative separateness of individuals.

The problem is that when you take out the everyone-is-a-kin premise from the thesis that one group's claim to nationhood has a greater claim to reason (as opposed to alternative ways of organizing a nation), the claim itself loses its purported normative force. This is one great hurdle faced by those who wish to build states around nations, and the fact that most societies are large and heterogeneous adds further complexity to state building.

In EPRDF Ethiopia the establishment of ethnic federalism epitomizes the problems just noted. Christopher Clapham states that "in reconstituting itself in ethnic terms," Ethiopia "has adopted what some might see as a peculiarly anthropological approach to state-building" (2002, 27). Ethiopia is believed to have set a dangerous precedent for other African states who struggle to reconstitute themselves into civic nations. "The belief that ethnicity is divisive and undermines national unity informs the constitutional and political discourse of many African states throughout the post-colonial period," writes Solomon Dersso (2012, 67). Accordingly, most pluralistic African states either directly prohibit or discourage the political mobilization of people on the basis of group identity, specifically along ethnic, religious, or linguistic lines. Interestingly enough, such a vision for establishing a civic nation is reminiscent of ideas derived from the eighteenth-century Enlightenment thinkers who with Ernest Renan declare that "to make politics depend upon ethnographic analysis is to surrender it to a chimera" ([1882] 1990, 14).

Ethnic, cultural, and religious plurality, and the politicization of those identities, are not facts in which Ethiopia differs from much of the rest of contemporary Africa. It differs precisely in conferring political salience to ethnic identity by going further than any African country to constitutionally declare that political sovereignty is invested in ethnic groups. An effort to recognize diversity and confer respect to identities through a national project of respectful accommodation is certainly a noble pursuit every pluralistic state should advance. This includes the recognition of the need to redress historic injustices as a precondition to strengthening the national fellowship and the reconstitution of the state as an act of affirmation. Needless to say, the making of the individual is inherently social in the sense that essential features of one's personality, the values one adopts, one's sense of self and dignity, and even one's perceptions are molded by and through membership to a community. To the extent that the most constitutive elements of personal identity are causally underpinned by membership to a community, according respect, recognition, and deference to the person inescapably requires a social framework where his/her group identity is recognized and protected. Moreover, it is often argued that "it is . . . only where their ethnic identity is recognized and protected that people with deep commitment to their ethnic identity can develop strong attachment to the state" (Dersso 2012, 72). There is some truth to the notion that the individual draws meaning for his/her life within the communal context and that respect for the latter is an indispensable element of respect for persons.

However, recognition-respect to ethnic identity does not necessarily require that the state share its sovereignty with ethnically identified groups and consequently permit a legalized path towards the politics of tribalism. Recognition and protection were not the underlying motives when, for instance, Art. 8 of the 1995 constitution declared that "all sovereign power resides in the Nations, Nationalities and Peoples of Ethiopia": its motives were founded on upholding the NNPs with an essentializing gaze. "When the state gazes at us—with its identity cards, educational stipulations, and other instruments of recognition," Appiah insists, "it invariably fixes and rigidifies a phenomenon that is neither fixed nor rigid" (2018, 97).

Appiah called this tendency by the state to turn the malleable into the primordial and to eternalize whatever commands respect and reverence the Medusa syndrome. He writes, "what the state gazes upon, it tends to turn to stone. It sculpts what it purports merely to acknowledge" (2018, 97). Evidently, ethnicity is principally what the Ethiopian state gazes upon and incidentally turns to stone. As a consequence, it is not the citizens but the identities they bear that must be convinced (through their vanguard organizations) that we are engaged together in a meaningful national project. The individual citizen is conceived as an avatar for his group's privilege or handicap; as he is expected to embody his group's standing within the body politic, so in the same way he is burdened with playing the archetype of his group's privileges or victimhood. The perils of such thinking have brought this country on the verge of collapse. Paradoxically, the case for ethnic mobilization has often been defended as part of the struggle for human dignity, when in fact part of the popular appeal of ethnic tribalism is owing to its contempt for liberal individualism and its attendant ideal of the dignity of man. In response to the ethno-nationalist's identification of their demand for political sovereignty with respect for human dignity, Arendt quipped, "No human dignity is left if the individual owes his value only to the fact that he happens to be born a German or a Russian [or an Oromo, Amhara, Sidama or Wolayta]" ([1951] 2017, 306).

Ethnic radicalism is not the anomaly but the logical consequence of the strategy to essentialize identities as immutable building blocks of the state supra-structure. Identities are complex, and to govern them one must first have a predefined list within which individuals are to be categorized. Reality defeats such strategy not only because it is reductionist in approach but also because the system cannot be sustained unless one resorts to the Procrustean technique of stretching or chopping what does not fit (for instance, the mere existence of individuals with mixed lineage or cultural heritage defeats the purpose of ethnic classification). As Appiah puts it, "To set out to govern identities is to set out to govern the ungovernable" (2018, 105).

What does it entail for the Ethiopian republic? The recognition of multiple sovereignties undercuts some essential components of a viable republic. That took the monopoly of force away from the basic structure of the state to a marketplace of identities where each identity competes for its share of the general will. It is like getting into marriage by contemplating divorce or by signing a divorce agreement, for one does not enter into such an important social institution in good faith without marital vows that emphatically declares, "Till death do us part." So, in the same way, the very idea of entering into a social pact with the understanding that a group can divorce from the pact whenever it is disenchanted by it will be as good as not having entered into the pact in the first place. The divorce metaphor admittedly implies that when two entities have grown apart and reached the point of no return, perhaps separation is the only viable option. That is also true of the relationship between national and subnational entities. However, the point I take issue with is the following: should marriage be taken seriously as a social institution of value, one does not base articles of marriage on articles of divorce, as each has a different logic to it. Analogously, a national constitution whose principal source of legitimacy is the recognition of subnational sovereignty collapses under its own weight. The structural changes brought forth by the constitutionally mandated ethnic federalism has not only disrupted the Ethiopian state as a viable republic but also brought changes to our values themselves. Such an attempt at redefining national sovereignty consequently compromises our solidarity as fellow citizens, and thus it is not only counterproductive but also self-defeating. For in modern democracies, as Andreas Eshete and many others have eloquently argued, it is fraternity/solidarity and the recognition of human moral equality that it engenders that underpins liberty. Freedom rests on that recognition of human moral equality and is reflected in our ability to instantiate equality of respect and moral concern between persons in our economic, social, and political institutions (Allen 2014). In a society seeking to do away with hierarchies based on social class, culture, and religion, establishing a federal structure that in all likelihood encourages what George Washington called "the ill-concerted and incongruous projects of faction" would consequently put a dent on that society's democratic aspirations.

It is evident that, because of our diversity and history, we Ethiopians are not a singular ethnographic entity with a single unifying *Volksgeist*. Our history is punctuated by frequent dominations by one another at every level of the sociopolitical hierarchy, where dominant traditions emerged while others were relegated to the domain of the irrelevant, the irreverent, or worse, pushed to oblivion. But that has not stopped us from thinking of ourselves as Ethiopians during the Italian invasion or at the Olympics—an enduring sense of patriotism often revealed during social crisis or when disaster strikes, when we witness injustices done, both in times of war and peace. All that has drawn us together over the centuries, living under different governments and sometimes by wrestling power away and using it against each other. That is the fabric with which Ethiopia is woven, and as such a republican aspiration should reflect that lived experience.

And a republic that relinquishes its monopoly of power—its sovereign virtue—will in effect not be able to properly recognize my mixed parentage and accord respect to my desire not to be identified with either of them as my political identity. Therefore, as far as I am concerned, to continue with this ethnic federalism where there is no "conceptual place where my value of being an individual with inviolability can be preserved" (Mekonnen 2018) would amount to "taxation without representation." What is to become of my future children, whose mixed lineage will likely include an element of identity across national boundaries? What common destiny is there for them to look forward to? A republic that systematically disenfranchises people who do not fit into some narrative of the folk does not generate "a civic creed that is both potent and lean—potent enough to give significance to citizenship, lean enough to be shared by people with different ethnic and religious affiliations" (Appiah 2018, 103).

To reiterate, the problem was not with the appeal for the recognition and accommodation of ethno-cultural diversity; the problem was the particular form in which such an appeal for recognition often takes, precisely the intellectual sophistry deployed to hold that ethnic identity passes for a politically viable national identity. As Francis Fukuyama succinctly puts it, "The problem was the narrow, ethnically based, intolerant, aggressive, and deeply illiberal form that national identity took" (2018, 128). At the heart of ethno-national reactive attitudes, a conflation of two conceptions of negative freedom, namely freedom as noninterference and freedom as non-domination, are found. The argument for the equal recognition and accommodation of ethno-cultural diversity is underpinned by the conception of freedom as non-domination. The proper remedy for historical domination is freedom understood as non-domination. Non-domination encompasses the rights of the powerless and the disenfranchised to limit the powers of the majority or the most powerful to impose its will on them, whereas appeals to freedom as noninterference are sensible when posited in relation to the basic rights to privacy, freedom of thought and conscience, and freedom of belief and worship—best understood as the rights of persons (regardless of whether the individuals' thoughts, beliefs, or conceptions of the good are patterned such that they are attached to identifiable groups or identities). In this case, conceiving freedom as noninterference could be justified as a source of collective rights only if it signifies an appeal for the effective protection of individual rights in a pluralist society. But in locating the seat of sovereignty on NNPs and further designing the federal structure along those lines, the constitution clearly utilizes a sense of freedom as noninterference, "which appears to be in tune not with federalism but with arrangements of a confederation type" (Eshete 2003).

Noninterference, in its political-sovereignty-implying sense, can seldom serve as an appropriate model for freedom that subnational entities can legitimately claim against the national entity under a liberal democratic framework. In contrast, Will Kymlicka argues that recognition of the cultural particularity up to noninterference in the political expression of particular cultures accords with a liberal theory of multicultural citizenship (1996). Kymlicka also insists that mere recognition of particular cultures and a preservation of formal rights to equal concern are insufficient for "citizens to want to keep a multinational state together." Citizens must, therefore, value "not just deep diversity in general, but also the particular ethnic groups and national cultures with whom they currently share the country" (1996, 191). Moreover, Kymlicka thinks that legal intervention against illiberal national communities by the federal state is impermissible, except in extreme cases of the kind that would justify international intervention.

Eshete observes two notable problems with that. One relates to Kymlicka's insistence that citizens must actively value diverse cultures and ethnic groups within the country. This indicates, Eshete replies, "a clear admission that national identity may be based on something other than a distinct cultural identity." For one to find a justified reason to value and promote a culture belonging to others, a reason one can also find acceptable from one's own particular point of view, there must be independent grounds for identifying with the others whose cultures one is compelled to promote. Shared past history along with pride in historical achievements could serve as powerful sources of an enduring sense of nationality, admittedly a view Kymlicka shares. Therein lies the shaky foundation on which Kymlicka's thesis for a multicultural liberal state is grounded. In admitting that a political community is not necessarily rooted in culture, Kymlicka's claim for the unique significance of culture in reconfiguring the liberal multicultural state consequently loses its normative footing. If the liberal approach to multiculturalism is not grounded in culture, it begs the question why, according to Kymlicka, cultural plurality holds a unique normative status in contrast to, for instance, religious plurality. His argument is simply that the pursuit of a meaningful life requires membership in a particular culture—a true statement in and of itself but one that does not mean that secure membership in a religious group does not equally confer a value system informing individuals to lead a life of their own choice. Consequently, there is no reason to suppose that "the separation of state and religion cannot serve as a model for the relation between the state and ethnic or cultural identity."(Eshete 2003, unpublished) Eshete's second counterpoint links brilliantly with the refutation of Kymlicka's dubious assertion that membership in a particular culture must be considered as constitutive to the liberal conception of justice. It relates to the idea of toleration in liberal societies. The separation of state and religion means that it is proper for liberal societies to act intolerantly towards illiberal religions that manifestly violate the rights central to liberalism. Since both religion and culture impose a conception of the good, Eshete argues, and quite rightly so, there is no ground for being tolerant towards illiberal cultures (2003).

Eshete, however, contends that the Ethiopian framework of federalism may be a nonideal but decisive political tool to transition Ethiopia to democracy. Considering the unfavorable conditions that marked its emergence onto the Ethiopian political scene, and under the backdrop of a unitary state that it has supplanted, during the transitional period it was not feasible to make a direct leap towards a liberal democratic framework. According to him, one of the major successes of Ethiopia's federalism is that it "has removed ethnic contest from the national political agenda. Admittedly, ethnic conflict is possible in regional states with significant cultural pluralism. Although ethnic parties predominate, ethnic issues do not predominate in the affairs of government" (Eshete 2003). His claims are neither grounded in facts about how the federal experiment actually worked over the last three decades nor consistent with the objections to Kymlicka that Eshete himself mounted. None of his concerns with the Ethiopian brand of federalism relate to the dangers of unfettered state (either federal or regional) control over people's lives and much less with group control and domination over the lives of individuals.

ALONG COMES *MEDEMER*

The term *Medemer* may strike as a recent entry into the Ethiopian political lexicon, but its origin may be traced back to a very old and neglected newspaper editorial about the meaning of being Ethiopian. As a concept that underscores a sense of unity in diversity as well as signifying the virtues of sacrifice and a sense of common purpose underpinning what it means to be Ethiopian, *Medemer* first figures in a brief editorial entitled ኢትዮጵያዊነት ("Being Ethiopian") in a 1942 edition of *Addis Zemen* newspaper. It reads: "ይልቁንም ዣሬ ጠላት ከለቀቀ በኋላ፣ ይህ ኢትዮጵያዊነት የሚባል ስም መደመርን እንጂ፣ መከፋልንም ፣ መቀነስንም አልወደደም ፡፡ ይህም አብቦ ለፍሬ የደረሰ ነገር ስለሆነ ፣ እንዳልበቀለ አድርጎ የየው ዘንድ ለማንም አይገባውም፡፡" ("Whereas, after the enemy has left, this notion of being Ethiopian has chosen unity (*Medemer*) instead of division or degeneration. Since it has already bore fruit, it wouldn't be proper for anyone to regard it as not having been blossomed.") The editorial further illustrates the triumphant moments in which Ethiopianism was displayed both during the Italian invasion, where everyone suffered gallantly for the sake of preserving freedom and independence, and in how Ethiopians conduct themselves in every aspect of their quotidian life.

Prime Minister Abiy deployed *Medemer* as an organizing concept that confers direction to the multifaceted efforts at responding to our current sociopolitical as well as economic predicament. The idea is meant to serve as an instrument for a purposeful confrontation of our past in ways that accord with a hopeful vision for the future. If recent history may be of any guide, anger and resentment at (real or perceived) indignities have proven to be a powerful catalyst that has shaped the trajectory of Ethiopian political discourse and action since the mid-twentieth century. The struggle for recognition underpinned the three consecutive revolutions Ethiopia went through since the 1960s, all the while proving Hegel's thesis that "the struggle for recognition was the ultimate driver of human history." One must note that not all demands for recognition have a claim to reason: Just because a certain political demand was presented bearing the language of recognition does not mean that it contains justified claims. Moreover, the precise content, as well as ultimate purpose for which such claims for recognition are made, determines their validity. Following Hegel, all struggles for recognition must finally assume the point of view of humanity: That is precisely why ethnicity-based demands of recognition in the form and content they figure in Ethiopia do not pass the test of Hegelian reason. Surely we have not yet figured out the practical steps we ought to undertake for an authentic mutual recognition to take place within the boundaries of the state. Philosophers mainly inform us of the warning signs of impending ruin; perhaps it is not traditionally within their purview to tell us exactly how to fix a broken social bond. Of the numerous admonitions given by Rousseau, the following is one to behold, for it perfectly captures our current predicament. He declared:

> When the state, on the verge of ruin, no longer subsists except in a vain and illusory form, when the social bond is broken in all hearts, when the basest interest shelters itself impudently under the sacred name of the public welfare [including freedom and dignity that are rendered banal], the general will becomes dumb; all, under the guidance of secret motives, no more express their opinions as citizens than if the state had never existed; and, under the name of laws, they deceitfully pass unjust decrees which have only private interest at their end. ([1762] 1998, 106)

If only we can repair the ruptured veins of our body politic, we will succeed in effecting an honest and credible mutual recognition sufficient to rescue the country from the cusp of ruin. Andreas Eshete argued that of the three revolutionary principles, it is fraternity that underwrites both liberty and equality (1981, 27–44). Engagement in a collective political project that works towards the protection of diversity and the fortification of cultural equality "does not engender equality; to the contrary, it presupposes solidarity" (Eshete 2003). A compelling path towards establishing a democratic republic must similarly be undertaken through the strengthening and emphatic reaffirmation of our fraternal relation. The term *Medemer*, therefore, comes in handy. It connotes the act of convergence, coming together with a purpose and vision for a common destiny, a daily mantra reaffirming what Appiah calls "a commitment . . . to sharing the life of a modern state, united by its institutions, procedures, and precepts." An internal document clarifying the value and normative force of *Medemer* declares, "ለአንድነት አንድ ዓይነትነት አይጠበቅበንም፡፡" (which can be interpreted as saying that our political unity is not underwritten by group commonality). The same document articulates *Medemer* as an umbrella term signifying the general normative approach to the idea of the citizen. It also specifically figures as a principle anchored on the notion of solidarity as well as in terms of specific prescriptions on how to cultivate civic duties. The document stresses the need to take charge of the country's future first by relinquishing hatred, mutual suspicion, and the desire for vengeance to settle historical scores and vanquishing the mental prison created by a tribal mentality.[8] Such understanding of civic fraternity,

Eshete would agree, "allows us to give expression to a form of moral sensibility that is witnessed in intimate domains of human fellowship" (1981, 43).

More importantly, *Medemer* appears to draw heavily from the rich cultural traditions of Ethiopia. It figures as a call for national reconciliation as signified by the age-old Ethiopian tradition of ringing the church bell. As tradition has it, a person who crossed the authority of the state and sought protection from punishment went to church and rang the church bell. The priests would then come, hear the person out and begin the process of pardon and reconciliation. *Medemer* seems to be that metaphorical bell citizens ring to begin the process of reconciliation and as a consequence safeguard the renewal of our social pact.

Moreover, the document spells out the idea in terms of specific prescriptions on how to carry oneself as an outstanding member of society, including a duty of respect for the dignity and rights of individuals in virtue of their humanity. To that extent, *Medemer* as a principle of fraternity "represents the diverse ways in which individuals are freely drawn together by their common humanity" without having to override the general dictates of morality that are not based on membership to a nation (Eshete 1981, 44). Such an expansive view of *Medemer's* normative reach appears to give moral gloss to the political conception of equality. The document also insists that the framework of *Medemer* does not merely delineate permissible acts of solidarity but, more importantly, directs at the process of cultivating one. Conceived more as a framework of thinking, *Medemer* figures as a principle of civic virtue, an idea of discourse ethics, a moral precept, and a doctrine of humanism. This is too much to pack into a single concept. The above described initial thoughts about *Medemer* also figure in Prime Minister Abiy's recently published book of the same title, albeit a more organized form. It asserts that *Medemer* is an indigenous philosophy tailor-made for charting our future (Abiy 2019, 49). While the book does not directly define *Medemer*—what it signifies, its basic tenets, precise substantive content, and normative boundaries—it enumerates what it aims at and is meant to remedy. *Medemer* is purposed at "preserving and expanding on recent economic and political victories, rectifying mistakes of the past, as well as securing the interest and aspiration of the future generation" (Abiy 2019, 36). Moreover, it is designed to serve as an antidote to polar thinking and citizens' sense of alienation. *Medemer* is also characterized by the values and principles that are claimed to be nested within it: national unity, respect and deference to citizens, respect for humanity as an end, and prosperity (Abiy 2019, 47–48). With respect to its choice of political ideologies, *Medemer* advocates that we strike the golden mean. It includes the choice between ethnocentrism and Ethiopianist political visions. It envisions a fair and secure political landscape where a reformed ethno-nationalism meets an inclusive Ethiopian nationalism halfway. In exchange for relinquishing a narrow interpretation of history towards a more inclusive account of Ethiopian identity and history, both conceptions of nationalism will find a conceptual space in which they can be mutually reinforcing instead of mutually exclusive. Despite its virtue of posturing, the problem with this constant search for the middle ground is that it lacks conviction.

Nonetheless, the idea seems to capture the basic truth that Ethiopia is not a fate but a project. However, it fails to underscore that (the politics of) ethnic identity is neither a fate nor a worthy project to pursue in a functioning republic. The official account of *Medemer*—by taking into account the views expressed in the book and other official documents such as Abiy's public declarations, working papers, and policy briefings—indicates that the overall narrative still sees the country through the EPRDF's ethnic prism; for it recognizes the political contiguity of ethnic groups, and one can say that the discourse is still caught under the spell of the "national question." With the official narrative increasingly drifting away from tangible constitutional reforms that include banning ethnic politics at the federal level, it is likely that *Medemer* may eventually turn out to be an empty slogan. In keeping with *Medemer*'s Aristotelian roots (and the maxim that virtue is the mean between two extremes), one workable, nonideal solution could be to redraw parliamentary representation from ethnic to geographically or historically based constituencies and at the same time to compel candidates for national public office to exclude ethnicity from their political programs. In exchange, one may permit political organizations on the basis of ethnicity at regional levels, which may foster more accountability and inclusiveness, especially in pluralistic regions.

Finally, as Rousseau once remarked: "If we wish to form a durable constitution, let us, then, not dream of making it eternal" ([1762] 1998, 89). The foundation of our social contract must constantly be renewed to reflect not only the path we've gone through but also our visions for the future.

The great struggle of the Ethiopian republic is balancing the legitimate demands of what Fukuyama calls *isothymia* with the imperative to prevent it from morphing into *megalothymia*. *Thymos* is a Greek concept signifying the part of the soul that desires the recognition of dignity: "Isothymia demands that we recognize the basic equal worth of our fellow human beings," whereas megalothymia represents "the desire to be recognized as superior" (Fukuyama 2018, 21–23). *Medemer* ought therefore to occupy that normative buffer zone where adequate recognition of dignity would serve as a formidable shield against megalothymia.

Regardless of the official interpretation of the concept, I must insist that, should *Medemer* hold any fundamental constitutional import, it must serve as a bulwark against the ongoing frantic enchantment with ethnic mobilization by poachers of resentment (and authors of self-help books on "how to kill a generation"). In effect, *Medemer* should crystallize into a *laïcité*—a constitutional principle for de-ethnicizing affairs of the state. It means nothing short of the birth of the third republic. If it is not the original intent, it certainly should be.

CONCLUSION

The national question has been the most potent tool for political mobilization; revolutionary wars were waged under its name, and it inspired the subsequent restructuring of the state and also figures prominently in the single most important constitutional provision. Paradoxically, it proved to be the Achilles' heel of Ethiopian republicanism. Other republics evolve over time, shedding some elements that are found to be unnecessary, unjust, or threatening to the civic order. The past not properly addressed often tends to come back to bite with a vengeance. The politics of identity, in its current form and content, displays the vengeful, deceitful, and resentment-ridden ideology on which it is predicated, whereas the recent spark of freedom and the spirit of renewal that have emerged on the Ethiopian political horizon require serious policy reform for their effects to endure across generations. If harnessed properly, *Medemer* thought has the potential to guide such a process. Then again, ethnic radicalism clouds over the spark of light that the winds of freedom have brought forth. If the new administration is to be accused of anything, it should be for its sins of omission. Despite all the

evidence, failure to take seriously the existential threat ethnic radicalism (of which the institutional essentialization of ethnicity has conferred legitimacy) posed to the state will likely have catastrophic consequences. It is, thus, pertinent to declare with Dylan Thomas:
Do not go gentle into that good night.
Rage, rage against the dying of the light.

NOTES

1. Modern European republicanism first emerged in late medieval and Renaissance Italy as an organizing theme for the resistance of the northern Italian city-states to absolutism, namely to emperors and papal authority. The spirit of republicanism later reemerged courtesy of two defining moments, the Dutch Revolt (1568–1648) and the English Revolution (1640–60), but eventually failed to establish enduring republics. For the latter, "Republicanism . . . remained essentially an ideology of protest in the face of restoration [of the monarchy], typically utopian or nostalgic in character" (Berenson, Duclert, and Prochasson 2011, 12).

2. For an elaboration of the colonial thesis from the Oromo nationalist point of view, see Holcomb and Ibssa (1990). Some Western scholars have also advanced the colonial thesis to undermine Ethiopia's continued freedom from colonialism, attributing our unconquerable soul to a rather insidious and cynical view that Menelik II saved imperial Ethiopia from falling prey to European colonization "by taking an active part in the scramble for Africa himself" (Toynbee 1965, 44; Schwab 1985, 5; see also Tidy and Lemming 1981; Gann and Duignan 1981). Cited in Tibebu (1996, 421). It is one thing to declare that the southward imperial expansion resembles colonial subjugation of "the other" but quite elusive and even more pernicious to underpin-to-undermine Ethiopia's freedom on being a willing participant to the same evil that European colonialism is rightly charged with. There is no moral equivalency between the claims. It almost beggars belief that one spreads such a spiteful and contemptuous view in the name of scholarship, when in fact it signifies a malignant effort to undermine such a remarkable feat by a black African nation.

3. For an exhaustive chronicle of the events that transpired during the dark days of the Red Terror, see Babile Tolla (1989).

4. Some historians are doubtful as to whether, except in a very general sense, there was evidently a significant connection between the 1960 coup attempt and the student radicalism that set in motion the 1974 revolution. For example, see Henze (2000, 254).

5. Citing Zewde (2002). See also Kebede (1999, 2008).

6. "Ethnic federalism includes ethnically defined national citizenship, self-determination on an ethnolinguistic basis as enshrined in the constitution, ethnically defined political representation and decision-making at all administrative levels and related policies" (International Crisis Group 2009, note 1).

7. Ethiopian federalism is often contrasted with multinational federations of the West (e.g., Switzerland, Canada, and Belgium). These three countries have been named as epitomes of multinational federations that Ethiopian federation can draw lessons from. But the devil is in the details, as fine margins decide the fate of a nation. In the first place, the three nations mentioned here are certainly multilinguistic federations, but to call them multinational would be a convenient simplification. Consider Switzerland as an example. It is a confederation of historically independent city-states and alpine mountain cantons; although the line separating the cantons is principally linguistic, historically the cantonal alliance also took religious form. But there is no national (in the sense of ethnic or tribal) divide that shaped the political configuration of contemporary Confederation Helvetica. There was no serious controversy over national identity, as theirs is a coming together type of (con)federation, and all subscribe to a deep sense of being Swiss. The Canadian and Belgian situation can also be described as linguistic, which also reflects historical patterns of the migration of distinct social groups. But the institutional design that, for instance, Canada has adopted bears little resemblance to our own, for ours rendered the legitimacy of basic institutions subservient to the sovereignty of NNPs.

8. *"መደመር ስንል ከቂም ከበቀልና ከጥላቻ፣ ለዘመናት ሲያባላን ከነበረው፣ ሲከፋፍልን ከኖረው ክፋት፣ ተንኮልና ምቀኝነት እንላቀቅ ማለታችን ነው። መደመር በዚህ ጊዜ መቃባበልን መላበስ ይሆናል።"* አምርታዊ ለውጥና መለያ መርሆቼ, ነሃሴ /2010, 47. It fell short of declaring with Ernest Renan that "forgetting and, I would say, historical error, is an essential element in the creation of a state" (*L'oubli, et je dirai l'erreur historique, sont un facteur essentiel de la création d'une nation*) ([1882] 1990, 8).

REFERENCES

Abiy Ahmed. 2019. *Medemer*. Los Angeles: Tsehai.

Allen, Danielle. 2014. *Our Declaration: A Reading of the Declaration of Independence in Defense of Equality*. New York: Liveright.

Arendt, Hannah. (1951) 2017. *The Origins of Totalitarianism*. New York: Penguin.

———. 1963. *On Revolution*. New York: Penguin.

———. 1977. *Between Past and Future: Eight Exercises in Political Thought*. New York: Penguin.

Appiah, Kwame Anthony. 2005. *The Ethics of Identity*. Princeton, NJ: Princeton University Press.

———. 2018. *The Lies That Bind: Rethinking Identity; Creed, Country, Colour, Class, Culture*. London: Profile.

Berenson, Edward, Vincent Duclert, and Christophe Prochasson, eds. 2011. *The French Republic: History, Values, Debates*. Ithaca, NY: Cornell University Press.

Clapham, Christopher. 2002. "Controlling Space in Ethiopia." In *Remapping Ethiopia: Socialism & After*, edited by Wendy James et al., 9–32. Eastern African Studies. Oxford: James Currey.

———. 1968. "The Ethiopian Coup d'Etat of December 1960." *Journal of Modern African Studies* 6, no. 4: 495–507.

Constant, Benjamin. 1819. *The Liberty of the Ancients Compared with that of the Moderns*. Lecture to the Athénée Royal of Paris.

Dersso, Solomon A. 2012. *Taking Ethno-Cultural Diversity Seriously in Constitutional Design: A Theory of Minority Rights for Addressing Africa's Multi-Ethnic Challenge*. Studies in International Minority and Group Rights. Leiden, Netherlands: Brill-Nijhoff.

Eshete, Andreas. 1970. "The Problem of Regionalism and Religion: Some Theoretical Considerations." ESUNA.

———. 1981. "Fraternity." *Review of Metaphysics* 35, no. 1 (September): 27–44.

———. 2003. "New Frontiers of Ethiopian Politics." Unpublished manuscript.

FDRE Office of the Prime Minister. 2018. አምርታዊ ለውጥና መለያ መርሆቹ, ነሃሴ /2010.

Fukuyama, Francis. 2018. *Identity: Contemporary Identity Politics and the Struggle for Recognition*. London: Profile.

Gann, L. H., and Peter Duignan. 1981. *Africa South of the Sahara: The Challenge to Western Security*. Stanford, CA: Hoover Institution Press.

Greenfield, Richard. 1965. *Ethiopia: A New Political History*. Praeger Library of African Affairs. London: Pall Mall.

Henze, Paul B. 2000. *Layers of Time: A History of Ethiopia*. New York: Palgrave.

Holcomb, Bonnie K., and Sisai Ibssa. 1990. *The Invention of Ethiopia: The Making of a Dependent Colonial State in Northeast Africa*. Trenton, NJ: Red Sea.

Human Rights Watch. 2005. "Targeting the Anuak: Human Rights Violations and Crimes against Humanity in Ethiopia's Gambella Region." March 23, 2005. https://www.hrw.org/report/2005/03/23/targeting-anuak/human-rights-violations-and-crimes-against-humanity-ethiopias.

International Crisis Group. 2009. "Ethiopia: Ethnic Federalism and Its Discontents." Africa Report No. 153, September 4, 2009.

Joireman, Sandra Fullerton. 1997. "Opposition Politics and Ethnicity in Ethiopia: We Will All Go Down Together." *Journal of Modern African Studies* 35, no. 3 (September): 387–407.

Kebede, Messay. 1999. *Survival and Modernization: Ethiopia's Enigmatic Present; A Philosophical Discourse*. Lawrenceville, NJ: Red Sea.

———. 2008. "Return to the Source: Aleqa Asres Yenesew and the West." *Ethiopian Review*, March 14, 2008. https://www.ethiopianreview.com/index/2097.

Kymlicka, Will. 1996. *Multicultural Citizenship: A Liberal Theory of Minority Rights*. Oxford: Oxford University Press.

Livesey, James. 2001. "The Culture and History of French Republicanism: Terror or Utopia?" *The Republic* 1, no. 2: 47–58.

Markakis, John. 2011. *Ethiopia: The Last Two Frontiers*. Eastern Africa Series. Woodbridge, UK: James Currey.

Mekonnen, Kebadu. 2018. "Opinion: The New Era of Transformation in Ethiopia and the Elephant in the Room." *Addis Standard*, September 5, 2018. http://addisstandard.com/opinion-the-new-era-of-transformation-in-ethiopia-and-the-elephant-in-the-room/.

Rawls, John. 2001. *The Law of Peoples: With "The Idea of Public Reason Revisited."* Cambridge, MA: Harvard University Press.

Reliefweb. 2019. "Ethiopia—Acute Humanitarian Crisis in Gedeo/Guji amid Ethnic Tensions and Renewed Displacements." WHO, Humanitarian Partners, ECHO Daily Flash, April 11, 2019. https://reliefweb.int/report/ethiopia/ethiopia-acute-humanitarian-crisis-gedeo-guji-amid-ethnic-tensions-and-renewed.

Renan, Ernest. (1882) 1990. "What Is a Nation?" Translated by Martin Thom. In *Nation and Narration*, edited by Homi K. Bhabha. New York: Routledge.

Rousseau, Jean-Jacques. (1762) 1998. *The Social Contract*. Translated by H. J. Tozer. Ware, UK: Wordsworth Editions.

Sen, Amartya. 2006. *Identity and Violence: The Illusion of Destiny*. New York: W. W. Norton.

Schwab, Peter. 1985. *Ethiopia: Politics, Economics and Society*. Marxist Regimes. London: Pinter.

Smith, Lahra. 2007. "Political Violence and Democratic Uncertainty in Ethiopia." United States Institute of Peace, Special Report, August 1, 2007. https://www.usip.org/publications/2007/08/political-violence-and-democratic-uncertainty-ethiopia.

Tibebu, Teshale. 1996. "Ethiopia: The 'Anomaly' and 'Paradox' of Africa." *Journal of Black Studies* 26, no. 4 (March): 414–30.

———. 2008. "Modernity, Eurocentrism, and Radical Politics in Ethiopia, 1961–1991." *African Identities* 6, no. 4: 345–71.

Tidy, Michael, and Donald Leeming. 1981. *A History of Africa, 1840–1914*. New York: Africana.

Tolla, Babile. 1989. *To Kill A Generation: The Red Terror in Ethiopia*. Washington, DC: Free Ethiopia.

Toynbee, Arnold J. 1965. *Between Niger and Nile*. London: Oxford University Press.

Tronvoll, Kjetil. 2000. "Ethiopia: A New Start?" Minority Rights Group International, Report, April 3, 2000.

Vaughan, Sarah. 2003. "Ethnicity and Power in Ethiopia." PhD thesis, College of Humanities and Social Science, School of Social and Political Studies, University of Edinburgh.

Zewde, Bahru. 2001. *A History of Modern Ethiopia, 1855–1991*. 2nd ed. Eastern African Studies. Oxford: James Currey.

———. 2002. *Pioneers of Change in Ethiopia: The Reformist Intellectuals of the Early Twentieth Century*. Eastern African Studies. Oxford: James Currey.

1.4 Ethiopia at the Juncture of Political Reform
A Gendered Analysis

Sehin Teferra

INTRODUCTION

In the last two years, Ethiopia has entered a period of deep transformation that has captured the imagination of the world. The sweeping reforms that Prime Minister Abiy Ahmed has introduced since taking office have ushered in a period of tangible changes in terms of respect for human rights and the opening up of the political space and have included the release of all political prisoners as well as the extension of peace offerings to armed opposition groups. Our new prime minister's transformation has had a distinct imprint on the state of gender relations in Ethiopia. Members of the Ethiopian women's rights movement were enthralled by the series of appointments that put Ethiopia on the front pages of international newspapers. Within a period of two months (October–November 2018), Ethiopia was bestowed its first gender-equal cabinet, with 50 percent of all ministerial seats occupied by women, including key posts such as the minister of defense (replaced in March 2019) and the minister of higher education and science. Furthermore, Ethiopia now has its first female head of state, a woman president of the Federal Supreme Court, and a woman president of the National Electoral Board.

It is with the recognition of these gains in terms of women's radically altered representation at the highest echelons of government that this chapter highlights the gaps through a gender analysis of the dynamic reforms that have transformed Ethiopia in profound terms. In the wake of the high praise that followed the appointments of our president and our women ministers, gender as a category of difference appears to have quickly lost relevance within the politics of the reform process. Although women constitute a numerical majority, comprising 50–51 percent of the Ethiopian population that is nevertheless politically marginalized, we surmise that gender has not been given due attention compared to ethnicity or religious identity. This chapter makes the argument that the structural gender inequality that consistently finds Ethiopia ranking in the bottom one-fifth of the world is not given the consideration that it deserves in the reform process due to the realities outlined below, followed by a discussion on the risks posed by such an absence of gender analysis. The chapter goes on to discuss potential avenues for adding a gender lens to the political-reform process, including an amalgamation of suggestions from the series of meetings held by representatives of the women's rights movement in the context of the reform process. Although the prime minister has not yet met with representatives of the women's rights movement or articulated an agenda for gender equality, the anticipation of the opportunity to meet with him has helped members come together on a joint agenda that will be reflected in this chapter. The series of meetings was held in the period between May 2018 and February 2019 and coalesced into a discussion on the areas of focus that needed to be reflected in the CEDAW (Convention on the Elimination of all forms of Discrimination against Women) Shadow Report that the Setaweet Movement copresented at the biyearly convention of the CEDAW Committee in Geneva in February 2019 (Setaweet Movement 2019).

THE CURRENT REFORM NARRATIVES ABOUT WOMEN

The narratives that are contained in many of the prime minister's speeches regarding women and in official statements that have emerged in the last year of reform deserve scrutiny from a gender-equality perspective. Although the appointment of women to the top positions in the land received well-deserved global attention, the various speeches in which the prime minister describes women as "loyal," "kind," and "above corruption" led to the fear that women have attained such high positions not because they, as half of the Ethiopian population, deserve representation by virtue of citizenry but as a special dispensation to aid a political agenda. For instance, when he first appointed a gender-equal cabinet, Dr. Abiy stated that "Ethiopian women had made a great contribution to restoring peace and stability, were less corrupt, respected their work, and could sustain the drive for change" ("Ethiopia's Abiy Gives Half of Ministerial Posts to Women," BBC News, October 16, 2018). In his first public address on International Women's Day (March 8, 2019), broadcast live at the African Union hall, the prime minister went on to emphasize that the role of Ethiopian women is to stop "brothers from different ethnicities from warring," and that Ethiopian women's *jegninet*, or heroism, lay in sustaining peace among men. The prime minister also made repeated reference to women as mothers, apparently conflating the two identities, and failing to discuss women as political subjects ("Prime Minister Abiy Ahmed Speech at International Women's Day," YouTube, March 8, 2019). As women's rights advocates, we question the choice of International Women's Day for such instrumentalizing statements by the prime minister. At the event, we would have liked to hear an outline of a gender-equal agenda or a recognition of Ethiopian women as citizens who often have no peace of their own, even in times of so-called peace. The narratives that come from the highest office in the land on who women are or what they do matters because it contributes to stultifying notions of femininity and masculinity that undergird gender inequality and gender-based violence. Ethiopian languages are rife with sayings that indicate the weakness and inferiority of women, and in most Ethiopian communities there are strict boundaries between the roles ascribed to women and men as well as gender norms that uphold the superiority of men in a largely patriarchal and religious society. Therefore, the representation of women by a prime minster who claims to stand for equality and justice needs careful consideration in order to not add to the unhelpful stereotypes about women and about the relationships between women and men. More recently, the newly minted Ethiopian Prosperity Party led by Prime Minister Abiy has started meeting with groups of women ahead of the official launch of its election campaign. This provides a pivotal opportunity for the prime minister and his party to frame gender equality as a political goal. The campaign trail provides the necessary terrain to talk *to* and not just *at* Ethiopian women and to invite their participation in politics beyond the roles limited by stereotypes of docility and motherhood.

A sincere effort to adopt a gender lens into its macro-policies, and to offer gender-progressive strategies would transform the reform process.

GAPS IN A GENDERED ANALYSIS

The National Machinery

The state machinery is insufficiently supported to mainstream gender across parallel ministries. In the recent shuffle of federal ministries, the Ministry of Women and Children has now been mandated to also serve youth, thereby covering over 75 percent of the population. This results in a further depoliticization of the mandate of the ministry, particularly when combined with the limitation in expertise in implementing gender mainstreaming and in monitoring gender-sensitive budgeting across line ministries, as per its mandate.

The current representation of women at the highest ranks of the executive branch of government at the federal level is impressive and includes one of the few gender-equal cabinets in the world. In the judiciary branch, Ethiopia now has its first woman president of the Federal Supreme Court, although at 20 percent of the judiciary, women are still underrepresented. In the legislative arm, the Federal House of Representatives is 38.8 percent women. There are variations, with the gender breakdown of the regional parliament in Tigray at close to 50 percent. In terms of institution building, the government, which has been in a state of deep reform in the past year, has augured the liberalization of media and the political space at large. We have seen the appointment of a woman as head of the electoral board who was previously a staunch opposition member and a political prisoner. Representatives of the nascent women's movement are encouraged by the political changes of the last year, as such reforms, when institutionalized, sustain the move towards democracy. However, there is a need to create a more welcoming environment for women in leadership positions within both the private and public spheres. In addition, despite the bold moves towards tangible democracy, including the release of political prisoners who, in the words of Prime Minister Abiy, "should not have been imprisoned in the first place," the narrative on women still lags in making women full political subjects, and we have yet to attain a gendered analysis of the human rights discourse.

Civil Society and Nongovernmental Organizations

The revised Charities and Societies Proclamation has rightfully overhauled the restrictions of the 2009 Charities and Societies Proclamation, which had received widespread condemnation for its restriction of civic engagements. The new proclamation has paved the way for enhanced engagement by civil society members on gender-equality issues. Therefore, organizations such as the Ethiopian Women Lawyers Association (EWLA) and the Network of Ethiopian Women's Associations (NEWA) are expected to fully return to their work of defending the rights of Ethiopian women. However, in the decade since the restriction placed on NGO funding and operations, many of the organizations with extensive experience in human rights work have lost most of their institutional memory and capacity, and it will take them time and decisive leadership to regain them. The failure to understand gender as a political category and the stark absence of gender justice and equality as a priority for the reform is a problem because it impacts the lives of Ethiopian women and girls in tangible ways and because it seriously undermines the efforts of the government to attain democracy as well as social and economic development gains. Research from all over the world demonstrates that countries that have better gender representation in political leadership benefit from the varied perspectives of a gender-balanced leadership (Marinósdóttir and Erlingsdóttir 2017), and we recognize that such sustained gains come from explicit commitments to equality as a desired goal in and of itself. The risk posed by the narratives that essentialize women is that it takes away from the gender-equality agenda that will commit Ethiopia, in the long term, to a consistent effort to invest in the leadership of women at all levels of government and to gender-equal policies that will ultimately contribute greatly to the government's commitment to economic growth and social development. The areas of life that are particularly affected by the absence of gender consideration are the weakened accountability of our social services, the general absence of the rule of law in women's lives and particularly on gender-based violence, as well as gaps in the education and health sectors, and lastly, the overt promotion of Ethiopian feminized labor to boost the country's status as a low-wage industrial destination.

Weakened Accountability in Gender-Based Violence and Violence against Women in the "New Ethiopia"

One of the unintended effects of the reform process is that with the effort to respect human rights and curb police brutality, there is, in effect, what appears to be a *de jure* suspension of the rule of law, with increased reports of crime and large pockets of insecurity in both urban and rural parts of the country. While this phenomenon is perhaps understandable as the growing pains of an infant democracy just charting its path, there is a startling absence of recognition that women and girls are disproportionately affected by the rise in insecurity and violence. During the reform process we have heard reports of gang rape and rape being used as weapons of ethnic conflict, with girls as young as nine and five gang-raped during the intra-community conflict in Burayu in September 2018. More recently, concerns of the international humanitarian community over the rate and process of the return of internally displaced persons have included a reflection of the reports of women and girls by armed gangs who caused the displacement of ethnic Gedeo women and men from West Guji. Following two rounds of returns since last April, which some observers considered premature, and after another bout of violence erupted in mid-December, fifteen thousand ethnic Gedeos fled West Guji again following the rapes of women and girls and the murders of community members. International media have reported that women and girls report being afraid to return while perpetrators are at large (Gardner 2019).

Even with the absence of active conflict, Ethiopian women often live in insecurity. During the reform period and between July 2018 and May 2019, thirteen women were murdered in Addis Ababa, with three of the murderers not facing justice, including Meaza Kassa's murderer, who eventually escaped police custody after his victim died of complications following his knife attack in February 2019. Another particularly gruesome case was of an engineer who was murdered—her body parts cut into pieces by her boyfriend in the Akaki sub-city of Addis Ababa. Other forms of gender-based violence also appear to be on the rise, while their prosecution is on the decrease; by its own account, over 90 percent of the rape cases that are reported to the Bole sub-city police department are dismissed for lack of capacity to investigate for evidence (Setaweet Movement 2019).

The absence of specific laws on gender-based violence, domestic violence, and sexual harassment is understood to contribute to the unchecked levels of gender-based violence in Ethiopia, which, according to a 2013 report by the Ministry of Women and Children's Affairs, affects up to 60 percent of Ethiopian women throughout their lifetimes. The Ethiopia Demographic and Health Survey (EDHS) 2016 sample shows that an average of 35.2 percent of women between fifteen and forty-nine have been affected by at least one form of physical, psychological, or sexual violence. The data and analysis provided in the EDHS sample are surprisingly low, which may indicate hesitancy on the part of respondents to disclose their experiences or perhaps a lack of understanding on the concepts of violence as articulated in the EDHS. "Women-and-Children's Desks" have been created throughout the government structure, including at police stations, and there are child-justice projects throughout the Ethiopian court system. In addition, women police officers are usually the first contacts for survivors of violence. While this structure has had some success in gender-responsive legal services, there is also a widespread mistrust of police in our communities, and there are reports of police officers who have allegedly raped women and girls, particularly sex workers (Ayele 2015).

The impunity enjoyed by the police has meant that incidences of sexual violence are further underreported. Lastly, a weak accountability system and lax punitive measures combine with criminal acts by the police to normalize the violation of the rights of women and girls. Furthermore, forms of violence that were not known or identified at the time the criminal code was formulated fourteen years ago, such as gang rapes and acid attacks, are now on the rise, and they are not sufficiently criminalized. Sexual harassment is yet to be well defined in the Ethiopian context, and marital rape has not been criminalized. The reform process, for all its promises on equality and justice, has not, as of yet, problematized gender-based violence or provided sufficient attention to the prevalent gender inequality that creates room for high rates of violence. In late 2018, the Setaweet team presented a case study of incidents of violence to a high-level working group that will make recommendations on reforms of procedures related to criminal law and anticipates some changes in how gender is treated as a category of difference within the procedures related to existing criminal law.

The gross violations of the rights of Ethiopian women and girls starkly undermine the state's commitment to eliminating discrimination. At this juncture of change to a more democratic order, the "new Ethiopia" needs to address gender-based violence as a matter of priority. Particular oversight by the new Ministry of Peace (headed by a woman)—which oversees the Federal Police as well as the attorney general—to implement existing laws with fidelity and ensure police accountability would be an important first step.

GENDER CONSIDERATIONS IN POLICIES AND STRATEGIES

Health-Care and Family Planning

The EDHS 2016 put fertility at 4.6 births per woman, down from 4.8 in 2011 and significantly lower than the 5.5 in 2000. Reducing maternal mortality has been of paramount significance for the government of Ethiopia in the last ten years. Births occurring at health facilities grew to 26 percent in 2016 from 5 percent in 2005, while the number of births attended by a skilled provider grew to 28 percent in 2016 from 6 percent in 2000. In addition, the EDHS indicates progress in terms of family planning services—in 2016, 36 percent of fertile women were using either a traditional or modern family planning method, compared to 8 percent in 2000. However, the EDHS has also shown that large segments of Ethiopian married and unmarried women still have unmet needs for family planning services.

The government deserves credit for rolling out an anti-HPV vaccination program for fourteen-year-old girls through the education system during this past academic year.[1] However, there is a resurgent resistance to vaccination, in Amhara Region in particular, which is affecting the deployment of maternal and child health services.

In addition, with the loss in funding of HIV-related interventions in response to the significant decrease in new infection rates (the current prevalence of HIV in urban Ethiopia is 4.1 among females and 1.9 among males), there is a risk that HIV infection rates might resurge, particularly with existing power inequalities between Ethiopian women and men and with high levels of sex work in urban areas.

Gaps in Women's Health Services

Women with disabilities are often underserved by the medical system, which fails to make facilities accessible both physically (with ramps, elevators, and disability-friendly toilet facilities) and through communication, including the availability of sign-language interpretation, proper signage, and reading material in braille. In addition, women with disabilities often complain of maltreatment by medical personnel who show them pity and do not provide the rightful access to health services they deserve. Reproductive health services are often the most difficult to access, with medical personnel often treating women with disabilities as devoid of sexuality, perpetuating the foregone conclusion that when a woman with a disability is pregnant, it can only lead to complications. In one report, issued by the Addis Hiwot Center of the Blind, a local NGO, violations of the reproductive rights of women with disabilities include unwarranted referrals to disability services, as opposed to the reproductive health services they sought; a visually impaired pregnant woman who received unsolicited advice to get an abortion; and a hearing-impaired mother who was fitted with a permanent contraceptive device without her consent (2016).

Furthermore, health-care providers in Ethiopia in general are inadequately prepared to deal with violence against women and girls, emergency care in the case of gang rapes, and acid attacks. For instance, according to the observations of feminist activists, gaps in emergency health care by referral hospitals in Addis Ababa and two regions have been implicated in the death or severe bodily impairment of the following young women in the last five years:

- **Hanna Lelango**: A sixteen-year-old who was gang-raped by five men and who died from an alleged infection in Addis Ababa in 2014.
- **Atsede Nigussie**: A twenty-four-year-old who had acid thrown in her face and lost sight in both eyes after a forty-day stay at Ayder Referral Hospital in Mekelle, Tigray Region, where she was given no care beyond the regular cleaning of her wounds. Although she was later referred to Yekatit 12 Hospital in Addis Ababa, she did not receive appropriate medical care there, either.
- **Chaltu Abdi**: A fourteen-year-old who died in August 2018 at Yekatit 12 Hospital following a stay of several months after being referred by Jugal Hospital in Harari Region for "burn injuries sustained

while cooking," although Chaltu's testimony to the advocates who spoke to her was that a flammable liquid was poured on her by her employer and his wife after Chaltu was repeatedly raped by him. It is not clear if medical negligence contributed to her unexpected death months after her injury. (Setaweet Movement 2019)

Beyond emergency care, the health-care system often fails women in terms of the delivery of quality services, with high incidences of reported rates of misinformation and malpractice. Regarding the care that Ethiopian women received during and after delivery between 2007–16, only 56 percent had their blood pressure, urine, and blood samples taken during an antenatal care visit, while only 44 percent received a postpartum checkup in a health facility after delivery and before discharge. Moreover, the results in health care that have earned accolades for Ethiopia in terms of reach of services have largely depended on the corps of female health workers who offer frontline services, including the provision of basic forms of contraception. The opportunities for advancement and the level of compensation offered to these women requires further analysis. Furthermore, observations by feminist activists in many parts of the country point to the neglect of responsibilities and corruption by medical personnel. Lastly, the political unrest of the past few years has left the health-care system in a dangerous state, affecting maternal and pediatric health-care delivery as services are suspended, with a high turnover of staff (Assefa et al. 2018).

EDUCATION

While Ethiopian primary education enrollment is nearly at gender parity (0.91), completion of the first cycle of primary education (grade five) is 75.1 percent for girls compared to 77.1 percent for boys; 52.2 percent of girls complete grade eight compared to 53.3 percent of boys. Girls start to drop out in high numbers from grade five on, and by the secondary school level, approximately 30 percent of students in grades eleven and twelve are female (Joshi and Verspoor 2013).

Persistent gender inequality, sexual harassment, violence against female students, gender-insensitive curricula that fail to challenge pervasive gender stereotypes, and the scarcity of women teachers contribute to the high rate of failure of girls. In addition, there are questions around the quality of data collected and analyzed by the Ministry of Education for its annual abstracts, which do not feature attrition rates for girls and boys, and there needs to be clarification as to whether the number of students who are counted in the enrollment data do in fact attend school regularly. According to research by the Population Council, child marriage was cited as a reason for nonattendance of school by 23 percent of girls in rural areas and by 16 percent in urban areas (2016). There is also some indication that with rampant problems with the quality of education as well as increasingly fewer job opportunities, formal education may be losing its value beyond the secondary school level. However, research also indicates that girls' education contributes to changing social norms around gender; for instance, educated girls become more likely to resist forced arranged marriages. Moreover, development practitioners assert that even basic literacy and numeracy obtained by young women and girls is an important attainment, helping them access better jobs and improved life skills.

Female Students with Disabilities

Although the Ethiopian education system has an inclusive policy towards disability and schools are prohibited from discriminating against students with disabilities, female students with physical and mental disabilities are underserved in terms of access due to a dismissive attitude towards disabilities by many teachers and administrators. Lack of physical access to dormitories and classrooms, as well as a shortage in teaching material in braille and of teachers who can interpret sign language, means that many female students with disabilities fall behind, and female students with intellectual disabilities are often under-taught. Girls with disabilities are exceptionally vulnerable to violence and sexual exploitation by teachers, other students, and their own family members. Difficulties with menstrual-hygiene management and inaccessible bathrooms make it difficult for girls with disabilities to attend school, which contributes to a high dropout rate (Pankhurst 2017).

Violence within Schools

Violence against female students is a major issue throughout the education sector. Sexual harassment, verbal and physical abuse, and the threat of abduction on the way to and from school make education an unsafe experience for many Ethiopian girls. Although corporal punishment in schools is now prohibited, research indicates that over 70 percent of all school-age children have experienced forms of violent punishment by teachers in a school setting (African Child Policy Forum 2016).

At the secondary as well as the tertiary level, reports of rape and gang rape in particular are becoming increasingly common, with scant attention given to the problem by school administrators. For instance, in December 2018, it took an online campaign of feminist activists in Addis Ababa for the administration of Jimma University to install a physical barrier between the women's and men's dormitories, after women students repeatedly posted on social media about being threatened with rape by male students. The problem was addressed after the health minister, who sits on the university's Board of Governors, intervened (Setaweet Movement 2019).

Future Trends

The recently revealed Ethiopian Education Development Roadmap (2018–30) is a comprehensive guide for major shifts within the education system from the pre-primary to the higher education segments. While heavily researched, the Roadmap, written by an all-male team, takes a cursory approach to gender-equality issues within education, except for occasionally noting that female enrollment lags slightly behind male, and a recommendation that primary education should be compulsory for all girls and boys. On the other hand, the newly appointed woman minister of science and higher education has unveiled an ambitious plan of a 50 percent representation of women an all boards of higher-education institutions, as well as the creation of a network of women scholars.

THE NEW LOW-WAGE FRONTIER: THE FEMINIZED LABOR OF ETHIOPIA

Ethiopian women are almost three times as likely to be unemployed as Ethiopian men, and their gross daily national income per capita is $1.16 as compared to men's $1.886. Women are also more likely to take jobs that put them in vulnerable positions that do not protect their basic labor rights. Women are paid 63 percent less than men for the same work (International Monetary Fund 2018). However, in the past two years, there have been encouraging trends in women's employment. The government has extended paid maternity leave to four months, although this has not yet been codified in the labor law and does not extend beyond federal employees. Government institutions are now mandated to have childcare facilities on site, and women government employees may bring their children with them on free public service buses. In addition, in rural parts of the country there are efforts to build childcare facilities as part of the Productive Safety Net Program, a major food-security program implemented by the government and supported by development partners. However, the percentage of women who can benefit from such policies is relatively low; most Ethiopian women who work for pay are hired by the informal sector. Furthermore, a large swath of poor Ethiopian women work as domestic workers, with a high level of insecurity and threats to their well-being. The supply and demand of domestic work has in the past decade been highly affected by the migration of tens of thousands of young women to countries of the Gulf region for domestic work—the relative decrease in the available pool has led to an increase in the payment offered to domestic workers and perhaps also to better treatment in people's homes.

Women with disabilities are particularly underserved by financial institutions, and they find it more difficult to obtain business loans. Despite the Right to Employment of Persons with Disabilities Proclamation, employers are reluctant to hire women with disabilities, and they usually fail to provide reasonable accommodation when they do. The Ethiopian government recognizes women as a major, if largely untapped, economic force. Accordingly, most of the jobs that are being created at the newly developed "industrial cities" within Hawassa, Kombolcha, and Mekelle and on the peripheries of Addis Ababa feature feminized and unskilled jobs in textile manufacturing. Cities like Hawassa have seen the opening of large industrial complexes that aim to generate a billion dollars a year in exports and which, when fully occupied, should create jobs for sixty thousand people—the majority of them women).

Gender-related issues that are arising out of the mobilization of so many women for work relate to the availability and quality of housing they are able to access, protection and safety issues, the health impacts of factory work, and the unintended burden of added household tasks on the women left behind in the homes of migrant workers. Lastly, a study of Ethiopian workers released in October 2016 by the US-based National Bureau of Economic

Research, conducted with the University of Oxford and the University of Chicago, found low-wage factories in industrial parks to be less desirable, more dangerous, and even lower paying than self-employment in the informal sector, with 77 percent of the study's cohort leaving factory jobs within the first year (Coren 2016). In addition, a recent *Forbes* article by Michael Posner (2019), assistant secretary of state for democracy, human rights and labor in the Obama administration, describes Ethiopia as the new "low-wage frontier—with the dubious distinction of offering the lowest pay anywhere in the worldwide clothing supply chain" and appeals to the corporations hiring these women to embrace a long-term investment model in order to make their production profitable and sustainable over time.

Posner argues that while corporations are beholden to their shareholders to make a profit, a sustainable model of longer-term wealth creation for corporations and for Ethiopia would entail increased wages, better training, and housing for the young women who leave their homes to work in the clothing factories. An argument from the Ethiopian side would agree with Posner's statement and appeal to a longer-term vision of job creation including livable wages and dignified work and living conditions for young Ethiopian women traveling from all parts of the country in search of work. A gendered analysis would go further and ask where the women go when they drop out of work in such large numbers, with a vision to avert a crisis from potentially swelled peri-urban areas, which we can expect to be populated by low-skilled young women with few resources for survival.

WOMEN WHO REQUIRE SPECIAL CONSIDERATIONS

Women in pastoralist areas are vastly underserved basic services and the protection of their rights. For instance, in the Education Development Roadmap, the suggestion is given that "pastoralist communities should be served with appropriate education services," without examining the complexities of providing education to girls within a mobile population. In addition, elderly women in all Ethiopian communities deserve better-tailored services.

While there is no clear definition as to which ethnic and religious groups may be classified as ethnic minorities in the Ethiopian context, Ethiopian Muslims have long complained of social and political exclusion in a country dominated, until relatively recently, by Orthodox Christianity as the state religion. Furthermore, certain communities, such as the Fuga, Gafat Beta Israel, Negede Weyto, Menja, Me'enit, and Gumuz, live amongst ethnic groups who treat them as inferior. Women and girls within these religious and ethnic groups may be understood to be doubly excluded.

AIDING THE REFORM PROCESS FOR GENDER EQUALITY: A CONCLUSION

The reform process still has time to adjust its priorities and narratives in order to be more gender-responsive to the needs of Ethiopian women. Engendering the political reform process would entail recognizing that gender-based violence and harassment is a serious impediment in the lives of too many Ethiopian women and is something that is on the radar of policy makers. The Education Development Roadmap, which will be put in practice as of the next academic year, requires a serious overhaul in terms of addressing the high rate of female dropouts and to combat pervasive gender-based violence experienced by female students, while fast-tracking women teachers and directors. The health sector needs to revitalize its efforts to respond to women's health-seeking options, further invest in community-based health workers, and strive to build on the gains made in reducing maternal mortality. Lastly, it is vital that the government, during the reform process, revise its views of Ethiopian women as "cheap labor," which may increase economic gains in the short term but which will ultimately harm women and Ethiopian society in general.

Members of the women's rights movement, led by NEWA, held three consultations with local civil society member organizations—including Setaweet—to outline the most pressing issues that we would like the reform process to focus on. They were identified as the following:

- A revision of the 1993 National Policy on Women into a policy on gender equality that reflects the complex realities of everyday Ethiopia and the multitude of challenges faced by Ethiopian women.
- The creation of a ministry whose mandate is gender equality and that is strongly supported in terms of budgeting and technical skills in mainstreaming gender across line ministries in order to meet international targets on gender equality.

- As civil society actors who have seen the gaps posed by weak legislation, we are encouraged, albeit with some reservations, by Ethiopia's adoption of the Maputo Protocol in late 2018. We would like existing laws to be reexamined from a gendered perspective, which would put Ethiopia on a stronger footing to eliminate all forms of discrimination. We particularly call for a new proclamation on gender-based violence, with a particular focus on domestic violence, gang rapes, acid attacks, and criminalizing sexual harassment and marital rape. We also hope to see a special commission that will inquire into gender-based violence and acknowledge its magnitude as a crisis.
- It is our hope that the education system and particularly the Education Development Roadmap receive a "gender overhaul" focused on the delivery of quality education for all girls and boys at all levels of the education system beyond the current focus on rates of enrollment. We ask that the state adopt a zero tolerance violence and harassment policy within schools and that it take swift measures to enact anti-sexual-harassment and anti-violence policies.
- As women's rights activists, we acknowledge the efforts of the government to create more employment opportunities for women. We hope to see in the coming few years a gendered analysis of all economic policies that views women as more than an economic resource. We hope to find policies, in particular with the ever-expanding industrial parks, that ensure the well-being and safety of women workers, while investing in much-needed economic growth for the country.
- The recognition of gender mainstreaming as a valuable technical skill that goes beyond representation and "adding women" and the investment in such skills across the executive branch of government and through line ministries.

This chapter has argued for the essential and urgent adoption of a gender analysis into the political reform process that is currently reshaping Ethiopia. It is imperative that the narratives and policies that are emerging out of the reform take into consideration the interests of 51 percent of the Ethiopian population to ensure not only that Ethiopian women finally attain full rights as citizens but also in order to unleash the full potential of women to contribute to the economic and social development of Ethiopia.

NOTE

1. Forms of cancers that affect women disproportionately, such as cervical and breast cancer, are on the rise in Ethiopia, with very limited medical services to help affected women.

REFERENCES

Addis Hiwot Center of the Blind. 2016. "Baseline Assessment on the Inclusiveness of Health Services to Persons with Disabilities of Two Governmental & Three Private Health Institutions in Arada Sub-City, Addis Ababa, Ethiopia." Addis Ababa: AHCB.

African Child Policy Forum. 2016. "The African Report on Child Wellbeing 2016: Getting It Right; Bridging the Gap between Policy and Practice." Addis Ababa: ACPF.

Assefa, Yibeltal, Dessalegn Tesfaye, Wim Van Damme, and Peter S Hill. 2018. "Effectiveness and Sustainability of a Diagonal Investment Approach to Strengthen the Primary Health-Care System in Ethiopia." *Lancet* 392, October 20, 2018.

Ayele, Sehin Teferra. 2015. "Agency and Sisterhood: A Feminist Analysis of Ethiopian Sex Workers' Experiences of, and Resistance to, Violence." Unpublished PhD diss., SOAS, University of London.

Coren, Michael J. 2016. "New Research Finds Sweatshops May Be a Necessary Evil in the Development of Economies." *Quartz*, October 7, 2016.

Gardner, Tom. 2019. "'Go and We Die, Stay and We Starve': The Ethiopians Facing a Deadly Dilemma." *Guardian*, May 15, 2019.

Institute for Security Studies. 2017. "Ethiopia Development Trends Assessment: Ethiopia Performance Monitoring and Evaluation Service (EPMES)," March 2, 2017. Addis Ababa: ISS.

International Monetary Fund. 2018. "The Federal Democratic Republic of Ethiopia." IMF Country Report No. 18/354, December 4, 2018. Washington, DC: IMF.

Joshi, Rajendra Dhoj, and Adriaan Verspoor. 2013. "Secondary Education in Ethiopia: Supporting Growth and Transformation." A World Bank Study. Washington, DC: World Bank.

Marinósdóttir, Magnea, and Rósa Erlingsdóttir. 2017. "This is Why Iceland Ranks First for Gender Equality." World Economic Forum, November 1, 2017. Cologny, Switzerland: WEF.

Pankhurst, Alula, ed. 2017. *Change and Transformation in 20 Rural Communities in Ethiopia: Selected Aspects and Implications for Policy*. Addis Ababa: WIDE.

Posner, Michael. 2019. "Why There Is a Need for a Long-Term Investment Model in Ethiopia." *Forbes*, May 15, 2019.

Setaweet Movement. 2019. "Gender at the Juncture of Political Reform." Shadow Report to the CEDAW Committee, Review of the 8th Periodic Report on Ethiopia, Suva, Fiji, February 2019.

Solomon, Desta. 2010. "Desk Review of Studies Conducted on Women Entrepreneurs in Ethiopia." Addis Ababa: Addis Ababa Chamber of Commerce and Sectoral Associations.

United Nations Development Programme. 2019. "Inequalities in Human Development in the 21st Century." Briefing Note for Countries on the 2019 Human Development Report. New York: UNDP.

1.5 Civil Society in Ethiopia
Reversing the Securitization of Civic Activism?

Camille Louise Pellerin

> Authoritarian regimes try to be responsive in a smart way. They don't have a safety valve for expression, and they risk that a little thing can become existential. There is no way to express frustration. Ethiopia is not a free country, and the government knows that its legitimacy depends on growth. For system survival, it tries to promote growth. But it tries to do this alone, and it doesn't work. The government cannot be insular and survive, but it hasn't understood this yet. It doesn't allow civil society to express itself, and it doesn't listen. This can be dangerous (Interviewee No. 46 2016).

As unwittingly predicted by my interviewee in spring 2016, the lack of space for civil society and the repressive rule of the Ethiopian People's Revolutionary Democratic Front (EPRDF) eventually contributed to the countrywide emergence of large-scale anti-government protests. Over the course of 2018, the unceasing protests forced the ruling coalition to implement political reforms. However, formal civil society organizations (CSOs) did not join citizens mobilization against EPRDF rule nor did they actively take part in the political transformation process that followed. The strict control that the EPRDF had established over CSOs prevented them from engaging in the public contestation of the ruling coalition, and the lasting impact of years of control affected CSOs' ability to take part in the political reform process.

The 5th of February 2019 marked an important change in the relationship between the EPRDF regime and CSOs in Ethiopia: the parliament passed the "Organizations of Civil Societies Proclamation No. 1113/2019" (CSOP), delivering on Prime Minister Abiy Ahmed's promise to adapt some of the country's legislation restricting citizens' democratic rights. While the legislative change provides a positive outlook for the country's political development, what seems to be conspicuously lacking is a thorough analysis of the administrative system preceding the new civil society law. However, in order to reform the existing system governing CSOs in Ethiopia beyond legislative changes and to understand why CSOs have not taken part in the political and social reform process yet, it is important to look back and analyze the political realities of civil society-state relations predating the political reform currently under way.

This chapter provides an overview of the relationships between the state and CSOs under EPRDF rule, covering the civil society legislation preceding the new proclamation (2009 and 2017). It explores the roots of the 2009 Charities and Societies Proclamation (ChSP), as well as its application, to analyze how it structured the relationship between the state and charities and societies in Ethiopia.[1] To contextualize the ChSP, the chapter briefly outlines the circumstances in which it was conceptualized before exploring the legal provisions of the ChSP, its drafting process, application, and impact. The chapter concludes with some reflections comparing both the drafting processes and contents of the new CSOP (2019) and the ChSP (2009).

The chapter is based on semi-structured and unstructured interviews with eighty-six interviewees (listed in Table 1.5.3) conducted in Addis Ababa, Adama, Hawassa, Sheshemane, and Arba Minch between November 2015 and April 2019. Informants included staff working at CSOs as well as employees at relevant public offices, civil society experts, and employees at international organizations.

REALIGNING CHARITIES AND SOCIETIES TO EPRDF POLITICS: A NEW LEGAL FRAMEWORK

In 2009, the Ethiopian government passed the ChSP, restructuring large parts of organized civil society in Ethiopia. The proclamation prohibited the use of international donor funding for activities related to democracy promotion and other rights-based activities and redirected the operations of CSOs towards development and relief activities. Research portrayed the law as a reaction to the involvement of a few NGOs in the 2005 election[2] and an attempt to close the associational space for civil society to prevent organizations from promoting democracy (Asnake 2011, 689f.; Burgess 2012, 166f.; Sisay 2012, 380). Dupuy, Ron, and Prakash (2015, 426) went as far as to state that "the ERPDF's real intention, after all, was to shut down political opposition, rather than to create a more vibrant civil society." While echoing the views of many CSOs and donor representatives in Ethiopia, most research failed to study the design of the ChSP and its long-term effects beyond the immediate political crisis of 2005 (Yitayehu 2010, 234ff.).

To understand the character of the ChSP, it is important to note that it was developed during the period starting the operationalization of the EPRDF's self-proclaimed "democratic developmental state" program that followed the legitimacy crisis revealed in the 2005 elections. Rather than through representation, the EPRDF aimed to build legitimacy via developmental achievements (Meles 2006). Within the developmental state, nongovernmental organizations (NGOs), according to the EPRDF, should mobilize capital for development interventions (Meles 2007), whereas mass-based associations were supposed to mobilize the population for economic and political development (EPRDF 2008a, 2008b). While the ChSP in theory provided a legal framework that coerced CSOs to align themselves with the EPRDF developmental state agenda, in practice, the ChSP was used to restrict their operations. The agency put in charge of overseeing CSOs exercised repression, and instead of focusing on mobilizing CSOs for the developmental state project, it prioritized to prevent contestation at all cost. This created conflict between the regulatory body of CSOs and different state organizations, especially at the local level, which wanted to cooperate with these organizations to implement the EPRDF's development plans.[3]

The ChSP was passed in 2009 and replaced provisions from the 1960 Civil Code that had regulated licensing and operation of CSOs since the reign of Haile Selassie (Proclamation No. 165/1960). The ChSP excluded only CSOs regulated by other laws, religious associations, and community-based associations and international/foreign organizations operating under specific bilateral agreements with the Ethiopian government (Proclamation No. 621/2009, Art. 3.2).

Complying with the definition of civil society put forward in the EPRDF's development plans (MoCB 2004; MoFED 2002, 2006), the ChSP categorized and regulated CSOs according to their (1) source of funding (foreign or local), and (2) their organizational structure (membership-based or not) (EPRDF 2008c). CSOs were divided into charities—organizations that benefit the community/public as a whole (Proclamation No. 621/2009, Art. 14)—and societies—membership-based organizations that work for the benefit of their members (Proclamation No. 621/2009: Art. 55). Furthermore, the proclamation differentiated between "Ethiopian" charities and societies, whose members were Ethiopian nationals and who did not receive more than 10 percent of funds from foreign sources; "resident" charities and societies, whose members were Ethiopian nationals and received more than 10 percent of funds from foreign sources; and "foreign" charities, whose members were foreign nationals and who received funding from foreign sources (Proclamation No. 621/2009, Art. 2).

According to the ChSP, the source of funding determined the type of activities that charities and societies could engage in. Only Ethiopian charities and societies were allowed to work on rights-related issues (Proclamation No. 621/2009, Art. 14.2 j–n), whereas resident and foreign charities and societies were limited to work on socioeconomic development issues (Proclamation No. 621/2009, Art. 14.2 a–i).

The justification provided by the EPRDF for the respective allocation of activities was:

> If it is an organization whose leaders and members are Ethiopian but run by foreign finance, it will still be controlled by foreign forces.... The proclamation is drafted in a way that the organizations that have an important role in our political activities are free from rent-seeking networks and requires that their source of income should be only their members and other Ethiopians and their internal organization should be democratic. (EPRDF 2008c)

While the source of funding was the prime criterion for regulating the activities of charities and societies, even their organizational status had some impact. Contrary to Ethiopian charities, Ethiopian mass societies, such as professional and women's and youth associations, were mandated to participate in the "process of strengthening democratization and election[s]" (Proclamation No. 621/2009, Art. 57.7), including voter education and election monitoring. Moreover, administrative requirements for mass societies were lower than for all other types of organizations regulated under the ChSP to facilitate their operations. The official reasoning for enabling mass societies to take on the responsibility of democracy promotion was that they represented their members' interests. However, given that they were formally tied to EPRDF structures, there existed a political motive for this decision (EPRDF 2008a, 2008c, 2011, 2015).

Contradicting the provisions of the Ethiopian constitution (Proclamation No. 1/1995, Art. 31), the ChSP understood freedom of association as a right reserved for citizens. All charities and societies (Ethiopian, resident, and foreign) could appeal to the agency's board regarding a decision taken by the agency, but only Ethiopian charities and societies "aggrieved by a decision of the board" could appeal to the Federal High Court (Proclamation No. 621/2009, Art. 104). The measure was justified by the EPRDF in the following way:

> On the occasion that the association is dissolved, they cannot sue the government in court for a violation of their right. This is because these foreign organizations have an opportunity to associate given by the government rather than a constitutionally provided freedom of association. (EPRDF 2008c)

Apart from the 90/10 directive (described above), another directive steering the operations of CSOs was the 70/30 directive (Proclamation No. 621/2009, Art. 88), which regulated the ratio of administrative cost to overall budget. CSOs were not allowed to allocate more than 30 percent of their overall funds for administrative costs, to make sure that 70 percent of the funds were transferred to the community. While the official reasoning was that the provision prevented corruption (EPRDF 2008c) and limited the amount of money spent on the salaries and benefits of international employees, it posed an obstacle to the operations of CSOs. Rather than enabling them to participate in the country's development and work with hard-to-reach populations, as foreseen in the EPRDF development plans, the accounting discouraged such work. Expenses related to working in remote areas (vehicles, staff relocation, etc.) were counted as administrative costs and not operational costs, as were training, monitoring of activities, and project infrastructure.[4]

The Drafting Process of the Charities and Societies Proclamation

The drafting process of the ChSP was integrated into the business process reengineering (BPR)[5] at the Ministry of Justice.[6] While the whole process seemingly started out technocratic, in reality former prime minister Meles Zenawi was not only the "architect of the EPRDF's civil society discourse" (Interviewee No. 1 2015) that differentiated between different types of CSOs and their respective roles and responsibilities in the developmental state project but also the "mastermind behind the law" (Interviewee No. 7 2016).

As part of the BPR, a group of three lawyers working in the civil service was appointed to review the CSO registration process and to provide recommendations regarding how to improve the law. A lawyer representing CSOs was also allocated but without substantially being able to influence the outcome of the drafting process. The working group was assigned two advisors from the civil service university, as well as several senior lawyers and young civil service graduates as support.

The team undertook several country visits in 2007 to study CSO legislation in Singapore, France, and Canada, among others.[7] Officially, the Singaporean law provided the blueprint for the ChSP (Mihret 2010, 2) and a high-level state representative stated that "the fundamentals of the law are solid, based on the NGO law of Singapore" (Yamamoto 2008b). A review of the Singaporean Charities Act and Societies Act suggested that although the ChSP provided for a country-specific approach to civil society, the Singaporean laws had inspired some provisions (Singapore Charities Act [Ch. 37] 1995; Singapore Societies Act [Chapter 311] 1966).

The drafting process itself was controlled by the Prime Minister's Office (PMO). The head of the working group, together with another group member and the minister of Justice, had to present the drafts regularly at the PMO. The prime minister and his chief of staff were directly involved in the drafting process, providing instructions for revisions and adding provisions to the drafts submitted. Some of the excessive provisions with respect to CSO operations, government oversight, and penalties were added by the prime minister's chief of staff. Documentation from the US embassy confirmed that the original draft of the ChSP did not include "the definition and restriction of NGOs receiving foreign funding" nor the excessive penalties added in later drafts (Yamamoto 2008b). While officially in charge of the drafting process, the working group and the minister lacked clear instructions with respect to their task and did not have enough political weight to influence the outcome of the drafting.

The late prime minister did not only control the internal processes of the drafting but also the external communications both with CSOs and international actors. Meles Zenawi summoned representatives from CSOs on several occasions to discuss the draft law, but these meetings increased animosity between state officials and representatives from civil society instead of fostering dialogue (Yamamoto 2008a–c). International actors tried to influence the drafting process through bilateral and multilateral meetings with prime minister Meles Zenawi and other high-level state officials. US, UK, and French ambassadors, for example, met Meles on four occasions in May, June, July, and October 2008 to discuss the drafts of the ChSP (Yamamoto 2008c–d). The international community tried to "kill or delay the bill," but they also attempted to influence its technicalities to make it less prohibitive (Yamamoto 2008e). While delaying the passing of the proclamation, international actors did not manage to fundamentally influence the proclamation's content (for a timeline of the drafting process, see Table 9.1) (Yamamoto 2008a, 2008f).

Despite repeated attempts of the international donor community and CSOs in Ethiopia to influence the provisions of the proclamation, the Ethiopian parliament (House of Federation) passed the bill in January 2009 (Yamamoto 2008g, 2009; Yitayehu 2010, 223f). According to documentation from the US embassy in Addis Ababa, the EPRDF government exercised pressure to ensure the passing of the bill. Documents stated:

> The ruling party has recently convened its parliamentarians to indoctrinate them on the party's version of reality in which civil society groups are "neo-liberal rent seekers" doing the bidding of the west to undermine the ruling party's democratic and

development agenda. . . . Speaker of Parliament Teshome Toga asserted that "there is no doubt that the law will pass because there is already consensus within the ruling party." (Yamamoto 2008h)

Table 1.5.1. *Timeline of the Drafting Process of the ChSP*

2007	2008	2009	2010	2011
Establishment of working group to review existing CSO legislation	Redrafting of the ChSP according to PMO requirements (Revised Drafts in May, September, November)	ChSP passed by the parliament after parliamentary hearings	Council of Ministers passed regulation 168/2010 further developing the ChSP	Eight directives for the application of the ChSP approved by the CSA board
Travel abroad to study international best practices	Meetings with Charities/ Societies to discuss the draft	Guidelines and templates for registration prepared	The agency became operational	
First Draft of the ChSP developed by working group	Meetings between the donor community (especially US, UK, and France) and Meles and other high-level officials	Drafting of directives for the application of the ChSP		
	ChSP final draft submitted to the Council of Ministers	Setting up of the agency		

The Establishment and Operation of the Charities and Societies Agency

The state body put in charge of implementing the ChSP was called the Charities and Societies Agency (ChSA) and was established in 2009. The ChSA was bestowed with substantial powers, including a quasi-judicial status deriving from its mandate to charge penalties. The agency acted as an investigator and prosecutor at the same time and, apart from the courts, it was the only state organization allowed to freeze financial assets. The ChSA had the power to interfere in charities' and societies' internal affairs, for example, through participation in their general assembly meetings (Regulation No. 168/2009, 3, Art. 24). Moreover, charities and societies were not allowed to dispose of any property or asset, as they were formally prevented from owning property, and the ChSA could at any time demand them to submit written documentation on their work (Directive No. 6 2011).

The PMO oversaw the establishment of the agency and validated directives and regulations produced as part of the operationalization of the ChSP (Directive No. 3 2011; Directive No. 4 2011; Directive No. 5 2011; Directive No. 6 2011; Directive No. 7 2011; Directive No. 8 2011; Proclamation No. 621/2009). The ChSA's first director and his deputy, together with other high officials, were responsible for the staffing of the agency. Some of the team members from the drafting group helped with the set-up of the agency, the preparation of documentation, directives and regulations, and the training of agency staff. They also supervised the initial reregistration process.

According to rumors, the agency was affiliated with the Ethiopian security apparatus. While difficult to corroborate with certainty, some individuals who had been working at the ChSA held that after its establishment, the ChSA was partly staffed with recruits from the police, the national security service, and the EPRDF politburo. The affiliation of the ChSA was transferred from the Ministry of Justice to the Ministry of Federal Affairs in 2010 (Proclamation No. 691/2010), also indicating a link to the Ethiopian security apparatus (Yohannes 2013a, 2013b).[8] Between 2012 and 2018 the ChSA was led by a former TPLF and EPRDF council member, former head of the Regional Security and Administration Bureau in Tigray, and board member of the Tigrayan veterans association. The change of ChSA directors was a clear indication that the handling of civil society was considered a security issue and a move away from addressing civil society concerns as part of the developmental state project. While the agency's first director was said to have operationalized the ChSP and executed Meles's instructions regarding human rights NGOs and others active during the 2005 elections, his successor went much further, targeting CSOs irrespective of their history, mandate, and political activity.

According to civil servants working at and with the ChSA, the agency provided reliable services to CSOs. Registration was said to be quick, and regular services like the monitoring of organizations' activities were provided to help them improve their operations. All ChSA employees interviewed stated that no CSO was discriminated against and that they interpreted the law in favor of them, not against them. While the interviewees stated that the law had improved the operations of CSOs, their attitudes, especially towards foreign and resident charities, were very negative, and they expressed a need for control over organizations' operations. Interviewees held that most foreign and resident charities were rent seekers, and many tried to illegally work on political issues with international donor finance. They recited the EPRDF discourse on neoliberal and rent-seeking organizations (EPRDF 2008c; Meles 2007), rather than reflecting on the role of charities and societies in the developmental state project that was detailed in development plans and the ChSP. Some suggested the need for even stricter legislation and higher punishments. None of the employees interviewed had a background in law and they lacked knowledge and understanding about the law, all providing differing interpretations of its provisions.

According to most CSOs interviewed, the agency did not apply the law but ruled by exception. The granting of licences and accepting CSOs' annual reporting depended on personal connections and organizations' history rather than on their adherence to the law. Staff at the agency lacked competence, and high staff turnover meant that CSOs needed to deal with different officers on a regular basis. Desk officers interpreted the ChSP in different ways, rendering reporting cumbersome. Although a history of political activism in many cases explained difficulties in obtaining and renewing licences, with the exception of Ethiopian societies, most CSOs reported problems in their dealings with the agency. According to the ChSP, CSOs could appeal the decisions of employees at the ChSA through contacting its board. However, few such cases were known and, according to the interviews conducted, none had led to the reversal of a decision taken by the agency staff.

The federal auditor general's report (2006 EC Budget Year) on the ChSA provided further insights into the administrative capacity of the agency. The report stated that the agency did not coherently apply the law and that high staff turnover led to a lack of skills among agency staff. It further revealed that roughly 50 percent of the staff at the agency had never undergone university training, and only 2.8 percent of the employees had obtained a master's degree and 47.7 percent a first degree. Contrary to its duties, the agency did not provide regular feedback to charities and societies on their reporting nor did it offer adequate training in these matters. It failed to communicate with other state organizations in charge of overseeing the work of CSOs. Documentation and knowledge management were found to be insufficient and, in many instances, the ChSA did not enforce the law (Federal Auditor General 2014).

The Impact of the Proclamation on Civil Society, Donors, and the State

The most visible impact of the ChSP was the sharp decline in the number of organizations in the category of Ethiopian charities, primarily human rights NGOs. Unable to substitute international funding with local funding, some closed down their activities, and others changed their mandate to development activities and registered as resident charities in order to apply for international grants.

Ethiopian societies were somewhat better able to deal with the ChSP than Ethiopian charities. However, within the category there existed differences, especially between Ethiopian societies and Ethiopian mass societies. The latter benefited from preferential treatment by the ChSA due to their direct link to state and EPRDF structures (EPRDF 2008a). However, the capacity of many mass societies remained very low due to a lack of financial and human resources, and most were unable to use their extensive mandate granted by the ChSP and detailed in the EPRDF documents. Ethiopian mass societies were sometimes able to negotiate exemptions for foreign funding of parts of their activities, but such practices were not institutionalized, meaning that they depended on a case-by-case negotiation and that privileges could easily be revoked.

The large majority of organizations on the agency's register in 2016 were resident charities, followed by foreign charities, primarily constituted of NGOs and some think tanks focused on socioeconomic development activities. While foreign and resident charities were working in areas of the developmental state project sanctioned by the EPRDF, they reported significant problems regarding their operation due to mistrust from state offices. This suggested that security concerns took primacy over developmental concern.

The ability of international donors to fund democracy promotion and human rights advocacy for charities and societies diminished significantly because of the ChSP. However, the EU and the World Bank managed to negotiate exemptions from the ChSP and were allowed to finance Ethiopian charities and societies working on democracy promotion and other rights-based activities (Brechenmacher 2017, 84f; Gebre 2016).[9] While funding exemptions saved some of the human rights NGOs in Ethiopia, the ChSA and other state organizations were involved in overseeing the implementation of the programs, limiting the donors' ability to work on issues or with organizations perceived as sensitive and/or political by the EPRDF.

The human rights NGOs and professional associations active during the 2005 elections were hit particularly hard by the ChSP. However, despite Meles's suggestion that "over 90 percent of NGOs will not be affected, only those NGOs/CSOs involved in domestic political activities" (Yamamoto 2008d), the operational environment became difficult for most charities and societies, with the exception of Ethiopian mass societies (see Table 9.2). The majority of resident, Ethiopian, and foreign charities reported problems regarding the ChSP and its directives. In the eyes of the ChSA, most resident and foreign charities and societies became potential suspects of illegally working on rights-related issues, and the use of words like "advocacy" or "empowerment" by these organizations sufficed to raise suspicion and trigger reprimand. Moreover, the ChSA suspected Ethiopian charities of illegally using international funding. Instead of effectively reducing financial mismanagement, the interpretation of the 70/30 directive meant that most charities and societies found it difficult, for example, to invest in construction of accessible office space and training of staff and monitoring of their activities. Moreover, it restricted their ability to work in remote areas because most costs associated with travel, communication, and project infrastructure had to be accounted for on the 30 percent operational budget.

Table 1.5.2. *Mandate and Funding Sources of Charities and Societies According to the ChSP and Relationship to ChSA*

	Source of funding	Type of organization	Mandate/ activities	Relationship with the ChSA
Ethiopian society	At least 90% local funding, with some informal exceptions for mass societies	Professional associations, interest-based associations and mass-based organizations	Political and development activities, election monitoring, and voter education for mass societies	Relatively unproblematic, especially for mass societies; however, some professional societies were suspected of illegally using international resources to work on rights-related issues
Ethiopian charity	At least 90% local funding	Human rights NGOs and think tanks	Political and development activities	ChSA suspected/feared illegal use of international resources, problems with 70/30 directive and recurring problems with licensing
Resident charity	More than 10% international funding	Development NGOs and think tanks	Development activities	ChSA feared/suspected clandestine pursuit of rights-based/political activities, problems with 70/30 directive, frequent problems with licencing and reporting
Resident society	More than 10% international funding	NGOs serving the interests of their members only (not third party)	Development activities	ChSA feared/suspected clandestine pursuit of rights-based/political activities, problems with the 70/30 directive, frequent problems with licencing and reporting
Foreign charity	International funding	NGOs and think tanks	Development activities	ChSA feared/suspected clandestine pursuit of rights-based/political activities, problems with 70/30 directive, frequent problems with licencing and reporting

Some resident and some foreign charities managed to negotiate an exemption from the ChSP. While the exemption allowed these organizations to work on rights-related topics with foreign funding, in exchange they had to renounce publicly criticizing the EPRDF. This meant that an organization could, for example, work on conflict resolution and justice issues, but without questioning the EPRDF's rule. To receive an exemption, resident and foreign charities needed to sign an agreement with a state organization, which in practice meant the Ministries of Federal Affairs and of Foreign Affairs and the PMO. The process of receiving an exemption differed between organizations and involved long negotiations. Several resident charities working on questions related to peace and justice obtained an exemption because their board members were also members of councils of elders and therefore respected traditional leaders.[10] Foreign charities relied on high-level EPRDF contacts for this matter. The agency was not mandated to oversee the work of organizations that had received an exemption, meaning that they were operating in a legal vacuum in which privileges could be revoked and organizations had no legal means to contest such decisions.

Securitization versus Developmental Politics: The Application of the ChSP across the Ethiopian State

The fact that the ChSA used the proclamation and its directive to restrict the work of CSOs—with the exception of mass societies—rather than mobilizing them for developmental efforts, caused conflict with other state organizations that relied on CSOs in their operations. However, given the head's position in the EPRDF and the agency's link to the security apparatus, it exercised more power than many ministries.[11] Many civil servants in ministerial positions and advisers to the prime minister were not able to force the agency to change its decisions. Two interviewees working at resident charities explained:

> No one dares to touch him [the ChSA's director]; he can do whatever he wants. You need to look at the party hierarchy, this is what determines who decides, not your position in the government. You see, someone like him, even a minister cannot tell him what to do. (Interviewee No. 55 24.10.2016)

> Two of our senior members are advisers to the prime minister. They are trying their best to help us, but they cannot. They got our

accounts reopened when the agency blocked them. But he [the ChSA's director] doesn't give us our licence, and they can't help with that. (Interviewee No. 36 17.10.2016)

Multiple cases existed where the agency restricted the operations of not only resident and foreign charities but also Ethiopian societies that worked jointly with state organizations. A well-known example concerned a key partner of the National Planning Commission (NPC) and the Ministry of Finance and Economic Cooperation (MoFEC). The agency wanted to force the organization to switch its status from resident charity (foreign funded and third-party serving) to Ethiopian society (locally funded and membership serving), although the organization was working on development research, not rights-related/political issues. Even high-level government officials were unable to solve the problem in favor of the resident charity in question. A foreign charity partnering with MoFEC and providing substantial funds for development projects had to leave the country as the agency revoked its licence and, despite attempts, MoFEC was not able to reverse the agency's decision. The Ministry of Health (MoH) was told off for channeling foreign funds to an Ethiopian society in an attempt to circumvent the 90/10 provision and had to withdraw the funds it had transferred to the organization in question. Moreover, another of the MoH's partners, a consortium of resident and foreign charities, was unable to receive its project funding from a foreign charity, as the ChSA prohibited sub-granting between charities/societies. The Ministry of Justice struggled to provide legal aid to poor people, as many of its key civil society partners in this work had been heavily affected by the ChSP. Those that were registered as Ethiopian charities and societies lacked financial resources, and many had registered as resident charities and were not allowed to work on the issue any longer.

The agency exercised much power at the federal level, ensuring that state organizations did not help CSOs to circumvent the ChSP. It prohibited federal state bureaus, for example, to work on rights-related issues together with resident charities and societies, even where state offices were interested in such cooperation. An interviewee working for a resident charity explained:

> During the first years we designed projects with human rights components and collaborated with government bodies to implement the projects. They did the human rights components, for example human rights trainings. Now the government

bureaus don't want to do that anymore. The bureaus said that they have been given a warning by the agency. They are not allowed to do human rights activities with NGO money. (Interviewee No. 31 10.02.2016)

Given its limited capacity to oversee the work of the over three thousand organizations registered by it, the agency had less influence on the work of CSOs at the local level. Many state organizations at the local level depended on CSOs for meeting their development targets assigned as part of the operationalization of the developmental state.[12] They cooperated particularly with resident charities in the provision of public services, but also in addressing selected rights-based issues, such as domestic violence and female genital mutilation which were officially reserved for Ethiopian charities and societies only. The ability of resident charities and societies to bring in international donor money provided them with negotiation power vis-à-vis state officials and led to a more flexible interpretation of the 70/30 and 90/10 directive at the local level, to ensure that they could operate and jointly address development challenges with state organizations. Conflicts among state organizations indicated the existence of disagreements over the role of CSOs in the operationalization of the developmental state program. While almost all state officials held that charities and societies should not work on political issues with donor money, many agreed on the need to work jointly with these organizations in the implementation of development initiatives.

The 2019 Civil Society Organizations Proclamation

As described above, the content of the ChSP and the way it was applied negatively affected the operation of CSOs in Ethiopia. Contrary to the ChSP, the new civil society proclamation was clearly inspired by an attempt to open the political space for civil society. This becomes particularly clear when comparing the drafting processes and the contents of the ChSP with the new CSOP.

Concerning the process, contrary to the drafting of the ChSP, the working group for the CSOP was primarily constituted of legal experts and civil society representatives, not civil servants. Rather than imposing a law on civil society, the drafting process was co-owned by civil society. A consortium of CSOs had submitted an assessment of the ChSP, its shortcomings, and the needs of the civil society sector already before the official drafting process for the new law started and the assessment formed the base for the new proclamation.

Instead of the PMO, the Attorney General's Office (AGO) oversaw the drafting process, also indicating that formal procedures rather than intraparty politics determined the process. While the ChSA and its former management heavily opposed both the drafting process as well as the new legislation, the AGO ensured that state offices did not interfere with the drafting process, leaving the working group in charge of the process. The working group organized consultation meetings with representatives from relevant federal and local government offices, but pushed back on some attempts of public officials to introduce more operational restrictions into the CSOP.

Consultations with CSOs in the country's different regions were conducted after the first draft was finalized to collect their input. Moreover, a large number of CSOs also attended the public hearing on the new CSO law at the House of Peoples' Representatives to make their voice heard and influence the final proclamation. CSOs managed to push for some legal changes during the hearing, most notably an increase of CSO representatives on the board of the new CSOs agency mandated to implement the CSOP. While most CSOs welcomed the legal changes, some CSOs lobbied against them and advocated for a more progressive opening of the civic space. While constituting a small minority, CSOs closely affiliated with the old political guard and those that had managed to negotiate formal exemptions and/or informal preferential treatments worried about how the new legislation would affect their operations.

Regarding the content, the most visible changes in the new legislation were the dismissal of the 90/10 provision, the curbing of the power of the ChSA, and an attempt to facilitate licensing and operation of CSOs. The ChSA was renamed the Agency for Civil Society Organizations (ACSO), and its oversight was transferred from the Ministry of Federal Affairs, responsible for security issues, to the AGO, in charge of enforcing human rights standards. This demonstrated a clear intent to reverse the securitization of civil society. Provisions for penalties and fines in case of violation of the law were removed, as were the quasi-judicial powers of the former ChSA, aimed at encouraging the setup of CSOs. Finally, a change of language from the terms "charities and societies" to "civil society" indicated a shift towards a more liberal definition of civil society and ended the legal favoritism in favor of mass associations affiliated to the EPRDF.

While the legal changes from the ChSP to the CSOP in theory ensure the freedom of association and the participation of CSOs in Ethiopia's political and economic development, their practical implications remain yet to be seen. The findings presented in this chapter and the fact that several civil servants and even some CSOs expressed concerns regarding the opening of the space for civil society during the drafting of the CSOP suggest that a key determinant of the future of civil society in Ethiopia will lie in the application of the CSOP. Changing the mindset of civil servants at the ACSO and other government entities involved in regulating CSOs will demand substantive training efforts to ensure changes in practice. While a change of leadership at the ACSO has signaled the willingness to reorganize government administration of CSOs, the new leadership has struggled to gain the support of ACSO (former ChSA) staff, that in its majority still features a negative attitude towards CSOs. Moreover, successful implementation of the CSOP will also depend on the attitudes of civil servants working in other public offices involved in overseeing the work of CSOs, for example, different regional and zonal bureaus (justice, women and children, health, labor and social affairs, etc.).

The nonparticipation of formal CSOs in the political protests from 2015 to 2018 and the reform process following the progressive political opening in 2018 also indicate that the problems created by the ChSP require more than a mere change in legislation. Formal CSOs have been surprisingly silent, and many seem to lack the ability to actively take part in the political transition under way. They appear unsure of how to develop and promote an independent agenda where before the EPRDF's priorities were the only valid ones to follow and some still fear possible negative repercussions for independent civic activism. Moreover, under the previous legislation, many CSOs became used to operating through state and party channels and the establishment of a level playing field and democratic rule of operations requires reorganization on the part of CSOs.

While the working group drafting the CSOP reached out to CSOs, their key partner has been closely connected to EPRDF circles. This raises some questions regarding the EPRDF's willingness to open up its relationship to civil society beyond the organizations that have been connected to the ruling coalition.

CONCLUSION

While the preamble of the ChSP suggested that the law was passed to ensure the contribution of charities and societies to Ethiopia's development and to guarantee citizens' right to association, the findings in this chapter suggest that the ChSA primarily used the proclamation to control charities and societies rather than to mobilize them as part of the EPRDF's developmental state program. In theory, the ChSP coerced charities and societies to align themselves to the EPRDF developmental state agenda and contribute to its fulfilment: resident and foreign charities and societies through securing external finance for socioeconomic development interventions and Ethiopian societies (professional and mass associations) through mobilizing the population behind the EPRDF. Ethiopian charities, essentially human rights NGOs, were also officially allowed to work on political issues, but their role was not further detailed. In practice, nearly all charities and societies interviewed, with the exception of mass societies, reported problems regarding their operations under the ChSP. While foreign and resident charities and societies and many Ethiopian charities were under higher scrutiny by the ChSA than Ethiopian societies, the latter could seldom make use of this due to their low human and financial capacity.

The new CSOP rectifies the key provisions of the ChSP that have restricted people's right to freedom of association and clearly intends to encourage such activity. While a change in the legislation is an important formal indication for democratic reform in Ethiopia, it is premature to make predictions regarding its impact on civil society. The way the law will be interpreted and applied will be key in determining the success of the legal reform. Moreover, it will need time for CSOs to (re)grow in the political realm that has only just started opening up. CSOs will need to prove their ability to participate in the political transformation process under way and the EPRDF, as well as opposition parties, their willingness to engage with civil society actors beyond those affiliated to particular political factions to facilitate such a process.

NOTES

1. With the adoption of the ChSP in 2009, the EPRDF has categorized CSOs falling under the proclamation into charities (third-party-serving organizations) and societies (membership-based organizations). The first category includes NGOs and think tanks, for example, while the second comprises, among others, professional associations and mass organizations.

2. Around the 2005 national elections, several donor-financed NGOs were involved in voter education, carried out election monitoring, supported opposition candidates, and participated in postelection protests.

3. A problem of decentralization in Ethiopia was that although the provision of public services such as health and education had been delegated to the *woreda* level, the majority of domestic revenue, foreign aid, and foreign direct investment (FDI) was collected and spent at the federal level (Markakis 2011, 241). This created a mismatch between obligations and financial capacity of local state organizations, leading them to turn to CSOs for support in the implementation of development plans.

4. A resident charity reported, for example, not being able to remodel its office to ensure accessibility for handicapped persons, as the financial costs would have exceeded 30 percent of administrative costs.

5. BPR was ongoing on a large scale in the Ethiopian civil service in the early 2000s (Tesfaye and Atkilt 2011).

6. The MoJ was in charge of registering CSOs between 1991 and 2010.

7. Both France and Canada were involved in the reform process at the Ministry of Justice and were therefore chosen as locations (Yamamoto 2008a).

8. The Ministry of Federal and Pastoralist Affairs was responsible for internal security questions, overseeing the police and prisons and being tightly linked to the security agency.

9. Officially the EU's civil society fund, the CSF II was granted an exemption on the grounds of the Cotonou Agreement, according to which EU-funded projects were considered third-country money

(hence local money, not international funding). However, it seemed that, rather than technical justifications, the amount of financial support provided by the World Bank and the European Union equipped them with a leverage during the negotiations for the exemption of their civil society funds.

10. The councils of elders (*shimaglewoch*) in Ethiopia are customary institutions that act as mediators between two parties in conflict. They exist in different regions and have significant social and political influence on communities (Gebreyesus 2014; Getachew 1998)1998. Despite the centralization of state power under EPRDF rule, elders have remained important political figures, especially in rural areas, and their support to the regime has proven crucial (Aregawi 2009, 227). After the 2005 political crisis, a council of elders, including personalities like former Harvard scholar Ephraim Isaac and pastor Daniel Gebreselassie, mediated between the imprisoned opposition politicians and the EPRDF (Yonas 2014, 36).

11. The power of public officials and, related to that, of the state organizations they were leading, depended on an individual's position within the EPRDF. The higher the ranking in the EPRDF hierarchy, the larger the power it could exercise vis-à-vis other public organizations.

12. See note 3.

REFERENCES

Aregawi Berhe. 2009. *A Political History of the Tigray People's Liberation Front (1975–1991): Revolt, Ideology, and Mobilisation in Ethiopia*. Los Angeles: Tsehai.

Asnake Kefale. 2011. "The (Un)Making of Opposition Coalitions and the Challenge of Democratization in Ethiopia, 1991–2011." *Journal of Eastern African Studies* 5, no. 4: 681–701.

Brechenmacher, Saskia. 2017. *Civil Society Under Assault: Repression and Responses in Russia, Egypt, and Ethiopia*. Washington, DC: Carnegie Endowment for International Peace.

Burgess, Gemma Lucy. 2012. "When the Personal Becomes Political: Using Legal Reform to Combat Violence against Women in Ethiopia." *Gender, Place & Culture* 19, no. 2: 153–74.

Directive No. 3. 2011. *A Directive to Provide for the Establishment and Administration of Charity Committee*. Addis Ababa: Charities and Societies Agency Director General, Ali Siraj.

Directive No. 4. 2011. *A Directive to Provide for the Establishment of a Charitable Endowment, Charitable Trust and Charitable Institution*. Addis Ababa: Charities and Societies Agency Director General, Ali Siraj.

Directive No. 5. 2011. *A Directive to Provide for Public Collection by Charities and Societies*. Addis Ababa: Charities and Societies Agency Director General, Ali Siraj.

Directive No. 6. 2011. *A Directive Issued to Provide for the Liquidation, Transfer and Disposal of the Properties of Charities and Societies*. Addis Ababa: Charities and Societies Agency Director General, Ali Siraj.

Directive No. 7. 2011. *A Directive to Provide for Income Generating Activities by Charities and Societies*. Addis Ababa: Charities and Societies Agency Director General, Ali Siraj.

Directive No. 8. 2011. *Directive to Provide for the Submission of Audit and Activity Reports of Charities and Societies and Charity Committees*. Addis Ababa: Charities and Societies Agency Director General, Ali Siraj.

Dupuy, Kendra E., James Ron, and Aseem Prakash. 2015. "Who Survived? Ethiopia's Regulatory Crackdown on Foreign-Funded NGOs." *Review of International Political Economy* 22, no. 2: 419–56.

EPRDF. 2008a. "The Significance of the Establishment of EPRDF's Women and Youth Leagues," translated by B. Bezawit. *Addis Raey: EPRDF's Ideology Magazin* 2, no. 2: 49–56.

———. 2008b. "Draft Report for the 7th EPRDF Congress," translated by B. Bezawit. *Addis Raey: EPRDF's Ideology Magazin: EPRDF's Ideology Magazin* 2 (Special Issue).

———. 2008c. "Behind the Charities and Societies Proclamation," translated by B. Bezawit. *Addis Raey: EPRDF's Ideology Magazin* 2, no. 3: 5–22.

———. 2011. *Report of the 8th EPRDF Congress, Presented to the 8th EPRDF Congress* (English version). Mekelle: EPRDF.

———. 2015. "The Decisions of Our 10th Congress and Its Strategic Contributions," translated by B. Bezawit. *Addis Raey: EPRDF's Ideology Magazin: EPRDF's Ideology Magazin* 5, no. 2: 6–53.

Federal Auditor General. 2014. *Report of the Federal Auditor General 2014—Charities and Societies Agency*. Federal Audit Report, translated by B. Bezawit.

Gebreyesus Teklu Bahta. 2014. "Popular Dispute Resolution Mechanisms in Ethiopia: Trends, Opportunities, Challenges, and Prospects." *African Journal on Conflict Resolution* 14, no. 1: 99–123.

Getachew Mequanent. 1998. "Community Development and the Role of Community Organizations: A Study in Northern Ethiopia." *Canadian Journal of African Studies* 32, no. 3: 494–520.

Markakis, John. 2011. *Ethiopia: The Last Two Frontiers*. Eastern Africa Series. Suffolk: James Currey.

Meles Zenawi. 2006. "African Development: Dead Ends and New Beginnings." Unpublished master's thesis, draft for discussion, Erasmus University.

———. 2007. "FT Interview: Meles Zenawi, Ethiopian Prime Minister." *Financial Times*, February 6, 2007.

Mihret Alemayehu Zeleke. 2010. "Civil Society and Freedom of Association Threatened?" Master's thesis, University of Oslo.

MoCB. 2004. *Civil Society Organizations' Capacity Building Program Design: Zero Draft*. Addis Ababa: Ministry of Capacity Building.

MoFED. 2002. *Ethiopia: Sustainable Development and Poverty Reduction Program*. Addis Ababa: Ministry of Finance and Economic Development.

---. 2006. *A Plan for Accelerated and Sustained Development to End Poverty (PASDEP)*. Addis Ababa: Ministry of Finance and Economic Development.

Regulation No. 168. 2009. *Council of Ministers Regulation to Provide for the Registration and Administration of Charities and Societies*. Federal Negarit Gazeta of the Federal Democratic Republic of Ethiopia.

Sisay Alemahu Yeshanew. 2012. "CSO Law in Ethiopia: Considering Its Constraints and Consequences." *Journal of Civil Society* 8, no. 4: 369–84.

Tesfaye Debela and Atkilt Hagos. 2011. *The Design and Implementation of Business Process Reengineering in the Ethiopian Public Sector: An Assessment of Four Organizations*. Addis Ababa: Organisation for Social Science Research in Eastern and Southern Africa.

Yamamoto, D. 2008a. *Meles on New CSO/NGO Law: Brace for Change* (Wikileaks Public Library of US Diplomacy No. 08ADDISABABA1593_a).

---. 2008b. *Draft Civil Society Law Clamps Down on Foreign-Funded NGOs* (Wikileaks Public Library of US Diplomacy No. 08ADDISABABA1223_a).

---. 2008c. *Prime Minister Meles Set on New CSO/NGO Law in Autumn* (Wikileaks Public Library of US Diplomacy No. 08ADDISABABA2105_a).

---. 2008d. *Ethiopia's CSO/NGO Law Ready for Parliament Approval* (Wikileaks Public Library of US Diplomacy No. 08ADDISABABA2846_a).

---. 2008e. *DRL a/S Kramer Notes U.S. Concern on CSO Law* (Wikileaks Public Library of US Diplomacy No. 08ADDISABABA2103_a).

---. 2008f. *Ethiopian Prime Minister Meles on 2010 National Elections, Draft NGO Law, and Ogaden Humanitarian Crisis* (Wikileaks Public Library of US Diplomacy No. 08ADDISABABA1259_a).

---. 2008g. *With CSO Law, GOE Tells Donors to Back Off* (Wikileaks Public Library of US Diplomacy No. 08ADDISABABA3100_a).

---. 2008h. *Engaging Parliament on CSO Law* (Wikileaks Public Library of US Diplomacy No. 08ADDISABABA3381_a).

---. 2009. *Ethiopia Passes Restrictive CSO Law* (Wikileaks Public Library of US Diplomacy No. 09ADDISABABA31_a).

Yitayehu Alemayehu Taye. 2010. "The State, Nongovernmental Organizations and the Making of the Charities and Societies Proclamation No. 621 of 2009 in Ethiopia—Historical and Institutional Perspectives." PhD diss., Northeastern University.

Yntiso Gebre. 2016. "Reality Checks: The State of Civil Society Organizations in Ethiopia." *African Sociological Review* 20, no. 2: 2–25.

Yohannes Woldegebriel. 2013a. "Are Business Associations Charities?" *Addis Fortune* 13, no. 680.

———. 2013b. "The Ordeals of Business Associations Registrations." *Addis Business*, April.

Yonas Berhane. 2014. *Mezard, Indigenous Conflict Resolution Mechanism in Northern Ethiopia: Assessing Rural Alamata Woreda, Tigray Regional State, Ethiopia*. Hamburg: Anchor Academic.

LIST OF INTERVIEWS

To guarantee anonymity, names and positions of informants have been omitted. Given the sensitive nature of the research, it was deemed necessary to guarantee the anonymity and confidentiality of sources. Interviewees have been sorted into relevant analytical categories, with rank and nationality indicated, where relevant and where there is no risk of revealing the identity of the person.

Table 1.5.3. *List of Interviews*

Number	Sector	Date(s) of Interview
1	Civil Servant*	24.10.2015, 13.11.2015, 27.01.2016, 22.08.2017, 30.10.2017, 15.03.2018
2	Consultant Charities and Societies, Ethiopian	10.07.2015,** 11.11.2015
3	Donor Representative, International	10.11.2015
4	Researcher, International	09.11.2015
5	Civil Servant, Public University	06.11.2015
6	Consultant Charities and Societies, International	10.11.2015, 09.02.2018
7	Civil Servant	12.11.2015, 29.02.2016

8	Consultant Charities and Societies, Ethiopian	11.11.2015
9	Civil Servant	12.11.2015, 24.05.2016, 30.10.2016
10	International Foundation, Director	12.11.2015
11	Donor Representative, International	13.11.2015
12	Civil Service Consultant, International	10.11.2015
13	Researcher, Ethiopian	15.11.2015
14	President, Ethiopian Resident Charity	16.11.2015
15	Civil Servant	17.11.2015
16	INGO, President	17.11.2015
17	Donor Representative, International	18.11.2015
18	Civil Service Consultant, Ethiopian	18.11.2015
19	Consultant, Charities and Societies, Ethiopian	19.11.2015
20	Consultant, Charities and Societies, Ethiopian	19.11.2015
21	NGO, Head of the Secretariat	20.11.2015, 09.06.2016, 01.11.2016
22	Civil Servant, Public University	22.11.2015
23	Civil Servant, Public University	23.11.2015, 17.05.2016
24	Donor Representative, International	23.11.2015
25	Donor Representative, Ethiopian	23.11.2015
26	Ethiopian Resident Charity, President	24.11.2015
27	Civil Servant	25.11.2015
28	Consortium of Resident and International Charities and Societies, President	25.11.2015
29	Ethiopian Resident Charity, Employee	26.11.2015
30	Ethiopian Resident Charity, Employee	27.11.2015
31	Ethiopian Resident Charity, Executive Director	10.02.2016
32	Ethiopian Society, Employee	10.02.2016
33	Consortium Resident and International Charities and Societies, Employee	16.02.2016
34	Civil Servant	17.02.2016, 23.03.2016, 19.05.2016, 15.06.2016
35	Civil Servant	17.02.2016

36	Ethiopian Resident Charity, Secretary General	18.02.2016, 17.10.2016
37	Ethiopian Society, Director General	19.02.2016
38	Civil Servant	22.02.2016
39	Ethiopian Charity, Employee	03.03.2016
40	Donor Representative, Ethiopian	08.03.2016
41	International Charity, Employee	16.03.2016
42	International Charity, Director	16.03.2016
43	Consultant, Charities and Societies, International	17.03.2016
44	International Foundation, Ethiopian	18.03.2016, 24.05.2016
45	Civil Servant	21.03.2016
46	Donor Representative, Ethiopian	22.03.2016
47	Chambers of Commerce and Sectoral Association, Member	30.05.2016
48	Civil Servant	20.06.2016
49	Civil Servant, Public University	01.06.2016, 28.06.2016, 23.02.2018
50	Ethiopian Resident Charity, Employee	03.06.2016
51	Ethiopian Charity, Director	13.06.2016
52	Politician	14.07.2016, 10.10.2016
53	Civil Servant***	18.07.2016
54	Donor Representative, Ethiopian	13.10.2016
55	Chambers of Commerce and Sectoral Association, President	14.10.2016
56	Ethiopian Charity, President	21.10.2016
57	Consultant, Civil Service, Ethiopian	24.10.2016
58	Ethiopian Charity, President	25.10.2016
59	Ethiopian Resident Charity, President	26.10.2016
60	NGO, Executive Director	27.10.2016
61	NGO, Project Manager	05.12.2016
62	Ethiopian Resident Charity, Executive Director	15.03.2017
63	Ethiopian Resident Charity, Executive Director	14.03.2017
64	Ethiopian Resident Charity, Executive Director	16.03.2017

65	Ethiopian Resident Charity, Employee	13.03.2017
66	Ethiopian Society, President	09.03.2017
67	Ethiopian Resident Charity, Employee	12.03.2017
68	Ethiopian Resident Charity, Employee	09.03.2017
69	Ethiopian Resident Charity, President	08.03.2017
70	Civil Servant	17.03.2017
71	Civil Servant	10.03.2017
72	Civil Servant	14.03.2017
73	Civil Servant	16.03.2017
74	Civil Servant	17.03.2017
75	Consortium Resident and International Charities, President	07.03.2017
76	Civil Servant	20.02.2018
77	Consortium Resident and International Charities, President	27.02.2018
78	Researcher, International	20.11.2015
79	Ethiopian Resident Charity, President	20.11.2015
80	Civil Servant, Public University	18.11.2015
81	Donor Representative, International	13.11.2015
82	Civil Servant	12.04.2019
83	Consultant, Charities and Societies, Ethiopian	12.04.2019
84	Consultant, Charities and Societies, Ethiopian	15.04.2019
85	Consortium Resident and International Charities, President	16.04.2019
86	Consortium, President	16.04.2019

* All interviews with informant No. 1 were conducted via Skype.
** Interview conducted via Skype.
*** Interview carried out by research assistant.

1.6 Choosing the Road and Smoothing the Bumps
The Media and Politics

William Davison

SUMMARY

Until the constitutional demands by Oromo protesters and the internal challenge from Oromo People's Democratic Organization (OPDO) reformists, Ethiopia was on a path to intensifying conflict. The resulting process of radical regeneration without regime change enhances the prospects for sustainable steps toward democratization, as the errors of the past can be discarded while the more solid foundations are built upon. Orthodox liberal frameworks suggest that conflict should reduce as differences are increasingly mediated through democratic procedures and institutions. But with this unexpected political opening, a polarized ideological landscape is now in full view, and it is one filled with partisan media and single-issue social media activists, including those who played a critical role in creating the opportunity for progressive change. That means that instability has continued and there are still significant risks of worsening conflict. To forge a path away from dangerous differences over identity and ideology and toward managed disagreement over policy and practices, objective journalism must, somehow, eventually drown out its sensational, seductive, and inflammatory competitor. That would help put Ethiopia on the path to competitive liberal politics rather than the road to anarchic conflict.

RECENT HISTORY

The previous two Ethiopian prime ministers, Meles Zenawi and Hailemariam Desalegn, referred to the essential role that democracy had to play in Ethiopia's survival as a nation. Their framing was that because of its diversity, democracy was essential to mediate differences and accommodate competing interests. But the ruling coalition of regional parties they chaired, the Ethiopian People's Revolutionary Democratic Front (EPRDF), had a particular interpretation of democracy. EPRDF doctrines presented the multinational federation it designed as democratic because minorities were granted the right to self-rule rather than having their identities suppressed, as in the past, and the political system as democratic because the party encouraged mass participation in development activities. Regardless of this ideological framing, EPRDF "democracy" did not produce a harmonious political settlement, and instead the system was often perceived as authoritarian and discriminatory. After the failed attempt at holding open elections in 2005, the EPRDF moved further away from liberal democracy and focused on its development program, while suppressing the opposition. This strategy also failed after Meles passed away in 2012 and fault lines grew in the EPRDF coalition, even as its political domination increased. In 2014 there was the first Oromo protest over a master plan for Addis Ababa's expansion and, after another electoral whitewash, in late 2015 public opposition broke into the open.

As the anti-government protests in Oromia and elsewhere in the country persisted sporadically in 2017, so moving into their fourth year, fears of Ethiopia descending into worsening conflict increased. One of the origins of those worries was this gulf in perception and narratives that had grown over decades between the EPRDF and its opponents. As a crude indicator of the media's role in amplifying this divide, there was the output of opposition-aligned foreign-based outlets and state-owned media. While Ethiopian Television rarely, if ever, uttered a critical word about the government, dissident channels such as Ethiopian Satellite Television and Radio (ESAT) infrequently, if at all, broadcast complimentary reports.

The uncritical approach of the public media was a faithful reproduction of the government's view of itself. Despite increasing admissions of maladministration, corruption, and stunted democratization, the government maintained that it was democratically elected and the rightful guarantor of the constitutional order and that any attempt to challenge it from outside the polling booth was therefore illegal. This standard conception of legitimate authority was accompanied by its political beliefs that EPRDF rule had brought protection and autonomy for previously threatened and marginalized ethnic communities and that the Ethiopian people overall had benefited from its pro-poor development policies.

The various opposition narratives diverged sharply on almost every single aspect of this official account. Whether based at home or abroad, campaigning on an ethno-national or pan-Ethiopian basis, leftist or liberal, all parties accused the EPRDF of decisively tilting the electoral landscape in its favor through a variety of authoritarian methods. These included unconstitutional restrictions on civil rights and ensuring—through a variety of formal and informal mechanisms—that EPRDF control was maintained throughout the government, economy, and society (Lyons 2014).

Adding extra toxicity to the debate, much of the opposition also argued that the EPRDF's multinational federal system and the state-heavy economic model that evolved under Prime Minister Meles was designed and dominated by the Tigray People's Liberation Front (TPLF) in order to secure Tigrayan hegemony over more populous groups, particularly the Amhara and Oromo. Opponents frequently argued that claimed economic gains were illusory and that the TPLF and its allies and supporters had disproportionately harvested the fruits of any progress (Bonsa 2015). They also said that the TPLF dominated the system despite formally equal power sharing, primarily through Meles's long rule and by controlling the armed forces and the federal security apparatus. Rather than agreeing with the TPLF and EPRDF that the system protected minority rights, critics focused on the alleged use of divide-and-rule tactics by the party from the minority Tigrayan group. Similarly, opponents did not give the EPRDF credit for creating a mass-based political movement that was able to get farmers to cooperate in development works and mobilize supporters effectively to participate in political events. They focused instead on coercive methods used to ensure participation, harassment of the opposition, clamping down on potential alternative sources of organizational power, and intolerance of dissent from the media or civil society, which all combined to produce noncompetitive elections.

One troubling consequence of this stark divergence in perspectives was that in 2015 and 2016 it was hard to imagine the government making concessions that would be considered significant enough to placate protesters. This was because the challenge to the EPRDF was an existential one. Demonstrators and foreign-based opponents were not making an appeal for compromise; they were risking their lives or focusing all of their political energies on trying to change a government that they considered illegitimate. As this was a zero-sum game, opponents set on total victory would have perceived any significant concession from the EPRDF as a sign of weakness ripe for exploitation—not as an olive branch from which a peaceful compromise could be cultivated. Therefore, the government seemed set to continue along its course rather than embolden such a threatening challenge by displaying vulnerability. That meant increasing attempts to suppress and repress the growing dissent that occurred in 2016, a strategy that hitherto had only led to increasing anger among opponents and worsening strife. This scenario tracked the established pattern since the 2005 parliamentary elections, when the EPRDF responded to a major challenge by shutting off most avenues of legitimate opposition, whether in party politics, civil society, or the media. As the opposition was excluded from all parts of the government in 2010 and 2015, most dissent was muzzled, often through prosecutions, and frustrations grew until the mass protests.

Since shortly after the 2010 election, where the EPRDF's dominance evolved into it governing a de facto one-party state, a national security state also grew in prominence, notably on matters relating to political repression. This appeared to be partly triggered—or perhaps encouraged—by the outbreak of pro-democracy protests in the Middle East known as the Arab Spring. If the US's draconian response to the attacks of September 11, 2001, provided authoritarian governments across the world with a justification for repression, the Arab Spring emboldened Ethiopian security operatives to take preemptive action against those they classified as potential agitators. This was when journalist and activist Eskinder Nega again fell afoul of the authorities, as he was imprisoned after lecturing and publishing on press freedom (Amnesty International 2011). By classifying the exiled counterparts of the few remaining domestic opponents as "terrorist organizations," it was easy for the National Intelligence and Security Service (NISS) to present links between civil dissenters and "terrorists," and there were few, if any, independent judges willing to push back against such crude tactics, which were flimsily supported by shambolic efforts at building evidence-based cases. The death of Meles, a skillful and fearsome political operator, in August 2012, further reduced effective oversight of the security services.

In a move that surprised many, even including some pro-government commentators, NISS went as far as arresting members of a blogging group, Zone 9, which, although oppositional, was not involved in provocative political activism. They were charged in 2014 under the all-encompassing terms of a 2009 anti-terrorism law, as were other journalists (Human Rights Watch 2015). One of the defendants on the Zone 9 charge sheet was Tesfalem Waldyes, a freelancer who was well known to the international press in Addis Ababa. The Zone 9 trial, along with the prosecution of two Swedish reporters on accessory to terrorism charges for embedding with the rebel Ogaden National Liberation Front (ONLF) in 2011, demonstrated to the media that nobody was safe—unless they stayed well outside what could be perceived as unacceptably critical reporting (Committee to Protect Journalists 2011). It should be noted here, however, that while Ethiopian journalists faced the very real threat of imprisonment during this period if they were perceived to have transgressed by NISS, foreign reporters were far more likely to face inconvenient yet brief detentions, and deportation was the likely worst-case scenario.

The shutout in the 2010 election could have had a galvanizing effect on the formal opposition, but the subsequent extinguishing of any lingering dissent meant instead that even more actors essentially gave up on the democratic process, as a wave of opponents had after the 2005 debacle. This led to a different form of opposition to the EPRDF, which first took shape in 2012 as members of the Islamic community objected to alleged unconstitutional interference in religious affairs, and US-based activists promoted a creative, dynamic program of peaceful civil resistance through Facebook (Davison 2012). That increased the prominence of online activists and demonstrated a successful model of opposition, although security operatives were soon able to control the growing movement by arresting a narrow and Addis Ababa-based leadership, wildly accusing them of trying to implement an Islamic state.

Lessons were learned and social media activism became an integral part of the Oromo protests. While doubtless that medium would have risen to prominence anyway with increasing Internet access, it became particularly important in Ethiopia, as other channels of critical information were closed due to growing government intolerance. Protests first occurred in 2014, although there had been similar previous bouts of discontent, for example in 2001 over the reversed decision to move Oromia's capital from Addis Ababa to Adama (Amnesty International 2005). But the protests began in earnest after the 2015 elections, when the EPRDF displayed either its desire for suffocating hegemony or its inability to control localized repression by, along with allied parties, capturing every single elected seat in the country, not only at the 547-member federal parliament but also in all regional councils. Building on the Muslim protests, the subsequent opposition movement was decentralized, with diaspora activists acting as hubs to receive information and then disseminate it, primarily from Facebook accounts with huge numbers of followers. This mode of reporting was far more influential than anything provided by the traditional media. While some activists claimed to adhere to high standards of accuracy through verification, there were plenty of reasons to doubt this, such as the unreliable activist allegations surrounding the 2016 Irreecha tragedy in Bishoftu, when more than one hundred people died at a cultural festival, mostly in a stampede. The response of the authorities was repression and suppression, the latter primarily involving shutting off Internet access.

If the government had wanted to reduce the impact of social-media-driven narratives, it could have facilitated access to reporters at this critical stage, but the opposite was the case. EPRDF desire for control and mistrust of private media meant that reporting was frequently interrupted, discouraging efforts to try. It was hard to understand the logic behind the government's attitude towards the media, as reporting from the field often led to a more nuanced understanding of the crisis, which was at odds with the binary presentation from activists. After failing to suppress and repress using routine methods, the government enacted a state of emergency in September 2016. This followed the intense and violent week of protests provoked by the tragedy at the Irreecha celebration and activist calls for "five days of rage" (Schemm 2016).

While the prospects looked grave during this period of the crisis, the saving grace for Ethiopia and, perhaps temporarily, the EPRDF, was the nature of the demands made by the most powerful protesting constituency, the Oromo. This can initially be illustrated by examining the more challenging nature of the next most significant strand of discontent, which was from Amhara. When the first mass protest in that region occurred in Gondar in August 2016, the focus of the complaint was alleged Tigrayan annexation of Amhara land (Davison 2016). This grievance went back to Ethiopia's previous transition, after the downfall of the Derg military regime in 1991. As the multinational federation emerged over the next four years of an EPRDF-orchestrated transitional administration, areas such as Welkait, Tselemte, and Tsegede, as well as Raya to the east, were incorporated into Tigray, when they had previously been part of provinces that became part of Amhara. The protests that occurred in 2016 were the result of decades of simmering discontent over a situation that grew into a major political challenge. Furthermore, constitutionally provided mechanisms for resolving disputes, such as referenda, were generally considered inappropriate by complainants, as the area was now populated by a strong majority of Tigrinya speakers. The litany of complaints about the wider situation included that it was the TPLF that had altered the demographics by resettling people into the area.

The critical point here is that the Amhara opposition surge partly represented a challenge to the governing system itself, as it argued that the process of constituting the federation was unjust. This included the allegation that genuinely representative Amhara elements were not part of the constitution-making process. The virulently anti-TPLF positioning was also in keeping with a strain of Amhara political thought that rejected the entire edifice of ethnic-identity politics that had dominated Ethiopian public affairs since the 1960s (Wondemagne 2016). This was partly because the "nationalities question" that arose, most famously discussed by Walleligne Mekonnen in his seminal 1969 essay, "On the Question of Nationalities in Ethiopia," was considered to be essentially "anti-Amhara." Given the nature of this challenge, it was hard to conceive the TPLF accommodating it, as doing so would not only result in the loss of Tigray's territory but also threaten to undermine the federal system that it had been instrumental in devising and of which it considered itself the primary guardian. Even though the Amhara Democratic Party (ADP, formerly known as the Amhara National Democratic Movement) has now partly adopted the protesters' territorial demands and the TPLF is considerably weakened, there is still no resolution to the issue, primarily because of the fundamental nature of the questions raised.

On the contrary, in Oromia, rather than rejecting ethnic federalism, protesters and activists instead wanted to deepen it—or, as it is sometimes put, to democratize the federation. The contemporary expression of long-standing Oromo grievances over marginalization boiled down to the perception that despite the constitutionally mandated self-rule for their region, there was not de facto autonomy. This overarching democratic concern was buttressed by more specific complaints, such as the alleged subservience of the OPDO, later the Oromo Democratic Party (ODP), to the TPLF within the EPRDF; federal government control of investment decisions in the region; the lack of economic benefits accruing to local people from those investments; and crucially, the rampant growth of Addis Ababa into Oromia, which was partly at the expense of Oromo farmers. These were often well-founded concerns and were popular in Oromia, especially after they were expertly packaged and promoted by social media activists.

Prior to the outbreak of protests, the government acknowledged chronic problems with maladministration and corruption, which it sought to address under the broad rubric of improving "good governance." Although they were radical and political, the Oromo complaints could also be placed under this umbrella. The infamous Addis Ababa-area "master plan"—the single most important catalyst of the protests—was always likely to rouse opposition, but it was also a failure of public administration, as there was insufficient consultation, political discussion, and media coverage as the blueprint was formulated. Likewise, investment in Oromia should have been handled with greater transparency and fairness, as corruption was frequently involved. The most political allegation was of OPDO subservience, but few people doubted that the Oromia wing of the EPRDF had rarely punched its demographic weight within the front.

The critical upshot of this was that the constitutional nature of the protesters' demands meant that there was an opportunity for OPDO reformists to make common cause with the public and call for change from within the EPRDF. This occurred right at the outset of the protests, in April 2014, when regional parliamentarians voiced their opposition to the master plan, an act that was in fact a trigger for initial demonstrations. After years of ensuing civil disobedience, which was met with the standard authoritarian repressive response, the OPDO's assertive stance entered a new phase when the regional council's speaker, Lemma Megersa, became chief administrator in October 2016 and Abiy Ahmed was appointed as one of his deputies.

These events set the stage for radical change under the EPRDF that had been hard to envisage before because of the existential nature of the challenge to the ruling coalition. Rather than the EPRDF and its opponents' differences leading Ethiopia down the path of worsening conflict as they both battled for supremacy, a less extreme option arose. The emergence of an assertive, oppositional OPDO, which sympathized with protesters who were making primarily constitutional demands, intensified pressure for reform within the EPRDF, especially as they allied with Amhara's ruling party leadership. And to complement this dynamic, when there was a need for new leadership to push through the reform agenda, Abiy, supported by Lemma, was ideally positioned to take the reins from Prime Minister Hailemariam.

As is now well established, Prime Minister Abiy and allies seized the opportunity that was presented to them in an ongoing dynamic political process, which is characterized both by continuity and change. The continuity stems from the fact that there has been no change of government; there has only been a new leader selected by the ruling party. Additionally, the EPRDF Executive Committee had decided in December 2017 to accelerate sluggish and half-hearted reforms, including by moving ahead with the release of political prisoners, although the initial implementation of this was also stuttering. The new leadership's more aggressive approach to this existing agenda led to significant developments, developments that were unimaginable under either of the previous premiers.

REGIME IMPROVEMENT

Rather than a violent and tumultuous process of regime change, there has been a radical process of regime improvement. That is potentially critical to Ethiopia's future stability, as it reduces the severity of the upheaval and allows Abiy's government to build on past achievements while shedding those practices and policies that have held the country back. That is a departure from the end of the imperial regime in 1974 and the demise of the Derg's military socialism in 1991, when new constitutional orders had to be constructed upon the ashes of the previous ones.

Consequently, in practice we have indeed seen significant elements of continuity. For example, in the economic sphere, while steps have been taken to reduce the debt burden by constraining public investment in infrastructure such as hydropower dams and railways, and there is a new phase of more ambitious privatizations, key developmental strategies of the EPRDF remain in place: the federal budget is still focused on social services such as education and health; the financial sector remains protected, at least for now, and directed towards long-term goals; and agriculture and manufacturing are still key planks of the growth strategy. Much the same can be said about Ethiopia's foreign policy, despite the rapprochement with Eritrea, which, of course, marks a departure. But whether it is in terms of pragmatically maintaining a wide array of bilateral relations with diverse partners, playing an active part in peacekeeping missions, or taking a leading role in regional affairs, there is more continuity than change. Rather than remaking its international approach from scratch, the new leadership is looking to improve bilateral relations, as with the ascendant Gulf powers, or increase its engagement with multilateral initiatives, as with plans to accelerate World Trade Organization accession and an assertive approach to the development of the African Continental Free Trade Area.

Those moves are part of an overall liberalizing approach where Abiy and allies appear to cleave closely to theories of democratic, or liberal, peace. These posit that democracies are less likely to go to war with each other; this was originally expounded in 1795 by Immanuel Kant in *Perpetual Peace*. As the Horn of Africa has been marred by closed autocratic or authoritarian regimes in Djibouti, Eritrea, Ethiopia, Somalia, Sudan, and South Sudan, there is a stated desire from Addis Ababa for this era to be marked by an opening of government and borders, as expressed by Abiy at his appearance at the World Economic Forum in Davos (2019). This agenda clearly faces challenges and will take many years, even if political circumstances are favorable.

In theory, the domestic arena should be less challenging for Abiy to influence, if he is able to maintain his popularity and power. Liberal theory generally suggests that democratic progress reduces the chances of internal conflict by producing institutions and processes that are suitable for mediating disputes and accommodating different interests. That is highly relevant for Ethiopia, where there are stark differences of opinion on the past, present, and future of the country. Most pertinently, these disagreements were expressed through views on a fractious EPRDF and its strained multinational federation, a model that is increasingly being challenged by resurgent opponents. Ideally, the unshackling of the opposition, civil society, and the media would mean a more dynamic marketplace of ideas rapidly developing that would allow a new consensus to emerge as diverse viewpoints coalesce around a compromise. This theoretical constructive exchange would be regulated by a bevy of new, or newly autonomous, democratic institutions. However, so far, this scenario has not materialized, raising the question of whether reducing conflict is a matter of continuing along the same trajectory for a longer period of time or whether Ethiopia is in fact not on the correct path to peace, despite the initial steps toward political and economic liberalization. Continuing, and perhaps even deepening, political polarization has accompanied the ongoing violence, which has become more intercommunal than state-society. While all actors have a responsibility to address the polarization problem, the traditional and social media have a particularly important role to play, as they are the conduits between the public and the political classes. But before addressing this critical issue of communication through the media, the nature of the polarization needs to be determined.

The changing character of the (now defunct) EPRDF under its new chairperson, Abiy, involved doctrinal repositioning from some member parties, as, for example, the ADP shifted away from revolutionary democracy, and the ODP, the renamed OPDO, tried to assert itself as a democratizing, liberalizing force. It should also be noted that the Southern Ethiopian People's Democratic Movement faced a major challenge from the Southern Nations, Nationalities and Peoples' zonal districts' demands for regional status, a process led by the Sidama (Davison and Kulle 2018). The front also appeared to discard a commitment to consensus-based decision-making, a process that may have begun after a minority of hardliners stymied Hailemariam's reformist inclinations.

The most significant EPRDF issue relating to polarization, which has been exacerbated by the media environment, has been the diminishment of the TPLF. This downgrading occurred in terms of the party's federal power—it now holds no cabinet posts—as well as its officials' influence in the security apparatus. The prosecution of officials from NISS, as well as Metals and Engineering Corporation (METEC) managers for corruption, exacerbated this loss of sway (Davison and Leake 2018). A perception has grown among the Tigrayan party—and, it appears, Tigrayans generally—that the prosecutions were politically motivated, as the two institutions were TPLF-dominated. This includes the charges laid against Getachew Assefa, the former head of NISS and a member of the TPLF politburo. Additionally, party leaders have expressed concerns over marginalization and "encirclement," arguing they were sidelined when the prime minister achieved a rapprochement with their long-term archrival, Eritrean President Isaias Afwerki. Those TPLF fears increased as Amhara elements ratcheted up the claims to Tigrayan territory.

The problem with this scenario is not that there has necessarily been any actual injustice suffered by the TPLF or its officials but that it has led to the relative isolation of Tigray, a lack of TPLF commitment to and participation in the enhanced democratization process, and an uptick in divisive rhetoric. This has reportedly led to increased Tigrayan solidarity with the region's beleaguered ruling party (Nebiyu 2019). The situation had a negative impact on EPRDF cohesion and collective decision-making, which would be dealt with most simply through the further sidelining of TPLF. However, if that results in the increasing isolation of Tigray or the disorderly disintegration of the EPRDF, then the federation as a whole is likely to suffer (the EPRDF has now been replaced by the Prosperity Party in a relatively orderly process, although the TPLF refused to join). In this area then, the fruits of radical change emanating from the relatively stable foundation created by the internal reform process have not yet materialized. Instead a liberalized scene threatens to accelerate progress down divergent paths, with even growing talk on the fringes of Tigrayan secession from the federation.

The other critical area of concern stems from the return of the gamut of Ethiopian political parties to the domestic scene. As a result of authoritarian methods to achieve overwhelming hegemony, the EPRDF had excluded a host of political actors. Previously exiled forces ranged from the ethnonational rebels of the ONLF to the former mayor-elect of Addis Ababa and proponent of liberal democracy, Berhanu Nega, ex-leader of Ginbot 7 and now the leader of a new political party. To try to irreversibly alter the problematic political dynamics this created, Abiy sought maximum inclusivity, which first meant ramping up Hailemariam's initial steps to release political prisoners. Soon accompanying this was a concerted effort to encourage all exiled political factions to return home, as long as they pledged to participate peacefully in the democratic process. These moves had the desired effect on the political atmosphere, contributing to a sense of liberation and progress while considerably enhancing the government's reputation, especially in the West. For example, the country went from being one of the world's worst jailers of journalists, according to the Committee to Protect Journalists' annual tally, to having no journalists in prison (Dahir 2018). The downside to the process, however, is that it has contributed to a wide-open transition where most actors seem to believe it is their moment to decisively shape the future direction of the country. Of course, this is not a problem if such legitimate ambitions are channeled through the electoral process and if those ambitions are not violently resisted by opposing factions, but there have already been incidents that have shown the risks. Paramount among these was the trajectory of releasee Asaminew Tsige, who allegedly orchestrated the assassination of Amhara and military leaders in June 2019 after he was promoted by the ADP to regional security chief in late 2018. Another striking episode was the return of Ginbot 7 and the Oromo Liberation Front (OLF), who held rallies within a week of each other in Addis Ababa in September 2018. Although they were joyous occasions for tens of thousands of supporters, there was also serious violence, and those clashes increased the tensions over the ongoing problematic issue of the administrative status of Addis Ababa (Nizar and Ermias 2018). Essentially, with the EPRDF's dominance threatened, other political actors have been emboldened, which is a necessary step in the process towards achieving inclusive democratic politics. This includes the Sidama and other southern nations, whose regional statehood demands are constitutional and emboldened by the political opening but could also cause further instability. Given the diverging ideologies now present in the political landscape, democratization is also a destabilizing process, as some disagreements stem from fundamentally different understandings of Ethiopian history and divergent visions for the country. Thus, despite the prime minister's efforts to inculcate a peaceful and loving political atmosphere, the opportunity he has provided has instead unintentionally increased tension and acrimony, as dormant fault lines have rumbled, such as over Addis Ababa. Liberalization has, so far, arguably contributed to deepening polarization.

OBJECTIVITY OBJECTIVE

Insofar as Ethiopia is politically polarized in the manner described, so is its media landscape. This important reality is both a cause and part of a potential remedy for the political challenges the nation faces, especially as there is so much opportunity for the growth and improvement of the media industry.

The government's accelerated democratization agenda partly means building stronger institutions to mediate differences peacefully, rather than having them play out through blood-soaked confrontations. As noted, given the ideological differences that exist, there are challenges to this. But there is ample space for the political discourse to become more policy-focused, which should have the desired effect of de-escalating the degree of confrontation. For example, for those that accept the constitutional promise of Oromia's "special interest" in Addis Ababa, there are obvious grounds for debate about how exactly that should be interpreted and articulated in law. This does not mean avoiding sensitive issues, such as the language of the federal government or political representation, but it could move the conversation away from binary debates about who owns Addis Ababa/Finfinnee. Instead, via media coverage, there is the opportunity to perhaps discuss what financial arrangements could be made for the disposal of Addis Ababa's waste in Oromia, clarify the issue of water management, look at what joint administrative arrangements are appropriate, or how Oromo culture could be promoted in the city. Discussions over details would undermine the extremes and provide a canvas for compromises to appear. Some argue that a vitriolic debate is too polarized to make this type of approach practical, but even if that is true, it is still the correct course to pursue.

All types of media formats and outlets clearly have a critical role to play in promoting and covering such discussions. But first, the ongoing democratization would ideally mean media narratives are decoupled from the nation's dramatic political oscillations, which might allow a more constructive use of the liberalized environment. Rather than acting as proponents or opponents, more outlets, and more journalists, should focus on informing the policy debate and providing critical scrutiny, even if they are generally in favor of whatever it is they are covering: a large-scale commercial irrigation project, security sector reforms, or maybe a regional state's efforts to boost tax collection. Currently, it is still too easy to accurately criticize much of the media as aligned with particular ideologies or actors and allowing its coverage to be led by those alignments, as has occurred to the detriment of the political conversation in the past.

As the country limbers up for its first competitive elections in fifteen years, minds are inevitably cast back to the previous one. Then, a dynamic, open environment led to acrimony and eventually chaos, and authorities portrayed chunks of the media as an accessory of the opposition. Perhaps through no fault of his own, an embodiment of that politicization was Eskinder Nega, who was one of the journalists jailed in the fallout from the 2005 elections. During his latest bout of imprisonment, which began when he was rearrested in September 2011, he was lauded by the international community, winning the 2012 PEN/Barbara Goldsmith Freedom to Write Award (PEN America 2018), although that was not a view subscribed to by his ideological opponents (Daniel 2012). Now, as part of the political reforms led by the prime minister, Eskinder is free again and very much back in the thick of the debate surrounding Addis Ababa and other issues (Eskinder 2019). Of course, nobody should deny campaigning journalism the right to publish, nor should journalists be restricted from participating in political discourse on social media, and here is not the place to dwell on disputed past allegations. But we may well question whether more fervent campaigning journalists are what Ethiopia's media most needs at this critical moment.

For certain, the debate between activists and journalists is not a new one, and it is not over. Nor, perhaps, will it ever be, as there will always be those who argue that the moral imperative to correct injustice outweighs competing considerations such as impartiality. The circumstance for activists is somewhat different, as they are focused primarily on promoting a particular cause. Of course, that does not mean they are unconcerned about facts, but it does mean they have objectives that could possibly justify a selective approach to them. Crudely put, sometimes the ends justify the means. How this balance is struck depends on the cause, the strategy, and the individual. Despite the constraints and frailties, journalists have a critical role in trying to make objective, dispassionate assessments. When they are perceived to not be sufficiently aligned with a particular narrative, there is a tendency to accuse journalists and media of having a hidden agenda. But the importance of striving for fairness and accuracy should transcend concerns about insults and conspiracy theories. Such responses are inevitable anyway in a polarized, passionate environment, when a failure to display the requisite sympathy is often perceived as allegiance with "the other."

These trade-offs between activist and objective journalism are hardly the sole preserve of a nascent democracy like Ethiopia where liberal pluralism has yet to be developed. Witness parts of the Anglosphere. For decades, a Chomskyan critique has identified mainstream journalism as supportive of a corporate-friendly status quo that is unwilling to challenge US power (Herman and Chomsky 1988). A more oppositional model—termed "adversarial journalism" by *The Intercept*—has gained strength since the invasion of Iraq and gone into overdrive during the Trump era. Now even more people identify the current administration as something that must be opposed rather than understood, which encourages campaigning-style journalism. To seek to understand the Trump voter perspective is to run the risk of being accused of complicity with fascism. Meanwhile, the president himself repeatedly identifies unsupportive media as "enemies of the people" or purveyors of "fake news."

The situation is not dissimilar in the UK, where society has been cleaved by the 2016 referendum decision to leave the European Union. As in Ethiopia, the polarization encompasses the media. Many people identify a few traditionally right-wing newspapers, such as *The Sun, Daily Mail*, and *Daily Telegraph*, as supportive of Brexit, with much of the rest of the media opposed. As opponents of departure consider withdrawal from the EU fundamentally flawed and damaging, they do not consider an equivocal, impartial stance to be sufficient. The debate even extends to the British Broadcasting Corporation (BBC), despite its global reputation as a relatively impartial and objective media outlet. The current polarization is such that Leavers call it the Brussels Broadcasting Corporation, while Andrew Adonis, a Labour peer campaigning for Brexit to be scrapped, labels it the Brexit Broadcasting Corporation (2018). Clearly, even developed liberal societies run the risk of polarization that is both driven by and reflected in the media. Recognizing the negative influence of polarization does not mean there is an obvious way forward in this highly contested area surrounding freedom of expression and extremism. Many would argue that there is a need to try to contain and control the excesses of the modern online media, as the current Ethiopian government appears inclined to do ("Ethiopia Issued Advisory on Social Media Hate Speech, Misinformation, Dissemination," *Borkena*,

May 30, 2020). But Ethiopia is emerging from a period when censorship and coercion was rife and instead needs to explore ways of incentivizing constructive, relatively impartial contributions.

Pure impartiality is, however, an almost impossible thing to achieve in practice and even more difficult in terms of perception, as has been frequently seen in Ethiopia.

EPRDF officials have expressed support for the development journalism approach, which is, broadly, that the media should play a role supporting progressive change (Mekonnen 2016). This was a counter-liberal proposal, as it partly argues that freedom for the media in practice means its manipulation by powerful private interests, as can undoubtedly be seen in the US, UK, Italy, and many other places. The BBC has been used as an example of the futility of the liberal media model in Ethiopia, with officials arguing that the publicly funded corporation was supportive of UK government interests in the same way Ethiopian state media was (senior government official, pers. comm., 2011). But this supposed mouthpiece was, for example, at loggerheads with the government over the BBC's critical coverage of the buildup to the Iraq War in 2003, which was symptomatic of the BBC's relative autonomy. More recently, Ethiopian commentators suggested that reporting by outlets such as the *New York Times* on the Ethiopian Airlines tragedy was slanted in the interests of Boeing.

Lumping all publicly funded media together or assuming that media from a particular country are acting in that country's interests seems to draw the wrong conclusion from the very real difficulties of achieving a perfectly nonpartisan media. It is of course true that all outlets, whether public or private, have an ideological perspective, and that is also impacted by the subjective inputs of reporters and editors—but this should not be used to justify a consciously skewed approach. Responsible media must strive for objectivity and impartiality by ensuring, for example, that they set out to report in an open-minded rather than prescriptive manner, they include a variety of perspectives, and they make a conscious effort to repeatedly reassess their own positions. Acknowledging inherent bias should not lead to fatalism about the limitations but should instead energize ongoing attempts to counter inbuilt prejudices.

The approach of the EPRDF has hitherto generally been to present the private media as potential opponents of broad-based development, as the commercial interests of economic elites supposedly drive coverage, and to downplay the potential of a liberated but constructive press. With that ideological baggage, there was little to stop the state- and party-owned media being purposed into offering coverage that was more propaganda than public interest. The framing of the "rent-seeking" private media contributes to a broader strategy of dividing the population into those that supported "development" and those who were "antidevelopment." In this manner, well-founded criticism by well-intentioned critics became tagged as irresponsible and politically motivated.

As an example of how this can be not just inimical to a free press but also counterproductive for the government, we can again look at the debate surrounding the Addis Ababa and surrounding Oromia Integrated Development Plan or, as it was more commonly known, the "master plan." The first major sign of stirring within the EPRDF was in 2014, when OPDO regional lawmakers voiced their objection to the plan, suggesting that there had not been enough debate and consultation (Oromia TV 2014). As we saw, that opposition spiraled into the Oromo protests, which contributed to the reform movement within the EPRDF and the current political opening driven forward by the prime minister. A lack of transparency and the discouragement of media scrutiny therefore contributed to the previous government's problems. This is because it is unlikely that opposition to the plan would have been so widespread and vociferous if there had been more and better media coverage of the process and thus a wider understanding of the facts.

The general problem was demonstrated by a host of personal experiences. I tried to begin covering the issue in 2014 outside the 6 Kilo campus of Addis Ababa University, where there was a protest by Oromo students. I was prevented from entering the campus by Federal Police and then bundled into a vehicle by a plainclothes officer. At the police station, an officer, absurdly, accused me of being an Egyptian spy—apparently because I had parked between the campus and the Middle Eastern country's embassy and therefore approached the protest from that direction. As the authorities demonstrated on many occasions, it seemed to think that suppressing information would deal with its problems. The opposite proved to be the case.

Rumors about the master plan spread, with the perception created that Addis Ababa was imminently going to expand to cover a huge area, stretching even as far as Ambo. Journalists who were in a position to offer corrective interpretations were provided limited information, allowing activists to set the agenda. And those activists in turn also pressured journalists, as at the tragic 2016 Irreecha celebration in Bishoftu. Reporting that many attendees died in a stampede, and not from gunfire from a military helicopter, was enough to earn the ire of activists. Journalists were either with committed activists or against them—precisely the same binary treatment meted out by the EPRDF government.

That indeed was a theme of my reporting experience in Ethiopia, as coverage of different topics for different outlets elicited starkly different responses. Allegations of corruption and pro-government bias poured forth if I reported for Bloomberg News on a generally positive economic program, such as plans to attract investment into manufacturing industries. But covering, for example, the highly politicized trials of Eskinder and others led to claims that I was part of an externally orchestrated neoliberal conspiracy that had the ultimate aim of replacing the government with one that was more compliant to Western interests. Rather than accurately reflecting the varied nature of the government's activities, it was often assumed that there was an agenda behind coverage. Journalists frequently confront these types of dynamics, as do all nonpartisan observers, and there is no easy answer to the predicament it creates. A relatively impartial position can always be construed as an attempt to justify abuse, part of a campaign to defend a particular cause, or as an example of false equivalence.

While it is true that objectivity is limited by personal opinions and experiences, that does not mean it is a better method of reporting reality to identify the oppressed and the oppressor and have conclusions flow from that judgment. Instead, it is important to try to assess every situation on its merits and disregard such preconceptions.

DEVELOPING STORY

In addition to these universal problems of subjectivity, there is also an inherent problem with international media coverage in Ethiopia, as the necessity to package stories for a distracted global audience lends itself to oversimplification and a lack of nuance. Rather than including caveats and counterevidence, there is a tendency to try to present a clean narrative, understandably arousing irritation from those who understand the intricacies of Ethiopian affairs.

Since August 2018 I have attempted to improve this situation by establishing the Ethiopia Insight website. The straightforward aim is to apply international standards to local-style coverage. By reporting and analyzing in relative depth, for example, the Sidama statehood movement or the Qemant identity question, there is room for all perspectives to be included and for some of the underlying issues to be explored (Davison, Solomon, and Kibreab 2018). Improving international understanding of such issues should be a positive contribution to the national political process. And there is also an opportunity to guard against sensationalism. For example, in March 2019, Ethiopia Insight published a translated nine-thousand-word version of a February 27, 2019, speech at Oromia's parliament by former chief administrator Lemma in which he goes into forensic detail about the myriad challenges of public administration in the region (Ermias 2019). Other media coverage, mostly via YouTube clips, had focused solely on some associated remarks from Lemma about resettling internally displaced Oromo in and around Addis Ababa, and that approach inflamed the debate. Here we see two starkly different approaches to a liberalized media environment that has also been changed by technological advances: the advent of online media offers unlimited space and increased autonomy for in-depth journalism, but it also drives sensational coverage via bite-size clips, as there is an intense battle for the attention of hyper-distracted audiences.

Since Abiy took office there has been a rapid and radical improvement in the media environment, as seen with the Committee to Protect Journalists' categorization. Furthermore, returned and released journalists have taken advantage of the liberalized environment to establish newspapers such as *Ethiopis, Fiteh,* and *Addis Maleda*. Reportedly, twenty-three publications and six privately owned satellite channels have been given licenses by the Ethiopian Broadcasting Authority since July 2018 ("Press Freedom in Ethiopia Has Blossomed. Will It Last?" *Economist*, March 16, 2019). There is also a more dynamic and wide-ranging political conversation on television and radio programs, an important bright spot in the emerging landscape. Government censorship has been dramatically reduced, and previously foreign-based media such as ESAT and the Oromia Media Network (OMN) have established local operations.

Caution here is in order, however, as this media opening replicates some of the potential problems raised by broader political liberalization. The two major satellite broadcasters built their reputations and audiences through fervent oppositional journalism, criticizing the abuses and injustices that they identified under previous administrations. In itself, that presents a problem, as the media operations are overtly political in nature, and it may be hard for them to remain as successful while evolving to a less partisan position. But this concern has actually intensified, as there is now considerable rivalry between camps associated with OMN and ESAT as their ideological differences come to the fore now that their previous common enemy, the TPLF, has been largely dealt with.

There is no easy solution for these types of volatile dynamics that are created by respecting the right to freedom of expression and that are somewhat exacerbated by Ethiopia's multilingual environment, as it encourages the creation of discrete audiences. Furthermore, it is futile to call on these politically passionate organizations to alter their editorial stances—there are, after all, substantive reasons behind their positioning. But what is worthwhile is to try to convince more and more people to appreciate that it is not just the freedom to opine that should be valued. It is also the importance of striving for impartiality, objectivity, fairness, and accuracy, as a growing appreciation of those qualities also offers the possibility of a more constructive debate going forward. And without it there is a danger that the media becomes increasingly adversarial, which is not the type of liberal discourse Ethiopia needs to see develop right now, given its existing fragilities.

Clearly, the problem of partisan commentary is further amplified on social media, where there is even less editorial control or expectation of impartiality. There is also even less opportunity for regulating the space, given the atomized nature of contributions. In March 2019 there was some discussion in Ethiopia of Egypt's 2018 law that classified social media accounts with five thousand followers or more as media outlets ("Egypt to Regulate Popular Social Media Users," BBC, July 17, 2018). There is now an online hate speech and "fake news" law being prepared that includes similar provisions. Rather than merely regressing to censorship, which is conceivable, the government should try to encourage responsible use of social media by all actors but particularly by the most influential. One possible way to try to reduce the risks of social media hate speech and false information is to have more users apply high standards and take a stand against perceived irresponsible behavior. Rather than allow social media to amplify negative traits, such as discrimination and suspicion, there should be an effort in Ethiopia to try to repurpose it toward encouraging positive ones relating to polite, evidence-based discourse. Such liberal values are needed to make the best of a liberated sphere.

Regardless of such concerns, the transitional period is so far characterized by a liberalized space and somewhat comparable with the post-Derg period, which also saw a flourishing of the press that continued through to the 2005 elections. A revision of the mass media proclamation is underway, which reportedly aims to make it less onerous to establish media and reduce punishments for regulatory infringements. These are important steps to creating a more favorable operating environment and eventually a strong, autonomous, constructive media, which would be boosted if donor-backed plans for a self-regulatory media council create a strong institution. The environment will also be markedly improved if a more independent judiciary develops, problematic laws such as the 2009 Anti-Terrorism Proclamation are revised, and other draconian provisions, such as those relating to defamation, are excised from the criminal code (Yesuneh 2018).

In the last year, there has also been a concerted central government effort to improve its communications, which has already paid dividends. Those close to former prime minster Hailemariam said his use of the media to announce the closure of Maekelawi was a deliberate attempt to make the policy a *fait accompli*, neutralizing hardliners (former adviser, phone interview, February 2019). Similarly, Abiy has used the media to great effect, initially creating unstoppable momentum in his bilateral dealings with Isaias, for example.

The modernization has involved increased use of social media, primarily Twitter, to announce policy measures and also the creation of a press secretariat at the Office of the Prime Minister. This was accompanied by the downgrading of the Government Communication Affairs Office (GCAO), leading to some concerns from journalists (Yared 2018). While it may be in the government's interests to centralize messaging, the media also needs empowered press officers at each federal ministry and at the sub-federal levels. That said, in one area of government communication there has been enhanced autonomy for regional actors, which, while generally positive, is partly due to intra-EPRDF tensions. Regional communication bureaus now brief against other states, sometimes using provocative language. That was seen in 2018 and 2019 in the disputes between Tigray and Amhara's governments over the Qemant identity issue and the Welkait and Raya areas. Prior to that, the late 2016 conflict between Oromo and Somali elements also involved a war of words between the two regional communication bureaus. Officials have also made divisive statements on their personal social media pages. These are problematic developments, as they have the potential to inflame the broader debate and demonstrate the need for strong management and the introduction of new operating procedures that are tailored to the newly liberalized environment.

An obstacle to more comprehensive reporting by private media has been the attitude of subregional officials to journalists, with claims that authorization from the relevant regional or the federal GCAO was insufficient to allow access. Those tendencies contribute to regional affairs receiving inadequate coverage, as it is simply harder than it should be for visiting journalists to get access and cover stories. Ensuring that local officials and security officers respect journalists' rights would be a positive contribution to the national democratic process, and there are concerns that this is not a priority, or even responsibility, of the press secretariat.

The focus on using the prime minister's office for government communications relates to a broader concern that the political opening and the transition are not inclusive enough. Moreover, constructive participation in the process can seem to be too closely linked to unambiguous support, partly because of the popularity of the prime minister. That is to say, unless fulsome support is expressed, there may be suspicion of "unhealthy" opposition. Instead, the process of democratization should mean a liberated political and media space where all views are welcomed, including constructive criticism.

This concern about continued cheerleading relates to the issue of polarization. An oft-repeated concern about Ethiopian politics is its regressively cyclical nature, as a power struggle throws up winners and losers until the winners eventually breed resentment and become losers. While there has been democratic progress and talk of reconciliation over the past eighteen months, there are also worrying signs of a perpetuation of zero-sum politics. As discussed, an area of concern is the outcast position of the TPLF and some of its former leaders. That is mirrored in the media sphere. Some social media activists are now ensconced in Mekelle delivering broadsides against the prime minister and his government, arguably using similar techniques as the foreign-based activists that criticized previous EPRDF administrations and the TPLF in particular. As with the TPLF itself, there is no argument here that there is any legitimacy to reckless stances, but there is a possibility that such isolation could breed unwanted political consequences if a rejectionist opposition grows. Whether perceived or real, injustice, marginalization, or oppression creates anger. As that anger grows, divisions also grow between those who share the anger and those who do not. At some point, people who are assessed to be insufficiently sympathetic are seen as in league with the enemy, which increases the risk of conflict. Ethiopia does not want to travel any further down that dangerous road.

CRITICAL MODERATION

While it is unrealistic to expect that there will be no implacable opponents of the new political dispensation, the media could have an important role to play in minimizing such rifts. That is because an approach that tends toward accuracy, objectivity, and impartiality necessarily means a more balanced perspective both on past and current administrations. Rather than shifting from one pole to the other, coverage would therefore reflect the stabilizing continuity that offers the current administration the opportunity to correct the mistakes of the past while building on the positive aspects of its predecessors' legacy. The media would therefore play a part in developing practices of inquiry and coverage that contribute toward an unconstrained but also constructive debate.

An area that needs improvement is the output of party-owned outlets such as Fana Broadcasting Corporation, which still often reports wholly uncritically. For example, rather than explaining any of the substantive issues behind the January 2019 political dispute in Somali Region, Fana reported, unsatisfactorily, that the prime minister had simply discussed regional development issues with the leaders of party and state ("Premier, Leaders of Somali Regional State Discuss on Dev't, Security Activities," *Somaliland Standard*, January 26, 2019). And after the *Addis Standard* reported on January 13 that the military undertook airstrikes in western Oromia, there was a virtual information blackout ("Ethiopia Defense Force Begins Airstrike in

Western Oromia; Says Targets Are OLF Military Training Camps"). While it is understandable that the government will continue to want to control the dissemination of information on conflict-sensitive topics, it is also vital that state- and party-owned media become more combative in the way that they deal with authorities.

Another area of concern was the role of Oromia Broadcasting Network (OBN) and other media in effectively providing supporting evidence to accompany the detention of officials from METEC and security agencies. Rather than merely amplifying the case being built by prosecutors, the role of the public media should be to critically assess the evidence. Uncritical narrations of official versions of events do nothing to assist long-term efforts to increase trust in public media. There were further concerns at OBN in February 2019 when former opposition journalist-activist Mohammed Ademo was fired from his relatively new role as director, reportedly after trying to introduce modernized and more combative and autonomous coverage of party and government affairs (Kaleyesus 2019).

While the government can directly impact the public media by relaxing controls and encouraging independence, it should take a more hands-off approach to the private media. Concerted efforts to improve the regulatory environment should be continued, but any efforts to guide or coerce coverage are undesirable and will probably prove counterproductive. Instead, the government could play its part in creating a healthier marketplace of ideas by releasing more information, making officials and projects more accessible to journalists, and constructively criticizing inaccurate or incomplete reporting, rather than chastising the media for its errors.

This can also be applied to policy. For example, it seems that a reasonable assessment of Ethiopia's corruption record would demonstrate that it had become a growing problem but that international donors still considered the government an effective spender of development assistance. On the macroeconomy, the growth record was strong, but certain areas, such as revenues from goods, have consistently disappointed, and there was also a related track record of delayed major infrastructure projects. The federal security apparatus was successful in preventing terrorist attacks, but it was frequently abusive and ultimately counterproductive in the way it dealt with peaceful domestic opponents. A sincere effort by the media to present all key facts—rather than cherry-picking those that fit a preconceived narrative—

lends itself toward such moderate positions. Through this type of evidence-based reporting, the media would become a constructive participant in the transition, advancing alternative viewpoints but not simply acting as cheerleader or naysayer.

Fundamentally, what could be acknowledged more is that unless someone is committed to propagating an absolutist position, attempts to chart a course between extremes should be welcomed. As elsewhere, the political situation in Ethiopia is multifaceted. To use crude examples, the government can be a protector and provider as well as a killer and a bully. A protester can be just and peaceful but also undiscriminating and violent. There will always be a need to have nonaligned observers bearing witness and sifting through the details of each incident. It is not siding with the powerful or sidling into activism to seek evidence and systematically provide opportunities for all sides to have their say, even if there is a history of dominance or dishonesty among subjects.

Part of the challenge now is to allow the media to freely perform its role as a constructive critic, which includes providing space for it to make inevitable mistakes, whether of fact or judgment. One of the current dangers is that the category of "anti-reform" becomes almost as abused as "antidevelopment" was by previous administrations. Criticism of aspects of the reform, if accurate, measured, and substantive, should instead be considered to be pro-reform, as constructive feedback will improve the process. Failing to appreciate legitimate criticism would repeat the errors of the past by boxing the media into one camp or another.

More objective journalism will not solve the ideological divisions, bitter disputes over contested histories, or myriad power struggles that confront Ethiopia. What it can do, however, is help create the conditions for conversations that can act as peaceful avenues to explore differences. Ultimately, the government's acceptance and encouragement of an autonomous, assertive, and critical media would be a vital part of the democratization process—and a failure to do so would mark a repetition of past mistakes.

REFERENCES

Adonis, Andrew. 2018. "There's Something Sinister about the BBC's Attitude to Brexit." *New European*, February 24, 2018.

Amnesty International. 2005. "Amnesty International Report 2005—Ethiopia," May 25, 2005. https://www.refworld.org/docid/429b27e07.html.

———. 2011. *Dismantling Dissent: Intensified Crackdown on Free Speech in Ethiopia*. London: Amnesty International Publications. https://www.amnesty.be/IMG/pdf/dismantling_dissent_afr250112011.pdf.

Bonsa, J. 2015. "Ethiopia's Economic Growth Borrows from ENRON's Accounting." *Africa at London School of Economics* (blog), Firoz Lalji Centre for Africa.

Committee to Protect Journalists. 2011. "Ethiopia Detains Two Swedish Journalists," July 5, 2011. New York: CPJ.

Dahir, Abdi Latif. 2018. "For the First Time in Decades, There Are No Ethiopian Journalists in Prison." *Quartz Africa*, December 13, 2018.

Daniel Berhane. 2012. "On Eskinder Nega: Setting the Record Straight." *Horn Affairs*, October 6, 2012.

Davison, William. 2012. "Muslims Accuse Ethiopian Government of Meddling in Mosques." *Christian Science Monitor*, May 31, 2012.

———. 2016. "Ethnic Tensions in Gondar Reflect the Toxic Nature of Ethiopian Politics," *Guardian*, December 22, 2016.

Davison, William, and Kulle Kursha. 2018. "As Southern Nations Break Free, Pressure Mounts on EPRDF." *Ethiopia Insight*, November 28, 2018.

Davison, William, and Leake Tewele. 2018. "Abiy Attacks Impunity as MetEC and NISS Officials Held for Graft and Torture." *Ethiopia Insight*, November 15, 2018.

Davison, William, Solomon Yimer, and Kibreab Beraki. 2018. "Violent Qemant Dispute Fueling Explosive Amhara-Tigray Divide." *Ethopia Insight*, December 16, 2018.

Ermias Tesfaye. 2019. "Lemma: 'Pushing Away Investment Will Not Help.'" *Ethiopia Insight*, March 18, 2019.

Eskinder Nega (@eskinder_nega). 2019. "Any attempt by the GOVERNMENT to CHANGE the demography of ADDIS ABABA and its surrounding areas is SOCIAL ENGINEERING. . . ." Twitter, February 26, 2019, 9:03 p.m. https://twitter.com/eskinder_nega/status/1100622337865641984.

Herman, Edward, and Noam Chomsky. 1988. "A Propaganda Model." Excerpted from *Manufacturing Consent: The Political Economy of the Mass Media*. New York: Pantheon. https://chomsky.info/consent01/.

Human Rights Watch. 2015. "Ethiopia: Free Zone 9 Bloggers, Journalists: A Year after Arrests, Drop Drop Politically Motivated Charges," April 23, 2015. New York: HRW.

Kaleyesus Bekele. 2019. "Mohammad Ademo Leaves OBN." *Reporter*, February 16, 2019.

Lyons, Terrence. 2014. "Big Tent: Ethiopia's Authoritarian Balancing Act." *World Politics Review*, February 18, 2014.

Mekonnen Hailemariam Zikargae. 2016. "Development Journalism as an Agent of Change or Meansto Political Power in Africa: A Focus on Ethiopian Perspective." *Sustainable Development in Africa* 18, no. 5: 30–39.

Nebiyu Sihul Mikael. 2019. "Is Tigray Really a Drop in the Bucket for Abiy's Administration?" *Ethiopia Insight*, January 17, 2019.

Nizar Manek, and Ermias Tasfaye. 2018. "Mob Killings Split Ethiopians as Political Fault Lines Test Abiy's Big Tent." *Ethiopia Insight*, September 26, 2018.

Oromia TV. 2014. "Addis-Ababa-Finfinnee Surrounding Master Plan Faces Fierce Opposition from Oromos." YouTube video, April 13, 2014. https://www.youtube.com/watch?v=MrWs8yJh5mY.

PEN America. 2018. "2012 PEN/Barbara Goldsmith Freedom to Write Award Winner Eskinder Nega Freed after Almost Seven Years in Prison in Ethiopia." February 14, 2018. New York: PEN America.

Schemm, Paul. 2016. "In Ethiopia's War against Social Media, the Truth is the Main Casualty." *Washington Post*, October 14, 2016.

Walleligne Mekonnen. 1969. "On the Question of Nationalities in Ethiopia." Haile Selassie I University, November 17, 1969. https://www.marxists.org/history/erol/ethiopia/nationalities.pdf.

Wondemagne Ejigu. 2016. "The Untold Plight of the Amhara People." *Untold Stories of the Silenced*, August 16, 2016. http://www.untoldstoriesonline.com/the-untold-plight-of-the-amhara-people/.

World Economic Forum. 2019. "Abiy Ahmed: A Conversation with the Prime Minister of Ethiopia (Davos 2019)." YouTube video, February 10, 2019. https://www.youtube.com/watch?v=x217KscqRro&t=13s.

Yared Tsegaye. 2018. "Newly Formed Press Secretariat Sees the End of Government Communication Affairs Office." *Addis Standard*, November 5, 2018.

Yesuneh Aweke Kabtiyemer. 2018. "Defamation Law in Ethiopia: The Interplay between the Right to Reputation and Freedom of Expression." *Beijing Law Review* 9: 381–400.

1.7 Transitional Justice and Reconciliation in Ethiopia's Hybrid Transition
The Case of the Reconciliation Commission

By Solomon Dersso

INTRODUCTION

The year that followed the assent to the pinnacle of power of Prime Minister Abiy Ahmed is characterized by a period of transition that involved not only a change of political leadership in Ethiopia but also the inauguration of major political, economic, and foreign policy reforms. Arguably, it is in the realm of politics that the country witnessed the most change during this period. In this respect, apart from the displacement of the Tigray People's Liberation Front (TPLF) from the center of power in the hitherto four-member powerful ruling coalition, the Ethiopian People's Revolutionary Democratic Front (EPRDF), the transition ushered in a new era of political liberalization involving the release of all political prisoners and the unbanning of exiled political parties and armed opposition groups.

As part of the effort to consolidate the newly opening political space and the journey for an inclusive and pluralist political order, Prime Minister Abiy and his government launched various reform initiatives. The legal reform process initiated with the establishment of the Legal Reform Advisory Council by the attorney general is one of them, and another such initiative that falls in this category is Proclamation No. 1102/2018, "A Proclamation to Establish a Reconciliation Commission."

The focus of this chapter, accordingly, is the form that transitional justice may take in Ethiopia's hybrid transition and the role of the Reconciliation Commission. Before delving into the focus of the chapter, it is important to begin this introductory section by clarifying the concept of transitional justice.

As aptly put in the African Union Transitional Justice Policy (AUTJP), transitional justice refers to the various (state-centric and community-based) policy measures and institutional mechanisms that societies coming out of violent conflict or repression or patterns of systematically unjust power relationships adopt through an inclusive consultative process in order to overcome past violations, divisions, and inequalities and create conditions for security, democratic, and socioeconomic transformation. Justice defined in a context of transition thus goes far beyond judicial forms of accountability and covers a wide range of political, institutional, and socioeconomic measures required for a transition destined to establish solid foundations for a just and inclusive political and socioeconomic order. Yet, the focus and nature of the transitional justice mechanism that a society implements to enjoy public legitimacy and have a prospect of success should be informed by the specific context of its transition.

THE NATURE OF THE TRANSITION THAT SETS THE CONTEXT FOR THE RECONCILIATION COMMISSION

Like other transitional justice processes, the establishment and context of the operation of the Ethiopian Reconciliation Commission is likely to have been shaped by the character of the transition that produced it. The history of transitional justice shows that, broadly speaking, it has been implemented in two forms. The first is the transition from conflict to peace, whether this comes about through a peace agreement, as in South Africa, Liberia, Sierra Leone, or Kenya, or through the victory of one of the conflicting parties, as in Ethiopia or Rwanda in the 1990s. In South Sudan, the current transition from conflict to peace is the kind for which the Revitalized Agreement on the Resolution of the Conflict in the Republic of South Sudan, chapter five, envisaged a system of transitional justice. The second form of transition is in the context of the overthrow of an authoritarian regime and a country's transition to a democratic system of government, which was common in Latin America and hugely influenced the discourse and practice of transitional justice. In Africa, a very good contemporary example of such a transition for which a transitional justice mechanism is currently in place is the Gambia. The various transitional justice experiences in Africa—from South Africa to Liberia, Sierra Leone, Kenya, and Tunisia—fall into either one of these two forms of transitions.

The current transition, in which the Ethiopian Reconciliation Commission is constituted as the preferred transitional justice mechanism, does not fit either of the above forms. It is not a negotiated transition as in South Africa in the early 1990s or the transitions that followed peace agreements in Liberia or Sierra Leone. It is not either a transition that resulted from the overthrow of the old regime like the transition Ethiopia witnessed in 1974 or the one that resulted from the military victory of the armed rebel groups over the Derg regime in 1991.

It is not a neat transition amenable to easy categorization. It is a transition that I would rather like to characterize as a hybrid transition.

Ethiopia's transition since the coming to power of Prime Minister Abiy is one that resulted from the ad hoc alliance of the protest movements in Oromia and Amhara (mobilized against the prevailing regime of the EPRDF) on the one hand and a portion of the membership of the EPRDF, the reformist block, on the other. It is a transition that brought to leadership positions the major reformist members of some of the coalition parties of the EPRDF. It is a hybrid transition that relies on the old EPRDF-based regime while trying to fundamentally reform it. It is thus not a transition that involves the overthrow of the old regime. It is rather a transition in which parts of the old regime are in the driver's seat. It is also one that is taking place in a context of both political and ethnic polarization threatening the shared social fabric of the people of the country. As such, it is a transition that faces the challenge of reforming the old regime and mending the divisions and conflicts feeding the political and ethnic polarization.

These features of the transition are not without major ramifications for its trajectory and the pursuit of transitional justice and reconciliation in Ethiopia. In particular, the choice of mechanism or combination of mechanisms to be used in pursuing transitional justice and, importantly, how such a mechanism or mechanisms are implemented is affected. As Awol

(2018) rightly points out, "Pursuing prosecutorial justice while at the same time promoting reconciliation of a highly divided society, particularly in a highly fragile setting . . . requires a strategic and holistic integration of the processes, as well as careful planning."

From South Africa's postapartheid transitional justice, which gave worldwide prominence to the use of a truth and reconciliation commission as a framework of transitional justice, to the experiences in Liberia, Sierra Leone, and Kenya, the choice of the transitional justice measure that a society in transition adopts constitutes an outcome of and a vehicle for the implementation of a (new) political settlement. In each of these countries, transitional justice was the result of a political agreement among various rival political forces who were parties to the conflict. As with many other countries, transitional justice in these countries was thus founded on, and constituted, only one element of the political/peace agreement, on which the entire transitional process is anchored. It is thus of paramount importance that a transitional justice process is anchored on a political/peace agreement/settlement.

Viewed from the perspective of the foregoing, there is little indication one finds to suggest that the Ethiopian transitional justice framework anchored in the Reconciliation Commission is founded on an identifiable political agreement. There does not seem to be any dispute about the value of establishing the commission. However, the lack of negotiation and agreement among the various political forces in the country on the its objectives, mandate, and expected role presents a major foundational gap.

THE ESTABLISHMENT AND MANDATE OF THE COMMISSION: CRITICAL REVIEW

Having clarified the preliminaries, in this section I wish now to examine substantive issues relating to the making of the commission and the content and scope of its mandate. In terms of the process of its making, the key issue to be discussed (beyond the question of some form of agreement highlighted above) involves the question of consultation and inclusivity in the process. Regarding the mandate of the commission, the analysis will address its material and temporal scope.

The Process of the Making of the Commission

It is imperative that it develops, as part of the transitional process, a well-thought-out approach for planning, designing, and implementing transitional justice and reconciliation. Both in terms of normative expectations and best practice standards, the most important process issue in the development of a transitional justice body such as a reconciliation commission is the creation of adequate platforms that solicit the input of various sectors of society, including victim groups, on the draft law establishing the transitional justice mechanism. Such a process is also required in terms of vetting the candidates for the membership of a transitional justice body like a reconciliation commission. These process issues have also been absent in the establishment of the commission and constitution of its membership.

In this respect, despite the fact that the value of the commission may not be contested, one of the striking features of its establishment is the conspicuous absence of process and, consequently, a well-thought-out and deliberated plan. The initiative on the commission and its establishment was managed as an affair that concerned the Office of the Prime Minister, with parliament playing a passive role. There was inadequate transparency on the background to and process for its formation. Unlike the process involving the review of various draconian laws, such as the civil society and charities law, there was no public consultation and participation on the law establishing the commission.

There was neither a public process nor clear criteria on the composition of the members of the commission. In other words, its establishment suffers from what may be called a process legitimacy deficiency. This lack of process is also reflected in the lack of clarity about its administrative and financial independence. While the proclamation envisages the establishment of a secretariat of the commission, it was unclear whether the secretariat operates as a special agency with its own budget and administrative arrangement or as a civil service body bound by the administrative and other institutional and financial regulations applicable to ordinary civil service bodies.

Another illustration of the poor preparation and process for the establishment of the commission is the quality of the drafting of the proclamation establishing it. The poor drafting of the proclamation raises questions on whether the role of the commission received the level of attention it deserved and how far the process and approach to its establishment and formation was rushed. There are variations in the Amharic and English versions of the proclamation. A case in point is the provision on the appointment of the head of office of the secretariat. While the Amharic version assigns the responsibility of appointing the head of the secretariat to the prime minister, the English version stipulates that the head is appointed by the chairperson of the commission.

Experience from relatively successful transitions in Africa and the world over shows that the elaboration of a transitional justice approach needs to be informed by key considerations for designing a legitimate and rule-based transitional justice and reconciliation process. I now turn my attention to these key considerations, focusing on the material and temporal scope of the commission's mandate.

Material Scope of the Mandate of the Commission

The first of these considerations or questions is our definition of the injustice to which transitional justice and reconciliation is to be applied as a response. One form of injustice is that which results from the nonrecognition of the cultural identity of certain groups or of the equal worth of such groups and the oppression accompanying it. Charles Taylor's famous work "The Politics of Recognition" (1994) is worth mentioning here as a great philosophical exploration of this theme. Another form of injustice is that which results from gender oppression. Another form of injustice involves socioeconomic marginalization and deprivation.

The injustice that often dominates the discourse on and practice of transitional justice results from the arbitrary use of state violence by state agents leading to the perpetration of serious human rights violations.

As stated in the proclamation, the scope of the commission's mandate is cast in broad terms. Article 5 stipulates that "the objective of the Commission is to maintain peace, justice, national unity and consensus and also reconciliation among Ethiopian peoples." The preamble makes reference to reconciliation "based on truth and justice the disagreement that developed among peoples of Ethiopia" and "identify and ascertain the nature, cause and dimension of the repeated gross violation of human rights." The concern is that the ambition of the proclamation may end up overloading the commission. Overloading can spread the transitional justice process thin and render it ineffective. Accordingly, the objectives of transitional justice should be adequately delimited.

Despite the broad terms in which the mandate of the commission is cast, close analysis of the proclamation establishing the commission cannot be said to preclude some delimitation. Indeed, such analysis reveals that the mandate of the Ethiopian Reconciliation Commission has two pillars or components. The first and perhaps most prominent relates to the social and political conflicts pillar or component—which is the core mandate focusing on the establishment of national reconciliation, peace, and cohesion. The other relates to gross violations of human rights. It thus addresses both the vertical relationship between the state and citizens and the tensions and violence between various communities, and hence on the horizontal dimension of the state-society relationship.

With respect to the pillar or component relating to gross human rights violations, it is important to identify its content/scope and its relationship to the first pillar or component. As becomes evident from a review of the terms of the proclamation, while this constitutes one of the components of the commission's mandate, it does not seem to be seen as standing in isolation from the first component. While its importance is visible and recognized, the proclamation does not seem to treat it on its own. No definition of what constitutes gross human rights violations is provided, as opposed to the definition of reconciliation specified in the proclamation.

Preambular paragraph two highlights the need for identifying and ascertaining the nature, cause, and dimension of the repeated gross violations of human rights as a means not only for ensuring respect for human rights but also for "reconciliation." While no direct reference is made to this pillar of the mandate under Article 5, which provides the objective of the commission, Article 6—which outlines its powers—stipulates under Sub-article 4 that the commission has the power to "make examination [sic] to identify the basic reasons of disputes and violations of human rights by taking into consideration of political, social and economic circumstances and the view of victims and offenders."

Unlike the laws of countries such as South Africa, Liberia, Sierra Leone, or Kenya that established similar commissions, the proclamation establishing our commission lacks details and hence suffers from major lacunae. One such lacuna is the absence of a definition of what constitutes gross human rights violations. As the law of each of these other countries shows, while there are commonalities in how gross violations of human rights are defined, there are also some variations. Under international law, gross human rights violations are often associated with systematic and large-scale violations of civil and political rights relating mainly to violations of the rights to life, bodily integrity, and liberty of the person. As a result, they exclude major deprivations involving socioeconomic rights such as deprivation of the right to health, the right to housing, and the right to land and livelihood, resulting, for example, from undue expropriation of land or forced displacement, which could be important in many contexts, including Ethiopia. They also don't cover major abuses of power by public officials involving embezzlement of public funds and grand fraud and corruption. Given that violations in our context at times tend to take identity dimensions, the violation of group rights should also be taken into account.

From the foregoing, "gross violations of human rights," for purposes of the proclamation, could thus be defined as systematic and widespread violations of fundamental human rights, including extrajudicial executions, torture, forced disappearances, sexual or gender-based violence, large-scale deprivation of socioeconomic rights, including, notably, dispossession of land and large-scale embezzlement of state resources, and massive violation of group rights, including massacre and displacement of members of targeted ethnic groups.

As with the social and political conflicts pillar, this pillar of the mandate will be implemented through convening hearings, document reviews, and the like. Thus, as stipulated in the proclamation, the commission will facilitate, initiate, and/or coordinate the gathering of information and the receiving of evidence from any person on such violations. However, as the pillar of the mandate that involves the determination of the existence of violations of legal standards, the methodologies to be used for this pillar could additionally involve forensic investigations and legal analysis.

As envisaged in preambular paragraph two and Article 6(4), the scope of its investigations is such that the commission must establish how and why such violations were committed; the identity of all persons, authorities, institutions, and organizations or groups involved in such violations; the identity of the victims, their fate or present whereabouts and the nature and extent of the injuries and harm they have suffered; and whether violations were the result of deliberate planning by the state or any other organization, group, or individual.

The Temporal Scope of the Mandate of the Commission

The second consideration relates to the temporal scope of the transitional justice and reconciliation. As with the substantive scope of the mandate, there is no clear provision in the proclamation on the period its mandate covers. The proclamation refers to "gross human rights violations in different time and historical occasions," thereby greatly widening the timescale. This issue of the commission's temporal scope is particularly important for the "gross human rights" pillar or dimension of the mandate. Just like the material scope, this has to be clarified through the implementation of legal instruments, notably regulation, through Article 19 of the proclamation.

Understandably, as the experience of countries such as South Africa and Kenya has shown, the temporal scope of institutions similar to our Reconciliation Commission covers different time periods. In the case of Kenya, it covered the colonial period and the independence period until the time of the 2007–8 postelection violent conflict. In almost all cases, while due account is given to considerations of practicability and efficacy, account is given to the historical origin violence and its legacies, as well as the political, social, cultural, and economic basis of the conflicts and attendant violations.

But while bearing in mind the lessons from the experience of others, as the commission seeks to clarify the temporal scope of its mandate, the expectation is that it would be guided by the terms and parameters set in the proclamation. In this regard, the question of particular importance is whether there are any hints that offer guidance for determining the temporal scope of the mandate. Although it can be said that there is generally open room in terms of timescale for the "social and political conflicts" pillar of the mandate, the question of temporal scope is particularly important for the "gross violations of human rights" pillar of the commission's mandate.

In this respect, one finds some useful hints that are expected to guide the commission in its endeavor to clarify—through a regulation under Article 19—the temporal scope of its mandate. These are particularly available in the preamble. The first reference to time that can be used as a basis for determining temporal scope is the phrase "for years" in preambular paragraph one. The phrase "for years" in this context is used in reference to the "disagreement that developed among peoples of Ethiopia" because of social and political conflicts. Clearly this phrase is principally addressed to the first pillar—the one concerning "social and political conflicts." Understandably, in this context, the phrase "for years" would obviously include the past couple of decades but is unlikely to be confined to those recent decades only. Understandably, the "social and political conflicts" have their antecedents in the political, economic, and sociocultural power dynamics of the country in the years preceding the past couple of decades. Additionally, it is not clear how limiting the definition of the phrase "for years" in this context would be, given the principal focus of the proclamation on moving the country forward and achieving reconciliation and national cohesion.

With respect to gross violations of human rights, the proclamation provides another hint under preambular paragraph three. Here the proclamation makes reference to "gross human rights abuses in different time and historical event [sic]." On the face of it, and using the ordinary meaning model of legal interpretation, the language "different time and historical event" seems to suggest a timescale that appears to be longer than the phrase "for years" reads on its own. As with the phrase "for years," the language "different time and historical event" would obviously cover the past couple of decades. Clearly, rather than a particular historical and political period, this language seems to cover various historical periods. As such, it also implies time and events beyond recent decades.

In terms of thus determining how far back we should go, further guidance should be sought from the objective to be achieved through this commission. Seen from this vantage point, the most important considerations for making the determination are the historical developments and time period to which the "social and political conflicts" and "gross human rights violations" dividing and bleeding the country can be traced. While from the perspective of "social and political conflicts" the historical developments and time period can be traced to the formation of the unitary form of state structure in Ethiopia, the perspective of "gross violations of human rights" and "different time and historical event" would also include the major incidents of human rights violations going as far back as the post-Italian-invasion period. Or it is possible to specify the focus of the "gross human rights violations" to the period going back to 1974. For purposes of gross human rights violations, going beyond this period would create, on account of the lapse of a long time, challenges in terms of collection of evidence and presence in life of the perpetrators and the victims.

It may be argued that such a long *durée* is not realistic to cover on account of various limitations. While this time period is not too long when compared to the temporal mandate of similar institutions, such as those in South Africa and Kenya, the concern is, however, legitimate. Yet this argument does not supersede the objective for which the commission was established. Importantly, there are ways of addressing the challenges that arise from such a timescale. Perhaps one effective approach for overcoming such challenges is for the commission to focus on investigating the major incidents of "gross human rights abuses" rather than trying to document all cases of such violations across different periods. One interesting precedent for this are the Red Terror trials instituted in the aftermath of the Derg's demise. Instead of probing the entire Derg era, the trials targeted only a particular incident that took place within a specific time period. The current commission may, taking cues from this experience, focus on specific major incidents of "gross violations of human rights" that took place, for example, since the end of the Italian occupation or from 1974.

In terms of whether the commission covers current events, all indications from the reading of the proclamation is that the commission is mainly tasked with addressing events prior to its establishment. As is common with legal instruments of this kind, their application runs until the time of their adoption. In that sense, the cutoff point for the application of the proclamation is the date on which it takes effect. The commission will thus not cover events since its establishment. It may cover such events only to the extent that they are directly related to events of the time period its mandate covers.

Within the framework of the foregoing paragraph, in limiting the temporal scope, experience shows that it might be prudent to leave the door slightly ajar for looking into issues prior to or after the time period specified in the legal instrument to be adopted for implementing the proclamation. A good example of this is the law establishing the Liberian Truth and Reconciliation Commission. It is thus possible to stipulate that "notwithstanding the period specified in the regulation, the Commission may, on an application by any person or group of persons on justifiable grounds, pursue the objectives set out in the proclamation, establishing it in respect of any other period preceding [say 1941 or 1974] or since its establishment."

The Form of the Remedial Measures of the Transitional Justice Approach

The next question is what approach to transitional justice and reconciliation is to be used. The issue that arises here is how a transitional society such as ours determines which factors matter for putting more or less emphasis on one aspect of the transitional justice approach (let's say, criminal prosecution) than on another (say, truth and reconciliation or institutional reform). The AUTJP states that "emphasis on one element of transitional justice should be equitable and hence not result in either impunity (by failing to ensure accountability) or full-throated revenge of victor's justice."

In a line that eloquently captures the weight of the dilemmas involved, the late chief justice of South Africa, Justice Ismail Mahomed, writing for the South African Constitutional Court in *AZAPO v. the President of the Republic of South Africa* (CCT 17/96; ZACC 16; (8) BCLR 1015; (4) SA 672; July 25, 1996) put it thus: Transitional justice involves a "difficult, sensitive, perhaps even agonizing, balancing act between the need for justice to victims and the need for reconciliation and rapid transition to a new future." The key for success is the approach that the society adopts for addressing this dilemma that often arises during transitions.

Given these features of the current transition, the question that one faces is whether a transitional justice approach of the kind pursued in the aftermath of the Derg, which, by virtue of its adversarial nature, necessarily produces losers, would befit the current objective conditions. That is, deciding whether an approach to transitional justice that focuses on criminal prosecution is the way to go. As Justice Albie Sachs of the South African Constitutional Court explains, "Courts are concerned with accountability in a narrow, individualized sense. They deal essentially with punishment." The result of such a judicial process, he rightly argues, is that "the social processes and cultural and institutional systems responsible for the violations remain uninvestigated" (2009, 84). Thus, in contexts whose core concern is addressing social conflicts and historically induced divisions and forms of overall state accountability, we need approaches that will attend to the concerns of victims and the wider society, such as reparations, rehabilitation, and truth telling. We also need approaches that address the broader national questions that foster interethnic rancor and impede peaceful coexistence and national reconciliation. In other words, the judicial would be utterly inadequate. This involves a more comprehensive conception of reconciliatory justice going beyond retribution—it consists of what Professor Makau Mutua calls principles that are "guided by their ability to heal; put victims at the centre; seek cooperation with perpetrators; understand abominations as injuries to social relations; de-emphasize the punitive or criminality of offenses and emphasize the causes of the abominations" (2011).

At the same time, as Awol (2018) rightly points out, if the past, characterized by state-sponsored acts of violence, is to be corrected and a culture of non-impunity and the rule of law is to take its place, it is imperative that transitional justice mechanism(s) combined with a measure of accountability against perpetrators, justice for survivors, and institutional reform to prevent recurrence are put in place. Depending on the degree of responsibility, this may entail the use of truth and reconciliation or national peace and reconciliation commissions of the kind used in South Africa, Sierra Leone, Liberia, or Kenya. While accountability in this instance may involve being named for violations and lustration, justice may include truth recovery, recognition, and reparations, as well as the restoration of civic trust and the building of social solidarity or cohesion.

A review of the proclamation of the commission shows, as stated in the preamble, that the commission "takes appropriate measures and initiate recommendations that enable for the lasting peace [sic] and to prevent the future occurrence of such conflict." Although the measures and recommendations that the commission can adopt with respect to addressing the violations, historical injustices, and conflicts are yet to be determined, there are certain formulations in the proclamation that offer useful clues that should guide the commission.

Specifically, it can be gathered from the proclamation that reconciliation constitutes the central framework. Unlike similar commissions in South Africa or neighboring Kenya, whose nomenclature involved, in addition to "reconciliation," "truth," and "truth and justice," respectively, the very designation of the Ethiopian commission is confined to reconciliation. The proclamation defines under Article 2(3) reconciliation to involve "establishing values of forgiveness for the past, lasting love, solidarity and mutual understanding by identifying reasons of conflict, animosity that are [*sic*] occurred due to conflicts, misapprehension, developed disagreement and revenge."

Article 5 of the proclamation states that the "objective of the Commission is to maintain peace, justice, national unity and consensus and also reconciliation among Ethiopian peoples." As these terms make clear, there is a particular premium put on the peace and reconciliation dimension of the commission's work.

While the proclamation does not provide details on how this pillar is to be implemented, there are a number of indications from the document. First, there is the element of truth, which is one of the themes used more than once in its preamble. The first preambular paragraph indicates that the reconciliation process is to be based on truth. Preambular paragraph four states that the commission is established on account of the necessity to have a "free and independent institution that inquire and disclose [*sic*] the truth of the sources, causes and extent of conflicts." It is interesting to note that the truth referred to in both of these paragraphs concerns what the proclamation calls "disagreement" (paragraph one) and "conflicts" (paragraph four).

Understandably, there may not be a single truth about conflicts in Ethiopia. Also importantly, as the South African Truth and Reconciliation Commission highlighted, truth does not consist only of factual/forensic/scientific truth. It can also consist of personal/narrative truth, social/dialogical truth, and healing/restorative truth as well. The methodologies that may be used for implementing this pillar have thus to be various. These may include analysis of primary and secondary documents on patterns, manifestations, and causes of conflicts in Ethiopia, statement taking, convening of hearings, and submission from experts such as historians and political scientists.

As Article 6 of the proclamation, which outlines the commission's powers, shows, it has the necessary authority to access documents (although those classified as secret remain off-limits), visit any premise of any institution, and subpoena witnesses. This means that the commission will be able to gather relevant information from all sources (including official sources by investigating public institutions) for establishing the various forms of "truth" about the disagreements and conflicts, as well as their causes. To this end, the commission is expected to provide various avenues, including: a) the provision of forums that facilitate the public acknowledgement of the sufferings that individuals and communities have endured due to gross human rights violations and political conflicts, and b) the establishment of as complete a record as possible of the facts relating to the social and political conflicts and gross human rights violations and the political, institutional, and socioeconomic conditions and circumstances that made such violations and conflicts possible.

Second, as part of its mandate to facilitate reconciliation and the mending of social divisions, the commission is also expected to initiate various measures, including a) the convening of national and community dialogue forums to deal with past and existing sources of polarization and tension, and b) the promotion through government and community-based initiatives of restorative measures. Per Articles 5(2) and (10), it will be responsible for convening intercommunity dialogue and reconciliation forums to chart ways of establishing reconciliation, harmonious coexistence, and national unity.

Third, pursuant to Article 5(3), the commission will be responsible for codifying shared principles and values of various communities in the country through intercommunity discussion forums as the basis for national reconciliation.

In terms of remedies for those affected by the violations, once again the proclamation seems to focus on the establishment of truth and the provision of narrative justice by providing victims the opportunity to be heard and to have public acknowledgement of their suffering. Thus, preambular paragraph two envisages that the commission is established to provide "victims of gross human rights abuses in different time and historical event [sic] with a forum to be heard." Similarly, Article 6(4) stipulates that the commission will draw on the views of victims (and offenders) in its examination to identify the reasons for human rights violations.

While it is true that this formula of accountability and redress of the proclamation establishing the Ethiopian Reconciliation Commission does not fit the template of the mainstream practice of transitional justice, with its emphasis on prosecution, truth, reparation, and non-recurrence, there is nothing that makes it wrong or normatively inadequate. The reading of the mainstream practice as being dogmatically prescriptive (and hence requiring that in all instances it has to take all these forms) is committing the error of a one-size-fits-all approach to transitional justice. Hence, the proposition that all societies in transition need all four dimensions of the mainstream transitional justice framework always in an equal measure is highly flawed and unhelpful. Such a proposition almost automatically removes due consideration of the context and principle of national ownership, robbing the members of the transitional society of the possibility of determining for themselves, based on their own assessment of the issues facing them, the form and focus of a transitional justice framework to fit their realities.

ISSUES TO BE ADDRESSED IN THE IMPLEMENTATION OF THE MANDATE OF THE COMMISSION

The other question that needs to be addressed in our consideration of transitional justice in Ethiopia is how to organize and administer the chosen approach of transitional justice. Experience from across the continent and other parts of the world shows that for a transitional justice approach to be not only successful at delivering its objectives but also legitimate, the process of its design and implementation has to be transparent, independent, and compliant with the minimum requirements of due process. This has to do with the standards that apply to the conduct of work of the commission in terms of investigation and collection of testimonies, as well as the protection of witnesses.

Past experience is another consideration. As we all know, transitional justice is not completely new to Ethiopia. An exercise in transitional justice was undertaken following the fall of the Derg. That exercise focused on the wrongs that happened during the Red Terror—the chosen mechanisms involved principally criminal trials, although they also used lustration, a form of restorative justice involving the reinstating of possessions taken away unjustly and memorialization, by erecting the "Red Terror" Martyrs Memorial Museum in the heart of Addis Ababa. The limitations from the transitional justice approach of the Red Terror trials, including the lack of evenhandedness of the process and the lessons from this experience should thus inform the design and implementation of any transitional justice and reconciliation process we may pursue in the context of the current transition.

As has already been imitated, the other question is which process should be followed in initiating, designing, and implementing transitional justice and reconciliation. When the transition is a result of negotiation, the parameters for pursuing transitional justice are set as part of the peace settlement. In Ethiopia's hybrid transition, there is no agreed upon framework on how to formulate and implement transitional justice. Questions abound on the ramifications of the lack of opportunity for participation of relevant stakeholders such as victim groups, civil society organizations, and the legal community in the planning and formulation of the transitional justice process and its monitoring.

Indeed, as experiences show and is appropriately underscored in the AUTJP, effective participation of the public is one of the most important success factors of transitional justice and the basis of legitimacy of the process. In this respect, the lack of public participation and consultation in the development of the law and the composition of the commission represents a missed golden opportunity in terms of establishing process legitimacy.

Related to the question of scope raised earlier is the issue of the objectives or purpose for which transitional justice is supposed to serve. Transitional justice can have either backward-looking and/or forward-looking objectives. If its objectives are simply punishing the wrongs of the past, such an objective is best addressed through the use of transitional justice that has criminal prosecution as its focus, as Ethiopia's experience with the Red Terror trials attests. If, on the other hand, its objectives are correcting the wrongs of the past and charting a common future, it needs to use a range of transitional justice measures including memorialization, truth revelation and record, reform of various state institutions, and the formulation of policies that include addressing human rights violations, gender oppression, socioeconomic deprivation, and the marginalization of youth. This question also depends on the consideration of whether the focus of transitional justice is on the perpetrators of violations, and therefore punishment, or on victims, and therefore recognition of the injustice they suffered, and healing, or the history and political system, and therefore on building a system of governance based on constitutionalism, the rule of law, and respect of the rights of all.

Its objective could also be either to address the wrongs that wreaked havoc on various sections of society or to create legitimacy for the new political system. Where it is used for achieving expedient political objectives, transitional justice is unlikely to deliver justice in a way that transforms the state-society relationship and creates the conditions for democratization and constitutionalism.

The final consideration is the care that should be taken to avoid the perils that come with transitions, such as the emergence of new grievances and deepening polarization. During transitions, the politics, the economy, and the social structure of the state tend to be in flux. Despite the demand of transitional justice for a rule-based approach, much of the changes may involve ad hoc measures, popular but extralegal or extra-constitutional actions, and purges lacking due process of law. This is particularly the case where transitions unfold without a common framework or negotiated roadmap. Another peril that comes with transitions is the susceptibility of transitional societies to external influence in their choice of the form of transitional justice and reconciliation approach.

CONCLUSION

From the foregoing exposition, it is clear that transitional justice and reconciliation is not an easy endeavor. For some of us it could be a topic that provokes memories of suffering and our experience of being wrongly violated and wrongly subjected to physical and psychological violence.

It could also be a topic that summons our sense of vengeance, our innate disposition of taking the law into our own hands, our retributive desire of meting out on our tormentors the pain and suffering they inflicted on us.

It is a subject that casts a shadow of trepidation and insecurity on the part of some of those perceived or real perpetrators of past wrongs or their associates. Depending on how it is framed and pursued, it could be a subject that may be politically mobilized by some actors for political score settling or engaging a country on a dangerous witch hunt.

It is also a subject fraught with major dilemmas arising from the imperative for balancing the demands of justice and reconciliation. These are demands which not only don't often sit in harmony but also at times could radically be opposed to each other during times of transition, which are characterized by their fluidity and uncertainty.

It is also a subject that is not always amenable to an easy and neat identification of responsibility. In a context such as ours, it brings the specter of attributing responsibility across a wider sector of society, depending on the temporal scope, going back generations despite the fact that not all sectors of society would bear the same level of responsibility. After all, the failures that resulted in the wrongs of the past are not simply products of individual culpability. Rather, they are in the main outcomes of societal and institutional pathologies, including a tradition of intolerance to and violent repression of dissent and political opposition, patterns of authoritarianism and patriarchal chauvinism.

If one simply follows the simple logic of criminal responsibility of the mainstream western-centric approach to transitional justice, then one would simply define those wrong acts as attributes of individual criminal behavior and conclude the question of transitional justice merely by applying criminal sanctions on the individuals thus blamed. In this respect, while the approach taken in the proclamation establishing the commission has avoided a particular approach, its inclination is rightly on broader issues of injustice.

Transitional justice is also a matter that calls all at once for both dispassion and empathy—dispassion because it is an ideal that should be pursued with fairness, evenhandedness, and a level of objectivity that a transitional society, a society in a fluid and polarized state of politics, should muster and empathy because the situation requires empathetic acknowledgement of the suffering that those who were wronged have endured.

It is also a subject that necessitates all at once the act of cursing and exorcising the wrongs of the past, acknowledging the suffering that those wronged endured, and showing magnanimity to those willing to own up to their responsibility and culpability. Thus, from the perspective of those who bore the brunt of the violations that the wrongs of the past caused, the challenge that transitional justice and reconciliation presents is beautifully captured by the Filipino poet J. Cabazares in "Discovering True Peace through Sincere Reconciliation":

> Talk to us about reconciliation
> Only if you first experience
> the anger of our dying.
>
> Talk to us about reconciliation
> If your living is not the cause
> of our dying.
>
> Talk to us about reconciliation
> Only if your words are not products of your devious scheme
> to silence our struggle for freedom.

Talk to us about reconciliation
Only if your intention is not to entrench yourself
more on your throne.

Talk to us about reconciliation
Only if you cease to appropriate all the symbols
and meanings of our struggle.

If pursued within the parameters of the foregoing considerations, transitional justice and reconciliation is also a subject that grants those who were wronged (victims or, to use more empowering language, survivors) the platform and opportunity to tell their stories in public and give their suffering public acknowledgement and thereby enable society to establish a record of the wrongs of the past through the voice of survivors and learn lessons for avoiding the conditions that make the perpetration of such wrongs possible. This is one of the roles specifically assigned to the Ethiopian Reconciliation Commission in the proclamation establishing it.

It is also a subject that offers society as a whole the occasion to see itself in the mirror, examine its various flaws, scars, and violent divisions, and apply the necessary corrective measures for removing the flaws, fully healing the scars, and mending the divisions among the members of society that the wrongs of the past sowed and nurtured.

This country owes to all those who have been wrongly abused and violated and to posterity that it enables the commission to pursue a transitional justice process that thoroughly, evenhandedly, and independently probes the full extent of the violations perpetrated, the category of individuals or political, professional, or ethno-cultural groups that suffered the most from the violations perpetrated, the persons who presided over the institutions used for perpetrating state violence, and the various conditions that made such systematic violence possible, including the failure of the justice system.

Seen from the vantage point of the foregoing and the review on the mandate and role of the commission, its establishment affords an opportunity that this country dearly needs for sensitively engaging with and addressing some of the major national issues that continue to challenge the emergence of a just, inclusive, and equitable democratic order in Ethiopia. At this point in time, whether the commission is able to deliver on its ambitious mandate remains to be seen. The preliminary analysis presented in this chapter on the process leading to the establishment of the commission and the nature of its composition leaves a lot to be desired.

REFERENCES

African Union. 2019. Transitional Justice Policy. Addis Ababa: AU.

Awol K Allo. 2018. "Navigating Ethiopia's Journey Towards Reconciliation and Justice." *Al Jazeera*, November 20, 2018.

Mutua, Makau. 2011. "A Critique of Rights in Transitional Justice: The African Experience." In *Rethinking Transitions: Equality and Social Justice in Societies Emerging from Conflict*, edited by Gaby Oré Anguilar and Felipe Gómez Isa, 31. Series on Transitional Justice 6. Cambridge: Intersentia.

Sachs, Albie. 2009. *The Strange Alchemy of Life and Law*. Oxford: Oxford University Press.

Taylor, Charles. 1994. "The Politics of Recognition." In *Multiculturalism*, edited by Amy Gutmann, 25–74. Princeton, NJ: Princeton University Press.

1.8 Restorative Justice Modalities
What Can Be Learned about Peace and Reconciliation from Imperial Ethiopia?

Charles Schaefer

Foundational to nation building is peacemaking, and integral to the latter is serving justice such that the form of justice promotes reconciliation. Prime Minister Abiy Ahmed's government established a Reconciliation Commission in December 2018 to do just that. The preamble for Proclamation No. 1102/2018 commits the commission to seek "truth and justice," "identify and ascertain" gross human rights violations, and provide a forum for victims "to be heard and perpetrators to disclose," all directed by an "independent institution" committed to seeking truth "to prevent the future occurrence of such conflict" (*Federal Negarit Gazette* Proclamation No. 1102/2018, February 5, 2019). Its intent is laudatory; its transitional justice theory is unclear.

This brief chapter makes an unabashed plea that Ethiopian policy makers and legal advisers associated with the new Reconciliation Commission but not limited to that institution consider adopting some of the ingenious, flexible, and infinitely adaptable legal remedies that were devised and tested in imperial Ethiopia. Too often successor regimes, whose country emerged from tyranny and gross human rights abuses, opt to import transitional justice modalities. The chapter divides transitional justice into its two constituent parts: restorative versus retributive justice.[1] After accessing the benefits and limitations of restorative (forgiveness) and retributive (punishment) justice, a critique against both will be made, paving the way for a strong argument to reject importing international legal procedures and instead modify and develop indigenous concepts of restorative justice that were used in imperial Ethiopia for hundreds of years. Ethiopian history certifies that plenty of mistakes were made, but from these mistakes corrections were decreed that substantively improved the manner in which restorative justice was adjudicated in order to bring reconciliation and promote enduring peace. Some scholars have coined "ethnojustice" as a term for advocating the indigenization of the peacemaking process (Branch 2011), but the sociopolitical examples they use do not have the historical depth or impute the legal wisdom that imperial Ethiopia imparts.

This chapter will conclude with five illustrations for initiating a restorative justice process that draws from lessons from Ethiopia's reconciliation history. Moreover, they demonstrate the ingenuity, flexibility, and adaptability of Ethiopia's restorative justice processes. As an added bonus, these five illustrations address many of the shortfalls associated with either form of transitional justice—restorative or retributive—and could be adapted to provide improved international understanding about effective tools for transitional justice. Ethiopia has an opportunity to substantively contribute new legal remedies into the discourse on transitional justice by digging into its rich legal history.

THE ETHIOPIAN RED TERROR TRIALS: RETRIBUTIVE JUSTICE'S FAILURE TO GENERATE RECONCILIATION

Retributive justice is often called "victor's justice." Ethiopia has already experienced retributive justice in the Red Terror trials. In many ways they were a failure. Beginning in 1976, Ethiopia experienced the ravages of the Red Terror, a period in which various revolutionary groups turned on one another, killing and brutalizing their foes in the name of their respective definitions of a purer Marxism-Leninism. Soon the Derg joined the carnage, but instead of killing out of ideological fervor, the Derg systematized the slaughter by methodically identifying students along with members of the intelligentsia and the ancien régime, executing them, and then recording in detail how they were eliminated. Wounds remained raw, and justice was thought to be the salve to bring about healing. But what form of justice?

The leadership of the EPRDF appeared to have selected a trial format well before entering Arat Kilo in 1991. According to Prime Minister Meles Zenawi, the decision "that a legal accounting of what happened was the best way to go" was taken during the last stages of the war against the Derg when victory favored the EPRDF. In an interview, Meles confided that truth commissions were unknown to them out in the bush[2] circa 1989–91, even though they were already employed in Latin America well before South Africa's Truth and Reconciliation Commission (TRC) began. Absent from Meles's comments were references to or even knowledge of Ethiopia's own long history of restorative justice. Speculation surrounding why the EPRDF leadership did not consider "traditional" forms of restorative justice remain clouded (Schaefer 2009). The period of 1989 through 1995 witnessed the collapse of the Soviet Union and, in its place, the ascendency of Western neoliberalism's insistence upon democracy, transparency, and accountability. Translated into the political and judicial realms, this meant holding free and fair elections and abiding by international law and the Geneva Conventions. To a great extent, the global trend during this period emphasized retributive justice carried out in either national or international courts to resolve all human rights abuses and bring about reconciliation (Teitel 2000). Certainly the United States exerted pressure on Ethiopia in this transitional period to opt for criminal prosecution, yet it appeared that the United States' insistence coincided with the EPRDF leadership's determination to try Derg officials in a court of law.

Trials were conducted throughout the country, though the most prominent 106 high-ranking officials of the Derg were tried in the flagship trial, *Special Prosecutor v. Colonel Mengistu Hailemariam et al.*, in Addis Ababa. The Special Prosecutor's Office (SPO) was given a dual mandate to bring Derg officials to trial and to record for posterity the massive human rights abuses perpetuated against the Ethiopian people, in order to educate citizens and prevent such a travesty from taking place in the future. (Recording the history of atrocity was to become a core element of truth commissions.) Twelve years later (1994–2006) the prosecution rested its case, the defense voiced their objections in a few months, and guilty verdicts were passed down, with appeals protracting the trial for two more years. In that excessively drawn out trial, infractions against international legal standards were abundant; these included detention without charge at the outset, legal problems in applying articles in Ethiopia's 1957 penal code, asserting the legality to define genocide to include social groups, and the appearance of impartiality when there was a revolving panel of judges that officiated over the trial but where not one judge was present from start to finish (Elgesem and Girmachew 2009).

What did the trials accomplish for the Ethiopian people? Did they bring about reconciliation and healing to a wounded nation? At the outset, expectations were high, especially as part of the dual mandate to invite victims to recount the abuses they suffered. But that invitation was ill conceived, for the number of people seeking to air their grievances overwhelmed the SPO, and the throngs waiting to tell their victim stories strained the courts (Vaughan 2009). Confined to a few courtrooms scattered throughout the country, the Red Terror trials, which lasted fourteen years, were hidden from and meaningless to the Ethiopian population. When finally the verdict was read, news reporters interviewing Ethiopians on the street found that there had been a dramatic shift away from viewing the Red Terror trials as mechanisms to bring about national reconciliation to an example of "victor's justice." As one Ethiopian put it, "Today's sentence makes a mockery of justice" (Reuters 2007). The trials did not bring about reconciliation. In employing retributive justice, a successor regime draws a "bright line demarcating the normative shift from illegitimate to legitimate rule" (Teitel 2000). For the successor regime, the task becomes defining "legitimate" by writing its own version of history to vilify the former regime and whitewash its own actions.

South Africa's TRC: Shortcomings of Restorative Justice

>Examples of restorative justice remained obscure until the 1995 TRC in South Africa. The TRC's foundation for applying restorative justice was built on the dynamic of applying *ubuntu*—an African understanding of identity that gives personhood by saying, "I am because you say I am," thereby emphasizing the primacy of human relationships. *Ubuntu* created the moral, legal, and institutional framework for the TRC; its conception of restorative justice appeared on the verge of ushering in a new vernacular for justice. Bishop Desmond Tutu's forceful, unapologetically Christian voice in favor of restorative justice is perhaps its most persuasive altar call, with all the Christian overtones appertaining (Tutu 1999; Appleby 2000).

Restorative justice is often viewed as a panacea, a guarantee to produce peace and reconciliation. Restorative justice tries to promote reconciliation by bringing perpetrator and victim together at a truth commission intended to bring societal healing through a power reversal associated with perpetrators asking for and victims granting forgiveness (Llewellyn 2014).

Once the TRC was underway, however, dissenting voices began to question the premise of offering amnesty for truth. The problem with the TRC was that Nelson Mandela and Desmond Tutu assumed restorative justice meant "forgive and forget," but giving amnesty to white apartheid perpetrators did not promote peace. What made amnesty particularly hurtful to victims of apartheid, over three-quarters of the population, was the absence of remorse and repentance on the part of many of the wrongdoers.

Academics as well as individuals working for the TRC analyzed each and every step in the forgiveness process. Almost every critique centered on the concept of forgiveness (Amstutz 2005; Krog 2000). Many decried the overly Christian conceptualization of forgiveness, which was less meaningful to South Africans professing African traditional religion, Islam, Hinduism, or Judaism. Others questioned the testimonies of apartheid security force personnel who may or may not have been genuinely contrite and how that gave rise to the perception of white impunity. Victims wondered aloud whether an apology was enough. "After a day's testimony in September [1997] from Harold Synman, [Steve] Biko's chief interrogator, Mrs. Biko said, 'There is nothing new. He is lying even more than in the inquest'" (2000).

Implicit throughout was the regret that perpetrators were not convicted and punished if they complied with the TRC.

Forgiveness was thought to be the central component of restorative justice, and this form of transitional justice was supposed to expedite reconciliation. But the TRC's understanding of forgiveness emphasized the here-and-now process involved in the power reversal inherent in forgiveness, which gave the forgiver, whether they were elite or lowly, the authority to forgive or not. Within the ideology of *ubuntu*, it was assumed that a one-time power inversion would rebalance South African society between black, colored, and white. To push forward, South Africans needed to forget the past and work towards a rainbow future, thus the "forgive and forget" mantra. Too much was made of societal reconciliation, for it promised to serve justice, provide a definitive mark in history between an abusive past and the beginning of a bright future, and promote national healing between races and classes. Everyone ultimately asked the question, Did the TRC produce national reconciliation? Few answered in the affirmative, many said "No," and even more obfuscated. As for reconciliation, it still appears elusive.

The desire to instantaneously correct the past and usher in a better future may be the problem for advocates of either form of transitional justice, for both want immediate and irrefutable results. An underlying assumption of transitional justice is that it is a one-time deal and that once justice is served the grievances never need be redressed. Much of the criticism of restorative justice revolves around the ambiguous nature of what it offers—apology, forgiveness, and amnesty—when reparations and prison sentences appear more concrete. By contrast, trials order punishment and sometimes offer compensation but seldom the qualitative, psychological satisfaction of an apology and the power shift that forgiveness can invoke. Imperial Ethiopian history provides a different narrative.

RESTORATIVE JUSTICE PRACTICED IN ETHIOPIA: A CALL FOR HISTORICIZING ETHNOJUSTICE

To repeat, imperial Ethiopian history provides a deeper, historically based narrative about restorative justice that rectifies many of the generally recognized shortcomings associated with restorative justice. First, Ethiopia's royal chronicles and ecclesiastic literature provide detailed information about peacemaking back to the time of Zär'a Ya'ecob and 'Amda Seyon. The *Kebrä Nägäst* and the more legalese *Fetha Nägäst* give historical substance to jurisprudence and the manner in which court decisions were integrated into nation building. This is in marked contrast to most African states that did not have a written language before colonialism (Van Donge 1998). Thus, Ethiopian history changes the underpinning of ethnojustice from a reconstructed ethnographic past to recorded legal rulings. Second, Ethiopia's understanding of forgiveness was conditional—forgive but never forget. This meant that grievances were constantly reassessed and justice itself was viewed as an ongoing process depending upon the contriteness of the individual or group. Third, restorative justice was not only a legal remedy but responded to sociopolitical demands that could demand apology, forgiveness, and amnesty under certain circumstances but order severe punishment or financial restitution under other situations. Its hallmark was ingenuity, flexibility, and adaptability.

Ethnojustice Without History

Restorative justice was developed originally in Latin American and then South Africa in the early 1990s, or at least that is what the literature ascribes. In the most famous case, TRC commissioners assigned to litigate apartheid's aftermath understood the meaning of *ubuntu* but had difficulty tracing its applicability in an obscure precolonial ethnography. Nelson Mandela and Desmond Tutu knew it existed but had no historical records to prove it and therefore retroactively invented a past in which it existed. The propensity to ascribe a modern legal remedy to a cloudy preliterate past is illustrated by *Gacaca* in Rwanda. *Gacaca*—literally "justice on the grass" in Kinyarwanda—was one form of grassroots customary dispute resolution (CDR) that existed in Rwanda by convening elders of a community to hear disputants and seek compromise or resolution; it had no historical mandate or legal writings, did not deal with state-level issues, and its legitimacy depended strongly on the community in which it operated (Africa Rights 2003; Biggar 2001). Yet because it was widely known among the population and for lack of an alternative, the Rwandan government seized upon it and modified, modernized, and gave it a mandate: "The *Gacaca* Law mandated the construction of a new hybrid judicial process known as the *Gacaca*—traditional in name, retributive in process and restorative in intent"

(Magnarella 2000; Meyerstein 2007; Pieper 2009). Unlike Ethiopia, in Rwanda a CDR institution had to be customized to fill the autochthonous void for a mechanism to administer justice and bring about national reconciliation. Ethiopia had time-tested instruments at the national level to reconcile foes through processes that line up closely with restorative justice.

The problem with restorative justice is that it has been co-opted by Western academics and legal scholars and has lost its African or Latin American origins. The term ethnojustice attempts to retrieve indigenous authorship. Arguing for it, Alan Branch states that ethnojustice "is based on the idea that in certain parts of the world, the most important, authentic identities are cultural identities, particularly traditional, customary, or tribal identities, and so participation should take place within this cultural framework or risk being rejected as an alien imposition" (2011). Alien imports can lead to the collapse of African values and ritual practices that enhance social harmony and undercut authority structures among elders and traditional leaders. Traditional reconciliation intended to rebuild the authority structures that war or civil strife challenged or destroyed (Branch 2011). This was certainly true in the case of restorative justice in Ethiopia, for it was premised on maintaining political stability. Even for the *shiftnät*, the pretext for rebellion was not social disruption but rather an alternate path to inclusion (Caulk 1984; Fernyhough 1986). But the case against ethnojustice is equally valid.[3] It presumes that the goal of ethnojustice is the reestablishment of traditional social order. The socioreligious diversity of Ethiopia—the old kaleidoscope depiction—begs the questions, Whose social order? Which ethnic group? In historical Ethiopia, traditions of restorative justice were pegged to the monarchy yet paradoxically display exceptional regional variety to accommodate religious and ethnic differences, while being recognized nationally. Ethiopia's historical record can and should be considered, for it is culturally relevant, yet shows considerable latitude.

Forgive but Never Forget

Most troublesome for restorative justice is the notion that forgiveness requires forgetting. The connection is long-standing. Barry Schwartz elaborates, "Society and its members must not only forgive; they must also forget." He adds, "On the collective, as opposed to the dyadic, level, however, it is the phenomenon of amnesty which best exemplifies the way a social system can be bound together by forbearance. This is because amnesty is the act of forgiving and forgetting the crimes of the collectivity, or, more precisely, part of a collectivity, for the expressed purpose of celebrating union.. ... Amnesty, or collective forgiveness, is in this sense the most radical affirmation of social integration" (1978). The parallels to Desmond Tutu's articulation of the role of amnesty for South Africa appear obvious (Tutu 1999) and are the insertion point of the "forgive and forget" thesis into restorative justice.

Forgiveness, particularly following the TRC's granting amnesty, was criticized for being a one-step deal, when those who lived in South Africa felt that forgiving was a never-ending process, especially by those who were asked to forgive wrongdoers. The type of forgiveness expected is viewed as unilateral forgiveness, which means that forgiveness is granted irrespective of whether the wrongdoers acknowledge their horrendous deeds, because forgiveness is therapeutic for victims, due to the fact that it is one of the few ways to bypass the sentiment of revenge by victims, and because "the teleology of forgiveness is reconciliation" (MacLachlan 2008; Murphy 2003; Roberts 1995). However, this presupposes forgetfulness or the pretense of forgetfulness. But in daily life in South Africa since 1994, where former apartheid officials and security personnel possess wealth, privilege, and protection, and blacks living in Soweto remain underemployed, poor, and preyed upon, it is exceedingly hard to forget the past, both the apartheid past and the reconciliation process that enabled unrepentant perpetrators to walk free. Again, the role of memory hampers forgiveness; thus, many South Africans ask: How can there be reconciliation when it is predicated on a unilateral understanding of forgiveness where the victims shoulder all the obligations and the perpetrators have impunity? The role of memory looms large.

Trudy Govier posits that forgetting does not ensure a return to a good relationship; rather, forgiving has constituent parts that argue against forgetting. First, forgiving is a process that forever requires work and constant revision; second, forgiving necessitates facing bitterness and anger and replacing those sentiments with positive ones; and third, foundational to forgiveness is trust, trust in the integrity of the other individual and trust that the process of forgiving, noted above, will be perpetually reenacted (2002). Central to all three constituent parts is the role of memory.

For Wole Soyinka, giving amnesty to perpetrators without their showing genuine remorse ensures that forgetting, and therefore reconciliation, is impossible. Pointing to instances from the slave trade to South Africa and Rwanda, Soyinka further breaks down forgiveness into two categories: moral and material (1999). The TRC and all the theoretical arguments for restorative justice advocate the moral arguments for atonement and therefore societal redemption, he claims, but these still leave out human agency—the feeling of betrayal black South Africans feel towards the amnesty given to privileged whites. Beyond theory, history is comprised of individuals experiencing, loving, hating, laughing, and weeping through life (Soyinka 1999), and under these circumstances the moral acts of atonement, be they genuine or not, are meaningless expressions. What Soyinka argues is that forgiveness has to be proven and a method to accomplish that is through forfeiting material—money, land, jobs. Only through reparations are the indignities of an abusive past righted (Soyinka 1999; Mamdani 1996). Memory is never erased, but through reparations, restitution can take place because perpetrators, too, will be remembering their material loss and in doing so the reasons for their loss, which returns full circle to the abuses they carried out. This ensures remembrance and dispels forgetting.

Ethiopian history tells us that Ethiopia made the mistake of "forgive and forget," particularly during the Zämänä Mäsafint. Because of the weakness of the center during the Zämänä Mäsafint, the effectiveness of Ethiopia's mechanisms to bring about social and political reconciliation through restorative justice was weakened such that the Yäju dynasty, for short-term expediency, emphasized "forgive and forget." I argue, however, that the forgetting exacerbated conflict and war for over eighty years during the Zämänä Mäsafint:

> How could a *ras*, twice or thrice defeated, be able to resume his position, reassert his patrimony over land and peasants, excise tax and tribute, use that income to procure arms, mobilize his subjects, and wage another war within one to five years with the ambition to topple the emperor, yet again, and assume the throne himself? (Schaefer, forthcoming)

Ethiopians learned from their mistakes, and, following Emperor Tewodros assumption to the throne, the refrain was "forgive but never forget." In other words, forgiveness is granted with conditions, and those conditions were never forgotten and had to be adhered to by the grantee. What Ethiopian history clearly demonstrates is that the forgetting component of "forgive and forget" was abandoned after 1855 because it rarely brought peace and stability. (If only practitioners and scholars of restorative justice in South Africa and elsewhere were familiar with Ethiopia's documented history, corrections could be made to the implementation of restorative modalities in other truth commissions.) The conditions upon which forgiveness were granted were part of the national memory that forced perpetrators to be accountable and atone for their misdeeds and therefore enabled forgiveness to take place and reconciliation to happen.

RESTORATIVE JUSTICE AS RESPONSE TO SOCIOPOLITICAL DEMANDS: FIVE LESSONS

To reiterate, Ethiopia's administration of restorative justice was never intended to be a legal remedy employing codified sentencing procedures; rather, it was a response to sociopolitical demands. Sometimes these demands required leniency that could order a submission ceremony or *werdat* (literally translated as shaming, dishonor, humiliation, obeisance) that featured the asking for forgiveness or clemency and the granting of conditional forgiveness. Under other circumstances, where the grantee abused previously agreed upon terms of forgiveness and, in so doing, brought social unrest or political rebellion, more severe punishments—including imprisonment and death—could be prescribed. Other remedies in nineteenth- and early twentieth-century Ethiopia included repair of harm agreements or financial restitution, which took many forms but primarily curtailed a wayward *ras* from taxing peasants working his tributary lands. The hallmark of Ethiopian traditions of restorative justice was ingenuity, flexibility, and adaptability.

While my forthcoming monograph, titled *Peace Not War: Traditions of Restorative Justice in Imperial Ethiopia*, historically assesses how restorative justice at the national level changed over two hundred years, five lessons can be pulled from it to illustrate how Ethiopian history should be acknowledged, studied, modified, and adapted to current conditions to promote durable peace and reconciliation.

Lesson 1: Justice in a public forum

The process involved in administering justice must be public in order to bring about compromise and buy-in. Technology has changed radically, but the need to consider oneself informed about the administration of justice by the state is a key component of restorative justice. The TRC held open forums for victims and perpetrators to describe abuses suffered or inflicted, and these sessions were televised for all to see. There was public support for amnesty in the early years because South Africans felt included in Mandela's vision of establishing a rainbow future. It fell apart when blacks looked around, observed the privileges that whites retained, and concluded there was not sufficient accountability. Part of the problem with the Red Terror trials was that most trials were held in obscurity. The principal trial in Addis Ababa was televised sporadically, yet as years passed, the duration and frequency of coverage swiftly dropped off. Most of the lesser, regional trials were conducted almost in secrecy. The Ethiopian public was unable to observe how justice was meted out; thus, the trials were deemed "a mockery of justice." How new truth commissions, court cases, or any other transitional justice forums are made public will require much thought and probably the incorporation of social media, including WhatsApp, WeChat, Twitter, Facebook, or more Ethio-inspired platforms like Mivasocial, but also reaching out through print, radio, and television, for the point is to reach as many people as possible. Bringing a transparent judicial process to the public is central to advancing national reconciliation.

In the nineteenth and early twentieth centuries, there was no communication technology, yet tried-and-true word of mouth, a proven communications form, was employed openly. Verbal accounts of the submission ceremony were taken back to remote provinces by local rulers, clergy, and peasants/soldiers who had witnessed the ceremony and were recounted to the public. People "living in the bush" stay remarkably current on news to the point that many development workers are bewildered over how quickly news travels. Imperial Ethiopia exploited this network.

The submission ceremony was a highly visual affair full of symbolism and spectacle (Orlowska 2009). The spectacle of justice being served was the news item that traveled to distant corners and was widely discussed by Ethiopians to inspire them to support the legitimacy of the crown. The victor and his retinue were often arrayed under an open tent or canopy, with the emperor or victorious *ras* in the center and aristocrats arranged in descending order of rank on either side in all their splendid regalia and lion-mane headdresses. Conversely, the defeated leader and his officers had to walk towards the tent hunched over according to rank. The ritual was choreographed to demonstrate superiority and inferiority, and those who submitted were expected to show diffidence and respect by physically humbling themselves. One way this was done was by draping a *shämma* tightly around his waist, leaving his shoulders bare as well as his whole face exposed. One definition of the Amharic verb *tattäqä* describes "folding a *shämma* around one's waist as a mark of respect" (Orlowska 2009). The *shämma* was an item of clothing worn by everyone for warmth; when working it was wound around the waist to free the arms for labor. Since the majority of the population was peasants, it became a symbol of subservience.

To accentuate shaming, an offender carried a heavy stone on his shoulders. "Generally the most culpable puts a large stone upon his neck, and, approaching the other, asks for pardon: the other, in saying to him 'May God forgive you!' ... A master ... contents himself, on forgiving his servant [inferior], with taking the stone from this neck and putting it into his hands" (Gobat 1834). Carrying a stone invoked servanthood, a clear sign of respect, repentance, and subordination, and a gesture for seeking forgiveness.

Figure 1.8.1 *Emperor Menilek and other courtiers at public ceremony under open tent.*

Source: Institute of Ethiopian Studies.

The submission of *Negus* Mikael after the Battle of Segale was held two times. The first was on the battlefield where *Negus* Mikael bowed before *Ras* Tafari, *Fitawrari* Habta-Giyorgis, and other members of the Shewan nobility after his defeat. The second time came at Jan Meda, where Empress

Zawditu and all the lords, retainers, soldiers, and urban population could watch. *Negus* Mikael, with pride and dignity, shouldered a stone, approached the empress's tent with humility and contriteness, and expressed loyalty to the throne, despite the fact that his son, *Lij* Iyasu, had been dethroned in a Shewan-inspired coup d'état. This is not the time or place to gauge the legitimacy or illegitimacy of the coup. What is noteworthy, though, is that the coup makers choreographed *Negus* Mikael's submission to demonstrate to the Ethiopian public the successor regime's use of restorative justice to bring peace and stability to a war-torn country. It was a visible, public affair.

That the terms and conditions placed on Mikael were rather harsh points to how fragile *Ras* Tafari and company viewed their regime, considering that *Lij* Iyasu was still loose in the countryside with an army of his own. That *Negus* Mikael nevertheless acknowledged and abided by those harsh terms points to the universal acceptance of restorative justice modalities. If wise and creative justice was able to smooth over Shewa's fractured state, with all its religious and ethnic undercurrents, then restorative justice appropriately and publically adjudicated may offer prospects for peace and reconciliation today.

Lesson 2: Forgiveness too freely given

Verdicts can be too lenient, too magnanimous. Amnesty or the propensity to forgive and forget can perpetuate animosity and rebellion. As stated above, the *Zämänä Mäsafint* is viewed as a period of incessant war, but by asking the question, Who fought the wars? research shows that it was the same cast of characters. On occasion, leaders were killed in battle, but rarely afterwards was vengeance served on a defeated lord, either in terms of physical harm or death, imprisonment, or even *gizot* (removal from his patrimony), for the whole land-tenure system was built on enduring patron-client relationships between *gult* and *rist* holders. Removing a lord could feasibly cause social unrest, curtail tribute sent to the emperor, and hinder the ability of the elites to recruit peasants/soldiers. Thus, this early form of the forgive-and-forget type of restorative justice was a conservative strategy to ensure the preservation of the sociopolitical status quo. This is nowhere better viewed than in the conflicts between *Däjazmač* Wəbe Haylä Maryam, the rebel, and *Ras bitwädäd* Ali II, the ruler of the Yäju dynasty.

There were many provincial *rases* who experienced submission multiple times, but none as poignantly as *Däjazmač* Wəbe (Rubenson 1978). He suffered the humiliation of the submission ceremony (*werdat*) multiple times, only to reconstitute his patrimony and try again and again to ascend the throne. Däjazmač Wəbe epitomizes the full range of restorative justice modalities and yet his recidivism, his constant thirst for more power, his lifelong aspirations for grandeur guaranteed that he remained a "thorn in the flesh" to the Yäju rulers—Yimam, Maryé, Dori, and Ali—from 1826 to 1855.

Däjazmač Wəbe is the ideal case study through which to question the hypothesis that restorative justice, when misapplied, can generate war and exacerbate political instability. Thrice defeated, Wəbe was able to resume his position, reassert his patrimony over his provincial lands, excise taxes on his peasants, use his tribute to buy firearms, rally his subjects, and fight three wars (1830, 1831, and 1842) to topple Yimam, Maryé, and Ali II in order to assume the imperial throne. In 1842, Däjazmač Wəbe had mobilized a powerful army and challenged *Ras bitwädäd* Ali at the Battle of Däbrä Tabor. After perhaps the bloodiest battle of the *Zämänä Mäsafint*, Wəbe won and sent Ali fleeing into the countryside. Yet in a surreptitious turn of events, finding Wəbe's victorious forces celebrating and thus out of formation, Bəru Aligaz mounted a surprise attack and routed the enemy. Wəbe was captured. In a shocking, incomprehensible, magnanimous gesture, Ali, upon being reseated on the Yäju *alga* by Bəru Aligaz, restored Wəbe to the governorships of Semen and Tigray. Irrationally, Ali gave Bəru Aligaz a minor governate to thank him for his loyalty.

It bears repeating that this traitor, this malcontent, this disloyal rival was forgiven and all his previous territories were restored, an example of forgive-and-forget restorative justice adjudicated most generously. The story goes that within the Yäju *chelot*, Wəbe's allies convinced Ali to return to the status quo and argued that restoring Wəbe was preferable to dealing with unknown rulers.

Lesson 3: Magnanimity in service of the state

Magnanimity does have its place under the right circumstances to promote the interests of the state. Recall that Ethiopia's manifestations of restorative justice were noted for their ingenuity, flexibility, and adaptability. The welfare of the state was always considered most important over some abstract notion of justice. This was due in part to the concept of *irq*. The ability to perceive contradictions and ambiguity in serving "justice" had metaphysical roots in Orthodox theology. The Ethiopian Orthodox Tewahedo Church did not appropriate Western ethical dualism—good and evil distinct and separate—rather, "the Ethiopian conception of dualism presupposes a non-essentialized and flexible other, and a compassionate self or soul. These two concepts are embodied in the idea of *irq*, which presupposes the possibility of negotiation and reconciliation between good and evil" (Yirga 2017).

Why did *Ras bitwädäd* Ali grant clemency to *Däjazmač* Wəbe Haylä Maryam after the bloody Battle of Däbrä Tabor? Perhaps Ali and members of his *chelot* possessed the foresight to estimate whether a particular action could lead to the goal of establishing peace and security, and the precaution to mitigate risky and foolish outcomes. Reappointing Wəbe governor of Semen and Tigray ensured peace in the northern provinces from 1842 to 1855.

Kassa Haylu brought a swift and inexorable end to the *Zämänä Mäsafint*. In 1853 he took on *Ras bitwädäd* Ali II, sovereign of the Yäju dynasty and suzerain over most of Ethiopia. In June 1853 Ali and Kassa fought their inevitable battle, and Kassa's military genius plus disciplined, battle-hardened soldiers overpowered Ali's forces at the Battle of Ayshal. There was only one holdout preventing Kassa from assuming an undisputed claim to the imperial throne and crowning himself Emperor Tewodros: *Däjazmač* Wəbe Haylä Maryam (Rubenson 1978). The same *Däjazmač* Wəbe who had thrice challenged the Yäju rulers for the throne; the same malcontent who blatantly disregarded summons to Ali's court in Däbrä Tabor; the same supplicant who had begged for forgiveness three times and had been granted unconditional pardons along with incomprehensibly generous rewards for his reluctant obeisance. And yet Ali's forgiveness appears to have paid off, for Wəbe remained loyal beyond the collapse of the Yäju dynasty.

Lesson 4: Cultural understandings of justice

A theme repeated in this chapter is that justice is culturally bedded, that perceptions of what is "just" in one nation do not necessarily speak to cultural understandings in another. Foreign ideas are just that, foreign. Rarely are they endowed with cultural meaning and symbolism. For the West, Lady Justice is depicted as blind to impart impartiality. Her inability to see prevents her from perceiving economic, kinship, or political ties that could cloud her judgment. Her duty is to adjudicate the case only on its legal merits—to determine whether an action was within the boundaries of the law but indifferent to human costs or societal repercussions.

In Ethiopia, justice is depicted as faceless but with eyes wide open to better assess the social, economic, and political implications of a case on an individual or society. Ethiopia's Lady Justice's identity known through facial recognition, in theory, is unknown, yet her eyes are able to discern everything. In Figure 15.2, Empress Zawditu epitomizes a faceless judge with eyes wide open. Her *netela* covers her face and head allowing only her eyes to be seen. Her identity, likewise, is theoretically unknown; thus, she is able to render a judgment, not as the empress with all the kinship, social ties and political pressures thereof and appertaining but as an unbiased human being. Her eyes wide open signify her willingness to consider broader sociopolitical implications.

Figure 1.8.2 *Empress Zawditu with Ras Tafari, left, hold court illustrating Ethiopian form of socially constructed justice "with eyes wide open."*

Source: Rosita Forbes, *From Red Sea to Blue Nile: An Abyssinian Adventure* (1925).

Verdicts in Ethiopia were not abstract renderings of case law, but socially constructed remedies. In historical Ethiopia, the *zufan chelot* (imperial court) had the unique ability to discuss each case based on its legal merits as well as on its social, political, and economic implications; thus, decisions were guided by what was best for the country to bring about reconciliation to the people and the state.

Shiferaw Bekele wonderfully describes how the *zufan chelot* functioned. The court was called into session when important issues of state needed to be addressed or in important civil or criminal cases. Once seated, the lower ranks in the *mäkwanent* (aristocracy) voiced their opinions, with more senior members following in order of rank. The emperor was the last to speak, and his word, ideally, reflected the consensus of the court and rendered equitable and impartial justice. Often the *afa negus*, the "mouth of the king" or chief justice, pronounced the judgment in civil or criminal cases, less often on issues of state where the emperor typically announced his decision. For those whose opinions were rejected, the fact that they were able to voice their views acted as a pressure valve—something analogous to parliament for modern states—and made them an integral part of the imperial court (Shiferaw 1990). The *zufan chelot* provided a forum for the emperor "to rally opinion and to mobilize support against rebels, conspirators and others who defied his authority" (Shiferaw 1990). Yet court procedure gave plaintiffs time to plead their case, seek justice, and request reinstatement scripted by the restorative justice protocols around forgiveness and atonement. The emperor was not removed from society, just the opposite: as the ultimate arbiter he or she was involved in civil and criminal cases on a daily basis.

The emperor, when deciding issues of state "with eyes wide open," sought the counsel of the *mäkwanent*, who in their own right were experienced judges. Indeed, *mäkwanent* is the plural of *mäkonnen*, which means governor or judge. As Samuel Gobat observed in the 1820s, midway through the Zämänä Mäsafint, political, judicial, and military offices were one and the same: "For all the governors are civil judges, and all the civil judges are military men" (1834). Transitional justice, whether retributive or restorative, could learn a lesson from imperial Ethiopia, for in matters of state, leaders from vastly different professions, experiences, and backgrounds were allowed to voice their opinions. Justice was culturally woven into the tapestry of the nation. While the verdict was given by the ruler or his or her representative, the decision was arrived at by consensus.

Lesson 5: Conditional forgiveness

Most important, terms associated with Ethiopia's form of conditional forgiveness were flexible; they allowed the state to modify its verdict in response to a perpetrator's willingness to abide by the terms set by the state. In other words, recidivism could be punished without remanding the case to court. Rejection of one-and-done verdicts allowed Ethiopians to mete out justice to best address people's changing definition of justice as circumstances change. Truth, unfortunately, can be rather fickle and circumstantial, and a truthful verdict given in a court or truth commission one year may be questioned five years later. This is particularly the case with "victor's justice" when a successor regime recasts the past to its own liking by promoting new, indelible truths. In less dramatic instances, having legal remedies that exhibited flexibility and adaptability was advantageous. One-and-done justice assumes that time served fulfills the requirements of the sentence—and it often does—but people's sense of justice changes; sometimes it becomes more vengeful, other times sympathy creeps in and it becomes more lenient. Restorative justice practiced in imperial Ethiopia had the capacity to move in either direction, for the terms and conditions were forged within a symbolic relationship between the public (the adjudicator of justice) and the perpetrator (those sentenced by the court/public), who were constantly reevaluating whether the terms were just and whether they were obeyed—the concept of atonement. *Ras* Alula represents how justice is like a pendulum swinging from lenient to punitive and back again as circumstances dictate.

Ras Alula's case shows how holding a big stick is compatible with conditions of forgiveness. Alula attached himself to the rise of *Däjazmač* Kassa Merča, a fellow Tigrayan, who took the coronation name Yohännes IV in 1871. As a dutiful general, Alula led Yohännes's troops into battle against the Egyptians at Gundät (1875) and Gura (1876). Recognized for his courage and brilliant military strategy, Alula was promoted to *ras* and henceforth functioned as both supreme military commander and trusted political councilor to Emperor Yohännes. In 1885 Alula defeated the Mahdists at Kufit on the border of Sudan (Erlich 2002). Two years later he crushed the Italians at the Battle of Dogali near Mitsawa, stopping Italy's colonial ambitions—at least for a while.[4] Still later, Yohännes recruited Alula to fight alongside him at Mätämma in March 1889 against the Mahdists. On the brink of victory, a stray bullet killed Emperor Yohännes, and the Mahdists claimed victory after a reassembled detachment overtook the funeral cortege, killed a number of senior Ethiopian notables, severed their heads, and paraded them along with Yohännes's head around Sudan (Zewde 2014). Ethiopia was in disarray.

Alula remained loyal to Yohännes's heir, *Ras* Mängäshä Yohännes, but more so to Tigrayan hegemony. Upon Menilek's coronation as *Negus Nägäst*, *Ras* Mängäshä agreed to travel to Addis Ababa and formally submit. *Ras* Alula, Yohännes's elder statesman and victorious general, had considerable influence over young *Ras* Mängäshä and did everything in his power to prevent Mängäshä from submitting to the emperor. Alula remained truculent, sometimes backing *Ras* Mängäshä for all the right reasons, other times going against Mängäshä, even to the degree of starting internal skirmishes in Tigray. Unbowed, Alula "reacted furiously and performed the traditional war dances, inciting everyone to shout anti-Shoan slogans" (Erlich 1996). One time, Alula absconded with four hundred rifles destined for Menilek and when reprimanded only returned two hundred, saying that the others were necessary to defend the homeland, when in fact he used them against Menilek's Tigrayan allies. Another time, he suggested *Ras* Mängäshä be overthrown if he submitted to Menilek (Erlich 1996). In between, multiple attempts were made to reconcile Alula into the body politic, yet with his recidivist tendencies, he resisted submission. Added together, Alula could have been indicted for high treason on multiple counts (Marcus 1975).

When Italian designs on Ethiopia developed into military incursions into Tigray, Alula had a change of heart and accompanied *Ras* Mängäshä to Addis Ababa in June 1894 to submit. Arriving in Addis Ababa, the Tigrayan contingent of *Ras*es Mängäshä, Alula, Hagos, and Woldä Mikael proceeded to Menilek's *gebbi*. Seated on his throne, wearing his crown and backed by his *mäkwanent* standing on each side in descending order, Menilek was prepared to pass judgment. Bent over in submission, Mängäshä, Alula, Hagos, and Woldä Mikael, each carrying a stone on their bare shoulders, proceeded towards Menilek, prostrated themselves before him, and asked for forgiveness. With one word, Menilek granted it. To dignify the occasion, all five sat in silence for approximately fifteen minutes while rifle and cannon fire saluted the reconciliation. Finally, the *Negus Nägäst* and the four *ras*es kissed the cross as a sign of peace (Erlich 1996). The terms of forgiveness, however, were still to be worked out.

Alula's terms were the most stringent. Alula was reconciled into the state as a loyal general once again, but this time more like a "salary man" given a stipend by the emperor to be ordered here and there at will. All his tributary lands in Märäb Melläsh were either ceded to the Italians or redistributed to other Ethiopian nobles. And *Ras* Alula agreed to all this. As a test of his loyalty, Menilek ordered Alula to take part in the Wallämo expedition and gave the great victor of Kufit and Dogali two hundred men to lead. A clear slap in the face! Yet with humility, Alula lived by the conditions set before him. As an obedient servant, Alula accepted Shewan hegemony and earned the trust of Menilek such that he became a close military adviser leading up to and through the Battle of Adwa, where he served with distinction. To an extent, Alula was reintegrated into the halls of power but never fully forgiven. Menilek continued to hold a big stick over Alula's head; always fearful of his decidedly Tigrayan ethic partisanship, Menilek never gave Alula a governorship nor allowed him to extract *gult* over large tracks of land. After Adwa, the pendulum swung back towards leniency but stopped midway, a political compromise Menilek and his *chelot* were willing to live with.

CONCLUSION

Prime Minister Abiy Ahmed writes that his PhD dissertation examines "issues which require a deep exploration that goes beyond describing the immediate causes of conflicts. Moreover, in part motivated by the theoretical and analytical discussions on the roles of social capital in the socio-political and economic settings . . . this study endeavored to analyze the makings and contributions of social capital in Ethiopia as it relates to traditional conflict resolution mechanisms" (2016). Ethiopia should be commended for having a prime minister conversant in the literature of conflict resolution and who himself contributed an investigation on Ethiopian-inspired and implemented mechanisms to resolve interreligious conflict. Cross-fertilization of Western and Ethiopian ideas and modalities is, of course, necessary, and that is observed in the citations and bibliography of Prime Minister Abiy's dissertation. Though less empirical, this chapter recommends that Ethiopians involved in bringing about national and/or ethnic reconciliation do the same thing. Certainly the burgeoning international literature on transitional justice should be studied, but interested parties, particularly those connected to the Reconciliation Commission, should look deeply at the historical record of restorative justice in imperial Ethiopia for the lessons that can be learned.

Circumstances in the twenty-first century are radically different from the imperial era; the lethality, scale, and collateral damage to innocent victims makes the limitations of imperial traditions' restorative justice appear antiquated and out of touch. Current issues like widespread political and ethnic oppression, endemic corruption, and state-sanctioned torture or disappearances will challenge the best political and legal minds to find remedies. But the intent of this chapter is not to provide recommendations on how to conduct post-atrocity truth commissions or trials, but to nudge policy makers and legal advisers to integrate some endogenously invented and vetted understandings of how to serve justice that were accepted by the Ethiopian population and that may promise better prospects for peace and reconciliation. The summation of this chapter suggests that legal remedies carried out at the national or regional levels to build enduring peace and reconciliation should exhibit the kind of ingenuity, flexibility, and adaptability that typified Ethiopia's imperial past. The lessons discussed above illustrate some thorny legal issues. First, assume that the administration of justice must be done in public view using the most appropriate media to ensure transparency. Second, acknowledge that granting general amnesties often does not resolve conflict but may defer or reignite it. Better for politicians and legal authorities to combine clemency with the potential for retribution that typified imperial Ethiopia's concept of "forgive but never forget." Third, always hold out that magnanimity can pay dividends to serve the state and the people. Fourth, recognize that justice is culturally defined and so consider appropriated Ethiopian understandings of justice like the concept of *irq* or the ability to perceive contradictions and ambiguity within the articulation of truth and justice (Yirga 2017). And fifth, apply flexibility to meting out justice, for one-and-done sentencing restricts justice to a time and place that five or ten years down the road appears unjust and offensive. Conditional forgiveness holds out the possibility of redress without remanding cases to litigation.

It would be appropriate to investigate Ethiopia's contribution to historically grounded restorative justice modalities in order to determine what could be modified and modernized to make the form of justice culturally relevant to the Ethiopian people and to furnish a model of ethnojustice for international jurists to study and, perhaps, modify for other transitional justice situations. Modification is, of course, key to adapting restorative justice modalities to current circumstances, but immutable understandings of the relationship between forgiveness and atonement define justice.

NOTES

1. An informed assessment of the relationship between transitional and restorative justice is found in the collection of articles in Kerry Clamp (2016). Sometimes a more logical line of argument is found in monographs; see Clamp (2014). For other assessments of this vast literature, see Elin Skaar (2012, 54–102); Kai Ambos, Judith Large, and Marieke Wierda (2009); and Patricia Lundy and Mark McGovern (2008, 265–92).
2. Interview by Kjetil Tronvoll with Prime Minister Meles Zenawi, January 16, 2002, Prime Minister's Office, Addis Ababa, quoted in Tronvoll, Charles Schaefer, and Girmachew Aneme (2009, 68).
3. Perhaps the first to articulate the pros and cons of African-based traditions of restorative justice was William Zartman (2000); also see, Rosalind Shaw, Lars Waldorf, and Pierre Hazan (2010).
4. The Battle of Dogali is best commemorated and historicized in the twenty articles published in Beyene Tadesse, Tadesse Tamrat, and Richard Pankhurst (1988).

WORKS CITED

Abiy, Ahmed. 2016. "Social Capital and Its Role in Traditional Conflict Resolution: The Case of Inter-religious Conflict in Jimma Zone of the Oromia Regional State in Ethiopia." PhD dissertation, Institute for Peace and Security Studies, Addis Ababa University, Addis Ababa.

Africa Rights. 2003. *Gacaca Justice: A Shared Responsibility*. Kigali: Africa Rights.

Ambos, Kai, Judith Large, and Marieke Wierda, eds. 2009. *Building a Future on Peace and Justice: Studies on Transitional Justice, Peace and Development*. Berlin: Springer.

Amstutz, Mark. 2005. *The Healing of Nations: The Promise and Limits of Political Forgiveness*. Lanham, MD: Rowman & Littlefield.

Appleby, Scott. 2000. *The Ambivalence of the Sacred: Religion, Violence, and Reconciliation*. Lanham, MD: Rowman & Littlefield.

BBC News. 1997. "Steve Biko: Martyr of the Anti-Apartheid Movement." December 8, 1997.

Biggar, Nigel. 2001. *Burying the Past: Making Peace and Doing Justice after Civil Conflict*. Washington, DC: Georgetown University Press.

Biko, Nkosinathi. 2000. "Amnesty and Denial." In *Looking Back, Reaching Forward: Reflections on the Truth and Reconciliation Commission of South Africa*, edited by Charles Villa-Vicencio and Wilhelm Verwoerd. London: Zed Books.

Branch, Adam. 2011. *Displacing Human Rights: War and Intervention in Northern Uganda*. Oxford: Oxford University Press.

Caulk, Richard. 1984. "Bad Men of the Borders: *Shum* and *Shifta* in Northern Ethiopia in the Nineteenth Century." In *Proceedings of the Second Annual Seminar of the Department of History of AAU*. Vol. I. Addis Ababa: Addis Ababa University Press.

Clamp, Kerry, ed. 2016. *Restorative Justice in Transitional Settings*. New York: Routledge.

———. 2014. *Restorative Justice in Transition*. New York: Routledge.

Elgesem, Frode, and Girmachew Alemu Aneme. "The Rights of the Accused: A Human Rights Appraisal." 2009. In *The Ethiopian Red Terror Trials: Transitional Justice Challenged*, edited by Kjetil Tronvoll, Charles Schaefer, and Girmachew Alemu Aneme. Oxford: James Currey.

Erlich, Haggai. 1996. *Ras Alula and the Scramble for Africa*. Trenton: Red Sea Press.

———. 2002. *The Cross and the River: Ethiopia, Egypt and the Nile*. Boulder, CO: Lynne Rienner.

Fernyhough, Timothy. 1986. "Social Mobility and Dissident Elites in Northern Ethiopia: The Role of Banditry, 1900–1969." In *Banditry, Rebellion and Social Protest in Africa*, edited by Donald Crummey. London: James Currey.

Gobat, Samuel. 1834. *Journal of a Three Years' Residence in Abyssinia*. London.

Govier, Trudy. 2002. *Forgiveness and Revenge*. London: Routledge.

Krog, Antjie. 2000. *Country of My Skull: Guilt, Sorrow, and the Limits of Forgiveness in the New South Africa*. New York: Three Rivers Press.

Llewellyn, Jennifer J., and Daniel Philpott, eds. 2014. *Restorative Justice, Reconciliation, and Peacebuilding*. Oxford: Oxford University Press.

Lundy, Patricia, and Mark McGovern. 2008. "Whose Justice? Rethinking Transitional Justice from the Bottom Up." *Journal of Law and Society* 35, no. 2 (June): 265–92.

MacLachlan, Alice. 2008. "The Nature and Limits of Forgiveness." PhD dissertation, Boston University.

Magnarella, Paul. 2000. *Justice in Africa: Rwanda's Genocide, Its Courts, and the UN Criminal Tribunal.* London: Routledge.

Mamdani, Mahmood. 1996. "Reconciliation without Justice." *Southern African Review of Books* 46: 3–5.

Marcus, Harold. 1975. *The Life and Times of Menelik II.* Oxford: Oxford University Press.

Meyerstein, Ariel. 2007. "Between Law and Culture: Rwanda's *Gacaca* and Postcolonial Legality." *Law & Social Inquiry* 32, no. 2: 467–508.

Murphy, Jeffrie G. 2003. *Getting Even: Forgiveness and Its Limits.* Cambridge: Cambridge University Press.

Orlowska, Izabela. 2009. "Performance and Ritual in Nineteenth-Century Ethiopia Political Culture." In *Proceedings of the 16th International Conference of Ethiopian Studies,* edited by Svein Ege, Harald Aspen, Birhanu Teferra, and Shiferaw Bekele. Trondheim, Norway.

Pieper, Daniel. 2009. "Reckoning with Past Atrocity: Truth, Retribution and Bureaucracy in Rwanda's *Gacaca* Tribunals." MSc dissertation, SOAS, University of London.

Reuters. 2007. "Life Sentence for Ethiopia Dictator." January 11.

Roberts, Robert C. 1995. "Forgivingness." *American Philosophical Quarterly* 32, no. 4 (October): 289–306.

Rubenson, Sven. 1978. *The Survival of Ethiopian Independence.* London: Heinemann.

Schaefer, Charles. 2009. "The Derg Trial versus Traditions of Restorative Justice in Ethiopia." In *The Ethiopian Red Terror Trials: Transitional Justice Challenged,* edited by Kjetil Tronvoll, Charles Schaefer, and Girmachew A. Aneme. Oxford: James Currey.

———. Forthcoming. *Peace Not War: Traditions of Restorative Justice in Imperial Ethiopia.*

Schwartz, Barry. 1978. "Vengeance and Forgiveness: The Uses of Beneficence in Social Control." *School Review* 86, no. 4 (August): 655–68.

Shaw, Rosalind, and Lars Waldorf, with Pierre Hazan, eds. 2010. *Localizing Transitional Justice: Interventions and Priorities after Mass Atrocities.* Stanford: Stanford University Press.

Shiferaw, Bekele. 1990. "Kassa and Kassa: The State of Their Historiography." In *Kasa and Kasa: Papers on the Lives, Times and Images of Tewodros II and Yohannes IV (1855–1889)*. Addis Ababa: Institute for Ethiopian Studies.

Skaar, Elin. 2012. "Reconciliation in a Transitional Justice Perspective." *Transitional Justice Review* 1, no. 1: 54–102.

Soyinka, Wole. 1999. *The Burden of Memory, the Muse of Forgetting*. New York: Oxford University Press.

Taddesse, Beyene, Tadesse Tamrat, and Richard Pankhurst, eds. 1988. *The Centenary of Dogali: Proceedings of the International Symposium, Addis Ababa-Asmara, January 24–25, 1987*. Addis Ababa: Institute of Ethiopian Studies.

Taddesse, Tamrat. 1972. *Church and State in Ethiopia 1270–1527*. Oxford: Oxford University Press.

Teitel, Ruti G. 2000. *Transitional Justice*. Oxford: Oxford University Press.

Tronvoll, Kjetil, Charles Schaefer, and Girmachew A. Aneme, eds. 2009. *The Ethiopian Red Terror Trials: Transitional Justice Challenged*. Oxford: James Currey.

Tutu, Desmond. 1999. *No Future Without Forgiveness*. New York: Doubleday.

Van Donge, Jan Kees. 1998. "The Mwanza Trial as a Search for a Usable Malawian Political Past." *African Affairs* 97, no. 386 (January): 91–118.

Vaughan, Sarah. 2009. "The Role of the Special Prosecutor's Office in the Red Terror Trials." In *The Ethiopian Red Terror Trials: Transitional Justice Challenged*, edited by Kjetil Tronvoll, Charles Schaefer, and Girmachew A. Aneme. Oxford: James Currey.

Yacob, Haile-Mariam. 1999. "The Quest for Justice and Reconciliation: The International Criminal Tribunal for Rwanda and the Ethiopian High Court." *Hastings International and Comparative Law Review* 22, no. 4.

Yirga, Gelaw Woldeyes. 2017. *Native Colonialism: Education and the Economy of Violence against Traditions in Ethiopia*. Trenton, NJ: Red Sea Press.

Zartman, William, ed. 2000. *Traditional Cures of Modern Conflicts: African Conflict "Medicine."* Boulder, CO: Lynne Rienner.

Zewde, Gabre-Sellassie. 2014. *Yohannes IV of Ethiopia: A Political Biography*. Trenton, NJ: Red Sea Press.

PART TWO

Economic Reform

2.1 From Histopia to Futopia: A Guide to a Successful Economic Transition in Ethiopia

2.2 The Case for the State-Private Partnership Model of Development for Ethiopia

2.3 The Political Economy of Land Policy in Ethiopia: Evolving Rationales and Challenges of State Ownership

2.4 Ethiopia Beyond Middle Income: Transforming the National Mindset

2.1 From Histopia to Futopia
A Guide to a Successful Economic Transition in Ethiopia[1]

Lars Christian Moller

INTRODUCTION

Ethiopia is at the early stages of a transition from a state-led economic model driven by public investment toward a more market-oriented model driven by private investment and productivity growth. This transition was initiated out of necessity, as the old model was becoming unsustainable, and out of choice, as a new leader embraced more political and economic freedom. A successful transition requires the reprogramming of a series of heterodox macroeconomic and structural policy choices that served Ethiopia well in the past, but which have become counterproductive today. In this chapter, it is argued that macro policies need to be geared toward achieving private sector credit growth, export promotion, and debt sustainability. Structural policies should seek to introduce more private sector participation and competition in key infrastructure sectors, including telecoms, energy, and trade logistics. Domestic reform efforts can be sustained through partnerships with the international community.Ethiopia has undergone substantial political change following a period of strong economic performance. The world has taken notice of the brave and far-reaching political reforms implemented by Prime Minister Abiy since assuming office in April 2018: from the peace process with Eritrea to the release of political prisoners, the opening of political space, and the refreshingly strong gender balance of the new government. At the same time, there have been important setbacks involving violence and several coup attempts. While significant challenges remain, there is hope that this could be a "Berlin Wall" moment for Ethiopia and the Horn of Africa. It is happening following fifteen years of record-high economic growth that transformed the economy and the country. At long last, Ethiopia is on the world map for all the right reasons. There could hardly be a better moment to take stock of what is happening in the country, reflect, and weigh in on the best way forward.

While groundbreaking and historic political reforms have been at the forefront of the agenda, it is now time to take a more careful look at the economic agenda. While nobody could expect any government to pursue more reforms over the first term than the Abiy administration has accomplished, there is a sense among some observers that more progress on the economic reform agenda is now needed. Several questions are being raised: What should be the role of government in the economy? Is Ethiopia still a developmental state? Does the government have a clear economic strategy?

Economic policy changes, since April 2018, consist of a series of moderate reforms along with ambitious policy announcements. Key measures implemented include: (1) legal and regulatory reforms to improve the management of state-owned enterprises (SOEs) in key strategic sectors (energy, telecoms, and logistics); (2) facilitating the use of public-private partnerships (PPPs) in infrastructure development; (3) electricity tariff adjustments to better reflect the cost of production; and (4) tighter fiscal policy, including the temporary suspension of new public investment projects and a freeze on new non-concessional external borrowing. Policy announcements made in June 2018, yet to be implemented, include an intention to partially privatize key SOEs such as Ethio Telecom, Ethiopian Airlines, Ethiopian Electric Power (EEP), and Ethiopian Shipping and Logistics Service Enterprise (ESLSE). While these reform efforts are impressive compared to the rigid and non-reformist policy stance under the previous Hailemariam administration (2012–18), continued macroeconomic and structural reforms are still needed to guarantee a successful economic transition.

As the Abiy administration assumed office, it faced primarily a political crisis rather than an economic one, and this partly explains the relatively stronger emphasis on political reforms. The new prime minister took charge of a country under a state of emergency after more than three years of anti-government protests and ethnic unrest and naturally focused mainly on political reforms. However, the political and economic agendas are intimately linked, especially when it comes to job creation. Moreover, economic challenges will become even more apparent in the years to come unless reforms are introduced. On the face of it, the Ethiopian economy seems to be doing relatively well. Economic growth remains above 7 percent, with inflation staying in the low double digits; the fiscal deficit is around 3 percent of gross domestic product (GDP). However, a closer look reveals that exports are performing very poorly, foreign currency shortages are endemic, and the external debt situation is highly challenging. While there is no economic crisis in sight, and a hard landing can still be avoided, decisive action is needed today across a range of policy dimensions.

The chapter is structured as follows: The section "Histopia: The Model behind the Ethiopian Economic Boom" reviews recent long-term economic performance and the economic model behind it. The section "The End of Histopia: Why the Model Was Not Sustainable" explains why this model is no longer sustainable and why a change of policy is needed. The section "Futopia: A Unique Blend" lays out the key strategic choices facing economic policy makers today and offers guidance. For ease of exposition and as a play of words, we refer to Histopia when describing the old economic model and to Futopia when referring to the new economic model. These terms are also anchored in the gradualist and pragmatic view that policy makers should not seek to implement Utopia, in which the economy is liberalized overnight.

HISTOPIA: THE MODEL BEHIND THE ETHIOPIAN ECONOMIC BOOM[2]

Ethiopia's economic development performance over the past decade has been one of the most successful among low-income countries (LICs). According to official data, the country achieved rapid and inclusive economic growth averaging 10.5 percent in 2004–18.[3] This was accompanied by substantial progress across a broad range of social and human development indicators. Between 2000 and 2016, poverty declined from 44 to 24 percent, income inequality remained unchanged—among the lowest worldwide—and life expectancy increased from 52 to 65 years. Given population growth of 2.4 percent per year, real GDP per capita increased by 8.1 percent per year between 2004 and 2018. This substantially exceeds per capita growth rates achieved during the monarchy (1951–73: 1.5 percent), under the communist Derg (1974–91: -1.0 percent), and in the decade as the country moved away from the planning economy (1992–2003: 1.3 percent). It also substantially exceeds regional and LIC averages over this period.

Agriculture was the growth engine at the beginning of the takeoff, but services gradually took over and were then complemented by a construction boom. Out of an average annual growth rate of 10.5 percent in 2004–18, services contributed by 4.4 percentage points followed by industry (3.2 percentage points) and agriculture (2.9 percentage points). A popular misconception that growth was driven by the well-publicized boom in light manufacturing is not borne out by the data, since this sector accounted for less than 5 percent of value added over this period, adding just 0.8 percent to the 2004–18 average annual growth rate.

Ethiopia's growth acceleration can be explained by the typical drivers that also help explain economic growth in other countries. In Moller and Wacker (2017), we present empirical evidence that public infrastructure investment was the single-most important growth driver, explaining 42 percent of the country's per capita growth in 2000–2013. In contrast to many countries in the region, the government deliberately emphasized public capital spending over government consumption in the national budget, and this was key for supporting growth. This was facilitated by declining military spending following the 1998–2000 war with Eritrea, giving rise to a "peace dividend." Growth was also supported by a conducive external environment reflecting positive commodity prices. Increased openness to international trade contributed to growth, as did the expansion of secondary education, though these effects were less pronounced. Macro-financial imbalances such as an overvalued exchange rate, low private sector credit, and high inflation held back growth somewhat. While growth drivers were typical, the way in which heterodox macro-financial policies accommodated growth, particularly via public infrastructure investment financing, was unique.

The strong growth contribution of infrastructure investment arises from a substantial physical expansion combined with the high returns to such investment. Ethiopia stands out during the 2000s for having registered very rapid physical infrastructure development. Using data for 124 countries over four decades, the country was among the 20 percent fastest in terms of infrastructure growth in 2004–14. Although this is partly the result of starting from a very low level, these infrastructure growth rates also exceed those of fast-growing regional peers with comparable income levels. As we do not know the true economic return to infrastructure investment in Ethiopia, we estimated their average returns from the 124-country sample. Given that public investment was concentrated in providing basic infrastructure such as energy, roads, and telecom, this growth effect seems plausible. Overall, Ethiopia's experience supports the notion that "getting infrastructure right" at the early stage of development can go a long way in generating high economic growth.

Heterodox financing arrangements supported one of the highest public investment rates in the world. Even if Ethiopia generally did not follow the recommendations of the Growth and Development Commission (2008), it did deliver the recommended impressive rates of public investment with the purpose of "crowding in" the private sector. Despite low domestic savings and taxes, Ethiopia was able to support high public investment in a variety of orthodox and heterodox ways. Orthodox policies included keeping government consumption low to finance budgetary public infrastructure investment as well as tapping external concessional and non-concessional financing to support SOE investments. Three less conventional mechanisms stand out: First, a model of financial repression that kept interest rates low and directed the bulk of domestic savings towards financing public infrastructure. Second, an overvalued exchange rate that cheapened public capital imports. Third, monetary expansion, including direct central bank budget financing, which earned the government seigniorage (inflation tax) revenues.

Financial repression helped direct savings toward financing of public investment at negative real interest rates. Ethiopia's banking sector is dominated by the state-owned Commercial Bank of Ethiopia (CBE), which accounts for about two-thirds of assets and deposits, although there are seventeen smaller private banks and the Development Bank of Ethiopia (DBE). The banking sector is closed to foreign participation, and the capital account is closed. Nominal interest rates were held low and stable over time, and high inflation resulted in negative real interest rates. CBE mainly finances public projects, typically executed by SOEs, through direct lending and bond purchases. Since 2011, the DBE has been partly financed by mandatory National Bank of Ethiopia (NBE) bill purchases by private banks. This policy aims to extend medium- to long-term loans to private priority projects, although more than half of bond proceeds were instead used to purchase treasury bills due to a lack of bankable projects. Prior to the 2011 NBE bill directive, a credit cap was in place, effectively setting a quantitative ceiling on private bank lending. To illustrate the effects of financial repression on public investment, it is noted that 70 percent of domestic savings are deposited in the state-owned CBE. About 60 percent of CBE net lending, in turn, goes to EEP to finance infrastructure investments in energy.

Ethiopia's exchange rate policy also facilitated the public investment. The Ethiopian birr is effectively pegged to the US dollar using a crawl-like arrangement or "managed float." For many years, the pace of the gradual nominal depreciation was relatively stable at 5 percent per year. One immediate macroeconomic benefit of this arrangement is the nominal price stability it generates. However, there is more to this system than meets the eye. First, from an economic point of view, it is not the nominal value of the birr that matters but its real value (adjusted for inflation differentials with major trading partners) and how it changes over time. Second, the choice of the US dollar as the nominal anchor for the birr implies that Ethiopia automatically experiences an arbitrary currency appreciation every time the dollar gets stronger, which occurred frequently in this period. As a result, the nominal exchange rate system produced a substantial and sustained real overvaluation of the local currency. To illustrate the potential magnitude of these effects, the real effective exchange rate increased by more than 50 percent between 2010 and 2014.

Public capital imports became artificially cheaper, and discretionary policy interventions ensured that public investment projects did not face forex shortages. There are multiple methods to estimate the extent of real exchange rate overvaluation. All methods consistently show that the birr was overvalued in real terms since the early 2000s (one method even shows permanent real overvaluation since 1951). Depending on the period of analysis and the method used, it emerges that the birr was overvalued between 10 and 30 percent in real terms. Returning to the financing of public investment, this overvaluation was a substantial advantage given the strong capital import content. An exchange rate overvaluation of 20 percent effectively amounts to a price discount on imports of a similar magnitude when measured in birr. Moreover, given the rationing system of foreign exchange that the government has in place, public capital imports were given priority and were not negatively affected by the chronic foreign exchange shortages hurting the private sector.

Direct central bank financing facilitated an inflationary and expansionary fiscal policy that supported central government public investment. In 2011–17, Ethiopia relied on central bank borrowing to finance about half of the domestic portion of the central government fiscal deficit, to the tune of about 1 percent of GDP per year. This policy of printing money helped sustain higher levels of budgetary public investment but at the cost of persistently high inflation.

THE END OF HISTOPIA: WHY THE MODEL WAS NOT SUSTAINABLE

There are four key reasons why the growth model of Histopia is no longer sustainable: debt, dollars, jobs, and credit. A common critique of the Ethiopian developmental state model has been that it was not sustainable. The basic premise was that the costs of the underlying policy choices would eventually outweigh their benefits. Policy makers were therefore encouraged to make changes before it was too late. Such periodic changes in the economic strategy of a country are only natural and necessary, as the experience of the East Asian countries amply demonstrates. The 2016a World Bank publication "Ethiopia's Great Run" lays out the case and proposes a set of "sustainability indicators" for policy makers to monitor closely to avoid a hard landing. These include debt sustainability, external competitiveness, credit/forex shortages, returns to investment, cost of financing, and inflation. As expected, most of these indicators have had an adverse trend over the past five years, reflecting that the current model has become more and more unsustainable.

Debt

The risk of external debt distress increased from "low" to "high" between 2014 and 2017. An intuitive way of illustrating the vulnerability of Ethiopia's external debt position is to monitor the risk rating of the Debt Sustainability Analysis (DSA) prepared annually by the World Bank and the International Monetary Fund (IMF). Following external debt relief, Ethiopia's risk rating declined from "moderate" in 2006–9 to "low" in 2010–14. However, given substantial volumes of non-concessional external commitments, especially from China, India, and a Eurobond issuance, this rating could not be sustained, increasing to "moderate" in 2015–16. Continued rapid loan disbursements and poor export performance led to a "high" risk rating in the 2017 and 2018 DSAs.

Rising debt risk was the result of a rapid rise in the external debt contracted at increasingly unfavorable terms. Ethiopia was an example of a country where the size of the combined public sector (central government and SOEs) fiscal deficit depended on the total amount of financing available. The more external creditors were willing to lend, the more willing Ethiopia was to borrow. The net financing of the public sector averaged close to 10 percent of GDP per year between 2012 and 2018, funded from an equal share of external and domestic sources. The government tapped into as much concessional external financing as possible but also resorted to non-concessional sources for SOE investments at less and less favorable terms. The external debt relief that Ethiopia had obtained in 2008–10 created the fiscal space to enable a renewed debt buildup. Total public debt increased from about 40 percent in 2010 to about 60 percent of GDP in 2018 (half of which is external). The Achilles' heel of Ethiopia's debt problem is that external debt stock and external debt service outweigh the country's capacity to earn foreign currency. As the DSA shows, the present value of the external debt stock and the external debt service (interest and principal) are too large compared with total projected export revenue. Moreover, the debt service to export ratio increased from 10 to 20 percent in 2011–17.

While public infrastructure investments generated growth returns, public investment management (especially project selection) had some flaws. Based on the available evidence, public investment management in Ethiopia was relatively good compared with relevant low-income and regional peers. While waste and corruption led to inefficiencies, public investments typically took place in productive infrastructure projects. However, not all projects had sufficiently strong economic merit. Government investment in large-scale sugar production facilities partly financed by Chinese non-concessional commercial loans exceeding $1 billion was a clear strategic mistake of previous governments. It did not follow the best-practice Maximizing Finance for Development principles to avoid government investment where the private sector could invest. The financial difficulties experienced by the Ethiopian Sugar

Corporation in 2015, which required government intervention, are illustrative. Railway investments also raise questions. While seemingly a meaningful and productive infrastructure investment, railways may not always be the most cost-effective transport solution, particularly in Africa. In general, the transit volumes must be very substantial to secure a positive internal rate of return of a project (coal mining is a good example). With regard to Addis Ababa Light Rail ($0.5 billion), passenger revenue is sufficient only to finance operating costs but not the underlying capital investment. Similarly, for the Addis Ababa–Djibouti Railway ($3.5 billion), the rail traffic assumptions used to justify the economics of the project were unrealistically high. Foreign creditors took no risks here as sovereign loan guarantees were in place. Undoubtedly the project will improve trade logistics performance, but this does not automatically imply that it was a good investment given the cost. Finally, Ethiopia does not always have the skills in project oversight and implementation to ensure that projects are completed to a high standard without delays. Poor contract management underpins the delays, which are partly responsible for the poor synchronicity of debt repayments and foreign exchange flows.

The public investment projects that were financed with external borrowing did not yield sufficient foreign exchange. Overall, public investment of Histopia demonstrates positive economic returns. However, these returns are often generated in local rather than foreign currency. Some projects arguably support foreign exchange earnings, such as prospective hydropower exports from the Grand Ethiopian Renaissance Dam (GERD) or trade logistics services of the Djibouti railway. Yet most investment projects implemented in Ethiopia, such as road and bridge, telecoms, and energy infrastructure, largely serve the domestic economy without substantially enhancing the export-generating capacity of the economy. This becomes a challenge when they are financed by expensive non-concessional foreign loans that need to be repaid in dollars or other hard currency. As a final consideration, Ethiopia may have been partly caught up in an intertemporal mismatch between the timing of the loan repayments and the timing of the returns to investment. In brief, the costs came sooner than the benefits. Prominent examples include GERD and the Djibouti railway. This issue generated substantial debate during the 2010s between supporters and skeptics of Ethiopia's aggressive investment and borrowing strategy. In hindsight, the skeptics were right.

Dollars

Permanent real exchange rate overvaluation introduces an anti-export, pro-import bias resulting in an external disequilibrium that erodes international reserves. As a low-income and capital-scarce economy, it is natural for Ethiopia to run a structural external current account deficit as it relies on capital imports. International reserves can be maintained only if enough foreign direct investment (FDI) and external borrowing can be obtained to finance the current account deficit. However, by artificially maintaining an expensive local currency, Histopia unnecessarily exacerbated its structural external imbalance. Imports became cheaper when measured in local currency. Exports became more expensive and less competitive on international markets. Anecdotal evidence that coffee growers and shoemakers preferred selling their products domestically rather than to export markets, considering the relative domestic and export prices, is illustrative. To maintain unchanged international reserves, Histopia had to resort to external borrowing at increasingly unfavorable terms, including direct borrowing by the central bank.

Rationing policies prevented a rundown of international reserves, but the resulting shortages hurt private economic activity. Ethiopia has traditionally held international reserves well below the recommended limits. Whenever the economy experienced foreign exchange shortages, reserves remained largely unchanged, typically at around two months of imports. Given the politically determined official exchange rate, the NBE supplied foreign exchange to the interbank market based on plans prepared at the beginning of the fiscal year, which considered estimates of supply and demand while maintaining a minimum level of reserves. Priority was given to critical imports (e.g., oil), public investment, external debt service, and imports for exporting firms. The rest of the economy, mainly the private sector, would then experience shortages and face substantial delays in applications for import permits. It substantially hampered private economic activity and investment.

In response to severe foreign exchange shortages, the government devalued the birr by 15 percent, but policy implementation proved insufficient and ineffective. The October 2017 devaluation was the right thing to do, but it was also too little and too late. If a 15 percent real devaluation could have been maintained, this would only have turned back the clock a few years on the real appreciation curve. Put differently, the real effective exchange rate remained overvalued even immediately after the devaluation. Moreover, the monetary tightening that should have accompanied the nominal devaluation was insufficient, repeating policy errors of the past during the previous devaluation in October 2010. Inflation remained between 10 and 15 percent, gradually eroding real gains. In addition, the NBE mistakenly temporarily halted the gradual 5 percent per year depreciation against the dollar. Moreover, the dollar continued to appreciate against other currencies over this period. As a result, according to the IMF (2018), the real effective exchange rate is largely back at levels before October 2017, and it remains overvalued by 12–18 percent.

Jobs

The current economic model is not generating enough productive jobs in the context of the rapid demographic transition. Ethiopia has a population of over one hundred million with about two million new entrants joining the labor market each year. The quality of jobs that the economy can generate to absorb new entrants is a critical success factor of economic strategy. Ethiopia's jobs challenge, ironically, is linked to its successful rapid demographic transition over the past three decades. Child and infant mortality started declining in the mid-1980s, while the fertility rate fell rapidly in the mid-1990s, partly in response to lower death rates. This shifted the age structure of the population, as more people were able to work. According to UN data, the working age population is projected to increase from 51 percent in 2005 to 58 percent in 2020 and will peak at 68 percent in 2055. A larger share of the working-age population means relatively more hands to work. Ethiopia's demographic transition is taking place faster than in the rest of Africa, owing to its more rapid decline in mortality and fertility. Improvements in female education had a particularly important impact on rapidly declining fertility, and this can be explained by the education reforms implemented in the mid-1990s.

The extent to which Ethiopia can benefit from its "demographic dividend" depends on how economically productive the additional workers are. Ethiopia's growth acceleration was supported by positive demographic effects. The economic takeoff coincided with a marked increase in the share of the working-age population, giving a positive boost to labor supply. Potentially, up to 13 percent of 2005–13 per capita growth can be attributed to this demographic effect. However, this estimate assumes that each additional person is gainfully employed, with average levels of productivity. To the extent that they are not, then this estimate would be too optimistic. For the youthful workforce to add value, they must be equipped with relevant education and skills, and the business environment must be such as to generate sufficient jobs to productively absorb the available labor.

One of the greatest failures of Histopia was its lack of support of private sector investment and job creation. Prior to 1991, Ethiopia was essentially a communist economy, and the private sector was nonexistent. Reforms implemented during the 1990s made the economy more market oriented, but the private sector remained meager. Economic activity was dominated by state-owned and party-owned enterprises. Until recently, most economic sectors were closed for private and foreign participation. As late as 2014, the government was opening new wholesale businesses (under the ALLE trademark) across the country while continuing to operate state-owned retail stores. Ethiopia's business environment trailed that of its peers, and the government showed little interest in improving it. The dialogue between the government and the private sector was either absent or hostile. Macrofinancial policies starved the private sector of critical credit and foreign exchange. In this context, it was extremely challenging for private businesses to open, operate, and succeed. As a result, the private sector was not strong enough to productively absorb the labor made available to it.

Despite policies to promote job creation in light manufacturing industries, the bulk of new jobs created in the 2000s were in low-productivity agriculture and services. Between 1999 and 2013, total employment increased from 25 to 40 million people. Agriculture absorbed three-quarters (11 million) of the new jobs while the services sector (largely informal and non-tradable) added 5.6 million. However, these sectors have relatively low labor productivity. Services productivity was somewhat higher than agriculture and giving rise to a static efficiency gain from structural change. Manufacturing employment increased by just 0.7 million, with the rest of the jobs created in "other industry," including construction. Inspired by East Asia, recent economic strategy rightly focused on creating productive jobs in light manufacturing. Eight industrial parks have become operational as of mid-2018, including the impressive Hawassa facility financed partly by the Eurobond issuance. While these manufacturing jobs are the high-productivity ones that the economy needs, the jobs created are counted in their thousands (a total of 56,000 so far). However, the jobs that need to be created are in their millions (2 million per year).

While an expansion of secondary and tertiary education aimed for Ethiopia to reap the demographic dividend, the strategy did not deliver the results policy makers were hoping for. The government implemented a substantial expansion of universities, technical schools, and secondary schools to educate the youth and make them ready to assume high-quality jobs in the labor market. As a result, large cohorts (millions) of better-educated youth entered the labor market year after year. But the quality of the education fell short, and the skills of graduates did not match the needs of the labor market. To some extent, the substantial absorption by the education system temporarily delayed labor market insertion. This had some benefits in keeping youth off the streets by placing them on school benches instead. But eventually, students began graduating in large numbers. Unable to find gainful jobs, these youth were left frustrated. These frustrations contributed to the subsequent political unrest.

Credit

Private firms need access to credit, the shortage of which was the major drawback of financial repression policies. By directing the majority of available domestic financial savings to finance public investment projects, the government starved the private sector for credit through the familiar "crowding out" channel. While public infrastructure investment helps firms become more productive, Ethiopian firms were relatively more concerned with getting access to credit. According to six different surveys conducted in 2011–15, credit is mentioned as the most binding constraint for firms. This suggests that the government made good progress in addressing the infrastructure constraint and now needs to pay more attention to alleviating other more binding constraints important to firms. Private sector credit to GDP in Ethiopia is a meager 10 percent, compared to about 50 percent in sub-Saharan Africa. The scope for financial deepening in Ethiopia is enormous, and this could be a future growth driver, as the example of the recent West Africa growth spurt amply demonstrates (Haile and Moller 2018).

The Ethiopian economy would benefit from a shift of domestic credit toward private firms where returns are relatively higher. If the aim of government policy is to enhance the productivity of private firms, then it is important to understand what the firm-level constraints are. If firms really need credit more than access to new roads or better telecommunications to grow and prosper, then government policy would need to support the alleviation of the relevant credit constraint at the firm level. Since public infrastructure investment is partially financed via the same domestic savings pool, infrastructure financing competes directly with the financing of private investment projects. It is indicative that the marginal return to private investment may well be higher than the marginal return to public infrastructure investment. Indeed, empirical estimates of these relative returns presented in World Bank (2016a support this assessment: at the margin, and in the presence of a domestic credit constraint, private returns (22.5 percent) are three times larger than public returns (7.5 percent) in Ethiopia.

FUTOPIA: A UNIQUE BLEND

A successful economic transition requires the reprogramming of a series of heterodox macroeconomic and structural policy choices. Macro policies need to be geared toward achieving private sector credit growth, export promotion, and ensuring debt sustainability. Structural policies should seek to introduce more private sector participation and competition in key infrastructure sectors, including telecoms, energy, and trade logistics. Domestic reform efforts can be sustained through partnerships with the international community.

Macro Policy

Sound macroeconomic management is a necessary condition for economic development. Histopia seemed to ignore this basic principle. Macro-financial policies that helped finance high public investment ultimately proved unsustainable. Ethiopia found itself constrained with debt and forex challenges. These challenges were foreseeable years earlier, but Histopia continued as if there were no hard constraints to economic strategy. Futopia will not repeat these mistakes. Instead it will undertake an adjustment of fiscal, monetary, exchange rate, and financial sector policies.

Fiscal policy should create fiscal space for sustainable physical capital spending over the medium term. Substantial infrastructure investment will remain a key element for Futopia, but it must be based on sustainable sources of financing. Histopia fell short on the latter, and as a result the Abiy administration had to implement a freeze on new public investment projects and on new non-concessional external loans. These short-term emergency measures were appropriate, but the challenge today is to design an exit strategy that would offer a sound basis for removing them. Specifically, the government needs to set annual fiscal targets that aim at reducing the external risk of debt distress rating from high to moderate over the medium term. Tax revenue mobilization should be the major plank of fiscal consolidation efforts, given how far Ethiopia lags from peers. A tighter fiscal policy must also be supported by appropriate exchange rate and monetary policies to support exports. If successful, this strategy would pave the way for gradually reintroducing modest amounts of non-concessional external borrowing and the financing of new public investment projects. The policy adjustment will be challenging, as growth and job creation will temporarily slow down, but there is no sustainable alternative. In the interim, policy makers need to resist the temptation of lifting the fiscal emergency measures prematurely.

Futopia would also need to place stronger emphasis on building human capital in addition to physical capital. A child born in Ethiopia today will be only 38 percent as productive when she grows up as she could be if she enjoyed complete education and full health. While Ethiopia's Human Capital Index is not too dissimilar from the averages for sub-Saharan African and low-income countries, there is still substantial scope for improvement. Children in Ethiopia can expect to complete 7.8 years of preprimary, primary, and secondary school by age eighteen. However, when years of schooling are adjusted for quality of learning, this is only equivalent to 4.5 years: a learning gap of 3.3 years. Students in Ethiopia score 359 on harmonized tests, on a scale where 625 represents advanced attainment and 300 represents minimum attainment. Long-term fiscal policy thus needs to be supportive of human capital formation by gradually enhancing tax revenue to finance public outlays to improve the quantity and quality of education. Effective public spending would help to support the economy's long-term productivity potential.

The introduction of a treasury bill market would help contain inflation in support of other macroeconomic policy adjustments. Histopia relied on printing money to sustain higher levels of public spending at the cost of persistently high inflation. In Futopia, this type of policy would need to be gradually phased out, as it contributes to unwarranted expansionary fiscal and monetary policies and undermines the desired adjustment of the real exchange rate. The government should introduce reforms to develop a market for government securities with market-determined interest rates. To this effect, the Ministry of Finance and Economic Cooperation could issue securities in gradually increasing volumes to finance the budget, which could be held and transacted by banks. In turn, the NBE would use interventions in this market to signal its interest rate stance, helping to better control broad money and credit growth. A deeper domestic debt market would also allow the public and private sectors to reduce reliance on foreign financing and serve as a buffer against volatile international capital flows.

Ethiopia needs a more flexible exchange rate policy aimed at correcting the overvaluation, improving reserve coverage, and reducing foreign exchange shortages. Futopia needs an exchange rate policy that supports exports and deters imports. This requires a real depreciation sufficient to bring the real exchange rate close to its equilibrium value. This can be achieved gradually over time by increasing the pace of nominal depreciation or through a one-off devaluation. The gains to competitiveness have to be weighed against the risks to debt sustainability, as a devaluation would increase the domestic currency value of external debt stock and service. According to the 2018 IMF/WB DSA, this imposes an upper limit of about 30 percent for a nominal devaluation. If the authorities wish to maintain some form of crawling peg, this should be linked to a trade-weighted basket of currencies, rather than solely relying on the US dollar, as Ethiopia does not trade much with the US. This would reduce the arbitrary appreciation pressures experienced in the past. Over time, the authorities could consider reactivating the interbank market and let the forces of supply and demand determine the daily rate. Central bank interventions could then be limited to smoothing excessive short-term fluctuations, as opposed to determining its long-term path. The government is encouraged to work closely with experts at the IMF to design and implement these reforms. This could be done in the form of technical assistance even outside a Fund program.

A more competitive exchange rate would bring important economic benefits. Recent empirical analysis conducted by the World Bank (2018a) provides strong evidence that a more competitive real exchange rate would provide an environment that is more conducive to manufacturing-led structural transformation, sustained growth acceleration, and improved external balance. For instance, a 10 percent devaluation of the real effective exchange rate would reduce the current account deficit by about 2 percentage points of GDP (through a 5 percent increase in exports and a 6 percent decrease in imports) and increase real GDP growth by more than 2 percentage points. However, the devaluation would also raise the cost of debt servicing and public foreign currency debt stock denominated in local currency.

Financial sector reforms are needed to address the challenge of low private sector credit. This would require a gradual move away from negative to positive real interest rates to better reflect the demand and supply for savings/credit and encourage an overall increase in formal financial sector savings. Savers would now finally have the financially attractive option of making deposits in banks, to the benefit of private investors with viable investment projects. This would *inter alia* reduce the current inefficient forms of saving associated with unproductive small-scale private real estate investments that result in the slow and incomplete construction of buildings scattered across Addis Ababa and other major cities in the country. Higher real interest rates would also make the financing of government spending, including on investment projects, more expensive and thus less attractive. The resulting effect would be more private investment and less government investment. As the returns to the former are much higher than the latter, there would be a positive economic impact. However, an increase in the real interest rate would also have negative impacts on public debt dynamics and reforms and would thus need to be introduced gradually to balance this trade-off.

Growth

Histopia achieved a growth acceleration through public capital accumulation, while Futopia would grow through private investment and rising productivity. Put simply, a country can grow by accumulating more factors of production (capital, labor) or by making these factors more productive. Histopia achieved capital accumulation through public infrastructure investments that in turn helped make the economy more productive. To illustrate, of the 8.2 percent average annual growth rate achieved in 2000–2010, capital contributed 2.4 percent and labor 2.4 percent, while total factor productivity growth was 3.4 percent. Futopia's growth would continue to automatically benefit from a growing labor force, owing to effects of the demographic transition. However, it would not be able to sustain the same rates of public capital accumulation as Histopia. This growth driver would need to be increasingly complemented with private investment (domestic and foreign), though private investment would be unlikely to match the levels of public investment of the past. Maintaining the past levels of productivity growth would also be challenging. In fact, annual TPF growth fell gradually from about 2.5 to 1 percent in 2010–19 (World Bank 2018a). Because of lower total investment (public and private) and lower productivity growth, we should expect lower economic growth in Futopia than in Histopia. On the upside, growth would now be much more sustainable.

Growth is likely to initially slow down, owing to the macroeconomic adjustment and before the positive effects of structural reforms pay off over the medium term. The necessary macroeconomic policy adjustment is likely to hold back short-term growth. Ethiopia already tightened fiscal and monetary policies somewhat in 2018. The "financial program" proposed here consists of a further tightening of fiscal policy in the form of an improved central government primary deficit as well as tighter monetary policy, such as reduced reserve money growth and reduced central bank budget financing. These measures would reduce aggregate domestic demand and lower the growth rate in the short term. This effect would be dampened by the real exchange rate adjustment, which should support external demand. Over the medium term, structural reforms to support private investment and productivity growth would eventually bring growth back at a sustained pace.

Structural Reforms

Interestingly, structural economic reforms have been largely absent from Ethiopia's recent story of success. Between 1991 and 2003, Ethiopia implemented wide-ranging market-oriented reforms but achieved relatively modest economic growth. Conversely, during the growth acceleration period between 2004 and 2014, major structural policy reforms were largely absent. As a result, Ethiopia lags behind sub-Saharan African peers in most reform dimensions. This is especially the case for the financial development, current account and capital account restrictions, and services trade restrictiveness.

Even modest structural reforms that close gaps with African peers would potentially have considerable impact on growth. Given that reforms matter for economic growth, and Ethiopia lags behind its peers, it is clear that there is substantial potential for growth through economic reforms. In World Bank (2016a) illustrative calculations demonstrate substantial growth dividends of reforms that liberalize the financial sector and reduce current and capital account restrictions. Such growth effects are the result of Ethiopia's lack of progress in this area compared to other countries. There are also considerable firm-level gains to be reaped from services sector liberalization, especially in credit, energy, and transport services. For example, if the access to credit conditions of Ethiopia were to match those of Rwanda, then firm labor productivity would increase by 4.3 percent. Similarly, if electricity conditions were to match those of Rwanda, the labor productivity gains would be close to 2.2 percent. Finally, matching China's transportation services would imply a productivity gain of 4.2 percent.

The government is developing detailed plans to implement the privatization program announced in June 2018. The broad outlines for the reform program, supported by Development Policy Financing (DPF) (World Bank 2018b), include strengthening competition in identified sectors and inviting foreign and domestic private investors to take stakes in key SOEs. The unbundling of regulatory, infrastructure operation, and service provision functions in sectors currently dominated by SOEs would encourage competition and create the conditions necessary for greater private sector participation. The proposed privatizations are a means of improving performance in sectors seen as having important network effects and raising financing for development. SOE governance reforms to support these plans are underway, including efforts to produce audited financial statements, critical to establish management performance objectives and conduct reliable financial oversight.

In the telecom sector, the government should introduce more competition by issuing additional licenses to reduce cost and improve quality. Ethiopia is one of the last three countries in the world (along with Eritrea and Djibouti) to retain a national monopoly on all telecom services, including fixed, mobile, Internet, and data communications. For many years,

Ethio Telecom's monopolistic control has limited the scope for innovation, restricted network expansion, and limited the services offered. As a result, customer service has been poor, and the development of new services, such as mobile money, has been slow. Opening the telecommunications sector for competition, attracting investment, and putting in place needed regulation are essential to enable a digital economy with a significant potential to boost competitiveness, increase exports, create job opportunities, and raise fiscal revenue. The government has already endorsed a set of policy decisions for telecom sector reform that allows for competition and foreign participation in the sector. These reforms need to be continued and accelerated to achieve better results for users.

Reform of the trade logistics sector will help reduce time and associated costs to import and export and will attract private (including foreign) investment in this sector. Inefficiencies in trade logistics represent a major challenge to Ethiopia's external competitiveness. The cost of shipping a twenty-foot container to Germany from Ethiopia is 247 percent higher than from Vietnam and 72 percent higher than from Bangladesh. The market for logistics in Ethiopia has the potential for expansion to become a multibillion-dollar sector that underpins competitiveness, creates jobs, and generates tax revenue for the government. Yet currently the logistics sector is dominated by the state-owned ESLSE, the only provider of multimodal services, whereby various transport modes are combined under the responsibility of one single transport operator, limiting scope for private participation and competition. Opening of the logistics sector is expected to attract FDI and help develop a new logistics services industry. An improved performance of the logistics sector ultimately will contribute to an increase in exports.

In the power sector, the government needs to shift from public to private investment and to improve cost recovery. Ethiopia is blessed with bountiful renewable energy resources, yet it has the third-largest electricity access deficit in sub-Saharan Africa and an electrification rate of 43 percent. Today, power generation capacity stands at 4,250 MW, with about 7,000 MW expected to come online by 2020 and over 15,000 MW by 2025. Virtually all the energy in Ethiopia is generated from renewable resources. The sector has invested over $10 billion in power generation, transmission, and distribution over the past decade to meet increasing demand (growing at 15 percent per annum). Following the 2018 PPP Proclamation, the private sector will take a central role as financier and implementer of new renewable energy generation plants and could participate in a complementary role in the rest of the sector value chain, as well as off-grid service delivery. However, the sector financial fundamentals are compromised by a stagnant tariff regime, lagging operational indicators, and an unsustainable debt management regime. Ethiopia recently increased the electricity tariff, which at $0.03/kWh was among the lowest in the region. Further tariff increases are needed, while taking into consideration the distributional and poverty implications, to improve the finances of the public utility and reduce subsidies.

External Anchors

Structural reforms are notoriously difficult to implement. First, reforms are politically difficult, so governments often implement them early in their mandate while they still have political capital. Second, the costs of reforms are experienced in the short term, while the benefits accrue in the longer term. Third, the costs and benefits to reform accrue to different interest groups. Fourth, in addition to political will and capital, governments must have the technical capacity to design and implement reforms. Conventional wisdom holds that reforms are easier to implement when economic growth is weak, when reforms have more immediate benefits (early wins), and when there is external pressure. Focusing on the latter, it is often argued that external anchors can help sustain domestic reform efforts.

The Ethiopian government should reach out to its international development partners for support in the reform process. In other words, it should try to create as much external pressure as possible to lock in the domestic reform agenda that it wishes to pursue. To illustrate, Eastern European EU accession countries were able to implement substantial political and economic reforms incentivized by the reward of ultimately joining the European Union. Countries aspiring to join the World Trade Organization (WTO) (e.g., China) or the Organisation for Economic Co-operation and Development (OECD) (e.g., Colombia) have experienced similar benefits. External anchors help drive the reform process forward when it is most difficult, keep the goals and the timelines clear, and ultimately offer reward in the form of membership or financial assistance. External agencies also offer relevant experience and technical expertise that can be useful when reforms are crafted and implemented. Risks include: (1) imposition of reforms or standards that the reforming country is not interested in and (2) *institutional mimicry* (i.e., building institutions and processes in weak states that look like those found in functional states). These risks can to some extent be mitigated if the country develops an indigenous and well-designed reform proposal that falls within the international standards and norms expected. International organizations are much more flexible in this regard than they used to be and contrary to what is commonly perceived.

To facilitate external support for an Ethiopian reform agenda there is an urgent need for the government to publish an economic strategy document and reform plan. More than one year into the Abiy administration it is noteworthy that this has not yet happened, given that strategy formulation has usually been a strength of past governments and the civil service. The government needs to clearly communicate its plan and articulate how development partners can most usefully support it. This plan should demonstrate a shared vision across government of reforms and constitute a base against which Ethiopian citizens and the international community can hold the government accountable.

Ongoing World Bank DPF offers an illustration of how the Abiy administration is working with the international community. The Ethiopia Growth and Competitiveness Programmatic Development Policy Financing was approved on October 30, 2018. It supports a reform program that is a subset of the overall government reform agenda. The structural reform program is organized around three pillars: (1) maximizing finance for development, (2) improving the investment climate and developing the financial sector, and (3) enhancing transparency and accountability. This three-year reform program was jointly designed by the government and the World Bank. The government must implement reforms every year of the program and will receive a general budget support disbursement when these reforms have been completed. So far, Ethiopia has received $1.2 billion in direct budget support for implementing the reforms of the first year of the program. The indicative triggers for years two and three of the program help create a line of sight for the reform effort, and the associated financing gives the government a financial incentive to implement its own reform program fully and on time.

The government could consider designing a macroeconomic program with the IMF. Ethiopia essentially needs to reset its macroeconomic framework as previously discussed. This includes the introduction of a medium-term fiscal framework with fiscal targets to exit high risk of debt distress supported by a flexible exchange rate policy and appropriate monetary policy. While the broad direction of this financial program is clear, it may be technically challenging for the government to design and implement it effectively without the support of relevant expertise from the IMF. Collaboration with the Fund, for instance through an Extended Credit Facility (ECF), would also bring the benefits of regular external credit disbursements to support the balance of payments. An ECF would be particularly helpful for the successful implementation of the World Bank DPF, which also has an adequate macro framework as one of its fundamental conditions.

Finally, Ethiopia should accelerate its application process for WTO accession. Ethiopia has been delaying a major reform effort for years, namely the process of joining the WTO and initiating the process of liberalizing its trade regime and services sector. The World Bank (2016a) presents an analysis of normative reform sequencing and country experiences that concludes that an appropriate next step for Ethiopia to accede to the WTO is to make a credible service offer that is acceptable to WTO members. In doing so, Ethiopia would follow the trodden path of reform also followed by East Asian countries, which starts with trade liberalization and gradually embraces financial sector liberalization. It has already taken the step of joining the Africa Continental Free Trade Agreement. Bolder steps need to follow.

CONCLUSION

To sum up the argument, we lay out the economic scenario of Futopia circa 2025. Real GDP is growing steadily at 7–8 percent following a temporary slowdown in the wake of recent macroeconomic adjustment and structural reforms supported by external partners. Growth and job creation are driven by private and public investment and improvements in productivity. Private business activity is underpinned by a healthy expansion of private sector credit and increased participation in new economic sectors previously under state monopoly, including telecoms, logistics, and electricity. Recent reforms have supported the sustainable financing of infrastructure investment from the private sector using PPP, complementing traditional public investment. The fiscal deficit is in line with the targets of the medium-term fiscal framework that successfully contained past fiscal excesses. It is financed through a well-functioning domestic treasury bill market and external borrowing. Exports are buoyant, supported by a competitive real exchange rate, and this has contributed to a reduction of external imbalances and an adequate level of international reserves. Inflation is contained to about 5 percent, owing to tighter monetary policy, including the suspension of central bank financing of the budget. The government continues to implement reforms to enhance competition and gradually reduce its role in the economy.

NOTES

1. This chapter was finalized in May 2019 and does not incorporate or discuss the macroeconomic effects of COVID-19.
2. This section draws upon World Bank (2016a; 2016b) and Moller and Wacker (2017).
3. The International Monetary Fund (2013) has argued that official growth rates may have been overestimated by as much as 3 percentage points in some years. Disputes over the numbers aside, there is an important agenda of strengthening statistical capacity with the view of improving the underlying macro and micro data that support economic policy analysis.

REFERENCES

Haile, Fiseha, and Lars Christian Moller. 2018. "Explaining the WAEMU Growth Spurt—The Role of Financial Deepening and Macro Policy." World Bank Policy Research Working Paper 8675. Washington, DC: World Bank Group.

IMF. 2013. "The Federal Democratic Republic of Ethiopia: 2013 Article IV Consultation." IMF Country Report No. 13/308. Washington, DC.

———. 2018. "The Federal Democratic Republic of Ethiopia: 2018 Article IV Consultation." IMF Country Report No. 18/354. Washington, DC.

Moller, Lars Christian, and Konstantin M. Wacker. 2017. "Explaining Ethiopia's Growth Acceleration—The Role of Infrastructure and Macroeconomic Policy." *World Development* 96 (August): 198–215.

World Bank. 2016a. "Ethiopia's Great Run: The Growth Acceleration and How to Pace It. Report No. 99399, November 2016. Washington, DC: World Bank Group.

———. 2016b. "Ethiopia: Priorities for Ending Extreme Poverty and Promoting Shared Prosperity." Systematic Country Diagnostic, March 30, 2016. Washington, DC: World Bank Group.

———. 2018a. "Ethiopia Economic Update: The Inescapable Manufacturing-Services Nexus: Exploring the Potential of Distribution Services." Washington, DC: World Bank Group.

———. 2018b. "Ethiopia Growth and Competitiveness Programmatic Development Policy Financing." Report No. PGD55, Washington, DC: World Bank Group.

---

* Comments from Carolyn Turk, Mathew Verghis, Jean-Pierre Chauffeur, Mame Fatou Diagne, Fiseha Haile, and two anonymous reviewers on a previous draft are gratefully acknowledged. The chapter was presented at Harvard Kennedy School on November 26, 2019, and the author thanks participants for their astute observations. The findings, interpretations, and conclusions expressed herein are those of the author and do not necessarily reflect the view of the World Bank Group, its board of directors, or the governments they represent.

2.2 The Case for the State-Private Partnership Model of Development for Ethiopia

Berhanu Abegaz

INTRODUCTION

Ethiopia is a very peculiar country, in its illustrious history as well as debilitating poverty, that frustrates easy cross-country comparison. Drawing instructive lessons from its hapless postwar experiments with every economic system known to man, I make a case here for an Ethiopian long-term development strategy whose institutional architecture is neither neoliberal nor etatist.

The preferred partnership model is one that is forged between a capable, nationalist, and market-friendly state on the one hand and an independent and entrepreneurial business class on the other. The division of labor between the state and the national capitalist class, economic theory tells us, should be dictated by the dynamic comparative advantage of each. In some time-bound activities, and especially in the accumulation-driven growth phase, the government may pragmatically lead; in most others, especially the productivity-driven growth phase, it ought to follow. Synchronizing built-up capability with domestic and global opportunities, the key to sustained and equitable growth from such an inauspicious starting point is what smart economic strategy or policy is all about.

The political economy of long-term structural economic reform, which by definition entails a significant alteration of the power balance in society, must contend with the endogenous interactions among economic ideas (ideology) and fundamental interests (power) (Mukand and Rodrik 2018). Considerations of the political feasibility of structural reforms (such as deep liberalization and large-scale privatization) must, therefore, figure prominently in policy analysis. Incentives must be pinned down for domestically unconstrained powerholders to accept momentous changes in the rules of the economic game that are socially good. This short note takes up the case for systemic or sub-structural reforms in the hope of showing what bold leaders, with cultivated support from a broad-based national coalition for meaningful change, can accomplish. I do not, however, presume that the current state elites are ready or able to assume this historic responsibility.

There are three alternative models or strategies of development that are most salient to a post-socialist Ethiopia (Abegaz 2018b; Hauge and Chang 2019). The first model is the existing *developmentalist state party* model whereby a vanguard political party manages to thoroughly capture state enterprises, party enterprises, and those private enterprises controlled by princelings, all of which operate within the framework of a crony market economy. This public-investment-driven model has delivered rapid growth for the past fifteen years. Given its self-limiting politics, overreliance on debt, supply-led investment in infrastructure, overreliance on a loyal kakistocracy, and understandable emphasis on exportables to finance a debt stock equivalent to 60 percent of GDP, it has a hard time sustaining long-term economic growth.

The second model is the *liberal private ownership* economy whereby state enterprises are limited only to the provision of basic public services and selected investment-intensive productive activities; all politically connected enterprises are curbed or dissolved, and a competitive market mechanism is enforced with secure property rights. In the absence of a strong bona fide private sector that can deliver on shared growth and constrain the excesses of predatory state elites or oligarchies, this strategy is clearly infeasible at this stage of Ethiopia's development. The template nonetheless provides a useful reference point for the debate on economic reform.

The third model is what I call a *state-private partnership* model, a suitably adapted version of the prototypical East Asian model whereby an evolving division of labor is forged between a growth-friendly state with limited capability and an enfeebled but profit-seeking private sector within a framework of a legitimately and appropriately regulated market economy. More broadly, this model entails three fundamental "separations" to ensure the productive use of mobilized economic rent: church/mosque and state, party and state, and ethnicity and state. This hybrid strategy moves us away from the self-seeking pathway of the neo-patrimonial state to a full-fledged liberal model. Sensible reforms can then turn the disadvantages of unbridled rent seeking and negative-sum competition into a bridge to the world of a mutually constraining and yet complementary dispensation between political society and economic society.

Space limitation compels me to be cryptic, but the key implicit assumptions must be pointed out at the outset. My conceptual framework focuses on state-business strategic relations to identify the circumstances that would tether high investment (via the mobilization of economic rent and foreign savings) and sustained economic growth. This chapter uneasily melds positive analysis by specifying the most relevant initial conditions that should inform the reform and normative analysis by pinpointing the institutional changes that may ideally undergird structural reforms. This way of thinking must grapple with a key challenge: how to design reforms that recognize the endogeneity of mutual constraints as well as beneficial alliances between an ideally autonomous and capable state and an independent and empowered business class (see Chen 2008 for a critical review of the literature).

For Ethiopia, a successful transition from embeddedness or capture that is revealed by the first model (the state taming business) to cooperation or collusion embraced by the third model (the state and business becoming competitive allies, AKA mutual hostages) is a fraught one. In this perspective, the existential angst of exclusionary ethnicism reveals itself in the ever-present floundering in the straitjacket of the contradictions between the productive use of economic rent to boost legitimizing growth and the patrimonial dissipation of rent to cement the loyalty of transactional constituencies. The analytical framework thereby calls for appraising the role of historical junctures, which fleetingly enable prepared citizens to tilt the balance in favor of a new political equilibrium that would ensure national survival and an economic equilibrium that would favor profit seeking over rent seeking.

There is no better time than now to debate the virtues of the competing strategies of economic transformation for Ethiopia. As the euphoria of potential regime change gives way to frustrations, it may sound vainglorious to offer a blueprint of deep structural reform while such elemental issues as peace, the security of property rights, and macroeconomic stability are increasingly becoming untenable. But we must keep our eyes on the prize, if only to stay prepared when political conditions permit a rethinking about a reconsideration of development strategy.

We will do well to remember at the outset Janos Kornai's (1990) "affinity principle," tethering forms of ownership with decision-making mechanisms: there is a strong congruence between state ownership and central planning, as well as between private property and market coordination. Hybrid cases (such as trying to marry state ownership with markets under market socialism or party-state control with private ownership under crony capitalism) are inherently contradictory and untenable in the long run.

KEY STYLIZED FACTS OF THE NONINDUSTRIAL ETHIOPIAN ECONOMY

Country peculiarities matter greatly for the design of reform strategy. Any sensible development strategy must recognize at the outset that Ethiopia remains an unbelievably poor, non-colonial country. The country's political elites have been reduced to engaging for a millennium in zero-sum extractive contests over the existing economic (mainly agricultural) surplus rather than in a positive-sum competition to nurture and protect wealth creators (Abegaz 2018a).

Let us now take a quick look at the unfavorable initial conditions and then proceed with the diagnosis and possible fixes. Ethiopia's multidimensional headcount poverty today stands at 82 percent, among the highest in the world, compared to 4 percent for Egypt (World Bank 2018). Some 26 million out of 110 million currently wallow in "extreme poverty," defined as living on less than $1.90 per day in 2011 prices. One in ten citizens sadly subsists on food aid in a typical year, and the ever-diminishing farm plots evoke the specter of livelihood "collapse" since they no longer provide an adequate livelihood for a fast-growing population.

Table 2.2.1. Poverty and Vulnerability Across the "Five Ethiopias" and Two Urban Centers, 2011

Economic region	Poor (%)	Vulnerable to poverty (%)	Household has a food gap (%)	Household experienced a shock (%)	Asset vulnerable (%)	Overall rank (%)	National population (%)
Moisture Reliable lowlands	45	75	31	87	26	1	2
Enset lowlands	29	47	36	75	57	2	18
Drought-prone highlands	28	43	25	46	50	3	33
Moisture-reliable highlands	32	42	13	63	13	5	42
Pastoral areas	31	52	21	31	16	4	2
Town/small city	26	27	9	52	41	6	7
Large city	22	23	4	28	0	7	12

Source: World Bank (2015a), Table 3.5. Ethiopia's 12 million farm households rely on rain-fed agricultural activities and, with rapidly declining land/man ratios, one in ten are permanently dependent on food aid.

Table 2.2.1 provides starkly telling measures of vulnerability for five agroecological zones and urban centers. The geographic distribution of poverty varies between urban (marginally lower) and rural, and across subnational units, with the highest levels recorded for Afar, Amhara, Southern, and Somali regional states. Per capita income in PPP terms stands at $2,500.[1] Economic inequality remains rather low (Gini = 0.33), thanks to the radical land reform of 1975–77 and the suppression of the formal private sector.

According to ILOSTAT, two-thirds of the 49-million-strong Ethiopian labor force in 2017 was self-employed, mostly in agriculture, compared to just 9.4 percent in industry. Of these, 4 percent (or 2 million, of whom 0.4 million had advanced education) were high-skilled, 62 percent middle-skilled, and 32 percent low-skilled. This rather dismal level of human capital would explain why Ethiopia's labor productivity is about one-ninth that of China's. Furthermore, based on the national labor force survey of 2013, one in ten members of the workforce had the status of employees (2 million in the public sector, 1.5 million of whom were in the civil service, and one-third of whom were women). Half the Ethiopian labor force (age 15+) was illiterate, 40 percent had basic skills, and 6 percent had intermediate skills—all well below the corresponding averages for Africa.

The informal rural economy of subsistence agriculture and petty trade provides livelihoods for 80 percent of the 110 million Ethiopians. Self-employment in nonfarm enterprises offers supplementary income for only 14 percent of the rural population. Proto-industrialization accounts for less than a quarter of total income—well below the 40 percent for Ghana and 50 percent for Bangladesh (EDRI and GGGI 2015; World Bank 2015b).

INSTRUCTIVE LESSONS FROM SUCCESSFUL GROWERS

The persistence of the twin evils of structural poverty and endogenous political misgovernance suggests that a robust growth engine remains elusive for Ethiopia. In this regard, the highly respected Spence Commission on Growth and Development (Spence 2012) identified the essential attributes of those developing countries that managed to achieve sustainably high and inclusive growth. These countries exhaust reallocation-driven growth before they shift to technology-driven growth by escaping the middle-income trap.

The first attribute of successful growers is *good leadership* (or accountable governance), which embraces enduring peace, adequate state capability, and inclusiveness. The second is respect for *market-led resource allocation*, with government followership playing a complementary role by correcting market failures, maintaining the social contract, and making up for missing markets.

The third quality is *future orientation*, as evidenced by a high rate and quality of long-term investment in human capital and critical public infrastructure to underwrite an industrial drive. To ensure a healthy 7 percent annual GDP growth rate for two decades or more, successful growers invest the equivalent of 25 percent of GDP—a level achieved by Ethiopia only after 2002 with massive foreign financing. The fourth attribute is *openness* to the global economy to judiciously access a bigger market for exportables and to benefit from a rapid diffusion of productivity-enhancing knowledge. The fifth and last quality is *macroeconomic stability* that is undergirded by sustainable fiscal and trade deficits. Ethiopia has until very recently had a respectable record of macroeconomic management, but adequate revenue mobilization (currently at 11 percent of GDP) and NBE autonomy have eluded it. Externally financed and public-sector-led infrastructural investment has so far undergirded respectable growth acceleration (Moller and Wacker 2017).

THE RENT-SEEKING PARTY-STATE MODEL OF DEVELOPMENT

Put simply, Ethiopia's post-WWII strategies of development have shifted from private-led under the imperial regime to state-led under the Derg and party-state-led under the EPRDF. In the last two cases, state elites have captured all state institutions, thereby blurring the line between private and public and between the political sphere and the economic sphere. With no prior experience in managing a modern economy, the political victors have consistently displayed a predictable proclivity to conduct grand politico-economic experiments that turned out to be initially promising but mostly disastrous in the end.

The Derg grappled with a regimented and anti-market war economy. The EPRDF has, for almost three decades, crafted a crony-capitalist economy that is captured rather than governed, as was the case with South Korea or Japan.

The ruling EPRDF has, for example, peddled the mutual embeddedness of party and state as a Nipponian grand bargain whereby the realization of democratic aspirations is to be deferred for a bread-for-all promise by the self-styled "revolutionary-democratic" developmental regime (Vaughan 2011; Zenawi 2012). This futile search for political legitimacy through public-sector-driven growth, relaunched with vigor after 2001, has brought a 7–8 percent GDP annual growth rate over the past fifteen years; an unprecedented level of institutionalized venality, including large inequalities among ethnic homelands; investment in an extensive network of roads and energy projects; high-value cash crops such as coffee, oilseeds, and sugar; expropriation of the land rights of especially urban and selected rural communities in the borderlands; and continued marginalization of the politically unconnected segment of the formal private sector. The politically influenced sphere consists of the MIDROC Ethiopia network of companies, the FDI-financed companies, and the bona fide domestic private enterprises. This multiheaded hydra can be simplified, for lack of good labels, as comprising two sets of profit-cum-rent-seekers: the amorphous "private sector" and the dominant "party-state sector."

A good chunk of the state enterprise sector inherited from the Derg has been privatized at a steep discount to the likes of MIDROC Ethiopia, EPRDF companies, military companies, FDI investors, and politically connected families. State enterprises still dominate the following sectors in terms of both output and employment: domestic and international cargo and passenger air service (EAL), power (EEP), telecommunications (Ethio-Telecom), banking (CBE and DBE), insurance, transportation (sea, road, and rail), engineering by military-owned companies, and critical subsectors of manufacturing. These for-profit state corporations, many with a higher level of productivity than private ones (World Bank 2015c), have been retained as cash cows or as instruments for the state-led development drive. Some are presently slated for hasty partial privatization.

Although the barriers to market entry to bona fide private competitors have eased in the last ten years, state and party enterprises jointly dominate key sectors (sugar, fertilizer, cement, financial services, telecom, and utilities), other holdings by the cadres and princelings, as well as by the MIDROC group, continue to have a substantial presence in many other sectors. The profoundly corrupt and incompetent Metals and Engineering Corporation

(METEC), for example, owns some seventy-five factories. METEC is a significant producer of military goods, a supplier of electromechanical works for the Grand Ethiopian Renaissance Dam (GERD), a contractor of the Yayu Coal Phosphate Fertilizer Complex in Illubabor, and a principal contractor for the Ethiopian Sugar Corporation. Its egregiously corrupt and inept practices, especially in the diversion or embezzlement of big loans from the state banks, are presently under legal scrutiny.

Parallel to the state-owned sector thrives a vast, ruling, party-owned business empire in the name of legally fictitious "private endowment" companies that is in fact firmly in the grabbing hands of the four coalition members of the ruling party (Abegaz 2013; Vaughan and Gebremichael 2011). Prominent among the EPRDF conglomerates is the cleverly named Endowment Fund for the Rehabilitation of Tigray (EFFORT or Timhit), with TPLF assets worth over $3 billion, which was formally established in 1995. EFFORT is by far the most prominent political conglomerate in terms of assets, number of subsidiaries, sectoral coverage, and supra-regional orientation. The junior partners of the EPRDF also own diversified for-profit companies (including banks) of lesser importance, again overseen by holding companies registered as endowments to contravene the prohibition of such faux charities by the 1960 Ethiopian Commercial Code. They are Endeavour (Tiret) of the Amhara Democratic Party; Tumsa Endowment, controlled by the Oromo Democratic Party; and Wondo Group, controlled by the Southern Ethiopia People's Democratic Movement. In a move that evokes the fate of KMT companies that disappeared (stripped away) as soon as a democratically elected government appeared in Taiwan, recent announcements point to the dissolution of EFFORT and Endeavour companies through contrived transfers to regional states, privatization, or illegal asset stripping.

The primary growth driver in this hyper-politicized economy is none other than the mainly debt-financed and inflation-financed public sector investment on exportables and physical infrastructure. Given the low level of national savings, some two-thirds of public spending (on roads, railways, hydroelectricity, sugar estates, education, and health) has been financed by large grants and soft loans (about $30 billion since 2002 along with a comparable level of domestic debt), large net private transfers (remittances projected to average $4–5 billion annually for 2011–18), a small stock of FDI

($6 billion), favorable commodity export prices that are moderating, favorable weather that cannot be relied upon, rising volumes of cash crop and service exports (EAL, resident international organizations, and underexploited tourism), and a massive monetization of the state-guaranteed or otherwise directed bank credit to politically favored borrowers, which has crowded out the independent (or non-comprador) private sector.

THE STATE-PRIVATE PARTNERSHIP MODEL OF DEVELOPMENT

A canonical modern capitalist economy is one that is private-led, profit-seeking, competitively disciplined, and innovation-oriented. A direct trajectory of transition from a state-stifled subsistence and semi-autarkic economy (Ethiopia today with a sizable non-traded sector) to a well-functioning and open-market economy is unlikely to materialize in the absence of a market-friendly state and a predominantly wealth-creating private sector.

The vulnerability of the Ethiopian economy to political shocks and climate shocks was such that it took almost two generations (1970–2015) to recapture the real per capita income attained in 1970. The most recent Country Assistance Strategy of the World Bank (2017), which is aligned with Ethiopia's Growth and Transformation Plan II (FDRE 2016), talks of Ethiopia as a country in the throes of a "dual takeoff" involving rapid growth and high public-service delivery. The Bank further notes that the need for bolstering this fragile growth engine, boosting structural change, and making growth more equitable requires two classes of deep reforms. The long-standing canned advice comprises (1) proper macroeconomic management, a better supply response by stimulating investment, and a focus on quality while extending basic public services to everyone; and (2) a shift from top-down, public-spending-driven growth to a sustainable financial model and a decentralized system of resource allocation.

There are three major areas of reform that require a serious recalibration of the development strategy for the incipient post-EPRDF economic order. They pertain to three areas: private-sector development, industrialization strategy, and regional growth engines (see Table 2.2.2).[2]

Given the inescapable realities outlined above, an Ethiopian partnership model for development will have to be based on sturdy pillars of structural or sub-structural reform. The partnership model self-reflectively embraces the few sites of efficiency and innovation within the state sector, replaces the mindset of capture and hostility toward the private sector with a market-friendly mindset, privatizes land and most state-party enterprises, and incubates dynamic small-scale and medium-scale industrial firms. Let's take up each briefly and prescriptively.

1. Nurture the independent domestic private sector to leadership:

That statist misadventures of economic modernization have enfeebled the domestic private sector is evident in the fact that there are only 250,000 registered small- and medium-sized enterprises in the urban areas, and the formal private sector accounts for just 4 percent of GDP and employs only 6 percent of the workforce (World Bank 2012). This is partly inherent in mass poverty itself. Risk-averse businesses are out of necessity oriented toward small-scale commercial and non-tradable activities where technologies are simple, fixed capital requirements are low, market demand is readily available, and risks can be minimized through short-term, high-turnover profit margins.

The urban-based formal private sector has haltingly discovered extraordinary opportunities in specialty coffee, sugar, processed meats, cut flowers, leather goods, winter vegetables, cultural goods for the diaspora, and textiles and garments. The state must then provide demand-led (rather than mostly supply-led) public infrastructure, development banking services, and human capital formation to accelerate movement along this trajectory. These far-sighted measures are critical for revitalizing the private sector by nudging the merchant class to become an industrial class by engaging in secondary processing activities, small exporters to grow into medium-sized ones with denser supply chains, and small farmers to specialize for the long-distance market. Appropriate price-stabilization and insurance schemes are paying off handsomely in many countries. The rub is that private-sector development needs a supportive state that is technocratically capable and disciplined enough to nurture a competitive and empowered business class.

Table 2.2.2: *Reconciling Ownership and Control for Ethiopian Economic Reform*

Ownership: Control:	State-owned enterprises	Party-owned enterprises	Privately owned enterprises
Government-driven allocation	Retain the most strategic enterprises; give them autonomy and force them to compete; privatize the rest.	Nationalize or liquidate party assets as appropriate.	Severe oligarchic and crony relations with bureaucracy or the ruling party.*
Market-driven allocation	Organize market-based *competition* and state-led *contests* for subsidies and government contracts.	Reregister as for-profit companies.	Foster a supportive but disciplining business climate to tame rent seeking and foster competition with emulation.

*   End state capture by the ruling party to prevent the entrenched political entrepreneurs from frustrating the structural reform process to retain economic rent, most of which is diverted from remittances, aid, and even loans.

2. Land to the tiller and the homeowner

The land reform of 1975 nationalized all land and rendered all Ethiopians the de facto tenants of an avaricious state. The land reform proclamation, resorting to the ambiguous language of "public ownership," facilitated the conversion of historically secure *rist-holders* (about two-thirds of the farm population) into supplicant use-right holders. Nor did it provide ownership rights to the sharecropping and renting *chisegna* (roughly half of the farmers in the south and a third in Wollo and Shewa). Concerning urban land and extra houses, a great deal of the nationalized real estate, it turned out, belonged to ordinary Ethiopians who relied on investment in real estate as the most secure form of long-term savings.

In the interest of optimal land use and high intersectoral labor mobility from least productive uses (subsistence activities) to more productive uses (industrial, off-farm, and modern commercial), households (with equal claims for women) should be given full ownership titles to the "farmland" they currently cultivate. Appropriate provisions for communal lands should be crafted in the seminomadic regions. Owners can then lease, mortgage, or sell their plots as they see fit. The subsequent gains in allocational efficiency will turn into productivity gains by allowing optimal farm sizes to emerge under the control of the most enterprising young farmers along with off-farm activities and cheaper food for those exiting direct farming (Abegaz 2004, 2015).[3]

Ending for good the imported and pernicious "revolutionary" culture of appropriating the hard-earned property of fellow citizens, after conveniently demonizing them as exploiters, is a tall order for state elites, since state ownership of land and the intimate tie between land and identity has been constitutionalized to legitimize pernicious contests by political entrepreneurs to siphon off the enormous capitalizable value embedded in urban and fertile agricultural areas. Constitutional reform has become the crux of the twinning of structural economic reform and systemic political reform in Ethiopia.

3. Pursue a balanced industrialization strategy

The EPRDF government has since 2002 become unusually ambitious and modernist by retreating from the core tenets of the so-called agricultural development-led industrialization (ADLI) (FDRE 2016; Oqubay 2015). One plan, well underway, is to invest $12 billion in irrigation and hydroelectric projects for both domestic agro-industrial use and regional exports. As an integral part of the politically sensitive multi-riparian Nile Basin Initiative, Ethiopia is also building Africa's largest dam, GERD, whose total cost is $4.5 billion. China has recently granted a loan of $1 billion for electricity transmission lines to neighboring countries when it is completed. The extensive road construction program underway is to be supplemented by an electrified national rail network of nearly three thousand miles. The estimated $6 billion costs will be financed mostly by the respective import-export and development banks of China, India, Brazil, Russia, and Turkey. Companies from each country carved out the construction contracts for one or more of the eight corridors.

One consequence of these initiatives is that, even in the face of such an ambitious development plan, dependency on Western aid ($40 billion in the past twenty-five years) is likely to diminish to less than one-third of total forex inflows. Currently, the BRICS have provided soft loans and grants that together amount to half of the average annual inflows of net official development assistance (ODA). As of 2017, diversified exports are beginning to net $3 billion annually, development aid of some $4 billion, FDI stock of $5 billion (out of the global stock of $2 trillion), and remittances in the $3–4 billion range. As we are discovering now, the combination of incompetence and egregious private diversion of state assets has frustrated timely project completion to generate the requisite foreign exchange earnings to timely service the large foreign loans. The fierce urgency of unsustainable dependence on foreign capital flows is rendering new tax and privatization policies hostage to questionable past commitments.

I have argued elsewhere that an urban-regional industrialization strategy is more appropriate for Ethiopia than ADLI, which is hopelessly anchored in subsistence agriculture or selected cash crops for export. The former melds selected regional growth engines and complementary industry-oriented peri-urban clusters such as special economic zones, specialized export processing zones, industrial zones and districts, and perhaps scientific parks. Manufacturing-based industrial takeoffs, with the capacity to create high-paying jobs far beyond the current 0.2 million, need to run on two legs—rural productivity growth and rapid urbanization (Abegaz 2018b; World Bank 2015c).

An illustrative urban-based, commercial-agriculture-linked Ethiopian industrialization is depicted in Figure 2.2.1. When we overlay the two-pronged industrial nodes over the three most productive agroecological zones (Qolla, Dega, and Woyna-Dega), we lay bare myriad complementarities in farm and nonfarm activities within each region and access to a broader array of ports in the Horn of Africa (EDRI and GGGI 2015).

Figure 2.2.1: Ethiopia's Urban and Regional Economic Growth Engines

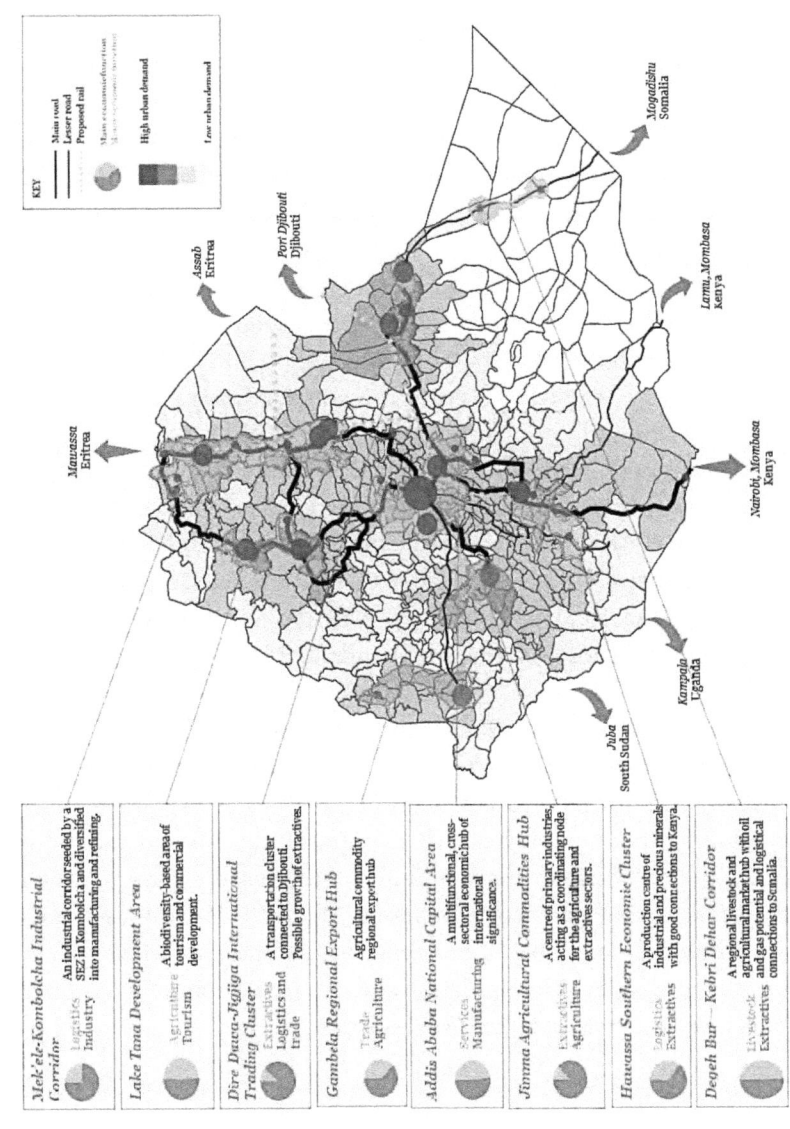

Mek'ele–Kombolcha Industrial Corridor
Logistics / Industry — An industrial corridor seeded by a SEZ in Kombolcha and diversified into manufacturing and refining.

Lake Tana Development Area
Agriculture / Tourism — A biodiversity-based area of tourism and commercial development.

Dire Dawa–Jigjiga International Trading Cluster
Extractives / Logistics and trade — A transportation cluster connected to Djibouti. Possible growth of extractives.

Gambela Regional Export Hub
Trade / Agriculture — Agricultural commodity regional export hub.

Addis Ababa National Capital Area
Services / Manufacturing — A multifunctional, cross-sectoral economic hub of international significance.

Jimma Agricultural Commodities Hub
Extractives / Agriculture — A centre of primary industries, acting as a coordinating node for the agriculture and extractives sectors.

Hawassa Southern Economic Cluster
Logistics / Extractives — A production centre of industrial and precious minerals with good connections to Kenya.

Degeh Bur – Kebri Dehar Corridor
Livestock / Extractives — A regional livestock and agricultural market hub with oil and gas potential and logistical connections to Somalia.

Source: EDRI and GGGI (2015), Figure D. Urbanization rate will double to 33 percent of the population by 2030.

Eight integrated agro-industrial regions stand out. Three of them are well established: (1) the Menagesha or Addis metro industrial-service hub is an enlarged capital region for an integrated special economic zone comprising industrial districts for SMEs, industrial processing zones for large-scale FDI, and a national distribution hub. A self-governing Addis Ababa region, which currently subsidizes other regional states, may very well need to have a fifty-mile radius to encompass much of southern Shewa (especially Nazret/Adama) and possibly the Awash dry port; (2) the Mekelle-Kombolcha-Dessie industrial corridor can integrate rather expansively the Mekelle-Adwa industrial complex, the emerging Dessie-Kombolcha industrial complex with a good agricultural hinterland, and also Woldya, which will be well connected by road and rail east-west (Assab-Djibouti-Metema) as well as north-south; and (3) the Dire-Dawa–Jigiga industrial and international trading cluster can link the first economic region and the mineral complex of the Ogaden and the Afar basin to three major foreign seaports—Assab, Berbera, and Djibouti.

The linchpin of urban-based industrialization has been the building of industrial parks, seven of which are in place at a cost of $1 billion (Oqubay 2015). These clusters have created some sixty thousand low-wage jobs along with disappointingly high labor turnover rates. Despite a large pool of laborers with secondary education, Ethiopia is still stuck at the lowest rung of the global supply chains and, hence, lackluster export earnings—at least for now.

The export-processing experiment has to be deepened by cultivating local sourcing of inputs, nurturing agro-industrial growth regions, pursuing a metropolitan approach to urban planning, and raising the quality of schools and upskilling those employed. Just as importantly, tailored and long-term financing of productive investment requires a rich set of commercial banks, development banks, and capital markets. What Ethiopia boasts, however, is a rather shallow bank-based financial system and a political system that does not encourage healthy emulation and competition among self-financing regional units that robust federalism requires.

SUB-STRUCTURAL REFORM: END VANGUARDISM IN FAVOR OF PARTNERSHIP

An ideologically post-EPRDF Ethiopia will, sooner rather than later, have to undergo a trifecta of transitions, especially since most of the parastatals have proved to be the commanding heights of blunder. The first is *political*—a transition from a strange mix of universalist-populist revolutionary democracy and self-limiting and exclusionary ethnocracy that fragments the national common market to a citizenship-based and pluralist system. The second is *economic*—a transition from nonindustrial destitution to a robust industrialization drive with an affordable social safety net for all. The third is *strategic*—a transition from a party-state-led development to a mutually constraining and empowering partnership between a growth-friendly technocracy and a profit-seeking business class.

The feather in the cap is a serious rethinking of the EPRDF development strategy that has long marginalized the legitimate private sector, privileged politically embedded and ethnicized business networks, and obsessed on raising foreign exchange to finance showcased development projects. The World Bank (2017, 2019) sums up the folly of the strategy of export-led commodity production and low-productivity services:

> Whereas structural transformation—the shift of economic activities and employment from low- to high-productivity activities—has taken place to some extent in Ethiopia, it has been driven by services. Ethiopia has only partly followed the traditional path of structural transformation often associated with East Asia, where a substantial rise in manufacturing (and away from agriculture) fueled the growth of economies such as China, Korea, and Vietnam. In Ethiopia, economic activity (output and jobs) has shifted from agriculture and into construction and services, mainly bypassing the critical phase of industrialization.

The superior agriculture-industry-services sequence of old Europe stands on three legs. One leg of the stool is close cooperation between a reasonably autonomous but accountable state and a competitive business sector with access to innovation rents and temporary protection. The liquidation of politically linked businesses, selective privatization of state monopolies, and enhanced freedom of entry into productive sectors are pivotal, as is a proper regulatory framework to discourage rent seeking and facilitate a competition-based market discipline on firms.

The second leg is a well-designed catchup industrialization strategy that is anchored in the emerging cities (which have better skill supply, public infrastructure, and initial demand for manufactures) as well as in locationally endowed or agriculturally rich regions. One by-product is a regionally balanced and equitable growth regime. The final leg of this development strategy is one that incentivizes the Ethiopian diaspora to invest and otherwise engage, which has a respectable stock of human capital, new ideas, and investible funds.

Despite an excellent start, the Abiy administration has yet to publicly provide a comprehensive roadmap of reform for the post-TPLF-led economy, including how it plans to manage the pro-market transition and WTO membership with all it entails for policy lock-in. Distilling the lessons of experience from similarly regimented post-socialist reformers, we can at least note that depoliticization of the economic sphere involves three blocks of serializable reforms: macroeconomic stabilization (S), market-building liberalization (L), and state enterprise and party enterprise privatization (P). We will not discuss speed (shock therapy versus gradualism) because of space constraints.

Concerning privatization, two challenges inevitably face the government: how best to privatize firms in an economy with a weak market and a weak private sector and how to sequence the three sets of reforms optimally. Underperforming state enterprises as well as party enterprises may be sold partially (say, the cargo division or the less-efficient domestic service of EAL) or wholly in an outright auction, management/employee buyout at a steep discount, or in a joint-venture arrangement. Hereby lurks the nagging problem of how to finance such large sales to the domestic sector with few assets in hard currency without a diversified domestic capital market. Selling to foreigners is an option, but it has its own baggage, including dependency and the reluctance of the new owners to inject the substantial new capital needed to modernize the privatized firms. Lastly, the hoped-for productivity gains will not materialize in the absence of a regulatory and enforcement system that impartially discourages unproductive rent seeking and selective asset stripping.

Worse still, if privatization proceeds are used to service ill-gotten foreign loans, the newly privatized firms cannot be modernized and readied for the more competitive environment they will hopefully face. This failure, along with the exchange of private monopolies for state monopolies in a poorly regulated market, has bedeviled post-socialist reformers in Eastern Europe and the former Soviet republics.

Greenfield privatization, with the right policy framework to incubate dynamic firms and support them to grow in size and market scope, often has a higher payoff. The cut-flower industry provides an inspiring example of private-sector innovation and market discovery.

These considerations tie into the choice between two sequencing options. One pathway is the S-L-P sequence that was widely adopted in central Europe, Vietnam, and China. This sequence is attractive where the political leadership enjoys a popular mandate to sell painful reforms to voters given the front-loaded pains and the back-loaded gains. The other is the S-P-L sequence adopted by Russia and Ukraine, where premature and large-scale privatization preceded the creation of a well-functioning market economy and led to massive state asset stripping and an oligarchic economy. The silver lining was that large-scale privatization drained the swamps and ensured the demise of the communist parties (Rohac 2013).

The last point worth making here is that a good strategy remains vacuous without (a) restraining the ongoing blatant land grabs in the Addis-Adama-Dire triangle, which accounts for over 60 percent of the formal-sector GDP, and (b) the right regulatory and policy frameworks. Let me mention illustratively pressing policy measures to address three seemingly insuperable problems:

A. Ensuring peace and stability:

Law and order and the predictability of government policy are not only elemental tasks for a viable state but are also the prerequisites for rapid economic growth. Investment in one's skills and businesses are a long-term commitment that abhors deep-seated political insecurity and policy uncertainty.[4]

B. Reducing the massive school-leaver unemployment and underemployment:

A program for school-to-work transition is urgently needed to help the half a million who annually graduate from the tenth and twelfth grades, and a further two hundred thousand at the tertiary level to acquire marketable occupational skills.[5] One nifty way of integrating academic knowledge and practical skills via the TVET model would be to establish model farms, model factories, and model offices as extensions of the schools. Internships with public institutions and the larger private companies will also help, as would small-business incubation through business planning, certification of marketable skills, and venture capital.

C. Stemming unsustainable livelihoods:

A legal framework to facilitate land leases and land sales along with training in craft skills and the provision of small credits will facilitate the emergence of optimal farms and the stimulation of off-farm and nonfarm activities in the countryside. Registration campaigns aimed at urban informal enterprises with promises of fair taxation, cheap electricity, and affordable telecom services and state support in the form of business training and credit provision will also be an excellent boost for small-scale industrial development and the private provision of affordable housing.

CONCLUSION

Appropriate institutions and an expanded policy space allow for the emergence of a competitive market. Reinvigorated participation in policy dialogue and self-regulation by the hitherto enfeebled chambers of commerce, sectoral associations, political parties, civic associations, academics, and think tanks are all known to prevent big policy mistakes or costly market distortions.

Political stability and policy predictability are preconditions for maximizing productive investment and, hence, robust economic growth. The root of this endemic uncertainty is the polarizing fusion of party and state that is tethered to an exclusionary ideology of ethnicism, which are intended to mask the political capture of high-profit activities in a nation of ethnic minorities. This structural defect in the political economy, though compatible with episodic growth, must somehow be eliminated for a robust growth engine to emerge.

Disruptive "big ideas" become decisive whenever incumbent rulers lose confidence and the excluded interest groups muster the courage and overcome coordination failure to fight for radical change. In developed economies, a coherent fusion of power and legitimizing ideology waxes and wanes depending on the relative strengths of the organized trinity: big business, big labor, and big government. In those middle-income countries that managed to industrialize, nationalist (albeit corrupt) politicians incentivize transaction politicians to spearhead a nationalistic development drive. In the case of present-day Ethiopia, however, ethnocentric politicians have raced to the bottom by resorting to a myopic mindset of exclusionary othering and absolutism as a mode of political mobilization by subverting preindustrial fusion of identity and land. Pluralism and contestability are vital for a culturally diverse country like Ethiopia on the verge of industrialization precisely because we do not know with certainty what strategies will work in the context of a rapidly changing world economy and transforming domestic economy.

That China and India, with per capita incomes no higher than Ethiopia's around 1970, have managed to make spectacular economic progress with the help of good leadership and sensible development strategies is awe-inspiring. A glimpse into Ethiopia's future evinces an immense set of challenges for reformers: linkage effects mean huge and simultaneous investment in power, finance, connectivity, and transportation are needed to render clusters of industries competitive; and mismatches must be handled adeptly (especially time and currency mismatches involving foreign financing and synchronization of the demand side and the supply side of investments). With a clear vision and sound strategy, however, it is possible to be free of poverty and tyranny within two or three generations.

NOTES

1. A reasonable benchmark for lower-middle-income status is $5,000–$10,000 in PPP terms rather than the ridiculously low and wide $1,000–$12,000 recommended by the World Bank.

2. The oft-mischaracterized East Asian developmental state boasts, as a hallmark of development, internally secure but externally threatened nationalist regimes that were selectively protectionist and interventionist but quintessentially pro-market. The African version of neo-patrimonial developmentalism (practiced in Ethiopia, Uganda, and Rwanda) is built instead around face-to-face patronage, seeks to supplant autonomous indigenous capital, and prefers to defy market fundamentals to compensate for the shallowness of the regimes' political base. The use of primordial loyalties for political mobilization and the deployment of state assets to cement patronage are essential features of nonindustrial societies where class cleavage is in its infancy (Fukuyama 2014).

3. All three postwar Ethiopian governments tried, with limited success, the shortcut strategy of sidelining the subsistence sector by establishing mega state and private plantations to boost foreign exchange earnings. While this shortcut makes sense in highly selective cases (most Ethiopian river valleys being non-navigable and requiring enormous investment to irrigate), a broad-based strategy of boosting agricultural productivity is what the country needs. Privatization of most urban land and rural land, under a competition-promoting regulatory environment, not only encourages investment in demand-driven real estate and the formation of a diversified investment portfolio but also is one of the few lines of defense for citizens against political and economic predation. Change in land ownership, among many others, is predicated on a new democratic constitution to decouple identity politics from land rights as the pivotal plan of a particular post-EPRDF dispensation (CCG 2018).

4. The change in leadership of the EPRDF from TPLF to OPDO (now ODP) that began in March 2018, despite commendable movements toward liberalization, has failed to carry out its responsibilities of maintaining peace and security in the country. The polarization of the civil service and security services along ethnic lines and the mounting

divisions within the ruling party has created strong incentives to intensify nonproductive rent seeking by exploiting the institutionalized identification of ethnicity with land and political authority. The economic impact has been the erosion of the common market and predation with guile.

5. It is interesting to note here that the entire stock of college-educated Ethiopians on the eve of the revolution was estimated to equal what Addis Ababa University graduates in one year (some ten thousand in 2019).

REFERENCES

Abegaz, Berhanu. 2004. "Escaping Ethiopia's Poverty Trap: The Case for a Second Agrarian Reform." *Journal of Modern African Studies* 42, no. 3 (September): 313–42.

———. 2005. "Persistent Stasis in a Tributary Mode of Production: The Peasant Economy of Ethiopia." *Journal of Agrarian Change* 5, no. 3 (July): 293–333.

———. 2013. "Political Parties in Business: Rent Seekers, Developmentalists, or Both?" *Journal of Development Studies* 49, no. 11 (September): 1463–83.

———. 2015. "A Pathway from Exclusionary to Inclusionary State and Market Institutions for Ethiopia." *International Journal of Ethiopian Studies* 9, no. 1 & 2: 37–66.

———. 2018a. *A Tributary Model of State Formation: Ethiopia, 1600–2015.* Cham, Switzerland: Springer.

———. 2018b. *Industrial Development in Africa: Mapping Industrialization Pathways for a Leaping Leopard.* Abingdon, UK: Routledge.

Chen, Ling. 2008. "Preferences, Institutions and Politics: Re-Interrogating the Theoretical Lessons of Developmental Economies." *New Political Economy* 13, no. 1: 89–102.

Citizens Charter Group (CCG). 2018. "A People's Transition Manifesto for a Democratic Ethiopia." *International Journal of Ethiopian Studies* 12, no. 1 (2018): 51–84.

Dercon, Stefan, and Douglas Gollin. 2019. "Agriculture's Changing Role in Ethiopia's Economic Transformation." In *The Oxford Handbook of the Ethiopian Economy*, edited by Fantu Cheru, Christopher Cramer, and Arkebe Oqubay, 449–67. Oxford: Oxford University Press.

EDRI and GGGI. 2015. *Unlocking the Power of Ethiopia's Cities: A Report by Ethiopia's New Climate Economy Partnership*. Addis Ababa: EDRI.

Federal Democratic Republic of Ethiopia (FDRE). 2016. *Growth and Transformation Plan II (GTP II, 2015/16-2019/20)*. Addis Ababa: National Planning Commission.

Fukuyama, Francis. 2014. *Political Order and Political Decay*. New York: Farrar, Straus and Giroux.

Kornai, Janos. 1990. "The Affinity between Ownership Forms and Coordination Mechanisms: The Common Experience of Reform in Socialist Countries." *Journal of Economic Perspectives* 4, no. 3: 131–47.

Hauge, Josten, and Ha-Joon Chang. 2019. "The Concept of a 'Developmental State' in Ethiopia." In *The Oxford Handbook of the Ethiopian Economy*, edited by Fantu Cheru, Christopher Cramer, and Arkebe Oqubay, 824–41. Oxford: Oxford University Press.

Moller, Lars, and Konstantin Wacker. 2017. "Explaining Ethiopia's Growth Acceleration—The Role of Infrastructure and Macroeconomic Policy." *World Development* 96 (August): 198–215.

Mukand, Sharun, and Dani Rodrik. 2018. "The Political Economy of Ideas: On Ideas Versus Interests in Policymaking." NBER Working Paper No. 24467, March 2018, Cambridge, MA: National Bureau of Economic Research.

Oqubay, Arkebe. 2015. *Made in Africa: Industrial Policy in Ethiopia*. Oxford: Oxford University Press.

Rohac, Dalibor. 2013. "What Are the Lessons from Post-Communist Transitions?" *Economic Affairs* 33, no. 1 (February): 65–78.

Spence, Michael. 2012. *The Next Convergence*. New York: Picador.

Vaughan, Sarah. 2011. "Revolutionary Democratic State-Building: Party, State and People in the EPRDF's Ethiopia." *Journal of Eastern African Studies* 5, no. 4: 619–40.

Vaughan, Sarah, and Mesfin Gebremichael. 2011. "Rethinking Business and Politics in Ethiopia: The Role of EFFORT, the Endowment Fund for the Rehabilitation of Tigray." Africa Power and Politics Programme Research Report 2. London: Overseas Development Institute.

World Bank. 2015a. *Ethiopia Poverty Assessment 2014*. Washington, DC: WBG.

———. 2015b. *SME Finance in Ethiopia: Addressing the Missing Middle Challenge*. Washington, DC: WBG.

———. 2015c. *4th Ethiopia Update: Overcoming Constraints in the Manufacturing Sector.* Washington, DC: WBG.

———. 2017. *Country Partnership Framework for the Federal Democratic Republic of Ethiopia.* Washington, DC: WBG.

———. 2018. *Poverty and Shared Prosperity 2018: Piecing Together the Poverty Puzzle.* Washington, DC: WBG.

Zenawi, Meles. 2012. "States and Markets: Neoliberal Limitations and the Case for a Developmental State." In *Good Growth and Governance in Africa: Rethinking Development Strategies,* edited by Akbar Noman, Kwesi Botchwey, Howard Stein, and Joseph E. Stiglitz. Oxford: Oxford University Press.

*Based on an invited paper for the *Ethiopia Forum*, sponsored by the African Studies Center of Michigan State University, April 2019. I am grateful to the participants and an anonymous referee for very constructive comments and suggestions.

2.3 The Political Economy of Land Policy in Ethiopia

Evolving Rationales and Challenges of State Ownership

Tom Lavers

INTRODUCTION

Land and property rights are foundational elements of economic theories of development. This is true of both new institutional economics and its concern with private property rights as the foundation of a market economy (Demsetz 1967; North 1990) and heterodox theories that highlight how the reallocation of property rights was an important capability of the East Asian developmental states (Chang 2009; Guan 2005; Kay 2002; Khan 2005). Yet the control of land has also always been a key feature of political authority as well as a vital economic and social resource in Ethiopia (Bruce 1976; Rahmato 2009; Hoben 1973) as elsewhere (Boone 2014; Lund 2008). Not only is land a key economic resource that is subject to competition over ownership and control, but competition for authority over land raises vital questions regarding the nature of state-society relations, citizenship, and belonging (Boone 2007, 2014).

This chapter argues that land has been central both to the economic models pursued under the EPRDF since 1991, playing distinct roles in Agricultural Development Led Industrialization (ADLI) and the "developmental state", and to the Front's political strategy for retaining power. Yet the limitations of land policy have been propelled to the forefront of political debates in the country as a result of the Oromo protests from 2014 to 2018 that, among many other factors, were motivated by high rates of landlessness and unemployment, the minimal compensation received by smallholders displaced by new investments, rapid urban expansion, and displacement of smallholders. While the reform process pursued in the last year has yet to confront the land question, the central political importance of these issues, growing interethnic conflict over land, and the economic reform process underway are likely to necessitate confronting this complex issue in the near future.

The political economy of land in Ethiopia is a multifaceted and complex topic and one that is closely related to a broad range of policy areas, including agricultural policy, migration, water resources, and urban development. Given the space constraints, this chapter can do no more than provide a brief reference to these related policy areas. Instead, this chapter attempts to provide a broad overview of the dynamics that have led to a series of interrelated challenges currently facing land policy and administration. The chapter then discusses some of the possible directions of change to the land policy, briefly assessing both their potential to address the key political challenges that currently exist as well as the political challenges such reform efforts would face. Unfortunately, there are no easy solutions. Any reform to this deeply political policy area would provoke considerable resistance and involve trade-offs. Nonetheless, the reality is that fast-moving events on the ground—both illegal land transactions and conflict and displacement—are rapidly running ahead of existing laws, highlighting the costs of inaction.

Following this introduction, the chapter briefly sets out the changing narratives used by the EPRDF to justify the policy of state land ownership, from the original Derg and TPLF land reforms to the ADLI strategy and then the "developmental state" under the EPRDF. The following section then outlines the key challenges facing land policy currently. The final section considers possible policy directions and the political ramifications of these.

CHANGING DEVELOPMENT MODELS AND SHIFTING NARRATIVES AROUND LAND IN THE EPRDF ERA

Land was originally nationalized by the Derg in 1975 under the slogan of "land to the tiller," while several of the insurgencies fighting the Derg, including the TPLF, carried out their own land redistribution programs based on similar rationales, as well as to consolidate their own political support (Berhe 2008; Chiari 2004; Young 1997). On coming to power in 1991, the EPRDF maintained and constitutionally enshrined the principle of state ownership and has sought to justify state land ownership in many different ways over the years, with the emphasis on different objectives and roles shifting over time (Lavers 2019a). In many ways, these rationales build on the socialist "land to the tiller" narrative but also go beyond this regarding the specific social, economic, and political roles land was expected to play in the national development strategy and politics.

First, state ownership was justified as a means of protecting smallholder farmers from displacement by market forces and thereby guaranteeing them access to an agricultural livelihood through the constitutional right to land free of charge. As Prime Minister Meles noted on several occasions, land was the only "social security" available to smallholders (Meles, cited in Marcus 1995); without the protection of state ownership, smallholders would risk displacement by market forces. Second, land policy was explicitly justified as a means of limiting class differentiation, building on the original "land to the tiller" narrative. Meles specifically questioned the idea common to new institutional property rights theory that the most efficient farmers would necessarily accumulate land, instead arguing that a land market would be subject to rent seeking (*Reporter*, "Interview—'I Have Never Heard of Any Convincing Reason as to Why We Should Privatize Land,'" May 3, 2000). Of particular concern was the specter of a return to something like the *neftegna-gebbar* system in which exploitative economic relations between landlords and tenants were overlaid on interethnic divisions. Third, and related to the previous rationale, was the use of state ownership as a means of allocating factors of production in line with the state's development strategy. ADLI built on the idea of the inverse relationship (Lipton 1993) of smallholders being more productive in their use of land than large-scale farmers—with state ownership as a means of ensuring that land (and, as a result, labor also) was directed to the most productive use: labor-intensive smallholder agriculture (MoFED 2003; TGE 1993, 1994). The aim of ADLI was to raise agricultural productivity through the supply of technologies such as improved seeds, fertilizer, and irrigation that raised productivity but did not replace labor, generating an agricultural surplus that could then be used to finance industrialization. While industrialization and urbanization were undeniably the focus of ADLI, in the short-term urban migration was discouraged, since it constituted a potential source of "economic, political and social instabilities" (MoFED 2002, 56). This brings us to the last main justification for state ownership: by limiting the land market and preventing displacement, the land policy encourages "farmers to remain on their land, thereby avoiding unproductive and potentially harmful labor mobility" that "may even be detrimental to peace and stability" (MoFED 2003, 27). This works to keep people in rural areas until such time as sufficient urban jobs are created for them to go to, primarily as a result of industrial expansion.

With respect to rural land, these various narratives were operationalized in constitutional provisions and a land policy that prohibited land sales, constrained land rental, and—according to the common understanding at the time—prevented the mortgaging of land, which could otherwise lead to default and displacement. The urban land governance system, though technically within the same constitutional constraints of state ownership, represents a very different land tenure system to that in rural areas. The urban leasehold system was originally introduced in the 1990s but revised and expanded in the 2011 proclamation (FDRE 2011). To a considerable degree, urban land administration approximates a market in land, with leaseholders allowed to borrow against and sell their leasehold, albeit that regional or city administrations retain significant powers to allocate land to priority uses, including infrastructure, industry, and housing, as well as to cancel leases where the leaseholder fails to develop it as intended.

What was described by the EPRDF leadership as a series of "armageddons"[1] in the early-to-mid-2000s gradually resulted in a reorientation of the development strategy, with ADLI evolving into the "developmental state" model through the PASDEP, GTP1, and GTP2 development strategies. These crises included the 2001 split in the TPLF leadership (Medhane and Young 2003; Paulos 2003), the 2002–3 food crisis (Lavers 2019b), and the 2005 electoral crisis, and they had direct implications for rural land tenure and the rationales used to justify state ownership. Alongside these changing development priorities, Ethiopia is also undergoing a major demographic shift with a rapidly growing population and, in particular, a large and rapidly growing youth population.

While consistent with ADLI in focusing on industrialization, promoting economic linkages between agriculture and emerging industry, and expanding the value chain within Ethiopia, the "developmental state" agenda, in many ways, constituted a marked shift from ADLI. New economic priority sectors include a range of agricultural investments, industrial parks, and a focus on high-potential smallholders, rather than a scale-neutral approach that characterized ADLI (MoARD 2010; MoFED 2005, 2010). Alongside these high-profile investments, analysis suggests that the main driver of economic growth to date has actually been massive public-debt-financed infrastructure investment in the form of roads, railways, and dams and an urban construction boom, particularly in Addis Ababa and the main regional cities (Moller and Wacker 2017).

The "developmental state" thereby has a number of important implications for land policy and the narratives used to justify it. First, the idea that land is a form of safety net and a mechanism of guaranteeing farmers a livelihood has been rapidly undermined by demographic changes, as well as coming into tension with the prioritization of new key economic sectors. With the exception of Amhara in 1997 (Ege 2002), there has been no land redistribution in most of Ethiopia since the late 1980s. The result is that more than a generation of Ethiopians living in rural areas have had no access to land through redistribution. Recent case studies emphasize the severity of land shortages (Rahmato 2018). At a national level, data are scarce and problematic,[2] but a rough calculation would suggest that somewhere in the region of 80 percent of the current Ethiopian population would have been under eighteen years old and thereby ineligible for land through redistribution in the late 1980s.[3] In addition to demographic shifts, the promotion of high-value horticultural investments in the Rift Valley and near-major regional cities, the promotion of industrial parks, massive infrastructure expansion, and support for rapid urban expansion have all entailed the displacement of smallholders—the central constituency under ADLI—to make way for alternate land users (Lavers 2012a, 2012b), further undermining the narrative of land as a safety net.

Second, the "developmental state" has involved a change in focus within the agricultural sector, from broad-based support to all smallholder farmers to focusing agricultural inputs and the support of the extension system on the most high-potential areas and high-potential farmers within those areas, while these farmers were subsequently enrolled as "model" farmers (Lavers 2013b; Lefort 2012). This change in emphasis has been mirrored with respect to changes to land tenure. Federal and regional land proclamations since 2000 have made redistribution all but an impossibility; first-level land certification was carried out during the 2000s with the aim of increasing tenure security and raising investment in agricultural production, and second-level certification is now underway[4]; Amhara regional state has led the way by first removing all restrictions on land rental (ANRS 2006), with the explicit aim of enabling effective farmers to rent in more land, while the less productive were expected to leave agriculture. More recently, Amhara has gone further in passing a proclamation that explicitly permits mortgaging of land to increase resources for investing in production (ANRS 2017),[5] while draft proclamations currently under consideration propose to follow suit both within the federal government and other regional administrations.

The result is that the previous rationales for state land ownership in the ADLI era are increasingly unjustifiable: state land ownership is no longer a means of guaranteeing a livelihood to more than a small proportion of the rural population; agricultural policy and land tenure are increasingly focused on promoting class differentiation, rather than limiting it. While state land ownership no doubt continues to limit further displacement and migration to a degree, it offers no means of keeping vast numbers of landless youth and adults in rural areas. This leaves one main justification for state ownership in the "developmental state" era that has increased greatly in significance: the use of state ownership as a means of allocating factors of production in line with state-defined development priorities— or, to echo the terminology of Ethiopia's "developmental state," a means of centralizing the state allocation of rents. Indeed, state ownership of land and control of the financial sector are perhaps the two most important levers of the Ethiopian "developmental state" model, providing the state with extensive powers to allocate land, capital, and, consequently, labor to priority purposes. An inherent requirement of this economic role is the current system for handling displacement and compensation. Current land laws provide the state with sweeping powers to expropriate land for any undefined "public purpose" (FDRE 2005, para. 3) and with minimal compensation that not only minimizes the cost to the state of expropriation but also constitutes a source of significant revenues, with the state receiving rents from investors and urban leasehold auctions that are far in excess of the minimal compensation payments made to displaced smallholders.[6]

State land ownership and, consequently, the discussion thus far has focused primarily on the highland areas where the majority of the Ethiopian population resides. The lowland periphery presents a quite distinct set of issues with respect to land tenure. Here, state ownership has always been a more problematic fit for livelihoods based on mobility, whether differing forms of agropastoralism—particularly in Afar, Somali, and southern Oromia and SNNPR—or flood-retreat agriculture and shifting cultivation in parts of SNNPR, Gambella, and Benishangul-Gumuz. Within national development strategies, the main emphasis has been to bring these populations in line with highland areas through large-scale settlement programs (MoFA 2008; MoFED 2003) while also prioritizing state infrastructural investments—particularly during the "developmental state" era—such as dams and private and state investments in large-scale commercial agriculture (Kefale and Gebresenbet 2014; Rahmato 2014; Kamski 2016; Lavers 2012b). Alongside the expansion of smallholder farmers from the highlands, the result for many living in these areas has been a growing challenge of limited access to land and water.

In addition to the distinct roles that land tenure was intended to play within the evolving development strategy, land tenure is also inherently linked to federalism and the "national question." The federal system was established as a means of providing self-determination for Ethiopia's nations, nationalities, and peoples, and land administration is one of the key responsibilities devolved to regional states. As such, federalism offers the possibility of ethnolinguistically defined regional governments administering key resources, including land, in their own interest. Yet federalism raises a range of important questions regarding the role of ethnicity in land administration. First, equating territory with distinct ethnolinguistic groups, even providing ethnic groups with the right to secession, implies a clear hierarchy between ethnic insiders—members of the ethnic group around which the region is defined—and outsiders, who belong to an ethnic group with a region or other administrative jurisdiction elsewhere in the country. As argued by Andreas Eshete,

> To confer the right to secession on national communities is to grant that a regional state's collective property rights take priority over the property rights of outsiders—nonmembers and federal government—in the region. What is now held by nonmembers can be legitimately taken by a seceding state. (2003, 21)

While the constitution and land proclamations emphasize Ethiopian citizenship and class—a willingness to farm the land—as the main criteria for accessing land, federalism provides a somewhat contradictory legal interpretation (Van der Beken 2009). Perhaps even more importantly, an extreme interpretation of federalism—that ethnolinguistic regions belong to the dominant ethnic group within them and therefore ethnic insiders have stronger claims to land than ethnic outsiders—remains an important narrative within public and, increasingly, political discourse (Lavers 2018). This narrative is then compounded by the institutional incentives built into the federal system. Comparative research in sub-Saharan Africa has clearly shown that land tenure regimes shape the form that conflict over land takes in a context of land shortages (Boone 2014). In the context of widespread land shortages and the narrative of the federal system that implies differentiation between the citizenship rights of ethnic insiders and outsiders, the likely result will be conflict along ethnic lines. Moreover, the reliance on referenda and "settlement patterns" as constitutional mechanisms for altering regional boundaries, whether in creating new regional states or altering the boundaries of existing ones (FDRE 1994, para. 47), provides incentives for interethnic violence and even ethnic cleansing to ensure that key votes are won. The result is that interethnic conflict over land and territorial boundaries has been a common theme under federalism (Kefale 2010, 2013; Adugna 2011; Tafesse 2007), with some arguing that this is the main source of conflicts in the country (Abbink 2006).

THE CURRENT CHALLENGES FACING LAND POLICY AND ADMINISTRATION

The events of recent years—both the protests beginning in Oromia in 2014 and spreading across the region and elsewhere in 2016–18, and the widespread outbreak of intercommunal violence and displacement in the last year or more—have brought underlying challenges facing the land tenure regime to the forefront of political debate. Though the political reforms launched in the last year have not yet sought to tackle the land issue, it is inevitable that the land question will arise on the reform agenda before long, given the central political and economic significance of land. At present, past approaches to land administration, shifting development strategies, and demographic changes have resulted in four daunting and interrelated challenges facing land policy, alongside the long-standing issue of how to raise agricultural productivity and what role land tenure should play.

The first challenge is that, despite constitutional provisions that provide peasants with the right to land (FDRE 1994, para. 40), land shortages across the country are widespread. As noted above, data on landlessness are extremely limited. The absence of redistribution for the last thirty years in most parts of the country, and for some twenty years in Amhara, means that many adults lack access to land except through the generosity of their parents or through limited rental markets. Recent studies have found that 38 percent of the population in three kebeles in Oromia lacked landholdings of their own (Adugna 2018), while nearly 25 percent in three kebeles of SNNPR (Abebe and Shanko 2018) and a total of 229,445 people in Tigray (Girme, Gebreogziabhert, and Gebru 2018) experienced the same. Even for those who do have access to land, through their own land or through rental, average landholdings have been in long-term decline, with the result that many have access to only very small "starvation plots" (Rahmato 1994, 37). Many landholders are forced to supplement their meager farm income with off-farm economic activities and support from the Productive Safety Net Program (PSNP) and/or humanitarian relief. The result has been growing landlessness and growing numbers of people with access to insufficient land to be able to support their families, resulting in increasing flows of urban migrants and the continuation of rural food insecurity (Lavers 2013a, 2019b).

The second challenge relates to the current system for expropriation and "compensation." This particularly concerns the rationale within the "developmental state" model of using state land ownership as a means of centralizing rents and allocating factors of production to priority economic sectors. For the "developmental state" to continue allocating land to priority economic sectors—whether agricultural investments, industrial parks, infrastructure expansion, and, as discussed in more detail below, urban expansion—modest rates of compensation are a necessity since this greatly reduces the costs of such investments. Yet low rates of compensation are a source of enormous and understandable resentment and were a notable flashpoint in the Oromo protests of recent years (Davison 2016). Displaced farmers have frequently found themselves impoverished as a result of the minimal compensation received, the high rates of inflation that quickly render such payments meaningless, and the challenges of finding suitable employment opportunities, especially given limited skills. This is regardless of whether or not the displaced farmers mismanage their payments, as often claimed by local government officials. Moreover, rural communities are well aware that the state is subsequently leasing out land to investors at rates that far exceed the minimal compensation paid to the original landholders, greatly enhancing their resentment.

The third and closely related challenge is that of urban expansion. Despite falling under the same constitutional provisions regarding state ownership, the present urban and rural tenure regimes differ markedly. While in rural areas land sales are prohibited, rental transactions are restricted and land cannot be used for collateral,[7] the urban leasehold system approximates a land market through the sale of leaseholds and rental and the right to use leaseholds as collateral to obtain credit. The result in peri-urban areas across towns and cities throughout the country is that on one side of the urban administrative boundary, under the rural administration, land is formally valueless since it cannot be bought and sold, while on the other side, under the urban administration, land can be worth an enormous amount of money. At the extreme of Addis Ababa, some land can be of an equivalent value to the most expensive cities in the world (Goodfellow 2017). Naturally, this issue is brought to the fore in the process of urban expansion that is taking place rapidly in towns and cities across the country, not least as a result of the growing rural landlessness discussed above. Urban expansion entails the rezoning of land from the rural administration to the urban one and, in the process, creating enormous value within the urban land market at the expense of displaced rural landholders, who receive minimal financial compensation and a small plot of land.

It is something of an irony of state ownership that, despite being justified under the "developmental state" narrative as a means of centralizing rents and limiting rent seeking, the land policy, and specifically the urban-rural division, has become one of the principal sources of rent seeking in the country. The enormous amounts of money involved have inevitably led to corruption in the process.[8] The challenge here is not merely that urban and rural areas have different tenure systems but that these different tenure systems and the extreme difference in land value that results are compounded by distinct rural and urban land administrations, who frequently fail to coordinate their activities and, at times, deliberately undermine one another, and the minimal compensation payments, which can be several orders of magnitude smaller than the land prices available through illegal land sales. To take the example of Adama, a series of expropriations over several years for urban expansion—the Addis Ababa–Adama Expressway, the Addis Ababa–Djibouti Railway, and the Adama Industrial Park—have been subject to compensation payments rising over time from 8 to 53 birr per square meter. In contrast, respondents suggest that land can be sold on the illegal land market for up to 1,000 birr per square meter. It can hardly be a surprise that many landholders in peri-urban areas are rushing to sell land as fast as they can before the state arrives.

The fourth challenge concerns the politicization of ethnicity and territory, as manifested in widespread intercommunal conflicts across Ethiopia, with land and territory frequently among the central issues at stake. In part, this explosion of conflicts relates to the weakening of central control that characterized EPRDF rule until 2012 and the emergence of political competition that has reopened suppressed debates and pent-up tensions across the country. In a context of extreme land shortages and a political system that provides incentives to mobilize along ethnic lines, the explosion of conflicts in recent years has frequently entailed attempts to displace supposed "ethnic outsiders" and to claim land for ethnic "insiders," with ethno-political leaders in many cases employing these divisive narratives as part of conflicts such as those along the Oromo-Somali border, between the Gedeo and Guji Oromo, the border between Wellega and Benishangul-Gumuz, and in Hawassa and other parts of Sidama. The demands for referenda on the creation of separate states for many of the ethnic groups in SNNPR are, furthermore, likely to exacerbate interethnic tensions, providing incentives to remove ethnic outsiders with referenda in danger of becoming ethnic headcounts. While these challenges are by no means exclusive to Oromia, the region does face certain particular challenges in that many towns and cities in Oromia have large non-Oromo populations as a result of historical legacies, while the classification of Addis Ababa as a separate city administration with special status provokes further resentment among many Oromo. The result is that urban expansion across Oromia has a particular interethnic dimension that is less common elsewhere, while the case of the expansion of Addis Ababa overlays the extreme challenges associated with massive urban expansion in the primate city onto the politically sensitive contradictions of the federal system.

Finally, it should be noted that, while it is perhaps not the most immediately pressing issue related to land, low agricultural productivity and limited commercialization remain important and long-standing challenges. For many observers, state land ownership constitutes a major obstacle by impeding a vibrant land market and limiting incentives to make long-term investments in increased productivity (Ali, Dercon, and Gautam 2011; Deininger and Jin 2006; Rahmato 2009). Official statistics show significant increases in agricultural productivity over the past two decades. Even if these are accepted as accurate,[9] there remains considerable potential for further progress. Indeed, this is exactly the motivation behind ongoing large-scale land registration programs, which aim to facilitate land rental markets and improve investment incentives.

THE POLITICAL CHALLENGE AHEAD: POSSIBLE DIRECTIONS FOR REFORM

There are, unfortunately, no easy solutions to the complex challenges described above. Not only is land policy unable and unsuited to resolving these problems on its own but any change to land policy would be a deeply contentious and political process. Nonetheless, what appears to be something of a change in direction regarding the economic development strategy, with a greater emphasis on markets rather than the state as the primary engine of growth, is likely to have implications for land tenure also. If the government does indeed act upon and extend recent announcements related to the privatization of state enterprises and liberalization of the economy, the liberalization of land tenure is likely to come onto the policy agenda also. Moreover, it seems highly likely that some donors, economic observers, and political parties, many of whom have pushed for land privatization in the past, will seize the moment to do so again. This section will briefly summarize some of the possible options open to the new administration, their potential to address the four challenges identified above—landlessness, inadequate compensation, urban expansion, and the ethno-politicization of land—and the political ramifications of such proposals.

The first option open to government is to continue more or less with the current direction of travel. Currently there are three relevant draft proclamations related to land administration under consideration by the federal government—a revised rural land proclamation, the revised compensation proclamation, and the revised urban lease proclamation. To the author's knowledge,[10] the proposed revisions constitute a relatively modest evolution from the existing proclamations. As discussed above, the rural land proclamation essentially brings the federal proclamation in line with reforms already undertaken in Amhara, the main changes being to remove long-standing restrictions on rental in order to facilitate a more vibrant land rental market and to explicitly enable the mortgaging of land as a means of accessing credit. These proposed reforms are closely linked to an ongoing, large-scale, second-stage land certification program and various agricultural policies.[11] The aim of these combined initiatives is to promote agricultural intensification, commercialization, and a vibrant land rental market.

In principle, agricultural intensification could enable more people to live off the land, and a land rental market could alleviate landlessness to a degree, with some landless households able to access land through rental. It is far from clear, however, that this would actually materialize in practice. One of the main justifications of the property rights theories underpinning these reforms is to promote land consolidation, since a market in land offers the most effective farmers a means of obtaining more land to expand their production, while the less effective farmers will be unable to compete and will gradually leave agriculture (Demsetz 1967; Joireman 2000; North 1990). A more critical interpretation would be that the wealthiest farmers (not necessarily the most effective) will accumulate land through market processes, while farmers (including some highly effective ones) who face external shocks (e.g., from weather or disease) will be forced to rent out land to make ends meet and will lose control of their landholdings (Chang 2009). In either case, the less well-off farmers—whether through limited access to land, agricultural labour (particularly female-headed households), oxen, and credit—are likely to gradually move out of agriculture. As such, proposed changes may contribute to increased productivity to a degree (though there is currently limited evidence for this) but at the likely cost of adding to the problem of landlessness.

Meanwhile, the draft compensation proclamation entails revising the calculation of compensation payments to displaced landholders and enhancing the provisions in place to rehabilitate them and their livelihoods afterwards. In terms of monetary compensation, the envisaged changes are modest. The present system that pays ten times the *average* annual harvest is to be adapted to pay fifteen times the *maximum* annual harvest from the past three years. While such a change, if approved, would result in an increase of 50 percent or more from current payments, it would do little to close the gap between compensation payments and the prices available for illegal land sales, which, as noted above, can be twenty times higher.[12] Ultimately, the reforms currently under discussion, alongside plans for agricultural commercialization, have the potential to raise agricultural productivity but would likely make landlessness worse, would barely make a dent in the problems of limited compensation and urban expansion, and would do nothing to address the politicization of ethnicity and land.

The original land reforms undertaken by the Derg, TPLF and other groups envisaged regular land redistributions as a key means of adapting landholdings to a changing population.[13] Land redistribution gradually fell out of favor as a result of the political upheaval induced by the 1997 Amhara redistribution (Ege 1997, 2002), arguments from neoclassical economists that the possibility of redistribution threatens tenure security and investment incentives and the growing shortage of land. Recent fieldwork in 2018 in rural areas of Amhara and Oromia suggests that for some young landless people, redistribution—either within smallholder communities or from agricultural investors to the landless—still holds considerable promise and a solution to their shortage of land and employment opportunities.[14] As argued above, however, state land ownership has long outlived its use as a safety net and a guarantee of land to rural households. As such, the land policy is poorly situated to address the interrelated challenges of land shortages, landlessness, and unemployment. Any move to return to land redistribution would be hugely politically contentious—as it was in Amhara in 1997, leading to intergenerational conflicts—and would damage commercially oriented smallholders while leading to widespread impoverishment, as has long been argued by Rahmato (1994, 1997, 2003). Given the shortage of available land, even recent moves in some regions to dispossess underperforming agricultural investors and return land to groups of landless youths cannot come close to addressing the needs of the vast number of young people who currently have no access to land. Over the past decade or more, local governments have sought to promote group activities by landless youths on communal land, engaging in beekeeping, forestry, and collective agriculture. Redistributing investment land appears to be a continuation of such efforts, which have been moderately successful at best, largely as a result of the shortage of available land. Land redistribution provides no more than a token of acknowledgement to landless youths, rather than any realistic solution to their problems.

For some opposition parties, economists, and donor agencies, state ownership has long been seen as a cause of low productivity in the agricultural sector, with privatization as the solution (Gebremedhin and Berhanu 2005; Nega, Adenew, and Gebreselassie 2002; Nega, Adenew, and Gebreselassie 2003). As noted above, the question of land privatization is likely to arise once again as part of the economic reform process and the campaigns for the 2020 elections. Yet privatization remains a hugely contentious issue that would provoke serious political opposition both within the EPRDF and many groups outside it. Moreover, it seems unlikely that a proposal to privatize land would meet the required thresholds to pass a necessary constitutional amendment, albeit that it might gain consideration as part of a broader constitutional revision that has been mooted in some quarters.

The argument in favor of privatization is that private property rights enhance tenure security and, thereby, incentives to invest in increased production; promote market exchange and accumulation of land by the most productive users; and enable landowners to use their land as collateral to access credit (De Soto 2001; Demsetz 1967). Privatization, therefore, rests on the same reasoning as recent tenure reforms in Amhara and proposed at the federal level. While the Amhara proclamation seeks to enhance tenure security through second-level certification, promote land rental markets, and facilitate access to credit, privatization would seek to strengthen these mechanisms through private property and land sales. While theoretically plausible, research across sub-Saharan Africa has repeatedly called this logic into question. Evidence is far from clear as to whether privatization actually enhances tenure security and investment or whether markets in land necessarily lead to more efficient allocation of resources, and studies repeatedly question the idea that privatization will improve access to credit

(Gilbert 2002; Kingwill et al. 2006; Lund 2000; Musembi 2007). Indeed, even the World Bank has moved away from advocating privatization as its default recommendation, acknowledging the importance of local contexts and that other tenure systems can provide the tenure security required to underpin investment (Deininger and Binswanger 1999).

In terms of the challenges outlined in the previous section, moreover, land privatization offers little potential to resolve the problems and may well make some of them worse. Certainly, privatization would offer no solution to the challenge of landlessness. Indeed, the explicit objective of privatization would be to promote land consolidation by the most effective farmers and, as a necessary corollary, the exit from agriculture of weaker farmers: privatization would exacerbate landlessness. Private property would presumably require the state and investors to pay market rates to smallholders to access land. As such, privatization would likely go some way to addressing the concerns of those threatened with expropriation—they would receive meaningful compensation. Moreover, a private market in land would allow the possibility that expropriated farmers could use the compensation they receive to buy land elsewhere, something that is not currently possible under state ownership. However, as a result, privatization would necessarily constrain the "developmental state" agenda, massively increasing the costs of expropriation for infrastructure development or expansion of existing industrial parks. It is also quite possible that privatization could limit demand for land from investors, since one of the main investment incentives provided by the government to attract investors to date has been through access to cheap land (Lavers 2012a). With respect to urban expansion, privatization would bring compatibility between rural and urban tenure systems and would thereby limit many of the opportunities for corruption and speculation in peri-urban areas. A private land market would also greatly facilitate urban expansion in many towns and cities, at the significant risk of large-scale displacement of rural landholders. It would also risk inflaming ethnic tensions, particularly in the areas surrounding Addis Ababa but also towns and cities across Oromia as ethnic outsiders acquired land through private markets.

Privatization would, therefore, be practically difficult to achieve and would bring very significant political and socioeconomic risks in exchange for highly uncertain economic benefits. A slightly more modest proposal that limits some of these risks to a degree would be to extend a leasehold system, similar to that already in place in urban areas, to rural areas as a whole or, perhaps, a broad area around major towns and cities. This leasehold system would have the advantage that it is consistent with the constitution—since such a system already exists in urban areas—and would bring greater continuity between rural and urban tenure systems that would limit corruption and speculation related to urban expansion. The leasehold system also offers the benefit of combining an increased role for land markets, reflecting the de facto situation on the ground in many peri-urban areas while retaining significant powers for state intervention to reallocate land and to ensure that it is used productively, as has already happened in urban administrations. Yet, a leasehold system would also face challenges: the promotion of a land market would likely exacerbate the problem of landlessness while facilitating urban expansion and, potentially, thereby feeding interethnic tensions in the surrounds of Addis Ababa and other towns and cities in Oromia.

The other main possibility related to the tenure system is to retain state ownership but to further revise the system for expropriation and compensation and to revisit the government structures for land administration. As noted above, the issue of minimal compensation in cases of expropriation has become a major issue in the context of the "developmental state" agenda and the emphasis on reallocating land to priority economic sectors. This is particularly problematic with respect to urban expansion in which the distinct urban and rural tenure systems, the minimal compensation payments, and the divided rural and urban land administrations combine to create the current problems. On the one hand, therefore, revisiting the compensation proclamation to significantly increase payments to expropriated landholders, closing much of the gap with the informal land market, would significantly reduce grievances and the incentives for corruption and speculation with respect to urban expansion. On the other hand, another possibility (that could be complementary but equally could be undertaken separately) would be to integrate rural and urban land administrations, creating a Federal Ministry of Land and Regional Land Bureau. At present, coordination between rural and urban administrations is frequently poor, and at points there is evidence of each administration intentionally undermining the other, with urban administrations expanding onto prime agricultural land while rural administrations approve developments that clash with urban expansion plans. An integrated land administration would offer the possibility of improved land administration and planning. It is important to note that Oromia is currently experimenting with an integrated regional administration but also that the region tried and failed to integrate rural and urban administrations back in 2010. Taking such a proposal forward to the federal level and to other regions would require careful planning and study. By creating an integrated land administration and revising the compensation system to provide meaningful compensation to displaced households and to limit the incentive to engage in illegal sales, such reforms could address the challenges presented by urban expansion and infrastructure development. Unlike the creation of a private land market (through either privatization or an extended leasehold system) however, an integrated administration and improved compensation would also retain the state's ability to plan urban expansion, including taking into account local political dynamics and sensitivities related to ethnicity. Yet such changes would be costly, massively increasing the cost of urban expansion and infrastructure development and removing one of the principal tools of the developmental state to direct the economy.[15]

As should be obvious from the discussion in this section, land policy alone cannot solve the interrelated challenges of landlessness and unemployment. Agricultural intensification could mitigate current challenges by enabling more people to earn a living from the land (although intensification could also lead to consolidation and exacerbate current land shortages). However, the only plausible long-run solution to rural landlessness lies in off-farm employment. Employment creation, alongside rising educational attainment and consequently rising aspirations of new entrants into the labor market, is, of course, another central challenge facing the government. While it is beyond the scope of this chapter, it is clear that limited employment creation is by no means an Ethiopia-specific problem and that there is no magic bullet in the form of industrialization or any other sectoral priority. Rather, the burden of employment creation will have to rely on employment in a combination of agriculture, the rural nonfarm economy, a growing industrial sector, and the service sector.

A final issue worthy of brief discussion is federalism and the politicization of ethnicity. There would appear to be no political possibility at this point that the current federal system could be replaced by a central state structure or that regional borders could be redrawn to remove their ethnic association. While it is not a plausible policy option, it should be reiterated, however, that the current federal system provides strong incentives for political mobilization along ethnic lines and consequently the refraction of conflicts and tensions through the lens of ethnicity. This dynamic is only likely to strengthen in the context of multiparty politics and competition between polarized political groups. At the time of writing, estimates suggest that more than two million Ethiopians are currently displaced by conflicts. While not all of these can be attributed to land, land is clearly among the central issues of contention in many instances. Political competition, including with significant ethno-nationalist movements in all the main regions and growing autonomy for regional administrations, holds very significant risks in terms of further rounds of interethnic violence and displacement. The room for maneuver and, perhaps, desire for legal changes to depoliticize ethnicity may be limited, consequently placing a great emphasis on political leaders at the federal and regional levels to provide stability and desist from inflammatory rhetoric.

There are undoubtedly benefits to incremental reform that avoid confronting the thorny political challenges associated with more substantive changes. However, the reality is that inaction means that the current situation is running ahead of the legal provisions on the land proclamation and the political challenges they entail are escalating. In many parts of the country, land in peri-urban areas and in the vicinity of expanding infrastructure such as roads is, de facto, privatized. Landholders facing the risk of expropriation and impoverishment as a result of minimal compensation payments are rushing to sell their land to make as much money as they can before the state arrives. Meanwhile, land shortages, landlessness, and unemployment are widespread, while federalism and the politicization of ethnicity contribute to conflict and displacement.

CONCLUSIONS

This chapter has argued that land tenure has been a central feature of both the EPRDF's economic development strategies and a source of political authority over the last three decades. Yet, the roles envisaged for land and the narratives used to justify state ownership have shifted considerably over time. The original land reforms conducted by the Derg, TPLF, and other groups were justified under the slogan of "land to the tiller." Yet, on coming to national power, the EPRDF provided an extended rationale for state ownership as a central part of ADLI, with land expected to protect smallholders against displacement by market forces, limit class differentiation, allocate land, labor, and capital to their most productive uses, and slow down the pace of urban migration in the interests of political stability. It is a central contention of this chapter that these multiple roles for land under ADLI have gradually given way to a dominant concern under the "developmental state," using state control of land (and finance) as a key mechanism of allocating factors of production in line with state-defined economic priorities. Indeed, the capacity of land policy to guarantee a livelihood to the rural population has long been exhausted, current policy focuses on promoting, rather than preventing, differentiation within the agricultural sector, and land tenure now provides only a limited break on urban migration.

The limitations of land as a policy tool—alongside the limited creation of employment, demographic changes, and the incentives of federalism—have resulted in a series of interrelated challenges facing land policy, namely high rates of landlessness and unemployment, resentment at the minimal compensation paid to smallholders displaced by the priority projects of the "developmental state," rapid urban expansion and displacement of rural populations, and growing levels of interethnic conflicts over land and territory. As a consequence, the land question is once again of central concern both as a result of the political pressure to address contemporary challenges and as part of the economic reform process initiated in the last year.

Yet, the chapter shows that there are no simple solutions to challenges associated with land. The past use of redistribution as a means of allocating landholdings to a changing population has long outlived its viability, while recent moves to return land from underperforming investors to young landless groups cannot be a solution for the vast majority of the landless. Likewise, however, calls for land privatization that are likely from some groups within Ethiopia and some development partners prioritize highly uncertain economic benefits at the risk of significant social and political challenges in terms of increased landlessness, unregulated urban expansion, and, potentially, interethnic tensions. Extending a version of the urban leasehold system to rural areas would rest on similar economic rationales but would face a lower political hurdle in terms of avoiding constitutional amendments and could combine a stronger role for markets while retaining significant powers for state intervention. Nonetheless, many of the challenges associated with privatization would likely apply also with a leasehold system.

Within the existing system of state ownership, there are plausible means by which reforms could address the challenges associated with compensation and urban expansion. Significant revision of the compensation system that closes the gap between compensation payments and the informal land market would significantly reduce opportunities for corruption and resentment against state-managed displacement, albeit at the cost of constraining the state's sweeping powers to reallocate land at present. In addition, restructuring land administration to integrate urban and rural authorities is an option that is worthy of careful consideration and study, given the potential to increase coordination with respect to urban expansion. The other issue of relevance to the political economy of land is the federal system. While federalism has problematic implications for the politicization of ethnicity and territory, it is, nonetheless, a political fact. There seems no plausible reversal of ethnolinguistic federalism in the near term and, indeed, the current tendency is towards greater regional autonomy. In the context of the centrifugal tendencies of federalism and the incentives that federalism provides for interethnic division and competition, great responsibility falls on the political leadership at the federal and regional levels to provide stability.

Ultimately, however, the challenges currently facing Ethiopia cannot be resolved through land policy and administration alone. Not only is land policy a rather blunt policy instrument, but as Ethiopia urbanizes and the economy transforms, the potential of land tenure as a distributional tool will diminish. Ultimately, the solution to the distributional challenges facing the country—mass landlessness and mass unemployment—can only be solved through increased off-farm employment creation within the rural nonfarm economy, the growing industrial sector, and, probably most important of all, the service sector, as well as enhanced social protection. Here Ethiopia is far from exceptional, with the challenge of employment creation and, particularly, creation of good jobs a common challenge facing developing and, increasingly, advanced economies also.

NOTES

1. See both the book by Bereket (2011) and an interview conducted with former deputy prime minister Addisu Legesse, Addis Ababa, October 2015.
2. There is no data on landlessness, and the lack of a census since 2007 means that demographic data are out of date and provide, at best, unreliable estimates of the scale of the problem.
3. In addition to land shortages, many studies highlight growing levels of land fragmentation as a major barrier to raising productivity and commercialization of agriculture (Nega, Adenu, and Gebreselassie 2002; Holden and Otsuka 2014). Nonetheless, recent work has disputed this dominant view, arguing that land fragmentation in Ethiopia may actually be compatible with higher levels of productivity and reduced food insecurity, since it enables households to diversify landholdings and mitigate risk (Knippenberg, Jolliffe, and Hoddinott 2018; Paul and Gīthīnji 2017).
4. First-level certification merely identified the neighbors to each plot of land and used physical markers such as trees and rocks; second-level certification attempts to map individual plots using GPS and other technologies.
5. For many years the widespread assumption was that mortgaging was unconstitutional, and this was certainly part of the narrative in the ADLI era. Subsequent legal discussion concluded that since there was no explicit prohibition of mortgaging, then it was legally possible.
6. Compensation is assessed at ten times the average annual yield for crops (FDRE 2007), but these pale in comparison to the resources generated by leases and auctions.
7. With the exception of Amhara as a result of a recent proclamation (ANRS 2017).
8. While land reform has been credited with limiting corruption and enabling the development of an effective bureaucracy in South Korea (You 2017) (one of Ethiopia's principal developmentalist role models), the reverse is taking place in Ethiopia, with state ownership

becoming a major source of corruption and inefficiency within the bureaucracy.

9. Some well-informed observers (Dorosh and Mellor 2013; Mellor 2014) do, though there is perhaps reason for some scepticism (Dercon and Hill 2009).

10. Having seen the draft rural land proclamation and from discussions with government officials of the key points under consideration in the draft being compensation and urban lease proclamations.

11. This includes a range of important recent initiatives to promote productivity increases, commercialization, and inter-sectoral linkages that are beyond the scope of the present chapter, including the Agricultural Growth Program, Agricultural Commercialization Clusters and the integrated agro-industrial parks.

12. The proposed compensation proclamation would also require the provision of training for displaced households to equip them with the necessary skills to find alternate employment or to set up small businesses. This is important but details remain scarce, while past experiences with top-down government training programs and defined livelihood pathways have not been uniformly positive (Di Nunzio 2015; Gebremariam 2017).

13. The other common approach being the resettlement programs conducted by the Derg and EPRDF from densely populated highlands to more sparsely populated lowlands. While EPRDF-era resettlement in the mid-2000s was less coercive and focused on intra-regional resettlement to reduce ethnic tensions, studies have found similar problems related to poor planning, hurried implementation, and a lack of meaningful participation from the resettlers (Hammond 2008; Pankhurst and Piguet 2009).

14. Interviews and focus groups conducted in West Gojjam, Amhara, and East Shewa and Arssi zones, Oromia, October 2018.

15. Admittedly, it may well be that the new administration intends to break from the "developmental state" model regardless.

REFERENCES

Abbink, J. 2006. "Ethnicity and Conflict Generation in Ethiopia: Some Problems and Prospects of Ethno-Regional Federalism." *Journal of Contemporary African Studies* 24, no. 3 (September): 389–413.

Abebe, Teketel, and Melessaw Shanko. 2018. "A Study of Selected Woredas in the Southern Region." In *Land, Landlessness and Poverty in Ethiopia: Research Findings from Four National Regional States*, edited by Dessalegn Rahmato. Addis Ababa: Forum for Social Studies.

Adugna, Fekadu. 2011. "Overlapping Nationalist Projects and Contested Spaces: The Oromo–Somali Borderlands in Southern Ethiopia." *Journal of Eastern African Studies* 5, no. 4: 773–87.

———. 2018. "Land, Landlessness and Rural Poverty in Oromia." In *Land, Landlessness and Poverty in Ethiopia: Research Findings from Four National Regional States*, edited by Dessalegn Rahmato. Addis Ababa: Forum for Social Studies.

Ali, Daniel Ayalew, Stefan Dercon, and Madhur Gautam. 2011. "Property Rights in a Very Poor Country: Tenure Insecurity and Investment in Ethiopia." *Agricultural Economics* 42, no. 1 (January): 75–86.

ANRS. 2006. "Amhara National Regional State (ANRS) – The Revised Rural Land Administration and Use Proclamation." *Zikre Hig* Proclamation 133/2006.

———. 2017. "The Revised Rural Land Administration and Use Determination Proclamation of the Amhara National Regional State." *Zikre Hig* Proclamation 252/2017.

Berhe, Aregawi. 2008. *A Political History of the Tigray People's Liberation Front (1975–1991): Revolt, Ideology, and Mobilisation in Ethiopia.* Los Angeles: Tsehai.

Boone, Catherine. 2007. "Property and Constitutional Order: Land Tenure Reform and the Future of the African State." *African Affairs* 106, no. 425 (October): 557–86.

———. 2014. *Property and Political Order in Africa: Land Rights and the Structure of Politics.* Cambridge: Cambridge University Press.

Bruce, John W. 1976. "Land Reform Planning and Indigenous Communal Tenures: A Case Study of the Tenure Chiguraf-Gwoses in Tigray, Ethiopia." PhD diss., University of Wisconsin–Madison.

Chang, Ha-Joon. 2009. "Rethinking Public Policy in Agriculture: Lessons from History, Distant and Recent." *Journal of Peasant Studies* 36, no. 3: 477–515.

Chiari, Gian Paolo. 2004. "Land Tenure and Livelihood Security in Tigray, Ethiopia". DPhil diss., Institute for Development Studies, University of Sussex.

Davison, William. 2016. "In Ethiopia, Anger over Corruption and Farmland Development Runs Deep." *Guardian*, January 18, 2016.

Deininger, Klaus, and Hans Binswanger. 1999. "The Evolution of the World Bank's Land Policy: Principles, Experience, and Future Challenges." *World Bank Research Observer* 14, no. 2 (August): 247–76.

Deininger, Klaus, and Songqing Jin. 2006. "Tenure Security and Land-Related Investment: Evidence from Ethiopia." *European Economic Review* 50, no. 5 (July): 1245–77.

Demsetz, Harold. 1967. "Toward a Theory of Property Rights." *American Economic Review* 57, no. 2 (May): 347–59.

Dercon, Stefan, and Ruth Vargas Hill. 2009. "Growth from Agriculture in Ethiopia: Identifying Key Constraints." Paper presented at Hilton Hotel, Addis Ababa: IFPRI.

De Soto, Hernando. 2001. *The Mystery of Capital: Why Capitalism Triumphs in the West and Fails Everywhere Else*. London: Black Swan.

Di Nunzio, Marco. 2015. "What Is the Alternative? Youth, Entrepreneurship and the Developmental State in Urban Ethiopia." *Development and Change* 46, no. 5 (September): 1179–1200.

Dorosh, Paul A., and John W. Mellor. 2013. "Why Agriculture Remains a Viable Means of Poverty Reduction in Sub-Saharan Africa: The Case of Ethiopia." *Development Policy Review* 31, no. 4 (July): 419–41.

Ege, Svein. 1997. "The Promised Land: The Amhara Land Redistribution of 1997." Trondheim University of Science and Technology Working Papers on Ethiopian Development 12.

———. 2002. "Peasant Participation in Land Reform: The Amhara Land Redistribution of 1997." In *Ethiopia: The Challenge of Democracy from Below*, edited by Bahru Zewde and Siegfried Pausewang, 71–86. Uppsala, Sweden: Nordic Africa Institute.

Eshete, Andreas. 2003. Ethnic Federalism: New Frontiers in Ethiopian Politics. Paper delivered at 1st National Conference on Federalism,n-Conflict and Peace Building, UNCC, Addis Ababa, May 5–7, 2003.

FDRE. 1994. "Constitution of the Federal Democratic Republic of Ethiopia (FDRE)." *Federal Negarit Gazeta*.

———. 2005. "Expropriation of Land Holdings for Public Purposes and Payment of Compensation Proclamation." *Federal Negarit Gazeta*, Proclamation 455/2005.

———. 2007. "Federal Democratic Republic of Ethiopia (FDRE) – Payment of Compensation for Property Situated on Landholding Expropriated for Public Purposes." *Federal Negarit Gazeta*, Council of Ministers Regulation, 135/2007.

———. 2011. "Federal Democratic Republic of Ethiopia (FDRE) – Urban Lands Leaseholding Proclamation." *Federal Negarit Gazeta*, November 28, 2011, Proclamation 721/2011.

———. 2018. "Land, Landlessness and Rural Poverty in Oromia." In *Land, Landlessness and Poverty in Ethiopia: Research Findings from Four National Regional States*, edited by Dessalegn Rahmato, 59–124. Addis Ababa: Forum for Social Studies.

Gebremariam, Eyob Balcha. 2017. "The Politics of Youth Employment and Policy Processes in Ethiopia." *IDS Bulletin* 48, no. 3 (May): 33–50.

Gebremedhin, Berhanu, and Berhanu Nega. 2005. "Land and Land Policy in Ethiopia in the Eyes of Ethiopian Farmers: An Empirical Investigation." In Proceedings of the Second International Conference on the Ethiopian Economy, Vol. 2, Ethiopian Economic Association.

Gilbert, Alan. 2002. "On the Mystery of Capital and the Myths of Hernando De Soto: What Difference Does Legal Title Make?" *International Development Planning Review* 24, no. 1 (March): 1–19.

Girmay, Gebreyohannes, Zenebe Gebreegziabher, and Girmay Gebru. 2018. "Land, Rural Poverty and Landlessness in Tigray." In *Land, Landlessness and Poverty in Ethiopia: Research Findings from Four National Regional States*, edited by Dessalegn Rahmato, 239–77. Addis Ababa: Forum for Social Studies.

Goodfellow, Tom. 2017. "Taxing Property in a Neo-Developmental State: The Politics of Urban Land Value Capture in Rwanda and Ethiopia." *African Affairs* 116, no. 465 (October): 549–72.

Guan, Xinping. 2005. "China's Social Policy: Reform and Development in the Context of Marketization and Globalization." In *Transforming the Developmental Welfare State in East Asia*, edited by Huck-ju Kwon, 231–56. Social Policy in a Development Context Series. Houndmills, UK: Palgrave Macmillan.

Hammond, Laura. 2008. "Strategies of Invisibilization: How Ethiopia's Resettlement Programme Hides the Poorest of the Poor." *Journal of Refugee Studies* 21, no. 4 (December): 517–36.

Hoben, Allan. 1973. *Land Tenure among the Amhara of Ethiopia: The Dynamics of Cognatic Descent*. Monographs in Ethiopian Land Tenure. Chicago: University of Chicago Press.

Holden, Stein T., and Keijiro Otsuka. 2014. "The Roles of Land Tenure Reforms and Land Markets in the Context of Population Growth and Land Use Intensification in Africa." *Food Policy* 48 (October): 88–97.

Joireman, Sandra Fullerton. 2000. *Property Rights and Political Development: The State and Land in Ethiopia and Eritrea, 1941–1974*. Oxford: James Currey.

Kamski, Benedikt. 2016. "The Kuraz Sugar Development Project (KSDP) in Ethiopia: Between 'Sweet Visions' and Mounting Challenges." *Journal of Eastern African Studies* 10, no. 3: 568–80.

Kay, Cristóbal. 2002. "Why East Asia Overtook Latin America: Agrarian Reform, Industrialisation and Development." *Third World Quarterly* 23, no. 6: 1073–1102.

Kefale, Asnake. 2010. "Federal Restructuring in Ethiopia: Renegotiating Identity and Borders Along the Oromo–Somali Ethnic Frontiers." *Development and Change* 41, no. 4 (August): 615–35.

———. 2013. *Federalism and Ethnic Conflict in Ethiopia: A Comparative Regional Study*. Routledge Series in Federal Studies. London: Routledge.

Kefale, Asnake, and Fana Gebresenbet. 2014. "The Expansion of the Sugar Industry in the Southern Pastoral Lowlands." In *Reflections on Development in Ethiopia: New Trends, Sustainability and Challenges*, edited by Dessalegn Rahmato, Meheret Ayenew, Asnake Kefale, and Birgit Habermann, 247–68. Addis Ababa: ISS.

Khan, Mushtaq H. 2005. *Review of DFID's Governance Target Strategy Paper*. London: Mimeo.

Kingwill, Rosalie, Ben Cousins, Tessa Cousins, Donna Hornby, Lauren Royston, and Warren Smit. 2006. "Mysteries and Myths: De Soto, Property and Poverty in South Africa." *IIED Gatekeeper* 124.

Knippenberg, Erwin, Dean Jolliffe, and John Hoddinott. 2018. "Land Fragmentation and Food Insecurity in Ethiopia." World Bank Policy Research Working Paper 8559.

Lavers, Tom. 2012a. "'Land Grab' as Development Strategy? The Political Economy of Agricultural Investment in Ethiopia." *Journal of Peasant Studies* 39, no. 1 (March): 105–32.

———. 2012b. "Patterns of Agrarian Transformation in Ethiopia: State-Mediated Commercialisation and the 'Land Grab.'" *Journal of Peasant Studies* 39, no. 3–4 (July): 795–822.

———. 2013a. "Food Security and Social Protection in Highland Ethiopia: Linking the Productive Safety Net to the Land Question." *Journal of Modern African Studies* 51, no. 3: 459–85.

———. 2013b. "The Political Economy of Social Policy and Agrarian Transformation in Ethiopia." PhD diss., University of Bath.

———. 2018. "Responding to Land-Based Conflict in Ethiopia: The Land Rights of Ethnic Minorities under Federalism." *African Affairs* 117, no. 468 (July): 462–84.

———. 2019a. "Distributional Concerns, the 'Developmental State,' and the Agrarian Origins of Social Assistance in Ethiopia." In *The Politics of Social Protection in Eastern and Southern Africa*, edited by Sam Hickey, Tom Lavers, Miguel Niño-Zarazúa, and Jeremy Seekings. Unu-Wider Studies in Development Economics. Oxford: Oxford University Press.

———. 2019b. "Social Protection in an Aspiring 'Developmental State': The Political Drivers of Ethiopia's PSNP." *African Affairs* 118, no. 473 (October): 646–71.

Lefort, René. 2012. "Free Market Economy, 'Developmental State' and Party-State Hegemony in Ethiopia: The Case of the 'Model Farmers.'" *Journal of Modern African Studies* 50, no. 4 (December): 681–706.

Lipton, Michael. 1993. "Land Reform as Commenced Business: The Evidence against Stopping." *World Development* 21, no. 4 (April): 641–57.

Lund, Christian. 2000. *African Land Tenure: Questioning Basic Assumptions*. London: International Institute for Environment and Development.

———. 2008. *Local Politics and the Dynamics of Property in Africa.* Cambridge: Cambridge University Press.

Marcus, Harold G. 1995. "A Breakfast Meeting with Prime Minister Meles," October 20, 1995, Ethiopian Embassy, Washington, DC. http://www.hartford-hwp.com/archives/33/008.html.

Mellor, John W. 2014. "Rapid Cereals Production Growth, 1997–2012, Ethiopia." *Occasional Paper* 33.

Milkias, Paulos. 2003. "Ethiopia, the TPLF, and the Roots of the 2001 Political Tremor." *Northeast African Studies* 10, no. 2: 13–66.

MoARD. 2010. "Ethiopia's Agricultural Sector Policy and Investment Framework (PIF) 2010–2020." Addis Ababa: Ministry of Agriculture and Rural Development.

MoFA. 2008. "Draft Policy Statement for the Sustainable Development of Pastoral and Agro Pastoral Areas of Ethiopia." Addis Ababa: Ministry of Federal Affairs.

MoFED. 2002. "Ethiopia: Sustainable Development and Poverty Reduction Program." Addis Ababa: Government of the Federal Democratic Republic of Ethiopia.

———. 2003. "Rural Development Policy and Strategies." Addis Ababa: Government of the Federal Democratic Republic of Ethiopia.

———. 2005. "Ethiopia: Building on Progress. A Plan for Accelerated and Sustained Development to End Poverty (PASDEP)." Addis Ababa: Federal Democratic Republic of Ethiopia.

———. 2010. "Growth and Transformation Plan (GTP)." Addis Ababa: Federal Democratic Republic of Ethiopia.

Moller, Lars Christian, and Konstantin M. Wacker. 2017. "Explaining Ethiopia's Growth Acceleration—The Role of Infrastructure and Macroeconomic Policy." *World Development* 96 (August): 198–215.

Musembi, Celestine Nyamu. 2007. "De Soto and Land Relations in Rural Africa: Breathing Life into Dead Theories About Property Rights." *Third World Quarterly* 28, no. 8: 1457–78.

Nega, Berhanu, Berhanu Adenew, and Samuel Gebreselassie. 2002. *Land Tenure and Agricultural Development in Ethiopia.* Addis Ababa: Ethiopian Economics Association/Ethiopian Economic Policy Research Institute.

Nega, Berhanu, Berhanu Adenew, and Seyoum Gebreselassie. 2003. "Current Land Policy Issues in Ethiopia." In *Land Reform: Land Settlements and Cooperatives*, edited by Paolo Groppo, 103–24. Rome: FAO.

North, Douglass C. 1990. *Institutions, Institutional Change and Economic Performance*. Cambridge: Cambridge University Press.

Pankhurst, Alula, and François Piguet, eds. 2009. *Moving People in Ethiopia: Development, Displacement & the State*. London: James Currey.

Paul, Mark, and Mwangi wa Gĩthĩnji. 2017. "Small Farms, Smaller Plots: Land Size, Fragmentation, and Productivity in Ethiopia." *Journal of Peasant Studies* 45, no. 4: 757–75.

Rahmato, Dessalegn. 1994. "Land Policy in Ethiopia at the Crossroads." In *Land Tenure and Land Policy in Ethiopia After the Derg*, edited by Dessalegn Rahmato. Trondheim: Centre for the Environment and Development, University of Trondheim.

———. 1997. *Manufacturing Poverty: Rural Policy and Micro-Agriculture*. Addis Ababa: Institute of Development Research, Addis Ababa University.

———. 2003. "Poverty and Agricultural Involution." In *Some Aspects of Poverty in Ethiopia*, edited by Dessalegn Rahmato, 1–15. Addis Ababa: Forum for Social Studies.

———. 2009. *The Peasant and the State: Studies in Agrarian Change in Ethiopia 1950s–2000s*. Addis Ababa: Addis Ababa University Press.

———. 2014. "The Perils of Development from Above: Land Deals in Ethiopia." *African Identities* 12, no. 1 (June): 26–44.

———, ed. 2018. *Land, Landlessness and Poverty in Ethiopia: Research Findings from Four National Regional States*. Addis Ababa: Forum for Social Studies.

Simon, Bereket. 2011. *A Tale of Two Elections: A National Endeavour to Put a Stop to an Avalanche* (In Amharic: *Ye-Hulet Merchawoch Weg: Nadan Yegeta Hagerawi Rucha*). Addis Ababa: Mega Enterprise.

Tadesse, Medhane, and John Young. 2003. "TPLF: Reform or Decline?" *Review of African Political Economy* 30, no. 97 (September): 389–403.

Tafesse, Tesfaye. 2007. *The Migration, Environment and Conflict Nexus in Ethiopia: A Case Study of Amhara Migrant-Settlers in East Wollega Zone*. Addis Ababa: Organisation for Social Science Research.

TGE. 1993. "National Policy on Disaster Prevention and Management." Addis Ababa: Transitional Government of Ethiopia.
———. 1994. "An Economic Development Strategy for Ethiopia." Addis Ababa: Transitional Government of Ethiopia.
Van der Beken, Christophe. 2009. "Ethiopian Constitutions and the Accommodation of Ethnic Diversity: The Limits of the Territorial Approach." *Issues of Federalism in Ethiopia: Towards an Inventory.* Ethiopian Constitutional Law Series 2: 217–300.
You, Jong-Sung. 2017. "Demystifying the Park Chung-Hee Myth: Land Reform in the Evolution of Korea's Developmental State." *Journal of Contemporary Asia* 47, no. 4: 535–56.
Young, John. 1997. *Peasant Revolution in Ethiopia: The Tigray People's Liberation Front, 1975–1991.* African Studies. Cambridge: Cambridge University Press.

2.4 Ethiopia Beyond Middle Income
Transforming the National Mindset

Kenichi Ohno

Ethiopia has experienced a spell of high growth in the last one-and-half decades, taking the country from widespread poverty and hunger to the status of a newly industrializing economy in Africa. The national goal of attaining lower middle-income appears within reach in the not-so-distant future. However, the going usually gets tough beyond middle income, and many latecomer economies slow down before attaining high income. Even in East Asia where industrialization has *on average* been successful, some economies rose straight to high income without stopping while others struggle with a middle-income trap or the future risk of it. Differences in long-term growth performance arise fundamentally from the mindset and capacity of national leaders, enterprises, and people, not so much from the size, starting point, or resource endowment of the national economy. Observing the Ethiopian economy and policies in the past twelve years in the framework of the Industrial Policy Dialogue, the author already detects symptoms of future trap possibility. An enhanced mindset campaign and policy improvement are required for Ethiopia to avoid a future trap and climb onto the high-income trajectory.

This chapter discusses the general features of middle-income traps, then presents concrete examples of mindset problems and attempts to tackle them, successfully or not so successfully, in selected Asian countries. With this background, the Ethiopian situation is analyzed and possible actions for transforming the national mindset are suggested from the perspective of Asian development experience.

THE MIDDLE-INCOME CHALLENGE

The World Bank Group classifies economies into low income, lower middle income, upper middle income, and high income according to the gross national income per capita of each economy. Data and thresholds are adjusted annually. Based on July 2018 data, which became effective in World Bank policy in July 2019, low income is $995 or less, lower middle income is between $996 and $3,895, upper middle income is between $3,896 and $12,055, and high income is $12,055 or more. As of 2018–19, distribution is as follows:

Low-income:	34 economies (15.6%)
Lower middle-income:	47 economies (21.6%)
Upper middle-income:	56 economies (25.7%)
High-income:	81 economies (37.2%)

Among the 218 economies thus classified, the largest group is high-income economies and the smallest group is low-income economies. If the two middle-income groups are combined, as is often done in popular discourse, the middle-income group becomes the largest, accounting for 47.2 percent of the total.

This classification system, created for World Bank lending policy but also used for target setting by many governments, is generous in the sense that it is biased toward high and middle income. High-income economies in this classification include many nations that are not exactly outstanding in their technological edge or economic impact on the global economy. They are a much broader category than what we normally regard as global industrial leaders or highly advanced nations. Moreover, there are usually more economies moving up than falling down in this classification in any particular year, so the distribution becomes even more top-heavy over time.[1]

Similarly, a movement from low income to middle income does not require particularly high policy competence or strong private dynamism. Any economy that has suffered from military conflict, political instability, or economic mismanagement and starts from a very low-income level, tends to register high growth for a decade or two simply by restoring stability, liberalizing private activities, integrating into the global economy, receiving international aid and foreign direct investment (FDI), and introducing new laws and institutions. After a national crisis, a spell of fast growth was observed in Vietnam, Cambodia, and Myanmar in Asia and Rwanda in Africa. Ethiopia, after the collapse of the Derg regime in 1991, and particularly in the last one and a half decades, can also be counted as a case of a one-time catching up to the lost income trajectory.

However, latecomer economies that maintain strong growth momentum at middle income and continue to climb to the highest income are few. Historically, among non-Western societies, Japan from the late nineteenth century and Taiwan, Korea, and Singapore from the 1960s onward are about the only such cases.[2] Two of them experienced a period of setback along the way—Japan due to World War II and Korea due to internal political turmoil in the 1980s—but these were caused by noneconomic crises rather than any fundamental defect in their economic dynamism.

Even in East and Southeast Asia, where high growth and technological progress are prominent *on average*, not all economies are high performers. Figure 1 shows the per capita real incomes of selected Asian economies relative to the United States.

Figure 2.4.1. *Catch-up Race in East and Southeast Asia (Per Capita Real Income Relative to the United States)*

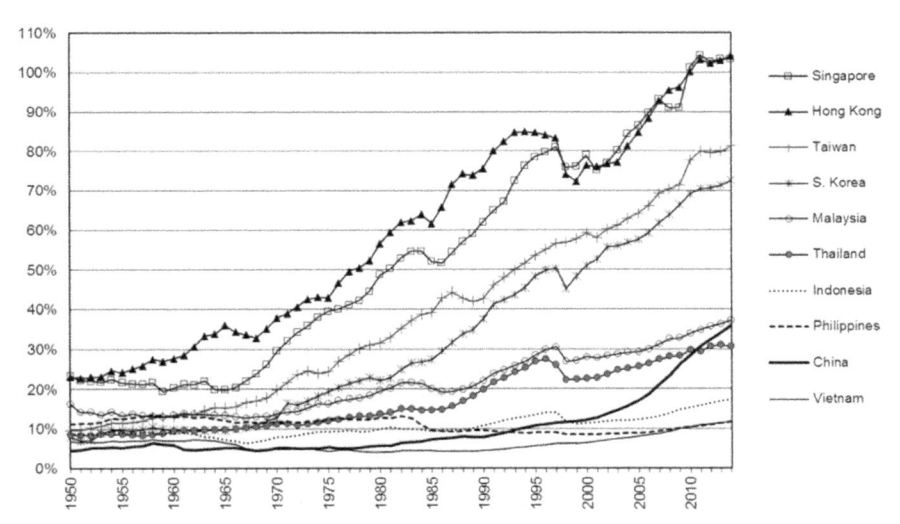

Source: Angus Maddison. *The World Economy: Historical Statistics*. OECD Development Centre, 2003; updated with International Monetary Fund World Outlook Database.

In the post-World War II period shown here, the two city economies of Singapore and Hong Kong rose rapidly to high income, even surpassing the United States in recent years. They never stagnated or slowed down at middle income. Their declines around 1998, also visible in other economies, reflect the severe but temporary effect of the Asian financial crisis in 1997–98. The economies of Taiwan and Korea also emerged strongly without stopping in the middle to join the highest income group.

Malaysia and Thailand, starting from the same position as Taiwan and Korea in the 1950s, are a different story. Their per capita income grew, but not fast enough to reach high income, even after a half century. Both are caught in middle-income traps, and their governments officially admit it. Below them are Indonesia and the Philippines, whose growth momentum is even weaker than that of Malaysia and Thailand. At their growth rates, it will take many centuries to catch up with advanced economies, if at all.

Then there are the two communist countries of China and Vietnam. The Chinese economy began to speed up in the 1980s and accelerated further around the turn of the millennium to rapidly move from low income to upper middle income. In comparison, the progress of the Vietnamese economy is less spectacular, though it, too, graduated from low income to lower middle income around 2008. Besides this, there are the latest comers, such as Cambodia, Myanmar, and Laos (data not shown), whose industrialization is far behind even that of Vietnam.

Why do economies diverge like this? Many answers are possible. But most fundamentally, the difference arises from whether the nation has citizens and enterprises that constantly accumulate skills, knowledge, technology, and the capacity to innovate. Among today's remaining latecomers, there are very few that are equipped with naturally dynamic human resources (if they were, they would have joined the high-income group long ago). For them, a strong private sector must be created by the government before it can be promoted and supported. But a latecomer government also faces problems of capacity, incentives, integrity, and stability, so it must first reform itself before the private sector can be helped and encouraged, a task that is never easy. This is the greatest difficulty in today's latecomer development.

Unless the government effectively overcomes this challenge, weak policy perpetuates a weak economy, and there is no escape from the trap. Visible policy improvement does not occur if the government introduces marginal changes but otherwise continues to operate as before. A clean break from the past is called for, and this usually happens, if it happens at all, when a new government is inaugurated. In Asia, the arrival of Chiang Kai-shek (Taiwan, 1949), Park Chung-hee (Korea, 1961), Lee Kuan Yew (Singapore, 1965), and Deng Xiaoping (China, 1977) marked a historical break in each society. By contrast, less successful countries such as Malaysia, Thailand, Indonesia, the Philippines, and Vietnam have never produced epoch-making leaders comparable with these four, even though they sometimes had relatively good prime ministers and presidents along with bad ones.

The situation of dynamic income divergence is illustrated in Figure 2. For a country that just overcame an internal conflict and/or terrible poverty and hunger, it is relatively easy to grow rapidly for a decade or two. Economic liberalization (ending suppression of the private sector), privatization, and global integration, along with necessary laws and institutions, are all that is required. Domestic firms increase in number, and official development assistance (ODA) and FDI flow in. This is essentially bouncing back to where the nation should have been had a crisis not occurred. In this initial stage, sophisticated industrial policy or competent technocrats who administer it are not imperative for generating growth. Domestic value creation remains small in this stage.

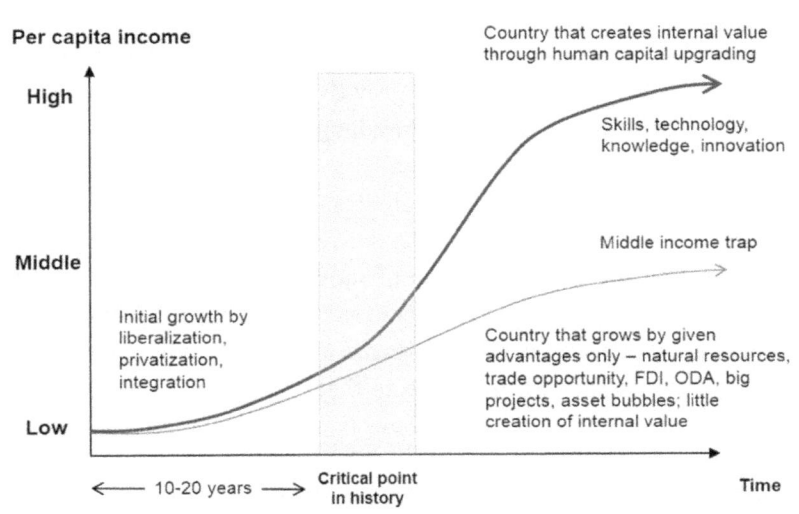

Figure 2.4.2. *Why Economies Diverge*

Source: adapted from the author's lecture, Policy Design and Implementation in Developing Countries, at the National Graduate Institute for Policy Studies.

However, when a nation reaches lower middle income, a critical moment arises. Growth begins to slow down *unless* domestic value creation is ignited and accelerated. Since most latecomers are without a strong private sector that can effectively compete internationally, the role of national leaders and technocrats becomes vital as a game changer and transformer of the private sector. This is an additional and much harder role for government to play than the tasks that confronted the governments of Japan, Korea, Taiwan, Singapore, or China when their industrialization began, because they already had an inherently strong private sector.

A middle-income trap can be defined statistically or analytically. Statisticians may define it as a situation where a country stays at least twenty-eight years in lower middle income or fourteen years in upper middle income, as proposed by Felipe, Abdon, and Kumar (2012). But policy makers need an analytical, not mechanical, description of a trap that can point to its possible causes and remedies. In the Asian context, Suehiro (2014) states that a middle-income trap arises when industrialization driven by low-cost advantages (cheap labor and big capital) comes to an end. Similarly, Kwan (2013) argues that a country unable to find new sources and patterns of growth will fall into a trap. In addition to these supply-side problems, Hara (2014, 2015) cites an inability to cope with gaping income gaps as an equally important cause of a trap. Tran (2010, 2013) and Tran and Karikomi (2019) point to the lack of high-quality institutions that generate new growth as a deeper cause of a trap. Consistent with Figure 2, all these arguments imply that a country at some point on its growth path enters a phase in which proactive policy response is required besides just liberalization, privatization, and integration.

We propose to define a middle-income trap as a situation where an economy is unable to create value beyond what is delivered by given advantages. Here, given advantages include endowment of natural resources, cheap and young labor, new trade opportunities as a result of opening up, inflows of FDI and aid, locational and geopolitical advantages, and asset bubbles, construction booms, and big infrastructure projects that superficially sustain growth. When these things drive growth, chances are that domestic citizens and enterprises are not creating much value. Furthermore, the presence of such advantages often diverts national attention from the accumulation of knowledge, skills, and technology due to various psychological, political, and economic reasons. Development in the true sense occurs only when value (GDP) is created and constantly augmented by domestic citizens and enterprises.

The curse of natural resources, also known as the Dutch disease, is well publicized. This maxim says that the existence of natural resources is a disadvantage for industrialization due to the reasons cited above. Laziness, diverted interests, corruption, and political lobbying will proliferate. Economists also warn that factor biases and currency overvaluation will emerge. This means that resource-rich nations face an additional task of overcoming these difficulties before they can introduce policies for domestic value creation. It is important to realize that all given advantages cited above, not just resource endowment, can cause similar problems and negatively affect industrialization. Another way to put it is that growth generated by given advantages is quantitative rather than qualitative. Effort, not luck, must drive the national economy.

DIFFERENCES IN NATIONAL MINDSET

Our working hypothesis is that a nation falls into a middle-income trap when the private sector is weak, and the government is unable to support it effectively. Other aspects, such as size, location, aid, FDI, and resource endowment certainly affect the development path, but they are not ultimate determinants of developmental success or failure. Any seasoned government official or business CEO knows the basic problems their countries face, and they even sense required policy actions to overcome them.[3] What they do not have is the practical knowledge of how such policies should be designed and implemented concretely, effectively, and in proper procedure, and how to build up political, administrative, and social capacity to constantly learn and strengthen such knowledge.

We can go one step further and ask, What produces a strong private sector and a capable government? Our tentative answer is it is the mindset that permeates the entire nation encompassing top leaders, technocrats, officials, experts, entrepreneurs, engineers, workers, farmers, and even students and pupils. Mindset is a broad concept. Here, our working definition is a state of mind that drives a human (or a collection of humans) to consistent action toward a desired goal.[4] Mindset is contrasted with capacity—skills, technology, knowledge, experience, and other qualities humans possess—which is a set of concrete tools for realizing development. Mindset and capacity are both needed as the subjective and objective conditions for national economic development.

At present, the author does not possess statistical evidence to prove the above statement. But after studying the policy-making methods of twenty-plus governments in Asia and Africa through policy research and dialogue, the author can offer many episodes that suggest this is the case. If one examines policy methods and contents in many countries long enough, differences in government capability are very clear just by checking key documents, interviewing responsible officials, hearing private voices, or witnessing a policy-making scene. These observations must be classified into different types, and possible causes and solutions for each must be explored. The current chapter remains narrative and issue raising without offering precise analysis, which is a task for the future.

Common features of vibrant and successful societies are pragmatism, willingness to learn, quick and effective action, risk-taking through trial and error, absence of bureaucratic fuss and delay, diligence, teamwork, commitment to quality, pursuit of public good, and passion for national development. Meanwhile, features unfit for economic growth include short-termism, selfishness, corruption, excessive bureaucracy, excessive materialism, inattention to detail, lack of persistence and resolution, lack of upward mobility, extreme individualism that rejects teamwork, and disregard of laws, rules, and contracts. These statements generally apply not only to business executives, engineers, and workers but also to national leaders and government officials who are supposed to assist the private sector.

In Singapore, technocrats are young, highly competent, competitive, fast-talking, and well paid. Information flows freely across ministries and divisions, as well as with the private sector and academia, without any bureaucratic hindrance. Meetings are short and to the point. Foreign visitors and researchers are welcomed, and meetings are quickly arranged without any official letter or protocol. On one occasion, a joint team of Japanese, Ethiopian, and Vietnamese officials visited the Research and Enterprise Division of the Ministry of Trade and Industry. After the meeting, we inquired about the Centre for Strategic Futures of the Prime Minister's Office, which had drafted a broad national strategy. The interviewee said that the Centre was in the same building, and he could take us there to see if the person in charge was available. He did so, and the responsible person was very happy to talk to us for fifteen minutes in a nearby tearoom before lunchtime. We were able to get sufficient information because his explanations were very fast yet comprehensive.

By contrast, government officials in Vietnam, where the author has advised for the last twenty-four years, generally lack capability and motivation and insist on excessive formality.[5] From 2006 to 2007, two Japanese motorcycle makers and the Ministry of Industry jointly drafted a motorcycle master plan. It took more than six months to pay a courtesy visit to a vice minister just to get approval for the project. He then set a very tight deadline, for which stakeholders worked very hard. After submission of the completed draft, the ministry revised it significantly and even added new export targets without telling the Japanese producers, which made them angry. But the responsible official assured us by saying, "Don't worry, Vietnamese master plans are never implemented." The Vietnam Industrialization Strategy initiative of 2011–13 was agreed to bilaterally at the prime ministerial level to boost six manufacturing sectors with Japanese cooperation. The Ministry of Planning and Investment and the "All-Japan" team had twenty-four sessions in all and spent enormous time, money, and energy.[6] But discussions never deepened because Vietnamese attendants changed every month and continued to ask basic questions about the purpose and scope of the project. We also spent far more time reporting the "progress" to higher-ups than drafting program substance. Finally, a deputy prime minister ordered Vietnamese ministries to speed up and finish the work without Japanese assistance, which ended bilateral cooperation and killed the initiative. On another occasion, when we took Vietnamese officials to Singapore for policy research, they never took notes and even skipped meetings for shopping.

In Taiwan, we visited the Industrial Development Bureau of the Ministry of Economic Affairs (IDB/MoEA). Up to the mid-1980s, MoEA was a command post of Taiwan's industrialization in a developmental state described as "governing the market" by Robert Wade (1990). By 2011, when we visited MoEA, its supreme power had waned, as large IT firms that relied little on official support emerged. But it continued to play important roles for small and middle enterprises (SMEs). MoEA officials were older and more relaxed than the Singaporean technocrats, but they were equally friendly and precise. Necessary information was gathered quickly, and our questions were answered promptly. Taiwan's industrial strategy was very simple and clear. It featured two policy tools of "industrial projects" commissioned by MoEA to expedite SME innovation and commercialization of R&D, and state management of various industrial estates—especially science parks but also export processing zones (EPZs) and industrial parks. Taiwan no longer offers any investment incentives except for R&D, and all firms, domestic or foreign, are subject to a uniform corporate income tax of 17 percent. In reality, Taiwan's industrial base is predominantly domestic, and FDI plays only a minor role. Taiwanese experts who established Kaohsiung EPZ in 1966 were later dispatched to Vietnam to create its first EPZ (Tan Thuan EPZ in Ho Chi Minh City). When we visited the management office of the latter without appointment, a Taiwanese official welcomed us with a big smile, served tea, and asked us to contact him any time if there were any further questions. Great hospitality to any visitor is the hallmark of highly competent industrial officials. Unexpected guests are never turned away.[7]

Indonesia has 264 million people, with per capita income of $3,540 (World Bank data 2017). The middle class is growing, with a great appetite for cars, processed food, and other consumer items, and FDI is attracted by this large and growing market. However, unlike neighboring countries in Southeast Asia, Indonesian manufacturing is domestically oriented, with little export. There is virtually no incentive for investors,[8] and licensing procedures are cumbersome. Although BKPM (the Indonesian acronym for the national investment agency) is relatively efficient, investors still need local consultants to fill out documents. Development policy is strongly driven by politics. Moreover, excessive decentralization carried out in 2001–3 hampers the implementation of technical and vocational education and training (TVET) and SME policies at the national level. Both domestic and foreign businesses complain bitterly that Indonesian policies are unpredictable, ambiguous, arbitrary, and uncoordinated, and too many ministerial regulations are issued without stakeholder consultation or any preparation period. Ministry of Industry officials we interviewed in 2014 were very friendly and invited us to lunch and dinner on two occasions, but their policy capacity seemed low. They were proud of a national exhibition center but could not explain much beyond this policy. Practically all industrial training is done by private firms or foreign NPOs. In infrastructure, there have been many grand plans, but implementation has been slow due to politics and administrative problems. Construction delays cause horrible congestion at Jakarta's roads, ports, and airports. MRT Jakarta, the first urban rail with Japanese cooperation, finally began a test run in March 2019. Compared with Addis Ababa Light Rail, which began operations in 2015 at much lower levels of income and urbanization than Jakarta, delays in Jakarta's urban transport construction are evident.

Both Korea and Malaysia learned car manufacturing from Japan, but their results were very different (Ohno 2013). In Korea, the learning curve was steep, and technology was quickly internalized. Hyundai received strong official support as well as technical assistance from Mitsubishi Motors of Japan initially, but it was soon able to send Japanese engineers home. In 1975, the Hyundai Pony, the first Korean-developed car, was produced. In 1986, Hyundai entered the American market with the Excel and set the record for selling the largest number of cars (126,000) in the first year of business in the United States. Koreans are now one of the top several global car producers and rivals for Japanese automakers.

In sharp contrast, Malaysia's learning curve was slow and incomplete. In 1983, as a pillar of a national heavy industrialization drive, Prime Minister Mahathir created Proton, a state-owned car company, and generously supported it with protection, subsidies, and policy attention. It also received technology from Mitsubishi Motors and learned design, engine, marketing, and other capabilities over time. It was the dominant car producer in the protected domestic market, but it did not become competitive enough for export. Malaysia continued to receive Japanese technical assistance for strengthening its local component industries. As import tariffs were subsequently lifted, domestic car demand shifted from Proton to foreign models. Proton faced the risk of bankruptcy and sought partnership with a number of global car giants, all of whom declined the offer. Finally, in 2018, Geely of China came to the rescue and bought 49.9 percent of Proton. Global automotive competition is very tough, and Proton's halfway learning did not produce success. Very different outcomes between Korea and Malaysia must be attributed to their national characteristics, not how Mitsubishi Motors taught them. This time, the difference was mainly in the absorptive capacity of CEOs and engineers rather than policy makers.

These are some examples of capable and not-so-capable nations in Asia. When we compare Singapore and Vietnam, Taiwan and Indonesia, or Korea and Malaysia, differences in learning capacity are obvious. We must start from the undeniable fact that not all nations are created equal in manufacturing mindset or policy capability.

ETHIOPIA'S TRAP RISK

According to World Bank data, Ethiopia's GNI per capita was $790 in 2018. To reach the lower-middle-income threshold of $996 by 2025, a simple calculation shows that real income per capita needs to grow 3.94 percent annually. Assuming population growth of 3.29 percent (actual data for the last decade), real GDP must grow at least 7.23 percent per annum. This conclusion may be affected by the creeping of income threshold or divergent trends in exchange rates and price deflators, but technical adjustments arising from them should be minor. If Ethiopia continues to grow at 7 percent plus or above in the next several years without any severe economic downturn, it is likely that lower middle income will be reached by around 2025. For low-income countries at peace and promoting economic liberalization, 7 percent growth is not a very high aspiration. Despite a recent slowdown, Ethiopia as a latest comer should have the potential to sustain such growth. However, this will be only the first step on a long road toward full economic development. As noted in the section "The Middle-Income Challenge," a middle-income nation must vigorously promote value creation in order to maintain growth momentum into high income.

Has Ethiopia prepared enough for this mission? By the standard of high-performing Asian nations, we must admit that it has done little so far. Policy effort must be doubled to transform the national mindset, avoid a future middle-income trap, and set the nation onto the high-income trajectory.

In 2008, Prime Minister Meles asked Japan to introduce *kaizen* to Ethiopia. In the following year, the Japan International Cooperation Agency (JICA) initiated kaizen cooperation, which is now in its third phase. The Ethiopian Kaizen Institute (EKI) was established, and its staff were trained. Ethiopia can now teach basic kaizen without Japanese assistance, and intermediate and advanced kaizen are currently being learned. Japanese kaizen was modified to the Ethiopian reality. The National Kaizen Award was created; Kaizen Month (September) was launched; master's and PhD courses in kaizen are offered at Mekelle University; citywide and regional kaizen movement is in progress; and Ethiopia began to teach kaizen to African neighbors as well as the African Union. These are great achievements. For JICA too, this was one of the most successful kaizen cooperation projects around the world. National enthusiasm for kaizen should be sustained far into the future.

However, kaizen is just one of the many methods for mindset transformation. More needs to be done to improve the Ethiopian mindset toward efficiency and high quality. Moreover, the spirit of kaizen—not just kaizen as a toolbox for eliminating waste—must be established firmly in the heart of every Ethiopian. This point was stressed many times by Prime Ministers Meles and Hailemariam.

Despite the good initial achievements in kaizen, there are signs that indicate Ethiopia is not yet ready for industrial excellence or global competitiveness.

First, the mindset of Ethiopian workers—and farmers who may become future workers—is still primitive. Ethiopian workers need higher awareness and more training in terms of literacy, dedication, sense of purpose and responsibility, time discipline, observance of work rules, attention to detail, teamwork, proper attire, reporting necessary things to supervisors, greetings and responses, and even the proper use of modern canteens and toilets. In most Asian countries, these are basic requirements for hiring new employees. In Vietnam, JICA is teaching workers to be more creative in finding possibilities for improvement in the workplace and suggesting solutions instead of being told what to do, having long-term career plans, and integrating personal welfare with the company's prosperity.[9] These are higher demands on workers that Ethiopians can adopt later after basic work discipline has been acquired. In agrarian societies, the introduction of modern industry usually requires a great transformation of traditional farmers into disciplined industrial workers. The problems mentioned above are not unique to Ethiopia, and this means Ethiopia can learn much by studying what other nations do to upgrade the mindset of farmers and workers.

Second, the capacity of middle- to low-ranking government officials is low. Although top Ethiopian national leaders have high aspirations and dedication to national development, officials on the ground are unable to map out policy details or carry out proposed policies effectively due to the lack of a proper mindset, knowledge, and experience. In Ethiopia, it is necessary to discuss policies at the ministerial or state ministerial level because officials below those levels do not possess the necessary mandate or information. This makes top leaders extremely busy while other officials remain idle. In most East Asian governments, there is no need to go to the minister frequently. Policies are discussed with middle-ranking officials who draft and implement them and therefore are well-informed. In the 1990s, two World Bank reports (1993, 1995) underlined the crucial importance of professional bureaucracy as one of the secrets of East Asia. To solve the problem of a missing "middle" and "bottom," Ethiopia needs a radical administrative reform that reduces the number of officials but enhances their capacity, authority, and motivation.

Third, policy must pursue quality rather than speed. Quality here means the ability to be implemented and effectiveness. We are frequently told that Ethiopia needs to quickly create jobs, eliminate poverty, and develop its economy, so policies must be drafted and implemented with great haste. Similar arguments are heard in other developing countries. Speed is required partly because of a passion for national development and partly because of the next election. But Japanese officials and experts are not convinced. In Asia, even high-capacity governments such as in Singapore and Taiwan take two to three years to draft a new policy or revise an important one, which includes time for initial brainstorming, consensus building, and preparatory studies.[10] A document may be drafted in a few weeks if officials work very hard, but that will hardly be sufficient to secure the strong support and ownership of key stakeholders, especially the business community, which is vital for effective implementation. Deep and practical research, trust building, and effective interaction with key stakeholders take time, and governments with little policy experience should take additional time to learn.

Figure 3 shows five necessary conditions for industrial policy to be able to be implemented and effective: (i) top leader(s) with proper vision and strong commitment, (ii) effective consensus building, (iii) efficient drafting, (iv) meaningful interaction with stakeholders, and (v) an overseeing agency with sufficient mandate and capacity. These conditions were extracted from the author's research on industrial policy formulation in over twenty countries in Asia and Africa. In high-performing governments such as Singapore and Taiwan, all these five conditions are satisfied.

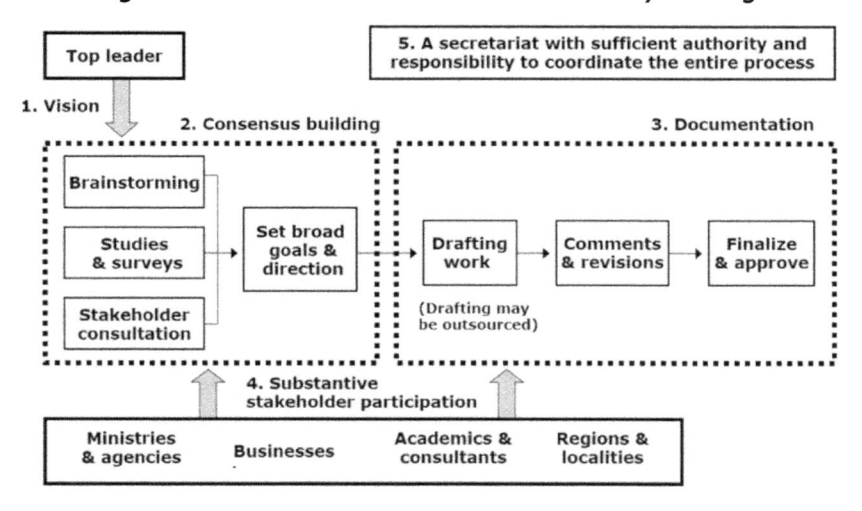

Figure 2.4.3. *Five Conditions for Good Policy Making*

```
                                 5. A secretariat with sufficient authority and
    Top leader                   responsibility to coordinate the entire process

1. Vision
              2. Consensus building                    3. Documentation

    Brainstorming
                         Set broad
    Studies             goals &          Drafting      Comments      Finalize
    & surveys           direction        work          & revisions   & approve

    Stakeholder                          (Drafting may
    consultation                         be outsourced)

                        4. Substantive
                        stakeholder participation

    Ministries                          Academics &    Regions &
    & agencies      Businesses          consultants    localities
```

Source: Ohno (2013), with slight modification.

In Ethiopia, many policies are created with very short deadlines. Trial and error is a legitimate strategy, and defective policies can be amended later. But it would be better to spend three years to forge a policy that is fully workable than quickly drafting policies that must be canceled later or revised frequently. In the latter case, many years pass before any visible result is produced on the ground. Quality over speed in policy making was one of the points the Japanese team stressed in Phase I of the Ethiopia-Japan Industrial Policy Dialogue. Ethiopia did not agree at that time, but Japan still wants to emphasize its importance.

Since April 2018, Dr. Abiy's government has launched many bold economic ideas and actions, such as state-owned enterprise reform, which includes the possibility of (selectively and partly) selling them; a wholesale review of past incentives for their cost-effectiveness, which includes the overhaul of automotive industry incentives, raising electricity tariffs in steps to a commercially viable level, a fresh look at the current industrial park policy, and a renewed interest in agricultural promotion. Many of these are coordinated with the World Bank, which provides necessary financial support. These are generally good policy directions. At the same time, they are all significant policy shifts that require good prior studies, careful consideration in project detail, and sufficient feedback from key stakeholders.

Great haste for political, economic, and external reasons is understandable, but these projects should be prepared with the utmost care so new policies, once implemented, should stay and produce expected results without the need to adjust them frequently or substantially. Singapore or Taiwan would spend at least a few years each for such policy initiatives.

METHODS FOR MINDSET TRANSFORMATION

Is a national mindset changeable? Is it a permanent feature reflecting the history and geography of each nation or a variable that can be adjusted by policy? We argue that a national mindset is difficult to change, but it is not impossible to modify it through proper policy design. Many methods have been tried around the world, and there are cases of full or partial success. It is worthwhile to study how these have been done in different countries. Some methods are universal, while others work only in certain cultural contexts. For this reason, selectivity and modification are required in transplanting a good model to any other country.

High-performing Asian economies also faced mindset problems, but they solved them relatively quickly. It may be argued that people in these societies had the potential to become productive to begin with, and policy fully developed it. In Japan, more than a century ago, the Survey of Industrial Workers by the Ministry of Agriculture and Commerce in 1901 found that Japanese workers were frequent job-hoppers, lacked work discipline, disregarded rules, saved little, and were only half as productive as American workers. By the 1910s, large firms began to replace traditional craftsmen with university graduates and offered them incentives for long service to promote skill accumulation and company loyalty. Wartime control in the late 1930s and early 1940s forced all firms and workers to stay with designated tasks and workplaces. After the war, especially in the 1960s, Japanese workers were highly disciplined and dedicated to the work and the company.

South Korea was initially considered a basket case. Kim and Leipziger (1993) report that Korea in the 1950s was a place heavily dependent on American aid and unfit for investment. Moreover, the Korean bureaucracy was a kind of spoils system. The World Bank (1993) agrees that as late as 1960 the Korean civil service was a corrupt and inept institution. But in the next two decades, it became one of the most reputable public sectors in the developing world. The transforming agent was General Park Chung-hee, who seized power in 1961 and started to run Korea with military discipline and severe punishment for incompetence and corruption. In 1970 he launched the Saemaul (New Village) Movement to galvanize farmers who were left behind by the nation's rapid industrialization. Every village in Korea was given bags of cement, guidance, and training to build something useful for village welfare. Results were monitored, and villages were rated. Some blame this as a top-down political show of President Park, but the fact that rural income rose significantly within ten years and sometimes even surpassed urban income must be duly acknowledged.

Singapore was aware of its productivity shortage at the time of its independence in 1965. It initially pursued labor-intensive manufacturing, but management-labor relations were tense. In 1979, Prime Minister Lee Kuan Yew delivered a speech lamenting that "workers here are not as proud of or as skilled in their jobs compared to the Japanese or the Germans." In 1981, Prime Minister Lee studied work practices at Japanese FDI in Singapore, visited Japan, and requested JICA and Kohei Goshi, chairman of the Japan Productivity Center (JPC), to teach productivity in Singapore. The National Productivity Council and the National Productivity Board were established, and the Productivity Movement was launched. JICA assisted with the Productivity Development Project from 1983 to 1990, which was Japan's first comprehensive cooperation for productivity improvement. After an initial period of building mutual trust and understanding, Singapore learned the Japanese method very well. It even started to teach productivity to other countries in the 1990s (JICA & GDF 2011).

Starting with Singapore, productivity and quality improvement projects—also known as kaizen—have become part of JICA's standard industrial cooperation. There have been at least twenty-seven such projects with significant size and duration in Asia, Africa, the Middle East, and Latin America, which are reported in the JICA Knowledge site. Smaller-scale courses, expert dispatches, factory diagnoses, and mini-projects for productivity improvement attached to larger projects are too numerous to list.

JICA's large productivity projects typically begin with a pilot project of thirty or so firms, then proceed to the establishment of a national productivity agency and staff training, nationwide implementation, and finally "privatization" (productivity activities are transferred to private firms, universities, and NPOs). In Ethiopia, the first three stages have been done. Apart from JICA, there are other Japanese organizations that teach productivity practices to the rest of the world, including the JPC, the Association for Overseas Technical Cooperation and Sustainable Partnerships (AOTS), and a large number of manufacturing firms and private consultants.

To launch a national productivity movement, awareness raising is critical. This is the first step in Japan's large-scale productivity cooperation. Awareness raising is needed not only for all workers and farmers to realize the meaning and importance of productivity but also for both Japanese and local officials in charge to overcome cultural differences and come to a common understanding of how productivity should be enhanced in the country. An awareness campaign, as a precursor to the national productivity movement, typically contains (i) the declaration of a national productivity movement by a top leader, (ii) designation of a responsible agency with a sufficient mandate, budget, and staffing, (iii) creation of a national slogan, logo, mascot, song, dance, etc., (iv) related events, including rallies, courses, speeches, seminars, conferences, TV and radio programs, and movies, (v) instruction materials such as manuals, books, magazines, web portals, and stories of productivity pioneers (with translations, if necessary), (vi) productivity awards and the publicizing of winners, and (vii) creation of a productivity month in which many events are held, including the top leader's speech and award ceremonies. This campaign should be followed by an action stage that includes Japanese experts coaching targeted factories in 5S and quality control circles, the training of domestic trainers, the creation of a national productivity model and teaching materials, and nationwide implementation. Ethiopia has already gone through this cycle.

However, a JICA-supported and kaizen-centered national productivity movement is not the only way to upgrade the national mindset. Governments, businesses, and researchers in many countries have tried various ways to inculcate efficiency and discipline into the heads and hearts of their citizens. A list of selected efforts is given below.

Productivity must be learned not only in workplaces but more broadly at home, in schools, and in every aspect of social and private life. A Japanese kindergarten would teach children to arrange shoes neatly, wash their hands, and put back toys after use. A century ago in rural Kyoto in Japan, Gunze, a private silk-reeling company founded in 1896, trained its young female workers with both skills and discipline, starting with "greet nicely, put your sandals in order, clean up," then proceeded to proper manners and sewing technique. Today in Vietnam, young workers going to Japan for three-year on-the-job training are given intensive lessons in Japanese language, Japanese manners and thinking, 5S, and career planning for six months prior to departure. In Singapore, military service is used as an occasion to teach young males not only order and discipline but also productivity.

The private sector often becomes a spontaneous and effective promoter of productivity. In Thailand, the Technology Promotion Association (TPA), a local private NPO, was established in 1973 by Thai returnees who studied science and engineering in Japan to disseminate Japanese-style thinking and manufacturing. For long, it has offered management, technical, and Japanese-language courses, published kaizen and other textbooks, and conducted firm consultation. In 2007, the TPA established the Thai-Nichi Institute of Technology (TNI), a long-planned university to teach Japanese-style manufacturing in both theory and practice, with a student capacity of four thousand. Graduates are very popular among Japanese FDI in Thailand. Management and financial resources remain local, with strong Thai ownership. Meanwhile, Japan assists the TPA and TNI from the sideline by dispatching experts, forging linkages with Japanese firms, and providing equipment. Today, Thailand has over two thousand domestic auto component suppliers that are competitive enough to work with global car giants and, through them, are linked with global value chains.

India's kaizen movement started with the establishment of Maruti Suzuki, a joint venture between the government of India and Suzuki Motor Corporation of Japan, in 1981. It revolutionized car manufacturing in India and has become the country's top passenger carmaker. Managers and engineers at Maruti Suzuki were trained, and local component suppliers were improved as required by Japanese quality standards. The Maruti Center for Excellence (MACE) at Maruti Suzuki, as well as AOTS and JPC in Japan, were instrumental in this training. An active network of kaizen-trained managers and engineers spontaneously emerged, facilitating knowledge sharing, mutual assistance, and the training of new recruits. The

Confederation of Indian Industry (CII) and the Automotive Component Manufacturers Association (ACMA) also contributed greatly to kaizen dissemination in India. CII was particularly important in spreading the practice to non-automotive sectors. Its headquarters in Delhi has a library that carries manuals and textbooks on kaizen (GRIPS Development Forum 2016).

Cambodia, one of the latest comers in Southeast Asia, faces the problem of labor quality. The majority of young factory workers are primary school graduates or dropouts or people who never went to school. Most are illiterate and unpunctual, and they lack teamwork and discipline. They are highly unproductive compared with Chinese, Vietnamese, or even Thai workers (who are known for their easygoing nature). A Japanese manager confessed that he was surprised at the extent of a lack of basic attitude and mindset in Cambodian workers, which was far worse than other light manufacturing nations. Meanwhile, the Cambodian government is weak and cannot be relied on to solve this problem. At Phnom Penh SEZ, large Japanese FDI firms cope with this problem in various ways. One automotive wire harness producer operates a private classroom within its factory to teach basic reading and attitude before operational training is given. One electronic component maker hires a Buddhist monk to preach efficiency to its workers because monks are more respected than Japanese bosses (GRIPS Development Forum 2016). Under a free and open investment policy, many Japanese investors come to Cambodia to produce high-quality pepper, cookies, and other high-end consumer items and souvenirs. But this way, technology and marketing remain Japanese, and value creation by Cambodians is close to nil.

In Sri Lanka, the apparel industry has over forty years of history. Sri Lanka is a leading OEM contractor for global high-end apparel markets, including brand-name lingerie for ladies. It can satisfy not only quality but also the ethical standards demanded by Western buyers. Even so, Sri Lankan workers were initially not so productive when the industry took off in 1977 with economic liberalization and the establishment of the country's first EPZ. Although workers were literate and spoke English, they were without proper life and work discipline. Young female workers from rural areas were dubbed "Juki Girls" for their inappropriate behavior. Top domestic apparel firms such as MAS, Brandix, Star Garment, and Hirdaramani, together with the Joint Apparel Association Forum Sri Lanka, tried hard to remove this stigma and reform workers' mindsets. MAS, the largest among them, which now hires ninety thousand employees in seventeen countries, has developed an internal system of worker training and applies it to all its factories around the world. Sri Lankan workers are now sufficiently skillful and disciplined for the high-quality goods they produce.

Global training programs are not unique to MAS. FDI garment firms of various nationalities bring their training systems to foreign lands to transform local workers. It is interesting to note that Velocity, DBL, and ITACA, which are three FDI garment firms recently starting operations in Mekelle, Ethiopia, are all satisfied with the quality of local labor, despite the usual claim that Ethiopian workers are unproductive (Ohno 2018). These firms apply the same worker training and incentivizing programs as in India, Bangladesh, and Italy, respectively, and produce good results in skills, efficiency, and discipline within six months of operation. Foreign mangers of these firms say Ethiopians are as efficient as Bangladeshi workers and better than Serbian ones. This points to the critical fact that Ethiopians are potentially productive, flexible, and trainable to become good workers, provided that proper training and incentives are given. They are gemstones that will shine with appropriate cutting and polishing. Since garment firms from different countries use different methods, proper training and incentives may not be one but many.

Finally, in Vietnam, an interesting mindset-change program is being developed by GKM Lean Management Institute, a private consulting firm. Dr. Nguyen Dang Minh, its executive, is an automotive engineer and management expert who gained seven years of work experience at the Production Technology Department of Toyota Motor Corporation headquarters in Aichi, Japan, before returning to Vietnam. He not only preaches the crucial importance of mindset (tam the in Vietnamese) but also offers client firms a practical and concrete program for transforming company-wide mindset. His method includes securing a full mandate and commitment from the general director, intensive discussions with the heads of all departments, assisted drafting of standard operations manuals by all departments, and the isolation of workers who do not cooperate. Details are a trade secret of the GKM Lean Management Institute. Since 2015, Dr. Minh has successfully transformed the mindsets of many Vietnamese firms, including Truong Hai Auto Corporation, the largest commercial vehicle assembler in Vietnam and a contract producer of Mazda and Kia passenger cars. In the service sector, his methods energized a labor-exporting company that trains young workers before they are dispatched to Japan for technical learning.

CONCLUSION

This chapter hypothesizes that a national mindset, among many other factors, is vital for the success of long-term economic development and overcoming middle-income traps. The general capacity to identify and solve problems effectively is more important than any particular problems or conditions from which a nation starts development. The mindsets of workers, engineers, managers, and farmers are all important, but the mindsets of national leaders and government officials are equally critical, as they must act as agents to encourage and support private dynamism.

This chapter also suggests that mindset can be learned and transformed, although how this can be done cannot be expressed in a concise formula or a one-size-fits-all model. The mindset issue is a very important yet difficult one for scientific research, and we are in the early stage of stating the problem and collecting random episodes. A more systematic collection, classification, and analysis of cases should be undertaken in the future. Nevertheless, this chapter has provided ample examples of mindset problems and attempted solutions from selected Asian economies, and these should give initial hints about how a national mindset may be transformed in latecomer economies in general and in Ethiopia in particular, where mindset improvement is desired in workers, government officials, and policy method.

NOTES

1. In the 2018–19 period, Argentina, Croatia, and Panama graduated to high income, and Armenia, Guatemala, and Jordan reached upper middle income. Meanwhile, Syria, Tajikistan, and Yemen fell back to low income. This suggests that the "high-income" group is not a very exclusive one, and low-income economies are often those that face internal war and conflicts.

2. This refers to high-income economies in the true sense with technological excellence and global economic impact, not a generous World Bank category of "high income." The economy of Hong Kong, now politically part of China, can be added to this list.

3. Once-popular growth diagnostics advocates tended to "discover" the difficulty of a national economy only superficially, saying, for example, that the fundamental problem of El Salvador was weak private response and that of Ethiopia was landlocked-ness. General statements such as these have little information value to development officials, who need to tackle concrete problems daily.

4. In labor surveys, the ability of workers can be divided into (i) technical skills such as cutting and sewing, (ii) cognitive skills such as literacy, basic math, and problem-solving, (iii) attitudinal (noncognitive) skills such as leadership, teamwork, tidiness, punctuality, and obeying orders, and (iv) personal characteristics such as emotion, openness, and agreeableness (Yamada et al. 2018). The mindset of workers can be defined as (iii) and (iv). However, this definition is too narrow for our discussion, which deals not only with workers but also managers, officials, and national leaders.

5. One may ask, Why then did Vietnam grow so remarkably in the last two and a half decades? The main reasons are trade expansion, ODA, FDI, asset bubbles, real estate booms, and the emergence of some active private firms (which are however not numerous or competitive enough). Policy contribution was close to nil.

6. In a more competent country, we would need three or four meetings altogether before finishing such a master plan, with far better content. We agreed to have many meetings with the ministry as part of a learning process for the Vietnamese government.

7. The same thing happened when our research team visited the management office of Vietnam Singapore Industrial Park in Binh Duong Province, Vietnam, without appointment. This industrial park was initially managed by the Singaporean government but now is under the provincial government of Binh Duong.

8. There are limited incentive packages for a small number of large FDI firms, but each applicant must negotiate individually with the ministry in charge because the budget for incentives is allocated to line ministries, not BKPM. Line ministries are not generous, because they want to save their budgets. This practically shuts out SMEs from getting any incentive. Asked why there was no broad incentive, a BKPM chairman once remarked, "The greatest investment incentive in Indonesia is our large population."

9. In the Japanese *kosen* (vocational college) system, creative engineers and technicians are systematically produced. Kosen conducts (i) technical education in knowledge and skills; (ii) teaching proper attitude and mindset; (iii) teaching creativity (just doing what is told is not acceptable); (iv) comprehensive assistance in students' job searches and internships; and (v) the college's own capacity building to offer these services.

10. For example, Taiwan spent about three years each to draft strategies to join the WTO, activate economic ties with mainland China, and revise the Industrial Statute (industrial policy law). This includes a comprehensive study by a think tank, stakeholder feedback, draft revisions, and parliamentary debate. By the time the policy was approved, necessary law and budget were ready.

REFERENCES

Felipe, Jesus, Arnelyn Abdon, and Utsav Kumar. 2012. "Tracking the Middle-Income Trap: What Is It, Who Is in It, and Why?" Levy Economics Institute Working Paper No. 715, Bard College.

GRIPS Development Forum. 2016. "Records of Ethiopia–Japan Industrial Policy Dialogue Vol. II: Policy Research in Third Countries," a report submitted to the government of Ethiopia, National Graduate Institute for Policy Studies.

Hara, Yonosuke. 2014. "Chushotoku no Wana wo Dou Traeruka" (How Middle-Income Traps Should Be Understood). *Kokusai Mondai* 633 (July/August): 1–4.

———. 2015. "Kaihatsu no Wana wo Dou Toraeruka: Asia Dynamism Saiko" (How to Interpret Developmental Traps: Reconsidering Asia Dynamism). Research Report, National Graduate Institute for Policy Studies, March.

Japan International Cooperation Agency and GRIPS Development Forum (JICA & GDF). 2011. "Kaizen National Movement: A Study of Quality and Productivity Improvement in Asia and Africa," Ethiopia–Japan Industrial Policy Dialogue Report.

Kim, Kihwan, and Danny M. Leipziger. 1993. *The Lessons of East Asia: Korea, A Case of Government-Led Development*. Washington, DC: World Bank.

Kwan, Chi Hung. 2013. "Chugoku Futatsu no Wana: Machiukeru Rekishiteki Tenki" (Two Traps of China: Facing A Historical Moment). Tokyo: Nihon Keizai Shimbun Shuppan Sha.

Ohno, Kenichi. 2013. *Learning to Industrialize: From Given Growth to Policy-Aided Value Creation*. Routledge-GRIPS Development Forum Studies. London: Routledge.

———. 2018. "Visiting Garment Factories in Mekelle: Preliminary Observations," Ethiopia–Japan Industrial Policy Dialogue Internal Report, December.

Suehiro, Akira. 2014. *Shinko Asia Keizai Ron: Catchup wo Koete* (Emerging Asian Economies: Beyond Catching Up). Tokyo: Iwanami Shoten.

Tran, Van Tho. 2010. *Vietnam Keizai Hatten Ron: Chushotoku no Wana to Aratana Doi Moi* (Economic Development of Vietnam: A Middle-Income Trap and New Doi Moi). Tokyo: Keiso Shobo.

———. 2013. *Vietnam Seicho Gensoku ni Chokumen: Souki no Wana Kaihi he Seido Kaikaku ga Kagi* (Vietnam Faces Growth Slowdown: Institutional Reform Is the Key to an Early Escape from the Trap), in *ASEAN Keizai to Chushotoku no Wana* (ASEAN Economies and Middle Income Traps), Japan Center for Economic Research, December.

Tran, Van Tho, and Shunji Karikomi. 2019. *Chushotoku koku no Wana to Chugoku ASEAN* (The Middle Income Trap from a China and ASEAN Perspective). Tokyo: Keiso Shobo.

Wade, Robert. 1990. *Governing the Market: Economic Theory and the Role of Government in East Asian Industrialization*. Princeton, NJ: Princeton University Press.

World Bank. 1993. *The East Asian Miracle: Economic Growth and Public Policy*. A World Bank Policy Research Report. New York: Oxford University Press.

———. 1995. *Bureaucrats in Business: The Economics and Politics of Government Ownership*. A World Bank Policy Research Report. New York: Oxford University Press.

Yamada, Shoko, Christian S. Otchia, Yuki Shimazu, Kyoko Taniguchi, and Fekadu Nigussie. 2018. "Interim Report: Bridging the Supply-Demand Gaps of the Industrial Workforce: Findings from a Skills Assessment of Garment Workers in Ethiopia," Skills and Knowledge for Youth (SKY) Research Project, September.

PART THREE

Federalism and Nation Building

3.1 Ethiopia in Change: Reinventing Narratives, Remaking a "Nation"

3.2 State of Ethiopian Federalism 2018–2019: Taking Intergovernmental Relations Seriously?

3.3 Conflict-Induced Internal Displacement in an Ethnolinguistic Federal State: Gedeo-Guji Displacement in West Guji and Gedeo Zones in Focus

3.4 Between Hope and Despair: Reflections on the Political Developments in Afar

3.1 Ethiopia in Change

Reinventing Narratives, Remaking a "Nation"

Shimelis Bonsa Gulema

INTRODUCTION

In May 2014, a small protest began in Ambo, a provincial town located some 120 kilometers west of Addis Ababa, Ethiopia's capital. The protest, and many others that followed, was directed against a decision by the Addis Ababa municipality to extend the boundaries of the city. The protest, which would assume a nationwide character, continued for the following four years and only subsided with the appointment in April 2018 of a reformist prime minister from Oromia, the epicenter of the resistance. The protest should be seen as part of a long lineage of protests representing a powerful critique of the Ethiopian state and the "nation" it embodies. However, the language of the protest and the way it was articulated showed the growing saliency of identity politics. It can be argued that the protests in general were fundamentally economic in nature but often conveyed in the emotive language of ethnicity. In short, what is being questioned, now or in the past, is Ethiopia's cultural and political identity and its place in the world. The answers to this question are rooted in the history of the "nation," especially its complicated and often contested origins, and the political economy that shaped its development.

This chapter discusses Ethiopia's contemporary moral and political crises and argues that this predicament is deeply rooted in the making of modern Ethiopia and in the ideologies and intellectual discourses that shaped the process. It interrogates the nature of modern Ethiopia nation-state building, the trajectory of its development, and the ideas and ideologies used to reorganize the process, especially since the 1960s. While identifying the structural and epistemic deficiencies of the Ethiopian "nation-state," the chapter makes a case for rethinking the way it was organized and the frameworks with which it was articulated. The main thrust of the chapter, therefore, is a critique of the politics and ideologies of the nation-making process. Its objective is to suggest an alternative way to analyze Ethiopia's social and political reality. It seeks to do so through a critical interrogation of Eurocentrism and its role in the production of Ethiopian knowledge and particularly the way history and historical knowledge is produced and used. The chapter underscores that rethinking the dominance of a Eurocentric episteme and the way we theorize and write history is critical to the political project of remaking Ethiopia as a progressive and inclusive nation.

What I will do in the following sections is twofold: one is to interrogate the making of modern Ethiopia and the structural crisis embedded in the process and the other is to analyze the ideological and intellectual frameworks that shaped the development, especially since the 1960s. The latter involves the main objective and contribution of this chapter, which is a critical discussion of alternative theoretical frameworks that includes a call for crafting a new Ethiopian history to foster a new Ethiopianism.

Theoretically, I argue that a Eurocentric mode of thinking and knowing shapes how Ethiopia perceives itself and is perceived by others but also informs discussions of Ethiopian history, politics, and development. The notion of exceptionalism or difference, which I will discuss in detail in relation to history, historiography, and knowledge production, has shaped Ethiopia's national psychology, or at least some parts of it, regarding the state's subjective perception of its place in the world, the nature of the Ethiopian state, the conduct of politics and diplomacy, and, not least, the production of knowledge. This idea, which has long organized discourse about Ethiopia, including writings by Hegel (1956) and a number of Western scholars, operates at two levels of "othering": one that others Ethiopia and Ethiopians from the West and the other from the rest of Africa. The former presents Ethiopia as a civilization comparable if not equal to the West and the latter as one that is distinct and superior to the rest of the continent. Both, however, de-subjectify Ethiopia, rendering it almost voiceless, although the country itself was complicit, intersubjectively, in creating and perpetuating the narrative of its difference or singularity.

The implication of this paradigm is that it prevents or limits a critical interrogation of modern Ethiopia and the entangled nature of its making within the framework of coloniality and global capital. It has engendered an understanding that underestimated the constitutive significance of the global capitalist economy that was deeply marginalizing or rejected coloniality as a framework of analysis. I call for an alternative framework that is critical of the notion of exceptionalism without, however, entirely emptying its theoretical and political potential; a structure of analysis that is also deeply cognizant of the specificities of the Ethiopian experience because of its unique location at the crossroads of multiple, at times overlapping, influences. I underscore ambivalence and entanglement as a prism to explore the complicated development of modern Ethiopia in the nineteenth and twentieth centuries.

"NEITHER AN EMPIRE NOR A NATION"[1]: THE MAKING OF MODERN ETHIOPIA

If the nineteenth century determined the *shape*[2] of Ethiopia, the twentieth century, arguably Ethiopia's "long century,"[3] could be said to have defined its *essence*.[4] Both represent two different but entangled aspects of a single process—nation-state building, which is the most seminal development of Ethiopia's modern history.[5] The complicated nature of this development engendered two essential questions, one over the nature of the polity as a political institution, serving as a source of order and structure, and the other over the cultural and political content of the nation as a national community. These questions about what Ethiopia is and what it wants to be informed the intellectual and political discussions of the first half of the twentieth century; they also organized Ethiopia's radical, and increasingly violent, political and ideological struggles since the 1960s. I argue that nation-state building has a much older and longer history in the country, going back to the early centuries of the common era (Adhana 1994), and Ethiopia, a thoroughly diverse society, could be said to have attained a degree of fundamental unity—a shared cultural world of values, myths, memories, and practices—among its culturally dominant groups, the Amhara and Tigrayans in particular, at least by the mid-nineteenth century. By then, however, this apparent unity, which led some to characterize Ethiopia as a nation, was put to the test by new dynamics: a deeper demographic and cultural heterogenization of the country because of the military expansions of the Ethiopian state and a gradual and peripheral incorporation into the global economy. Reconstructing Ethiopia a nation-state in response to a deeply changing landscape, both domestic and global, became the centerpiece of Ethiopia's political development since the late nineteenth century.

There are two different ways of interpreting this emerging dynamic that shaped the development trajectory of Ethiopia's complicated identity. In the first case, Ethiopia emerged as an empire (Holcomb and Ibssa 1990) and the task for its leaders, which was the paradox of the late nineteenth century, was to simultaneously undo an older, yet tenuous, "nation" unified by economy, culture, and history, and inscribe the contours of a fundamentally unequal "empire," engendering a new challenge in the process: to transform an "empire" to a nation that is both modern and national, which are inclusive. In the second, which is my argument, the Ethiopia that materialized after and as a result of the developments of the nineteenth century was neither an empire nor a nation, which is a simplistic binary, but somewhere in between, simultaneously containing the qualities and elements of both structures.

However, discussions about Ethiopia's cultural and political identity are often constrained by the use of concepts and frameworks that are theoretically sterile and politically limiting. One of the fundamental questions that has for long pervaded much of the political and intellectual discussions of Ethiopia and the Ethiopian state is whether Ethiopia was an empire, consisting of thoroughly different and subjugated communities, or a nation, which, despite the many differences among its constituent parts along the axes of history, culture, and traditions, enjoyed an essential unity. Ethno-nationalists, as well as radical or progressive intellectuals, argue that empire captures the political character of the Ethiopian state since the late nineteenth century. For others, such as mainstream nationalists, Ethiopia was a nation not so much in terms of a common language, culture, ethnicity, or psychological makeup as in terms of sharing a legacy of history and memories forged over the centuries and a deep understanding of a shared existence. What is needed to overcome this analytical deadlock, which also constrains the political imagination, is to create an alternative vocabulary and frameworks of social analysis that is expansive enough to capture the complexities embedded in the construction of the Ethiopian state.

Notwithstanding the differences in the naming and meaning of what Ethiopia is, what is critically missing is Ethiopia as a civic (rather than ethnic) nation—an imagined community of citizens of diverse backgrounds, unified by a willingness to live together. A political project with this objective requires a fundamental reorganization of the ideological ethos of the state, which was deeply embedded in the Judeo-Christian traditions of highland Ethiopia, but also creating the material conditions to imagine or enable extended connections or solidarity among strangers. This would involve creating a network of urban centers, a national economy, and institutions such as school systems that could spearhead the nationalization enterprise. The answer was to be found in modernization, which, it was asserted, would bring the nation so desired into existence. I argue, at the risk of simplification, that the quest for modernity was Ethiopia's most important political project in the twentieth century.

Inadequacy and the Specter of Lagging Behind: The Quest for Modernity

> የዛሬው የኢትዮጵያ ንጉስ ስራ እንደ የድሮቹ አይደለም። የዚህ ዓለም ንግስት በድሮ ዘመን ድንቁርና ነበረች። ዛሬ ግን የማትቻል ብርቱ ጠላት ተነሳችባት እርስዋም የኤሮጳ አእምሮ ትባላለች። ለርስዋም ቤቱን የሚከፍት ከበረት ይጨምራል ቤቱን የሚዘጋባት ግን ይደመሰሳል። ኢትዮጵያችን የኤሮጳን አእምሮ የተቀበለች እንደሆነ የሚደፍራት ጠላት የላም። ያልተቀበለች እንደሆነ ግን ትፈርሳለች ወደባርነትም ትገባለች።

> The task awaiting the present Ethiopian king [*Lij* Iyasu 1913–16] is not like that of his predecessors. In the old days, Ignorance had held sway. Today, however, a strong and unassailable enemy called the European mind has risen against her. Whoever opens his door to her [i.e., the European mind] prospers; whoever closes his door will be destroyed. If our Ethiopia accepts the European mind, no one would dare attack her; if not, she will disintegrate and be enslaved. (Gebrehiwot Baykedagn, quoted in Bahru 2002, 110)

This exhortative statement by Gebrehiwot Baykedagn, one of Ethiopia's reformist intellectuals of the early twentieth century, reveals the urgency with which modernity was sought after. Although there was no consensus on the pace and depth of change and the source and character of modernity, the conviction among the elites and within the progressive branch of the

Ethiopian leadership was that modernization was the key to building a country that was both modern and national but also to overcoming the sense of inadequacy and ever-present specter of lagging behind. Many of the early twentieth-century intellectuals saw the lack of material progress, more than anything else, as Ethiopia's existential challenge. They saw modernity as a key to resolving the country's development predicament, a revelatory teleology that would restore Ethiopia back to history as a member of the civilized world. Exposure to the West and its material achievements, as in the case of the 1924 visit to Europe by *Ras* Tafari Mekonnen, the future Emperor Haile Selassie, was a particularly sobering reminder that Ethiopia, although ancient with a cherished history, was dangerously backward. If the Adwa victory cemented a sense of exceptionality, the short-lived Italian occupation of Ethiopia (1936–41) brought to sharp relief, at least for some of the political and cultural elite, that to modernize was also to survive the onslaught, material and even epistemic, of the West. Intellectuals articulated the need, even urgency, for change, which Emperor Haile Selassie (1930–74) championed as long as such a change strengthened the monarchy without undermining the material and ideological basis of the state.

What followed, at times in fits and starts, was a process to modernize. The twentieth century could, in fact, be seen as Ethiopia's "age of rationalization," a reference to state-led projects to reorganize politics, government, economy, and foreign relations, thereby reconstructing the nation, all without essentially destabilizing the foundations of Ethiopia's imperial system. Examples of these measures include the centralization of administration, the creation of a modern bureaucracy, the building of a national army, the production of national symbols (anthem, flag, language, national history), the codification of laws, the rise of a network of transport and communication, the emergence of a national system of schools, the beginnings, albeit incipiently, of a national economy, and the establishment of a national urban system centered in the capital.

Urban centers, particularly Addis Ababa, emerged as crucial spaces to compose (and impose) visions, often statist and authoritarian, of nation and modernity. Cities as principal structures of modernity emerged as the cauldron where a modern nation was constructed, reinforced, and reflected. The urban became a site where nation met modernity, in which the latter was produced and reproduced in the social and physical spaces of the former. The planning of cities, like the building of schools and an army, was also aimed at creating new subjectivities—"new Ethiopians" (አዲስ ኢትዮጵያዊ/ት) and "a new Ethiopianism" (አዲስ አትዮጵያዊነት)—that were urban, national, and modern. But what kind of Ethiopianness and Ethiopianism?

Nevertheless, Ethiopia's encounter with modernity was deeply problematic and largely unsuccessful on many grounds, not least ideological, which I will discuss in detail in later sections. The first has to do with context or Ethiopia's unique historical location, which engendered its dependent development on the periphery of global capital. A country that escaped the colonial onslaught found itself entrapped by coloniality, which informed the trajectory of its political economy and epistemic development. Ethiopia's ambivalence and complicated entanglement with the world, the West in particular, generated a political and cultural reality, which some refer to as "acolonial" (Marzagora 2018), that is uniquely Ethiopian, at least in Africa, and reflected in the social, even psychic, forms of the nation. This is evident in Ethiopia's simultaneous embrace and rejection of the world, its incoherent dependence, its incomplete independence, and its shaky claims to exceptionalism. "The Hyphenated-Ethiopian," by Solomon Deressa and Gedamu Abraha (1969) offers a critical commentary on the contradictions of the modern Ethiopian man and by extension the country as a whole—the precarious condition of being suspended between tradition and modernity and between past, present, and future.

Internally, the need to modernize was confronted by the understanding of the deep material inadequacy of the nation. A traditional political economy that was changing, albeit slowly, under the pressure of global capital could not, therefore, escape the logic of a fundamental crisis in the larger political project of modernization. What this meant was that the quest for modernity would lead, as it eventually did, to large-scale exploitation, dispossession, and disenfranchisement. Violence, which was embedded in the modernist project elsewhere, also attended Ethiopia's modernist undertaking, enabling the exploitation of the peasantry, including the appropriation of his/her labor, which at times involved outright and violent predation. Such was in the nature of a predatory state like Ethiopia's and couldn't have been avoided in the absence of alternative sources of capital. Ethiopia's incorporation into the international economic system, necessitated in part by the need to modernize, facilitated the entry of capital, ideas, and goods but also created the conditions for Ethiopia's dependency and the intensification of its poor. The imperial expansions of the nineteenth century, for instance, were in part driven by Ethiopia's derivative modernization and marginal incorporation into the global economy. They brought millions into the emerging empire-state but only as subjects of the state, oppressed as a class but also as members of distinct communities, especially those in the south.

What decades of Ethiopia's encounter with modernity engendered finally was the intensification of the incoherence, and consequently the contradictions, of Ethiopia's political economy. The crisis of Ethiopia's development and the moral-political bankruptcy of its leadership was evident in the most outrageous of ways: the appalling disparity between town and country, with the urban, Addis Ababa in particular, representing the largest concentration of wealth, power, and resources. By the time the imperial regime was nearing its end, the fundamentals of a failed state and an unsuccessful modernity were firmly entrenched, all leading slowly but inexorably to a revolution, arguably Africa's bloodiest.

Ethiopia's predicament—its backwardness and the inequality and poverty of its people—required, it was argued, reinventing the country as a modern and democratic nation, transforming its people from subjects to citizens and unleashing their energy for economic self-sufficiency. The great intellectual debates of the twentieth century and the embrace, albeit selectively, of the West (የአው ርፓ መንገድ) and its ideas of modernity were based on a narrow, largely economistic, conception of development—the achievement of material progress—and were devoid of discussions about fundamental questions of popular sovereignty, social justice, freedom, equality, and secularism. These enquiries remained marginal or even elided in Ethiopia's intellectual and political discourse until the 1960s. The fight for modernity—ensuring material progress but also guaranteeing fundamental rights—had to await the rise, since the 1960s, of a progressive generation, whose analysis exposed Ethiopia's structural crisis: a backward country, a deeply authoritarian state, and a profoundly unequal nation. They believed that revolution, not reform, would deliver modernity and a thorough restructuring of state and society. Only a radical ideology, socialism, could achieve such a systemic overhaul, a break from an oppressive and chronically unequal system, and a reinvention of Ethiopia on a foundation of freedom, equality, social justice, and economic development. The experiment was revolutionary, and the changes it brought were in many ways transformative, whether that was the Derg's redistributive justice or the EPRDF's ethnic federal experiment.

Yet, the deeply contentious nature of the changes, their incompleteness, inconsistencies, and, not least, their simultaneous and contradictory effects of empowering and disempowering, created a perpetual condition of precariousness in the nation, heightening the fear that the country is teetering on the precipice of social and political catastrophe. Notwithstanding the social and material progress registered during the "revolutionary" regimes, poverty and inequality remained deeply entrenched, and the state remained oppressive, denying people the freedom to exercise their rights. Both "revolutionary" regimes, like their counterparts elsewhere, pledged to deliver popular sovereignty and socioeconomic justice but failed in both. Part of the crisis of Ethiopia's fifty years of revolutionary experiment has to do, in part, with what Andreas Eshete, in reference to the socialism of the Derg, calls "costly illusions" (2013, 14)[6] that put uncritical faith in the transformative power of an avowedly revolutionary regime and its equally radical measures. The reality has been starkly different. Ethiopia's postimperial regimes have become more repressive, enabled by their access to technologies of coercion and control. There was no fundamental change to the deeply illiberal nature of the Ethiopian state or a check on its infraction of the rights of the "citizens," even when it was expanding them, at least in theory and often out of political expediency. What emerged instead was a cannibalistic system bound to the dictates of global capital while furthering the predaceousness of the state. The state's authoritarian development practices have alienated and, in many cases, impoverished the poor in whose name it seized state power.

There is no denying the fact that there has been an expansion of the scope of freedom in Ethiopia, largely as a result of the revolutionary measures of the past fifty years. At the same time, though, the experience of that same period showed the reversibility of those freedoms, which for that matter were not always respected. These contradictory trajectories, to simultaneously empower and subjugate, created a precarious condition of citizens without citizenship (like constitutions without constitutionalism), whereby the rights citizens are endowed with and recognized, at least in legal terms, are continuously circumscribed through political actions. If we consider freedom, an idea that organized the political and intellectual struggles of post-1960 Ethiopia, to be the most fundamental attribute of a citizen and citizenship, where does an ordinary Ethiopian stand? A critical interrogation of the question of citizen and citizenship is particularly significant when state ideologies seek a Faustian bargain with their "citizens," under which the quest for economic prosperity is used to justify or require a sacrifice of democratic rights and values.

The Making of a Nervous Nation: The Crisis of Analysis

Ethiopia combines a curious mix of absolute pride as an exceptional nation of divine chosen-ness with a deep sense of incompleteness, not to mention the siege mentality deeply entrenched in the history and psyche of the nation. It is a proud country but a nervous nation as well. Ethiopia's current nervousness, which is unlike its age-old fears of falling behind (and the urgency of catching up) that shaped much of early twentieth-century thinking and politics, stems from a growing worry over its very survival as a country. Descriptions of Ethiopia as a country at a historic crossroads or even on the edge of the abyss have permeated public discourse and intellectual discussions. Deepening poverty and inequality, corruption, interethnic strife, mass displacement, and extrajudicial killings render a powerful commentary on the state of contemporary Ethiopia—the widening fissures, the threat they pose to peace and stability but also the possibilities they offer for renewal and reconstruction.

As I argued earlier, Ethiopia's current crisis, which essentially is a crisis as much of nation building as it is of economic development, was created and has a genealogy that goes back to the rise of modern Ethiopia, when a deeply predatory state expanded the scope of its predaceousness to the south. Part of this process was the south's contradictory development—its economic centrality to the new state as a source of resources but also its systemic marginality in the emerging nation-state engendering a convergence between class and "national" oppression. These emerging structural fractures of the Ethiopian state were, therefore, deeply political-economic but cultural in nature as well. While the cultural is not a simple reflection or extension of political economy, one can argue that identity politics in Ethiopia, as elsewhere, is used more often as a vehicle for the expression of fundamentally economic struggles.[7]

It was also stated earlier that Ethiopia's intellectuals sought to address the country's malaise, although their interpretations and prescriptions differed, resulting from their dissimilar ideological predispositions. This ranges from the more development-focused approach of the early twentieth-century to the structuralists of the post-1960s period, which has since set the fundamental patterns of social change in the country. As transformative as they were, the changes, however, have fallen short of addressing fundamental questions of progress, freedom, justice, and equality. Take, for instance, the EPRDF's experiment with ethnic federalism, which is radical in many respects. Its recognition of cultural autonomy involving a maximalist understanding of the right to self-determination has reorganized Ethiopia as a polyethnic and multicultural nation. Yet, the ethnic federal arrangement, which entails the ethnicization of politics, has equally deepened the fractures embedded in the nation's fabric, not to mention its constant mutilation through repressive laws and administrative practices.

Shaping Ethiopia's future especially in a context of intensely divisive discourses and politics, therefore, requires a critical interrogation of what we have dreamt and achieved and what went wrong, at least in the last fifty or so years. In particular, we need to reexamine the kinds of questions we have been asking, the interpretive frameworks and concepts we have deployed, and whether they were grounded in a deeper understanding of Ethiopia's conditions—its complicated histories, traditions, and experiences.

The question of what went wrong is more about diagnosis than about prognosis, the way in which Ethiopia's condition and its ailments are examined and remedies are prescribed. As stated elsewhere, the policies of the Derg and the EPRDF were far-reaching in many cases. The nationalization of land and state control of allocation and distribution broke the material basis of the imperial state, whereas the elevation of ethnicity as the singular organizing principle broadened the political space by empowering formerly marginal communities (while at the same time disempowering those who were not captured by the ethnic framework, including people of mixed backgrounds). The former saw Ethiopia's crisis and its resolution through the prism of class; for the latter, the privileging of ethnicity was an answer to what some consider as modern Ethiopia's "birth defects." But how did we arrive at these conclusions? Or did the crises of Ethiopia, structural and deep-seated, call for revolutionary measures shaped by a radical socialist ideology?

Messay (2008, 190) argues that Ethiopia's socioeconomic problems are not enough to explain the birth of a revolutionary mind and subsequent radical measures. For him, it was the radicalism of the elite's analysis, not of the problems, that needs to be explained. He does so by attributing the elite's epistemic crisis to cultural dislocation and their embrace, often uncritically, of the Western canon, its theory of history, and its ideas of progress. Instead of provincializing modernity, which is a result of a specific spatiotemporal experience, the educated class accepted it as a universal and universalizing norm. The West's, like Hegel's,[8] epistemic violence is partly mediated through the construction of a Manichaean opposition between tradition and modernity in which the former—and the non-Western other it represents—is considered backward and needs to be overcome through rupture in favor of the latter, which is the West's self. The result is alienation and uprootedness instead of a critical appropriation of culture and a belief in a break with the past and tradition as a sine qua non of modernity.

A chronicle of Ethiopia's last fifty years demonstrates how rupture[9] as a paradigm was used to give meaning and mandate to the state or to rethink history and organize politics. A deeper analysis, however, shows there were also essential continuities in the fabric of the country in the midst of a break the revolutions produced. One such example is the deeply authoritarian nature of the Ethiopian state, which remained intact or was even reinforced by the tools of a revolutionary ideology.

The implications of Ethiopian elites' epistemic acculturation are enduring and significant. They range from a new conception of history and historicity to a radical reorganization of politics, economy, and ideology. One cannot disentangle the political and cultural reinvention of Ethiopia from the ideological orientation of its leaders, who in most cases were products of a Eurocentric or westernized education. Eurocentrism enjoys considerable epistemic dominance, which, in some instances, has immobilized alternative intellectual practice in the non-Western world. Notwithstanding, to attribute the radicalism of the Ethiopian intelligentsia or the revolutionary nature of their measures to their elitism and cultural dislocation is to miss the radicalizing power of the deep structural crises of the country—its backward economy, its repressive politics, and its alienating cultural life. Radicalization was a process (Bahru 2014, 135) involving the deepening of social crisis and hardening the positions of different social actors (Balsvik 1985, 160).[10] It was more than a result of the adoption of Marxian thought, which was never deeply entrenched among the student leadership (Love 1986).

WHAT IS NEEDED?

What is at stake at the present is the future of an ancient but deeply polarized country and its capable but misgoverned people. The question is how to create a country that is democratic and inclusive, where every citizen and group has a stake in its future, an Ethiopia that is at peace with itself and with the world. The awakening that attended the arrival of a new group of leadership in the country has created a sense of optimism and a belief in the possibilities for a turnaround. At the same time, the last year since the election of the prime minister, Dr. Abiy Ahmed, has once again laid bare Ethiopia's deep fissures and its complex challenges. Now is the right time to ask critical questions, examine our complicated experiences, confront Ethiopia's inconvenient truths, and build on the legacy of the fight for economic and social justice, freedom, and equality.

While deep structural and institutional changes are imperative for the efficacy of transforming Ethiopia, they won't be viable if they are not attended by a fundamental rethink or review of how we know what we know about Ethiopia and its predicaments. My argument, which I discuss elsewhere in the chapter, is that there is a crisis with modern intellectual practice in Ethiopia, which largely is rooted in its deep Eurocentric upbringing and reflected consequently in its problematic interrogation of the Ethiopian condition. History and historical knowledge, in particular, require our dispassionate interpretation, especially as they have become intensely, at times violently, contested. This partly results from the presentism(ness) of the past. Current struggles on history are rarely about the past, which is never really past, but about the present and future (Baldwin 1968, 106). In the following, I will address two related themes, one on the need for a de-colonial system of knowledge production and the other on history as a discipline and profession, its place in knowledge production, its relation to politics, and its role in shaping current public discourse.

"Decolonizing the Mind"[11]: In Search of a New Epistemic Structure

The curious word in the title is decolonizing, and a reader might be forgiven for asking what the term has to do with Ethiopia, for the conventional wisdom is that there is no link between the two. Ethiopia's peculiarity, at least in Africa, has to do with its arguably "exceptional history"—a country with a distinct historical experience, which is partly a result of its location at the crossroads of multiple influences from within and without, the latter including African, Asian (Middle Eastern, Indian), and European inspirations. One can even argue that the "idea of Ethiopia" is a product not just of Ethiopian imagination[12] but also of imaginations from other areas, the West in particular. There is in fact a convergence between a Eurocentric conception of Ethiopia and Ethiopia's Semitist "great tradition," both placing the country on a pedestal of exceptionalism as a place "in rather than of Africa" (Hegel 1956, 117),[13] a "black Caucasian" distinct from and better than the rest of Africa, if not Europe.[14] Ethiopia (or at least its leaders) saw itself and was seen by many others, the West included, through a paradigm of difference, even as a separate civilizational space. Its "great tradition," enshrined in the *Kebrä Nägäst* and other documents, and its Adwa victory were deployed as instruments of validation.[15] The epistemic and material implications of this creative imagination are profound.

Ethiopia's "exceptionalism" claim raises more questions than answers, but a critique of its ideological and cultural premises and practices should not drain its epistemic possibilities, say, for instance, as a foundation for an alternative and counterhegemonic narrative. The singularity narrative has the potential to open up new avenues to interrogate and resist the West, its Eurocentric assumptions, and its universalist claims. One example is the Ethiopian critique of the West, its search for alternative modernity or attempts to negotiate Europe's colonial/colonizing modernity. An early representative of this mode of thought is *Negadras* Gebrehiwot Baykedagn, and I argue that Ethiopia's conception of itself, not just his travels, studies, and experiences, appear to have informed Gebrehiwot's early critical inquiry, notwithstanding its occasional yet dangerous Eurocentric slippages (Messay 2016) into the domains of political economy, capitalism, dependency, coloniality, and modernity (Alemayehu 2002; Bahru 2002; Caulk 1979; Gebrehiwot 1995,

2015; Salvadore 2007). Another is Ethiopia's—and its narrative's—place in subaltern cultural and political imaginations and its role in the global anti-colonial and anti-imperialist struggles. Suffice it to mention the unmistakable bond between Ethiopia on the one hand and Rastafarianism, Ethiopianism, pan-Africanism, and Afrocentrism on the other.

At the same time, we need to ask what the metanarrative of exceptionalism has done to us, not just for us. What kinds of questions and thoughts has it concealed from us in institutions and structures? Has it given us or denied us the ability to ask those questions, interrogate those thoughts, including those that were sexist, misogynistic, patriarchal, even racist but also those about power, capital, neoliberal development, and their embodied implications? A deeper interrogation of Ethiopian exceptionalism exposes its complicity, both epistemic and embodied, with tyrannical power and the consequences of tyranny. The notion of singularity, which simultaneously includes and excludes, is empowering but also subjugating. Singularity often slips into ideas of manifest destiny and civilizing missions, eerily akin to similar ideas in the West that were used to organize the unequal relationship along the axes of class and identity (racial, ethnic, religious) between Ethiopian rulers and their subjects. One cannot help but notice how current discourses, especially on social media, on questions of Ethiopia's cultural identity and belonging, among others, tap into these deeply sedimented and embedded stories and narratives.

Let's briefly elaborate what the narrative of exceptionalism signifies, especially in the context of contemporary politics and discourse. It has been argued that Ethiopian exceptionalism is fundamentally the exceptionalism of highland, Judeo-Christian, and Semitic-speaking Ethiopia, the region and culture which is constructed as the bedrock of Ethiopia's civilization. Such a culturized political imagining and construction of Ethiopia, as the space "burdened with history" (Adhana 1994; Hegel 1956; Jesman 1963), is implicated in otherizing and concealing the rest of the country—their cultures, histories, traditions, and knowledge. A cultural bifurcation of Ethiopia into a civilized north and a backward south (Ullendorff 1973), which localizes a global cultural division between the West and the rest, informs and legitimates the current politics of autochthony or indigeneity, in which people are divided into indigene or native (*nebar*) versus strangers or settlers (*safari*). Interestingly, reverse discourses that, as "representatives" of marginalized communities, claim to be counterhegemonic, use the same logic and language and reproduce the same binaries and exclusions (Asafa 1993).[16] Contemporary Ethiopia is littered with evidence of the embodied violence such a simplistic opposition entails or enables in the form of the demonization, marginalization, displacement, and killing of people considered different or alien, at times animalized beings,[17] in a way unnervingly reminiscent of Rwanda on the road to the genocide.[18]

Externally, the narrative of Ethiopian exceptionalism led to an ambivalent and complicated entanglement with the world, both the global south (notably Africa) and the West. This is evident in Ethiopia's simultaneous embrace and rejection of the world, its incoherent dependence, its incomplete independence, and its insulation from crucial discussions of colonialism and the "coloniality" (Quijano 2000, 23) of knowledge production and through them issues of poverty, inequality, global capital, and neoliberalism. While recognizing the existence of a long tradition of critical inquiry going back to the early twentieth-century,[19] the dearth of sustained and deep conversations between, and within, Ethiopian scholars and scholars from the global south (particularly Africa) has impoverished intellectual and political practice in Ethiopia.

There are at least two ways to interpret the contradictions of Ethiopia's claims to singularity, its epistemic withdrawal from decolonial inquiries, and simultaneous dependence on and rejection of the West. One is the contrast this has with the fundamentals of modern Ethiopia's historical constitution through an ambivalent and complicated negotiation with, rather than instead of, global capital. What shaped the development trajectory of modern Ethiopia are its marginal location in the global economy and its encounter, albeit unacknowledged, with coloniality, all in spite of its claim to exceptionalism. The brutal reality is that Ethiopia's independence is circumscribed by, and its complicated development takes place under, a constant, often seductive and subjugating gaze of global capitalism and capitalist modernity.

The other is what Mamdani calls "history by analogy" (1996, xviii-xix)[20]—the production of knowledge within the West's epistemic structures by pursuing the leads and examples, models and paradigms in the history of Europe, using the West as a prototype. One cannot disentangle the modern condition of Ethiopia, Africa, by extension—their ambivalent identity, the incoherence of their derivative modernity, the fragility of their institutions and structures—from the epistemic violence of this deracinating quest to understand, or rather explain away, Ethiopia and Africa in the "shadow of Europe," the former always trying to catch up and emulate the latter.

Min Yishalal (what should we do)? While underscoring the historical specificity of the Ethiopian experience, embedded in the idea of exceptionalism, one can argue that there is a need, even urgency, for Ethiopia to decolonize its episteme. A decolonial option (Mignolo 2010)[21] entails de-linking Ethiopian scholarship from its Eurocentric-Semiticist inheritance and relinking[22] it with critical subaltern/postcolonial conversations, including postcolonial African studies. A quest for epistemic vernacularism is an ambitious objective but one that is not possible or even necessary, especially in a world which the West, through its epistemic and material dominance, names and shapes.

What Ethiopian scholarship needs is more than overcoming its orientalist-Semiticist birthmarks but, more importantly, the positivist-historicist philosophy of history that structures and legitimates it. The question at stake is the very idea of history, historiography, and historical knowledge and its organizing and legitimating ideologies and methodologies. The task is to overcome a double yet overlapping challenge—a Semiticist and Eurocentric historiography and its abundant Hegelian and Rankean (Ranke 2011) constitution—and develop an alternative historiography. Achieving the latter will create the capacity for a critical inquiry into Ethiopia's contemporary condition, its place in the world, and its future trajectory.

A decolonial epistemic structure, as an inter- and transdisciplinary exercise, offers the vocabulary, concepts, and frameworks required in the production of a knowledge that liberates and empowers. At the heart of this exercise in decolonization is the ability to appreciate the complexity and interconnectedness of our lives but also our struggles for liberation. Such an understanding enables us to ask the right questions and devise the modalities and strategies that can be used in a broader temporal-spatial scale. It allowed the articulation of oppression in imperial Ethiopia as internally connected, intersectional (although the issue of gender was at times peripheral), but also rooted in the political economy of global capitalism as the main source of immiseration. The struggles then, like today, were transnational and used the language of global solidarity against capital's incursions to essentialize, homogenize, and compartmentalize. Such a legacy of critical inquiry and imbricated struggle has the capacity to inform and shape contemporary identitarian politics, which have fragmented and impoverished national political life and narrowed avenues for a more connected struggle that goes beyond divisions on the basis of class, ethnicity, gender, sexuality, religion, and region.

Beyond Binaries: In Search of a New Historiography

Part of the project of decolonizing knowledge and knowledge production in Ethiopia is to produce a new critical historiography that enables a new political imagination. This requires addressing the crisis of historical inquiry as a discipline and profession, as it informs and animates contemporary political and intellectual discourses. At the heart of the crisis is not just the binarization of discourse but its homogenization, in which a single narrative becomes hegemonic, assuming the force of Truth while eliding other truths, memories, and histories. 'Every history hides another history,' in the process engendering a hegemony as well as a homogeny of truth. Discourse constructed as such and likewise informing and legitimating political practice is the germ of Ethiopia's current predicament and the source of its precariousness.

To homogenize, that is to produce a one-dimensional metanarrative, is a deeply authoritarian political and intellectual endeavor. The evidence is none other than Ethiopia's intensely divided and convoluted politics. A case in point is the intellectual and political debates of the 1960s and 1970s. Much of the discussion was organized and reproduced within the framework of the class-ethnicity binary, although there were arguments over whether or not the two imbricated or were analytically distinct or if one of them, often class, subsumed the other. An important feature of the Ethiopian left was to transpose categories of class oppression for group oppression, just like French critical theorists had done in the 1960s. Representing the struggles of the time in the singular and singularizing language of class or ethnicity or as a contest between the two concealed other forms of oppression and resistance structured along questions of gender, sexuality, religion, and region.

Since 1991, ethnicity has been empowered as the single most important framework to order and legitimate Ethiopian politics and political participation. Article 8:1 of the Constitution of the Federal Democratic Republic of Ethiopia places all sovereign power "in the Nations,

Nationalities and Peoples of Ethiopia" and Article 39:5 defines a nation, nationality, or people as "a group of people who have or share a large measure of a common culture or similar customs, mutual intelligibility of language, belief in common or related identities, a common psychological makeup, and who inhabit an identifiable, predominantly contiguous territory." What followed was the passing of several intensely contested policies, including the institution of ethnic federalism, the ethnicization of administrative boundaries, and the privileging of groups and group rights. The implications of all these are enormous.

To begin with, privileging ethnicity, the ethnicity of the father at that, as the only marker of identity pivotal for citizenship and politics, entrenches patriarchy and marginalizes other equally important frameworks and categories with which people define themselves and organize their social and political lives. Ethiopians, especially those that subscribe to nonethnic and cosmopolitan identifications, are put in danger of being disenfranchised, with limited access to the political process. Giving precedence to a primordial definition of ethnicity engenders a narrow understanding of ethnicity that ignores the social and historical constitution of identity and its unbounded, overlapping, and malleable nature. Such an objectivist conception of ethnic groups as fixed entities or primordial givens ignores the flux in ethnic identification (Eller and Coughlan 1993; Jenkins 1997, 51). The result is the erasure of people with mixed ethnic ancestry while imposing intra- and interethnic homogeneity at the expense of the rich multiplicity of social affinities and affiliations. The formation of ethno-political entities—such as regional states and political parties—empowers, even invents, (primordial) ethnic identities while creating ethnic (and effectively citizenship) hierarchies in which some are considered natives and indispensable and others as immigrants and expendable.[23]

On the other hand, the same argument—of homogenizing, primordializing—applies to other equally powerful categories of articulation such as nation, nationalism, and the civic-ethnic variations of nationalism. More often, nation and nationalism are constructed as two distinct, bounded, and fixed categories organized around notions of organic and inorganic, liberal and illiberal, and civic and ethnic oppositions (Brubaker 2004, 133). Such binaries represent an attempt by scholars, not least political elites, to "come to terms with the normative ambivalence and empirical ambiguity surrounding the protean phenomena [that is nation and nationalism] ... to domesticate these normatively and empirically unruly phenomena, to impose conceptual and moral order on them, to subsume under a convenient formula" (Brubaker 2004, 146). In other words, this is an attempt to conceptualize or organize a complex world through a simplistic prism into a monochrome of races and ethnicities.

In Ethiopia, the nation is rendered primordial, often using the language of immutability and timelessness while ignoring its social and historical construction, its malleability, incoherence, and fluidity. Nation or "nationness" (Brubaker 1996, 13) is conceptualized as a fixed, bounded, real, substantial, and enduring entity rather than as a variable, constructed, contingent collectivity. It is composed as civic, which transcends and is privileged over all other affinities and affiliations along the axes of race, ethnicity, religion, gender, and sexuality. Conceived as such—a civic nation based on common citizenship—Ethiopia and its civic nationalism are seen as being endowed with liberal, voluntarist, universalist, and inclusive characteristics. On the contrary, ethnicity and ethnic nationalism are coupled with illiberalism, particularism, and exclusiveness. A question one may ask is how civic or pan-Ethiopian is Ethiopia's purportedly civic or pan-Ethiopian nationalism, especially in light of its fundamentally ethnic and cultural origins and characteristics?

What such discourse and the politics it shaped has done is to impair political and intellectual debate and practice, to occlude rather than clarify, and to confound efforts at conceiving alternative ways of knowing and organizing. Equally significant is their capacity or tendency to omit, deny, or conceal discussions about fundamental questions of political economy, poverty and inequality, neoliberalism, and global capital. In short, the way ethnicity, nation, nationalism, and ethnic and national identities are conceptualized[24] and politically empowered through legislative, administrative, and fiscal measures has proven to be theoretically bankrupt, analytically obscuring, and politically restricting. The crisis of Ethiopian intellectual and political imagination is exposed through the embodied violence it generated in the form of mass displacement and killings, to name just two. There should not be any reason more urgent than this to make a rethinking of the whole experience.

A critical revisiting of the road we have traveled so far, which the new political opening seems to allow, should enable a different intellectual and political imagination. One such case is to envision ethnicity (and the making of a nation and national identity) as a process, practice, and cognition and shift the emphasis from groups to group making, identity to identification, class to classification, and gender to the process of gendering (Brubaker 2002, 168; Bourdieu 1991, 223–24). Another is to restructure the infrastructure of the ethnic federal arrangement through a critical interrogation of what is working, what is not, and what is the best way out. Of crucial significance in both cases is to probe the homogenizing and essentializing discourses and practices, confront misleading binaries and their analytical and normative ambiguities, discern the slippages that occur in the process, destabilize and transcend structures that are limiting, and formulate new and liberating conceptualizations.

At the risk of simplification, I argue that political discourse in contemporary Ethiopia is organized along the analytic binary of civic versus ethnic nationalisms, each representing two different forms of organization. The former, a byword for pan-Ethiopian nationalism, is based on civic-citizenship and the latter on ethnicity and thus eliciting contrastingly distinct, often mutually exclusive, interpretations and loyalties. Both nationalisms are constructed as internally coherent, homogeneous, bounded, and fixed entities, although in reality they intersect and overlap and are considerably varied and dynamic.

Currently, mainstream, often uncritical, pan-Ethiopian and ethno-nationalisms shape the language and content of Ethiopia's public discourse. Pan-Ethiopian nationalism has gone through several permutations over the years. One component is the progressive antiestablishment tradition, which was rooted in the student movement and tried, albeit in vain, to redefine the nation on ideas of equality, solidarity, and freedom. It was, however, an exception, and a weak, albeit crucial, counter to the nationalism that is older and deeply embedded in the institutions, structures, and discourses of the state. This is a nationalism whose logic is essentially provincial—a result of a specific historical and cultural experience—but in spite of which constructed all the principal signs and symbols of the nation. Reasoning in the name of nation building or national survival, pan-Ethiopian nationalism valorizes Ethiopia's achievements, struggles, and sacrifices, especially in defending against foreign aggression, while glossing over the agonies of the nation, which include the atrocities its intensely patriarchal state committed against the poor, peasants (Afawarq 1908, 233–34), women, minorities, and members of different ethnic and religious communities (Donham and James 2002). The state, with the connivance of nationalist intellectuals, has been able to compose and impose a one-dimensional metanarrative of the past, in the process eliding or justifying its morally indefensible practices.

Ethno-nationalists, whose raison d'etre is to present a counterhegemonic narrative, often end up reproducing the tools and logic of the nationalist discourse. Immensely successful in exposing the "civic-ness" of mainstream nationalism while reifying their own, ethno-nationalists engage in building intra-ethnic homogeneity and making boundaries vis-à-vis others. One example is to claim autochthony or historical precedence (Triulzi 2002, 286), reversing the dominant or state-framed nationalism's assumptions while fortifying a native-versus-immigrant opposition. The tradition of the Habeshas as indigenous to Ethiopia is now contested by an inversionary mythology that constructs non-Habeshas as the natives. The latter draws on an antiestablishment historical scholarship[25] that offers a rival, not least invented, account of the past.

The contest over Addis Ababa, between mainly "pan-Ethiopian" and Oromo nationalists, encapsulates current national conversations over identity politics and the totalizing and essentializing impulses of the debates. It demonstrates how history or varying conceptions of it are implicated in the process, informing and being informed by current intellectual and political discourses.

For the "ethno-nationalist school," which I use for lack of a better term,[26] what organizes its discourse and politics is the contention of historical and historiographical erasure. Two periods are particularly significant in shaping Oromo historical memory and its modern political practice; one is the sixteenth century,[27] which, as the narrative goes, marks the beginning of a continuous and effective Oromo presence in the area of what is today Addis Ababa and its surroundings (or broadly speaking, the old medieval provinces of Šäwa, Damot, and Gafat). The other is the nineteenth century, which includes two important episodes: the era of early Šäwan kings, Sahle Selassie (1813–47) in particular, in the first half of the nineteenth century, and the time of Menelik (as king of Šäwa (1868–89) and Ethiopia (1889–1913)) in the latter half of the century. If earlier Šäwan kings began expanding into Oromo-inhabited areas of Šäwa, one of which, led by Sahle Selassie, in fact lasted for a quarter of a century, King Menelik consummated the process by occupying the lands and subjugating their inhabitants. The Oromo, like other subjects of the Ethiopian empire, were now subjected to various forms of state practices, including eviction, that came upon the foundation of Addis Ababa. Dispossession, which, since then, occurred within and in the environs of the city, emerged as an integral part of the fabric and history of the capital. Its most recent manifestation was the removal of Oromo peasants that attended the physical expansion of Addis Ababa, especially in the years leading to the unveiling of the city's latest (tenth) master plan in June 2013.[28]

The "pan-Ethiopianist" camp, which includes a motley of groups and interests,[29] offers a contrasting interpretation of the past that privileges historical antiquity and, on that account, claims precedence when it comes to questions of ownership and belonging in the city or defining its cultural and political identity. It speaks of a longer and older historical presence in the contested area and, specifically, the existence of a medieval capital called Bärara and other towns in the area, including Entoto, but also the site of modern Addis Ababa. It views the expansion of the imperial Ethiopian state in the nineteenth century as a recapturing of areas lost long ago. It cites stories and legends[30] as well as contemporary documents and archaeological ruins of long-defunct settlements and buildings. The latter include a pentagonal medieval fortress surrounded by a 520-meter-long stone wall and a number of large, round stone towers and deep ditches cut into the solid rock (Vigano 2016; Gleichen 1898, 210–11; Powell-Cotton [1902] 2009, 564).

The above discussion points to a past that was immensely complex, not least chaotic, and a country that was irreversibly transformed as a consequence. Old kingdoms crumbled and their inhabitants dispersed; at the same time, new populations moved in, bringing with them distinct cultures and political and economic organizations. Central Ethiopia, Šäwan in particular, was the site where this complex historical drama played out, often violently, changing the region and the country in the process. However, the way this period and its history are remembered and interpreted today, selectively for a large part, demonstrates the entanglements between memory and history, history and politics and between past, present, and future. It shows how the past informs our present and future and how the present dictates our conception of the past and the way we remember and forget it.

The two contrasting narratives outlined above consider history as the source of their claims and the legitimacy thereof but offer very different interpretations of the past, which in turn speaks to the nature of sources used and the quality of scholarship involved but also the intrusion—often disruptive—of politics and political calculations in the production of historical knowledge. Such an instrumentalist use of history extends to equally passionate and contrasting renderings of the present, especially Ethiopia's constitution—the way it was crafted and ratified, its contentious provisions, and the political reorganization it generated. A common thread that ties both discourses, which I contend has important implications, historiographically or for the way history as a discipline is understood, is their rejection of the evolving, multiple, and nonlinear nature of historical progress or the entangled character of Ethiopia's historical experience.

The two accounts valorize origin and claim autochthony, although they contest the historical depth of each one's claim and at times disregard movement and interaction, which has always been a central theme in Ethiopian history. Citing history or their own interpretation of the past as evidence, a growing number of intellectual and political elites—many being ethnic entrepreneurs—demand a redress of historical injustice as key to building a nation at peace with itself and the world. Such an undertaking entails setting the historical record straight, although that is easier said than done; making reparations (which might involve atonement, giving recognition, and paying respect to "natives" who might now be extinct or dispersed); renaming places; granting special privileges; and, in extreme cases, restoring land and rights to autochthons, although who counts as the autochthon is a matter of intense debate (Amba YeTenat ena Meremer Ma'ekel 2017).[31] In a way, this quest could be seen as a genuine attempt to confront the past and rectify the wrongs, which are plenty, and is a necessity to build a country that is fair and equal. At the same time, it could also be viewed as a political project that aims to shape the rules of belonging and create a hierarchy of citizenship and entitlements by dividing citizens into natives (*näbar*) and immigrants (*mäté*).

Such a reductionist understanding of history and historiography informs and animates Ethiopia's contemporary political debate and is partly responsible for the rise of a politics of nativism and exclusion. The language of *näbar* and *mäté* and the opposition and hierarchy it engenders mean empowerment and entitlement for one and the lack thereof for the other, who are compelled to lead precarious lives as a result, which includes forced evictions and violent attacks. The enabler is a radical political order that, since 1991, authorized several hotly contested policies—the institution of ethnic federalism, the politicization of ethnicity and administrative boundaries, and the privileging of groups and group rights over individual rights. What seems to be the case is that a radical political experiment that promised to end injustice ended up creating new ones.

The Case for a National History

> If we historians fail to provide a nationally defined history, others less critical and less informed will take over the job for us.[32] (Degler, quoted in Lepore 2019)

This is what Carl Degler, a Stanford historian, warned his fellow historians at the annual meeting of the American Historical Association in 1986. It was a reaction to the abandonment, at least in the US, of the study of the nation in favor of issues smaller or bigger than itself, like social groups, their cultures and experiences or transnational structures and global processes. For a nation to survive, however, a shared history is fundamental, and historians, rather than charlatans and tyrants, are the ones to write it. The case for a national history now is stronger and more urgent than ever, especially in a country like Ethiopia, where its very relevance, desirability, or possibility is being questioned. When a nation totters on the brink of civil war and political entrepreneurs replace writing critical history with manufacturing myths, prejudices, and hatreds, what better antidote exists than a common history as the basis for a shared future? The depth of the crisis may force some to think that it is too late or even unnecessary to write a common history or for historians to make a difference. However, it is that gravity of the situation we are in but more importantly the understanding that our history, lives, and destiny are deeply interconnected that should give us a reason to try to find a way out. There is no other option but to craft a new Ethiopian history, one that can foster a new Ethiopianism. But what is this new Ethiopian history and Ethiopianism, and what should they look like?

Writing a national history is a foundation for creating a country that is truly national—that is inclusive, fair, and equal for all. This is particularly significant when there are deeply divided and divisive understandings of the past and conceptions of the future. At the heart of this undertaking is defining what modern Ethiopia is and what it wants to be. Ethiopia, and its nationalism, is distinct, if not exceptional, from many other nations. Historic Ethiopia could be seen as a nation with a state but its modern successor, at least since the late nineteenth century, is different: a state without a nation. The question, therefore, is how to turn the state into a nation, which a long and complicated endeavor. This requires a new conception of Ethiopian history that is acutely decolonial and informed by the more generative idea of entanglement, within and without. One of its tasks is to inscribe Ethiopia's profoundly intertwined history, a history that underscores that we are a multicultural pluralistic society unified by shared histories and destinies but also recognizes the specificities of our experiences (oneness if not sameness). Composing Ethiopia's national identity, especially in the context of competing ideas of the state, constitutes the substance of Ethiopia's modern political and cultural history.

The last twenty-nine or so years represent the continuation of the struggle over the cultural and political definition of Ethiopia. The difference now is that ethnicity is introduced as a privileged organizing principle competing with, or even at the expense of, what is often referred to as civic or pan-Ethiopian nationalism. The contest currently is largely between the forces of an emboldened ethnic nationalism and those that claim to represent civic nationalism, which has been in retreat. Although a progressive tradition exists and animates both nationalisms, contrary to the simplistic opposition between a bad ethnic or illiberal nationalism and a good civic or liberal nationalism, both engage in the production of metanarratives that are totalizing and hegemonic, drawing on similar methodological and philosophical traditions and needing and feeding each other in the process. Pan-Ethiopian nationalists offer a national history that leaves out the origins, reality, and endurance of inequalities, whereas ethno-nationalist elites write a history that ignores the entanglements key to the making of the nation. The former, it is claimed, seek to write a story of consensus and the latter of dissensus,[33] thus simultaneously enabling a pluralist and richer understanding of the past while complicating the task of writing a national or nationalizable history or fostering a sense of national consciousness. A new Ethiopia or Ethiopianism—the future—imagined and enabled through such divided memories and histories of the past can be liberating and empowering. It can also be a recipe for exclusion.

The challenge is not that there are contrasting ideas of Ethiopia or competing nationalisms about it, both of which can be made better and more inclusive, but that the nationalisms in Ethiopia today are of a different variant: nationalist populism, representing a potent convergence of (civic and ethnic) nationalism and populism.[34] Populists stem from and draw on both ethnonationalist and pan-Ethiopianist streams, are often antiestablishment and opposed to political pluralism, and hold beliefs that cross over into nativism, in the process mainstreaming discourses and practices that are exclusionary or could lead to violence. One needs only to see the everyday embodied violence Ethiopians experience or the poisoning of public discourse through a politics of exclusion-inclusion mediated through native/settler, host/guest, and north/south dichotomies.

In the end, the question is, what should a new Ethiopianism and a new Ethiopian history look like? Nationalism, in its civic and ethnic formations, is here to stay, and the task for us as a country is to reconcile the two and make each better, fair, and inclusive. As Degler argues, building better forms of nationalism and a better country requires better nationalists and, more importantly, a new or renewed national contract between leaders and citizens. History informs and animates this crucial political project, but how it is written matters. As I have written elsewhere, a radical reading of Ethiopia as a coherent entity risks the danger of homogenizing the nation's diverse histories and experiences. An extreme interpretation of the notion of plurality, on the other hand, complicates the task of making sense of the nation. The challenge is what kind of history to write: One that subsumes complexity and heterogeneity under a single dominant "national" history or one that fragments a shared history into the experiences of bounded and separate groups? A way out would be to de-compartmentalize discussions of Ethiopia to show how its constituent parts are all tied in a complex web of interdependence and relationships. Such an undertaking valorizes the specificities of local experiences while constructing a composite nationalism, national identity, and history.

We need a "third space of enunciation" (Bhabha 1994, 37–38)—contradictory and ambivalent but also fundamentally inclusive, transcultural, and transcendental in nature—as a foundation for building a new nationalism and a new national history. The history we need to write is not nationalist but one that is national or "national, *anti-nationalist*" (Bhabha 1994, 56).

However, writing a national history, especially in the context of a country that is polarized and born in contradiction, also requires a moral, human rights discourse[35] (Abena 2008; Weyeneth 2001). Such an approach, which is missing in Ethiopian historiography, offers an alternative to an idealized or sanitized national history that erases or rationalizes human suffering as the collateral damage of the quest for progress or nation building. It can broaden our understanding of the past and give us the capacity to confront, redeem, and transform it and make provision for the future. Bringing the notions of morality and empathy in the writing of history will allow individuals and groups who have suffered injustice to demand a place for their memories of violence and abuse within the national history. Whitewashing or obliterating histories of violence and human suffering while selectively monumentalizing certain battle sites, specific figures, and key events will impoverish us as a nation without giving us the opportunity for a moral reckoning. What we need is not simple remembrances but critical reflection, understanding, and a political compromise to fight the corrosive powers of polarization.

NOTES

1. This is the title of my second book project, which is in progress.
2. By *shape*, I am referring, among others, to the wars against foreign aggression, the territorial campaigns, and the subsequent agreements to delimit the borders of the country. All these gave Ethiopia its modern shape, although that changed with Eritrea's secession, and put the country squarely on the map of the world.
3. The notion of the "long century," often used to refer to Europe's consequential nineteenth century (such as Eric Hobsbawm's "long nineteenth century," which spans 1789–1941, but also other periods like Fernand Braudel's "long sixteenth century," which spans 1450–1640), is employed here in reference to the formative developments that defined the social, cultural, and political character of modern Ethiopia. The "long" in the "long century" is less about the length of the period and more about the depth of the changes in the period. The concept of the "long century" is an adaption of Braudel's (1966) notion of *longue durée*, an expression used in the French Annales school of historical writing that gives priority to long-term historical structures, spanning several centuries, and focuses on analyzing historical trends and patterns. Other authors who pioneered the *longue durée* approach include Marc Bloch and Lucien Febvre. See Hobsbawm (1962, 1987).
4. *Essence* or *content* (of the nation) here represents the transformative processes that helped constitute what Ethiopia was or became, organized the cultural and social stuff that gave meaning to the "nation," and defined the ways in which it saw itself and was seen by others. These developments include, but are not limited to Ethiopia's incorporation, albeit marginally, into the global economy and the international system, its steady yet complicated entanglement with the ideas and goods of modernity, and the revolutionary experiments that reorganized state and society in the country since the 1970s.
5. For a sociological, albeit controversial, exploration of the process, one is referred to Donald Levine (1974).
6. Andreas's analysis is made in the context of the student movement and the socialist experiment of the Derg period but it, I argue, is relevant

to understanding the current manifestation of that same revolutionary experiment, the EPRDF, and the Ethiopian condition over the last twenty-eight or so years.

7. To say that economy is a fundamental factor in the upsurge of nationalism and populism does not diminish the significance of demands for recognition (*isothymia*). Fukuyama (2018) in fact argues that "Much of what passes for economic motivation is . . . actually rooted in the demand for recognition," dignity, and respect.

8. Hegel (1956, 99) defines Africa as "the unhistorical, undeveloped spirit, still involved in the conditions of mere nature."

9. The notion of rupture as revolution or a break from what preceded it (which could be a social/political formation, an epistemological tradition), is common in Marxist literature. An example is Hegel, in the *Philosophy of Right*, writing, "What is rational is real; and what is real is rational," which is an argument for the rationality of the world as it is (his specific case being liberalism, private property, market economy, and capitalist social relations), while rejecting the need for rupture or revolutionary rupture as a way to change society. For Marx, this argument is problematic, as the institutions that according to Hegel represented the embodiment of freedom and rationality do not resolve fundamental contradictions (of a one-sided and unequal society) but intensify them in a few ways and rupture, a revolutionary break, is needed to transform society.

10. For more on the link between structural conditions and student radicalization, see Kiflu Tadesse (1993) and John Markakis and Nega Ayele (1986).

11. This subtitle is adopted from Ngugi wa Thiong'o, *Decolonizing the Mind: The Politics of Language in African Literature* (Harare: Zimbabwe Publishing House (Pvt.) Ltd., 1981).

12. This assertion requires some interrogation that has a double implication—how Ethiopian is this "Ethiopian imagination"? The "Ethiopianness" of this imagination refers to the cultural politics in the constitution of the modern idea of Ethiopia. Who are included in this process and who are not and what is the role of the world, especially the West, and global capital in the making of this idea?

13. See also Czeslaw Jesman, *The Ethiopian Paradox* (Oxford University Press, 1963).
14. For detailed discussions about ideas of Ethiopia's singularity and the place of the West in their production, one is referred to the following works of Messay Kebede (1999), Teshale Tibebu (1995, 1996), and Harold Marcus (1971).
15. Likewise, Ethiopia's multiple citations in the scriptures (the Bible, Koran, and Hadith), the antiquity of its history and the achievements thereof (script, architecture, to cite a few), and its repeated successes against foreign aggression gave the country a powerful symbolic resonance and made it the inspiration for global black liberatory political imaginations. See Fikru Negash Gebrekidon (2005) and Joseph E. Harris (1994).
16. This is a reference to the inversion of the logic of exclusion (reverse ethnocentrism or "anti-racist racism"), which is to use the same signs and symbols of the "oppressor" to fight it, which includes defining, classifying, demonizing, marginalizing, and obliterating the "enemy." Northerners, or *Habeshas* (or speakers of Semiticized languages), are thus defined as "foreigners," "immigrants," and "settlers," not just to southern Ethiopia but also to Ethiopia as a whole. The cultural and historical link with the Middle East (Israel or Arabia) which became the stuff of the "great tradition" to legitimate the north's dominance and its claim to superiority is now inverted and used to otherize it, challenge its belonging, and demand its exclusion or expulsion. A case in point is the intense dispute, at times violent, over Addis Ababa, which is littered with tropes that tap into deeply contested memories, histories, and historiographies over who is the autochthon and who is the stranger and who has the precedence to name and own the place. Social media abounds with polarized debates about the city, but I cite two extensive works on the subject: Amba Yatenat ena Mermer Ma'ekel [Amba Center for Study and Research] (2017) and Tsegaye R. Ararsa (2016).
17. This refers to the use of terms such as *temch* and *jib* (hyena).
18. Mamdani (2001, 203) traces the making of the genocide, which includes the Hutu othering, rather animalizing, the Tutsi minority as

cockroaches (*inyenzi*). Dehumanized as such and constructed as sub- or less than human, the Tutsi were easily subjected to indiscriminate atrocities. In Ethiopia, occasional use of similar terms with the same effect presages a potential slide into a dark abyss.

19. The evidence is found in the works of Gebrehiwot (2015) in the 1920s, the intellectuals of *Berhanena Selam*, a major newspaper (1925–35), and the radically creative and critical minds of the 1960s and 1970s.

20. Reasoning by analogy offers a new way of examining the modern African condition, the intimacy of colonialism and coloniality, and their suffocating and oppressive power or claim to explain the world. At the same time, though, the implication of this perspective is to reduce the global south to little more than a passive spectator of European drama, a barren or empty space for the enactment of European history, and a product or reflection of European imagination. The Ethiopian/African is thus devoid of agency, the ability to subvert, make fun of, or manipulate the West, exploit its incoherence, deficiencies, and fears. An alternative argument is to see the making and writing of modern Ethiopia (and the global south), especially the last fifty years, as a product of global entanglement and part of a global human history (although one might ask how global is this global history). There is no denying that Ethiopia's political leaders or its intellectual elites were mesmerized by the West, its material progress, and were willing to learn from it. However, they were equally aware of its constraining powers and used their agency, albeit limited, to manipulate, subvert, and resist. While recognizing the merit of analogy, we should not lose sight of the power, and the empowering capacity, of this dialogic encounter between Ethiopia and the world (or the West and the rest).

21. See also Mignolo and Walsh (2018) quoted in Surafel Wondimu (2018, 26).

22. I use the term "relink" in recognition of the presence of early critical inquiry in Ethiopia going back to the early twentieth century and more concertedly in the late 1950s and 1960s. Many Ethiopians, especially those exposed to the radical, often Marxist, literature of the time showed a deep understanding of issues of racism, class oppression, global capital, imperialism, and neocolonialism. A review

of contemporary cultural and political productions by people like Tsegaye Gebre Medhin, Skunder Boghossian, Solomon Deressa, and Gebrekirstos Desta, as well as those in the student movement and the political groupings that materialized in later years, demonstrates that critical discourse permeated discussions of the time. See Shiferaw Bekele (2004). For detailed discussions, see Surafel Wondimu (2018) and Elizabeth W. Giorgis (2019).

23. The idea that the EPRDF-led government composes and/or imposes primordial ethno-national identities (through discourse and practice) shouldn't conceal its simultaneous instrumentalist use of identity politics. Suffice it to mention two examples to demonstrate this pragmatism, ambivalence, or evolution: the manipulation, even manufacturing, of ethnic identities and the invention of a region (SNNPR) contrary to the principle of convergence or equivalence between ethnic-group identity and polity.

24. Here the issue is not so much about the reality of primordialism as it is about the analytical construction of primordialism by ethnic entrepreneurs and scholars. What needs to be interrogated is analytical primordialism, the discourse through which the primordialism of ethnicity, nation, and ethnic and national identities is created and legitimated.

25. Some of the most prolific examples of an expanding subaltern scholarship are works by Oromo, Somali, and Sidama intellectuals. See Asafa (1993) and Holcomb and Ibssa (1990). For more on this historiography, see John Sorenson (1993).

26. The "ethno-nationalist–pan-Ethiopianist" opposition is problematic, to say the least. To begin with, the binary, simplistic as it is, assumes these groups to be bounded, coherent, and inflexible. There is a whole spectrum of opinions and positions within these two "camps," which themselves are internally heterogeneous and which the binary doesn't represent. On the other hand, this binary creates the impression that ethno-nationalists are antithetical to pan-Ethiopianism and vice versa. In actuality, both camps are not necessarily antagonistic or mutually exclusive; there are ethno-nationalists who are also pan-Ethiopian nationalists (ethno-nationalist pan-Ethiopianists) and pan-

Ethiopianists who don't see any contradiction with espousing ethno-nationalism. The reality is more complex, but what is clear is that both assumptions are incomplete, if not entirely wrong, and both camps present their own conceptions of Ethiopia and Ethiopian identity. There are instances of rejections of one position by the other but there are also many cases in which positions and interests intersect and interlock. For discussions on groups and grouping, see Brubaker (2004).

27. Although recent scholarship, especially the works of Mohammed Hassen, takes back Oromo presence in central Ethiopia, including Šäwa in the fourteenth to fifteenth centuries, the majority of available evidence points to the sixteenth century, and the wars and population movements the period saw, as one that fundamentally changed the trajectory of Oromo and Ethiopian history. See Hassen (1990, 2015). See also the thorough work by Merid Wolde Aregay (1971). A historically valuable, albeit contested, account of the Oromo movement was provided by a contemporary Ethiopian monk called Abba Bahrey (1959 E.C.). An English translation is available in Beckingham and Huntingford (1954).

28. The tenth master plan was in the works for quite some time, but the impetus to speed up the process came after the electoral debacle of 2005, in which the ruling party lost Addis Ababa, winning only 1 out of 135 seats. But the deeper roots of the master plan go back to the Derg's (1975–91) 1984 plan for a metropolitan city.

29. There is a tendency among members of the "pan-Ethiopianist camp" to conflate the Ethiopian state with the Amhara or present the former as a distinctly Amhara institution. The result of such merging is to claim historic Bärara, which was a multiethnic urban space, as an Amhara town.

30. See *Dersanä Urael* (1985 E.C.), a sixteenth-century book written by *Aqabe Se'at* Yohannes, a functionary in the palace of Lebne Dengel (1508–40). The book offers a historical account of medieval Ethiopia and its provinces, including Wäräb, where the imperial seat, Bärara, was found. See also *Dersanä Raguel*, a book written during the reign of Menelik that narrates stories of a medieval town (possibly Bärara), the dispersal following its destruction, and the link with Entoto; André

Caquot (1957); and *Tsehafe Te'zaz* Gebre Selassie, *Tarikä Zämän Zädagmawi Menelik Negusä Nägäst Zä Ityopiya* (History of the Reign of Menelik II King of Kings of Ethiopia) (1959 E.C.). The latter writes about a long-held tradition about Entoto as the seat of King Dawit (1380–1413) and its eventual reconstruction under a descendant of the king, a prophecy allegedly fulfilled by Menelik in 1881 when Entoto "once again" became an imperial seat of the kingdom of Šäwa, a prominent part of Ethiopia until 1889, when its king became the emperor of Ethiopia.

31. The paper's overall argument is that there is a historical link between Bärara and modern Addis Ababa and that the region, which includes the medieval provinces of Wäräb, where Bärara is said to have been located, as well as Gafat and Šäwa, were integral parts of the medieval kingdom until they were overrun in the sixteenth century, first by the forces of *Imam* Ahmad ibn Ibrahim and then the Oromo. What happened then and in the following centuries was a massive process of dispersal and dispossession but also extinction, as in the case of the Gafat people. Any discussion of autochthony and subsequent claims of special interest and entitlement should therefore be based on a full accounting of this complex history, the implication of which being those whose ancestors were in the areas first should enjoy equal, if not more, rights and access as those who live there or make special claims to them (because of current political dispensation). Such a reading of history thus raises very pertinent questions regarding history and historical knowledge, historiography, and sources: What is history and its relationship to memory? What are historical sources? How do we understand and interpret them? How do we write history? More specifically, who and what is native and who is not? What does historical injustice, in this particular case, mean? What does rectifying historical injustice entail? What does reparation like look like and how does it occur? What is the danger of privileging some memories, histories, names, and personalities while concealing or even erasing others?

32. While the quotation is intended to stress the responsibility of professional historians, especially now, one might also take it to ask for some of its assertions: What is a nationally defined history, and who

defines such a history, especially when professional historians become not just national but also nationalist historians?

33. One can also argue that a narrative of dissensus can help generate a varied understanding of the past and the writing of a richer national history.

34. One can be a nationalist without being a populist, the latter being someone who claims that he/she alone represents the "real people," takes control of the nation on behalf of the people or restores it to ancient greatness.

35. The notion of human rights and humanity is more complicated and has been used in exclusionary terms that privilege the humanity and rights of certain groups and regions (the West) as well as some rights at the expense of others (notably the non-Western world). We need to ask questions like what the content of this humanity and these rights is, what they are, and whose and which humanity and rights are privileged and concealed or suppressed. For a detailed discussion of human rights, see Hannah Arendt, "'The Rights of Man': What Are They?" *Modern Review* 3:1 (1949b), 24-36; Giorgio Agamben, "Beyond Human Rights," *Means Without Ends: Notes on Politics* (Minneapolis: University of Minnesota Press, 2000), 15-26 and his *Homo Sacer: Sovereign Power and Bare Life* (Stanford: Stanford University Press, 1998); Chrisoph Menke, Brigit Kaiser and Kathrine Thiele, "The "Aporias of Human Rights" and the "One Human Rights": Regarding the Coherence of Hannah Arendt's Argument," *Social Research*, Vol. 74, No. 3 (2007), 739-762

REFERENCES

Abba Bahrey. 1959 E.C. *Zenahu Le Gala Le Aba Bahrey ze Tsafo Be Lesane Ge'ez*. Addis Ababa: Institute of Ethiopian Studies.

Abena Ampofoa Asare. 2008. "The Ghanaian Reconciliation Commission: Reparation in a Global Age." *Global South 2*, no. 2 (Fall): 31–53.

Adhana Haile Adhana. 1994. "Mutation of Statehood and Contemporary Politics." In *Ethiopia in Change: Peasantry, Nationalism and Democracy*, edited by Abebe Zegeye and Siegfried Pausewang, 12–29. New York: Bloomsbury Academic.

Afawarq Gabra Yasus. 1908. *Ityopya: Guide de voyageur en Abyssinie*. Rome.

Alemayehu Geda. 2002. "The Gebre-Hiwot Model: A Pioneer African (Ethiopian) Development Economist." *Ethiopian Journal of Development Research* 24, no. 1: 1–28.

Amba Yatenat ena Mermer Ma'ekel [Amba Center for Study and Research]. 2017. "Addis Ababa Barara Nat, Bararam Addis Ababa" [Addis Ababa is Barara, Barara is Addis Ababa], *Nehase* 2009 [August 2017].

Andreas Eshete. 2013. "Modernity: Its Title to Uniqueness and Its Advent in Ethiopia." From the lecture "What is 'Zemenawinet'?: Perspectives on Ethiopian Modernity." *Journal of Northeast African Studies* 13, no. 1: 1–18.

Asafa Jalata. 1993. *Oromia and Ethiopia: State Formation and Ethnonational Conflict, 1868–1992*. Boulder, CO: Lynne Rienner.

Bahru Zewde. 2002. *Pioneers of Change in Ethiopia: The Reformist Intellectuals of the Early Twentieth Century*. Eastern African Studies. Oxford: James Currey.

———. 2014. *The Quest for Socialist Ethiopia: The Ethiopian Student Movement, c.1960-1974*. Eastern Africa Series. Oxford: James Currey.

Baldwin, James. 1968. "Unnamable Objects, Unspeakable Crimes." In *Black on Black: Commentaries by Negro-Americans*, edited by Arnold Adoff, 173–81. New York: Macmillan.

Balsvik, Randi Rønning. 1985. *Haile Selassie's Students: The Intellectual and Social Background to Revolution, 1952–1977*. East Lansing: African Studies Center, Michigan State University.

Beckingham, Charles F. and G. W. B. Huntingford, eds. 1954. *Some Records of Ethiopia, 1593–1646, Being Extracts from the History of High Ethiopia or Abassia by Manoel de Almeida, together with Bahrey's History of the Galla*. London: Hakluyt Society.

Bhabha, Homi K. 1994. *The Location of Culture*. London: Routledge.
Bourdieu, Pierre. 1991. *Language and Symbolic Power*, translated by Gino Raymond and Matthew Adamson. Cambridge: Polity Press.
Braudel, Fernand. 1966. *The Mediterranean and the Mediterranean World in the Age of Philip 11*, vol. 1. Second revised edition. Paris: Armand Colin.
Brubaker, Rogers. 1996. *Nationalism Reframed: Nationhood and the National Question in the New Europe*. Cambridge: Cambridge University Press.
―――. 2002. "Ethnicity Without Groups." *Archives europeennes de sociologie* 53, no. 2 (November): 163–89.
―――. 2004. *Ethnicity Without Groups*. Cambridge, MA: Harvard University Press.
Caquot, André. 1957. "L'homélie en l'honneur de l'archange Raguel (Dersanä Raguel)." *Annales d'Ethiopie* 2.
Caulk, Richard. 1979. "Dependency, Gebre Heywet Baykedagn, and the Birth of Ethiopian Reformism." *Proceedings of the Fifth International Conference of Ethiopian Studies*. Edited by Robert L. Hess, 569–81. Chicago: University of Illinois.
Donham, Donald L., and Wendy James, eds. 2002. *The Southern Marches of Imperial Ethiopia: Essays in History and Social Anthropology*. Eastern African Studies. Athens: Ohio University Press.
Eller, Jack David, and Reed M. Coughlan. 1993. "The Poverty of Primordialism: The Demystification of Ethnic Attachments." *Ethnic and Racial Studies* 16, no. 2 (April): 183–202.
Fikru Negash Gebrekidon. 2005. *Bond Without Blood: A History of Ethiopian and New World Black Relations, 1896–1991*. Trenton, NJ: Africa World Press.
Fukuyama, Francis. 2018. *Identity: The Demand for Dignity and the Politics of Resentment*. New York: Farrar, Straus and Giroux.
Gebrehiwot Baykedagn. 1912. "Ate Menilek-na Ityopya" [Emperor Menilek and Ethiopia]. Asmara: Berhan Yihun.
―――. 1995. *The State and Economy in Early Twentieth Century Ethiopia: Gabrahiwot Baykadagn*, translated by Tenker Bonger. Lawrenceville, NJ: Red Sea.
―――. 2015. (*Negadras*), *Mengestena Ye-Hezb Astedader* [Government and Public Administration]. Addis Ababa.

Giorgis, Elizabeth W. 2019. *Modernist Art in Ethiopia*. Athens: Ohio University Press.

Gleichen, Lord Edward. 1898. *With the Mission to Menelik, 1897*. London.

Harris, Joseph E. 1994. *African-American Reactions to War in Ethiopia, 1936–1941*. Baton Rouge: Louisiana State University Press.

Hassen, Mohammed. 1990. *The Oromo of Ethiopia: A History, 1570–1860*. African Studies Series. Cambridge: Cambridge University Press.

———. 2015. *The Oromo and the Christian Kingdom of Ethiopia: 1300–1700*. Eastern Africa Series. Woodbridge, UK: James Currey.

Hegel, G. W. F. 1956. *The Philosophy of History*. Translated by J. Sibree. Dover Philosophical Classics. New York: Dover. First published 1899.

———. 1967. *Philosophy of Right*. Translated by T. M. Knox. Oxford: Oxford University Press.

Hobsbawm, Eric. 1962. *The Age of Revolution: 1789–1848*. London: Weidenfeld & Nicolson.

———. 1975. *The Age of Capital: 1848–1875*. London: Weidenfeld & Nicolson.

———. 1987. *The Age of Empire: 1875–1914*. New York: Vintage.

Holcomb, Bonnie K., and Sisai Ibssa. 1990. *The Invention of Ethiopia: The Making of a Dependent Colonial State in Northeast Africa*. Trenton, NJ: Red Sea.

Jenkins, Richard. 1997. *Rethinking Ethnicity: Arguments and Explorations*. London: Sage.

Jesman, Czeslaw. 1963. *The Ethiopian Paradox*. London: Oxford University Press.

Kiflu Tadesse. 1993. *The Generation: The History of the Ethiopian People's Revolutionary Party, Part I*. Silver Spring, MD: Independent Publishers.

Lepore, Jill. 2019. "A New Americanism: Why a Nation Needs a National History." *Foreign Affairs*, March/April.

Levine, Donald. 1974. *Greater Ethiopia: The Evolution of a Multiethnic Society*. Chicago: University of Chicago Press.

Love, Robert S. 1986. "Marxian Method and Historical Process in Modern Ethiopia." In *African Historiographies: What History for Which Africa?* edited by Bogumil Jewsiewicki and David Newbury, 179–88. Sage Series on African Modernization & Development. Thousand Oaks, CA: Sage.

Mamdani, Mahmood. 1996. *Citizen and Subject: Contemporary Africa and the Legacy of Late Colonialism*. Princeton Studies in Culture/Power/History. Princeton, NJ: Princeton University Press.

———. 2001. *When Victims Become Killers: Colonialism, Nativism, and the Genocide in Rwanda*. Princeton, NJ: Princeton University Press.

Marcus, Harold G. 1971. "The Black Men Who Turned White: European Attitudes toward Ethiopians, 1850–1900." *Archiv Orientalni* 39, no. 15: 155–66.

Markakis, John, and Nega Ayele. 1986. *Class and Revolution in Ethiopia*. Trenton, NJ: Red Sea.

Marx, Karl. 1976. *Capital*, vol. 1. Harmondsworth, UK: Penguin.

Marzagora, Sara. 2018. "Nationalism: The Italian Occupation in Amharic Literature and Political Thought." In *The Horn of Africa and Italy: Colonial, Postcolonial and Transnational Cultural Encounters*, edited by Simone Brioni and Shimelis Bonsa Gulema, 141–66. Oxford: Peter Lang.

Merid Wolde Aregay. 1971. "Southern Ethiopia and the Christian Kingdom, 1508–1708, with Special Reference to the Galla Migrations and Their Consequences." PhD diss., University of London.

Messay Kebede. 1999. *Survival and Modernization, Ethiopia's Enigmatic Present: A Philosophical Discourse*. Lawrenceville, NJ: Red Sea.

———. 2006. "Gebrehiwot Baykedagn, Eurocentrism, and the Decentering of Ethiopia." *Journal of Black Studies* 36, no. 6: 815–32.

———. 2008. *Radicalism and Cultural Dislocation in Ethiopia: 1960–1974*. Rochester Studies in African History and the Diaspora. Rochester, NY: University of Rochester Press.

Mignolo, Walter D. 2010. "Introduction: Coloniality of Power and De-Colonial Thinking." In *Globalization and the Decolonial Option*, edited by Walter D. Mignolo and Arturo Escobar, 1–21. London: Routledge.

Mignolo, Walter D., and Catherine E. Walsh. 2018. *On Decoloniality: Concepts, Analytics, Praxis*. Durham, NC: Duke University Press.

Powell-Cotton, Percy Horace Gordon. (1902) 2009. *A Sporting Trip through Abyssinia*. Reprint, Whitefish, MT: Kessinger.

Quijano, Anibal. 2000. "The Coloniality of Power, Eurocentrism, and Latin America." *Nepantla: Views from the South* 1, no. 3: 533–80.

Ranke, Leopold von. 2011. *The Theory and Practice of History*. London: Routledge.

Salvadore, Matteo. 2007. "A Modern African Intellectual: Gabre-Heywat Baykadan's Quest for Ethiopia's Sovereign Modernity." *Africa: Rivista Trimstrale di studi e documentazione dell'Istituto italiano per L'Africa e L'Oriente* 62, no. 4 (December): 560–79.

Shiferaw Bekele. 2004. "A Modernising State and the Emergence of Modernist Arts in Ethiopia (1930s to 1970s) with Special Reference to Gebre Kristos Desta (1932–1981) and Skunder Boghossian (1937–2003)." *Journal of Ethiopian Studies* 37, no. 2 (December): 11–41.

Solomon Deressa and Gedamu Abraha. 1969. "The Hyphenated Ethiopian." *Addis Reporter* 1, no. 7 (February): 10–15.

Sorenson, John. *Imagining Ethiopia: Struggles for History and Identity in the Horn of Africa*. New Brunswick, NJ: Rutgers University Press.

Surafel Wondimu. 2018. "Decolonial Embodied Historiography: Female Performing Bodies, Revolutions and Empire in Ethiopia." PhD diss., University of Minnesota Twin Cities.

Teshale Tibebu. 1995. *The Making of Modern Ethiopia: 1876–1974*. Trenton, NJ: Red Sea.

———. 1996. "Ethiopia: The 'Anomaly' and 'Paradox' of Africa." *Journal of Black Studies* 26, no. 4: 414–30.

Thiong'o, Ngugi wa. 1986. *Decolonizing the Mind: The Politics of Language in African Literature*. London: James Currey.

Triulzi, Alessandro. 2002. "Battling the Past: New Fragments for Ethiopian Historiography." In *Remapping Ethiopia: Socialism & After*, edited by Wendy James, Donald L. Donham, Eisei Kurimoto, and Alessandro Triulzi, 276–88. Eastern African Studies. Athens: Ohio University Press.

Tsegaye R Ararssa. 2016. "The Special Interest: The Affirmation of Denial." *Addis Standard*, January 18, 2016.

Ullendorff, Edward. 1973. *The Ethiopians: An Introduction to Country and People*. London: Oxford University Press.

Vigano, Marco. 2016. "The Missing Tower at the Entoto Royal Citadel, in Three Photographs from 1897," December 20, 2016: 8–25. (https://www.academia.edu/30552555/The MissingTower_Tower_At_the_Entoto_Royal_Citadel_in_three_photographs_from_1897).

Weyeneth, Robert R. 2001. "The Power of Apology and the Process of Historical Reconciliation." *Public Historian* 23, no. 3 (August): 9–38.

3.2 State of Ethiopian Federalism 2018-2019

Taking Intergovernmental Relations Seriously?

Yonatan T. Fessha

INTRODUCTION

Lenin supposedly said that "there are decades where nothing happens; and there are weeks where decades happen." This aptly describes the dizzying political sea change that Ethiopia has been going through since April 2, 2018, the day that saw the election of Abiy Ahmed as prime minister. Since then, the country has witnessed political reforms that, if sustained, will soon herald a new era of democratization and human rights. As many Ethiopians, and those that follow developments in Ethiopia would agree, it has been a year of breaking news.

If there has been one constant constitutional topic that caught the attention of many in the last two years, it is the federal arrangement. It has been the subject of heated debates. It is often condemned as the cause of the country's miseries or lauded as the only hope of a constitutional avenue that can save a country on the brink of the abyss.[1] For some, it is an aspect of the constitution that is not subject to negotiation.[2] For others, it must be a central element of the constitutional reform that must happen and happen soon.[3] The way the debate on federalism is framed shows that, even after twenty-eight years of living under a federal constitution, the federal solution that the country has adopted has remained extremely controversial.

This chapter does not aim to address the major debates on Ethiopian federalism. That, I guess, is not the aim of this book. As part of a book that reviews the political and legal reforms introduced in the last two years, it focuses on major federalism-related developments that have unfolded since the election of Abiy Ahmed as prime minister. The aim is to reflect on the developments and analyze what those developments say about the state of federalism and intergovernmental relations in Ethiopia.

THE CHANGING LANDSCAPE OF INTERGOVERNMENTAL RELATIONS

One of the major observations that one can make with regard to developments affecting the state of Ethiopian federalism probably has to do with intergovernmental relations. In the twenty years of Ethiopian federalism, there has not been a single reported case of intergovernmental dispute (Gedion and Idris 2017). The Ethiopian People's Revolutionary Democratic Front (EPRDF), the ruling coalition party, controlled every state government and every seat of the federal parliament. Any dispute between a state and federal government or between state governments was addressed through party channels. More importantly, democratic centralism, the cardinal operating principle of the ruling party, required that decisions made by the executive committee of the ruling party were followed and implemented both by federal and state officials (Fessha 2019a). Ethiopia might have a federal constitution, but it is not, strictly speaking, a federation.

But things are changing quickly in the Ethiopian federation. It started almost four years ago when the youth in Oromia, the largest state in the federation, took to the streets protesting against the Addis Ababa Master City Plan, which they believed was part of a policy to drive the Oromo out of the capital city, taking their lands and threatening their cultural survival (Chala 2016). It quickly morphed into a protest against the domination of the Tigray People's Liberation Front (TPLF), one of the four parties that form the EPRDF. It did not take long before this fault line divided the ruling party itself, releasing the tension that was simmering within. The new political reality quickly led to the displacement of the TPLF as the most influential member of the coalition, through an alliance between two other members that claim to represent the two largest ethnic groups in the country, the

Oromo and the Amhara. It also led to the emergence of the Oromo People's Democratic Organization (since renamed the Oromo Democratic Party (ODP)) as a major player in the coalition and its leader, Abiy Ahmed, as the leader of the coalition and the country.

The orderly way in which the EPRDF handled the transition of power within itself prompted some to admire the resilience of the party as an institution. That might now turn out to be a premature assessment. Or perhaps the developments that ensued following the appointment of the new prime minister might have disrupted the way the party operates. But the cracks within the ruling party are more visible than ever. More disturbingly, this has morphed into public intraparty hostility. The TPLF and ADP have literally traded insults through a series of well-prepared public statements that, one must add, are unbecoming of political leaders that claim to represent citizens (*Addis Fortune*, "The War of Words Between TPLF and ADP," July 13, 2019). The bromance between the ODP and ADP, the two powerful members of the coalition that helped displace the TPLF as influential members of has also not lasted long, as tensions started to emerge over the fate of Addis Ababa and important federal appointments (Abebe 2019; International Crisis Group 2019). It has become not uncommon to hear members of the two political parties engage in public spats. Democratic centralism has been dying slowly. Intergovernmental relations are no longer as cordial and quiet as they were.

FEDERAL INTERVENTION

The strained relationship between the federal government and some of the state governments became more evident when, on the morning of August 4, 2018, federal troops took over key positions in Jijiga, the capital city of the state of Somali, one of the constituent units of the Ethiopian federation (BBC, "Violence as Troops Deploy in Ethiopia's Somali Region," August 4, 2018). Heavily armed military vehicles were stationed outside the state parliament, the offices of state government, and the state TV station. It was a federal intervention. In some respects, this should not have been surprising. Federal interference in Ethiopia is the rule, not the exception, particularly in the state of Somali. Numerous state presidents have been appointed and removed at the whims of the federal government (Samatar 2004). This is, however, the first time that the federal government had to send its army not to control unrest and "public disturbance" but to impose its will on a state government. In a move that is unprecedented in the history of intergovernmental relations in Ethiopia, the Tigray state government, which is controlled by a party that is a member of the ruling party, openly condemned the federal government's actions in Jijiga. In a public statement, it characterized the federal actions as an "irresponsible and illegal use of force" that threatens the federal system and called for their immediate halt (*Borkena*, "Tigray Regional State Issued Vague Statement on the Situation in Jijiga," August 5, 2018).

The federal constitution and law allow federal interventions in three particular cases (Art. 62(9), FDRE Constitution; Federal Proclamation 359/2003). The first, which may include the of the Ethiopian Federal Police and National Defense Force (ENDF), is the deterioration of security situation in the state (Art. 51(4), FDRE Constitution, Part Two; Federal Proclamation 359/2003). This, however, can only happen upon the request of the state government. Violations of human rights can also be used as grounds for federal intervention (Art. 55(16), FDRE Constitution; Part Three, Federal Proclamation 359/2003).[4] Although the request or consent of the state government is not a requirement for federal intervention under such conditions, the federal intervention is limited to giving directives to the state government to arrest the violators of human rights and does not involve the deployment of federal forces.

The ground that gives room for a more extensive form of federal intervention is when there is a threat to the constitutional order (Art. 62(9), FDRE Constitution; Part Four, Federal Proclamation 359/2003). The failure of the state government to comply with the directives of the federal government to stop the serious violations of human rights and bring those responsible to justice is regarded as an act that endangers the constitutional order and warrants federal intervention. But it goes beyond that and includes armed uprisings, disturbances of the peace, and the security of the federal government, as well as resolving conflicts between states by resorting to unpeaceful means. It also includes any activity or act that is "carried out by the participation or consent of a regional government in violation of the Constitution or the constitutional order" (Art. 12, Federal Proclamation 359/2003). What makes this federal intervention extensive is also that it does not require the request or consent of the state government and includes the deployment of federal forces. At the same time, this is an intervention that can only happen with the blessing of the House of Federation, the second chamber of the Ethiopian federal parliament, which also supervises the intervention once it takes place.

When the federal government ordered its army to take over key positions in Jijiga, it was clear that it was not doing so upon the request of the state government. Although the state of Somali is not known for peace and stability, there was also no reported case of armed uprising or disturbance of the peace and security of the federal government. What the unconfirmed reports present as a trigger for the actions of the federal government is the decision of the state government to declare secession from the federation.[5] Assuming this is true, the question is whether a declaration of secession amounts to a threat to a constitutional order.

Perhaps in a country like Spain, where the autonomous region of Catalonia recently declared secession, one can have a debate as to whether that amounts to a threat to the constitutional order ("Catalan Separatism Is a Challenge for Europe," *Daily Sabah*, November 14, 2019). But Ethiopia is not Spain, where the constitution indicates the indestructability of the country. Ethiopia is a country that has constitutionalized secession (Art. 39, FDRE Constitution). When a council of the state government gathers to debate and even decides to declare secession from the federation, it is exercising a constitutional right. It is not posing a threat to the constitutional order. After all, there is a long way to go before effecting secession. The constitution outlines a number of conditions that must be fulfilled before a majority vote in a referendum—let alone a declaration by a state council—leads to the creation of an independent state. There was no indication as to whether the state government had decided to ignore those procedural requirements and declare secession unilaterally. If that was the case, perhaps that would have posed a threat to the constitutional order and justified federal intervention, even then only with the blessing of the House of Federation (Art. 62(9), FDRE Constitution; Part Four, Federal Proclamation 359/2003). But still, there is no indication that this was the road the state government opted to take.

Perhaps the federal government should have allowed the council to proceed with its deliberations, if indeed there were any, or waited until the state government made its intentions known to the public. Even in a country like Spain, a country that, like Ethiopia, has faced the threat of secession and where, unlike Ethiopia, the constitution emphasizes the indestructibility of the country and does not recognize secession as a constitutional right, the parliament of Catalonia was allowed to make its views known. Only after that did the Spanish government invoke the constitution to take over administration of the region and arrest those responsible for committing what the Spanish government regards as the Catalan government's "conscious and systematic rebellion and disobedience" (Burgen 2017). Perhaps that is the road that could have been taken in Ethiopia as well. It was only after the federal government managed to convince or force the president of the state to resign that the federal government declared that the ENDF had taken over the state upon the request of the new acting state president. Clearly it was an attempt by the federal government to attach a badge of constitutional federalism to actions already underway.

Somali is a state where the actions of the federal government are seen with suspicion. Political integration of this region in the Ethiopian state remains, to say the least, tenuous. To remove the leader of the state, however unpopular that government might be, only adds to the narration of political marginalization and continuous domination by northern rulers imposing their will on the Somali people (Samatar 2004). Given the recent conflicts that claimed the lives of many along the Oromo-Somali border, one could also easily interpret the actions of the federal government as part of an Oromo war against the Somali people. It is no surprise that footage from the riot and protest in the city shows some residents chanting "Down, Down, Oromo." And, of course, the state government commands a heavily armed force of not less than twenty thousand special police officers in the volatile border area of the Horn of Africa.[6]

A negotiated political solution would have also helped the country avoid the death and destruction that followed immediately after federal troops moved to control key institutions of the state government. It would have also given the federal government enough time to take, as a measure of last resort, comprehensive action that considers not only the need to take control of key public institutions but also the safety of the residents of the state. The seemingly noncommittal and ambivalent intervention of the federal government has given supporters of the state government space and time to incite and mobilize local youth against the inhabitants of the state who are not ethnic Somali (Dahir 2018a).

Currently, the new leadership of the state—headed by Mustefa Omer, reportedly handpicked by the prime minister himself—seems to be enjoying a cordial relationship with the federal government. Intergovernmental relations seem to be smooth and not conflictual. The state is also enjoying unprecedented levels of peace and stability. It is not clear if the actions of the federal government in July 2018 have reset the mode of intergovernmental relations. The impression one gathers so far is that the state government is being run by leadership that is confident and competent enough to assert its autonomy and intergovernmental relations that make unwarranted federal intervention difficult, if not impossible.

THE CONFUSED FEDERATION

The federal system itself has not remained unaffected. The major political shift that followed the three years of protest have brought death to (or at least severely weakened) democratic centralism, which relegated state authorities to being implementers of the federal government. A cacophony of competing voices is now coming from the ruling party. The subnational governments, in particular the four large state governments, are increasingly asserting their powers and interests. This is palpable for anyone who takes the time to watch the TV stations owned by the state governments. As mentioned earlier, the state government of Tigray has declared the actions of the federal government in the state of Somali illegal. The state government of Amhara has publicly expressed its unhappiness with the situation in a neighboring state, namely Tigray, and has called for the intervention of the federal government. In the last two years, the two state governments have engaged in a war of words, with tensions rising along their borders (*Addis Fortune*, "The War of Words Between TPLF and ADP," July 13, 2019). As a result, there are plenty of signs of a federal system that is coming to life, albeit sometimes with undesirable consequences. One such undesirable consequence has been the confusion of mandates, evident in the flurry of actions and activities that have unfolded in the last two years.

In 2018, Isaias Afwerki, president of Eritrea, received delegates from Ethiopia (ENA, "Eritrean President to Visit Amhara Regional State," November 7, 2018). This would not normally make for big news, as receiving dignitaries usually forms part of the itinerary of a head of state, but in this case it was a major news item and, one may argue, understandably so. These are two countries that have been in state of war for the last twenty years. But there is another reason why the visit should have attracted unusual attention. It was not the delegates of the national government that paid a visit to the Eritrean president, it was a delegation of the Amhara state government, one of the nine state governments that make up the Ethiopian federation. They asked the Eritrean president to visit the Amhara state. The Eritrean president returned the favor by visiting the state.

This is not the only act of a state government that recently drew unusual attention. For some of the state governments 2018 was a busy year. Earlier in 2018, the president of Oromia was in the Eritrean capital, negotiating a peace deal agreement with a rebel force that was fighting for the self-determination rights of the Oromo people (Ashenafi 2018). A week after that, the delegates of the Amhara state government were in the same capital negotiating a peace deal with another rebel force that claimed to fight for the rights of the Amhara people (ENA, "ADFM to Pursue Peaceful Political Struggle," August 17, 2018). Later that year, the president of Oromia signed what looked like a peace agreement with one of the rebel forces, marking the end of hostilities (Ethiopian Embassy 2018). There are no indications that the leaders and members of these two state governments were acting on behalf of the national government.

The state government of Tigray was in the news when it arrested forty fully armed men who arrived in its capital. Apparently, they were members of the Federal Police, and the state government was not sure why they were coming to the state. They arrested them on the grounds that they had entered the state "without the permission" of the state government. The federal force, according to the state government, was "unnecessary since there was nothing that is out of control for the state government nor the state government requested help from the Federal government. . . . We had to communicate with the Federal government to figure out why they came to [the state] and were made to stay until we reach common understanding with the Federal government," the official added (BBC, "Violence as Troops Deploy in Ethiopia's Somali Region," August 4, 2018). The implication, it seems, is that the Federal Police can enter the territories of state government only under limited circumstances and often with the permission of a state government.

Exercising Autonomy?

The actions of the state government might seem a departure from the recent past, where state governments, despite their constitutional powers, were simply acting as implementing agents of the federal government. The events might be easily interpreted as indications of state governments coming into their own and asserting their autonomy, vowing to no longer serve as the administrative arm of the federal government. And that would have been a very good development. Unfortunately, that is not what is happening. What we are witnessing is state governments blurring the constitutional responsibilities of federal and state governments. As the following paragraphs argue, they are probably violating the constitution and acting on matters that are normally left to the national government.

In most federal countries, foreign affairs is a business left to the national government. On the main, subnational governments cannot enter into a relationship with other countries. This is largely due to the widely held understanding that "the representation of a country's general collective interests, especially in matters of high politics such as diplomacy, defence, and national security was seen as transcending the division of powers due to the need to present a common front toward foreign states" (Michelmann 2009). Of course, increasingly, subnational governments in some federal systems are given a say when the national government enters into multilateral commitments that have the capacity to affect powers that are left to subnational governments. In some countries, subnational governments may even have treaty-making powers and might be part of the national delegation that represents the country in some international organizations. Those are, however, the exceptions. The rule remains that foreign affairs are the competencies of the federal government. Ethiopia is no exception. The powers and functions of the federal government listed under Article 51 of the constitution includes foreign relations. When the Amhara state government invites and receives the president of Eritrea, it is engaging in foreign affairs, thereby intruding into the sphere of the national government. Of course, the federal prime minister traveled to the state to receive the Eritrean president. That was probably done to attach a badge of federal affairs to an event that was originally conceived as an affair of the state government.

The same is true with national defense. That is usually the exclusive responsibility of national governments, including in Ethiopia, as per Article

51 of the constitution. That obviously includes declaring a war and making a peace deal. The leaders of state governments negotiating a ceasefire and signing a peace agreement is again an instance of state governments exercising another function that belongs to the national government. After all, those rebel forces were not waging a war against state governments. They were fighting the national army. Even if the state governments were acting on behalf of the national government, it is not clear why the state governments were chosen to make the negotiation rather than officials of the federal government. They could have, of course, joined as members of the negotiating team. It was odd to watch the minister of Foreign Affairs sitting next to the president of a state government as a junior member of the delegation.

Furthermore, it is not accurate to suggest that the Federal Police can enter into the territories of state government only under exceptional circumstances. That is confusing the intervention powers of the federal government with the run-of-the-mill responsibilities of the federal government. It is true that it is only under limited circumstances that the federal government can intervene to take over—wholly or partially—responsibilities that are normally left to state governments. In addition to those intervention powers, however, the federal government has its own powers on a wide range of matters that require it to operate across the territories of state governments. After all, the power of the federal government is not defined by territory but by functional areas. And, according to Article 51 of the constitution, the federal government is authorized to enact and enforce criminal law. The federal government does not require the permission of the state government to arrest a suspect in a federal criminal investigation. Courtesy and effective criminal law enforcement strategy might require intergovernmental coordination and information exchange with relevant state officials. But that is not the same as requesting permission.

The tensions between the federal government and the state government of Tigray reached another level when the former, through an act of parliament, decided to establish the Administrative Boundaries and Identity Issues Commission (Ezega News, "House Approves Bill to Establish Boundary and Identity Commission," December 20, 2018). From the preamble and the rest of the proclamation that established the commission, one can gather that its stated purpose is to ensure that a neutral and professional body provides recommendations with respect to the prevention and resolution of issues of administrative boundaries, self-government, and identity questions that repeatedly occur between regions. That is not how the state government of Tigray understands the purpose of the commission to be (International Crisis Group 2019). The concern on the part of Tigray, it seems, is that the commission will be used to undermine the position of Tigray with respect to some of the territories that currently form part of Tigray but are contested by political formations belonging to Amhara. In a move that is unprecedented in the history of Ethiopian federalism, the state government petitioned the House of Federation, challenging the constitutionality of the law that established the commission (Addis Maleda 2019). The decision of the state government to petition a formal body signifies not only the arrival of an open season of intergovernmental disputes but also the fact that the party channel is no longer able to contain intergovernmental disputes, as a result of which governments are resorting to formal dispute resolution mechanisms. This, of course, is not necessarily a bad beginning, and, given the political culture of the country, if anything, it needs to be encouraged.

The Unhealthy Federation

Yet these actions of the state governments are not the real problems. What is worrying is the fact that these are symptoms of the unhealthy state of affairs that the federation finds itself in. They reveal the serious tensions that characterize the Ethiopian federation. The visit to Asmara by the Amhara state government is not necessarily as motivated by the desire to promote harmony between the two countries as it is by the desire to score political points against Tigray. The action of the state of Tigray that arrested members of the Federal Police is also an indication of the mistrust that has developed between the federal government and the state government. The mistrust further deepened with the Tigray state government accusing the federal government of an "ethnic crackdown" (Reuters, "Powerful Ethiopian party accuses government of ethnic crackdown", November 20, 2018). What is more alarming is the war of words that is going on between the Amhara and Tigray state governments. One may even easily describe the situation as a state of war (*Addis Fortune*, "The War of Words Between TPLF and ADP," July 13, 2019; *Addis Standard*, "TPLF Threatens to Distance Itself from ADP; Demands Independent Investigation into Assassinations and a Clear Decision on General Elections," July 11, 2019; *Addis Standard*, "As

War of Words Escalate ADP Unleashes a Barrage of Criticism on TPLF," July 12, 2019). When one takes into account the fact that these are state governments that do not only have a bureaucracy and the state machinery to act as an independent force but also command the armed militia as a form of special police force, it is evident that a clear and present danger is hanging over the Ethiopian federation. The situation is compounded by the absence of an intergovernmental mechanism that can facilitate dialogue and peaceful resolutions of intergovernmental disputes. In fact, matters that should be resolved through intergovernmental negotiations and behind closed doors are now allowed to fester through demonstrations and wars of words that only serve to deepen the rift among communities.

It is a good development that state governments are increasingly asserting their powers. But this must not come at the expense of constitutional federalism. The federal government must find a way to convince state governments not to continue blurring the responsibilities between the two levels of government, lest the country ends up with a de facto confederation. And that is not necessarily far-fetched. Some are already pondering over the establishment of a de facto independent Tigray state (Temare 2019). After all, most of the state governments already command armed forces, and some are conducting foreign relations.

CONCLUSION

These are better days for the Ethiopian federation. The days when Ethiopia is a federation in name only might be coming to an end soon. A cacophony of competing voices is coming from the state governments. The best evidence for that comes from the state of Tigray, run by a political party that was, until recently, an influential member of the ruling party and is now demanding that the federal government respect the constitution. The decision of member parties of the ruling coalition and the affiliate parties, with the exception of the TPLF, to merge and create a single national party, namely the Prosperity Party (*Borkena*, "Ethiopia's Prosperity Party Officially Formed in the Capital Addis Ababa," December 1, 2019), some argue, may reduce or eliminate the cacophony of voices coming from the state governments. As noted by Yohannes Gedamu (2019), "A new unified party would mean that decision making systems within the party hierarchy could be more centralised" and, arguably, that translates into less conflictual intergovernmental relations. But that assumes that the new party, following in the footsteps of its predecessor, will dominate the federal and all state governments. That is not guaranteed and probably unlikely. With the coming of democratization, the federation will inevitably be characterized by political pluralism, with the possibility of state and federal governments controlled by different political parties. When that happens, the intergovernmental disputes and tensions that are already emerging are likely to be louder and more frequent. There are, therefore, enough indications that Ethiopians now live in an era when they must take the federal experiment seriously. It is highly likely that Ethiopians will no longer be living in a country that is governed by a ruling party that religiously follows democratic centralism.

Meanwhile, the same developments mean that Ethiopians are also heading to an era when the party channel is no longer available to manage intergovernmental disputes. That could be because there is no longer a dominant ruling party that is able to enforce democratic centralism but different political parties that control federal and state governments. Therefore, intergovernmental relations will have to be managed outside the party structure through institutions and processes established by law, ad hoc, informally, and/or based on the will of the parties involved. The important point is that a culture of intergovernmental relations emerges as one of the principles that guides the operations of the federation. That also helps to imbue the federal system with a culture of dialogue and negotiation. That way, the federal government will avoid sending the national army to the capitals of state governments to achieve its goals, however legitimate those might be.

Moreover, as to whether the opening of the democratic space and the newly found autonomy that the state governments are asserting is leading to constitutional federalism, there is no clear answer as yet. The intervention of the federal government in the state of Somali that led to the removal of the state government seems to represent a continuity of the era of a federal government that is leading from the center. Given that a new dispensation that promises democratization and respect for the rule of law is on the horizon, the Jijiga situation was an opportunity to show that the decisions and actions of the federal government are guided by constitutional federalism and that the days of pseudo-federalism are gone. The resignation of some of the leaders in the SNNPR from their positions in state and local governments, after being asked publicly by the federal prime minister to do so, suggests again that accountability of state governments still runs back to the federal government, rather than the state council to which they are politically accountable. The ruling party of the state of Afar, after meeting with the prime minister, agreed to change the leadership of their state government. Yet what is becoming increasingly clear is that the ability of the federal government to interfere in the affairs of state governments seems to depend on the political position of the state government within the ruling party and the federation. A de facto asymmetry is probably taking root in the Ethiopian federation. It is clear that it is no longer possible for the federal government to easily dictate and interfere in the affairs of some of the state governments in the way that previous federal authorities have done. The successful campaign of the Sidama to have their day in a referendum to vote for their own state and to do so with the support of an overwhelming majority and despite the clear wishes of the federal government is another indication of the changing mode of relations between the federal and state governments (Fessha 2019b).

The best hope for true federalism in Ethiopia lies in the many indications that the conditions that made it possible for the federal government to function in a manner that flouts the basic principles of constitutionalism may no longer be present. The media is now relatively free. In an apparent celebration of the fact that there are no imprisoned journalists in today's Ethiopia, the 2019 edition of the United Nation's World Press Freedom Day took place in Addis Ababa. The judiciary is now headed by a prominent women's rights activist. The electoral commission is now led by a former judge and leading opposition figure who was once jailed and exiled for her role in the disputed election of 2005 that led to the deaths of hundreds of people. A committee of independent experts has been established to revise laws that undermined human rights and democratization. Topping the agenda of the committee are the 2009 Charities and Societies Proclamation that has now been replaced by a law more friendly to civil society, as well as the media laws and the 2008 anti-terrorism law, which are also in the process of being revised. With the arrival of organized groups and institutions that are independent of the state, the days of constitutionalism might be around the corner. When that happens, the federal government may not find it easy to function in a way that is indifferent to the constitutionally entrenched federal structure.

FUNDING

This project has received funding from the European Union's Horizon 2020 research and innovation programme under the Marie Skłodowska-Curie grant agreement 752098.

ENDNOTES

1. Arguably, politicians and activists that claim to represent the majority of the population in the country insist that the only road to peace and stability is via multinational federalism. As noted by Gebreluel (2019), "The regional states of Oromia, Tigray, Somali and even Amhara—historically the bedrock of the unitary nationalism—are all dominated by ethnic nationalist ruling parties and ultranationalist opposition parties." For a detailed defense of the current system, see also Weldemariam (2019). Others may not disagree with the wisdom of adopting a federal system but insist that the ethnic nature of the federal arrangement has exacerbated, if not created, ethnic divisions. This includes pan-Ethiopian political parties like the Ethiopian Citizens for Social Justice, which champions "citizen-based politics" and a federal system based on geographical and administrative convenience, and some of the parties that claim to represent the Amhara ethnic group and possibly the majority of the urban electorate (Lefort 2019).

2. The Oromo Democratic Party, formerly known as the Oromo People's Democratic Organization, released a statement indicating that the federal system is not subject to negotiation (Mulugeta 2019). This was also echoed by other political parties and movements that claim to represent the interests of the Oromo.

3. A number of opposition political parties, including the Ethiopian Citizens for Social Justice and even the Amhara Democratic Party (formerly known as the Amhara National Democratic Movement), a member of the ruling coalition party, would like to see constitutional reform as part of the democratization process. It is not clear, however, if they would want to see this happen before the election scheduled for May 2020.

4. According to Art. 7 of Proclamation No. 359/2003, "An act of violations of human rights shall be deemed to have been committed where an act is committed in the Region in violation of the provision of the human rights stipulated in the Constitution, and the law enforcement agency and the judiciary are unable to arrest such violations of human rights."

5. Other reports indicate that it has to do with the attempts of the special force of the state of Somali to disrupt a meeting by the members of the Somali community in Dire Dawa, who were condemning the gross human rights violations being committed by the state government. For more, see Caniglia (2018).

6. Under the current arrangement, "each village, or 'kebele,' chairman heads a militia consisting of, on average, fifty armed men. Each region commands its own police, including thousands or even tens of thousands of constitutionally dubious 'special police' equipped with combat weaponry" (Gardner 2019). Arguably, this is unconstitutional, as the constitution only allows state governments to maintain a police force tasked to maintain law and order. The problematic nature of allowing the states to have control of heavily armed special police forces is well explained by Mustefa Omer, the acting president of the state of Somali: "One of the biggest mistakes made along the way [was] creating autonomous security structures in the regions. No country can survive that" (*Addis Standard*, "The Interview: Displacement Crisis Not a Precursor for a Very Bad Future but Residue of a Very Bad Past: Mustefa Omer," May 15, 2019).

REFERENCES

Abebe, Adem K. 2019. "The Threat of Intraethnic Strife in Ethiopia." *Al Jazeera*, November 1, 2019. https://www.aljazeera.com/indepth/opinion/threat-intraethnic-strife-ethiopia-191028144228231.html.

Addis Maleda. 2019. "የትግራይ ክልል የማንነት እና ወሰን ጉዳዮች እንዲታገድ የፌዴሬሽን ምክር ቤትን ጠየቀ." *Addis Maleda*, October 21, 2019. https://www.addismaleda.net/archives/7472.

Ashenafi, Neamin. 2018. "GoE, OLF Sign Peace Agreement in Asmara." *Reporter*, August 11, 2018. https://www.thereporterethiopia.com/article/goe-olf-sign-peace-agreement-asmara.

BBC. 2018. "በመቀሌው አሉላ አባነጋ አውሮፕላን ማረፊያ የተያዙት የፌደራል ፖሊስ አባላት እንዲመለሱ ተደረገ." BBC, August 17, 2018. https//www.bbc.com/amharic/news-45225643, August 17, 2018.

Burgen, Stephen. 2017. "Catalonia: Spanish Government to Impose Direct Rule." *Guardian*, October 21, 2017. https://www.theguardian.com/world/2017/oct/21/spain-prepares-to-seize-powers-from-catalonia.

Caniglia, Mattia. 2018. "Ethiopia: Recent Turmoil in the Somali State Region Risks to Jeopardize the Security and Political Situation as Ethnic Tensions Spread across the Country." ESISC. December 11, 2018. http://www.esisc.org/upload/publications/briefings/ethiopia-recent-turmoil-in-the-somali-state-region-risks-to-jeopardize-the-security-and-political-situation-as-ethnic-tensions-spread-across-the-country/Ethiopia%20-%20Mattia%20Caniglia.pdf.

Chala, Endalk. 2019. "Ethiopia Scraps Addis Ababa 'Master Plan' after Protests Kill 140." *Guardian*, January 14, 2016. https://www.theguardian.com/world/2016/jan/14/ethiopia-addis-master-plan-abandoned.

Dahir, Abdi Latif. 2018a. "Ethiopia's New Premier Is Now Facing His First Major Domestic Challenge." *Quartz Africa*, August 6, 2018. https://qz.com/africa/1349015/violence-and-looting-as-ethiopia-troops-enter-somali-ogaden-region/.

Ethiopian Embassy. 2018. "ODP and OLF Agree to Work Together." https://ethiopianembassy.be/2018/11/15/odp-olf-agree-to-work-together/November 15, 2018.

Fessha, Yonatan. 2019a. "A Federation without Federal Credentials: The Story of Federalism in a Dominant Party State." In *Decentralisation and Constitutionalism in Africa*, edited by Charles M. Fombad and Nico Steytler. Oxford: Oxford University Press.

———. 2019b. *"Voting for Internal Secession: Federalism and Ethnicity in Ethiopia."* *VerfassungsBlog,* November 28, 2019. https://verfassungsblog.de/ethnicity-based-federalism-in-ethiopia/.

Gardner, Tom. 2019. "Ethiopia Awaits: Abiy Ahmed and the Struggle to Keep Ethiopia Together." *Africa Report,* October 11, 2019. https://www.theafricareport.com/18565/abiy-ahmed-and-the-struggle-to-keep-ethiopia-together/.

Gebreluel, Goitom. 2019. "Should Ethiopia Stick with Ethnic Federalism? And Is the Current Federal System Encouraging Ethnic Violence?" *Al Jazeera,* April 5, 2019. https://www.aljazeera.com/indepth/opinion/ethiopia-stick-ethnic-federalism-190401092837981.html.

Gedamu, Yohannes. 2019. "Sidama Vote First Step in Long Process of Change in Ethiopia." *The Conversation,* November 21, 2019. https://theconversation.com/sidama-vote-first-step-in-long-process-of-change-in-ethiopia-127525.

Gedion, Hessebon T., and Abduletif K. Idris. 2017. "The Supreme Court of Ethiopia: Federalism's Bystander" In *Courts in Federal Countries: Federalists or Unitarists?* edited by Nicholas Aroney and John Kincaid, 165–92. Toronto: University of Toronto Press.

International Crisis Group. 2019. "Preventing Further Conflict and Fragmentation in Ethiopia." July 19, 2019. https://www.crisisgroup.org/africa/horn-africa/ethiopia/preventing-further-conflict-and-fragmentation-ethiopia.

Lefort, René. 2019. "Political Shake-up and Localism Can Edge Ethiopia Forwards." *Open Democracy,* May 29, 2019. https://www.opendemocracy.net/en/political-shake-and-localism-can-edge-ethiopia-forwards/.

Michelmann, Hans, ed. 2009. Introduction to *Foreign Relations in Federal Countries.* A Global Dialogue on Federalism, vol. 5. Montreal: McGill-Queens's University Press, 3–8.

Mulugeta, Melat. 2019. "Current Federalism System Not Up for Negotiation—ODP." *Mereja,* February 20, 2019. https://mereja.com/index/266377.

Reuters. 2018. "Powerful Ethiopian Party Accuses Government of Ethnic Crackdown." November 20, 2018. https://www.reuters.com/article/us-ethiopia-politics/powerful-ethiopian-party-accuses-government-of-ethnic-crackdown-idUSKCN1NP1JN.

Samatar, Abdi Ismail. 2004. "Ethiopian Federalism: Autonomy Versus Control in the Somali Region." *Third World Quarterly* 25, no. 6: 1131–54.

Temare, Getachew Gebrekiros. 2019. "The Republic of Tigray? Aydeln, Yekenyeley!" *Ethiopia Insight*, September 28, 2019. https://www.ethiopia-insight.com/2019/09/28/the-republic-of-tigray-aydeln-yekenyeley/.

Weldemariam, Alemayehu. 2019. "Ethiopia's Federation Needs Reviving, Not Reconfiguring." *Ethiopia Insight*, January 10, 2019. https://www.ethiopia-insight.com/2019/01/10/ethiopias-federation-needs-reviving-not-reconfiguring/.

3.3 Conflict-Induced Internal Displacement in an Ethnolinguistic Federal State

Gedeo-Guji Displacement in West Guji and Gedeo Zones in Focus

Nigusie Angessa

INTRODUCTION

Post-1991 Ethiopia is an ethnolinguistic federal state made up of different nations, nationalities, and people. This political administration was introduced in the country's political history to address long-standing discontent against unitary government as well as access to and control over resources (especially political resources) among the various ethnic groups in the country. The intention of the system was to bring internal peace and stability by addressing long-standing ethnic questions; however, despite the benefits the federal system brought for the nations, nationalities, and people in the country, intergroup tensions have increased both in scope and intensity more than at any time before. The recurrent intergroup tensions have raised the sense of insecurity among different ethnic lines in the country in general and between those who share administrative boundaries in particular. Ethnic tensions and intergroup conflicts have remained the major challenges to both the twenty-five-year-old Ethiopian federal system and the current reform process since their inception. This chapter argues that intense ethnic conflict is usually caused by collective fears for the future which, in turn, emanate from a lack of trust and genuine interactions among the diverse groups in the country. The chapter justifies this argument by presenting the case of the Gedeo-Guji conflict as a practical example and shows how the system that was introduced to defuse ethnic tensions has changed the origins, trends, and dynamics of intergroup conflict in the country. The article presents demographic threats, identity politics, and the symbolic value of land coupled with institutional paralysis as structural causes of conflict-induced internal displacement, whereas information failure, lack of credible commitment, security dilemmas, and bad memory are the key factors that have intensified intergroup rivalry and the intensity of internal displacement in the region. To reach these conclusions, the text first describes the background of the study by analyzing the nature and dynamics of interethnic relations between the Gedeo and Guji in post-1991 Ethiopia. Next, the chapter describes the sociocultural context of the Gedeo and Guji communities, which is followed by an analysis of the underlying root causes and triggering factors for conflict-induced internal displacement in East and West Guji zones. The chapter finally analyzes the factors that have exacerbated internal displacement among the two groups.

BACKGROUND OF THE STUDY

Post-1991 Ethiopia is an ethnolinguistically based federal state made up of different nations and nationalities. This new feature of the state was crafted after long-time confrontation with the old unitary state in general and seventeen years of guerrilla fighting with the Derg regime in particular. In 1991, the coalition of the Eritrean People's Liberation Front (EPLF) and Ethiopian People's Revolutionary Democratic Front (EPRDF) overthrew the Derg regime. In 1994, the EPRDF introduced the ethnolinguistically based federal system to bring internal peace by defusing ethnicity and ethno-regional tensions as a source of armed upheaval. Based on this, the country's political system was redefined, and sovereignty was vested in the country's nations, nationalities, and peoples with the presumption that recrafting the old state would serve as the answer to the ethno-regionally based conflicts and inequalities that marked Ethiopia before 1991

(Hagmanna and Abbink 2011). Moreover, the system was also believed, in due course, to solve the "national question"—the inequalities in power, cultural prestige, and resources between the various ethnolinguistic groups (Abbink 2006). This system has given recognition to different ethnic, religious, and linguistic groups in the country. The federal system has also guaranteed to every nation, nationality, and people the unconditional right to self-determination; the right to speak, to write, and to develop its own language; the right to express, to develop, and to promote its culture; and the right to the full measure of self-government (Ethiopian Constitution 1995, Article 39:1–3). However, contrary to these benefits, tensions among different ethnic groups have increased more since the emergence of the federal system than at any time before (Abbink 2011; Asebe 2007). Ethnic-based claims and counterclaims over pocket administrative boundaries and the contested referendums conducted to address such contestations have eroded the long-standing social capital among different ethnic groups who have lived together for decades. The referendums that were conducted in different parts of the contested areas, instead of bringing lasting peace, ended up intensifying conflict between the competing groups. These social conundrums severely threatened the system that was designed to defuse ethno-regional tensions. According to Clapham, the new approach to the nationality question has prompted a set of often violent conflicts over the ownership or demarcation of the newly established territorial units, which range from full regions for the larger nationalities to district jurisdictions for the smaller ones (2006, 148).

Ethnic tensions and other related social conundrums, therefore, are not new phenomena. The problems are endemic and deep-seated in the country's sociopolitical arena since the emergence of the Ethiopian ethnolinguistic federal system. The polarized debate on the role of ethnicity in Ethiopian politics as a trigger of ethnic tensions was there since the Ethiopian Student Movement in the 1960s (Merera 2006), continued in the post-1991 Ethiopian political and constitutional debate, and has remained a point of departure among the political elites (Abbink 2015; Bahru 2000; Clapham 2006; Vaughan 2011; Yonatan 2010). Ethnicity has also remained a contested domain in state-society relations in Ethiopia and embedded in the political economy of the country (Yeshtila, Kjosavik, and Shanmugaratnam 2016). However, tensions have been heightened partly, if not completely, by the divergent views and polarized debates on the role of ethnicity in the Ethiopian political arena, which could not be reconciled—at least up to now. The magnitude and intensity of the problems have increased recently due to instability in the internal political system, weakened local administration, lack of institutional capacity to reinforce law and order at the grassroots level, and power contention. The intensified violent conflicts between the Somali and Oromo ethnic groups in eastern Ethiopia and between the Gedeo and Guji in the southwestern part of the country can be cited as practical indicators for these gaps.

This chapter presents the results of a field-based study that dealt with the ethnic tensions between the Gedeo and Guji communities, which has been highly politicized and caused the displacement of a large number of people from their places of origin. Data for the study were generated from regional, zonal, and *woreda* government officials and conflict-prevention and early-warning experts of the Oromia Regional State and the Southern Nations, Nationalities, and Peoples' Region (SNNPR), displaced people from both ethnic groups, elders, *Gada* fathers, women, youth, and religious leaders. Data was also generated through focus group discussions and key informant interviews. Information regarding the number of displaced people due to conflict was obtained from the offices of woreda administrations and finance and planning bureaus. During the fieldwork, the most affected woredas and *kebeles* of both West Guji and Gedeo zones were also visited. The study reveals the driving forces behind conflict-induced internally displaced people (IDPs) from West Guji zone (most affected zone), Oromia Regional State, and Gedeo zone of SNNPR by analyzing the trends, dynamics, causes, and consequences of ethnic tensions between the Gedeo and Guji communities in West Guji zone of Oromia Regional State.

SOCIOCULTURAL CONTEXT OF THE GEDEO AND GUJI COMMUNITIES

The Gedeo and Guji have a long-standing history of coexistence. Before 1991, both ethnic groups were under one administrative unit known as Sidamo Province (*Sidamo Kiflehager* in Amharic). However, since the establishment of the federal system, the two ethnic groups have been split into two and put under two regional states—the Guji under Oromia

Regional State and the Gedeo under SNNPR. In the current political structure of regional administration, the Guji administer East and West Guji zones, whereas the Gedeo administer Gedeo zone. However, regarding the settlement, a large number of Gedeo communities have been living in the two Guji zones, and a significant number of Guji communities have been living in Gedeo zone. West Guji zone, from where many Gedeo have been displaced, was carved out of the highland woredas of Borana zone in September 2002.

The Guji and Gedeo have histories of both conflict and peaceful coexistence. The Gedeo people identify themselves with the Oromo ethnic group, particularly with the neighboring Guji people, in such a way that today's Gedeo and Guji people descended from the same ancestors (Asebe 2007; Tadesse 2002). There is a long-standing oral narrative that the Guji, the Gedeo, and the Borana are ancestrally from the same family. Almost all of the respondents, including the Gada leaders, stated that the Guji, the Gedeo, and the Borana groups were from apical ancestors called Urago, Daraso, and Bor, respectively, and were children of the same father. The Abba Gada takes the view that these three brothers were living together at a place called Badda Wixii, around the current Hadiya zone of SNNPR. There is still strong evidence for a shared identity between the two groups; however, the written literature in this regard is very scant. The Gedeo and Guji people are highly intermingled communities that have developed shared language, history, and culture. The two communities have their own languages: *Afan Oromo* for the Guji and *Gedeogna* for the Gedeo, both of which fall under the Cushitic group of languages. The Guji predominantly use Afan Oromo as their mother tongue, while the Gedeo in West and East Guji zones use both Gedeogna and Afan Oromo. However, in West and East Guji zones, Afan Oromo serves as a working language and a medium of interaction for both groups. On the one hand, both the Gedeo and the Guji have the same political, military, economic, ritual, and juridical organization, known as the Gada system (Asebe 2007). The Gada system is still strong and most respected by both groups. They also have a common intergroup conflict resolution and transformation system called *Gondoro,* which is still used to resolve conflicts between the Guji and Gedeo. No other ethnic groups use this system to resolve their conflicts. Women of the two communities have a common economic support system called *Jaalaa.* The two communities have intermingled through marriage. A significant number of people at the woredas who were affected by ethnic tensions are Protestant by their religion and worship together in the Kalehiwot Church.

Through interactions and long-time coexistence, the two communities started to influence one another. The agriculturalist Gedeo taught the Guji farming and sedentary life, while the pastoralist Guji taught the Gedeo animal rearing. The two communities have developed socioeconomic interdependence and skills and commodity exchanges for decades. They also share common means of livelihood (coffee, *Ensete (False Banana)*, and livestock production). However, the Guji have a large area of land, while the Gedeo are characterized by high population density and lack of enough cultivable land. The Gedeo's socioeconomic well-being has been affected by this extreme population density, which has resulted in a high influx of Gedeo to Guji zone in search of cultivable land and related jobs, which gradually led to permanent settlements in the zones, and which, in turn, changed the demographic pattern of Guji zone, especially in some woredas of West Guji zone, where many Gedeo were displaced due to the 2018 ethnic tensions.

GEDEO-GUJI CONFLICT DYNAMICS

Interactions between the Guji and Gedeo can be characterized by both a history of peaceful coexistence and a history of conflicts. According to Asebe (2007), the Guji belong to the Oromo ethnic group and share significant markers of ethnicity such as language, religion, shared memory of history, similar traditional practices, and even a common psychological makeup with the neighboring Arsi and Borana Oromo clans; however, these markers of ethnicity could not curtail warfare among these clans of the same ethnic group. On the contrary, the Guji have had more harmonious and friendly periods of interaction with the Gedeo, who may be considered "distinct" on the basis of such criteria. Due to their long-time coexistence, the Gedeo and Guji have developed different identity makeups in common; and according to elder respondents, the ordinary people did not consider themselves as distinct ethnic groups, especially before the emergence of an ethnolinguistic federal system in the Ethiopian political administration. Thus, the influx of Gedeo communities to Guji areas was not considered a serious threat to their

Guji brothers. Of course, there were intermittent conflicts between the two ethnic groups, mainly due to differences in their livelihood strategies. The elders and the Gada father have a view that their ethnicized power politics, identity-based claims and counterclaims over administrative boundaries, and resource-based competitions (both political and economic resources), as well as considering themselves as distinct ethnic groups ("us"-"them" perspectives) due to ever-increasing ethnic narratives, are recent phenomena brewed by the political and business elites situated within the ethnolinguistic political system. In addition to these, the shift of the Guji livelihood strategy from pastoralism to agropastoralism contributed to reshaping the pattern and dynamics of competition for land and redefined the conflicts between the Gedeo and Guji. This, in turn, has gradually created a security dilemma between the two groups. The heightened identity politics and territoriality in the region have also played a significant role in reshaping intergroup relations between the Guji and Gedeo.

Insights from focus group discussions and key informant interviews indicated that recurrent territorial rearrangements by successive governments have also created continued discontent between the Guji and Gedeo groups. The discontent with territorial rearrangement basically emanated from two grounds: 1) dividing members of the same ethnic group into two administrative regions, and 2) the Guji felt that they were dominated by the Gedeo on "their own land," while the Gedeo felt they were denied their constitutional rights to rule themselves in areas in which they assume dominance, which in turn ethnicized the political environment (Asebe 2007) and heightened intergroup tensions around the two since 1991. Discontent with territorial delineation and strong demand for self-government resulted in the 1995 and 1998 referendums, which ended in violent conflicts and related calamities. Especially after the 1995 referendum the Guji felt betrayed by their Gedeo brothers because the Guji lost some of their localities through the referendum. Thus, the efforts made by the government to resolve the problems by delineating the administrative localities to the competing ethnic groups through the referendum could not bring any lasting solution to the problems; rather, it heightened ethnic tensions. Thus, the 2018 tensions between the Guji and Gedeo communities were not a new phenomenon. They were an extension of the 1995 and 1998 unaddressed contestations over administrative localities between the two communities. What makes the recent tensions different from the previous ones are their intensity and magnitude.

According to the elders, the Guji-Gedeo conflict even dates back to the Haile Selassie regime, when the regime resettled the Gedeo on the then-vacant place traditionally called Tef Meret (ጤፍ መሬት) which the Guji claimed as their grazing land. This resettlement, which was done to create space for the overpopulated Gedeo, led to contestations with the Guji, who used the land during the dry season for pasture. Due to this discontent, the elders ascertained that there were intermittent intergroup conflicts during that time, too. Land-related conflict between the two groups also continued during the Derg regime. However, almost all of the respondents stated a belief that the two groups were managing their conflicts by themselves through their own customary mechanisms. According to these elders, the conflict passed to a new phase after the 1995 referendum, which was conducted to address the Guji's deep discontent with being politically dominated by the Gedeo, cultural uncertainty, territorial isolation from their ethnic members, and economic powerlessness with regard to their own resources (Asebe 2007). According to the elders, the implementation process of the 1995 referendum ended up with deadly conflicts, mainly because both parties were not ready to accept the referendum. Without properly addressing the root causes of the 1995 violence, a similar effort was made in 1998 to conduct a referendum on disputable localities, which in turn led to a relapse of the conflict. Economic interests of Gedeo politicians on the one hand and Guji's strong demand for territorial integrity and defense to their land rights on the other complicated the 1998 violence (Asebe 2007). As Asebe notes, regardless of other possible causes of interethnic tensions, the "new experiment" of ethnic policy played a central role in the changing Gedeo-Guji conflict dynamic. Gedeo and Guji elders confirmed this idea. In general, the 1995 and 1998 post-referendum violence took away individuals' lives and property and distracted the long-standing social capital between the groups. The 2018 conflict and associated internal displacement was, therefore, the result of these two outbreaks of violence, which were not transformed but rather contained by the government security apparatus.

When the regional states were constituted for the second time in 1995, identity-based deadly conflict erupted between the two groups in some contested localities of both Oromia and SNNPR. An effort to resolve the conflict through a referendum was not successful, and the expected peace between the two communities was not ensured. However, claims and counterclaims over some administrative localities continued. To address the problem once more, a committee was established to reinitiate the referendum process. However, due to intensified violence that erupted again between the two groups and led to great loss of life and the displacement of hundreds of thousands, the referendum was not conducted. This attempted referendum also failed to resolve the underlying causes of the tensions between the two groups. Thus, almost all of the respondents stated that neither the first nor second referendum was conducted successfully. Instead, the referendum efforts created a big rift between the Guji and Gedeo. In this process, business and political elites, in order to ensure their political and economic upper hand, played their part to construct narratives and counter-narratives that could erode the social capital that had held the two communities together for a long period of time. The Gedeo have been construed as land-grabbers, while the Guji have been portrayed as oppressors of the Gedeo. Any dispute on land or land use between individuals or households has been ethnically galvanized and become a collective issue pitting the two communities against each other. Interpersonal conflicts have been considered as interethnic conflicts. Consequently, fear and frustration have developed over time. Trust and positive attitudes toward one another have been weakened. Deep-seated grievances from both sides have also accumulated over the last twenty-five years. These accumulated and unaddressed social problems, together with weakened institutions and lack of the rule of law, finally led to the 2018 large-scale conflict between the two communities.

These two referendum attempts, according to the respondents, did not bring the intended result and ensure peace; rather, they led to further instability and human insecurity. Local administrators also have the view that the post-referendum situation played its part in reshaping the intergroup relationship between the Gedeo and Guji, which in turn changed the intensity and dynamics of the conflict between the two groups. Two major causes were mentioned by both community representatives and local administrators who participated in this study. The first cause that changed the intensity and dynamics of the conflict, according to the respondents, was that both groups developed a win-lose mentality after the referendum. Competing interests of local administrators over disputable localities was stated as the second cause that intensified the conflict. It also became difficult for all parties (the community and government officials) to wholeheartedly accept the results of the referendum. The major driving factor behind this was more of symbolic politics than social and/or economic, as many of the respondents stated. As Jenkins notes, attempts by political and business elites to construct counter-identities as part of the challenges against an ethnic order generated interethnic tensions. For these groups, a "we" cannot be defined except as distinct from a "they." Ethnic identities in this frame of thinking are borne in opposition and carry an abstract potential for conflicts. To make identity markers more dramatic, these groups construct collective memories in the form of myths, symbols, and legends about events and actors (2010). The current Gedeo-Guji conflict can also be seen exactly through this lens. On the other hand, politics in general manipulates people's myths, symbols, and emotions, while "symbolic politics" mainly focuses on arousing emotions rather than addressing real interests (Kaufman 2001). Thus, as Kaufman rightly puts it, prejudiced symbolic politics and insecurity feed off each other. Ethnic prejudice and hostility, in turn, make people more likely to see the other group as threatening, while feelings of threat and insecurity contribute to the success of efforts by elites to stir up ethnic extremism (2001). In this context, myth and symbols (especially land as a symbolic value) have been used to widen the ethnic gap between the Guji and Gedeo. For decades, events and actions were given a particular meaning by defining enemies and heroes, victims and perpetrators, and tying ideas of right and wrong to people's identity. These myths also have been emotionally charged and gradually widened the "we" and "they" perspectives. Symbolic politics, manipulative elites, and claims and counterclaims over political administration at the contested localities of West Guji zone remained unresolved for decades. These, in turn, increased levels of mistrust and suspicion among members of the two communities as well as a sense of marginalization among the Gedeo, especially the youth who reside in the Guji zones. It was a cumulative effect of these social problems that resulted in the 2018 massive internal displacement and human suffering.

UNDERLYING ROOT CAUSES AND TRIGGERING FACTORS FOR CONFLICT-INDUCED INTERNAL DISPLACEMENT IN THE GUJI ZONES

Different factors can be considered as causes for the Gedeo-Guji conflict. In pre-1991 Ethiopia, contestation over land was the central cause of recurrent Guji-Gedeo conflicts. In the past, land-related conflicts between the two groups were managed at two levels: minor disputes by the elders or customary leaders and violent ones through the Gondoro system. However, the introduction of the federal system added identity politics to the already existing stiff competition over land, which in turn changed the nature, intensity, magnitude, and dynamics of conflict between the two groups, making it difficult for customary institutions to deal with such complex conflicts. The 1995, 1998, and 2018 conflicts were the biggest Gedeo-Guji violent conflicts, where the former led to the latter and caused by identity-based contestations in administrative localities. As stated elsewhere, the influx of a large number of Gedeo into Guji areas already changed the demographic pattern in the current West Guji zone. In some localities, like Kercha woreda, for instance, Gedeo claim a majority. As a result, the zone remains a point of contention between the two communities when it comes to political administration. It has been a place where recurrent questions of self-administration have been raised and cost thousands of human lives, large-scale property damage, and recurrent displacement. From this perspective, Toft (2003) states that ethnic solidarity in geographically segregated areas facilitates the social construction of ethnic identities, which in turn are mobilized by charismatic ethnic leaders who construct new identities and challenges to state power. The same is true for Gedeo-Guji tensions.

In this context, the federal system by itself may not be a problem. However, its handling and the understanding of the people who have been governed by this system have serious problems. Before the emergence of the ethnolinguistic federal structure, the Gedeo used to get access to Guji land either through land rent or sharecropping. At that time, land was essential primarily for livelihood. But after the enactment of the new system of governance, access and control over land has become a critical issue—it has become not only a source of livelihood but also a precious commodity on which all the constitutional rights and policy provisions are put into effect, guaranteed, and exercised. The symbolic values of land increased, and the right to get access to and control over land has been redefined. This, in turn, changed the nature and pattern of interactions between those who claim ancestral ownership of land and those who hold it. This is mainly because land has become the most important economic and political resource and a major existential and identity aspect for the people who occupy it. For the Gedeo communities who flood the Guji zones, land has a high economic value and is a guarantee to sustain themselves and their families. For the Guji communities, land has become an important economic asset. More than its economic values, land has symbolic and historical meaning and forms the basis of their social and cultural existence. But behind both, there is also the political interest of elitists like the local political class, business groups, and some educated people who have assumed power. These perceptions not only linger today as defining the heritage of the group but also have tended to develop into a basis for exclusive identity formation, as can be seen from the numerous territorial conflicts between the groups that have come to style themselves discursively in ethnic terms (Abbink 2006). These perceptions, which emerged with the new governance system, have continued up to these days as the underlying causes for recurrent ethnic tensions between the Gedeo and Guji.

The competition between Guji and Gedeo political and economic elites heated ethnic tensions and made the ordinary and innocent people pay an unnecessary cost. Government officials from both regional states who participated in this study accepted that in West and East Guji zones, stiff competition, delegitimization, and ethnic polarization were increasing among local political elites and businessmen of both the Gedeo and Guji. According to their view, Gedeo elites felt that the Guji administration was not treating them the way their Guji fellows were treated in business and political affairs; however, the Guji elites did not accept this. In this polarization, one denies the legitimacy of the other when it comes to access to local political leadership. For example, in some contested localities of Kercha, Abaya, Birbirsa Kojowa, Bule Hora, Hambela Wamena, and Gelana woredas of Oromia, the Gedeo claim a majority over the Guji. Thus, they claim the right to administer themselves, teach their children in their mother tongue, and promote their culture freely. However, this is unacceptable for the Guji, who claim they gave their own land to the Gedeo in good faith. They also believe the Gedeo have no right to claim special woredas for self-administration on Oromo soil, because the constitution of the Oromia Regional State does not contain such a provision. From this perspective, the regional constitution under Article 2 recognizes Oromia as a geographical area wherein the Oromo people and the other people who choose to live there have settled. On the other hand, Article 5 of the same constitution states Afan Oromo as the region's working language, while Article 8 names the Oromo people as the owners of ultimate power. However, the regional constitution is silent about the provisions for nationality administration for those interested in living in the region and recognized under Article 2, as in the case of Article 73 of the 1994 revised constitution of the Amhara National Regional State.

On the other hand, focus group discussions indicated that businessmen from both groups were also in competition to bring their own people to power. According to respondents from the Gedeo, their businessmen felt ill-treated and were asked to pay high taxes by the local administrators, who were all Guji. They also felt that Gedeo businessmen were systematically discouraged from engaging in business, while Guji businessmen were given preferential treatment. Others expressed the view that Gedeo businessmen were asked to pay high taxes that did not take into consideration their actual income, whereas nobody asked Guji businessmen to pay taxes. Thus, Gedeo business elites believed that bringing some people from their ethnic group to power would help them avert what they thought was preferential treatment, especially at the kebele level. To meet their goals, business elites organized their own supporters along ethnic lines, especially from youth groups, and mobilized them against one another. Focus group discussions and key informant interviews revealed that these groups existed both in the community and in government institutions such as schools. Community representatives shared the view that local administrators of both regional states directly or indirectly took part in this grouping.

The Gedeo who live in the Guji zones felt that irrespective of their population size, they were marginalized in the local administration. Those who participated in this study took the view that they were not represented either at the woreda or kebele level. They also felt that they were deprived of their constitutional rights to self-administer, promote their culture, and educate their children in their mother tongue, which they said was submitted to the Oromia Regional State and allowed by the same, but they did not blatantly articulate their intentions for a referendum. The Gedeo community representatives who participated in this study also mentioned that Oromia informed the local administration to handle the case, but no document was shown to us during the course of the fieldwork. The Guji, on the other hand, understood the Gedeo's demand as a step toward a referendum and a systematic way of taking away their land, which has symbolic value to the Guji. The Guji have developed a bad memory from the previous two referendum attempts and the annexation of some of the localities to SNNPR. The Guji could not get a guarantee from the Gedeo that the recent request for mother tongue education and other related issues would not end with conducting a referendum, as was the case in 1995 and 1998. Due to the lack of proper information exchange and previous bad memory, the Gedeo request for democratic rights could not be taken positively among the Guji.

Conflict entrepreneurs as well as business and political elites used this as a good opportunity to divide the two communities. Interviews with local administrators and elders indicated that those who could not gain access to resources (especially political and economic resources) either at the individual level or in groups, both from inside and outside government structures, played their role to aggravate the conflict. Those who developed vested interests to ensure power with the pretext of self-rule were determined to create new power relationships with those who had already secured political power. Instigating conflict was seen among some, though not all, as a prerequisite for protecting perceived or real collective injustices. The conflict entrepreneurs mobilized their groups by convincing potential members of the community, mainly youth, that the mobilization was to avoid the perceived disastrous effects of the other group mobilizing. Specifically, conflict entrepreneurs from the Gedeo side mobilized their group to ensure the constitutional rights (particularly self-rule and the right to develop their language and culture) of those who live in the Guji zones, while conflict entrepreneurs from the Guji mobilized their groups to avert what they perceived as a disastrous effect on their core identity values, in other words, land that had not only economic but also symbolic value. The political and economic elites used the situation as an environment conducive to the consolidation of political and economic power, respectively. To this effect, the ordinary people were fed inaccurate, incomplete, uncertain information about one another. The level of misunderstanding between the two groups was widened by design so as to provoke the ordinary people to make potentially "wrong" choices based on unverified information such as conducting a referendum and a plot to attack. Everything, including displacement, has been ethnicized; data on IDPs have been reported in an exaggerated manner. Political and social activists used IDP cases for their own agenda. Those who gained access to the media propagated the case as an ethnic conflict, while the case, as explained above, is more elitist than ethnic. Thus, a collective social problem that brewed in the political system has been manifested as if it is an ethnic hatred between the two groups, who still have strong social-psychological and emotional connections to one another. In general, conflict-induced internal displacement from the Guji and Gedeo zones resulted from the cumulative effects of long-standing ethnic polarization, which gradually led to ethnically motivated political mobilization and ended up as interethnic tensions. If things continue in this way, the problem may continue to flare up, and its spillover may result in more harm, not only on the two ethnic groups but also on others who live in neighboring localities.

These polarities among elite groups increased the level of distrust between the Gedeo and Guji communities, which in turn increased tensions between the two communities. Formal institutions weakened due to the previous youth-led violence and riots against the government and absence of the rule of law at the grassroots level served these groups to play ethnic cards as they wanted. The high contraband movement, proliferation of firearms, and movement of armed groups in the area complicated the situation and jeopardized the human security of the Gedeo who have been living in the Guji zones. To increase the level of intergroup fear, distorted and unverified information about preparations for more attacks was disseminated to them through anonymous mobile calls and SMS. As a result, intergroup tension, fear, and frustrations escalated. This in turn resulted in the displacement of hundreds of thousands of people from their places of residence and the destruction of houses and schools, on top of other human rights violations. The tensions displaced both the Gedeo and Guji from their places of residence, though much has been said only about Gedeo displacement. On the other hand, it was witnessed during field visits and also confirmed by the respondents of this study that a significant number of Gedeo hid themselves in Guji houses. Similarly, a large number of Guji who were displaced from different kebeles of the Gedeo zone in fear of revenge attacks hid themselves among Gedeo families in the Gedeo zone.

Local administrators and security and administration experts of both regional states have a view that, compared to the previous conflict-induced internal displacements, the 2018 one was the largest in number, widest in geographic scope, and has been highly politicized and ethnicized. Efforts were made to triangulate this view with quantitative data regarding the number of IDPs due to the conflict. However, aggregate data obtained from West Guji zone, Gedeo zone, and the sum of data collected from the respective woredas do not match. Data obtained from West Guji zone estimated the total number of internal displacements up to 250,000, whereas data from Gedeo zone and its woredas took the number up to 800,000. Due to conflicting data, it became difficult to specify the exact number of IDPs from both groups, but one can understand how serious the situation was from the number of temporary shelters prepared. Due to relentless efforts made by the federal and regional governments as well as other nongovernmental organizations, almost all of the displaced people were returned to their places of residence, though few have been done on the ground so far to ensure peace and human security of the returnees. The destruction of property and other vital facilities complicated the lives and livelihood of returnees.

FACTORS THAT EXACERBATED INTERNAL DISPLACEMENT

According to Lake and Rothchild (1996), information failure, problems of credible commitment, and security dilemma are the three key factors that contribute to the development of ethnic conflict. Similar factors contributed to the 2018 Gedeo-Guji tensions. From the very beginning, there was information asymmetry between the Guji and Gedeo regarding administrative issues, which in turn triggered recurrent demands from the Gedeo side for a referendum. There was also the lack of a credible commitment from both sides to reveal their own interests and fears to one another, and the lack of genuine interactions over incompatible goals raised the level of suspicion between elites, which in turn put the two communities in security dilemmas. The study identified different issues in connection to these causes.

The rumor to conduct a referendum on contested administrative localities spread throughout West and East Guji zones. The Guji community, especially youth groups, became furious with the Gedeo, who they perceived as settlers on their ancestral land. As a result, cases of intimidation were reported from some rural kebeles where a large number of Gedeo were living. For example, in December 2018, an elderly Gedeo man was found dead in a coffee-processing house owned by a Guji businessman in Sire Saba kebele of Kercha woreda, West Guji zone. In response, the Gedeo demonstrated, disrupting operations at the coffee-processing house. In connection to this, the Gedeo suspected of the crime were put in prison. Some Gedeo respondents argued that more than sixty-five people were sentenced to five to eight years in prison. Finally, the situation escalated and led to the displacement from West Guji zone of thousands of Gedeo, who escaped to Gedeb woreda of SNNPR in fear of a revenge attack. Attempts were made to return the IDPs back home. However, before these IDPs fully returned, a second round of displacement occurred in March 2018. On March 27, 2018, the Guji fired bullets into the sky the whole evening to express their happiness at the selection of Dr. Abiy Ahmed as the head of the EPRDF. The Gedeo, who already feared violence, considered the incident as war against them (this view was also repeated during the televised conversation with the prime minister while he visited the displaced Gedeo in March 2019). On the same evening, hundreds of thousands of Gedeo from East and West Guji zones left their homes and rushed to the adjacent Gedeo woredas. A large number of people were displaced from Kercha and Birbirsa Kojowa woredas of West Guji zone and entered Gedeb, Yirgachefe, and Kochore woredas of Gedeo zone. In early April 2018, another incident triggered mass displacement of the Gedeo community from West Guji zone. On April 9, 2018, some Gedeo youths were beaten at Mileda Buqisa kebele of Kercha woreda because they were seen on the street wearing their cultural costumes for the Easter holiday. Some Guji groups took that as an attempt to organize the community for a referendum. This, in turn, increased tensions in the community. Out of fear and frustration, a large number of Gedeo left East Guji zone and entered the camps prepared for IDPs.

Efforts have been made several times both by formal and customary institutions to restore peace between the two groups. However, the broken social capital has not yet been maintained. There is a long way to go to restore intergroup trust and positive attitudes. Politicization and ethnicization of the problem have complicated the situation and made it difficult to resolve tensions amicably. The Gondoro system, which is supposed to be performed only once for one conflict, was carried out twice at Kercha woreda to restore peace, but this could not prevent the problem from relapsing and escalating to the wider context due to the role symbolic politics played. For a long time, almost all of the suspected perpetrators of the conflict were not brought to justice and tried. According to some respondents, some of the people who instigated the tensions were in the community, and some were even engaged in the government structure. This created fear and distrust among the IDPs to return home. However, after a long deliberation between the two regional states and the federal government, efforts were made to bring some of the conflict instigators from both sides to justice. Almost all of the displaced people returned to their previous places of residence. However, the causes of the problem have not yet been fully addressed; the social-psychological rupture created between the two groups due to the conflict has not yet been treated, and cultural reconciliation attempted by the Abba Gadas has been stifled by a lack of genuine political commitment to address the root causes of the conflict, which may even drive a relapse of the conflict in the future, mainly because the advocators of self-administration from the Gedeo side still believe that, apart from returning the IDPs, their questions have not been answered. In general, the measures taken so far are on the effects of the problem. The accumulated root causes are still contained as they were in the past. Thus, there is no guarantee for conflict-induced displacement not to recur.

CONCLUSION

This study revealed that lack of good governance and rule of law, unequal treatment in government sectors (especially at the kebele level), lack of equal opportunity for the two ethnic groups (especially employment opportunities), lack of diversity-management skills, and lack of participatory and inclusive political leadership at the local administrative level, together with institutional paralysis are the major causes for identity-based frictions in the woredas where the two ethnic groups lived together. In 2018 and the years before, the EPRDF encountered widespread discontent and civil disobedience from grassroots movements, especially youth groups. To comply with public demands, the party was engaged in renovating itself through a rigorous reform process. In this course of action, the government could not deliver what was expected of it in all aspects, especially in the social security arena. After the reform period, the new teams at the federal and regional levels became soft in countering civil disobedience through timely interventions; this, in turn, made the governments invisible in terms of ensuring law and order as well as peace and security at the grassroots level. Failure to do so created a conducive environment for the invisible hands and interest groups that wanted to create more pressure on federal and regional governments by creating identity-based narratives that played divisive roles in the community. These two problems—the government's laissez-faire approach and manipulative elites coupled with power contention—exacerbated ethnic tensions between the Gedeo and Guji communities and resulted in a large number of IDPs.

In general, intergroup tensions in Ethiopia, like those between the Guji and Gedeo communities, may be used as a political agenda to heat a political debate in power politics; however, it could never be solved by making an internal political reform and/or changing a party leader. Whoever comes into power, the problem continues to be used by the interest groups to ignite political tensions because the intergroup tension observed so far has been brewed in the constitutional gaps both in principle and practice. This constitutionally driven intergroup problem requires a constitutional solution, part of which could be a constitutional amendment. The 2018 ethnic tensions between the Gedeo and Guji communities, therefore, is not a problem borne of and grown up after the reform process but rather is an indicator of the EPRDF's long-standing diversity governance deficit as well as a lack of capacity and genuine political commitment to ensure a culture of peace and peaceful coexistence among diverse identity lines, as well as a failure to ensure reliable law and order at the grassroots level. Current ethnic tensions between the Gedeo and Guji communities and other related tensions have existed since 1991. However, these problems were not addressed properly. Instead, they were contained forcefully by the security apparatus of the system. These restrained, long-standing intergroup tensions have flared up both in scope and intensity during the current political reform process.

To bring a lasting solution to such problems, displacement issues should be seen in a humanized way without any ethnicization and politicization. In the case of the Gedeo-Guji tensions, the elites should give a chance to the wider community and allow the two groups to solve their own problems through their customary institutions. The issue of referendum, which has been witnessed as a divisive and risky business, should be closed once and for all. Instead, the collective good memories of the two ethnic groups should be reactivated. It is only through the empowerment of the two groups and their rich institutions that sustainable peace will be ensured at the contested areas in West and East Guji zones. The customary institutions may not address the underlying political causes of the conflict. To address this, there should be genuine political dialogue among the interest groups from both Oromia and SNNPR. Any action that does not involve customary institutions and interest groups from both regions may contain the problem for a while, as was done before, but will not transform the tensions to peaceful coexistence, since the underlying structural causes of the problem remain salient, and the competing groups will remain in conflict cycles.

REFERENCES

Abbink, Jon. 2006. "Ethnicity and Conflict Generation in Ethiopia: Some Problems and Prospects of Ethno-Regional Federalism." *Journal of Contemporary African Studies* 24, no. 3: 389–413.

———. 2011. "Ethnic-Based Federalism and Ethnicity in Ethiopia: Reassessing the Experiment After 20 Years." *Journal of Eastern African Studies* 5, no. 4: 596–618.

———. 2015. "The Ethiopian Revolution After 40 Years (1974–2014): Plan B in Progress?" *Journal of Development Societies* 31, no. 3: 333–57.

Asebe Regassa Debelo. 2007. "Ethnicity and Inter-Ethnic Relations: The 'Ethiopian Experiment' and the Case of the Guji and Gedeo." MA thesis, University of Tromsø.

Bahru Zewde. 2000. "A Century of Ethiopian Historiography." *Journal of Ethiopian Studies* 33, no. 2: 1–26.

Clapham, Christopher. 2006. "Ethiopian Development: The Politics of Emulation." *Commonwealth & Comparative Politics* 44, no. 1 (March): 108–18.

Hagmanna, Tobias, and Jon Abbink. 2011. "Twenty Years of Revolutionary Democratic Ethiopia, 1991 to 2011." *Journal of Eastern African Studies* 5, no. 4: 579–95.

Jenkins, J. Craig. 2010. "Ethnic Conflict." In *The Oxford International Encyclopedia of Peace*, vol. 2., edited by Nijel J. Young. Oxford: Oxford University Press.

Kaufman, Stuart J. 2001. *Modern Hatreds: The Symbolic Politics of Ethnic War*. Cornell Studies in Security Affairs. Ithaca, NY: Cornell University Press.

Lake, David A., and Donald Rothchild. 1996. "Containing Fear: The Origins and Management of Ethnic Conflict." *International Security* 21, no. 2 (Autumn): 41–75.

Merera Gudina. 2006. "Contradictory Interpretations of Ethiopian History: The Need for a New Consensus." In *Ethnic Federalism: The Ethiopian Experience in Comparative Perspective*, edited by David Turton. Addis Ababa: Addis Ababa University Press.

Tadesse Kippie Kanshie. 2002. *Five Thousand Years of Sustainability? A Case Study on Gedeo Land Use (Southern Ethiopia)*. Heelsum, Netherlands: Treemail.

Toft, Duffy. 2003. *The Geography of Ethnic Violence: Identity, Violence, and Their Indivisibility of Territory*. Princeton, NJ: Princeton University Press.

Vaughan, Sarah. 2011. "Revolutionary Democratic State-Building: Party, State and People in the EPRDF's Ethiopia." *Journal of Eastern African Studies* 5, no. 4: 619–40.

Yeshtila Wondemeneh Bekele, Darley Jose Kjosavik, and Nadarajah Shanmugaratnam. 2016. "State-Society Relations in Ethiopia: A Political-Economy Perspective of the Post-1991 Order." *Journal of Social Sciences* 5, no. 48: 1–19.

Yonatan Tesfaye Fessha. 2010. *Ethnic Diversity and Federalism: Constitution Making in South Africa and Ethiopia*. London: Routledge.

የኦሮምያ ብሔራዊ ክልላዊ መንግስት. የተሻሻለው የ 1994 ዓ.ም. የኦሮምያ ክልል ሕገ-መንግስት.

3.4 Between Hope and Despair
Reflections on the Current Political Developments in Afar

Abubeker Yasin

INTRODUCTION

The post-1991 political order in Ethiopia was reconstructed by the TPLF/EPRDF along lines of ethnic federalism intended to bring about democracy, economic development, and lasting peace in the country. The Federal Democratic Republic of Ethiopia, constituted itself in nine regional states with the intention of reducing political conflict and developing power from the center to regional states. On this ground, the Afar Regional State, like other regional states, was established to exercise self-determination rights as enshrined in the Ethiopian constitution.

The Afar people, who witnessed the suppression and exploitative policies of previous regimes, welcomed the promises of the TPLF/EPRDF to congregate in their own *kilil*/regional state. This move heralded a new political beginning for Afar. Initially, through the Afar Liberation Front (ALF), new Afar subordinate elites ruled the region.

Dissatisfied with ALF disobedience and a skirmish relationship in 1997, the TPLF/EPRDF began to think about a new political formula that engineered the merger of five political parties to produce the ANDP (Afar National Democratic Party) and installed Esmail Ali Siro as chairman. Gradually, the TPLF/EPRDF began to negate the promise of self-governance for the Afar people and revealed its true colors.

The Afar were denied their democratic rights to establish a new political party to compete against the ruling ANDP. The demand of Afar intellectuals to have an alternative political party was downplayed by one of the senior advisors and minister of Federal Affairs during the Meles Zenawi administration, Abay Tsehaye, who said the "EPRDF will never give birth to twins, and in case it happens, we will never raise both" (Yasin 2008).

The Afar region is dubbed a "backward" region in Ethiopia, even by its own state makers. Explaining the experience of the Afar under the EPRDF, Markakis (2011) opines that no significant progress was made under federalism towards political integration and that this is the last frontier that needs to be crossed in the nation-state building process and more battles will have to be fought on this front.

Developmental policies in the Afar region reflected political and strategic government interests in the expropriation of natural resources. Large areas of grazing land are allocated to the state and foreign commercial companies to cultivate sugar plantations and minerals. In this light, the Afar pastoral livelihood has suffered under ill-planned and executed development projects (Mu'uz 2015). Afar are excluded from the salt-mining sector in Afdera and Dobi. The salt industry has been dominated by highlanders and people close to power. An exposition of the major economic players and their respective power positions in the production and distribution of salt reveals the continued marginalization of the Afar despite the strong rhetoric of self-determination in post-1991 Ethiopia (Dereje 2011). Hence, the local people are worried about the economic insecurity that threatens their livelihood. The net result of these development interventions is dispossession of Afar lands, ultimately leading to their political disempowerment (Dereje 2011).

The Eritrean-Ethiopian War has had a devastating impact on the Afar community during the last twenty years. As a result, the Afar region has been a military zone controlled by the Ethiopian state. For geo-political reasons, the need to address the Afar conflict with Issa/Somali falls on deaf ears, so as not to disappoint Ismaïl Omar Guelleh's regime in Djibouti. Indeed, because of subordinate and compliant local Afar elites, the Afar people couldn't effectively negotiate their own interests. As a result of the domestic source of discontent and resentment, a call for reform has become imperative.

This contribution examines how the reform process at the national level has played out in the Afar and reflects on the way forward to deepen the intended reform process in the context of the region.

PLACING AFAR

The Afar people, historically divided by colonial powers, straddle the Horn of Africa states of Ethiopia, Eritrea, and Djibouti, an area commonly referred to as the Afar Triangle. The Afar Triangle extends from the Bouri peninsula to the foot of Tigray and the Amhara highlands in the west. In the south, it goes from East Djibouti city along the railway line through Erer to Awash Station. In the west, the two joints form a vertex seventy-five kilometers northeast of Addis Ababa at Namale Fan (Yasin 2008). The Afar have a distinct cultural and linguistic identity of their own. Predominantly Muslim, they speak a common language, Qafar af, a language from the Cushitic family. The Afar homeland comprises geo-strategic areas with an abundance of natural resources that have attracted the encroachment of both colonial and Horn of Africa states.

The Afar people have a well-defined political and social organization based on a system of traditional governance. They have more than five sultanates and *makabons* (traditional leaders). According to Markakis (2011), the founding principle of Afar society is blood kinship; the building block of its social structure is the patrilineal descent group or clan. It is estimated that there are more than a hundred clan-families among the Afar, each comprising a pyramidal structure of smaller lineage groups with its own identity, territory, and leadership. As a political and social reality, the clan pattern helps to maintain social balance and serves as a means of defense to external threats.

In Ethiopia, the Afar are located in the Northeastern part of the country and have their own national regional state organized under five zones, thirty-four districts, and two city administrations. Geographically, the region shares international boundaries with Eritrea and Djibouti. Internally, it borders the regional states of Tigray in the North, Oromia and Somali in the South, Amhara in the West, and the Republic of Djibouti in the East. The estimated size of the region is 100,860 square kilometers. The 2017 Afar population projection of the Ethiopian Central Statistical Agency is 1.8 million, a number expected to rise with the coming census. Most of the population lives in rural areas. Afar land is mostly hot and ranges from semiarid to arid, gaining minimum rainfall annually. As a result, the region faces frequent drought.

The Awash River, the second-longest river in Ethiopia (700 km), and the main road that stretches from Addis Ababa to Djibouti and Eritrean ports runs through the Afar homeland and serves as a lifeline to the Ethiopian economy. The region possesses undeveloped land, water, mineral resources, and potential for tourism and geothermal energy. As a result, state-making projects like the Tendaho Dam and the Kessem Sugar Factory, as well as large mineral companies, have been established in Afar territory.

The majority of the Afar people engage in seminomadic pastoralism. They keep various types of livestock, including camels, cattle, sheep, and goats. Movement in search of pasture and water is a typical lifestyle. They use hardy, well-adapted breeds and sophisticated herd movements and grazing strategies. Resource depletion due to recurrent droughts and other external pressures is a serious problem that has greatly diminished the size and composition of family livestock, which in turn has resulted in the deterioration of living standards (Tadesse and Yonas 2007).

THE WIND OF HOPE AND NEW PROMISE

After years of political violence, Ethiopia has begun to see a new dawn in its quest for a bright future. Either from inside or outside, "the egg" has been broken to enable the demands and dreams of the people to come true. The rise to power of Prime Minister Abiy in April 2018, and his reform agenda, wasn't imagined by many who yearned for political reform. Ethiopia has witnessed a political earthquake that has resulted in promising political openness and transition to a democratic system. The salvo of reforms he fired off created a positive shock of which whole swaths of the public had been dreaming (Lefort 2018). The conducive political environment created so far has enabled many Ethiopians to breathe fresh air and plant seeds of hope for the future.

The political change ignited in the center, however, has not reached all regions in Ethiopia at an equal pace. With the arrest of Abdi Mohammed Omar (Abdi Illey) of the Somali region, many people in Afar wished the wind of hope would reach them swiftly, too. In the meantime, after twenty-seven years of silence, many Afar youth protesters secured a pioneering window of opportunity on state-owned media (EBC Amharic) on July 26, 2018, to demand change, and they continued to protest peacefully. During his visit to emerging regions, Abiy Ahmed reached out to the presidents of regional states to quickly embrace the change.

The leadership of the ANDP, which runs Afar politics, failed to understand the inevitability of the coming change and the warning of Abiy Ahmed. Compelled by the mounting demands of young Afar protesters, slowly but surely the president of the Afar regional State, Siyoum Awal and the forty-five central committee members of the ANDP were summoned for an urgent meeting in Addis Ababa. In November 2018, the Abiy administration in clear terms informed Siyoum Awal that change has come and is unstoppable. Through Abiy's administration spokesman, the Afar people were informed about the decay of the ANDP leadership, which had failed to give strategic leadership, renew internal organizational democratic practices, and had permitted the prevalence of antidemocratic elements. Many people were taken aback to hear the many self-criticisms of Afar leaders in Addis Ababa. However, this move enabled many Afar to be ecstatic and feel confident about the intended change on the way.

Though at a snail's pace, the Afar people accepted the political change with euphoria, as they had been looking for an opportune moment to get rid of oppressive rule. As a region that lags in development, even among emerging regions in Ethiopia, Afar rank the lowest on all human development index, living in a fragile and disaster-prone environment with deteriorating livelihoods, snared in the web of local, regional, and international conflicts (Yasin 2008). Fear politics fall apart; the Afar people, for their part, felt they would also enjoy the signs of a liberal and open political space observed in the country and hoped to see their demands and aspirations met.

The shift of balance in political power from the TPLF, the organization that created the ANDP and oppressed the Afar people through local elites, more than anything else ushered the Afar in euphoria . The Afar people felt that the time had come to be ruled by their own sons and daughters, who could be elected through the ballot box.

Soon after, the Afar Youth Movement (Xuko Cina), who were organized to fight against injustice and consisted mainly of young Afar, intensified their peaceful struggle against the region's governing elites. The Afar Youth Movement ignited their struggle on social media (mainly Facebook), held several demonstrations, and was inspired nationally by the wave of popular movements like Qerro, Fano, and others.

Prime Minister Abiy Ahmed's pledge in May 2018 to support Afar economic growth, as well to end political marginalization, came as a piece of good news. Lefort (2018) predicted that for the first time in Ethiopia's history, these peripheral areas could in the future have a real say at the central level. The removal of seventy-two old guards with "honor" from the top leadership of the ANDP through the urgent 7th ANDP conference in December 2018 in Samara, the capital city of the Afar region, consolidated the hopes of the Afar people for the desired peaceful change process.

During the ANDP conference, "new" leaders substituted for the old guards and formed a central committee, comprised of forty-five members. The incumbent construction Minister of Ethiopia, engineer Aisha Mohammed, was installed as the leader of the ANDP, while Awal Arba became president of Afar Regional State. Both leaders that were preferred by the ANDP and the central government, pledged they would work for the betterment of Afar's future, and promised cooperation with opposition parties, Afar youth, intellectuals, and the diaspora community. In her acceptance speech, Aisha Mohammed vowed that she would work hard to develop the Afar region from its current state of "backwardness." In a similar vein, Awal Arba promised to enact radical reforms to meet the Afar people's quest for development.

TOWARDS A NEW BEGINNING

A change whose time has come compelled the ruling elites in Afar either to accept it or face mounting pressure from the central government and continued protests from the people. The December 2018 conference came about after a meeting with Prime Minister Abiy Ahmed in Addis Ababa, when ANDP leadership urgently called for the previously delayed conference to take place. The conference brought over five hundred members of the ANDP together and served as an entry point to discussions on how to receive the change process that had commenced at the national level and ponder the measures to be taken to redress the fault lines within the ruling party.

At the conference, party leaders confessed that they had utterly failed to properly lead the Afar people. Aisha Mohammed's interview with FBC in December 2018 attested that the ruling leadership ended up in a strategic failure, as they had failed to embark on timely change; as the result, the region was performing below expectations. Among others, Aisha put the cause of the ANDP's inability to lead mainly on widely practiced rent seeking and a power struggle between the leadership that was grounded in clanisim.

After the removal of the seventy-two old guards from the party leadership, the "new" administration focused on revisiting government structures and attempted to inject new blood into the party by bringing some educated youth to leadership positions. The newly elected administration is said to have taken into consideration a new formula involving educational background, clan, regional, and pastoralist composition while selecting some of the newcomers.

The post-Siyoum administration has released Afar youth protesters who ended up in jail and welcomed Afar opposition parties such as the Afar People's Party (APP) and the ALF by allowing them to meet their supporters in a gathering hall. Meanwhile, the new administration entered a peace agreement in Asmara, Eritrea, with a rebel movement, Afar Ugugumo, in March 2019 that struggled for the Afar cause for over forty years. With a window of opportunity secured, Afar intellectuals and youth are exercising their freedom of speech through an Afar TV channel and the right to peaceful demonstration. Reformation of the security sector is underway. To this end, with the support of the Ethiopian National Defense Force, the Afar Liyu Police, a paramilitary group once used as an instrument of repression, have undergone renaissance training, and eleven of its leaders have been identified as abusers of power.

CONTINUITY OF OLD TRICKS AND THE PEOPLE'S DESPAIR

Despite creating real hopes to see political change and the commencement of some measures on the path to political liberalization, the central government's approach to bring about a change in real terms remains a concern. It has chosen the same old top-down tactic in pursuing politics. While summoning the Afar leaders to urgently come to Addis

Ababa and embrace the change process, the Abiy administration failed to make a deeper and more genuine consultation process on how to embrace the change process.

During his visit to Samara in May 2018, Prime Minister Abiy preferred to sit only with members of the ruling Afar party, which provided him with continuous applause while he delivered his speech, in which he called Afar "Ugaz" and "Garad" (the title of the Issa/Somali sultanate). Rather than connecting with incumbent Afar leaders, Abiy should have taken a different approach by listening to the voices of educated elites, youth, and clan leaders and candidly discuss the predicaments of the Afar people. The Afar youth who demonstrated in the presence of Abiy to make their voices heard ended up in jail. Abiy's approach to Afar revealed his political calculation or the expediency of avoiding the TPLF threat; this had a devastating impact on the Afar people, as they couldn't make use of this new political opportunity for real reform. Despite his achievements nationally, Abiy Ahmed seems to have fallen into an illusory trap.

On the other hand, the ANDP, which drives politics in the Afar region, has from the outset attempted to embark on political reform without properly assessing its inner organizational culture and taking appropriate measures to break from the past. The approach of the ANDP caused concern, as it did not rigorously diagnose problems or clearly define the reforms to be initiated and the direction to be taken in a participatory and inclusive method. In a hurry, the ANDP has attempted to embrace reform in the absence of policy, strategy, and due political communication. It failed to reinvent itself to better manage the change process and serve the Afar people. A democratic deficit still haunts the organization. Despite its rhetoric, the new leadership couldn't craft a road map towards satisfying the people's demand for change, and it seems to be too late to commence a public dialogue through which to build trust.

The reality on the ground revealed that the ruling party, which took the lead in the reform attempt, was distrusted by the people, as it was the party that held political power for over twenty years and failed to solve the problems of the Afar people. The legacy of the party in terms of the political approach it pursued, weak leadership, and lack of direction, now faces a litmus test from the people.

The change process played out at the national level has not begun in Afar Regional State from a clean slate, as the people expected it to. During the 7th

ANDP conference, the need to embrace the change was, from the outset, met with a bitter struggle for power between change supporters and those who still wanted a grip on power. The political culture of the ANDP served as fertile ground for the political elites to play the dirty game of politics. The old guards in the party, in their bid to be elected again, have injected money and played clan, regional, and networking tactics, which is the usual modus operandi of politics in the Afar region. Unsurprisingly, the presidium committee members of the conference, who were entrusted to do justice while selecting new central and executive members, misused the power to their advantage.

As a result of the power struggle, the old guards again secured the opportunity of being selected and/or replaced by their supporters, kith, and kin as "new" members of the central and executive committees of the ANDP. After the farewell and recognition of certificate bestowed to them, the old and ineffective guards are back as "new" leaders to lead the change process. They are both the members of the executive and central committees, with significant supporters in the government structure. A leap in the dark shaped and impacted the course of the reform process.

At the expense of education, leadership skills, and the people's mandate, the new administration opted for regional and clan quotas in bringing individuals to leadership posts, an approach which already has served as a divide-and-rule tactic. Then and now, clan is used as a political instrument to allocate posts in government structure. In terms of representation, the selected leaders represent their clan. Indeed, this move has impacted civic politics and in turn led to the absence of good governance. The political elites make use of clan as a shell to accumulate power and resources and to position themselves against other clans. Clanism is shaping the political behavior of the Afar people. At this juncture, clanism has significantly impacted unity among the Afar and this, in turn, assisted the ruling elite to stay in power.

The resurgence of Afar-Issa/Somali conflict on December 25, 2018, adds to the discontent of the Afar people at large. The intractable conflict with Issa/Somali that killed many in the past is consuming much of the energy and focus of the new leadership. They are under increasing pressure from the Afar people to defend Afar land before a reform process. The Afar feel insecure about the continuous encroachment of Issa/Somali onto their land. The Issa/Somali encroachment to Afar land is more than a competition over scarce pastoral resources.

A war between Afar and Issa/Somali is in full swing and has left many dead. According to Ahmed Sultan, who is the head of the Afar Peace and Security Bureau, the Issa/Somali attack on Afar is believed to have the backing of external actors (Afar TV, October 16, 2019). The verdict of the federal government, which ordered the special Afar paramilitary force to pull out of the Issa-inhabited hamlets (Adaytu, Undafuo, Gadamaytuin) of Afar, and the call of the current president, Awal Arba, for a political solution to mitigate the conflict, dashed the hopes of many Afar.

The central government of Ethiopia seems to be concerned more about road security than the human security of the Afar people. We can't think of real political reform, democratization, and stability without properly addressing this protracted conflict. The failure to resolve the conflict attests to the continuity of the previous approach.

As a structural fact, rampant corruption poses a profound threat and impediment to political reform in Afar Regional State. In the past twenty-eight years, corruption has become a way of life and a means for leaders to satisfy their hunger for wealth and power. Because of an absence of effective autonomous structures with the strength to check corruption, political elites engaged in high and sometimes egregious levels of corruption, increasingly diverting people's resources for personal gain. The "new" leadership, entrusted to bring about change, has a record of misappropriating the annual budget. A lack of political will to fight corruption by the incumbent leadership has been observed so far. Politics of the belly and neo-patrimonialism are government practices in Afar. Hence, the people are wary of the intended change .

The political reform attempts underway in Afar are not led by capable political leaders who are educated enough or who have the capacity to design a clear and conscious road map for political reform and thereby improve the lives of the Afar people. The leadership lacks political maturity and qualities that could earn them trust among the people. No bold and tangible measures have so far been taken to bring about meaningful change. The performance of the "new" leadership remains below expectations.

The leadership has failed to change their mindset and build institutional capacity to embrace reforms and bring young and educated leaders with the requisite skills to leadership positions that could change the lives of the Afar pastoralist community. So far, the new administration hasn't been able to reach out to the rural community and listen to their demands and aspirations. Basic demands for good governance have yet to be met. As such, through peaceful demonstration, Afar youth protesters in all districts of the region are revealing their disenchantment with the ruling class.

The wind of hope that blew over Afar have begun to fade away. The new administration's maneuvering tactics and way of handling the change process so far have dashed the people's hopes, desires, and needs for a bright future. As a result, the Afar People are saying that ,though the locust has gone, it has already laid its eggs.

The people expected that the new administration, while embarking on political reform, would opt for a democratic approach in pursuing politics. The popular expectation was to see the reinvention of the ruling party and to be led by capable and legitimate leaders who could understand the needs and aspirations of the Afar people. More particularly, the people expected that the corrupt leaders who exploited and suppressed the people would face justice, but so far no measures have been taken against them. Equally, the hope that natural resources appropriated by political elites would be returned to the people has proven to be in vain.

Despite a "new" crop of leaders, as German philosopher Friedrich Schiller wrote, "the great moment has found a little people" in Afar who are unwilling or incapable to lead the change process.

THE OUTLOOK

The changing political landscape in Ethiopia, accompanied by the political liberalization that has ensued since April 2018 through Prime Minister Abiy Ahmed, has created a swath of hope for Ethiopians. An unprecedented window of opportunity has opened to transition from dictatorship to democracy. The wind of hope have gradually reached regional states in Ethiopia such as Afar. After twenty-eight years of heavy-handed interference from the central government and exploitation by local Afar elites, the Afar people welcomed the ignited political reform to come out of the current predicament it finds itself in. The Afar hope for a brave new world shifted into high gear when the administration in Afar made a new promise to bring about the desired change.

The embryonic reform attempts underway in Afar are an appreciable move as fear-based politics fall apart but the people have much despair on the way, considering how the political reform has been managed from the outset. The failure of the ruling party to reinvent itself in order to properly manage the change process, the inability to define the reform and its direction, and the coming back of old guards after the farewell all makes for an incapable political leadership that is not in a position to craft a road map for the intended reforms. As a result , the hope of the Afar people are dashing.

The political reform in Afar will not be an easy journey, as the road towards democratization is bumpy and long. Indeed, due to political tactics pursued in the past twenty-eight years under TPLF/EPRDF rule, Afar lags behind all regional states in Ethiopia and carries all the burden. Managing a change in the hitherto marginalized region requires wise political decisions.

Political reform in Afar calls for an appropriate assessment of what went wrong and why while pursuing a politics that impoverished and haunted the lives of many people. Learning from history will help us to not repeat past mistakes and move towards a better future. The success of initiated reforms depends heavily on a political leader who is educated and politically mature enough to lead by example. Above all, servant leadership could gain acceptance and recognition from the people by understanding the needs and aspirations of the Afar people, being capable enough to craft a policy and strategy that transforms their prevalent condition for the better, and by being able to act with self-confidence - this should be a priority. The leadership should have the political will to open a political space, solve the structural challenges that derail the change process, and steer the Afar people to a bright future.

The Afar people should be the owners of the political reforms they earned through hard choices to attain the demands and benefits of their democratic citizenship. The people, from whom popular sovereignty derives, deserve primacy in the democratic process. Power belongs to the people. The reforms, if they are to be successful, require legitimacy and high acceptance from the Afar people. Putting the people and their welfare back at the center of political decision-making is of paramount importance.

The neglected traditional governance system of the Afar people needs to be encouraged and maintained given that it could help in consensual decision-making and public participation. If fairly managed, traditional governance can have a significant impact on democracy, peace and conflict, and socio-economic development. As it is a given reality, we can opt for dual polities: both traditional and modern forms of governance in realizing the Afar people's demands and aspirations. On an equal footing, clan, which is a foundation of Afar political and social organization, must be taken into account as a critical variable while leading the people. We can't do away with the clan, as it will remain the eternal and immutable bedrock of Afar society. Rather, we should wisely use it to achieve equilibrium in Afar society for stability but not as a political instrument to divide and rule. Past wrong deeds created by the misapplication of the clan system must be redressed to create a united community.

The Afar regional government must rebuild itself to be responsive enough to citizens' concerns and aspirations. To this end, a clear definition and direction of reform is required to wisely manage the change process. The region should familiarize itself with a basic ethos of democratic principles and lay the groundwork for good governance practice. In this regard, the reform effort needs to be conducted in a participatory approach and with proper implementation and monitoring mechanisms. For Afar Regional State, dialogue and consensus as guarantors of sustainable and sufficient reform with a commitment of political leadership must be made with political and socio-economic actors. Political imagination and tolerance are essential to navigate through differences.

On the way towards democracy, ensuring democratic rights in a region that underwent bad governance will be indispensable. Universal principles of democracy, the rule of law, popular legitimacy, participation, inclusion, freedom of expression, freedom of association, freedom to compete for political office, free media, and the right to vote must be guaranteed. Civil society organizations, which are absent from political space in Afar, should be created to ensure popular participation and government accountability. In a similar vein, institutional backing of reform is sine qua non for endurable and legitimate reform to happen. The Afar people's destiny should not rest on the goodwill of leaders. In the long run, institutions are the guarantors of the future for a hope to prevail.

Recent moves to expand and unify the EPRDF on November 16 and 21, 2019, towards the new Prosperity Party and merge the affiliated parties in the Afar, Benishangul-Gumuz, Gambella, Harari, and Somali regions into the fold is regarded warily by many Afars. Primarily, before their decision to join the Prosperity Party, Afar leaders utterly failed to consult with the people they represent and also failed to negotiate to protect Afar interests. This is again another wrong premise to embrace the change process. All members (557) of the now-dissolved ANDP overwhelmingly approved the merger plan without any preconditions. Afar youth and educated elites were excluded from the plan. Through their interview on Afar TV, the new leaders interpreted the genuine concern of the Afar people as a sign of weak faith emanating from poverty.

The Afar people are not against the merger, but the idea has not been clearly defined as to what it means in real terms. The Afar are concerned that the new plan will compromise their self-governance rights and representation in the federal government and might also set the stage for a return to the previously abusive system of centralization and homogenization. For the Afar, though national unity shouldn't be compromised, the merger plan is a premature idea whose time is yet to come. They are of the opinion that before embarking on the plan, the engineers of the Prosperity Party should have carefully thought about the current pressing challenges that need to be addressed, both at the national and regional levels. Past injustices and inbuilt problems, primarily, should have been addressed properly. The means, not the end, should justify the matter. The Afar are in quest of full regional autonomy that guarantees their political, social, and economic rights. The merger issue shouldn't be left only for the incumbent political leaders to decide. Through creating a platform and pressure groups, concerned bodies must play their part to bring about a panacea and shape the destiny of the Afar people.

REFERENCES

Abiy Ahmed. 2018. "Ethiopia - Prime Minister Abiy Ahmed Full Speech in Semera, Afar Region." YouTube, June 28, 2018. https://www.youtube.com/watch?v=-N2rgbCLt78.

Dereje Feyissa. 2011. "The Political Economy of Salt in the Afar Regional State in Northeast Ethiopia." *Review of African Political Economy* 38, no. 127 (March): 7–21.

Lefort, René. 2018. "Ethiopia: Climbing Mount Uncertainty." *Ethiopia Insight*, October 21, 2018.

Markakis, John. 2011. *Ethiopia: The Last Two Frontiers*. Oxford: James Currey.

Mu'uz Gidey Alemu. 2015. "The Geopolitics and Human Security of the Afar in the Post-Cold War Period." *African Journal of Political Science and International Relations* 9, no. 6 (June): 225–53.

Tadesse Berhe and Yonas Adaye. 2007. "Afar: The Impact of Local Conflict on Regional Stability." Institute for Security Studies/CPRD Paper.

Yasin, Mohammed Yasin. 2008. "Political History of the Afar in Ethiopia and Eritrea." *Afrika Spectrum* 43, no. 1: 39–65.

PART FOUR

Foreign and Security Policy

4.1 Ethiopia's Defense Reform Agenda: Progress and Challenges

4.2 Eritrea-Ethiopia Rapprochement: Benefits, Issues, and Challenges

4.3 Neither Old nor New: Ethio-Eritrean Relations through the Dawn of Change in Ethiopia

4.4 Ethiopia's Engagements with Its Fragile Neighbors: An Examination of the Concept and Application of Buffer Zones as a Security Strategy in Ethiopia's Relations with Somalia

4.1 Ethiopia's Defense Reform Agenda
Progress and Challenges

Ann M. Fitz-Gerald

INTRODUCTION

Ethiopia's post-April 2018 political settlement has brought about change across the security sector and, most notably, within the Ethiopia National Defense Force (ENDF). Under the leadership of Prime Minister Abiy Ahmed, the new government has made wide-ranging changes at both the strategic policy and operational levels of the defense force. Although some aspects of the reforms were arguably "in train" prior to the change in political leadership, other initiatives are new, wide-reaching, and have been most felt in the areas of human-resource-based institutional structuring, leadership and governance, and oversight. Such reforms are in line with the strategic direction laid down by the new prime minister in the commitments communicated at the start of his tenure and resonate with the way in which Ethiopia seeks to move forward with a clear boundary between politics and the military.

Although the issue of defense reform is not a new phenomenon for the government of the Federal Democratic Republic of Ethiopia, both the magnitude of the recent change and the pace at which the change has occurred risks triggering a number of potential sensitivities among those groups who are most affected by the change. Moreover, the strength and sustainability of the individual reforms will depend on the extent to which the reforms remain aligned with, and supported by, a clearer direction taken on Ethiopia's wider national security agenda.

This chapter will examine existing thinking on defense reform and what accounts for successful defense and "security sector reform" (SSR) outcomes. It will then analyze some of the key aspects of Ethiopia's defense reforms before and after the country's April 2018 political transition and discuss areas of progress as well as ongoing challenges and recommended initiatives in moving forward. The chapter is supported by empirical data based on fieldwork in Ethiopia as well as a range of published primary and secondary sources.

THE IDEA OF "DEFENSE REFORM" AND ITS APPLICATION IN PRACTICE

The idea of defense reform was popularized as a domain that warranted further academic research following the defense reforms in central and Eastern European countries after the fall of the Berlin Wall in 1989. These ideas combined with the field of "civil military relations," which was further extended to influence the thinking on wider SSR, which evolved in the early 1990s. In essence, by approximately 2010, guidance and good practice for institutional defense reform was supported by two knowledge domains: civil military relations and SSR. As defense reform became a significant aspect of the wider SSRs pursued by most transitional societies, defense reform experiences influenced the various guidelines subsequently published by a number of international organizations and think tanks.

The changing strategic environment for peace and security after the turn of the millennium evolved thinking on defense reform even more. An ambitious global development agenda, the emergence of smaller conflicts, border incursions, and new emerging threats, including counterterrorism, trafficking, counter-radicalization, and cyber warfare, served as just some of the trends that characterized the changing landscape for defense. As such, and despite not being made so obvious by the predominantly "post-conflict"-based literature, defense reform was initiated in both the Northern and Southern Hemispheres.

During this period and based on the well-researched and undisputed relationship between security and development, international development organizations began working more closely with security actors. The World Bank's work examining the link between military expenditure and poverty, the physical security fears of impoverished communities, the relationship between "war economies" and the "poverty trap," and calls for more "comprehensive" approaches to security all led to the further broadening of national security and international security concepts. Based on their more collaborative work with other security-relevant actors, what were once very autonomous international development agencies began to act more like departments of state. These interactions and newly interdependent relationships led to more comprehensive security sector policy agenda, including SSR.

Although a consensus on definitions of the terms security, security sector, and SSR has now been achieved,[1] agreement on guidance and principles for supporting "successful" SSR outcomes has been less harmonious (Fitz-Gerald 2017). In many cases, due to the large internationally sponsored investment in SSR research in the late 1990s and early 2000s, the work of the SSR policy world outstripped the pace of academic research on the subject. With the policy literature in the lead, key international organizations began producing guidance to inform both the strategic and operational aspects of what they felt constituted effective SSR. To date, this guidance appears to fall into one of two categories—guidance directed at implementation and delivery (that is to say the "operational" side of reform programs) and guidance in the form of principles for strategic engagement (Fitz-Gerald 2017). Although this international strategic and operational guidance published by organizations such as the UN, OECD, and DCAF covers similar areas, in practice the guidance is quite different. On the basis of the existing SSR policy literature, it is therefore quite difficult to develop useful guidance that can be applied to a range of different defense reform contexts. Indeed, scholars such as Westerman (2017) have argued in support of the need for "subfields" supporting defense reform that are more appropriate to specific contexts and cultural practices in which defense reform is being implemented.

On the other hand, organizations like the UN (UN Security Council 2014) and the AU (African Union Commission 2014) developed policy frameworks for SSR and supporting operational guidance. The AU guidance was informed by lessons learned from a number of different African defense and security reform experiences across the continent and was consolidated by the African Security Sector Network, headquartered in Accra, Ghana. Both sets of guidance touch on some principles of SSR, including "effective and accountable security," "ownership and commitment of the States and societies involved," "integrity of motive, accountability, resources and capacity," and the importance of long-term commitment and monitoring (UN Department of Peacekeeping Operations 2012, 14). The guidance resonates with the broad principles published by the OECD-DAC (OECD 2005, 2007) as well as the work of the Geneva-based International Security Sector Advisory Team (ISSAT), which outlines three overarching objectives for SSR (to be accountable to the state and its people; effective, efficient, and affordable; and respectful of international norms, standards, and human rights) and three core principles (local ownership; effectiveness and accountability; and holistic, political, and technical) (2016).

The SSR norms and frameworks notwithstanding, it could be argued that SSR as a concept is still fraught with tensions and contradictions and has not been hugely successful in Africa (Abrahamsen 2016; Fitz-Gerald 2017; Jackson 2011). A large part of this failing has been blamed on the way in which SSR principles have emerged from the liberal peace paradigm and the Anglo-American and Westphalian tenets of state building. Westerman (2017) also observed the lack of consideration given to experiences other than immediate post-conflict transitions in the SSR literature and the potential utility of learning from defense and security reforms that have been ongoing in dynamic national settings for years, including in countries like Israel. It is also the case where some of the more interesting and locally driven (versus internationally imposed) defense and security reform processes have not been as well documented based on the availability of research for lesson learning and policy development for regions where the international community has been involved. As a result, relatively successful defense reform experiences in countries like Israel, and earlier disarmament, demobilization, and reintegration experiences in countries like Ethiopia, have simply not made any significant appearance in the literature until recently and, despite the relative success of these programs, have had little impact on the development of SSR principles and guidance to date.

In addition to the questions that remain on the success of SSR experiences to date, it has also been argued that the development of security sectors in many African countries does not align well with the assumptions of how the "security sector" is more universally defined and referred to. A number of African scholars have also questioned the extent to which more mainstream principles of civil military relations can be easily transferred to the African continent, where military loyalty to civil authorities and the military's "non-role" in national politics do not reflect either past experience or, in some cases, ongoing practice (Ebo 2005; Ngoma 2006). SSR principles also assume an existing interface between security-relevant ministries and civil society groups, whereas the reality has been a difficult at best and nonexistent at worst relationship between the two groups, due to past perceptions that civil society was antiestablishment in nature.

Based on the shortcomings of both the SSR and CMR discourse in terms of its separate or combined application in a non-Western context, challenges exist in developing guidance and criteria to inform and evaluate SSR programs. However, based on existing work, three general thematic areas could be identified under the headings accountable, suitable, and sustainable (Fitz-Gerald 2017). The broad-based framework emerging from these areas is outlined below and implies that successful SSR requires both a top-down and bottom-up approach. Whereas the bottom-up approach ensures that the foundation and assumptions for SSR in different countries are considered, top-down ownership and direction encourages both sustainability and defense reforms that are led by strategic-level national security policy.

Table 4.1.1 *Framework for a Successful SSR*

Accountable	Suitable	Sustainable
All actors must be partners in the undertaking, with the local population having trust in the integrity and motive of both local leaders and international donors.	Objectives must be based on democratic norms and internationally accepted human rights principles and on the rule of law. They should seek to contribute to an environment characterized by freedom from fear.	A clearly defined, long-term strategy and plan, which provides for sufficient resources and capacity, must be put in place from the start.
The security system should be managed according to the same principles of accountability and transparency that apply across the public sector, in particular through greater civil oversight of security processes.	The objectives must be developed jointly with partner governments and civil society and based on an assessment of the security needs of the people and the state. Delivery plans must be flexible and tailored to the local context.	The objectives must be developed jointly with partner governments and civil society and based on an assessment of the security needs of the people and the state. Delivery plans must be flexible and tailored to the local context.
Well-understood monitoring and evaluation processes must be put in place from the start to track SSR progress and to make amendments to plans as necessary.	Broad consultation must take place among donor government departments as well as close coordination with other donor governments, international organizations, and a wide range of local actors to ensure that the various stakeholders' objectives do not conflict.	An integrated and multi-sectoral approach to ensure that any individual project undertaken fits into and interacts with the wider security and justice system. SSR practitioners must retain a holistic vision of security and justice development.

Source: Fitz-Gerald, Westerman, Macphee (2017).

EVALUATING ETHIOPIAN DEFENSE REFORMS IN THE CONTEXT OF WIDER SSR

Ethiopia required SSR based both on its past history of violence and control and its need for modern-day institution building according to the new federal system of governance. Since the reign of Menelik II, and even through the era of Emperor Haile Selassie (1930–74), Ethiopia had relied on a strong military to ward off successive attempts at colonization. Under

Haile Selassie's leadership, contests with neighbors over bordering and disputed territory (e.g., the Ogaden and Eritrea regions) gave prominence to the military's role supporting internal security. Resistance to colonization also meant that the systems and institutions of the colonial masters across the rest of Africa had little to no influence on the way Ethiopia developed its society and methods of governance. This left the country in a position to develop its own national approaches to military security during both dynastic periods. The Derg regime that deposed Haile Selassie arguably gained its strength from the resources and influence afforded to it under the emperor but subsequently pursued a seventeen-year regime characterized by oppression and terror. The military strength that had been preserved under these successive regimes also emerged by way of a national effort to manufacture weapons and armaments. By the time the Tigray People's Liberation Front's (TPLF) revolutionary army overthrew the Derg in 1991 and developed a coalition-based government under the Ethiopian People's Revolutionary Democratic Front (EPRDF), the notion of a "national military" was a concept that required rebranding and needed to demonstrate a service to the country, versus a regime.

A more contemporary approach to both SSR and defense reform in Ethiopia emerged around the turn of the millennium. While this period was already ten years into the EPRDF's leadership, it could be argued that the first ten to fifteen years of the newly developed ENDF's post-Derg experience almost wholly focused on the disarmament, demobilization, and reintegration of armed militia groups that either supplemented or opposed the TPLF's efforts to victory and, to a much lesser extent, the war with Eritrea. This left an already under-resourced new armed forces with little capacity to support broader institutional development.

A discussion emerged in 1997–98 during a time when Ethiopia's internal and external security issues and threats were recognized as complex and dynamic and had real implications for the peace and stability of the state. The fragility of Somalia, the instability generated by a number of extremist movements and terrorist organizations operating in the region, the uncertain and unstable governance system in Eritrea, its border conflict with Ethiopia, election-related domestic violence, and other security threats raised the importance of reform in the government's national security organizations. These reforms prompted the drafting of the 2002 national security white paper (the Foreign Affairs and National Security Policy and Strategy—FANSPS) and the subsequent creation of a national security advisor and a National Security Council. Until the production of the FANSPS, and not unlike most of its Western counterparts at the time, Ethiopia had no experience of any integrated national security policy or mechanism.

In addition to a mandate supporting poverty reduction, Ethiopia's FANSPS also presented democratization and good governance as key national goals (Federal Democratic Republic of Ethiopia 2002). These three strategic goals were reflected in the country's 2006 Plan for Accelerated and Sustainable Development to End Poverty (PASDEP)[2] as well as its successor documents, entitled Growth and Transformation Plan (GTP I, 2010–15, and GTP II, 2015–19). While this suggested good strategic alignment between national security and development, it also begged the question as to whether or not, mindful of the interdependent relationship between security and development (Spear and Williams 2012), the 2002 analysis underpinning the FANSPS continued to inform the more recent thinking on national development. Similarly, it could also be argued that, for a country that had been steadfast in its approach to updating subsequent iterations of its national development strategy (PASDEP/GTP I/GTP II), it was peculiar not to observe a similar level of planning and commitment supporting an evolving FANSPS.

To date, a successor document to the FANSPS has not yet been produced by the government. At the time of writing, although this issue was being discussed, this is an essential element of the strategic direction that is not only required for defense guidance but also the guidance for the wider range of security actors, including the National Intelligence and Security Service (NISS), the Ministry of Justice, and the federal and regional police. Irrespective of the urgency in making such legislative changes, and despite the laudable measures taken in expediting the exercise, the recent submission of the new 2019 national security legislation has gone forward in the absence of a new national security framework, strategy, or policy. This suggests that, despite the passing of some much-needed legislative changes informing the way the security sector operates, these amendments have still been shaped and informed by the former strategic context of the previous national security strategy and that further legislative changes will be required. Appropriate sequencing would normally call for the publication of a national security strategy or policy followed by a review of existing legislation and an evaluation of the extent to which the current legislative framework supports the intended strategic policy direction. Similarly, the initiation of far-reaching defense reforms in the absence of an agreed upon and approved overall national security policy framework also risks a lack of policy coherence. While it is realistic for governments to, based on necessity, initiate these measures in parallel, the exercises should be tightly linked and mutually reinforcing.

Arguably, one further challenge that could stymy the process of national security strategy development is what could be described as numerous potentially competing organizations with a mandate for national security analysis and planning. Based on the way in which the FANSPS combined the concepts of national security and foreign policy, efforts within the Ministry of Foreign Affairs to produce a successor document to the 2002 FANSPS had emerged prior to the 2018 political transition (EPRDF state minister, interview, May 2017). In parallel to this, ongoing analytical work continued in the national security advisor's office in the Office of the Prime Minister at the same time as the unveiling of the new Ministry of Peace, mandated to provide leadership and strategic direction to all security-relevant ministries. Based on the regional turbulence in areas such as Raya, Gondar, Hawassa, and Wollo since the new political settlement, like other elements of the new federal government the Ministry of Peace has been forced to run before it has learned to walk. That said, with strong civilian leadership and a growing cadre of civilian employees and established offices in Addis Ababa, it is arguably best placed to lead on strategic planning for, perhaps, not just "national security" but rather on "national peace and security."

The FANSPS called for a focus on human resources (rather than material resources) in the development of the armed forces and also sought to relate defense capability requirements to the national economy (van Veen 2016, 35). In the years that followed, a commitment was made to the development of knowledge and skill sets across all levels of the armed forces. This was reflected in the creation of the National Defense University concept introduced in 2010 (Mulugeta 2017) and with the country's efforts to avail of donor funding for the purposes of training and education. The emphasis on the military's role in the development of the national economy further bolstered the capacity of the Metals and Engineering Corporation (METEC), a parastatal conglomerate that was run by the military.

The emphasis on human resource development also led to a focus on new structures, systems, and procedures, thereby giving way to more comprehensive institutional reforms. Structural changes to the ENDF also led to the appointment of a civilian minister (who had not formerly held a senior role in the military) and the development of a new defense research and transformation unit. Although Ethiopia has not produced a formal defense policy or strategy, it became one of very few countries on the African continent to develop a defense doctrine based on its largely conventional warfare and counterinsurgency experience to date. This doctrine development exercise was based on numerous discussions and considered debate on the country's experience and the implications for the current environmental trends impacting defense.[3] With very few other African countries mirroring this capability for doctrine development, and with such demands for African peacekeeping currently facing the African Union (Fitz-Gerald 2017), one could argue that Ethiopia has much to offer to its fellow African partners in terms of their collective preparation for ongoing and future peacekeeping and stabilization interventions.

With a significant thrust of Western support for defense reform, international funding has directly supported the ENDF's priority of professionalization through education and training. Between 2004 and 2009, while this provision took the form of many short courses and training delivered by external experts, the ENDF also remained determined to professionalize through award-bearing postgraduate education (Macphee and Fitz-Gerald 2014). Its rationale supporting this direction was that the institution would benefit from comparative views, approaches, and models from across the globe and, secondly, that this effort could support capacity development of the country's existing universities, particularly those that formed the newly developed National Defense University.[4] Defense leaders also prioritized the development of English-language skills, which became a mechanism not only for enhancing regional and continental interoperability but also for the selection of officers on a range of foreign staff college and UN peacekeeping opportunities. This support has been ongoing since 2003–4 and still continues today.

It could therefore be said that defense reforms that were given priority by way of objectives outlined in the FANSPS had a positive impact on development. The emphasis on the new "people's armed forces," the significant downsizing of the military, professionalization through education and skills development, and military support to economic development through METEC all contributed to many of the development-related goals laid out in both the FANSPS and PASDEP/GTP documents. However, where the outcome of defense reforms has undergone further scrutiny is in evaluating the extent to which it has supported the country's democratization agenda. In this context, the four areas that continue to fall under the microscope of international media and human rights organizations relate to accountability and oversight of the armed forces, the division of roles and responsibilities between the military and the police, corruption, and the role of the military in politics.

Whereas the Ethiopian Ministry of National Defense (EMOND) had developed an internal accountability system characterized by a general six-point framework on which it reports quarterly and on which its performance is evaluated regularly by the parliamentary defense and security committee, there have been concerns over the generality of this framework and in the ministry's lack of transparency surrounding appointments (van Veen 2016). Feedback from respondents supporting this research indicated that, irrespective of the increased ethnic representation across mid- to senior officers between 2010 and 2018, the promotion of Tigrayan officers was still happening at a faster rate than non-Tigrayan officers whose experience and achievements had satisfied criteria for promotion (mid-ranking and senior ENDF officers, interviews, May 2018). Other areas of concern have related to the defense budget, the relationship between EMOND and METEC and off-the-books defense budgeting. Prior to 2018, there was also concern with the dominant voice of the ministry projected from the "uniformed" side of the building as opposed to the office of the defense minister, whose remit was to provide political direction and leadership for all uniformed personnel.

At the operational level, responses from the security forces to the protests and demonstrations in different parts of Oromia and Amhara between 2015 and 2017 suggested that a top-heavy approach was still being taken by security forces to quell opposition and dissent ("Ethiopia Declares State of Emergency as Deadly Protests Continue," *Guardian*, October 9, 2016). This issue questioned the extent to which commitments made in the constitution to demonstrate peacefully and to enable popular voices were genuine. The callout to federal forces to overstep the regional security authorities did not offer good optics, albeit were seen to be required as a result of the weak capacity at the regional level to manage such protests and demonstrations. As one interviewee for this research stated, "If the regional security forces of Oromia were left to manage the situation [rather than the military], the post-demonstration situation would have been much worse" (anonymous, interview, August 2017). With both international and national media referring generally to the behavior of "the security forces," it was difficult during this protest period to ascertain how the behavior of the security forces broke down into the activities of the regional police, federal police, military, and other special units. These ongoing generalizations, the lack of evidence supporting the generalizations, and the current polarized positions of political groups risked leading to certain perceptions about the military. The outcome also made for a difficult set of dynamics to be reconciled and something that only more pluralistic, regular, and inclusive debate and discussion on security policy could address.

The long history of the military's role in politics is linked with the party affiliation that senior members of the armed forces have maintained with the EPRDF and its various coalition party members. Described by Mulugeta (2017) as a "politico-military form of hybrid leadership," one could argue that the existing political partisan nature of the military is a product of recent history and a culture that would perhaps, with more diverse ethnic representation across all levels, diminish into something less political and more professional over time. Feedback from a number of interviewees, including former senior officers themselves, suggested that while its historical roots and role remain unquestioned and embedded in the country's political culture, there is a widespread view that even prior to the 2018 political transition the dominant influence of the TPLF within the armed forces had been reduced and would need to diminish further.

The role that the military plays in support of economic development has also placed question marks over possible links between the security forces and corruption. Although interviews supporting this research suggest that corruption among the Ethiopian security forces is "petty" in nature and has tended to have involved the police more than the military, the historic role of the military in the economy, and its role in large parastatal companies like METEC, has led to questions being asked about the privileged access that senior members of the armed forces have had to economic benefits. Arguably, the model of the military being involved in economic development is one that has been used in other emerging Middle Eastern and Eastern economies and is not new. However, METEC's production of defense-related armaments, as well as a wide range of manufactured products for civilian use, led to questions concerning the full transparency of defense spending, as well as the degree to which the security forces benefited financially from this affiliation and the economic fruits of regular commercial activity. Respondents from EMOND acknowledged the important role played by METEC not only during the EPRDF era but even in its previous incarnation in support of the Derg, during which time the government aspired to be self-sufficient in its production of small-scale armaments.

Irrespective of these positive contributions, feedback from respondents indicated that a view still existed in many parts of the population that regards the senior cadre of military officials as having favorable access to the economic fruits of its development efforts. One could argue that, in a Western context, inevitable economic benefits accrue to those who have held senior posts in government. However, when this phenomenon becomes superimposed onto the existing economic culture of parastatal leadership, as well as a dominant ethnic-based group whose senior positions represent a longer-term outcome of a liberation struggle, both the situation and the lingering perceptions become inevitable.

The final area of concern under the theme of accountability is the limited public debate and discussion on security, justice, and human rights, the result of which leads to questions surrounding the transparency of security policy. This issue is undoubtedly linked to the 2001 proclamation that prevented the development of civil society organizations (CSOs) in the areas of human rights, security, and justice, and the imprisonment of reporters and bloggers over more recent years (Davison 2015). In some respects, the lack of government interface with civil society on issues relating to national defense and security runs counter to the experience of the late prime minister Meles Zenawi, who invited feedback from a number of Addis-based academics during the drafting of the 2002 FANSPS (Mulugeta Gebrehiwet, interview, May 2012, Addis Ababa). Neither does the practice align with the commitment made by EMOND to professionalize its institution through higher education, which, to some extent, indicates respect for research and knowledge in the field. In 2016, the previous government had made efforts to respond to calls for more transparency and public debate by introducing the "People's Forum," where senior government panels consulted with leading sectoral-based actors (i.e., transportation, health) on a quarterly basis and that sought to engage with sectoral leaders and opinion makers (van Veen 2016). However, despite these positive developments, issues such as defense, national security, and justice were not included in this initiative and, therefore, were not subject to public debate.

In parallel to these developments and ongoing observations, Ethiopia's regional and international influence continues to strengthen, a reputation that has accrued over the past ten years. In addition to its role as lead troop-contributing nation for UN peacekeeping missions, Ethiopia also currently holds the chair position for the Intergovernmental Authority on Development and served as a nonpermanent member of the UN Security Council between 2017 and 2019. Following the 2015 report by the UN High-Level Independent Panel on Peace Operations, the international peacekeeping role that Ethiopia now leads will take on additional significance in the proposed new era of strategic partnership between the UN and AU. Experience from its leadership of the first-ever nationally commanded and structured UN Interim Security Force for Abyei (UNISFA), and the ongoing feedback this mission provides to the UN, has had a significant influence on the debate on the future of UN peacekeeping missions. The dialogue it has generated with UN technical assistance missions on issues concerning the further development of the UN mandate in Abyei has offered wider lessons influencing the future of UN mandate development (former UNISFA commander, interview, 2015).

In summary, prior to the political transition in April 2018, the ENDF enjoyed a better reputation for its external international engagement in comparison to the reputation they appeared to enjoy inside the country. While the former was based on its prolific involvement in, and leadership of, international peacekeeping missions (and the assistance it offered to the immediate region), the latter appears to be focused on a lack of institutional transparency and accountability, its links to the economy, its role in internal security, and perceived high levels of corruption. The final section of this chapter will examine ways in which the reform measures taken by Prime Minister Abiy's government thus far have addressed these areas.

ETHIOPIA'S DEFENSE REFORM AGENDA POST-APRIL 2018

Since the April 2018 political transition, changes have impacted the defense leadership hierarchy. A new chief of the General Staff, General Seare Mekonnen, replaced General Mohammed Yonus ("Samora"), who had been in office since 2001. Following the tragic assassination of General Seare Mekonnen in June 2019, General Adem Mohammed, former director-general of NISS (and, prior to that, former chief of the Ethiopian Air Force), was appointed to the position. Other senior officers whose age of retirement had been extended under the former leadership were immediately retired or had their periods of extension significantly reduced. For officers who had remained in the rank of full colonel or higher, some of whom had existed in these ranks for periods of ten years, a decision was taken that either promotion or retirement would be required after being in the rank for five years. Following another (unusually) long-term appointment that had survived a number of cabinet shuffles, the former defense minister, Siraj Fegessa, was replaced initially by Motumo Mekassa (Oromia), who was then replaced by Aisha Mohammed (Afar) and, in April 2019, by the former Oromia regional president Lemma Megersa. With the new prime minister's emphasis on the armed forces being a force for the people and loyal to the "government of the day" (Kiram 2018), the profile of the minister's office is now being strengthened. While there has never been a significant cadre of civilian policy officials present in the ministry, plans appear to be focused on the recruitment of a new "delivery unit" that will be focused on meeting key performance indicators (KPIs) underpinning intended reforms.

In addition to change within the ministry, the House of Peoples' Representatives approved the addition of a navy and a cyber and space command, in addition to the three existing commands: the air force, special forces, and ground force. Structural change is also being applied further down at all levels of command. With the disbandment of the Central Command and the reintroduction of the regional brigade system, regional, battalion, company, and unit command structures will now only include one officer from each ethnic group. More specifically, this means that each member of the four-member management committee at each level of command—including the commander, the deputy commander (head of operations), head of administration, and head of logistics—will all be different in terms of ethnic background. The intention is to build a more representative professional force that reflects all of Ethiopia's nations, nationalities, and peoples, thereby projecting a more "national" ENDF that represents all of Ethiopia's regional states.

The prime minister has also addressed the military's role in the strategic, operational, and financial management of METEC as a state-owned and state-run conglomerate. Twenty-seven officers from the former METEC management were gathered and arrested for acts of corruption and embezzlement during their term as METEC employees ("Ethiopia also Arrested 27 METEC Employees, Police Officials," Reuters, November 12, 2018). This purge included the arrest of Brigadier General Kinfe Dagnew, former chief executive of METEC ("Attorney General's List of Detainees in Relation to Alleged Corruption," *Reporter*, November 13, 2018). In addition to the suite of METEC arrests, the organization was restructured to have its production of military equipment and matériel come under EMOND and its production of civilian and commercial equipment and matériel stay under METEC. As a result of METEC not meeting the milestones of many of the country's megaprojects, and to address internal efficiencies in the organization, approximately 25 percent of the staff was laid off on "administrative leave" ("METEC to Lay Off Workers," *Reporter*, September 8, 2018).

Around the same time, arrests of thirty-six members of NISS were made on alleged grounds of human rights abuses and corruption. The Federal Police commissioner was apprehended, and a warrant for the arrest of the former Director-General of NISS was issued (Aaron 2018).

It is more questionable as to the extent to which the intellectual debate on defense and security issues in Ethiopia has benefited from the involvement of CSOs. Based on the past culture where CSO organizations were perceived by government as antiestablishment—a trend that was common in many African countries—it is still difficult to find any CSOs based in Addis Ababa that focus on issues relating to Ethiopia's defense and national security institutions. Although Addis Ababa University hosts the renowned Institute for Peace and Security Studies, the organization's peace and security remit is very broad and focused on continental and global challenges, including border security, trafficking, countering violent extremism, and continental and regional policy frameworks. Arguably, some of the more credible media organizations in the country have really led the effort to provide informed commentary on national defense and security issues. In addition to reporting more regularly on these themes, they have also reached out to credible global experts to provide informed commentary.

The above notwithstanding, EMOND has called for the review of the current training and education curriculum in order to evaluate the extent to which this reflects the current strategic environment and the missions, tasks, and activities in which the ENDF are now involved. Until 1998, the experience of the ENDF was based on counterinsurgency, a campaign that shaped the strategy to overthrow the Derg. This left the armed forces somewhat unprepared for the conventional warfare challenges faced during the 1998–2000 Eritrean-Ethiopian War. Now, after another twenty years, the challenges the ENDF faces have less to do with conventional warfare and more to do with issues concerning the movement of contraband, terrorism, riot control, and insurgencies led by highly mobile insurgents. It is the intention of EMOND to design and develop training and educational material that reflect the realities of the current strategic environment. This is particularly important in the absence of any AU continental or regional doctrine that is not African in nature and that has not been influenced by the peacekeeping and stabilization experiences of very different colonial and NATO-led missions (Fitz-Gerald 2017).

Perhaps the greatest challenge facing the security forces of the country is to support the capacity and development of the federal and regional police forces and ensure the primacy of these internal security forces for addressing internal security issues. As is the case for most developing countries, there is a difference in the institutional strength and operational competencies between the federal and regional police forces, with the former institutionally stronger and more professionalized than the latter. The high degree of regional autonomy exercised by regional state governments, particularly with regard to security, has not provided a conducive environment for the sort of "partnered" relationship required between the federal and regional forces. As a result of this, and even due to the weak capacity of the federal police themselves in managing some of the large-scale protests and low-level violence that has emerged in regions such as Amhara, Oromia, Tigray, and the Southern Nations, Nationalities, and People's over the past three years, clarity on roles and responsibilities—and closer cooperation—between the military, federal police, and regional police forces must be encouraged. Through the leadership of EMOND, the new government has already taken measures to emphasize the importance of the military obeying, coordinating, and planning with the civilian authorities in supporting common goals. Ensuring that these forces have the appropriate skills and knowledge to support their respective constitutional remits will support more seamless security sector cooperation.

As is the case for other African countries, the growth in the contribution to international peacekeeping missions, and the military "buildup" this will bring, will just need to be carefully balanced with appropriate national military requirements, as well as the unilateral roles that the ENDF has pursued in support of their own national security interests in the region, including training support to the Somali Armed Forces (Albrecht and Haenlein 2016).

DEFENSE REFORM IN ETHIOPIA—TOWARDS SUCCESSFUL OUTCOMES?

In applying the suitability-sustainability-accountability framework from Table 10.1, the data on Ethiopia summarized above indicates that some elements underpinning successful SSR are being achieved, whereas further efforts should be made in other areas to target important gaps.

In terms of "suitability," one could argue that the existence of the FANSPS is a positive contribution to the country's national security architecture, particularly as it was a "homegrown" exercise and not one imposed by donor efforts, similar to a high number of other African experiences. However, this policy paper is woefully outdated and provides very little in terms of guidance for national defense. As EMOND has made significant progress in terms of reviewing and developing new curricula and material for future defense training and education requirements, the analytical efforts supporting this exercise should feed into not only a wider policy discussion on national security but also either a parallel or subsequent defense policy exercise. This is particularly important during a time when different security institutions, such as NISS, with its new national security legislation, continue to pursue reforms independent of any overarching national security framework. The new Ministry of Peace is well positioned to lead on clarifying higher-level national security objectives that a new defense strategy could support.

What is common to all of these exercises is the need for deep and effective evidence-based analysis and a team that can keep this analysis ongoing in a very fluid national and regional security environment. As defense ministries typically lack the ability to undertake the scale of analysis necessary to inform their strategic visions for the future, it is important for the security-based ministries to engage with appropriate CSOs with the mandates to inform these types of debates. Such engagement would also support the "accountability" pillar of the Table 10.1 framework and lend positively to the notion of a "people's," as opposed to a "regime's," institution. Moreover, as the institution seeks not only to evolve its training and education curriculum but also its defense doctrine, operational guidance, and rules of engagement to reflect the contemporary exigencies and operating environment, "analysis" will be an important area for future investment. As a number of media representatives and academics currently make up the epistemic community supporting an evidence-based discussion on defense and security, the government should open space to supplement its analytical efforts and include these experts in roundtable debates and seminars or even through "closed" meetings by "invitation only." This civil society engagement also provides an opportunity for EMOND to share information on how it is currently performing against its designated KPIs which, if positive, could work in support of the institution's reputation with the population.

Also, in terms of "suitability," the government should be commended for its efforts to extract the military from the operation of national commercial enterprises and the economic rents that flow from these organizations. This enhances governance and transparency of the defense institution and demonstrates a reduced conflict of interest in the institutional mandate of the military and in the profit-making interests of the economy. However, the merging of the defense-related industries and factories under EMOND will drive an expectation of defense budget transparency and open-source reporting on defense industry activities. Perhaps the most optimal way of taking these initiatives forward links back to the need for a defense policy that includes clear strategic objectives that subsequently inform KPIs and milestones that reflect targets for each of the reporting periods.

In terms of "sustainability," the restructuring of the brigade system and the early retirement of many officers entering their "extended" contract beyond statutory retirement will help provide opportunities for others and remove the bottlenecks. Even a sizeable number of serving officers who are not yet close to retirement will inevitably be faced with early retirement due to the lack of positions to accede to for any one ethnic group under the new command structure policy. However, based on the global experience of these sorts of demobilization programs, it is important for the government to provide sufficient incentives to support the departure of early-retired officers, most of whom are Tigrayan. Bearing in mind the current tension between the federal government and the Tigray regional government and the arrests and detainments of former TPLF officials, the government should ensure that a strategic approach is taken to support this demobilization effort. Not doing so may risk some skilled and experienced—yet, in some cases, possibly disgruntled—officers to support a more "securitized" Tigray region. With the recent peace dividend with Eritrea, and with plans to access the coastline for both trade and the development of a navy, Tigray provides an important gateway to enable these opportunities. As such, the government may consider leveraging the knowledge and skill sets of some of the early-retired officers to support the development of microenterprises in both Tigray and other less developed areas of the country. A well-thought-out system, as opposed to a "one-off" solution, will be required to support this displacement, as this phenomenon is likely to be ongoing for a further ten years, until a more balanced and representative system is in place.

CONCLUSION

This chapter has examined the general approach that Ethiopia has taken to aspects of defense reform to date, both prior to and following the 2018 political transition of the EPRDF leadership. The framework used to guide the analysis was informed by the academic literature on defense and security reform, whose theoretical underpinnings are supported by literature on both civil military relations and wider SSR. In this context, ongoing defense reforms and residual challenges were analyzed in terms of the suitability, sustainability, and accountability pillars of a framework guiding successful SSR outcomes.

The analysis illustrated that aspects of both the past defense reform agenda and the new current agenda go some way to address these three general issues and, in some areas, may be further extended to bring about a more comprehensive approach to defense reform. Critical to this will be the development of a defense strategy/policy that supports the overall direction for national peace and security. In addition, the development of a civilian cadre within the defense ministry and a healthier partnership with research centers of excellence can ensure that strategic policy moving forward is evidence based and well debated and discussed. Lastly, a well-informed, comprehensive defense policy framework with clear strategic defense objectives can also inform the development of effective KPIs, on which the future performance of the defense institution can be evaluated.

NOTES

1. The DCAF definition of SSR neatly brings all of the various definitions together when it describes it as "the process through which a country seeks to review and enhance the effectiveness and the accountability of its security and justice providers" (DCAF 2012, 5).
2. PASDEP became the government of Ethiopia's label for its internationally funded Poverty Reduction Strategy Program (MoFED 2006).
3. Based on discussions with the former EMOND director of training, Addis Ababa, February 6.
4. The National Defense University colleges included accredited institutions specialized in areas such as engineering, logistics, management, and medicine.

REFERENCES

Aaron Maasho. 2018. "Ethiopia Arrests Ex-Deputy Intelligence Chief in Corruption, Rights Crackdown." Reuters, November 14, 2018. https://www.reuters.com/article/us-ethiopia-politics-idUSKCN1NK079.

Abrahamsen, Rita. 2016. "Exporting Decentred Security Governance: The Tensions of Security Sector Reform." *Global Crime* 17, no. 3–4: 281–95.

African Union Commission. 2014. African Union Policy Framework on Security Sector Reform (SSR). Asssembly/AU/Dec.472(XXX). Para 21. https://issat.dcaf.ch/content/download/60132/986021/file/AU_SSR_policy_framework_en.pdf.

Albrecht, Peter, and Cathy Haenlein. 2016. "Fragmented Peacekeeping: The African Union in Somalia." *RUSI Journal*, March 11, 2016.

Davison, William. 2015. "Ethiopia's Crackdown on Dissent Drives Opposition to Push for 'Freedom First.'" *Guardian*, June 11, 2015. https://www.theguardian.com/global-development/2015/jun/11/ethiopia-crackdown-dissent-drives-opposition-push-freedom-first.

DCAF. 2012. *SSR in a Nutshell: Manual for Introductory Training on Security Sector Reform.* http://issat.dcaf.ch/content/download/2970/25352/file/ISSAT LEVEL 1 TRAINING MANUAL - SSR IN A NUTSHELL - 5.3.pdf.

Ebo, Adedeji. 2005. "Towards a Code of Conduct for Armed Security Forces in Africa: Opportunities and Challenges." Policy Paper 05, DCAF, Geneva.

Egnell, Robert, and Peter Haldén. 2009. "Laudable, Ahistorical and Overambitious: Security Sector Reform Meets State Formation Theory." *Conflict Security & Development* 9, no. 1: 27–54.

Federal Democratic Republic of Ethiopia. 2002. "Foreign Affairs and National Security Policy and Strategy." November 2002. Addis Ababa: Ministry of Information, Press & Audiovisual Department. https://chilot.me/wp-content/uploads/2011/08/national-security-policy-and-strategy.pdf.

Firsing, Scott. 2014. "Thinking through the Role of Africa's Militaries in Peacekeeping: The Cases of Nigeria, Ethiopia and Rwanda." *South African Journal of International Affairs* 21, no. 1: 45–67.

Fitz-Gerald, Ann. 2012. "Thematic Review of Security Sector Reform (SSR) to Peacebuilding and the Role of the Peacebuilding Fund." New York: United Nations Peacebuilding Support Office. https://www.un-.org/peacebuilding/sites/www.un.org.peacebuilding/files/documents/ssr2_web.pdf.

———. 2017. "Towards a Common Doctrine for African Standby Force-Led Peace Operations." *International Peacekeeping* 24, no. 4: 616–38.

Greene, Owen, and Simon Rynn. 2008. "Linking and Co-ordinating DDR and SSR for Human Security after Conflict: Issues, Experiences and Priorities." Thematic Working Paper 2, Centre for International Cooperation and Security, University of Bradford.

Hoeffler, Anke. 2014. "Can International Interventions Secure the Peace?" *International Area Studies Review* 17, no. 1: 75–94.

International Crisis Group. 2016. "Ethiopia: Governing the Faithful." Briefing Paper No. 117/Africa, February 22, 2016.

ISSAT. 2016. "SSR Overview." Last modified 2020. Accessed July 11, 2016. http://issat.dcaf.ch/Learn/SSR-Overview. Geneva: DCAF.

Jackson, Paul. 2011. "Security Sector Reform and State Building." *Third World Quarterly* 32, no. 10 (November): 1803–22.

Kiram Tadesse. 2018. "PM Abiy Urges Respect for Rule of Law." Afro 105.3 FM, August 20, 2018. http://www.afro105fm.com/afrofm.com/2018/08/20/pm-abiy-urges-respect-for-rule-of-law/.

Knight, Mark. 2009. "Social Sector Reform, Democracy, and the Social Contract: From Implicit to Explicit." *Security Sector Management* 7, no. 1 (February): 1–20.

Krause, Keith. 2007. "Towards a Practical Human Security Agenda." DCAF Policy Paper No. 26. Geneva: DCAF.

Le Roux, Len. 2006. "Challenges for Defence Planners in Africa: Ensuring Appropriate, Adequate, Accountable and Affordable Armed Forces." *African Security Review* 15, no. 4: vi–viii.

Macphee, Paula-Louise, and Ann Fitz-Gerald. 2014. "Multiplying a Force for Good? The Impact of Security Sector Management Postgraduate Education in Ethiopia." *Peace Education* 11, no. 2: 208–24.

McCandless, Erin. 2012. *Peace Dividends and Beyond: Contributions of Administrative and Social Services to Peacebuilding*. New York: United Nations Peacebuilding Support Office.

MoFED. 2006. "Ethiopia: Building on Progress; A Plan for Accelerated and Sustained Development to End Poverty (PASDEP)." https://www.afdb.org/fileadmin/uploads/afdb/Documents/Policy-Documents/Plan_for_Accelerated_and_Sustained_(PASDEP)_final_July_2007_Volume_I_3.pdf.

Mulugeta Gebrehiwot Berhe. 2017. "The Ethiopian Post-Transition Security Sector Reform Experience: Building a National Army from a Revolutionary Democratic Army." *African Security Review* 26, no. 2: 161–79.

Ngoma, Naison. 2006. "Civil-Military Relations in Africa: Navigating Uncharted Waters." *African Security Review* 15, no. 4: 98–111.

OECD. 2005. *Security System Reform and Governance: A DAC Reference Document.* DAC Guidelines and Reference Series. http://www.oecd.org/dac/conflict-fragility-resilience/docs/31785288.pdf.

———. 2007. *OECD DAC Handbook on Security System Reform (SSR): Supporting Security and Justice.* https://www.eda.admin.ch/dam/deza/en/documents/themen/fragile-kontexte/224402-oecd-handbook-security-system-reform_EN.pdf.

Sedra, Mark. 2010. "Towards Second Generation SSR." In *The Future of Security Sector Reform*, edited by Mark Sedra, 102–16. Waterloo, ON: Centre for International Governance Innovation.

Short, Clare. 1999. "Security Sector Reform and the Elimination of Poverty." Speech delivered at Centre for Defence Studies, Kings College, London, March 9, 1999. http://www.clareshort.co.uk/speeches/DFID/9 March 1999.pdf.

Spear, Joanna, and Paul D. Williams, eds. 2012. *Security and Development in Global Politics: A Critical Comparison.* Washington, DC: Georgetown University Press.

UN Department of Peacekeeping Operations. 2012. *The United Nations SSR Perspective.* Security Sector Reform Unit, Office of Rule of Law and Security Institutions. https://peacekeeping.un.org/sites/default/files/ssr_perspective_2012.pdf.

UN Security Council. 2014. Resolution 2151, Maintenance of International Peace and Security. S/RES/2151, April 28, 2014. https://www.un.org/en/ga/search/view_doc.asp?symbol=S/RES/2151(2014).

UN SSR Task Force. 2012. *Security Sector Reform Integrated Technical Guidance Notes.* New York: UN.

van Veen, Erwin. 2016. "Perpetuating Power: Politics and Security in Ethiopia." *Clingendael*, October 11, 2016. https://www.clingendael.nl/publication/perpetuating-power-politics-and-security-ethiopia.

Westerman, Ian. 2017. "Too Much Western Bias? The Need for a More Culturally Adaptable Approach to Post-Conflict Security Sector Reform." *Defense and Security Analysis* 33, no. 3: 276–88.

Wrong, Michela. 2014. "Why Are Africa's Militaries So Disappointingly Bad?" *Foreign Policy*, June 6, 2014. https://foreignpolicy.com/2014/06/06/why-are-africas-militaries-so-disappointingly-bad/.

4.2 Eritrea-Ethiopia Rapprochement

Benefits, Issues and Challenges

Senai Woldeab

INTRODUCTION

The Eritrea-Ethiopia rapprochement, formally cemented by the peace agreements signed in Asmara (July 9, 2018) and Jeddah (September 16, 2018), is one of the most noticeable geopolitical scores of 2018 in the Horn of Africa. Mainly linked to the coming into power of Ethiopian Prime Minister Dr. Abiy Ahmed Ali, the results of the rapprochement have been felt in the Horn and may even be contributing to shaping the geopolitics of both sides of the Red Sea and beyond. Given the velocity and extent of its already noticeable marks, some form of initial—and critical—analysis can be made of this rapprochement. This chapter intends to discuss and analyze the benefits that have been and can in the near future be reaped from the rapprochement, the issues that need to be raised in understanding and narrating the rapprochement, and the challenges that can face the realization of the ambitious goals of the peace agreements. The analysis centers on the thesis that domestic, regional, and international factors have contributed, and will continue to contribute, to each of the three angles of assessment identified by this chapter.

1. GENESIS AND CAUSES OF THE RAPPROCHEMENT

Genesis of the Rapprochement and Its Ripple Effects

In his inaugural speech before the Ethiopian parliament on April 2, 2018, Ethiopia's new prime minster, Dr. Abiy Ahmed, extended an olive branch to Eritrea and its leaders and said:

> With the government of Eritrea, we want from the bottom of our hearts that the disagreement that has reigned for years to come to an end. We will discharge our responsibility. While expressing our readiness to resolve our differences through dialogue, I take this opportunity to call on the Eritrean government to take a similar stand not only for the sake of our common interest but also for the common blood relations between the peoples of the two countries. (Hussein 2018)

On the contrary, on May 14, 2018, the Eritrean government, in response to what it perceived to be an anti-Eritrea meeting between Abiy and then Sudanese leader Gen. Omar Hassen al-Bashir, issued a strongly worded statement rejecting an agreement between Ethiopia and Sudan "to extend support to what they termed as Eritrea's armed opposition groups in order to enable them to properly execute their objectives" and provide them with material support and requisite facilities. In short, as far as Eritrea was concerned, Abiy appeared to be continuing the hostile policy his predecessors followed against it ("Press Statement," *Eritrea Profile*, May 16, 2018; Mumbere 2018).

On Tuesday, June 5, 2018, the Executive Committee of Ethiopia's ruling coalition, the Ethiopian People's Revolutionary Democratic Front (EPRDF), issued a statement in which it promised to fully implement the Algiers Agreement, the December 2000 peace deal that formally ended the two-year border war (1998–2000) between the two countries, and the ruling of the Eritrea-Ethiopia Boundary Commission (EEBC), which was established under the Algiers Agreement (EBC 2018). At least in Asmara, where the author was when the June 5 call was announced, there was, therefore, uncertainty as to whether the Eritrean government, given its May 14 statement, would reciprocate the call with an unconditional welcome.

On Wednesday, June 20, 2018 (Eritrean Martyrs' Day), two weeks after the call from the EPRDF Executive Committee, Eritrea's president, Isaias Afwerki—standing at the gate of the Martyrs' Cemetery before members of his party and government, representatives of the international diplomatic community, and thousands of citizens—surprised the audience by pronouncing that he accepted the EPRDF's call. Citing the hitherto positive impact of the presidency of Donald Trump and the demise of "vultures" in Ethiopia, Isaias announced that he would be sending representatives to Addis Ababa because the shenanigans of the Tigray People's Liberation Front (TPLF) could aptly be described as "game over" ("President Isaias's Speech on Martyrs' Day," *Eritrea Profile*, June 23, 2018).

A whirlwind of diplomatic, public, and regional acts of rapprochement ensued in what looked like a snowball effect of the speeches in Addis Ababa and Asmara. Asmara hadn't witnessed such a flurry of visits by foreign dignitaries in over two decades.

June 2018

Eritrean Foreign Minister Osman Saleh and Presidential Advisor Yemane Gebreab arrived in Addis Ababa on June 26 and were warmly welcomed ("Senior Eritrean Delegation Winds Visit to Ethiopia," *Eritrea Profile*, June 30, 2018). In his speech, delivered in Amharic, Yemane said, "We do not look like we have been separated for twenty years."

July 2018

The Osman-Yemane visit was reciprocated by Abiy Ahmed's historic trip to Asmara on July 8–9 ("Prime Minister of Ethiopia Dr. Abiy Ahmed Visits Eritrea," *Eritrea Profile*, July 11, 2018). This first landing of an Ethiopian Airlines airplane at Asmara's airport was preceded by a near-dreamlike waving of Ethiopian flags in the streets of Asmara and other Eritrean cities. On July 9, the two leaders signed a five-articled Joint Declaration of Peace and Friendship ("Joint Declaration of Peace and Friendship between Eritrea and Ethiopia," *Eritrea Profile*, July 11, 2018). Immediately after his return to Ethiopia, Abiy met UN Secretary-General António Guterres in Addis Ababa and formally requested the UN Security Council lift the sanctions that had been imposed on Eritrea since December 2009 in response to Eritrea's allegedly disruptive involvement in Somalia and its conflict with Djibouti. Five days later, an Isaias-led high Eritrean delegation was ecstatically welcomed in Addis Ababa and Hawassa, and the Eritrean embassy was symbolically opened at the very building it occupied two decades before ("President Isaias Afwerki's Official Visit to Ethiopia; Eritrean Embassy in Addis Ababa Reopens, *Eritrea Profile*, July 18, 2018).

On July 18, African Union (AU) Commission Chairperson Moussa Faki Mahamat released a statement wherein he praised the peace deal as "a major and historic contribution to the stabilization and sustainable development of the Horn of Africa region" (African Union 2018).

On July 24, Abiy Ahmed and Isaias Afwerki were conferred the Order of Zayed, the highest award of the UAE in recognition of their work for peace between the two nations ("President Isaias on Official Visit to the UAE and Saudi Arabia, *Eritrea Profile*, July 25, 2018).

On July 28, Asmara welcomed Somali President Mohamed Abdullahi Mohamed, and on July 30 the two leaders signed a Joint Declaration on Brotherly Relations and Comprehensive Cooperation (Eritrea Ministry of Information 2018a). They also established a Joint High-Level Committee of Eritrea and Somalia ("Somali President Conducts a Three-Day Official Visit in Eritrea," *Eritrea Profile*, August 1, 2018).

August 2018

On August 13–15, a senior Eritrean delegation visited Somalia and held discussions with Somali leaders ("Senior Eritrean Delegation Concludes Visit to Somalia," *Eritrea Profile*, August 18, 2018). On August 22, South Sudanese President Salva Kiir Mayardit conducted a two-day visit to Asmara to discuss bilateral and regional developments ("President Salva Kiir Conducts a Two-Day Working Visit in Eritrea, *Eritrea Profile*, August 23, 2018).

September 2018

On September 5–6, the leaders of Ethiopia, Somalia, and Eritrea held a tripartite summit in Asmara and issued a Joint Declaration on Comprehensive Cooperation Between Ethiopia, Somalia and Eritrea (Eritrea Ministry of Information 2018c). They also established a Joint High-Level Committee of their foreign ministers ("Leaders of Eritrea, Ethiopia and Somalia Hold

Tripartite Meeting," *Eritrea Profile*, September 8, 2018). As a result, the three foreign ministers visited Djibouti on September 6 and delivered a joint message from the three leaders to the president of Djibouti, Ismaïl Omar Guelleh. Guelleh welcomed the message from the three leaders and in particular expressed his willingness to restore relations with Eritrea, which had broken down following a border clash in June 2008 (Eritrea Ministry of Information 2018d) Hassan and Kimball 2008).

In the early hours of September 11, the Geez New Year, Abiy and Isaias opened the Debay Sima-Bure common border that lies on the road that connects the Eritrean port of Assab and Addis Ababa. Then both leaders flew to the common border of Serha-Zalambessa and celebrated the holiday at the common border. That same morning, the common border, which had been dubbed the most fortified border on the continent, was opened, and people from both sides swarmed to embrace each other and visit long-separated relatives and friends. A massive movement of people and goods ensued ("Roads Connecting Eritrea and Ethiopia Re-Opened, *Eritrea Profile*, September 12, 2018; Ahmed 2018; Al Jazeera 2018).

On September 16, in the presence of Saudi King Salman bin Abdulaziz, Crown Prince Mohammed bin Salman, and UN Secretary-General Guterres, the Eritrean and Ethiopian leaders signed, in Jeddah, a seven-articled Agreement on Peace, Friendship and Comprehensive Cooperation ("Agreement on Peace, Friendship and Comprehensive Cooperation Between the Federal Democratic Republic of Ethiopia and the State of Eritrea," *Eritrea Profile*, September 19, 2018) and were honored with the Order of Abdulaziz Al Saud medal, the kingdom's highest civilian honor ("President Isaias Afwerki and Prime Minister Abiy Ahmed Presented with Highest Saudi Arabia Award," *Eritrea Profile*, September 19, 2018; Associated Press 2018).

Reflecting on the peace deal that he had just witnessed, Guterres remarked, "There is a powerful wind of hope blowing across the Horn of Africa," adding, "We have seen a conflict that has lasted for decades, ending, and that has a very important meaning in a world where we see, unfortunately, so many conflicts multiplying, and lasting for ever" (UN News 2018).

On September 17, in what has been called a historic meeting, Djibouti's Guelleh met Eritrea's Isaias, and the two leaders, although without signing a formal document, promised to restore relations ("Meeting of Presidents Isaias and Ismail Omar Guelleh," *Eritrea Profile*, September 19, 2018). Following his Jeddah honoring, Isaias once again visited Abu Dhabi, on September 19, and discussed the new developments in the Horn of Africa with UAE Crown Prince Mohammed bin Zayed Al Nahyan ("President Isaias Met and Held Talks with Crown Prince of Abu Dhabi," *Eritrea Profile*, September 21, 2018).

October-December 2018

In what may be the first official visit by a Western leader in more than two and a half decades, Italian Prime Minister Giuseppe Conte arrived in Asmara on October 12 for a one-day stay. Conte's visit was added Italian (or perhaps European) flavor to the rapidly accelerating dynamics in the Horn ("Italian Prime Minister Conducts Official Visit to Eritrea," *Eritrea Profile*, October 13, 2018). Three days later, Isaias flew to Addis Ababa for his second official trip after the rapprochement ("President Isaias Conducts Official Visit to Ethiopia," *Eritrea Profile*, October 17, 2018).

The Eritrean and Somali presidents then visited Ethiopia, this time in Bahir Dar and Gondar, on November 9–10, where they and Abiy signed a joint statement for an inclusive regional peace and cooperation (Eritrea Ministry of Information 2018e).

On November 14, the UN Security Council unanimously lifted the sanctions on Eritrea, conditioned on a six-monthly review of progress (Nichols 2018). The Eritrea Ministry of Information responded by releasing a press statement titled, "The Question is not 'Removal of Sanctions': It is why sanctions in first place?" (Eritrea Ministry of Information 2018b).

On December 4, US Assistant Secretary of State for African Affairs Tibor Nagy met Isaias in Asmara as part of his visit to the Horn ("President Isaias Holds Talks with US Assistant Secretary for African Affairs," *Eritrea Profile*, December 5, 2018). On December 13, Isaias paid working visits to Somalia and Kenya ("President Isaias on Working Visit to Somalia and Kenya," *Eritrea Profile*, December 15, 2018) and continued on to the UAE ("Presient Isaias Returns Home Concluding Working Visit to UAE," *Eritrea Profile*, December 22, 2018).

At the end of December, in what appeared to be an odd move, Eritrea closed the two key border crossings to Ethiopia (Adi Kuala-Rama and Serha-Zalambessa) without informing the Ethiopian government (Xinhua 2018). While some speculated that the move could have been prompted by concern over the possibility of Eritrean opposition groups crossing over from

Ethiopia, where they had been stationed for many years (Kidane and Plaut 2019), the Eritrea Ministry of Information posted an article on its website stating that "the unstructured border crossing in some areas was partially restricted for legal arrangements" (Weldemichael 2019).

2019

The partial closure of the border may have been one of the reasons for a relative cooling of high-level engagements between Eritrea and Ethiopia during the first two months of 2019. Nevertheless, on March 3, 2019, Asmara welcomed Abiy and Kenyan President Uhuru Kenyatta, where they discussed tripartite and regional peace and cooperation. The next day, Abiy and Isaias flew to Juba, where they met President Salva Kiir and discussed the acceleration of peace in South Sudan and regional integration at large ("President Isaias and Prime Minister Abiy Visit South Sudan," *Eritrea Profile*, March 6, 2019). Abiy and Somali President Mohamed Abdullahi next flew together to Nairobi to discuss the Kenya-Somalia maritime boundary dispute (Shaban 2019a). On March 18, Eritrean Foreign Minister Saleh and Presidential Advisor Gebreab traveled to Hargeisa and discussed bilateral and regional matters with Somaliland President Muse Bihi Abdi (Horn Diplomat 2019). Between late March and April 10, Saleh and Gebreab also visited Mogadishu, Cairo, and Riyadh along the same mission (Shaban 2019c). The Somali president responded by paying Asmara his second visit on April 24 (All Africa 2019).

Towards the third week of April, Eritrea extended its December 2018 partial closure of the border to all crossings (Shaban 2019d). The entire border remains closed as of the writing of this chapter. No official explanations have been given. The range of speculations extend from the security concerns mentioned above to the need to include border crossings as part of the cross-border trade agreement that is yet to be finalized between the two countries.

The Domestic Elements of the Equation

It can be argued that the rapprochement was brought about by a combination of domestic and external factors. Following is a brief description of likely domestic factors in Ethiopia and Eritrea that may have contributed to the rapprochement. It is true that there were attempts during the 2002–

2016 period to resolve the conflict between the two countries. However, Bereketeab (2019) argues, and this author also believes, that it is the maturing of objective and subjective conditions in Ethiopia and Eritrea's apparent trusting of the Abiy leadership that brought forth the rapprochement.

Ethiopia

By objective conditions in Ethiopia it is meant to refer to key events that occurred at the national level since 2015 and their ripple effects that likely contributed to Abiy's offer of peace to Eritrea. These include the popular uprisings mainly in Oromia and later Amhara (Dinberu 2018), the dip in the economy, social unrest and human and proprietary insecurities, and communal infightings (Bruton 2018). Another key domestic factor could be the internal split within the EPDRF and the reaction of the public to the series of state-of-emergency declarations (Maru 2018). One may argue that the Ethiopian leadership was urged to settle the deleterious tension with Eritrea to focus on solving these increasingly damaging internal problems.

The overall contribution of the key leaders also merits attention. The rapprochement came following the resignation, on February 15, 2018, of Prime Minister Hailemariam Desalegn, perceived by Eritrea's leaders as following in the footsteps of his predecessor, Meles Zenawi, who passed away in the midst of heightened tension with Eritrea. The series of steps taken by the newly elected Abiy Ahmed were carefully studied by Asmara, and such moves as Abiy's welcoming of the hitherto Eritrean-based anti-regime forces attracted Asmara's attention. The warm welcome of Abiy's actions by Ethiopians and the international community could have given Asmara the hope that a friendly partner might have been put at the helm of power in Addis Ababa. Added to this was Abiy's inaugural speech in parliament (followed by his party's June 5 call) and the general perception in Eritrea that the new leader showed sincerity, honesty, and seriousness in his determination to end the stalemate with Eritrea. To the Eritrean leadership, Abiy may have appeared, unlike Hailemariam, to be at least independent of, if not winning over, the TPLF's influence—a very crucial precondition for Asmara's engagement with the new regime. It is not disputed that Isaias's reference to "vultures" and "scavengers" whose "game is over" was directed at the TPLF.

Eritrea

Eritrea's experience of increasing the economic, social, and political costs of the UN-imposed sanctions was a likely factor in its quick embrace of Abiy's call for peace. The country suffered from severe depletion of its human capital, especially the youth, since the early 2000s, and has been subjected to seriously consequential investigations of its human rights record at continental and international platforms. With Ethiopia's active participation, Eritrea was isolated from regional and continental platforms (Andemariam 2015). Eritrea's leaders attributed the absence, delay, or suspension of many governance and developmental agenda (such as embarking upon constitutional governance, limiting of the indefinite term of the national service program, travel restrictions, and the lifting of import, construction, and related permit restrictions) to Ethiopia's continued opposition and Western conspiracy. As far as Asmara was concerned, Addis was the central player in initiating, maintaining, or facilitating the all-front attacks against the very survival of Eritrea, its people, and government (Bereketeab 2013; Mengisteab 2014; Permanent Mission of Eritrea to the United Nations 2012). The Eritrean government accused the Ethiopian leadership of harboring, funding, and encouraging diaspora-based opposition groups, although it did the same by training and stationing thousands of anti-EPRDF Ethiopian fighters inside its territory (Abbink 2003; Lyon 2009). Asmara saw no, or less, merit in the narratives attributing Eritrean problems to the country's policies (domestic and foreign) or the decisions of an autocratic government. Asmara perceived these accusations as ruses to implement a Washington-concocted plan to overthrow the Eritrean government. Therefore, Eritrea's leaders may have concluded that a peace deal with Abiy's Ethiopia would vaporize the unfounded narratives previously invented by the TPLF regime and contribute largely towards erasing Eritrea's problems.

The Regional-Global Dynamics Involving the Rapprochement

The domestic wing of the rapprochement tells only half of the story. It may be argued that regional and global developments in the Horn, the Red Sea, the Arabian Gulf, and beyond also contributed to, and will in turn be affected by, the rapprochement.

The Arab Spring that started in late 2010 and spread from Tunisia to Oman, Yemen, Egypt, Syria, Morocco, and Bahrain resulted in deep divisions within the members of the Gulf Cooperation Council, mainly between Saudi Arabia, the UAE, and Bahrain on one side and Qatar on the other. The former three countries plus Egypt (together identified as the Quartet) started to accuse Qatar of supporting political Islamic groups, especially the Muslim Brotherhood, that were active in the revolts occurring throughout the Middle East and North Africa. Slowly the contention developed into political and economic rivalry as each group worked to increase its influence and attract partners in the Arabian Gulf, the Red Sea region, and beyond (International Crisis Group 2019). In June 2017 the tension mounted into a serious crisis when the Quartet and several other countries severed diplomatic relations with Qatar and banned Qatari airplanes and ships from using their territories. They issued a list of thirteen demands to Qatar as a precondition to reverse their course against it. Qatar then deepened its relations with Turkey and strengthened its alliance with Iran. As immediate neighbors to the Gulf tension, countries on the African side of the Red Sea started to be involved in the rising tension. Mostly involved in this progress were Eritrea, Djibouti, Sudan, and Somalia, with Ethiopia appearing to remain neutral (Kinninmont 2019).

Qatar was already heavily involved in the Horn. It brokered a mediation process to settle the border dispute between Eritrea and Djibouti by also stationing its peacekeepers at the border between the two countries. It also had invested in Sudan and was very active in the anti-Mubarak revolt in Egypt. It mediated tensions between Eritrea and Sudan (Mesfin 2016). Similarly, the Emirati Dubai Ports World remained active in Djibouti after establishing a joint venture with the Djiboutian government for a thirty-year concession to operate the Port of Djibouti. With the rise in tension between the Quartet and Qatar, Eritrea and Djibouti sided with the Quartet in 2015, and Qatar abandoned the mediation process by also withdrawing its troops from the Eritrea-Djibouti border (Al Maashi 2017, 50; Al Jazeera 2017). Saudi Arabia and the UAE, therefore, found a space to fill in once Qatar lost its footing in Eritrea and Djibouti. Eritrea provided an air base for UAE warplanes to bomb Yemen's Houthi fighters who, allegedly supported by Iran (and by association, Qatar), have been fighting against the Saudi-UAE-supported government of Abdrabbuh Mansur Hadi.

As an example of the continued relevance of regional dynamics to the Eritrea-Ethiopia relationship, on April 4, 2019 the Eritrean government, in a strongly worded press release, accused a Qatari-Turkish-Sudanese alliance of facilitating and financing the establishment of a fundamentalist Islamic Eritrean organization, the Eritrean Ulama's League/Eritrean Rabita-i Ulama, and in general of working to thwart the achievements of the Eritrea-Ethiopia rapprochement (Jawhar 2019).

Moreover, peace between Eritrea and Ethiopia is important in combating terrorism in this part of the world. The Red Sea continues to be an increasingly important strategic corridor in global economic flow,[1] and this necessitates holding foot in the key ports on both sides of the Red Sea (Suakin, Port Sudan, Massawa, Assab, Tajurah, Djibouti, Hargeisa, Berbera, Aden, etc.). The Red Sea is also an important corridor for China's Belt and Road Initiative and an important foothold for asserting its military presence on the global stage. The same applies to Russia, which has a continued interest in remaining relevant in the Middle East by stationing itself in the Mediterranean and Red Sea areas. Moreover, the Red Sea, linked to the Arabian Gulf, remains a crucial space in the tension between the United States (including Israel and Saudi Arabia) and Iran (Al Maashi 2017; Bayram 2018; de Waal 2018; Snyder 2018, 2019; T. G. 2018).

The sum of all these factors is that the countries that aim to assert and increase their influence in the Red Sea had to address, or actively participate in solving, problems in the Red Sea neighborhood. It was therefore likely for this reason that the US, UAE and Saudi Arabia actively worked for around a year through back channels to settle the conflict between Eritrea and its influential neighbor Ethiopia (Fick and Cornwell 2018; Manek 2018).

2. BENEFITS

The benefits to be reaped from this rapprochement can be looked at from the individual country, bilateral, and regional perspectives.

Ethiopia

Ethiopia has gotten relief from Eritrea acting as safe haven for opposition forces. Already the Patriotic Ginbot 7, the Oromo Liberation Front, the Ogaden National Liberation Front, the Tigray People's Democratic

Movement, the Afar Liberation Movement, and the Gambella People's Liberation Movement have laid down their arms and returned to Ethiopia to participate in the political process (Bereketeab 2019; Shaban 2019b).

Ethiopia and Eritrea have, in the Asmara and Jeddah Agreements, agreed to respect each other's sovereignty and territorial integrity and not to interfere in each other's internal affairs. In relation to this, the long-held academic, historical, legal, and political debate as to whether or not Ethiopia can rightfully access Eritrean ports (especially Assab) and through them the sea (Kahsay 2007; Asrat 2014; Fessahatzion 1999; Milkias 2003, 52) can now rest because both countries can, as mandated by international law of the sea, peacefully negotiate terms of Ethiopia's access to Eritrean seaports.

Eritrea

Eritrea's immediate benefits are the relief from the twenty-year-long strain on its human capital, mainly the youth, and the opportunity to refocus its energy on development, institutionalization, and constitutionalism. Eritrea can now work on taking these measures to redo an image tainted by such labels as "the North Korea of Africa" (T. G. 2018), a "geopolitical pariah in the Horn of Africa" and "prickly and difficult to deal with" (Müller 2015), and a "bad neighbour" and "exporter of instability" (Mosley 2014).

Eritrea's long isolation from the Horn and beyond seems to be over, and it can now be reabsorbed as a more active player in the regional political system (Woldemariam 2019) and use its strategic location in the Red Sea as an influence and catalyst to bring about positive change in the region.

Eritrea may also have been offered an opportunity to enhance its human rights achievements, hitherto low rated by the international community, by curing the deficiencies admitted to by the government.

Eritrea and Ethiopia

To these countries, which for the last two decades have been engaged in a nearly zero-sum game of hostilities, diplomatic maneuvering, and proxy war, the benefits are not difficult to discern. Eritrea accused Ethiopia of trying to asphyxiate it through a trilateral alliance with Yemen and Sudan ("Ethiopia-Sudan-Yemen Alliance a 'Conspiracy', Eritrea's FM," *Sudan Tribune*, January 8, 2004). The author recollects that when opposition to Sudan's al-Bashir started to grow, a "look-who-has-the-last-laugh" picture started to circulate on social media showing Eritrea's Isaias having a superlative laughter with the pictures of al-Bashir, with Ali Abdullah Saleh and Meles Zenawi on his side. At least between Eritrea and Ethiopia, one can hope that the time for such vindictive politicking will quickly pass. A spirit of peace and trust has now been given a chance and awaits institutionalization and consolidation. In an exciting twist of events, Eritrea's chargé d'affaires to the AU and the UN Economic Commission for Africa, which was humiliatingly escorted out of an Intergovernmental Authority on Development (IGAD) meeting at the Sheraton Addis by Ethiopian guards in August 2011 (Andemariam 2015), has posted a happy picture with Prime Minister Abiy aboard an Ethiopian Airlines airplane!

At least since Emperor Yohannes IV, the territory of and the situation in Eritrea has played a key role in Ethiopian affairs. Yohannes's missions to confront rebellion of the locals in Eritrea, as well as the series of battles against the Egyptians and Italians in Eritrea, is partly attributed to his weakening and his death at the hand of the Mahdists in March 1889 (Zewde 1991, 42–59; Erlich 1996; Yohannes 1991, 31–49). Eritrea and Eritrean soldiers and spies were involved in the historic 1896 battle at Adwa between Emperor Menelik II and the Italians (Milkias and Metaferia 2015). Troops stationed in Eritrea (the Second Division) were instrumental in ending Emperor Haile Selassie's regime in 1974 through a series of mutinies and acts of insubordination in Asmara (Tiruneh 1993; Lobban 1976, 373). The liberation forces from Eritrea, in cooperation with the TPLF, removed the Marxist regime, the Derg, in May 1991. Arguing that Eritrea had played some role in bringing about the shift within the EPRDF in 2018 may also hold some water (Bereketeab 2019, 32). The same argument also applies to the impact on Eritrea of events and regimes in Ethiopia. Therefore, the new rapprochement has opened an atmosphere where Eritrea can play a positive, enforcing role in Ethiopia's quest for internal peace and transformation and vice versa.

As envisaged in the Asmara and Jeddah Agreements, both countries have created opportunities for joint economic, cultural, social, security, and other works together. Moreover, they can learn from each other's development and governance experiences.

The Region

With the increase of diplomatic visits to the capitals since the Eritrea-Ethiopia rapprochement, the region appears to be gathering one of its scarcest supplies: trust and friendship among the leaders. The Eritrea-Ethiopia conflict has long been blamed as the major stumbling block retarding the achievement of regional integration and economic development, at least that envisioned by IGAD (Bereketeab 2012; Dersso 2014; Healy 2009). The Eritrea-Ethiopia rapprochement has provided IGAD and countries of the Horn with a welcome challenge to resume/reinvigorate their long-decelerated integration projects.

Moreover, with Eritrea and Ethiopia at the fulcrum of this new wave of peace, each country can serve as a mediator in resolving disputes that the other may be involved in. For instance, Ethiopia has promised to ease the tension between Eritrea and Djibouti and seems to have succeeded in keeping Eritrea and Somalia close to each other. Likewise, Eritrea, given its ties with the Somali people during the struggle for its liberation, can also mediate the historic tension between Ethiopia and Somalia. With its apparent neutrality in the Saudi/Emirati-Qatari tension, Ethiopia can work to reconcile Eritrea and Djibouti with Qatar and reactivate the Eritrea-Djibouti mediation process that Qatar suspended in 2015. Eritrea can play an active role in bringing Ethiopia and Egypt together in their tension regarding use of the Nile River. Such a mediatory role can be (and has already been) extended to beyond the countries, as Ethiopia has tried to work on solving the maritime dispute between Kenya and Somalia. Eritrea and Ethiopia can similarly work together in easing tensions between Sudan and South Sudan.

3. ISSUES

In this section the author proposes the issues that must be raised as we try to narrate and understand the Eritrea-Ethiopia rapprochement. These issues, it is hoped, will help us understand the rapprochement comprehensively and objectively. These are: (1) the trigger to the rapprochement; (2) the peace formula; and (3) institutionalization and transparency.

What Triggered the Rapprochement?

A reference has already been made to Bereketeab (2009), who points at the maturity of objective and subjective conditions (Ethiopian) and the concomitant trust factor (Eritrean). These factors lead us to ask some fundamental questions as to what caused this rapprochement that has the potential to cut the Horn of Africa's historic Gordian knot of conflicts, mistrusts, and often bloody battles (Yoel 2018).

One may ask whether the rapprochement was mainly caused by the ripening of domestic factors in both countries or was an extension of the policies of regional and global powers whose interests required the settlement of the Eritrea-Ethiopia dispute. Some writers (Bereketeab 2019; Woldemariam 2019) hold that a mix of both factors, without the need to apportion them, contributed to realization of the rapprochement. The involvement of the UAE, US, and Saudi Arabia has been noted above. Alongside considering external factors, it may also be asked whether the economic, political, and reputational damage caused as a result of the repeatedly renewed 2009 UN sanctions against Eritrea played a role in convincing Eritrea to accept Ethiopia's offer.

Within domestic factors, the contribution of the respective peoples of the two countries, including those living at the common borders, and the personalities and decisions of the elites should also be examined. As far as Ethiopia is concerned, how much of a factor was the popular uprising of 2015 in bringing the rapprochement? As far as Eritrea is concerned, did the serious depletion of its youth to years of migration, and as a result being one of the highest per capita refugee-producing countries in the world, translate into necessitating the rapprochement?

The Peace Formula

The Asmara and Jeddah Agreements contain a number of points that define the nature of the peace embraced by the two countries.

The Asmara Declaration has five articles that (1) announce the coming to an end of the state of war between them; (2) mandate both countries to cooperate in political, economic, social, cultural, and security issues; (3) announce the resumption of links in transport trade, communications, and diplomacy; (4) pledge the implementation of the decision on the boundary between the two countries; and (5) commit both countries to jointly endeavor to ensure regional peace, development, and cooperation. The Jeddah Agreement essentially copied the Asmara Agreement, with slight additions. Article 2 adds defense, trade, and investment to the areas of cooperation listed in Asmara. Article 3 calls for developing joint investment projects, including the establishment of joint special economic zones. Through Article 5, both countries pledge to work for global peace and security on top of the Asmara commitment to regional peace and security. Under Article 6, both countries will strive to combat terrorism as well as trafficking in people, arms, and drugs in accordance with international covenants and conventions. Under Article 7, a High-Level Joint Committee, as well as subcommittees as required, will be established to guide and oversee the implementation of the agreement.

A number of questions come to mind as one reads these two agreements.

Firstly, what is the legal relationship between the two agreements? Are they independent or complementary of each other? That the Asmara document is called a "Declaration" of peace and friendship and the Jeddah document is called an "Agreement" of peace, friendship, and comprehensive cooperation may be read to make the latter superior in its weight, owing to: (a) the nomenclature attributed to it (agreement versus declaration); (b) its comparatively larger scope; or (c) even its being attested to by a head of state (the Saudi king) and the UN secretary-general. Or, on the contrary, is the Jeddah document an embodiment of, and therefore subjected to, the preceding Asmara document that declared the principles for the peace negotiated by the two countries? According to one highly placed source in Asmara, the Jeddah Agreement was a mere formality to recognize Saudi efforts to bring about the peace deal; hence, no textual or legal scrutiny is needed to compare the two agreements, and the Asmara declaration suffices to be considered the real peace formula. Given the larger similarities between the two documents, however, a midway answer seems appropriate; that is, both documents are in essence the same and hence must be read as one package.

Secondly, one may inquire about the legal status of these documents. That they were formally signed by the leaders of the two countries may be held to be enough to consider them as legally binding. But are they treaties per se? Despite the identifiers used to name the two documents (Declaration and Agreement), a convincing argument may be forwarded to consider the documents treaties, or one treaty as such. According to the Vienna Convention on the Law of Treaties, a treaty is defined as "an international agreement concluded between States in written form and governed by international law, whether embodied in a single instrument or in two or more related instruments and whatever its particular designation" (Article 2(a)). Every state possesses the capacity to conclude treaties (Article 6) by persons representing it, including heads of state and heads of government (Article 7(1) and (2)(a)). Whether an agreed-upon document is a treaty or not is determined by the nature of the agreement, not by how the signatories name it. Thus, the Asmara and Jeddah documents can be accepted as treaties since they are international agreements concluded between the two countries in writing to bind their relations under the new era of peace. However, it must be noted that to have the full force of binding law, such documents may need to be further approved or "domesticated" under respective constitutional or institutional processes. Absent these processes, the signed documents may be devoid of their legal status and be relegated to being considered declarations of intent or written reflections of foreign policy that the signatories commit to implement. This issue merits lengthy analysis beyond the scope of this chapter.

Thirdly, regardless of whether the two agreements are treaties or signed instruments/declarations of intent and policy, their relationship with the Algiers Agreement needs to be thoroughly discussed. It is true that the EPRDF Executive Committee communicated to Eritrea its desire to implement the Algiers Agreement and unconditionally accept the border commission's ruling. According to an informal discussion the author had with a senior Eritrean diplomat, it is mainly because of this commitment to the Algiers Agreement that the Eritrean government positively responded to the call. In fact, when pressed by members of the Ethiopian parliament to elaborate his and his party's call to Eritrea, Prime Minister Abiy responded that he was merely implementing the very agreement that his predecessors had begun to implement under a legal authorization they received from the same parliament (Government of Ethiopia Proclamation 2000).

But that seems where the reference to the Algiers Agreement ends, at least at the level of the texts of the Asmara and Jeddah Agreements. It is known that the widely discussed Algiers Agreement (e.g., de Guttry, Post, and Venturini 2009) had three components: delimitation and demarcation of the boundary by a border commission (Article 4); addressing the negative socioeconomic impact of the border crisis and setting the damages by a claims commission (Article 5); and investigating the origins of the conflict by an independent body appointed by the secretary-general of the Organisation of African Unity (Article 3). Moreover, the International Committee of the Red Cross was given the responsibility to cooperate in following up on the conditions of prisoners of war and other victims of the conflict (Article 2). The United Nations Mission in Ethiopia and Eritrea was constituted to monitor and patrol a demilitarized zone between the two countries. According to Plaut (2016, 41), the Algiers Agreement, the institutions it created, and the other relevant institutions made up a "a gold-plated peace agreement, drawn up with the best of intentions by skilled negotiators from across the globe." The works of the Eritrea-Ethiopia Boundary Commission (EEBC) and Claims Commission (EECC) were concluded in 2002 and 2009, respectively, but they remain unimplemented. The investigating body has not been constituted.

However, the Asmara and Jeddah Agreements (Articles 4 and 4, respectively) identify, for implementation, only the works of the EEBC. There is no mention of payment of EECC awards to each country by the other and of the investigating body. It is not clear whether this was intentional. It needs to also be mentioned that the Asmara and Jeddah Agreements declare the "end of the state of war between the two countries" and that the Algiers Agreement had similarly so declared (Article 1). Were the two countries therefore in a "state of war" between December 2000 and July 2018? Does it mean that, as far as the two governments are concerned, the Algiers Agreement did not avert a state of war that continued from before December 2000 until July 2018? If so, have the Asmara and Jeddah Agreements replaced the Algiers Agreement, except the ruling of the EEBC?

A more sensible reading of the relationship between Algiers and the two 2018 agreements would be to consider the latter as logical continuations of the former. The Algiers Agreement was limited mainly to ending the conflict and bringing the countries back to normalcy (Bereketeab 2009) by addressing key issues of their conflict (investigating causes, clarifying the border, and paying damages). In short, the Algiers Agreement may be perceived as focusing on the *past*. The 2018 agreements build on this and appear to be focusing mainly on the *future* by laying the groundwork for cooperation in many areas (trade, investment, tourism, defense, security, and regional and global peace). If the 2018 agreements are considered as continuations of and therefore constituting one big peace package with the Algiers Agreement, it behooves both governments, as a matter of legal obligation and historical responsibility to their people and posterity, to dwell on the two apparently forgotten Algiers components (investigation and damage) so this bloody chapter in their common history gets a proper and responsible closure.

Institutionalization and Transparency

Institutionalization and transparency will prove to be two indispensable tools as the page now turns to implementing the commitments and achieving the "lofty objectives" (see fourth recital of the Preamble to the Jeddah Agreement) of the peace process ("Agreement on Peace, Friendship and Comprehensive Cooperation Between the Federal Democratic Republic of Ethiopia and the State of Eritrea," *Eritrea Profile*, September 19, 2018). It is expected that all necessary legal, institutional, and personnel arrangements are being made on both ends. Over and above the need to process the rapprochement through constitutional/institutional legitimization mechanisms, the people of both countries need, as of right now, to be updated through formal and informal channels on the progress of the peace process.

4. CHALLENGES

Given the above-narrated context within which it was concluded, the rapprochement cannot be expected to be immune to challenges. Some potential challenges are discussed below.

Expectations

Given the paucity of documents and public explanations of the details of the peace process, it is difficult to ascertain whether expectations from both governments are coinciding. It is natural that both governments do look at the peace process mainly from the perspective of their own interests.

At least the following respective interests need to be harmonized in order for the peace process to move smoothly. These are the interests of the Eritrean and Ethiopian governments; the interests of the Eritrean and Ethiopian public (especially those at the border between the two countries), which may or may not coincide with those of the governments; and the interests of the neighboring countries in the region as well as that of the superpowers that have stationed themselves on and around the Red Sea. Expectations of these various actors may be low or high depending on the angle from which they look at the rapprochement. As the two governments embark upon implementing the peace, they need to recognize and be sensitive to said interests and incorporate them in the process as much as is practically possible.

Sensitive Issues

Given the historical, social, cultural, religious, military, and emotional factors involved in the bloody history of Eritrea's independence from Ethiopia, a couple of "sensitive" issues that need careful handling come to mind.

Eritrea launched a three-decade-long armed struggle against Ethiopia to be an independent country. The struggle cost close to one hundred thousand Eritrean and hundreds of thousands of Ethiopian lives. It is therefore expected that steps taken by the two governments under the 2018 agreements that touch upon the social, political, economic, defense, and security interests of the peoples of both countries will be carefully watched and every step monitored. Actions, words, phrases, gestures, and even quips from any person or institution of influence on both sides have been taken seriously and meticulously scrutinized and discussed in small and large gatherings. Bereketeab (2019, 39) warns us:

> Any illusions concerning the nature and scope of the relationship should be exposed: there must be a clear understanding of what is meant by assertions such as "we are one people" or "the border has no meaning," and by phrases such as "integration and unity," "reconciliation," etc. Most of the time, these have different meanings for Eritreans and Ethiopians.

An alternative approach to realize the expected Eritrea-Ethiopia multilevel integration is to make it part of similar processes at the regional or continental levels. An ambitious, aggressive Eritrea-Ethiopia-alone integration process may prove "too fast."

There is also the other sensitive issue of access to the sea and ports. What is contentious is not the fact of Ethiopia needing access to the sea per se but the claims, some based on disputable historical and legal narrations, of Ethiopia's sovereign and unencumbered right to access the Red Sea and Eritrean ports (Kahsay 2007) as well as the thorny political statements made around this issue (Asrat 2014; Milkias 2003, 52). Confusion abounds in this issue since, mainly, two concepts get frequently confused: the right of access to the sea under international law and right of access to make use of ports in adjacent maritime territories. The issue of the non-absolute (Bayeh 2015) right of landlocked states to the sea, their enjoyment of sea resources and transit rights as well as the conditions of the grant of such rights have long been settled by the now-customary rules of the United Nations Convention on the Law of the Sea (Preamble recital 5, Articles 17, 58(1), 69, 70(3)(c), 82(4), 87(1), 90, 124–132, 140–141, 148, 152(2), etc.) and by case law (e.g., the recent judgment of the International Court of Justice in *Obligation to Negotiate Access to the Pacific Ocean (Bolivia v. Chile)*) (International Court of Justice 2018).

It is not the purpose of this chapter to discuss these issues in further detail. Politics and the not-so-comprehensive grasp of the international rules governing access to the sea and use of ports aside, however, the act of balancing Ethiopia's rights vis-à-vis Eritrea's maritime sovereignty must be handled with careful consideration of applicable international norms and under transparent arrangements that guarantee mutual benefits.

Impact of Domestic Problems and Policies

Bereketeab (2019) does not hide his concerns on the impact of Ethiopia's internal unrest in derailing the peace process. Eritrean officials have also not shied away from airing such beliefs as well. For instance, Eritrean officials, in numerous public discussions they held with mid- to high-level officials and the public in April 2019, repeatedly stated that they would assist in stabilizing the domestic unease in Ethiopia so both countries can equally reap benefits from the peace process. Bereketeab identifies a number of such Ethiopian domestic challenges: youth impatience to see immediate change; provocation by entities who may have lost advantages as a result of the 2018 change in Ethiopia; bringing security and military forces fully under the control of the new political leadership; and the tension between federal and state governments, especially the Addis-Mekelle divergence and its impact on the chemistry among Addis Ababa, Mekelle, and Asmara. Arguably

Bereketeab (cf. Bereketeab 2019, 37) concludes that "it seems only a matter of time before the EPRDF splits." Regardless if such a split occurs, it is undeniable that Ethiopia's domestic problems will negatively impact the peace process.

The most important domestic challenge from the Eritrean side will be the pace at which the country returns to national aspirations and programs long withdrawn, suspended, or retarded for reasons attributed to the border war and the subsequent isolation of the country. These include ending the de facto indefinite term of the national service; producing and practicing a national constitution; reactivating the national assembly; improving key infrastructure; addressing housing, employment, water, electricity, and energy issues; and revitalizing health, education, and other social services. At the moment the country, whose potentials and resources have for the last two decades been consumed to aggressively defend what it perceived as an existential threat, has welcomed this cooperation process with a partner (i.e., Ethiopia) with an asymmetrical demographic, economic, and diplomatic leverage. Eritrea knows it needs to quickly catch up in order to equally share the benefits of the peace with Ethiopia.

Bereketeab (2019) rightly points out the impact of the differing political and economic policies and practices of both countries. Surely both countries have promised to develop joint investment projects, including the establishment of joint special economic zones. Joint economic work by two sovereign states will require some matching of the economic principles that the two countries have adopted. Abiy's economic policy appears to be more open to private sector participation than his two predecessors (Barber and Pilling 2019; Wilson 2019). Eritrea has decidedly inclined towards collective interest, distribution of resources, and aggressive government and party intervention in the market to implement the policy of social justice (Government of the State of Eritrea 1994; People's Front for Democracy and Justice 1994). Although reconciling these apparently different economic and political ideologies and practices is not an obligation or indispensable factor in realizing the common trade and economic objectives of the rapprochement, it can be mentioned with some certainty that the differences can retard the progress and may eventually translate into diplomatic rupture. Many, including the late prime minister Meles Zenawi (2011), had argued that serious differences in economic and, mainly, in monetary policies and practices were the main factor in the outbreak of the 1998 border war (Abbay 2001; Bereketeab 2009, 39). If true, we may witness a slowing of the progress of the rapprochement.

Refugees

According to the United Nations High Commissioner for Refugees, there were at least 175,000 Eritrean refugees in Ethiopia by November 2018, and the influx of these refugees, a large proportion of whom are unaccompanied minors, increased after the signing of the peace deal in July 2018 (Jeffrey 2018). According to a highly placed source in Asmara, both governments have, as in the pre-1998 years, in principle agreed to allow citizens of the other country to live and work as if they were nationals of the host state. Ethiopia's revised Refugee Proclamation no. 1110/2019 provides adequate protection and rights to refugees. It has adapted the standards, definitions and principles of international refugee laws. To date, most Eritreans who have been granted asylum all over the world base their asylum requests on claims of violations of fundamental human rights (to worship, movement, employment, expression, etc.). The granting of refugee status to the tens of thousands of Eritreans in Ethiopian refugee camps could mean Ethiopia accepting a situation of violation of rights in Eritrea. If so, will Ethiopia's continuing to grant refugee status to Eritreans—which it promised to provide under no discrimination (Article 4)—affect the up-and-coming smoothening of the relationship between the two countries? This may happen in the reverse as well.

Related to the issue of citizens of one country living in the other will be the case of agreeing on extradition as well as the rights and limitations of opposition individuals, groups, or parties of one country visiting or meeting in the other.

Implementation

Both governments have admitted that the peace deal intends to achieve "lofty objectives" (Jeddah Agreement, recital three of the Preamble). Implementing joint cooperation in eight areas (political, security, defense, economic, trade, investment, cultural, and social fields) is a genuinely ambitious intent by the standards of these two countries facing various domestic challenges of their own.

Although both governments may submit justifications, there is a discernible delay in implementation of some basic steps at the time of writing this chapter (thirteen months after the Jeddah Agreement). For instance, except for an explanation on the Eritrean side (i.e., that the TPLF is actively hindering its implementation), both governments have not indicated how they intend to move forward with implementation of the border ruling.

Although there are indications that it may have been constituted, the public is yet to know if the High-Level Joint Committee envisaged by the Jeddah Agreement has been established and started its deliberations.

The common borders were opened at different times at the Omhajer-Humera (western), Adi Kuala-Rama (central), Serha-Zalambessa (central), and Debay Sima-Bure (southeastern) crossings. They have all been closed as of April 2019. The closing may have to do with border security or the need to properly regulate the movement of goods and vehicles as well as customs and immigration, but in the absence of an official explanation, this is all speculation. As trade will prove to be one of the most important elements of the cooperation, the serious issue of the common/differentiated use of the respective currencies of both countries must be thrashed out.

CONCLUSION

By all standards the Eritrea-Ethiopia rapprochement was remarkable not only in the way it was brought forth but also by the immense atmosphere of cordiality and peace diplomacy it has triggered in the Horn and the hope it has breathed into the African continent at large. It has been cited as the main reason for awarding the 2019 Nobel Peace Prize to Prime Minster Abiy Ahmed (Norwegian Nobel Committee 2019). Although some (e.g., Bereketeab 2019, 44) have argued that this rapprochement lends credence to the mantra "an African solution to African problems," it may be an understatement to brush aside the role that the actors in the broader region played in making the rapprochement a reality. Nevertheless, if properly seized, the new peace fervor can have the potential of reversing with equal vigor the many opportunities lost to this hostile corner of the world.

Given the two decades of conflict and hostility between the two countries at all levels, it may be early, or rather unreasonable, to start feeling pessimistic about the slow progress of implementation of the peace deals.

Implementation, however, needs to be heavily reliant on institutionalization of the process and transparency and not on the urge of the otherwise powerful state and its leaders. A feeling of "we have been down that road before" could loom if the pre-1998 style of cooperation that was heavily reliant mainly on trust and the personal rapport of leaders repeats itself. The same feeling can arise if progress of the peace is not publicized at frequencies more than the reporting during the years of war and tension.

This much-sacrificed-for peace cannot be sustained if it is not based on curing previous errors (including, perhaps, addressing respective violations of the Algiers Agreement between 2002 and 2018; see Measho 2019) and building on previous commitments (e.g., all elements of the Algiers Agreement). A "let us forget the past and just move on" formula did not previously warrant the avoidance of conflict.

Finally, if this peace is to be sustained, greater emphasis must be had on inculcating its spirit on the new generation of both countries who carry the chance to shape up a brighter future.

NOTE

1. One source (Snyder 2018), for instance, states that:

   Today some 20 percent of global trade by volume passes through [the Red Sea]. In 2016, nearly 17,000 vessels crossed from the Red Sea to the Mediterranean Sea or vice versa through the Suez Canal (there is no consolidated organization that measures all Red Sea traffic), transporting approximately 820 million tons of cargo. Most of the maritime trade between Asia and Europe—about $700 billion annually—traverses it. Access to the Red Sea, and therefore to the Suez Canal, substantially shortens shipping times, making it easier and cheaper for China and the rest of Asia to sell to Europe.

REFERENCES

Abbay, Alemseged. 2001. "Not With Them, Not Without Them: The Staggering of Eritrea to Nationhood." *Africa* 56, no. 4: 459–91.

Abbink, Jon. 2003. "Ethiopia-Eritrea: Proxy Wars and Prospects of Peace in the Horn of Africa." *Journal of Contemporary African Studies* 21, no. 3: 407–25.

African Union. 2018. "Statement of the Chairperson of the Commission on the Relations between Eritrea and Ethiopia." July 16, 2018. http://www.peaceau.org/uploads/auc-com-ethiopia-and-eritrea7-16-2018-eng.pdf.

Ahmed, Hadra. 2018. "Ethiopia-Eritrea Border Opens for First Time in 20 Years." *New York Times*, September 11, 2018. https://www.nytimes.com/2018/09/11/world/africa/ethiopia-eritrea-border-opens.html.

Al Jazeera. 2017. "Why Did Qatar Leave the Djibouti-Eritrea Border?" June 18, 2017. https://www.aljazeera.com/indepth/opinion/2017/06/qatar-army-djibouti-eritrea-border-170618100118290.html.

———. 2018. "Ethiopia-Eritrea Border Opens for First Time in 20 years." September 11, 2018. https://www.aljazeera.com/news/2018/09/ethiopia-eritrea-border-opens-time-20-years-180911082008249.html.

All Africa. 2019. "Eritrea: Somali President Pays His Second Visit to Eritrea Since 2018." April 24, 2019. https://allafrica.com/stories/201904240583.html.

Al Maashi, Haifa Ahmed. 2017. "From Security Governance to Geopolitical Rivalry: Iran-GCC Confrontation in the Red Sea and the Indian Ocean." *Asian Journal of Middle Eastern and Islamic Studies* 11, no. 4: 46–63.

Andemariam, W. Senai. 2015. "In, Out or at the Gate? The Predicament on Eritrea's Membership and Participation Status in IGAD." *Journal of African Law* 59, no. 2 (June): 355–79.

Asrat, Gebru. 2014. *Sovereignty and Democracy in Ethiopia*. Gaithersburg, MD: Signature Book Printing.

Associated Press. 2018. "Ethiopia, Eritrea leaders Sign Peace Accord in Saudi Arabia." September 16, 2018. https://www.cbc.ca/news/world/ethiopia-eritrea-accord-saudi-arabia-1.4826101.

Barber, Lionel, and David Pilling. 2019. "'My Model Is Capitalism': Ethiopia's Prime Minister Plans Telecoms Privatisation." *Financial Times*, February 24, 2019. https://www.ft.com/content/433dfa88-36d0-11e9-bb0c-42459962a812.

Bayeh, Endalcachew. 2015. "The Rights of Land-Locked States in the International Law: The Role of Bilateral/Multilateral Agreements." *Social Sciences* 4, no. 2 (April): 27–30.

Bayram, Mürsel. 2018. "The Fact and Fiction in Eritrea's Middle East Policy." *International Journal of African and Asian Studies* 43: 67–76.

Bereketeab, Redie. 2009. "The Eritrea-Ethiopia Conflict and the Algiers Agreement: Eritrea's Road to Isolation." In *Eritrea's External Relations: Understanding Its Regional Role and Foreign Policy*, edited by Richard Reid. London: Chatham House.

———. 2012. "Intergovernmental Authority on Development (IGAD): A Critical Analysis." In *Regional Integration, Identity & Citizenship in the Greater Horn of Africa*, edited by Kidane Mengisteab and Redie Bereketeab. Suffolk, UK: James Currey.

———. 2013. "The Morality of the UN Security Council Sanctions Against Eritrea: Defensibility, Political Objectives, and Consequences." *African Studies Review* 56, no. 2: 145–61.

———. 2019. *The Ethiopia-Eritrea Rapprochement: Peace and Stability in the Horn of Africa*. Policy Dialogue No. 13. Uppsala, Sweden: Nordic Africa Institute.

Bruton, Bronwyn. 2018. "Ethiopia: End Game?" *Atlantic Council*, February 14, 2018. https://www.atlanticcouncil.org/blogs/africasource/ethiopia-end-game.

Dersso, Solomon. 2014. "East Africa and the Intergovernmental Authority on Development." Mapping Multilateralism in Transition no. 4. International Peace Institute (October). https://www.ipinst.org/wp-content/uploads/publications/ipi_e_pub_igad.pdf.

de Guttry, Andrea, Harry Post, and Gabriella Venturini, eds. 2009. *The 1998–2000 War Between Eritrea and Ethiopia—An International Legal Perspective*. The Hague: T.M.C. Asser Press.

de Waal, Alex. 2018. "Beyond the Red Sea: A New Driving Force in the Politics of the Horn." *African Arguments*, July 11, 2018. https://africanarguments.org/2018/07/11/beyond-red-sea-new-driving-force-politics-horn-africa/.

Dinberu, Tefera. 2018. "Ethnic Nationalism Must Be Replaced by Ethiopian Nationalism." *ZeHabesha*, October 10, 2018. https://www.zehabesha.com/ethnic-nationalism-must-be-replaced-by-ethiopian-nationalism/.

EBC. 2018. "Ethiopia Decides to Fully Accept Algiers Agreement." June 5, 2018. http://www.ethiopia.gov.et/-/back-ethiopia-decides-to-fully-accept-algiers-agreement-ebc-june-5-2018.

Eritrea Ministry of Information. 2018a. "Eritrea-Somalia Joint Declaration on Brotherly Relations and Comprehensive Cooperation." July 30, 2018. http://www.shabait.com/news/local-news/26772-eritrea-somalia-joint-declaration.

———. 2018b. "The Question Is Not 'Removal of Sanctions': It Is Why Sanctions in First Place?" July 30, 2018. http://www.shabait.com/editorial/press-release/26794-press-statement.

———. 2018c. "Joint Declaration on Comprehensive Cooperation between Ethiopia, Somalia and Eritrea." September 5, 2018. http://www.shabait.com/news/local-news/27003-joint-declaration-on-comprehensive-cooperation-between-ethiopia-somalia-and-eritrea-.

———. 2018d. "Foreign Ministers of Eritrea, Ethiopia and Somalia left for Djibouti." September 6, 2018. http://www.shabait.com/news/local-news/27004-foreign-ministers-of-eritrea-ethiopia-and-somalia-left-for-djibouti.

———. 2018e. "Joint Statement of the Bahr Dar Meeting between the Leaders of Ethiopia, Somalia and Eritrea." November 10, 2018. http://www.shabait.com/news/local-news/27384-joint-statement-of-the-bahr-dar-meeting-between-the-leaders-of-ethiopia-somalia-and-eritrea.

Erlich, Haggai. 1996. *Ras Alula and the Scramble for Africa: A Political Biography: Ethiopia & Eritrea, 1875–1897*. Trenton, NJ: Red Sea Press.

Fessahatzion, Tekie. 1999. "Explaining the Unexplainable: The Eritrea-Ethiopia Border War." *Eritrean Studies Review* 3, no. 2: 227–41.

Fick, Maggie, and Alexander Cornwell. 2018. "In Peace Between Ethiopia and Eritrea, UAE Lends a Helping Hand." Reuters, August 8, 2018. https://www.reuters.com/article/us-ethiopia-eritrea-emirates-insight/in-peace-between-ethiopia-and-eritrea-uae-lends-a-helping-hand-idUSKBN1KT1QX.

Government of Ethiopia. 2000. "Peace Agreement Between the Government of the Federal Democratic Republic of Ethiopia and the Government of the State of Eritrea Ratification Proclamation No. 225/2000." *Federal Negarit Gazette*, 7th year, no. 7, December 8, 2000.

Government of the State of Eritrea. 1994. Macro-Policy. November 1994. http://www.eritreadigest.com/wp-content/uploads/2018/03/Eritrea-macro-policy.pdf.

Hassan, Omar, and Jack Kimball. 2008. "Nine Dead in Djibouti-Eritrea Border Clashes." Reuters, June 12, 2008. https://www.reuters.com/article/us-eritrea-djibouti-idUSL1236173020080612.

Healy, Sally. 2009. "Peacemaking in the Midst of War: An Assessment of IGAD's Contribution to Regional Security." Working Paper no. 59. Royal Institute of International Affairs, Crisis States Working Papers Series no. 2 (November). http://eprints.lse.ac.uk/28482/1/WP59.2.pdf.

Horn Diplomat. 2019. "Eritrean Delegation Arrives in Somaliland for High Level Talks." March 18, 2019. https://www.horndiplomat.com/2019/03/18/eritrean-delegation-arrives-in-somaliland-for-high-level-talks/.

Hussein, Hassen. 2018. "Full English Transcript of Ethiopian Prime Minister Abiy Ahmed's Inaugural Address." April 3, 2018. https://www.opride.com/2018/04/03/english-partial-transcript-of-ethiopian-prime-minister-abiy-ahmeds-inaugural-address/.

International Court of Justice. 2018. *Obligation to Negotiate Access to the Pacific Ocean (Bolivia v. Chile)*. General List no. 153, October 1, 2018. https://www.icj-cij.org/files/case-related/153/153-20181001-JUD-01-00-EN.pdf.

International Crisis Group. 2019. "Intra-Gulf Competition in Africa's Horn: Lessening the Impact." Middle East Report No. 206, September 19, 2019. https://d2071andvip0wj.cloudfront.net/206-intra-gulf-competition.pdf.

Jawhar, Jamal. 2019. "Eritrea Accuses Qatar, Turkey of 'Subversive Acts'." *Asharq Al-Awsat*, April 5, 2019. https://aawsat.com/english/home/article/1665896/eritrea-accuses-qatar-turkey-'subversive-acts'.

Jeffrey, James. 2018. "Eritrea-Ethiopia Peace Leads to a Refugee Surge." *New Humanitarian*, November 15, 2018. https://www.thenewhumanitarian.org/news-feature/2018/11/15/eritrea-ethiopia-peace-leads-refugee-surge.

Kahsay, Abebe T. 2007. "Ethiopia's Sovereign Right of Access to the Sea under International Law." LLM thesis, University of Georgia School of Law (copy with author).

Kidane, Selam, and Martin Plaut. 2019. "Eritrea and Ethiopia: A Year of Peace, a Year of Dashed Hopes." *African Arguments,* July 8, 2019. https://africanarguments.org/2019/07/08/eritrea-and-ethiopia-a-year-of-peace-a-year-of-dashed-hopes/.

Kinninmont, Jane. 2019. "The Gulf Divided: The Impact of the Qatar Crisis." Chatham House, The Royal Institute of International Affairs, Research Paper, Middle East and North Africa Programme, May 2019. https://www.chathamhouse.org/sites/default/files/publications/research/2019-05-30-Gulf%20Crisis_0.pdf.

Lobban, Richard. 1976. "The Eritrean War: Issues and Implications." *Canadian Journal of African Studies* 10, no. 2: 335–46.

Lyon, Terrence. 2009. "The Ethiopia-Eritrea Conflict and the Search for Peace in the Horn of Africa." *Review of African Political Economy* 36, no. 120: 167–80.

Manek, Nizar. 2018. "Saudi Arabia Brokers a New Ethiopia-Eritrea Peace Deal." Bloomberg, September 17, 2018. https://www.bloomberg.com/news/articles/2018-09-17/ethiopia-eritrea-leaders-sign-peace-accord-in-saudi-arabia.

Maru, Mehari Taddele. 2018. "The Old EPRDF Is Dead, Can Its System Be Saved? Five Steps to Save the Federation." *Ethiopia Insight,* October 3, 2018. https://www.ethiopia-insight.com/2018/10/03/the-old-eprdf-is-dead-can-its-system-be-saved-five-steps-to-save-the-federation/.

Measho, Hanna. 2019. "When *Pacta Is Non Sunt Servanda*: State Responsibility for the 16 Years of Unenforced History of the Algiers Agreement Between Eritrea and Ethiopia." LLB thesis, School of Law, College of Business and Social Sciences, Eritrea, May 3, 2019 (copy with author).

Mengisteab, Kidane. 2013. *The Horn of Africa.* Cambridge, UK: Polity.

Mesfin, Berouk. 2016. "Qatar's Diplomatic Incursions into the Horn of Africa." Institute for Security Studies, Iss. 8, East Africa Report, November. https://issafrica.s3.amazonaws.com/site/uploads/ear8.pdf.

Milkias, Paulos. 2003. "Ethiopia, the TPLF, and the Roots of the 2001 Political Tremor." *Northeast African Studies* 10, no. 2: 13–66.

Milkias, Paulos, and Getachew Metaferia. 2005. *The Battle of Adwa.* New York: Algora.

Mosley, Jason. 2014. "Eritrea and Ethiopia: Beyond the Impasse." Chatham House, April 1, 2014. https://www.chathamhouse.org/publications/papers/view/198954.

Müller, Tanja. 2015. "Singled Out? Eritrea and the Politics of the Horn of Africa." *WPR*, September 17, 2015. http://www.worldpoliticsreview.com/articles/16715/singled-out-eritrea-and-the-politics-of-the-horn-of-africa.

Mumbere, Daniel. 2018. "Sudan, Ethiopia Accused of Agreeing to Support Armed Eritrean Opposition Groups." *africanews*, May 16, 2018. https://www.africanews.com/2018/05/16/sudan-ethiopia-accused-of-agreeing-to-support-armed-eritrean-opposition-groups//.

Nichols, Michelle. 2018. "U.N. Security Council Set to Lift Eritrea Sanctions on Wednesday." Reuters, November 12, 2018. https://www.reuters.com/article/us-eritrea-sanctions-un/u-n-security-council-set-to-lift-eritrea-sanctions-on-wednesday-idUSKCN1NH2C2.

Norwegian Nobel Committee. 2019. "The Nobel Peace Prize for 2019." October 11, 2019. https://www.nobelprize.org/prizes/peace/2019/press-release/.

Permanent Mission of Eritrea to the United Nations. 2012. "Peace and Security in the Horn of Africa: Eritrea's View." April 16, 2012, p. 2. http://www.eritreaembassy-japan.org/data/Peace_and_Security_in_the_Horn_of_Africa_Eritrea's_View.pdf.

Plaut, Martin. 2016. *Understanding Eritrea: Inside Africa's Most Repressive State*. New York: Oxford University Press.

People's Front for Democracy and Justice. 1994. "Hagerawi Charter Ertra" [The National Charter of Eritrea], adopted by the 3rd Congress of the EPLF/PFDJ, Naqfa, February 10–16.

Shaban, Abdur Rahman Alfa. 2019a. "Ethiopia PM's Key Regional Moves in Space of Three-Days." *africanews*, March 7, 2019. https://www.africanews.com/2019/03/07/ethiopia-pm-meets-all-horn-leaders-in-three-days-save-djibouti//.

———. 2019b. "Eritrea Peace Talks Between Ethiopia Govt—Afar, Gambella Opposition Parties." *africanews*, March 15, 2019. https://www.africanews.com/2019/03/15/eritrea-peace-talks-between-ethiopia-govt-afar-gambella-opposition-parties//.

———. 2019c. "Eritrea Diplomacy Hits Top Gear: Team Visits Mogadishu, Cairo, Riyadh." *africanews*, April 11, 2019. https://www.africanews.com/2019/04/11/eritrea-diplomacy-hits-top-team-visits-mogadishu-cairo-riyadh/.

———. 2019d. "Eritrea Shuts All Borders with Ethiopia—Unilaterally." *africanews*, April 23, 2019. https://www.africanews.com/2019/04/23/eritrea-shuts-all-borders-with-ethiopia-unilaterally//.

Snyder, Xander. 2018. "The Red Sea, Where Alliances Shift with the Tide." *Geopolitical Futures*, February 8, 2018. https://geopoliticalfutures.com/red-sea-alliances-shift-tide/.

———. 2019. "New Alignments in the Horn of Africa." *Geopolitical Futures*, April 10, 2019. https://geopoliticalfutures.com/new-alignments-horn-africa/.

T. G. 2018. "Why Eritrea Is Called Africa's North Korea." *The Economist*, August 14, 2018. https://www.economist.com/the-economist-explains/2018/08/14/why-eritrea-is-called-africas-north-korea.

———. 2019. "Why Are Gulf Countries So Interested in the Horn of Africa?" *The Economist*, January 16, 2019. https://www.economist.com/the-economist-explains/2019/01/16/why-are-gulf-countries-so-interested-in-the-horn-of-africa.

Tiruneh, Andargachew. 1993. *The Ethiopian Revolution 1974–1987: A Transformation from an Aristocratic to a Totalitarian Autocracy*. Cambridge: Cambridge University Press.

UN News. 2018. "'Wind of Hope' Blowing through Horn of Africa Says UN Chief, as Ethiopia and Eritrea Sign Historic Peace Accord." September 16, 2018. https://news.un.org/en/story/2018/09/1019482.

Weldemichael, Simon. 2019. "Disinformation and Its Impact on Society." Eritrea Ministry of Information, April 6, 2019. http://www.shabait.com/categoryblog/28293-disinformation-and-its-impact-on-society-.

Wilson, Tom. 2019. "Ethiopia Looks to Young Technocrats to Lead Ambitious Reform Drive." *Financial Times*, June 5, 2019. https://www.ft.com/content/38c9e736-7e49-11e9-81d2-f785092ab560.

Woldemariam, Michael. 2019. "The Eritrea-Ethiopia Thaw and Its Regional Impact." *Current History* 118, no. 808: 181–7.

Xinhua. 2018. "Ethiopia Says It Has No Information on Border Restrictions Imposed by Eritrea." December 28, 2018. http://www.xinhuanet.com/english/2018-12/28/c_137703009.htm.

Yoel, Benjamin. 2018. "The Ethiopia-Eritrea Peace Deal: Why Now?" *Ifriqiya* 4, no. 5: 1–5.

Yohannes, Okbazghi. 1991. *Eritrea: A Pawn in World Politics*. Gainesville: University of Florida Press.
Zenawi, Meles. 2011. "Interview with Assenna." February 25, 2011. https://es-pl.com/video/9lrjPhT1A7M/voice-of-assenna-interview-with-pm-meles-zenawi-of-ethiopia-feb-25-2011.html.
Zewde, Bahru. 1991. *A History of Modern Ethiopia, 1855–1974*. London: James Currey.

4.3 Neither Old nor New

Ethio-Eritrean Relations through the Dawn of Change in Ethiopia

Awet T. Weldemichael

INTRODUCTION

The coming to power of Prime Minister Abiy Ahmed in April 2018 represents a watershed moment in modern Ethiopian history that is already leaving its mark on the future of the wider region. Dr. Abiy represents the dazzling changes that have since rescued Ethiopia and the region from the edge of the precipice. He also presides over the ominous continuity that contributed to bringing the country to the verge of total chaos that catapulted him to power. Nowhere are these contradictions more apparent than in Ethiopia's thawing relations with Eritrea.

After a bloody two-year border conflict and seventeen years of "no peace, no war" under two previous premiers, not only did Prime Minister Abiy persist in calling for a new page in Ethio-Eritrean relations, but he took nearly everyone by storm and made it happen. What is especially noteworthy is that he did so without giving in to Asmara's two-decade-long position, that is, implementation to the letter of the April 2002 ruling of the Eritrea-Ethiopia Boundary Commission (EEBC). On the reverse of that shining performance, however, lies an unpromising prospect for that relationship due to Ethiopian domestic dynamics and factors that are uniquely Eritrean.

This chapter analyzes the bold and courageous moves of Dr. Abiy's government that made the Ethio-Eritrean rapprochement possible. It also examines the real and discombobulating prospects of the newly normalized relations stalling or even backsliding on the altars of narrow and excessive personal, regional, and/or national self-interest. Suspended above the potentially paralyzing contradictions between promising rapprochement and the prospect of its stagnation and reversal is the decisive role of the United States, Saudi Arabia, and the United Arab Emirates in the ongoing changes. This chapter analyzes the interests and roles of these and other foreign actors and the interests of Eritrea and Ethiopia (individually and jointly). It concludes with a call to a change of both course and discourse in order to institutionalize the relations of these two sisterly countries and put them on a more promising, stable footing.

THE HISTORICAL BACKGROUND IN BRIEF

Following the UN-mandated merger (without plebiscites) of the former Italian colony of Eritrea with imperial Ethiopia, Ethiopia undermined Eritrea's autonomous status under that federal arrangement. After all efforts to maintain local autonomy failed, Eritreans rose up in arms and waged a thirty-year war between 1961 and 1991 (Tesfai 2016). During the second half of that war, the Eritrean People's Liberation Front (EPLF) scored incremental military, diplomatic, and political gains against the military dictatorship of Mengistu Hailemariam that had overthrown Emperor Haile Selassie in a September 1974 coup d'état. The EPLF's strategic genius rested on the alliances that it struck with several Ethiopian rebel movements that it deemed would become "democratic alternatives" to the succession of repressive governments in Addis Ababa (Berhe 2009; Markakis 1987; Weldemichael 2014; Young 1997). The Tigray People's Liberation Front (TPLF) in northern Ethiopia was salient among these insurgents in the Ethiopian heartland.

From the Eritrean point of view, the EPLF's relationship with the TPLF rested squarely on the premise that upon defeating the Ethiopian government the Eritrean people would exercise the right to self-determination and independence. At no point did the TPLF question or do anything to undermine that premise. Nevertheless, its initial goal of seceding from Ethiopia and forming an independent Tigrayan republic strained the relationship between the two armed movements at the outset. Nearly a decade later, their relationship broke down due to a number of factors, among them political ideology and military tactics and strategy (Weldemichael 2014; Young 1996). During the subsequent four years of hiatus in their comradeship, the EPLF kept calling on all progressive Ethiopian movements to form a unified front (Voice of the Broad Masses 1985) that was realized with the formation of the EPRDF in 1989 with EPLF collaboration (see Hussein and A. 2017 for a recent Ethiopian perspective).[1] Eritreans also supported non-EPRDF forces such as the Oromo Liberation Front (OLF). In the end, Eritrean elite mechanized, commando, and security units and logistics teams helped spearhead the advance against Derg forces inside Ethiopia and all the way into Addis Ababa in May 1991.

Nevertheless, the TPLF continued to diminish the role of their one-time senior Eritrean allies during the final push against the Derg (1989–91) to no more than small technical assistance, in the same fashion that the EPLF minimized their Tigrayan partners' contributions against the large-scale Derg offensive inside Eritrea in 1982. Confidential sources of the time indicate that EPLF departments expected to receive anywhere between three thousand and five thousand TPLF fighters to aid in the defense of Eritrean positions against Addis Ababa's famed Red Star campaign (dubbed the Sixth Offensive among Eritreans). In the end, the number of TPLF fighters who actually arrived in Eritrea and held positions and fought alongside their Eritrean comrades was around three thousand. Similarly, EPLF mechanized and infantry units played an important role in breaking a stalemate at the February 1989 Battle of Shire that had threatened to unravel prior TPLF advances against the Derg (Melake 1994). In nearly all major southward offensives that the TPLF subsequently launched against government positions as they marched toward Addis Ababa, EPLF heavy artillery batteries helped in neutralizing government long-range weapons and offered cover to their side's infantry assaults.[2]

To legalize the military outcome, the EPLF decided to hold the first-ever referendum in Eritrea in which voting-age Eritreans would take part. To minimize the immediate and long-term effects on Ethiopia of Eritrea's likely separation, Eritreans agreed to delay the vote by two years and granted Ethiopia unfettered access to the Eritrean ports of Massawa and Assab (Cohen 2000). The new interim president of Ethiopia and EPRDF Chairman Meles Zenawi initially hesitated and prevaricated on giving Ethiopia's open support to the process and outcome of the Eritrean referendum, claiming that he "faced stiff Amhara resistance" to Eritrea's independence. Worried and impatient, the president of the Provisional Government of Eritrea, Isaias Afwerki, instructed his envoy in Addis Ababa to assure Meles that they stood by him and he should not fear any force (confidential pers. comm.).

The public display of the close ties between President Isaias and Prime Minister Meles obscured and often overshadowed the efforts to institutionalize the relationship between their two countries. A formal pact was signed in 1994 that included joint defense commitments and cultural and educational exchanges. A joint ministerial high-level committee met several times until 1998 to work out the details of the pact and hammer out incipient misunderstandings and immanent differences between the states. Meanwhile, President Isaias grew increasingly impatient with and started to scoff at Prime Minister Meles for his slower—if not necessarily more deliberative than Isaias's—process of deciding on and implementing their agreements, some of which were not only verbal but also casually communicated indirectly thus, "Just tell Meles...."

As the ties at the highest level started to show signs of strain, monetary and economic policy differences between the two countries also came out to the open in such a way that served and empowered warmongering provocateurs who had been lurking close to the surface in both countries. Officials of the Tigray regional state (*kilil*) toured Eritrea and, in the words of then regional president Gebru Asrat, came back alarmed by what they believed was Eritrea's building of its military capacity through its national service program. Convinced that Eritrean strength was a threat to Tigray and to the TPLF, the joint defense and other pacts notwithstanding, some members of the TPLF leadership, among them Gebru Asrat, entrapped Meles's government in an open conflict with Eritrea that they helped engineer (Asrat 2014a, 2014b). On the Eritrean side, a few army generals, who had direct access to President Isaias and on whom the president increasingly relied as he distanced his most seasoned lieutenants, are said to have kept prodding the president into "putting Meles in his place," purportedly saying he had started to look down on the president.

When the 1998–2000 war broke out between the two countries, the same TPLF leaders were instrumental in Ethiopianizing the localized clashes by touring all corners of the country to hold flag ceremonies that steered national sentiment among Ethiopians and enlisted them into the revving war machine against Eritrea.[3] Whereas TPLF cadres assured their subordinates and recruits that they would march into Asmara,[4] their topmost generals—among them Chief of Staff General Tsadkan Gebretensae—pushed for the forceful seizure of Assab for Ethiopia (Semeneh 2019). Perhaps the worst mistake with both immediate and long-term scars was the branding of all Eritreans as enemies and subjecting them for commensurate treatment in a bid to "break the backbone of Eritrea," as at least one senior TPLF official put it on one occasion. Although all that failed and the war stalemated at the strategic level, Ethiopia gained a tactical upper hand at the cost of more than a hundred thousand lives, destruction of property and infrastructure, and loss of incalculable opportunities on both sides.

The war came to an end with the signing of the December 2000 Algiers Agreement that stipulated the formation of three bodies: an investigative commission (Article 3), a boundary commission (Article 4), and a claims commission (Article 4) (Agreement 2000). The entity entrusted with carrying out the investigation on "the incidents of 6 May 1998 and on any other incident prior to that date which could have contributed to a misunderstanding between the parties regarding their common border, including the incidents of July and August 1997" was neither established nor has the issue been raised by either side (Agreement 2000). To this day, the root causes of—and ultimate responsibility for—this most destructive war has not been conclusively established in an honest, impartial study. Between mid-2003 and late 2005, the Eritrea-Ethiopia Claims Commission rendered its series of decisions, including blaming Eritrea for initiating the fighting in May 1998, which both Eritrea and Ethiopia accepted and agreed to abide (Permanent Court of Arbitration, n.d.(a)).

Meanwhile, in April 2002, the EEBC, the first of the three entities, announced its binding verdict that by and large took a middle position but awarded Eritrea the previous little-known border town of Badme that was at the center of the conflict (Permanent Court of Arbitration, n.d.(b)). Ethiopia rejected the decision; having later failed to alter the final verdict, it demanded negotiations as precondition to its implementation, that is, demarcation. Eritrea insisted that per the binding agreement, before there could be negotiations Ethiopia needed to vacate all territories that have been deemed Eritrean. For nearly two decades, the relationship between the two peoples and countries practically froze over this matter.

FAILURES AND BREAKTHROUGHS OF PEACE INITIATIVES

There were several attempts to break the impasse between Eritrea and Ethiopia. The closest any of them reached to achieving peace between the two countries was when an initiative between late 2008 and early 2009 extracted the late Prime Minister Meles's commitment to unilateral Ethiopian withdrawal from occupied Eritrean territories and President Isaias's written assurances to immediately normalize relations—with all its security, political, and economic implications. An individual intimately known to both leaders pressed Prime Minister Meles to take the initiative. On getting Meles on board, this mediator enlisted the support of a colleague of the same stature as himself to approach Isaias, who also provided written assurances to Meles's demands in return for unilateral withdrawal to allow the full implementation of the 2002 EEBC ruling. All fell apart when Libya's Muammar Gaddafi took over as African Union chairman (during its 12th Summit, in Addis Ababa) and sought to strongarm both men into a solution by traveling from the AU summit to Massawa, where Isaias lived at the time (confidential pers. comm.).

The next time something got close to the 2008–9 near breakthrough was in 2016, when the EPRDF leadership quietly decided to fully accept and implement the 2002 EEBC ruling in a bid to ease tensions along the border and normalize relations with Eritrea. Senior EPRDF officials claim that they reached that decision upon concluding that they had sufficiently weakened Eritrea and President Isaias. Nevertheless, two other factors had far more to do with the policy change of the Ethiopian ruling coalition. First, the mounting domestic pressure on the government following the 2015 spontaneous unrest (first in Oromia, then in Amhara) demanded the government's undivided attention. That challenge had to be contained before it spiraled out of control and linked up more directly with the Eritrea-supported Ethiopian opposition that had grown increasingly stronger and bolder in confronting Addis Ababa in multiple arenas. This new pressure reinforced the persistent demands of the people of Tigray to end the state of war in their region and restore peaceful relations with their kith and kin across the border in Eritrea.

Second and equally important, the dramatic changes across the Red Sea and the Gulf of Aden triggered parallel changes in the disposition of countries on the African side of those waters. More specifically, with the escalation of the Gulf Cooperation Council (GCC) countries' war in Yemen and Djibouti's sudden termination of Saudi and Emirati military presence in its territories in May 2015, the Saudi-led coalition found an eager replacement in Eritrea that had been seeking to break out of its isolation (Mello and Knights 2016). Ethiopia grew concerned about the UAE's subsequent establishment of a state-of-the-art military base near the port of Assab. Prime Minister Hailemariam Desalegn's warning about it to the Emiratis and Saudis in late 2015 ("Hailemariam Desalegn Warns Saudi Arabia and UAE," *ECADF Ethiopian News and Views*, December 2, 2015), however, opened the doors to those countries' mediation between Ethiopia and archrival Eritrea.

Although rumors abound that large quantities of Saudi and UAE monies went into the mending of the Ethio-Eritrean fences, details remain cloudy. Whatever the veracity of claims of money exchanging hands or funds flowing in one direction or another, the wider regional context of the EPRDF's 2016 discreet decision regarding the border and overall relations with Eritrea is unmistakable. At least one known personality who had his ways with the Eritrean leader hand-delivered the EPRDF's new position with a request to normalize relations. Noting the TPLF's continued dominance of the EPRDF and that the Tigrayan leadership had Prime Minister Hailemariam under its thumb, Asmara persisted in its position: Ethiopia had to first withdraw its troops from Eritrean territories to enable demarcation of the border before normalization could start. In a bid to move the Eritrean government, in April 2017 Prime Minister Hailemariam publicly hinted at Addis Ababa's changed approach that he said was going to "emphasize on creating sustainable peace" ("Ethiopia to Have New Policy Direction on Eritrea?" *Ezega News*, April 23, 2017). Without changes in the TPLF's preponderance in his government, however, Asmara remained unmoved—at least publicly—until his resignation.

Meanwhile, with the change of government in the United States, the Eritrean government found a more favorable audience with, on the one hand, seasoned career diplomats who had gone unheard in previous administrations and, on the other hand, a hawkish team of policy advisors of the new Trump administration bent on confronting China in the Horn of Africa (White House 2018). Through Egyptian facilitation since at least late 2017, Asmara and Washington—in parallel to previous Saudi and Emirati quiet harmonization of dispositions—hammered out the details of the restored relationship within an integrated region. In the words of Donald Yamamoto, seasoned US diplomat in the Horn of Africa and newly appointed ambassador to Somalia, "You can't have peace in East Africa without peace in Eritrea, Ethiopia, Djibouti, Kenya, Somalia, Tanzania. They're all interrelated, and I think they can all benefit from a vibrant economic program. And that's what we're trying to do, not just for Somalia, but for the whole region" (Solomon 2018).

For that to happen, Hailemariam Desalegn's government had to unshackle itself from the stranglehold placed on it from within. Failing to do so while in office, it appears, the prime minister sought to make that happen by making way for someone who could. Hailemariam's closely guarded decision to resign the premiership in February 2018 came as a shock to many, but it opened the gates for the tectonic changes that catapulted Dr. Abiy Ahmed and the Oromo People's Democratic Organization (OPDO, since renamed the Oromo Democratic Party (ODP)) to the helm in Addis Ababa. As Team Lemma, as it was fondly called among the public after OPDO/ODP Chairman Lemma Megersa, quickly and publicly distanced itself from the TPLF, the latter saw its national significance shrink to its home base in Tigray.

In his inaugural address to the Ethiopian House of Peoples' Representatives, newly sworn in Prime Minister Abiy Ahmed called for the need to resolve the dispute with Eritrea and that he would not spare any effort to that effect. Two months later, on June 5, the EPRDF Executive Committee publicly announced its decision to abide by and fully implement the 2002 EEBC ruling on the border issue with Eritrea, which in effect was more than making public its 2016 decision. After two weeks of total silence from Asmara, President Isaias announced on June 20 that Eritrea was dispatching a delegation to Addis Ababa in order "to know the current situation directly and in-depth and chart a [joint] program for the future" ("President Isaias Afwerki's June 20, 2018 Speech" 2018).

The immediate and impromptu response on the part of Abiy Ahmed showed his commitment to peace with Eritrea. In a video recording in Tigrinya (one of the Eritrean government's two working languages), he celebrated President Isaias's decision and assured him that the Eritrean delegation would be received well—not as guests but as brothers. Composed of Foreign Minister Osman Saleh and Presidential Advisor Yemane Gebreab,

Eritrea's first delegation to Ethiopia in two decades was indeed accorded a reception normally reserved for a visiting head of state. The month of July saw what no one expected a few weeks prior: Prime Minister Abiy visited Asmara on the 8th, and President Isaias visited Addis Ababa on the 14th. Ten days later, on July 24, both traveled to the UAE to receive the country's highest honor in a ceremony that made it appear among the Arab royals as if Isaias were an elder interlocutor to the much younger Abiy. On September 16, a similar ceremony took place in front of the Saudi royals in Jeddah. These diplomatic theatrics showed an overreliance on the Middle East, which can be disenchanting to other Africans, especially in East Africa, as well as to an Africa-centered agenda. The absence of IGAD and African Union representatives at the signing ceremonies in front of the Saudi and Emirati royals was indeed glaring.

On the ground, things immediately changed for the better faster than any system or institutions could be put in place to sustain them. By far the best and immediate dividend of the budding relations between the two countries was the ability of families and friends to communicate directly by telephone and later in person. On July 8, direct telephone connection was restored after two decades of interruption (Fitsum 2018a). Ten days later, Ethiopian Airlines resumed direct flights between Addis Ababa and Asmara, and both countries lifted visa requirements for each other's nationals (Maasho 2018). On September 11, the two countries opened border crossings at Bure and Zalambessa ("Ethiopia-Eritrea Border Opens for First Time in 20 Years," Al Jazeera, September 11, 2018), and on January 7 at Humera-Omhajer (Shaban 2019). These bold moves enabled the fulfillment of one of the most basic human needs and brought to public display long bottled up pure human emotions when families and friends, who had not spoken to or seen each other for two decades, got to speak, embrace, and sob on each other's shoulders; others got on their knees to kiss the feet of their long-missed loved ones. These heartwarming scenes and the admirable political courage that made them possible were, however, matched by problems that started to pop up shortly afterwards.

While the thawing relationship between Ethiopia and Eritrea is a cause for celebration, its dizzying speed and the intimate personal dynamics that appear to have developed between the two leaders have since become a source of as much concern. At the very least, many Eritreans started to get wary of Asmara's new relationship with Addis Ababa; they grew concerned at the high stakes involved for their country and have now grown resentful at the opacity of what has—or has not—happened. The person of Dr. Abiy—his courage, strength of personality, and consistency about peace—and his first visit to Eritrea was electrifying among Eritreans (in the country and abroad). While residents of Asmara thronged the streets between the airport and presidential palace in the city center to receive him, Eritreans elsewhere were glued to television screens to watch the spectacular scene. Fitsum Arega captured the sentiment on both sides when he tweeted: "From The Airport to the State House in #Asmara's streets, the Ethiopian delegation was greeted & received with overwhelming joy & love by the kind people of Eritrea. The yearning for peace was palpable & we'll decidedly move forward for the good of our people" (2018b). Such spontaneous outpouring of reception that Eritreans showed Dr. Abiy (and his delegation) was indicative of two things: first, their long craving for peace; and second, their hope and trust that Abiy would deliver. More than six months later, many are uncertain about the first and as many have already been frustrated with the latter, all because Prime Minister Abiy does not seem to have an Eritrea strategy, while his Isaias strategy is on full display—as discussed below.

On the first Ethiopian Airlines flight to Asmara on July 18, former Prime Minister Hailemariam led a large delegation that was widely touted as Ethiopian investors prospecting for investment potential in Eritrea to signal the nature of the budding relationship (Mumbere 2018). That came as a shock to many Eritreans and experts of Eritrea because in the preceding years inordinate government interventions and draconian restrictions had crippled the Eritrean economy. Eritrean investors had either lost their investments in the country or kept their capital out of the country due to government arbitrariness and the greed and corruption of powerful officials—all in the absence of the rule of law. The service sector had been starved of cash following the change of currency in late 2015. Many businesses had to contend with ruinous penalties for purported violations of the subsequent clumsy monetary policy.

As if the news of Ethiopian investors coming in when Eritreans had their hands tied behind their backs was not shocking enough, more was to come with the opening of the overland border crossing. Small-scale traders flooded into Eritrea with the opening of the border, which had a negative moral/psychological outcome in spite of its immediate positive impact. Basic consumer goods across Eritrea dropped sharply with the opening of the country to Ethiopian imports. Nevertheless, Eritreans—business people or not—were outraged by the free rein that the government gave Ethiopians, mainly Tigrayans, to operate in Eritrea while the stringent government restrictions continued to apply against Eritrean businesses; local transporters had ceased operations for lack of fuel and spare parts, while Ethiopian vehicles transported passengers locally.[5]

Resistance to what many Eritreans viewed as humiliating came in earnest and in different forms. In preparation to receive the first large Ethiopian delegation that Hailemariam Desalegn led, the Eritrean government ordered open businesses that it had previously shut down as penalty for purported violations. The Eritrean National Chamber of Commerce, which had over the previous years been hollowed out of any substance, was also ordered to open, as were some ministries deemed of interest to the visiting Ethiopian delegation. While the small private businesses had no choice and made do with last-minute preparations to open for service, senior officials of the chamber of commerce and directors general of some ministries are said to have refused to show up for work while the delegation was in town. It is said that Dr. Abiy is not disposed to paying attention to such signals nor to listening to warnings that Eritrea lacks the institutions and infrastructure and that the Eritrean government neither enjoys the legitimacy nor has the capacity that it once had. Nevertheless, it is possible that the prime minister either feels that his government has no choice but the current course or that he actively sticks to that approach as a deliberate, self-serving strategy, taking advantage of Eritrea's severely weakened position and cleverly disguised behind the façade of regional integration and synergy, that is, *Medemer*.

In order to further unpack the spiraling contradictions in current Ethio-Eritrean relations, the remainder of this chapter will look more closely into the most relevant aspects of the political dynamics in Eritrea and Ethiopia separately before examining Prime Minister Abiy's genius and good fortune, as well as the prospects and pitfalls of his approach. It will particularly analyze how Dr. Abiy's Isaias-centered strategy restored the Eritrean president to statesmanship that he had long lost while, according to many Eritreans, injuring Eritreans' dignity in the intermediate term and potentially undermining their hard-won sovereignty in the long term. The following critical review should not be taken as intent on diminishing Dr. Abiy's well-deserved acclaim for the rapid positive changes unprecedented in Ethiopian history.[6]

BETWEEN PEACEMAKING AND VENGEANCE

With all the powers concentrated in his hands in the past two decades, President Isaias calls meetings of his cabinet of ministers, whenever and wherever he wished, mostly to listen to his own policy papers—and occasionally to hear pro forma presentations from some or all of his ministers. Surrounded by survivalist individuals adept at justificatory postmortems of his actions and inactions, he progressively distanced himself from sound policies and praxis—both domestic and foreign. His own follies had left him effectively isolated at home and abroad. For several years preceding the changes in Ethiopia, he busied himself with personally overseeing the dubious construction of a dam at Adi-Halo, outside of Asmara, where he mostly sequestered himself during regular working hours. What little day-to-day affairs of the country remained he insouciantly left to a handful of lieutenants—including very junior personal peons—all locked in carefully orchestrated and paralyzing mistrust, rivalries, and tensions.

At the heart of President Isaias's tragic descent from the exalted status of a liberation hero and statesman to one of widespread opprobrium and isolation was the border war with Ethiopia and, more specifically, the conflict with the TPLF.[7] He understandably continues to feel aggrieved about it and to seize every opportunity to strike at the TPLF for the damage. The rise of Abiy Ahmed to the premiership not only offered one more such mighty opportunity but was also an irresistible moment to seek vindication and revive a decayed statesmanship. In his June 20 address, when he announced Asmara's acceptance of Addis Ababa's overture for peace, President Isaias lambasted the TPLF in the same breath. He condemned it as a vulturine scavenger and declared that its "game [was] over." In his swift positive response, Prime Minister Abiy ably and noticeably skipped the president's attack on a member of his governing coalition and former senior partner. With the uptick of anti-TPLF vitriol across Ethiopia, Isaias's appearance of wanting to exact vengeance against the TPLF and Abiy's silence on the matter—either in the interest of the pursuit of peace or to partake in Isaias's dangerous brinkmanship with regard to the TPLF—sent off alarm bells within the Tigrayan organization.

In spite of its initiation of the process to resolve the dispute with Eritrea as a necessity, the TPLF immediately started backpedaling on the matter. It ultimately revived and held on to Addis Ababa's old position of renegotiating the disputed border. TPLF officials continue to argue that the peoples on both sides of the border know their territories and should be consulted in the resolution of the border issue—if not left alone to resolve it themselves. Short of that, according to the TPLF position, there would not be any territories changing hands, a position that remained a deal breaker for Eritrea until mid-2018. The fact that the Ethio-Eritrean border had been decided by international law and is under the purview of the federal government in Addis Ababa did not deter the TPLF.

In an impressive show of political agility, Asmara prioritized strengthening ties with Addis Ababa—as did Addis Ababa with Asmara—over having the occupied territories vacated and the border demarcated per the 2002 international ruling. Having preposterously announced during his welcome of Prime Minister Abiy to Asmara on July 8 that Eritrea had not lost anything and had regained what rightfully belonged to it, the border became a nonissue to President Isaias and his government. Bent on making the erstwhile senior EPRDF partner and regional administrator in Tigray pay for its past deeds and misdeeds, President Isaias has since shunned the TPLF and Tigray region while dealing with Addis Ababa as well as with the regional states surrounding Tigray, that is, Amhara and Afar. So determined was the Eritrean president that he did not wish to open the Zalambessa border crossing with Tigray in September 2018, preferring instead to only open the Bure crossing connecting the Ethiopia heartland to the port of Assab through the Afar region/*kilil*. Similarly, during the opening of the Humera-Omhajer border crossing further west along the common border with the Tigray region, Isaias is said to have not wanted Tigrayan regional administrator and TPLF Chairman Dr. Debretsion Gebremichael to attend the ceremony. It was a credit to Abiy's ways with his Eritrean counterpart that the two governments were spared those embarrassing—possibly even dangerous—diplomatic situations. Beyond contradicting the rhetoric of peace, synergy, and integration, the president's total disregard of a region that shares the longest border with Eritrea does leave the peace along the border in limbo.

The overall inter- and intra-regional tensions within Ethiopia[8] speak to the shriveling authority of the federal government and bode ill for the country's internal stability. When repeatedly pressed on the question of the border, Prime Minister Abiy stated that the two countries were in a state of "conflict transformation," whereby negotiations on the most divisive issues are deferred to a more opportune future date. The border remains to be one such divisive issue due to the TPLF's refusal to budge and the federal government's inability to enforce its will. Dr. Abiy is facing difficulties in exercising effective command over the federal forces in Tigray (along the Ethio-Eritrean common border), much less implement the 2002 court ruling and hand over territories to Eritrea. Having been quietly denied the prerogative of rotating out of the region some of Ethiopia's heavy weaponry and elite units early on during his tenure, six months later TPLF-spurred Tigrayan civilians twice scuttled the relocation of federal units by openly blocking their movement; when some federal units were eventually rotated out, the regional units moved in to fill their place (confidential consultations). This is tantamount to a constitutional crisis, as it undermines the division of powers between the federal government and regional states, although the Ethiopian military official denied it in front of parliament.

For its part, Eritrea is now a shell of its former self as previously indicated, due to a combination of the consequences of the wars and postwar challenges, as well as government actions and inactions. The indefinite national service—and attendant violation of human rights of citizens—has proven to be the worst mismanagement and downright abuse of the country's human resources. The consequent flight of large numbers of Eritreans from their country has severely degraded its wo/manpower. Misplaced government priorities, incompetent policy formulations, and inexplicable punitive interventions practically paralyzed the private construction and service sectors in what appear like deliberate policies to emaciate local financial capacity. All that combines with the country's decayed administrative institutions and corroding infrastructure to render Eritrea weak in negotiations and an unreliable partner in carrying out and sustaining constructive engagements.

Astutely aware of Eritrea's weaknesses and President Isaias's Achilles' heel, and seemingly convinced that he could get a grip on Isaias during the few years he expects the president to be around, Dr. Abiy crafted a savvy strategy centered around the person of the president. His repeated breaking of protocol to address President Isaias with short-form names of endearment, his well-orchestrated display of public adulation of the president (be it on Isaias's arrival in Addis Ababa or during the ceremonies in Hawassa and at the millennium), his formal references to him as an elder statesman (in Asmara), and the literal kissing of the president's hand (during the UAE ceremony) can be assumed to have been calculated steps that have, at least for the time being, successfully charmed the Eritrean head of state. While through such flattery lifting the president out of his isolation at the Adi-Halo dam construction/supervision site to a position of regional statesman, Dr. Abiy scored a strategic security concession for Ethiopia from Asmara, that is, neutralizing the Eritrea-based armed Ethiopian opposition movements, which also had the effect of further diminishing Isaias's threat potential.

Over the preceding two decades of hostilities and tension, both Ethiopia and Eritrea had come to host their rival's preexisting opponents, foster the rise of new opposition groups, and prod groups and individuals to organize against the rival government. In this regard, Asmara's record outshined by far that of Addis Ababa's under the TPLF-dominated previous government. Ethiopia hosted a number of armed and unarmed Eritrean opposition groups that were kept under strict orders of the Tigray-dominated Ethiopian security apparatus. All Ethiopia-based Eritrean opposition were kept on a very short leash that not only left them weakened but also humiliated and ultimately incapable of posing a meaningful threat to the Eritrean government. After the normalization of relations in July 2018, all that the federal Ethiopian government did to assure the Eritrean government was to notify Ethiopia-based Eritrean opposition groups to cease operations, which they had no choice but to comply with.

By contrast, Ethiopian opposition movements in Eritrea were in a relatively better relationship with their host from the get-go. Asmara thus hosted and actively supported some of Ethiopia's most capable opposition forces that had the potential to destabilize or even overthrow the government in Addis Ababa. That was especially the case in the wake of the popular unrest across Ethiopia since 2015, which helped prompt the Ethiopian government to seek peace with Eritrea in the first place. So the first substantive thing Abiy sought—and Isaias clearly agreed to—was to take Eritrea-based Ethiopian opposition forces out of Eritrea and into Ethiopia through negotiated agreements.

In August 2018, all Ethiopian opposition movements in Eritrea in quick succession signed such agreements with various Ethiopian government bodies and left Eritrea for Ethiopia. On August 7, the OLF signed an agreement with the president of Oromia, Lemma Megersa, and Ethiopian Foreign Minister Workeneh Gebeyehu before going back to Ethiopia. On August 16, a large delegation from the Amhara regional state government visited Eritrea and signed a reconciliation agreement with the Amhara Democratic Forces Movement (ADFM) that enabled the latter to return to Ethiopia in September to peacefully carry out its political work. Unlike in the other movements that signed agreements with their respective regional state governments, and consistent with President Isaias's refusal to engage the TPLF and Tigray regional government, neither the TPLF nor the Tigray regional government's representative came to Eritrea to fetch the Tigrayan armed opposition group in Eritrea. Instead, the federal-level director of the Ethiopian National Intelligence and Security Service, General Adem Mohammed, traveled to Asmara on August 28 to sign an agreement with the Tigray People's Democratic Movement (TPDM) faction that had remained in Eritrea and brought it back to Ethiopia less than two months later.

MEDEMER, A NEW DISCOURSE OF AN AGED IDEOLOGY AND REVIVING PRAXIS?

Beyond the abovementioned dynamics, some unsettling developments and destabilizing discourse have emerged with the thawing of Ethio-Eritrean relations, which is otherwise welcome. To begin with, many aspects of the budding relationship is still shrouded in secrecy. It is as if Prime Minister Abiy Ahmed and President Isaias Afwerki are in some kind of surreptitious relationship, which an exiled young Eritrean journalist perceptively noted that, "Since July 2018, [Isaias] Afwerki has met with Abiy [Ahmed] nine times while he has only met with his Cabinet ministers once" (Zere 2019). Likewise, despite the many meetings, Dr. Abiy has hardly spoken about their substance nor has he elucidated the planned projects beyond generalities. Such secrecy has not only become of immediate concern to citizens—especially worrisome to Eritreans—but also risks undermining the legitimacy of whatever agreements are being inked in the long term. Moreover, the secrecy surrounding the agreements between the Ethiopian government and its former armed opposition movements in Eritrea does not bode well for sustainable peace within Ethiopia itself.

The opacity of the dealings between Addis Ababa and Asmara, the Eritrean president's deafening silence about any of its immediate and long-term tangible aspects, and the Ethiopian prime minister's nonchalant talk about integration have failed to adequately inform citizens of Eritrea and Ethiopia. Spokesperson Fitsum Arega's timely updates were the most detail that has been disclosed about the ongoing deal. In a July 8 tweet, for example, Fitsum reported: "HE PM Dr Abiy after his discussion with HE President Isaias confirmed the normalization of Ethio-#Eritrea relations will start in earnest—flights will resume, utilization of the sea ports will start & the two countries will re-open embassies in each other's capital" (2018c). More than six months after the signing of the declaration of peace and friendship between Eritrea and Ethiopia in July 2018, no further details of the understandings, memoranda, and/or agreements between the two countries have been fully and formally disclosed. No one, for example, seems to know the conditions under which Ethiopia rehabilitated the highway (with sixty of the seventy kilometers inside Eritrea) that connects Assab to Ethiopia.[9] Nor the terms of the construction of railways between central Ethiopia and Massawa, the feasibility study of which Italy reportedly promised to fund ("Italy to Fund Ethiopia-Eritrea Railway Feasibility Study—Abiy," *africanews*, January 22, 2019), which the prime minister's office announced via Twitter on January 21: "PM Abiy Ahmed was received by H.E. Giuseppe Conte in an official welcoming ceremony. The two counterparts held bi-lateral & agreed to take their cooperation to the next level in the Addis Ababa - Massawa railway line" (Office of the Prime Minister 2019). Nor the Emirati plan to build oil/gas pipelines from the Ethiopian hinterland to the Eritrean coast (Obulutsa and Fick 2018). Yet Ethiopia's ambassador to Eritrea, Redwan Hussein, recently announced that the two countries had concluded their studies to lay the ground for implementation following parliamentary approval ("Ethiopian, Eritrean Leaders Set to Sign Detail Deals," *New Business Ethiopia*, February 20, 2019).

While there is no parliament to speak of in Eritrea, the speaker of Ethiopia's House of Peoples' Representatives, Tagesse Chafo, told Ethiopian media outlets in February 2019 that no agreements had been signed with Eritrea because agreements come to the parliament for approval and none had. In the context of Eritrea's weakness, President Isaias's diminished vitality and significance, and his possible sense of indebtedness to Prime Minister Abiy, the latter, many Eritreans fear, seems to have succeeded in ramming down Eritrea's throat potentially unfavorable deals unbeknownst to Eritrean citizens—or even the Ethiopian public for that matter. Such secretive work beneath the thin veneer of publicized regular meetings and fanfare about the peace deal seems to confirm lagging institutionalization of the ongoing process that some observers have cautioned against (Gebreluel 2018). The risks and pitfalls of a strategy centered around individuals, in this case the two leaders, are far too great to overlook. Dr. Abiy has at least once assured his audience that ultimately the Ethiopian and Eritrean peoples, and not himself and/or President Isaias, are the guarantors of the peace. But it is not clear how these two peace-loving peoples are expected to play that role when they are uninformed about and effectively shut out from the agreements that are being negotiated and/or signed.

Moreover, Abiy Ahmed's rhetoric—in his speeches and interviews—has subtly appealed to tropes of Ethiopian expansionism, and more specifically to the still-present sentiments toward Eritrea's Ethiopian-ness and the wish among segments of the Ethiopian elite to see its independence reversed. During his maiden speech in Asmara on July 8, the prime minister told the stunned and admiring Eritrean president and invited guests that Ethiopia had tried every weapon of war to bring Eritrea to its knees and failed. What has not been tried, he said, was the naturally occurring love. The electrifying mood of the moment did not lend itself for somber reflection of what was being said, but one could not help wonder whether that meant the objective remained the same—that Eritrea was still prey, except that this time the weapon was love. Soon afterwards, Dr. Abiy left nothing to the imagination as he got straight to the point in front of another rapturous audience in Addis Ababa. On President Isaias's first post-normalization visit to Ethiopia and celebrations at the Millennium Hall, Abiy told the audience in black and white that when Isaias and he are united, Ethiopians get the Eritrean port of Assab: "እኔና ኢሱ ስንደመር፥ እኛ ዓሰብን እንካፈላለን!"

This has to be seen against the backdrop of the ongoing rehabilitation of the image of former Ethiopian dictatorial rulers who had been the bane of Eritreans and many Ethiopians alike. Emperor Haile Selassie told Eritrean elders gathered in Asmara on his behest that Ethiopia had no interest in the people of Eritrea but their land: "ኤርትራ መሬትዋ'ንጂ ሕዝቧ አያስፈልገንም!" His guileful strategy of acquiring Eritrea and retaining it through crude scorched-earth counterinsurgency war, which, among other things, saw hundreds of villages razed to the ground and their inhabitants killed or dispersed, lived up to his declaration.

Likewise, for the subsequent seventeen years, Colonel Mengistu Hailemariam's military junta came to power declaring that they would fight the Eritreans to the last man standing. Although in the end he cowardly fled to a long-planned cushy exile, his dictatorship pursued the war with unprecedented intensity on the battlefronts and heretofore unseen brutality against the civilian population across the country. Dr. Abiy's casual speak of even Mengistu's possible return from exile in Zimbabwe and former Prime Minister Hailemariam Desalegn's visit with the former dictator in Harare shortly after returning from Asmara are especially unsettling not only to Eritreans but equally to Ethiopian victims of Derg-era bloodletting. Although the tweet has since been deleted, the former prime minister was indiscreet about his meeting when his official handle (@PMHailemariamD) captioned their picture together: "I met former president of Ethiopia, colonel Mengistu Hailemariam. I wish to see more former heads of government and state in my country contributing their parts in different capacity after peaceful transition of political power" (see also, BBC 2018; Associated Press 2018).

Such nonchalance at the new center of power about past suffering seems to have invited jingoistic revisionist talk in Ethiopian media outlets about the painful years of the Derg military dictatorship. An example of this is the disgraced former commander of the 16th "Sentiq" Mechanized Brigade—and subsequently of other mechanized formations—of Ethiopia's Second Revolutionary Army in Eritrea, Brigadier General Kassaye Chemeda. Not only was he reprimanded in 1982 for failing to give timely and meaningful reinforcement to badly hit infantry units but also several times afterwards his elite mechanized units were routed at the hands of Eritrean insurgents. The last such defeat he suffered was in March 1988, after which he was implicated in one of the Ethiopian army's most egregious atrocities. Following the destruction of Ethiopia's Nadew Command at Afabet, soldiers who either escaped the carnage or had not entered the fray congregated in neighboring villages. Brigadier General Kassaye's own autobiography places him in the villages of Shebah and Sheib when both were razed to the ground and hundreds of Shebah's residents and nearly every one of Sheib's more than four hundred inhabitants were massacred in cold blood. It does not augur well for peace between the two peoples and countries for figures such as him to feel comfortable to publicly and unrepentantly brag about having beaten the Eritreans to the gates of Nakfa, irrespective of the historical record.[10]

The vast majority of Eritreans have been scarred by the wars of those previous governments in Addis Ababa. Eritreans who came of age—or were born—after Eritrea's independence also endured the trauma of war with Ethiopia during the 1998–2000 conflict and subsequent tensions with occasional outbreaks of fighting along the border. It thus becomes all the more important that the budding peace between the two countries trickles down to average Eritreans through mechanisms of purposive confidence building. That must necessarily include acknowledging many Eritreans' traumatic experiences with Ethiopia, honoring the victims of deliberate Ethiopian government actions, and respecting (in words and actions) their hard-earned independence and sovereignty. For the peace to be sustained and flourish it has to be buttressed by grassroots backstopping without precluding the imperatives of state-to-state dealings.

CONCLUSION: CHANGING COURSE AND DISCOURSE

A year is too short to make a conclusive assessment of a single national project, let alone of managing a country (of more than a hundred million people) in transition with numerous domestic and external engagements, both challenges and opportunities. Even then, the performance of Dr. Abiy Ahmed's government during his first year in office outshines the record of many other governments during their entire tenures stretching over several years and in some cases decades. Yet a great many shortfalls remain, too many to overlook or be complacent about lest they neutralize the accomplishments and forestall further progress. The promising new chapter in Ethio-Eritrean relations under Abiy's tutelage is one such project. Because good neighborliness, active cooperation, and mutually beneficial, incremental, and transparent regional integration between Ethiopia and Eritrea—and the rest of the countries in the Horn of Africa—is as crucial as peace and good governance within each of them.

Both Ethiopia and Eritrea have their respective complex domestic challenges that have already impacted their improving relations and are likely to determine their long-term trajectory and outcome. On top of that, they are located in a region of global geopolitical significance that has drawn the interest and active involvement of more powerful regional and global powers, which is not always in the interest of the local populations. Although the alignment of US, Saudi, and Emirati interests helped spark anew peaceful Ethio-Eritrean relations, the two leaders and governments have to be wary of overreliance on external support and influence—for they are the shifting sands of international diplomacy. No sooner had the GCC countries' rivalry with Iran and their war in Yemen set the Ethio–Eritrean rapprochement quietly in motion than the friction among them burst to the open and threatened that very process.

One way to shield the gains so far achieved and those that are yet to materialize from external manipulation is for both Ethiopian and Eritrean citizens to own the process and determine the outcome of peace building and cooperation between their two countries. For citizens to play that role, the first thing they require—and must demand and get—is the right to information as to what is being negotiated and signed in their respective names. The parallels that some analysts draw between the current Abiy-Isaias dynamics and the past Meles-Isaias relationship are not far-fetched. Yet Ethiopia and Eritrea are now in uncharted waters, and the burden of institutionalizing this promising new relationship has to be shared with actively engaged civic society groups through transboundary solidarity and social, cultural, economic, and other bridges. The starting point for both countries should be an end to secrecy and ushering in more transparency in their dealings. The change of course in this regard will inevitably be followed—if not accompanied—with a change of discourse to one that recognizes and respects the rights, experiences, and current state of the two peoples in their respective countries before thoughtlessly speaking of them—or rushing to lump them together—as a single people.[11]

NOTES

1. Whereas the strained EPLF-TPLF relationship had been restored for almost a year and active military cooperation resumed, the EPLF released hundreds of ethnic Oromo prisoners of war who went on to form the Oromo People's Democratic Organization (OPDO), which joined the emerging EPRDF.

2. During the seven short years of euphoria and hyperactivity following the 1991 victory, these stories of shared sacrifices and many others, including the tale of Eritrean commando (security) signals and logistics teams across mainland Ethiopia, did not receive the attention they deserved. As the 1998 conflict broke out, the shared history became not only the first victim but also the basis of mutual acrimony, with each side downplaying the contribution of the other while magnifying one's own.

3. Ethiopian Broadcasting Corporation transmitted these events live beginning in mid-1998 and throughout the war.

4. Several interviews conducted with Ethiopian POWs and aired in Eritrea bear this, as do remarks by ranking members of the TPLF/EPRDF leadership.

5. Although the borders have since been closed, neither the closure nor the process through which it was effected have allayed the concerns and anger of many Eritreans.

6. An era in Ethiopian history when there are no political prisoners, jailed journalists, direct or proxy wars with neighbors and when its government has half of its ministries run by highly skilled, experienced, and professional women while other women hold other critical non-ministerial posts, is a proud moment not just for Ethiopians but also for northeast Africans—and all Africans for that matter.

7. Crucial issues of difference—and even conflict—between Eritrea and Ethiopia as separate entities cannot be denied. The limited scope and purpose of this chapter, however, relegate a comprehensive analysis of the entirety of Ethio-Eritrean relations of the past six decades to a future date and project.

8. These include but are not limited to the violent flare-ups within the Oromia region, the bloody altercations between Oromo and Somali forces, and the unpublicized clashes between militias from the Amhara region and Tigrayan forces in October 2018.

9. According to the state-owned Ethiopian media that broke the news, this road repairing cost more than 120 million birr.

10. This is especially unsettling at a time when Eritreans and Ethiopians are best served by healing wounds, honoring the experiences of victims, and respecting one another to sustain the precarious peace between their two countries emerging on the horizon. Let alone deliberate targeting of civilians and their abodes such as he was involved in, even the battlefronts that Kassaye Chemeda took part in (and lost) involved large-scale loss of human life, material possessions, opportunities, and good will for the peoples of both Eritrea and Ethiopia.

11. Whereas Prime Minister Abiy repeatedly invoked the blood ties between the Eritrean and Ethiopian peoples to speak to their oneness, President Isaias put it plainly in an unscripted address at the luncheon prepared to welcome him to Addis Ababa on July 14: "Anyone who, from now onwards, speaks of the people of Eritrea and the people of Ethiopia as two peoples is only someone who does not know the truth."

REFERENCES

"Agreement between the Government of the State of Eritrea and the Government of the Federal Democratic Republic of Ethiopia." 2000. UN Peacemaker, December 12, 2000. https://peacemaker.un.org/eritrea-ethiopia-agreement2000.

Asrat, Gebru. 2014a. *Sovereignty and Democracy in Ethiopia*. Washington, DC: Signature Book Publishing.

———. 2014b. Interview. Tigrigna VOA News, September 23, 2014. https://tigrigna.voanews.com/a/author-gebru-asrat-part-2/2459770.html.

Associated Press. 2018. "Ex-Ethiopian Dictator Mengistu Meets Former Leader in Harare." August 2, 2018. https://www.news24.com/Africa/News/ex-ethiopian-dictator-mengistu-meets-former-leader-in-harare-20180801.

BBC. 2018. "Why a Photo of Mengistu Has Proved So Controversial." August 2, 2018. https://www.bbc.com/news/world-africa-45043811.

Berhe, Aregawi. 2009. *A Political History of the Tigray People's Liberation Front (1975–1991): Revolt, Ideology, and Mobilization in Ethiopia*. Los Angeles: Tsehai.

Cohen, Herman J. 2000. *Intervening in Africa: Superpower Peacemaking in a Troubled Continent*. New York: St. Martin's.

Fitsum Arega (@fitsumaregaa). 2018a. "For the first time after two decades, a direct international telephone connection between #Ethiopia and #Eritrea is restored today." Twitter, July 8, 2018, 7:10 a.m. https://twitter.com/fitsumaregaa/status/1015961261509697536.

———. 2018b. "From The Airport to the State House in #Asmara's streets. . . ." Twitter, July 8, 2018, 3:33 a.m. https://twitter.com/fitsumaregaa/status/1015906612702310401.

———. 2018c. "HE PM Dr Abiy after his discussion with HE President Isaias. . . ." Twitter, July 8, 2018, 2:35 p.m. https://twitter.com/fitsumaregaa/status/1016073362030907392.

Gebreluel, Goitom. 2018. "Ethiopia and Eritrea's Second Rapprochement." Al-Jazeera, September 18, 2018. https://www.aljazeera.com/indepth/opinion/ethiopia-eritrea-rapprochement-180918135547856.html.

Hussein, Hassen, and Mohammed A. 2017. "Ethiopia: Is OPDO the New Opposition Party? An Appraisal." November 11, 2017. https://www.opride.com/2017/11/11/ethiopia-is-opdo-the-new-opposition-party-an-appraisal/.

Maasho, Aaron. 2018. "Ethiopian Airlines Says Will Resume Flights to Eritrea's Capital on July 17." Reuters, July 10, 2018. https://www.reuters.com/article/us-ethiopia-eritrea-airlines/ethiopian-airlines-says-will-resume-flights-to-eritreas-capital-on-july-17-idUSKBN1K00J4.

Markakis, John. 1987. *National and Class Conflict in the Horn of Africa.* Cambridge: Cambridge University Press.

Melake, Tekeste. 1994. "The Battle of Shire (February 1989): A Turning Point in the Protracted War in Ethiopia." In *New Trends in Ethiopian Studies: Papers of the 12th International Conference of Ethiopian Studies, Volume II: Social Sciences,* edited by Harold G. Marcus, 963–80. Trenton, NJ: Africa World Press.

Mello, Alex, and Michael Knights. 2016. "West of Suez for the United Arab Emirates." *War on the Rocks,* September 2, 2016. https://warontherocks.com/2016/09/west-of-suez-for-the-united-arab-emirates/.

Mumbere, Daniel. 2018. "Historic Ethiopian Flight Welcomed in Eritrea with Cheers." *africanews,* July 18, 2018. https://www.africanews.com/2018/07/18/historic-ethiopian-flight-is-welcomed-in-eritrea-with-cheers/.

Obulutsa, George, and Maggie Fick. 2018. "UAE Plans Oil Pipeline from Ethiopia to Eritrea in Latest Horn of Africa Move." Reuters, August 10, 2018. https://www.reuters.com/article/us-ethiopia-eritra-pipeline/uae-plans-oil-pipeline-from-ethiopia-to-eritrea-in-latest-horn-of-africa-move-idUSKBN1KV0VS.

Office of the Prime Minister (@PMEthiopia). 2019. "PM Abiy Ahmed was received by H.E. Giuseppe Conte in an official welcoming ceremony. . . ." Twitter, January 21, 2019, 7:24 a.m. https://twitter.com/PMEthiopia/status/1087370320628076546.

Permanent Court of Arbitration. n.d.(a). "Eritrea-Ethiopia Claims Commission." Accessed March 7, 2019. https://pca-cpa.org/en/cases/71/.

———. n.d.(b). "Eritrea-Ethiopia Boundary Commission." Accessed March 7, 2019. https://pca-cpa.org/en/cases/99/.

Solomon, Salem. 2018. "New US Ambassador to Somalia Sees Path to Peace, Prosperity." Voice of America, November 24, 2018. https://www.voanews.com/a/newus-ambassador-to-somalia-sees-path-to-peace-prosperity/4672810.html.

Semeneh Bayfers. 2019. "Lt. General Tsadkan Gebretensae Interview." Walta TV, January 1, 2019. https://www.youtube.com/watch?v=4iZM-RGfmUy0.

Shaban, Abdur Rahman Alfa. 2019. "Ethiopia-Eritrea Officially Open Border Crossing Point." *africanews*, January 7, 2019. https://www.africanews.com/2019/01/07/abiy-afwerki-officially-open-ethio-eritrea-border-along-tigray-region/.

President Isaias Afwerki's June 20, 2018 Speech. 2018. EriTV, June 20, 2018. https://www.youtube.com/watch?v=qwRApE7LE5Y.

Tesfai, Alemseged. 2016. *Eritrea: From Annexation to Revolution, 1952–1962*. Asmara: Hidri Publishers.

Voice of the Broad Masses. 1985. "The EPLF and Its Relationship with the Democratic Movements in Ethiopia." Tigrigna. January 31–February 2, 1985 [copy of transcript available with the author].

Weldemichael, Awet T. 2014. "Formative Alliances of Northeast African Insurgents: The Eritrean Liberation Movement and the Ethiopian Armed Opposition Between the 1970s and 1990s." *Northeast African Studies* 14, no. 1: 83–122.

White House. 2018. "Remarks by National Security Advisor Ambassador John R. Bolton on the Trump Administration's New Africa Strategy." Remarks. December 13, 2018. https://www.whitehouse.gov/briefings-statements/remarks-national-security-advisor-ambassador-john-r-bolton-trump-administrations-new-africa-strategy/.

Young, John. 1996. "The Tigray and Eritrean Peoples Liberation Fronts: A History of Tensions and Pragmatism." *Journal of Modern African Studies* 34, no. 1 (March): 105–20.

———. 1997. *Peasant Revolution in Ethiopia: The Tigray People's Liberation Front, 1975–1991*. Cambridge: Cambridge University Press.

Zere, Abraham T. 2019. "Eritrea's Diplomatic Offensive?" *Africa Is a Country*, March 11, 2019. https://africasacountry.com/2019/03/eritreas-diplomatic-offensive?fbclid=IwAR0rRdbJO99bMeYM8TeibfUktb-6B03ym590R6ciA6brBNkJdJ6tzm8SbB3I.

4.4 Ethiopia's Engagements with Its Fragile Neighbors
An Examination of the Concept and Application of Buffer Zones as a Security Strategy in Ethiopia's Relations with Somalia

Abdeta Dribssa Beyene

INTRODUCTION

The primary duty of the nation-state is to ensure security and stability for its citizens. But states vary in capacity of delivery. In this regard, state capacity in realizing territorial control (Herbst 2000) and state penetration into society (Mann 1986) determine whether the states in question can fulfill this. Compared to other regions, state capacity and development remain abysmal. Terrorist outfits and insurgencies, such as Al-Shabaab, have flourished, threatened, and attacked adjacent states, forcing measures that have had serious consequences. When actors using ungoverned spaces in failed states present a grave threat to the security of neighboring countries, neighboring states are forced to create mechanisms to fend off threats. In order to address the security challenges that stem from the vacuums of state failure, neighboring states have had to intervene in the affairs of their unstable neighbors by establishing buffer zones and sustaining them. In Somalia, the Ethiopian government has developed strong linkages with regional administrations as well as the Somali Federal Government (SFG). Some in the international community may view these efforts as undermining the de jure central government established in Mogadishu. The first strategy that states deploy to manage threats is to strengthen relatively stable areas and engage their administrations. The second strategy is the creation of buffer zones to deal with threats emerging from these states. The areas either directly occupied or governed through proxies are a means of denying terrorists and rebel groups the ability to control someone else's territory and establish a base of operations. The relatively strong state projects power beyond its borders. Sufficient capacity to administer the territory is a necessary condition for buffer zones to be effective security measures.[1] This chapter investigates Ethiopia's mechanisms of fending off threats stemming from Somalia.

The Horn of Africa is an extremely volatile region, and some of the countries are fragile, with weak government institutions and even, at times, without any institutions at all in areas they claim to control. Some are considered failed states. These states are sources of insecurity and other threats to their neighbors. They mutually reinforce their weaknesses as they spend resources to undermine each other, worsening the situation as these countries of the Horn engage in tit-for-tat war directly or through proxies. One can see a pattern of "reciprocal intervention" depending on the threat level. Threats may arise through ideological underpinnings, economic interests, or big power rivalries, as the Horn has witnessed for millennia, whereby fragile states in the region end up being proxies. These engagements have over time impacted significantly the capacities of states in the region to fully govern their territories. Some of these states attain mere de jure sovereignty, while de facto they are replete with ungoverned spaces. Ungoverned spaces that are not administered invite insurgent groups and other non-state actors that exploit this void to plan attacks against adjacent countries, as they can operate without fear of the host government's intervention. The presence of many failed states in the Horn, the most notable of which are South Sudan and Somalia, as well as civil wars and intermittent crises, characterize the political landscape. Regional collaboration and cooperation remain feeble. Even with existing changes, institutional cooperation at the regional level is not on the horizon. However, bilateral engagements might lead to further strengthening existing regional cooperation institutionally.

Fragile and failed states have a combination of territories that their governments have no control over or where other actors, indigenous or extraneous, contest their monopoly of control. These territories may be totally empty, ungoverned spaces or might have fledgling local administrations that are barely linked with the central government or even stand in direct contradiction to the central authority. Non-state actors, armed and unarmed, whose objective is to challenge the peace and stability of the state concerned or other states in the neighborhood, might have taken over these spaces. The areas might have weak structures that either willingly accommodate or are coerced to harbor non-state actors that contest the state's monopoly of violence at the center or that of other states in the neighborhood.

Apart from underscoring the fundamental security framework that Somalia's neighbors deploy in engaging with the country, this chapter tries to probe questions such as: What makes a buffer zone an important instrument to fend off threats? How did Ethiopia manage the buffer zone to engage failed states like Somalia, given the ongoing changes in the region and beyond? What are the challenges in aligning the interests of other external actors in Somalia, and how are these critical challenges to peacemaking in Somalia? How did the Gulf Cooperation Council crisis impact developments in Somalia, and is there a mechanism to address this? What does this mean for Ethiopia and the entire Horn? Finally, the chapter makes some suggestions on the way forward. This chapter uses the framework of buffer zones to address the fundamental state securitization issue and the questions indicated above, explaining how a state uses this mechanism to fend off threats.

THE CONCEPT OF THE BUFFER ZONE

All states are apprehensive about their internal and external security (Frisch 2002), and security and state survival remain critical in the Horn of Africa, even if the region is not alone in this. State security has remained a major factor in interstate relationships in the Horn; ensuring security for the state and its population is not only a priority per se but also a raison d'être for any administration or government. In the Horn of Africa, the physical structures of territory, government, and state are evident, and the notion we see in some publications (Wilson and Donnan 1998) that assert that state borders are obsolete does not appear to be applicable here. States and their structures have strengthened in the face of the perception that people are freer or more forced to slip through the constraints of territorially based politics; this is yet to have much significance in the Horn of Africa. It is within this context that states in the region create various mechanisms to ward off threats.

One of the mechanisms states in the Horn of Africa create to fend off threats from groups challenging their monopoly of coercion and engaging in undermining peace and stability through the use of ungoverned spaces in adjacent areas is the establishment of buffer zones around their borders. A buffer zone is first and foremost a space, a certain geographical area designated or created to serve certain political, security, or other purposes in which the creation and management realizes a political order across borders directly or through proxies. The creation and sustenance of these buffer zones have serious implications for international norms in interstate relations. In this context, the why and how of buffer zones and their implications remain critical. Moreover, state behavior in the creation and sustenance of a buffer zone informs policy makers of other countries and organizations of the variables they have to take into consideration when formulating policies related to their interests.

Hence this chapter makes a systematic inquiry into buffer zone sustenance and triggers of collapse. The concept of the buffer zone is, inevitably, deeply entwined with matters of state security and questions of sovereignty, and they are critical instruments in understanding how conflicts in the Horn of Africa display two prominent features: a local dimension and a tendency to become intertwined with regional and superregional competition. These intrastate and interstate dimensions of conflict have affected people's lives as well as relations between states. Viewed from below, the role of ideology and the dynamics of domestic politics have determined the character and evolution of continuous crisis in the region (Medani 2012). At the same time, this domestic turmoil and the interlinkage with developments across the border challenging the rules and norms governing interstate relationships— and the spillover—is considered one of the main explanations for the continuation of turmoil in the region (IGAD 2009). Viewed in geopolitical terms, the interests of superpowers and other external actors have made the Horn of Africa susceptible to what Aalen (2014) calls a network of multilevel proxy wars, hence triggering local actors to get involved in the creation and sustenance of buffer zones.

This process features many complex interactions, and figuring it out has been likened to peeling an onion (Markakis 2003)—when one peels away the domestic aspect of the crisis, one uncovers the regional aspect of the problem underneath; and if one goes further, one will find superpower interactions playing their part. Christopher Clapham (2013) shares this view as well. He asserts that "the Horn of Africa is an extremely complex region, in which layers upon layers of potential problems are piled one on top of another." Lionel Cliffe (1999), on the other hand, highlights the fact that almost all conflicts in the Horn since the 1970s originated internally but were amplified by a pattern of "mutual intervention," as internal conflicts, due to lack of democracy, subjugation, and poverty, were somehow linked to insurgencies' support in neighboring states.

In sum, this linkage between domestic turmoil, regional proxy wars, and superpower interventions challenges fundamental elements of a Westphalian notion of sovereignty, including the right to self-determination, legal equality, and nonintervention in internal affairs. At the same time, the domestic turmoil of so-called failed states—Somalia, for example—poses threats to neighboring countries as a result of the multilayered dynamics. For instance, as indicated earlier, Ethiopia has adopted a two-pronged approach in Somalia, supporting reliable and capable partners within this failed state while also creating buffer zones to deny adversaries territory and control. The first strategy revolves around partnering with actors within a failed state that have demonstrated the ability to govern, albeit over small swaths of territory, and the second relates to direct engagement through peacekeeping or in collaboration with existing structures or unilaterally (Mesfin and Beyene 2018).

The use of buffer zones is an important issue, and the central focus, because the ways this device is used sheds light on how political authorities in the region manage their relations (and engage in conflicts) in an environment that includes (1) states that exhibit widely varying domestic capacities and organizations of authority and (2) regional susceptibility to involvement in proxy wars and other interference on the part of external actors.

In any event, it is clear that proxy wars in this context have further intensified the pressure on states to establish mechanisms to deal with such challenges. State survival remains a critical matter in the Horn of Africa. States, therefore, have been forced to create alternative mechanisms to defend themselves from other states or from non-state actors that organize opposition to undermine their monopoly of power or the sovereignty of the state they govern from within or without. Such mechanisms are, of course, numerous. Howe (2001), for example, identifies three military strategies that African states use to address threats to their present existence, given the wider structural constraints on their choices. Howe indicates that these strategies are regional intervention forces, private security companies, and Western-sponsored upgrades of state militaries—and he argues that all of these are likely to fail unless African states emphasize indigenous military professionalism. But Howe misses the other mechanism that this chapter outlines, a tool with a growing significance in helping to control pressures on a state, both internal and external—that is, the creation and management of buffer zones. This mechanism is working successfully for some states; for others, it is not very effective, but it is still employed. All states do not use buffer zones, and those states using buffer zones do not use them everywhere. Some states neighboring failed states establish buffer zones, while others do not. What explains these variations?

Buffer zones, neutral areas designed to prevent acts of aggression and mitigate or neutralize potential conflict between hostile nations, can be established in a shared territory or created unilaterally through force and monitored exclusively by one state or through proxies in non-shared areas in relatively weaker states or on the other side of enemy territory that harbors a threat to the stronger state. Although it is not the intent to go into full details of the causes of such threats here, it will be necessary to indicate how those threats reveal themselves within a state or through cross-border activity in the course of buffer zone creation and maintenance in the context of asymmetrical capabilities.

These threats can emerge from rebel groups, Islamist movements, and other armed groups organized in neighboring states, often in territories that are outside the control of local state authorities. This presents a particular dilemma, as recognized sovereign authorities may lack the capacity and political will to exercise this control. Conventional tools of international relations, such as pressuring a national government to fulfill the obligations of its sovereignty, either are ineffective or not applicable in a context in which a state lacks a government with the capacity or political will to exercise even minimal control over its territory and armed groups within it. This domestic turmoil is integral to contentions and power plays within local elite politics that reflect the fragmented character of political authority in many countries. Most countries in the Horn of Africa[2] have been going through acute political, social, cultural, and economic crises, and these, together with policy responses to them, have contributed to this internal fragmentation and instability. Failure by these states to solve these crises and conflicts, and their subsequent inability to provide protection and basic social services to the majority of their respective peoples, can build popular support for various non-state armed groups, as communities look beyond the state for protection or are given such protection through informal institutions such as clans and subclans.[3] The governments of these states are responsible for generating other vectors of regional instability such as recurrent wars and famines, absolute poverty, and disastrous diseases. These problems have often led to substantive revolts, which in turn have invited forceful reprisals, driving the rebellion and its civilian supporters or sympathizers into neighboring states (Jalata 2004). The civilians and the rebels become refugees, changing identities as necessary for survival while extending the reach of some of these networks of instability.

ETHIOPIA'S ENGAGEMENT IN SOMALIA

Since the creation of the Somali state in 1960, Ethiopia-Somalia relations have gone through a number of sensitive periods and tantrums. Somalia claimed to reestablish a "Greater" Somali state, bringing all Somali-speaking territories together, as it declined to recognize colonial borders with its neighbors. This position mellowed in the 1980s, but even current political leaders in the south continue to entertain it. Obviously, the spread of Somalis across borders and the regional elites' ambitions to go beyond borders and create realities on the ground to gain power and wealth will continue to be a challenge, and one cannot see a change on the horizon in this regard. The process of state formation, colonial legacies, and subsequent policies of the governments in power have created animosities among the people and driven them to interstate wars. Big power rivalry in the Horn played its role as well. It is no exaggeration to say that the people of Ethiopia and Somalia are victims of these realities and remain at the receiving end, plunged into conflict again and again.

Similarly, state policies in self-defense or otherwise, the role of others in the neighborhood in supporting irredentist rebels, tit-for-tat measures between the two states, and insurgencies organized in the name of religion have all played large roles in the conflicts between Ethiopia and Somalia. Somalia's territorial claims triggered two major wars with Ethiopia in the 1960s and 1970s, dragging in Cold War actors and their satellites. Ethiopia's treatment of its own people adjacent to Somalia's territories contributed to the problem. Since development was neglected, as the area was considered more or less a military backyard, the Somali Region attracted a lot of attention and, at times, brought more critiques than praises, becoming a headache for policy makers. Due to the wars of the 1960s and 1970s, the region remained a military zone until the fall of the Derg regime, and Ethiopia's treatment of its own Somalis did not change much until the late 1990s. The Ethiopian People's Revolutionary Democratic Front (EPRDF) began to change the dynamics and brought about a paradigm shift, providing self-governance rights to the people in the region, spearheaded by a regional government. Over time, the regional government managed Ethiopia's internal insurgencies in the area and allowed Ethiopia's military to engage beyond its borders.

But the combination of challenges of the internal insurgencies and threats from adjacent areas made the creation of sustainable peace and security in Ethiopia's Somali Region difficult. Armed internal actors with cross-border links would undermine Ethiopia's security, particularly when insurgents had access to adjacent territories in Somalia. The border areas are simply too porous, long, and difficult to allow full control of insurgent groups' movements. Nevertheless, Ethiopia resisted engaging militarily in Somalia from 1991, following the collapse of the Somali state, until 1995. The EPRDF's recognition of the historical baggage of both countries and the sympathy of the EPRDF leadership to Somalia deriving from the latter's support in the fight against the Derg, plus the mandate IGAD and the Organisation of African Unity gave Ethiopia all contributed to the restraint. But the historical divide between the two countries remained deep, making Ethiopia's genuine efforts suspicious in the eyes of Somalis and others.

Eventually, when a series of bombings carried out at Addis Ababa's Ghion Hotel and in the eastern city of Dire Dawa created turmoil in the country, the Ethiopian government had to reconsider its policy of positioning forces only at the border. Ethiopia made three critical unilateral interventions in Somalia. The first decisive action followed an assassination attempt on the late Abdul Majid Hussein, an Ethiopian cabinet minister, for which al-Itihaad al-Islamiya (AIAI), a terrorist organization that organized attacks on Somali-inhabited Ethiopian territory, claimed full responsibility. Ethiopia's army destroyed AIAI's training camps inside Somalia's Gedo region in a conventional military engagement in 1995. But even if the military operation dismantled AIAI's armed forces, the group understood that continuing the military confrontation would be difficult and costly, so it simply shifted its activities into controlling businesses in the economic and social sectors. Some of the veteran AIAI fighters continue to play a role in the politics of Somalia to this day. The second intervention took place in 1998, when a conventional threat emanating from the border conflict with Eritrea turned to proxy warfare, since Eritrea tried to undermine Ethiopia through Somalia's actors. Ethiopia's third major intervention came in 2006.

This third intervention is considered one of the critical junctures that shifted politics toward support of the Somali Transitional Federal Government (TFG): removing the Islamic Courts Union (ICU). The ICU had become an imminent threat not only to the TFG but also to Ethiopia's national interests. And so, in that operation, Ethiopian forces swiftly dislodged the ICU fighters in a series of conventional battles, forcing the collapse of the ICU's command and control. The ICU forces fled the front, Mogadishu, and the surrounding areas, allowing the installment of the TFG in Mogadishu.

In their history as neighbors, Ethiopia and Somalia have long had a tit-for-tat approach: a "strategy of cooperation" or competition "based on reciprocity," to address respective challenges or to undermine each other (Axelrod 1984, 1997). They employed various strategies and mechanisms to manage their differences and the threat of rebels infiltrating their borders. Buffer zone creation and maintenance, the position of which might vary in intensity and space, remains one of the most important tools that governments deploy for fending off threats. With a view to reinforcing buffer zones, Ethiopia and Somalia have supported each other's proxies, apart from the two conventional wars between their armies before Somalia's collapse in 1991. Ethiopia supported opposition groups fighting Siad Barre's government in Somalia; these included the Somali National Movement (SNM), Somali Salvation Democratic Front (SSDF), United Somali Congress, and others.

Meanwhile, Somalia's strategy involved groups such as the Tigray People's Liberation Front, Eritrean People's Liberation Front (Reno 2003), Ogaden National Liberation Front (ONLF), Islamic Front for the Liberation of Oromia, and Western Somali Liberation Front (WSLF). This support was manifested in two different ways: arming non-Somali Ethiopian groups and creating and infiltrating Somali groups with the direct authority of Somalia's army (Mohamed 1997). Groups such as the WSLF and the Somali Abo Liberation Front were created and infiltrated Ethiopian territories. The groups did not have autonomy (Tareke 2000). Somalia also served as a proxy for extra-regional countries with stakes in the region, incorporating their plans and getting compensated for it. Egypt, in particular, has used Somalia in this way, in return facilitating support from other Arab countries.

The two countries went to war in 1977, whereby the major Cold War actors had a significant role when Somalia invaded Ethiopia, but the Somali forces were driven out of Ethiopia's Ogaden region after Somalia was defeated in 1978. The peace agreement that Siad Barre and Mengistu Hailemariam signed on March 22, 1988, in Djibouti signified the formal end of the conflict, and a subsequent agreement that was signed on April 6, 1988, in Mogadishu helped the countries create buffer zones along their common borders. In this agreement, both sides resolved to sort out problems related to the border, to desist from assisting their proxy rebel groups, and to withdraw their forces twenty-five kilometers from the common border—effectively creating a buffer zone. It is critical to note here that both states agreed to create the buffer zone for different reasons, and so no third party, to monitor the area, was indicated in the agreement. Although some attribute the effort to IGAD and then-president of Djibouti Hassan Gouled Aptidon, in fact the two leaders took the initiative to make peace directly, negotiating and signing a treaty to sustain their positions (Mohamed 1997).

Mengistu Hailemariam, then the Ethiopian leader, was trying to uphold a regime that was under serious threat from Tigrayan and Eritrean liberation fighters in the north. He needed to reposition the forces of the eastern sector facing Somalia to the north. Mengistu, therefore, encouraged the peace deal with Siad Barre, as the government would be able to move troops to northern Ethiopia. Siad, on the other hand, believed that the treaty would deprive the clan-affiliated Somali rebels of Ethiopian support, leading to their eventual collapse (Mohamed 1997). In fact, the implementation of the

Ethiopia-Somalia peace agreement did not work out as well as envisaged. Ethiopian security elements in the eastern military command, which were heavily involved in organizing anti-Siad Somali forces, felt the deal was a betrayal of their Somali colleagues, notably the SNM. The SNM was the most active of the Somali rebel groups and engaged in fierce fighting against Siad (Ambassador Fisseha Yimer, interview). Following the agreement, the SNM quickly relocated its fighters from Ethiopia to northern Somalia, seizing Burao, in the eastern part of Somaliland,[4] and strengthening SNM forces inside Somalia. Somalia launched a violent response from Mogadishu and Hargeisa against the SNM and its main constituency, the Issaq clan, through military bombardments that forced some four hundred thousand people to flee into Ethiopia. The SNM military victory and the way southern groups treated the former became the basis for Somaliland's aspirations for independence and, at the same time, planted the seeds of disintegration in the former Somali republic (Yusuf Ahmed Bobe[5] interview).

The treaty also left Ethiopian officials—engaged with other Somali opposition movements Ethiopia supported—with a dilemma.[6] The SSDF had been weakened following Ethiopia's arrest of its entire leadership due to political disputes related to Ethiopia's Somali Region, and the SSDF was in no position to take advantage of the weakened Siad, and hence Ethiopian military commanders did not do much. But the SNM that was fighting Siad's regime in the north had the capacity to continue to expand its control in northwestern Somalia (now known as Somaliland) and was threatening the regime in Mogadishu; Ethiopian army officers were in a difficult situation to withdraw their support to the SNM.[7] Within two years, the regimes in both countries had lost their wars against their respective armed opponents and were removed from power, rendering any dispute over the implementation of the agreement moot, although the agreements concluded between governments legally remain intact irrespective of whether those who signed them exist or not. The agreement became practically irrelevant to the existing situation in the relations between Ethiopia and Somalia.

Changes in Ethiopia in 1991 and a State Collapse in Somalia

Following the demise of the Derg in 1991, the EPRDF-led government engaged Somali political leaders in a series of efforts to resolve their differences in an effort to save the latter from devastation.[8] Ethiopia organized the first face-to-face meeting in Bahir Dar, following which Somali political leaders representing fifteen factions gathered for the National Reconciliation Conference in Addis Ababa on March 15, 1993. The meeting was one of the most successful of the series of conferences held on Somalia, producing the Addis Ababa agreement, which committed the fifteen factions to a national reconciliation process and a procedure for establishing the Transitional National Council and relevant government institutions. Following this breakthrough, the UN Security Council endorsed Resolution 814 (1993), expanding the United Nations Operation in Somalia (UNOSOM) and agreeing to deploy a peacekeeping force of some twenty-eight thousand troops (UNOSOM II), giving it a mandate to restore peace, law, and order and help reestablish a national government. The UN, in fact, tried to reestablish a central government (Geshekter 1997), but since this created suspicion among those in Somaliland, the UN was asked to leave the northwestern areas (UN Res. 814).

UNOSOM II was not only the largest peacekeeping force in the UN's history but also the most ambitious in having a mandate to systematically resort to coercive methods to enforce the disarmament of all factions and warlords in Somalia to ensure lasting peace and stability (UN Res. 814). Those who advocated a much more coercive role for the UN, and critics of the Addis Ababa agreement, argued that the talks produced a rushed and vaguely worded agreement that sparked tensions between the UN and some armed factions over whether the creation of district- and regional-level councils were to be implemented by those who signed the agreement or whether they should follow a bottom-up process. Armed conflict broke out between General Mohamed Farah Aideed's faction and UN peacekeepers, which derailed the mission and blocked the agreement's implementation. Conflicts of interest within UNOSOM helped Somali factions manipulate the situation, making the implementation of the Addis Ababa agreement extremely difficult.[9]

The UN and US forces on the ground engaged in a manhunt exercise when differences emerged in the implementation of the agreement and following the deaths of twenty-four Pakistani UN peacekeepers, after which the Security Council (UN Res. 837) decided to detain all those responsible, including Aideed, and eventually a $25,000 bounty was placed on his head (Woodward 2006). The ensuing skirmishes led to the deaths of eighteen

American marines and the shooting down of two Black Hawk utility helicopters.[10]

This had disastrous consequences for Somalia and the region at large. Ethiopia tried to create an understanding between the UN, the US, and other international actors on the one hand and Somali leaders on the other, but none of these efforts succeeded. When all efforts to calm the situation failed, Ethiopia engaged the UN and the US to try to keep them from making disastrous mistakes. The UN peacekeeping mission ran into major difficulties, and first US troops and then the UN mission withdrew. The UN peacekeeping effort ended without success in 1995. Somalia became the beginning and the end of the peace enforcement doctrine that then UN Secretary-General Boutros Boutros-Ghali advocated. Following the withdrawal of UN forces, Somali factions started another round of civil war that eventually got General Aideed killed.

Following the departure of UN peacekeeping forces from Somalia, Ethiopia embarked on another effort to bring the warring factions and other political actors together, this time in the resort town of Sodere, in eastern Ethiopia, in 1996. Participants wanted to establish a government for Somalia, but they were finally persuaded by Ethiopia to agree to establish an alliance, called the National Salvation Council (NSC), with a co-chairmanship arrangement. In order to create a framework to accommodate Aideed's group, the establishment of a government was postponed. But all of this came to naught after Egypt tried to reconcile the NSC leadership with Aideed's group. Following the death of his father, Aideed took over salballar—meaning broad-based government in the Somali language—but neither he nor his group secured recognition and legitimacy.

Ethiopia openly objected to what Egypt was doing at that time. Rather than bringing the two groups together, Egypt divided the NSC leadership and created an alliance between those who broke from the NSC and Aideed's group. Egypt did not expect that two of the leaders of the NSC who walked out of the negotiations would matter much. Colonel Abdullahi Yusuf Ahmed and General Aden Abdullahi Nur (aka Gabyow) revealed how the 1997 Cairo agreement became yet another failed peacemaking effort for Somalia. But the Cairo fiasco could be looked at as a critical juncture that ensured the demise of the Bossaso conference planned as a larger national reconciliation to establish Somalia's national government but also as an event that shaped

Somali politics, pushing the country toward decentralization and federalism and making a centrally controlled unitary government history.

The first brick of federalism was laid in Puntland following the Cairo conference. Peace efforts that followed the Cairo event began underscoring federalism as one of the pillars of reconciliation among Somalis. But this sequence, unfortunately, is ignored in most of the literature that explains the ongoing developments in Somalia's federal arrangement.

Ethiopia's Military Engagement in Somalia and the African Union Mission in Somalia (AMISOM)

As indicated earlier, state securitization and peacemaking continue to remain the major framework for Ethiopia's engagement in Somalia. Whatever has been done on the security side is aimed at supporting peace efforts and addressing threats that undermine these. Ethiopia's military engagement in Somalia, in concrete terms, took different turns, depending on the threat level from groups posing a military challenge to Ethiopia or partners in Somalia. Due to sensitivity related to historical relations between Ethiopia and Somalia, the EPRDF-led Ethiopian government refrained from engaging militarily until 1995.

In 1998, Ethiopia engaged for the second time when groups that were used for a proxy war against Ethiopia threatened Ethiopia's security from Baidoa and the surrounding areas. Ethiopia destroyed these forces and handed all seized arms to the Rahanweyn Resistance Army, which changed Somalia's local politics for good. Ethiopia's third major military engagement with Somalia took place in 2006. Developments following the 2004 peace conference in Kenya that established the Somalia TFG and the subsequent refusal of the warlords to allow the relocation of the TFG, plus the emerging dynamics following the ICU takeover of southern Somalia, triggered this engagement. Warlords that could not attain power in the mediation process resisted the TFG's relocation to Mogadishu in 2004, and the ICU controlled the area after defeating them all. Understanding the context in which Ethiopia decided to engage militarily at that time is critical.

Although IGAD coordinated the mediation, it did not prepare for a security challenge like government relocation to Mogadishu, and this proved problematic. The first challenge came from warlords opposing the TFG's relocation, and, recognizing its mistake, IGAD made an effort to deploy a peace support mission to realize the move. However, it failed to secure backing from partners. The opportunity then was squandered. Subsequently, however, the TFG moved to Jowhar, a place controlled by a warlord who then made the work of the TFG difficult, forcing relocation to Baidoa. Neither move resolved the TFG's problems. While the TFG was in Baidoa, there was a confrontation between warlords and the ICU, engineered in Mogadishu. The warlords lost, and the ICU took over Mogadishu and quickly expanded throughout the remaining southern areas of Somalia, including Kismayo.

In Somalia, there were mixed feelings about the ICU takeover. Although the ICU and the sanctions imposed intimidated Somalis, there was some nuanced optimism about the takeover. The Nairobi-based international media were quick to create a positive narrative. Most Somalis were not certain about the ICU's next moves, whether it would pursue peace and national reconciliation or use military force to coerce the areas it controlled. While ICU determination to continue its military engagement helped strengthen its position, the takeover was further facilitated by a lack of cooperation and coordination between the countries of the region and their international partners and their failure to understand the political realities in Somalia. This made it possible for the ICU to project a formidable challenge to the peace and stability of the subregion and beyond the region's boundaries.

Indeed, the regional implications were immediate and extensive, as ICU leaders almost at once began to reinstate the irredentist "Greater Somalia" agenda, creating emotional connections with Somali-speaking peoples in the region that few had expected or anticipated. Ethiopia originally did not shed tears for the defeat of the warlords, as they had been obstacles to the relocation of the Somali government from Nairobi to Mogadishu in 2004. Indeed, Ethiopia saw the ICU's takeover as an opportunity at first. It had, of course, remained deeply engaged with the problems of Somalia and worked with the ICU to help them resolve their differences with the TFG peacefully and ensure that the ICU would not allow others bent on undermining Ethiopia's security interests to use territories under their control, but subsequent developments forced Addis Ababa to reconsider its previous position. Following the failures of the international community to consider IGAD's proposals and the threats the ICU posed, Ethiopia managed to unilaterally address the emerging challenges quite effectively.

At the beginning, Ethiopia took part in a parallel engagement with the ICU to encourage a peaceful resolution of the differences with the TFG on the one hand and simultaneously continued to strengthen the capacity of the TFG on the other. In 2006, Ethiopia conducted a series of meetings with the ICU leadership in various cities, including Nairobi, Khartoum, London, Djibouti, and Dubai, and made it clear to them that Ethiopia was prepared to live with an Islamic government in Somalia. This was on the condition that the ICU respected international law governing interstate relations and did not allow areas under its control to be used by elements that would undermine Ethiopia's national security interests. One issue was Somali irredentism, which several ICU leaders had publicly supported. The ICU immediately interpreted the desire of Ethiopia for engagement as a weakness and, on record, declared jihad against Ethiopia. The ICU claimed that its forces would pray in Addis Ababa within a month.

In 2006, there was pressure on Ethiopia to avoid military engagement from all corners. Ethiopia's leaders also did not want to engage militarily. But the ICU made the situation difficult and untenable, and Ethiopia eventually deployed a strategy—defensive engagement—that forced the ICU to attack Ethiopia's positions in waves and led to the former's eventual collapse. At the end of the day, faced with the ICU threat to the remaining Ethiopian buffer zones in Somalia and repeated TFG requests for Ethiopian support, Ethiopia could not avoid engaging in a war of the ICU's own making in December 2006. Fortunately, the first round of war was over in a matter of days. Given the numerous allegations that have been made about Ethiopia carrying out the US's "war on terror" agenda, it is worth underlining that Ethiopia was strongly advised by the US not to get involved in Somalia, as it ran the risk of a crisis like the US's engagement in Iraq.

The US pointed to the difficulties it was facing in Iraq as an example of the possible dangers and implications of yet another failure in the war on terror, provided Ethiopia lost. The US was less concerned about the security threat that the extremist groups posed to Ethiopia and the entire region. Certainly, after Ethiopia won the war, the US media painted a very different picture. And, undoubtedly, the US provided critical support in the UN Security Council to avoid any kind of international condemnation or scrutiny of the conduct of war.

The international community's response was muted at best, neither supporting nor opposing, while the international media promptly launched a campaign claiming that US Special Forces were embedded to assist Ethiopian forces on the ground. None were. In fact, the swift conclusion of the war surprised the US, who were interested to learn how Ethiopia had succeeded. Despite this, the war continues to be understood as an Ethiopian bid to help the war on terror. The US neither agreed to Ethiopia going into Somalia nor to its later withdrawal from Somalia, as some US officials later made clear on the record.

In fact, Ethiopia could have withdrawn from Somalia immediately after removing the ICU in December 2006. Indeed, it would have preferred to do so. But there were requests from clan elders and the TFG calling for protection since "their ICU government" had collapsed and the TFG needed time to build up its capacities with either assistance from Ethiopia or elsewhere. Unfortunately, the opportunity the presence of Ethiopian forces created for stabilizing the situation in Mogadishu was squandered. The TFG, immediately after relocating to Somalia, began abusing residents and failed to provide the necessary leadership. Internal power struggles immediately took center stage.

Since Al-Shabaab was weakened on the ground at that time, Ethiopia began contemplating withdrawal in 2008. As the international community was not prepared to share the burden with Ethiopia and took the latter's continued stay for granted, Ethiopia made known its decision to vacate. Ethiopia's numerous attempts and pleas to convince "Somalia's partners" to strengthen the capacity of the TFG so it could withdraw fell on deaf ears. All sorts of reasons were produced to avoid providing support. One wonders how much money was spent trying to build up TFG security forces afterwards and how much would have been saved if Ethiopia's proposals had been supported in 2007.

Ethiopia withdrew in 2009, openly announcing that it would only reenter Somalia under two conditions: if AMISOM forces were threatened or if Al-Shabaab took over Somalia. This clear position remained a deterrent for a long time. Ethiopia was then asked to join AMISOM, and it has continued to play its role in this regard since 2013. Since their deployment, Ethiopia's AMISOM contingents have covered the largest sector, and there are no threats posed from those areas. They remain one of the most resilient and successful forces within AMISOM Security Service. As AMISOM's drawdown began, Burundi withdrew its one thousand troops by the end of February 2019. This withdrawal was not related to Somalia but to developments in Burundi's domestic politics to which the international community reacted. Since Burundian forces were deployed in areas where the population density is very high, their withdrawal had serious consequences.

On March 1, 2019, Al-Shabaab detonated two consecutive blasts on Maka Al-Mukarama road in Mogadishu; several people were killed and properties destroyed. This called for the international community to review the way it formulated AMISOM's withdrawal. There was also talk that Somalia's neighbors intended to train more than thirteen thousand troops for the SFG. The leadership in Mogadishu will have a hard time providing leadership. This plan might help but will not solve the problem. Unless the SFG works in tandem with the Federal Member States (FMS) and addresses Somalia's fault lines, the possibility of Somali security forces dealing with Al-Shabaab effectively is highly unlikely.

The fault lines in the security institutions of the SFG also call for a careful handling of AMISOM's withdrawal. The Somali National Army (SNA), Somali Police Force (SPF), and National Intelligence and Security Agency that AMISOM mentors and international advisers train and support provide security in Somalia, and there is a plethora of challenges these agencies face. For example, there is an ongoing challenge within the SFG security structures related to salary and other benefits and biometric registration. The SFG is arguing that all members of its security organs must register so that SNA members will be properly paid and take orders from the SFG leadership. The registration is also intended to rein in the problem of ghost soldiers and corruption in the SNA and to reorganize the army with a proper command and control to address the challenge of faction leaders and businessmen who give orders to militias and paramilitaries, who should be taking orders from the leadership of the SNA or SPF only to carry out fighting and policing.

It is a well-known fact that a warlord or a businessman controls the decision to move a contingent within the SNA from elsewhere and determines the relocation and where they will be deployed. Informal institutions play the greatest role in the way soldiers behave in training and combat as well. A large number of army commanders and their soldiers are refusing biometric registration. Some believe that the act is intended to purge a significant part of the army to create a balance between clans. The evacuation of the militias from a number of their military bases in March 2019 was related to this and reveals the mistakes the SFG committed in this connection. As militias are based in their respective FMS states, each with their own command and control, the SFG's intention to use biometric registration as an instrument of control will have serious security implications. This is already beginning to cause the security structure's collapse, as the militias are vacating certain areas, allowing Al-Shabaab to quickly fill in. Added to this, Al-Shabaab's infiltration of the SFG military and police units facilitates the fill-in. Government ministries and their respective leaders do not operate as institutions. Instead, each one takes its own militia and security detail, exacerbating the situation and making the SFG leadership's political will to address these challenges questionable.

Transition and Change in Ethiopia and Implications for Somalia

The recent changes in Ethiopia were taken positively in Somalia. This emanates from the expectation that Ethiopia will impact Somalia's peace efforts positively through engaging all stakeholders. Somalis have understood that federalism is not necessarily a bad idea and has helped them solve some of the country's problems. They expect that changes in Ethiopia will further enhance federalism, with the leadership engaging the SFG and FMS and encouraging them to come together and bridge their gaps. While this was their expectation, Ethiopia's decision at the highest level of the political leadership to focus on the SFG, rather than bringing all stakeholders together, has undermined that confidence. Somalis expect that Ethiopia would bring together Somalia's actors to sort out their differences, rather than completely siding with the SFG, whose legitimacy is de jure, while having a limited capacity. Given the fact that Ethiopia-Somalia relations carry a lot of baggage, one would expect the new leadership in Ethiopia to take this into consideration. One cannot simply start afresh, free from what Ethiopia and Somalia have done previously: tit-for-tat proxy wars to undermine each other with outcomes that radically changed the region's power configurations in the 1970s and 1980s, resulting in the collapse of the Somali state. Then Ethiopia's leaders, through mandates from the neighborhood or Africa, have been trying to support Somalis as they address their challenges. It is, therefore, impossible to de-link Ethiopia's new leadership from this history.

Indeed, Ethiopia's decision to fully back the SFG following changes in Ethiopia, at the expense of the real or perceived abandonment of the FMS, was interpreted as the continuation of the old policy of "weakening Somalia," emphasizing that the historical baggage remains alive and could reveal itself anytime.

Ethiopia's overall policy for the last twenty-seven years centered on security and deployed various instruments to fend off threats rather than impose Ethiopia's will. Military engagements had specific political objectives for Somalia: either inducing a power balance for reconciliation or forcing parties to abandon military options to resolve differences. But Ethiopia's policy towards Somalia was not a one-time affair and evolved over the years. The policy was not dogmatic but rather dynamic. That is why, when consecutive efforts to have a government at the center failed and Somalis created local-level administrations in relatively peaceful areas, Ethiopia cultivated relationships with regional administrations across the border and developed a shared interest. While Ethiopia would fend off threats emanating from elsewhere, the local administrations would strengthen their own capacities to govern. Both would address common security threats and ensure the smooth movement of goods and people across the common border, which, at the same time, explains how Ethiopia's policy towards Somalia evolved over the years.

Given these relationships, Ethiopia's engagement should not aim to choose one side over another in contestations between the FMS and SFG. Getting involved in that choice should not be the framework of thinking, since the contestations have serious security implications for Ethiopia. Somalia finds itself in a situation that has the capacity to sustain itself for a long time because there is a lack of consensus among stakeholders at various levels, locally and beyond. This means that actors on the ground should be encouraged to come together and address the country's problems, without forcing Ethiopia to side with this or that actor.

The changes in Ethiopia have resulted in amendments to some of the country's laws, including the proclamation related to terrorist and freed groups that were considered to be involved. These changes have implications for the way Ethiopia engages its neighbors, including Somalia. Ethiopia's decision to make changes to its internal rules through its legislature—including amendments to the anti-terrorism law—removed the Oromo Liberation

Front (OLF), ONLF, and Ginbot 7 from the list of terrorist organizations. The first implication is that countries that were cooperating in this context do not need to follow their previous policies. This put Ethiopia and its leaders in a position to raise issues of integration and greater collaboration. But for this to be taken seriously, Ethiopia must address its fault lines internally.

To take the situation back to Somalia, changes in Ethiopia have impacted the relevance of the FMS and hence they feel abandoned, as if they are no longer relevant for Ethiopia's security. But Ethiopia's cooperation with Somalia's stakeholders extends beyond the pursuit of the OLF, ONLF, Ginbot 7, and other groups. There are critical issues that we need to take into account in our relationship with Somalia, beyond rebel groups. Save terrorism, there are other challenges that demand cooperation with Somalia's actors at all levels. The major threats of arms trafficking, illegal immigration, and contraband trade, as well as the problem of fending off threats from terrorists such as Al-Shabaab and the Islamic State in Somalia continue to exist.

There are doubts among Somalia's stakeholders that Ethiopia and the international community will continue to engage with both the SFG and FMS so that they harmonize their positions and become more proactive in shaping a realistic approach in Somalia. Somalia's stakeholders wonder whether outsiders will contribute to further polarization instead. Ethiopia, the region, and the international community, with some having their interests at the forefront irrespective of the circumstances, have continued to engage with Somalia all along. The Somali stakeholders are pushing back against the changing realities on the ground. Although this is an issue one might need to contemplate further, a major crisis is emerging in relation to the SNA and biometric registration. The government, to address the challenges of identifying its soldiers and to control ghost soldiers and double registrations, implemented strict fingerprinting and related data collection, on which huge resources have been misappropriated. The measures have generated debate within Somalia, and international partners have expressed support.

There have been major challenges encountered in the process of implementing Ethiopia's policy in Somalia. Somali stakeholders view Ethiopia's role differently. The expectation of the current political leadership in Somalia and its potential areas of cooperation with Ethiopia are huge. But for the two countries, the major merits or drawbacks of Ethiopia's peace efforts in Somalia depend on how Ethiopia manages its relations with all actors and how much it leverages them to partner in peace on the ground. That is why understanding the historical context of relations between Ethiopia and Somalia is critical.

After efforts to produce a national government acceptable to all Somalis in 1993 and 1995 failed, Somalia's politics shifted to a "building blocks" approach and saw the emergence of local-level governance structures. The 1998 administration that Puntland State of Somalia created remains monumental in this regard. Although some Somali observers argued that Puntland was just a reaction to Cairo and would not be able to sustain itself, Puntland surprised most and became a reference point. Obviously, the creation of Puntland created tension with Somaliland, particularly in the areas of Sool and Sanaag, since both administrations' positions were mutually exclusive. Hargeisa was forced to be much more accommodative of its eastern enclaves in its power and resource sharing. Since 1998, Ethiopia, on the other hand, has embarked on engagement with Somalis and adjusted its policy to fit realities on the ground, supporting relatively peaceful areas and their administrations in a bottom-up approach and, at the same time, supporting all efforts towards reconciliation at the national level. Since establishing a national government for Mogadishu faltered when challenged by external actors, adjustments were needed to Ethiopia's policies toward strengthening administrations and managing threats in collaboration with these administrations.

For Ethiopia, managing these problems in Somalia required the continuation of the two-pronged approach indicated above, that is, supporting islands of peace that have been partners in peace and peace building through proper governance and strengthening them as buffer zones while in parallel supporting the peacemaking effort at the national level. These strategies are complementary and reinforce each other.

Ethiopia's strategy has been most evident vis-à-vis Somaliland and Puntland. This was further enhanced following the adoption of a federal constitution in Somalia. Ethiopia engaged in the creation and sustenance of the emerging FMS on the basis of that constitution. All these administrations provide basic levels of order and security to their populations locally. Cooperation with Ethiopia helps the administrations to develop capacity, enable their citizens to travel easily, and engage with other partners that share similar views. Obviously, since there is harmonization of interests and identification of common threats, Ethiopia's support plays a critical role in limiting the extent to which other foreign governments must intervene in the internal affairs of these authorities when engaging them over matters of mutual concern—security, in particular. Of course, this was not without problems. Extremist groups and those that use this context to generate a national rhetoric got the opportunity to expand their base and remain viable. But for Ethiopia, the choice was between allowing the entire territory of Somalia to be used by those bent on undermining Ethiopia's security and allowing small enclaves to resist while governance structures are eventually built brick by brick. This was a trade-off, and this reality has allowed Mogadishu-based governments at the center to manipulate emotions as they see fit within the country, since some Somalis from the center perceive this as interference in the internal affairs of Somalia, which presents a structural challenge from the center in Mogadishu.

Since this brings to the fore redistribution of power without consent from Mogadishu, decentralization within a Somali context undermines the monopoly of coercion of the center. This explicit political framework for supporting these local administrations is meant to achieve Ethiopia's underlying policy objective, which is to implicitly strengthen the creation of buffer zones through the development of realistic local partners and administrations in order to address Ethiopia's security concerns and, at the same time, those of its partners. The basic premise is that these administrations are institutionally linked to the society they administer. The clan members and their kith and kin govern the area, and those intending to serve as others' instruments are quickly identified and neutralized. Ethiopia began providing capacity building in support of these administrations to deter the expansion of AIAI after 1995 and Al-Shabaab after 2009 into places where there exists relative peace and stability, as well as to fend off other threats and deter the infiltration of insurgent groups that target Ethiopia's security.

To realize collaboration concretely, institutions that enhance cross-border collaborative frameworks are put in place, providing avenues for the security institutions of both sides to exchange information periodically and conduct joint operations whenever the need arises. Since there is continuous interaction and movement of the peoples of both countries, these frameworks are critical in ensuring a smooth flow around the border. Ethiopia, in fact, has maintained its relationship with administrative setups along the entire eastern border of Ethiopia's Somali Regional State.

If this territory were not properly secured on both sides of the border, elements bent on destabilizing Ethiopia directly or used as proxies could pose a serious security threat to Ethiopia. Taking lessons from others that have suffered is critical. But this is not a policy that will remain in place forever. Ethiopia's securitization of threats may alter, and this would change the kind of engagement that is called for. It should be underscored that Ethiopia benefits immensely from the deterrence that results from the relationship and collaboration with these administrations and the center. There is no alternative to this for the time being.

Since the destabilization of these regions would have serious implications for Ethiopia's security, Ethiopia also provides a political context in which the challenges these administrations face are addressed peacefully. Encouraging the administrations of Somaliland and Puntland, as well as the newly established administrations to work with the SFG to resolve all outstanding issues through dialogue and peaceful means, should continue to be the bottom line in Ethiopia's engagement with these authorities. The premise is that any military clash threatens to create a situation that could be manipulated, creating ungoverned spaces in the area, which in turn would have spillover effects for Somaliland, Puntland, and the other FMS—and Ethiopia as well.

The process of engaging with these administrations in tandem within this context is another challenge and a security dilemma. Managing these administrations through the provision of capacity building creates natural competition. Since the SFG and FMS on one side and Puntland and Somaliland on the other have discontinued communication, they interpret any support for either side as supporting one against the other. This is where political engagement at the leadership level with all the administrations becomes critical, and Ethiopia has been doing this all along, irrespective of Mogadishu's fierce opposition. In fact, Ethiopia continues to provide a guarantee of response and support when a threat comes from all sorts of actors.

Ethiopia engages regional administrations and ensures cooperation if possible or avoids war between its collaborators through offering capacity building and engagement and withdrawing them when necessary. This method was continuously deployed with Puntland and Somaliland so that both refrain from fighting around their disputed border regions of Sool and Sanaag. Ethiopia might need to continue with respect to the FMS and SFG to avoid armed confrontation. If collaboration is achieved, synergy could be created between them to fight Al-Shabaab. Obviously, the policy sometimes falters, as Puntland and Somaliland, as well as the SFG and FMS, engage in a short-lived military confrontation and agencies involved might fail in handling differences neutrally and efficiently. At times, Ethiopia explicitly informs the parties that it is ready to engage directly to restore order, hence playing the deterrence role. Engagement with other FMS states is much more closely related to supporting the various actors working together and to coordinating with the international community so that the SFG can channel resources fairly, mainly to the FMS. Concrete collaboration to jointly fight Al-Shaabab is yet to be achieved.

Current Changing Dynamics in the Horn, the Role of the Gulf, and Its Implications

The change that has taken place in Ethiopia and the normalization of relations between Ethiopia and Eritrea with the support of the Gulf countries have created an opportunity that could transform the Horn. If Ethiopia and Eritrea address all the gray areas in their relations, this could change the political landscape in the region. If Ethiopia and Eritrea work a visible synergy to revitalize IGAD, harmonize positions in Gulf-Horn relations, and work significantly on other security issues, tremendous ground could be covered in moving the region toward peace. Ethiopia addressing its internal challenges following the changes also creates better opportunities in relations between the countries of the Horn. Ethiopia's decision to remove the OLF, ONLF, Ginbot 7, and others from the terrorist list and allow their return home means that the basis of the relationship between Ethiopia and its neighbors has changed dramatically to new avenues of cooperation. The countries will focus on cooperation for regional integration and contribute even more to the peace and stability of the subregion. With a hopeful trajectory in the process of this ongoing change, the Horn of Africa could be a region whose partnership will increasingly be sought by various global actors, with better opportunities to attract foreign direct investment and address challenges of unemployment, thus creating better conditions for improving the current economic situation (Tekeda 2019).

It is for all of these reasons that changes in Ethiopia and the normalization of relations between Ethiopia and Eritrea have the potential to signify a gigantic historical transformation in the Horn of Africa, with immense positive implications for the region and those outside it that are affected positively or negatively by what takes place here. One must expect that if the process of transformation moves smoothly, the process of peacemaking in Somalia may be sped up as well.

CONCLUSION

Somalia's woes continue, though there are obvious improvements in areas where regional states are established and are functioning well. But the tug of war between stakeholders continues, and that is further polarized since resources coming from elsewhere are reinforcing them. One obviously wishes that Somalia's internal stakeholders come to an agreement on major issues, consider the suffering of their people, and create a semblance of peace in their country. It is absolutely immoral to derive comfort from Somalia's continuous challenges. But if Somalia's actors remain divided and contestation endures, a relationship with all in a reasonable way would provide the opportunity to bring them together. This should be understood both in reality and in perception, as the latter matters in Somalia politics. Alienating any actor, or even giving that impression, keeps the opportunity for peace further away. Hence, since buffer zones provide the opportunity to pacify areas, engaging all stakeholders remains central in managing ungoverned spaces that other non-state actors have been using or may potentially use for destabilizing purposes. Practical application and realities on the ground, for all intents and purposes, make this a valid policy. Of course, the policy framework and its adaptation have to be constantly revised and recalibrated, taking into consideration the evolving dynamics and challenges in Somalia. Moving forward, building consensus between the SFG and FMS remains critical if Somalia is to achieve a sustainable peace and stability. Tilting the balance of forces on the ground to one of them, without consensus, would be a futile exercise, since the basis of the SFG and FMS are strong, and they have to come together to fight the common enemy: the extremist groups.

REFERENCES

Aalen, Lovise. 2014. "Ethiopian State Support to Insurgency in Southern Sudan from 1962 to 1983: Local, Regional and Global Connections." *Eastern African Studies* 8, no. 4: 626–41.

Axelrod, Robert. 1984. *The Evolution of Cooperation*. New York: Basic Books.

———. 1997. *The Complexity of Cooperation: Agent-Based Models of Competition and Collaboration*. Princeton Studies in Complexity. Princeton, NJ: Princeton University Press.

Clapham, Christopher. 2013. "Why Is the Horn Different?" Rift Valley Institute, October 28, 2013.

Cliffe, Lionel. 1999. "Regional Dimensions of Conflict in the Horn of Africa." *Third World Quarterly* 20, no. 1: 89–111.

Frisch, Hillel. 2002. "Explaining Third World Security Structures." *Strategic Studies* 25, no. 3: 161–90.

Gebru Tareke. 2000. "The Ethiopia Somalia War of 1977 Revisited," *International Journal of African Historical Studies* 33, no. 3: 635–67.

Geshekter, Charles. 1997. "The Death of Somalia in Historical Perspective." In *Mending Rips in the Sky: Options for Somali Communities in the 21st Century*, edited by Hussein M. Adam and Richard Ford. Lawrenceville, NJ: Red Sea.

Herbst, Jeffrey. 2000. *States and Power in Africa: Comparative Lessons in Authority and Control*. Princeton Studies in International History and Politics. Princeton, NJ: Princeton University Press.

Howe, Herbert M. 2001. *Ambiguous Order: Military Forces in African States*. Boulder, CO: Lynne Rienner.

IGAD. 2009. "Peace and Security." Annual Report, 46–62. Djibouti: Inter-Governmental Authority on Development.

Jalata, Asafa, ed. 2004. *State Crises, Globalisation and National Movements in North-East Africa*. London: Routledge.

Mann, Michael. 1986. *The Sources of Social Power, Volume 1: A History of Power from the Beginning to AD 1760*. New edition. Cambridge: Cambridge University Press.

Markakis, John. 2003. "Ethnic Conflict in Pre-Federal Ethiopia." Paper delivered at 1st National Conference on Federalism, Conflict and Peace Building, United Nations Conference Center, Addis Ababa.

Medani, Khalid Mustafa. 2012. "The Horn of Africa in the Shadow of the Cold War: Understanding the Partition of Sudan from a Regional Perspective." *Journal of North African Studies* 17, no. 2: 275–94.

Mesfin, Seyoum, and Abdeta Dribssa Beyene. 2018. "The Practicalities of Living with Failed States." *Daedalus: Journal of the American Academy of Arts & Sciences* 147, no. 1 (Winter): 128–40.

Mohamed, Mohamed-Abdi. 1997 "Somalia: Kinship and Relationships Derived from It." In *Mending Rips in the Sky: Options for Somali Communities in the 21st Century*, edited by Hussein M. Adam and Richard Ford. Lawrenceville, NJ: Red Sea.

Reno, William. 2003. "Somalia and Survival in the Shadow of the Global Economy." Working Paper Number 100. QEH Working Paper Series—QEHWPS100. February 2003. Oxford Department of International Development, University of Oxford.

Tekeda Alemu. 2019. "On African Approaches and Policies to Prevent and Counter Violent Extremism." Paper presented at a conference organized by the European Institute of Peace, entitled "Move Slow and Mend Things: Learning from Successful African P/CVE Approaches." March 2019.

Wilson, Thomas M., and Hastings Donnan. 1998. "Nation, State and Identity at International Borders." In *Border Identities: Nation and State at International Frontiers*, edited by Thomas M. Wilson and Hastings Donnan, 1–30. Cambridge: Cambridge University Press.

Woodward, Peter. 2006. *US Foreign Policy and the Horn of Africa*. US Foreign Policy and Conflict in the Islamic World. London: Routledge.

ENDNOTES

1. Mesfin and Beyene (2018) thoroughly explain the concept of the buffer zone and how countries deploy it in "The Practicalities of Living with Failed States," from which most of the arguments are adopted here.

2. For the purpose of this chapter, the Horn of Africa includes Djibouti, Eritrea, Ethiopia, Somalia, Sudan, South Sudan, and Kenya.

3. Somalia is a good example in this connection. Even if Somalia has a government in Mogadishu and various regional federal member states, Somalis mainly depend on security protection from their clans and subclans, whose informal institutions determine the behaviors of individuals within communities. Clan and subclan collaborations go beyond security and related insurance systems.

4. Somaliland has remained independent since the SNM took control of the territory but has failed to secure international recognition so far.

5. Former SNM senior official and a former minister of information for Somaliland.

6. The Ethiopia-Somalia peace agreement, initiated by the two leaders on the sidelines of the IGAD meeting, was signed in April 1988 in Mogadishu.

7. The author did not find a clear answer whether the SNM moved to Somalia with or without the support of the Ethiopian army. SNM veteran Yusuf Ahmed Bobe insists that the SNM moved into Somalia without support from the Ethiopian army, independent of whatever the Ethiopian military officers thought about the impact of the agreement between Mengistu and Siad, recognizing that Mengistu would put their leader under arrest and dismantle the SNM, affecting operations and threatening the group's survival. Ambassador Fisseha Yimer asserts that the SNM would have faced serious logistical challenges in traveling all the way to Somalia and capturing Burao without the Ethiopian military's support but states that the action might have been taken without explicit orders from the commander in chief of Ethiopia. But when Mengistu addressed the Ethiopian people, he indicated that Somalia's collapse was of his own making and said that he was expediting the collapse of the regime in Khartoum. However, the latter

worked out in reverse eventually, as his own regime was ousted with Sudan's assistance.

8. Ethiopia's efforts in the 1990s emanated from a commitment to peace and gratitude to the Somali people who hosted the Ethiopian rebel group leaders, many of whom used Somali passports and obtained financial and logistical support from Somalia during the struggle against the Derg. But those efforts did not achieve their ultimate objective of peace. On the one hand, the Somali faction leaders failed to unite and on the other hand, the international community was not united on how to address the crisis in Somalia. This generated competing and contradictory efforts, creating an opportunity for forum shopping. A US-led humanitarian intervention in 1992, which the UN peace enforcement mission followed, ended in absolute failure, triggering a withdrawal of the UN peace enforcement mission from Somalia in 1994. Similar reconciliation efforts did not make progress. While the frustration continued, a developing Islamic insurgency brought a new dimension into the security dynamics, triggering a different response.

9. The archives of the Ministry of Foreign Affairs indicate the details of the efforts and the engagements made at that time.

10. A lot has been said about this incident; *Black Hawk Down*, a 2001 film directed by Ridley Scott, recreated the events.

Contributors

Abdeta Dribssa Beyene, PhD, is the executive director of the Centre for Dialogue, Research and Cooperation (CDRC). His professional experience began with Ethiopia's Ministry of Foreign Affairs, which included serving as director general for African Affairs until 2012, head of the Conflict Early Warning and Response Unit (April 2009–November 2010), chief of the Cabinet at the Ministry of Foreign Affairs (July 2006–August 2008), Ethiopia's Special Envoy to Somalia (August 2008–March 2009), and head of the Ethiopian Trade Office in Hargeisa (April 2002–June 2006), as well as officer for Somalia and Ethiopia's neighboring states. He also served as chief of staff of the IGAD-led Mediation Team for the Republic of South Sudan and briefly for the Joint Monitoring and Evaluation Commission to oversee the Agreement to Resolve the Conflict in South Sudan. He holds a PhD from Northwestern University.

Abubeker Yasin hails from the Afar pastoralists of Ethiopia, holds an MA in international relations from Addis Ababa University, and is a cofounder of Samara University, where he currently lectures in the College of Social Sciences and Humanities.

Ann Fitz-Gerald, PhD, is a professor of international security and the director of the Balsillie School of International Affairs in Canada. Prior to commencing her PhD, she completed degrees in commerce, political science, and strategic studies. She has worked in the financial sector and with the Government of Canada's Ministry of Foreign Affairs and held posts at the Lester B. Pearson Canadian International Peacekeeping Training Centre and NATO Headquarters. In addition to course director and deanery appointments, in 2018 she became the university's director of Defence and Security Leadership. Ann has worked regularly in Ethiopia for the past sixteen years.

Awet T. Weldemichael, PhD, LLM, is professor of history and Queen's National Scholar at Queen's University in Kingston, Ontario, and Hubert H. Humphrey Distinguished Visiting Professor at Macalester College in Saint Paul, Minnesota. He most recently authored *Piracy in Somalia: Violence and Development in the Horn of Africa* (Cambridge University Press, 2019).

Berhanu Abegaz, PhD, is professor of economics at the College of William & Mary. He specializes in development economics and comparative economics. His latest books are *A Tributary Model of State Formation: Ethiopia, 1600–2015* (Springer, 2018) and *Industrial Development in Africa: Mapping Industrialization Pathways for a Leaping Leopard* (Routledge, 2018).

Camille Louise Pellerin, PhD, is researcher and lecturer in development studies in the Department of Government, Uppsala University. Her research and teaching interests span political participation, civil society-state relations, democratization and political institutions in Africa, economic development, and public sector reform. Camille obtained her PhD in development studies from the London School of Economics and Political Science in 2019, based on her monograph *The Politics of Public Silence: Civil Society-State Relations under the EPRDF Regime*. Camille, together with colleagues, has been awarded a research grant by the Swedish Research Council for the project *Shades of Civic Activism: State-Labour Relations in India and Ethiopia in 2020*. Her latest article, "The Aspiring Developmental State and Business Associations in Ethiopia—(Dis-)embedded Autonomy?" was published by the *Journal of Modern African Studies*.

Charles Schaefer, PhD, is professor of international studies and history at Valparaiso University in Indiana. He grew up in Ethiopia as the son of missionaries. His mentor in graduate school was Donald Levine, and a publication that foregrounds this chapter that he coedited and authored is *The Ethiopian Red Terror Trials: Transitional Justice Challenged* (James Currey, 2009).

Christopher Clapham, PhD, is based at the Centre of African Studies, University of Cambridge. His most recent book is *The Horn of Africa: State Formation and Decay* (Oxford University Press, 2017). He has also written on the Haile Selassie and Derg regimes.

Dereje Feyissa holds a PhD in social anthropology from Martin Luther University. He has been a research fellow of Osaka University, the Max Planck Institute, and the University of Bayreuth Centre of International Excellence "Alexander von Humboldt." Currently he is a research and policy advisor to the Life & Peace Institute in Uppsala, Sweden. Dereje has extensive experience in research on a wide range of topics, such as ethnicity and conflict, religion and politics, the political economy of development, and borderland studies. He is the author and coeditor of several books, as well as numerous articles in peer-reviewed journals and edited volumes.

Kebadu Mekonnen Gebremariam, PhD, is assistant professor of philosophy at Addis Ababa University, where he teaches social and political philosophy. Prior to that, he worked as a visiting scholar at the World Health Organization's Department of Ageing and Life Course, developing an ethical framework for the WHO's global strategy on ageing and health. Kebadu received his PhD from the Center for Ethics at the University of Zurich. He also holds an MA in political and economic philosophy from the University of Bern and a BA in philosophy from Addis Ababa University. He is presently working on a monograph entitled *Human Dignity and Moral Rights*, which is an extension of his doctoral dissertation.

Kenichi Ohno, PhD, is a professor at the National Graduate Institute for Policy Studies, Tokyo. He obtained a BA and MA in economics from Hitotsubashi University, Tokyo, and has an economics PhD from Stanford University. He worked at the International Monetary Fund and taught at the University of Tsukuba and Saitama University before taking up his current position. His main interest is comparative study on industrial policy formulation and its execution in Asia and Africa. He has conducted regular policy dialogue with Vietnam (since 1995) and Ethiopia (since 2008). His recent books include *Learning to Industrialize: From Given Growth to Policy-Aided Value Creation* (Routledge, 2013), *The History of Japanese Economic Development* (Routledge, 2018), and the coedited *How Nations Learn: Technological Learning, Industrial Policy, and Catch-Up* (Oxford University Press, 2019).

Lars Christian Moller is a manager at the Macroeconomics, Trade and Investment Global Practice, Africa Region, the World Bank Group, Washington, DC. Between 2012 and 2015, he was the lead economist and program leader for Ethiopia, based in Addis Ababa. He can be contacted at lmoller@worldbank.org.

Mamo E. Mihretu is a senior adviser on policy reforms to the prime minister of Ethiopia and Ethiopia's chief trade negotiator. Prior to taking his post in 2018, Mamo was a senior project manager at the World Bank Group from 2010 to 2018 and has more than sixteen years of experience in economic policy reforms. His past roles include lecturer at Addis Ababa University and other Ethiopian academic institutions. Mamo studied leadership, public administration, and economic development at the Kennedy School of Government at Harvard University. Additionally, he completed his postgraduate studies in law at the Universities of Pretoria and Amsterdam.

Melaku Geboye Desta is professor of international economic law at Leicester De Montfort Law School in England (since 2013), currently on leave working for the United Nations Economic Commission for Africa (ECA) as principal regional advisor in regional integration and trade. From 2001 to 2013 Melaku served as lecturer/senior lecturer and reader in international economic law at the University of Dundee, Scotland. Between January 2016 and September 2018, Melaku also served as senior technical adviser to the CEO of the APRM Secretariat in Johannesburg. Melaku is a lawyer by training and holds a PhD in international economic law. Melaku has published widely in the fields of international economic law and policy, with a particular focus on the interests of developing countries in general and those in Africa in particular. Melaku has consulted for a number of international organizations and national governments and served as arbitrator in international disputes. Melaku is a founding coeditor of the *Ethiopian Yearbook of International Law* (EtYIL), which has been published annually since 2016.

Nigusie Angessa is a program manager at the Peace and Development Center in Ethiopia. He recently coauthored "Challenges in Managing Land-Related Conflicts in East Hararghe Zone of Oromia Regional State, Ethiopia" (*Society & Natural Resources*, 2017), "Transforming Technocratic Practitioners' Thinking Toward Responsible Management of Land-

Related Conflicts: Experience from Eastern Ethiopia" (*Research in Post-Compulsory Education*, 2017) and "Integrating Reflective Problem-Solving and Mindfulness to Promote Organizational Adaptation toward Conflict Sensitivity" (*Transformative Education*, 2017).

Sehin Teferra, PhD, is the founder of Setaweet Movement, an Ethiopian feminist network that strives for gender justice. A Mo Ibrahim Scholar, Sehin has authored, most recently, a chapter in *Feminist Parenting: Perspectives from Africa and Beyond* (Demeter, 2019).

Semir Yusuf, PhD, is a senior researcher in the Horn of Africa Programme at the Institute for Security Studies, Addis Ababa. His research focuses on conflict and peace studies, transition politics, authoritarian politics, and Ethiopian studies. Yusuf obtained his PhD from the University of Toronto in comparative politics and development studies. His MA and BA were in political science and international relations. Prior to joining the ISS, he taught political science at different universities, including Addis Ababa University and the University of Toronto.

Senai W. Andemariam, PhD candidate at Maastricht University, is a former judge and now an assistant professor at the School of Law in Asmara, Eritrea. He earned his LLB from the University of Asmara and his LLM from Georgetown University as a Fulbright Scholar. He is a member of the editorial team of the *Journal of Eritrean Studies*. He has published with reputable journals at Oxford University Press, Cambridge University Press, Brill, De Gruyter, Aethiopica, and others. He has recently presented parts of this chapter at the African Studies centers at the Universities of Oxford and Cambridge.

Shimelis Bonsa Gulema has a PhD from UCLA and is currently an associate professor of history and Africana studies at Stony Brook University. His research interests include modern and contemporary African history and politics, with a focus on Ethiopia and the Horn of Africa. He has published his research findings as monographs, articles, and book chapters.

Solomon Ayele Dersso, PhD, founding director of Amani Africa—a policy research, training, and consulting think tank—is a recognized legal scholar and peace and security analyst with specialization in, among others, transitional justice. Adjunct professor at Addis Ababa University College of Law and Governance Studies, he led the drafting of the African Union Transitional Justice Policy and the African Commission on Human and Peoples' Rights Study on Transitional Justice. He serves as editorial board member of the *International Journal of Transitional Justice* and has been appointed as a member of the Ethiopian Reconciliation Commission.

Tom Lavers is a senior lecturer (associate professor) in politics and development at the University of Manchester's Global Development Institute. His research focuses on how land tenure, agrarian change, and social policy shape state-society relations and has been published in leading journals in the field. His most recent book is the coedited *The Politics of Social Protection in Eastern and Southern Africa* (Oxford University Press, 2019, open access).

William Davison is a British journalist and political analyst who is based in Addis Ababa. He was Ethiopia correspondent for Bloomberg News from 2010–17 and also published news analysis regularly for *The Guardian*, Al Jazeera, the *Christian Science Monitor*, and other international media. In August 2018, William established Ethiopia Insight website, which, under his management, has rapidly become one of the foremost sources of English-language analysis and commentary on Ethiopian affairs. Since April 2019 he has been the senior analyst for Ethiopia at the International Crisis Group and has so far been the main author of prominent ICG reports on Ethiopia's transition and the Sidama regional statehood campaign.

Yonatan T. Fessha (LLB, LLM, PhD) is a professor of law at the University of the Western Cape in South Africa. His teaching and research focuses on examining the relevance of constitutional design in dealing with the challenges of divided societies. He has published widely on matters pertaining to but not limited to federalism, constitutional design, autonomy and politicized ethnicity. His publications include *Ethnic Diversity and Federalism: Constitution Making in South Africa and Ethiopia* (Routledge, 2016) and the coedited *Federalism and the Courts in Africa: Design and Impact in Comparative Perspective* (Routledge, 2020). He has contributed to constitution-building projects, including in Sudan, South Sudan, and Yemen. He was a Michigan Grotius Research Scholar at the University of Michigan and recipient of the Andrew W. Mellon Postdoctoral Fellowship in the Humanities. He is currently a Marie Curie Fellow at the Institute for Comparative Federalism at Eurac Research.

Index

A

Abay Tsehaye, 446
Abaya, 434
Abdi Mohammed Omar (Abdi Illey), 24–25, 448
Abdi, Muse Bihi, 495
Abdulaziz Al Saud medal, 493
Abdulaziz, Salman bin (king), 30, 493
Abiy Ahmed: Afar and, 449–52, 455; CSOs and, 142; defense and, 463, 476–77, 537; economy and, 263, 270, 292, 347, 510; Eritrea and, 30–32, 449, 489–97, 501, 505, 512, 523, 530–43, 545n11; Isaias Afwerki and, 30, 32, 190, 491–95, 501, 530–40, 543, 545; liberalization and, 178–81, 188–92, 455; *Medemer* philosophy of, 86, 112, 114–17; media and, 188–91; Mengistu Hailemariam return and, 541; Nobel Peace Prize and, 512; reconciliation under, 221, 241; reforms under, 249–51, 448, 476–77; rise to power of, 2, 31, 60, 177, 199, 373, 403–4, 439, 448, 489, 523, 534; TPLF and, 496, 534; transition under, 50, 177, 199–201, 250–51, 403–5, 448, 455, 541–42; women and, 123–26
absolutism, 59, 61–62, 65, 73, 117n1, 194, 295
ACMA (Automotive Component Manufacturers Association) (India), 352
ACSO (Agency for Civil Society Organizations), 157–58. *See also* ChSA
Adama, 142, 174, 290, 293, 311
Addis Ababa agreement, 559–60. *See also* Somalia
Addis Ababa–Djibouti Railway, 257, 311
Addis Ababa Light Rail, 257, 343
Addis Ababa Master City Plan, 405. *See also* master plan (Addis Ababa)
Addis Ababa University, 186, 297n5, 478
Addis-Adama-Dire triangle, 293
Addisu Legesse, 322n1
Addis Maleda, 188

587

Adem Mohammad (general), 477, 538
Aden, Gulf of, 528
Aden, port of, 499
ADFM (Amhara Democratic Forces Movement), 410, 538
Adi Kuala-Rama (border), 494, 512
ADLI (Agricultural Development Led Industrialization), 287–88, 301–6, 320, 322n5
Administrative Boundaries and Identity Issues Commission, 412–13
Adonis, Andrew, 184
ADP (Amhara Democratic Party), 24, 101, 175, 179, 181, 405, 409, 413–14
Adwa, Battle of, 241, 366, 374, 501
AESM (All-Ethiopia Socialist Movement), 95–96. *See also* MEISON
Afan Oromo, 427, 435
Afar, 26–28, 102, 280, 290, 307, 416, 445–59, 477, 535
Afar-Issa/Somali conflict, 28, 446, 453–54
Afar Liberation Front, 445, 451
Afar Liberation Movement, 500
Afar Liyu Police, 451
Afar National Democratic Party, 28, 445–46, 449–53, 458
Afar People's Party, 451
Afar Youth Movement (Xuko Cina), 449–50
Africa: colonial, 39, 44, 46–47, 469; defense in, 466–67, 472, 478, 480, 556; Eritrea-Ethiopia rapprochement and, 512, 531; Ethiopia and, 374, 376; ethnic pluralism and, 51, 105; governing elites of, 46; Hegelian definition of, 390n8; Japan and, 345–46, 349; political transition in, 56–57, 72, 201–2, 204; postcolonial, 42, 63, 65, 71, 377; precolonial, 227; railways in, 257. *See also* Horn of Africa
African Continental Free Trade Area, 178, 271
African Security Sector Network, 466
African traditional religion, 225
African Union, 42, 345, 465, 472, 476, 479, 492, 528, 531
African Union Mission in Somalia, 562, 565–66
African Union Transitional Justice Policy, 200, 210, 215
Afrocentrism, 375
Agency for Civil Society Organizations, 157–58. *See also* ChSA
Agreement on Peace, Friendship and Comprehensive Cooperation between Eritrea and Ethiopia, 30, 493, 504, 507. *See also* Jeddah Agreement
Agricultural Development Led Industrialization, 287–88, 301–6, 320, 322n5
agriculture: commercialization of, 62, 64, 322n3; economic growth and, 178, 252, 260,

291, 304; labor and, 280, 318; land use and, 303, 306–7, 313, 315–16; subsistence, 19, 41, 288; technology and, 64

agropastoralism, 307, 429. *See also* pastoralism

Ahmad ibn Ibrahim (imam), 395

Ahmed, Abdullahi Yusuf (colonel), 561

Ahmed Sultan, 454

AIAI (Al-Itihaad Al-Islamiya), 33, 557, 571

Aideed, Mohamed Farah (general), 560–61

Air Force, 477. *See also* ENDF

Aisha Mohammed, 450–51, 477

ALF (Afar Liberation Front), 445, 451

Algiers Agreement (2000), 490, 505–7, 513, 527

Al-Itihaad Al-Islamiya, 33, 557, 571

Ali II (*ras bitwädäd*), 234–36

All-Ethiopia Socialist Movement, 95–96. *See also* MEISON

Al-Shabaab, 33, 549, 565–67, 569, 571, 573

Ambo, 187, 361

Amhara Democratic Forces Movement, 410, 538

Amhara Democratic Party, 24, 101, 175, 179, 181, 405, 409, 413–14

Amhara (people), 171, 363, 394n29, 405

Amhara (region): constitution of, 102, 435; EPRDF and, 177, 201; Eritrea and, 410–11, 413, 526, 535, 537–38; ethnicities in, 102–3; hegemony of, 95; land use and, 305–6, 309, 313–15, 322n7; poverty in, 280; protests in, 473, 480, 496, 528; regional disputes and, 24, 410, 545n8; regional government of, 417n1; resistance to vaccination in, 130; Tigray and, 175, 191, 409, 413, 545n8; TPLF and, 180

Amhara National Democratic Movement, 175. *See also* ADP

Amharic, 46–47, 85, 95, 203–4, 233, 491

AMISOM (African Union Mission in Somalia), 562, 565–66

ANDP (Afar National Democratic Party), 28, 445–46, 449–53, 458

Andreas Eshete, 96, 108, 110–11, 113–14, 307, 369, 389n6

Annales school, 389n3

anti-republicanism, 10, 91

anti-terrorism law, 60, 173, 190, 416, 568

Anuak massacre, 103

AOTS (Association for Overseas Technical Cooperation and Sustainable Partnerships), 350–51

apartheid, 225–27, 229

Appiah, Kwame Anthony, 10, 104, 106–7, 109, 113

Aptidon, Hassan Gouled, 558

Arabian Gulf, 30, 497–99

Arab Spring, 56, 172, 498
Arendt, Hannah, 88, 96, 103, 107
Argentina, 355n1
aristocracy, 62–65, 75n5, 87, 238
Armenia, 355n1
Asaminew Tsige, 181
Asfaw Wossen (crown prince), 99
Asmara, 413, 490–97, 501, 509, 511, 523, 527, 529–41. *See also* Asmara agreement; Eritrea; Isaias Afwerki
Asmara agreement, 30–31, 489, 500–1, 503–6
Assab, port of, 290, 493, 499–500, 525, 527, 529, 535, 539–40
assimilationism, 96
Association for Overseas Technical Cooperation and Sustainable Partnerships, 350–51
AU (African Union), 42, 345, 465, 472, 476, 479, 492, 528, 531. *See also* AMISOM; AUTJP
authoritarianism: democratic institutions and, 58; EPRDF and, 66, 170–71, 176–77, 180; government responsiveness and, 141; history of as impediment to democracy, 8, 217, 368–69, 372; homogenization and, 378; in Horn of Africa, 178; justification for, 42, 172; in Kenya, 58; relapse to, 67, 70, 77n16; revolutionary warfare and, 65, 72; rule of law and, 76n13; structural and institutional factors for, 59; transition to democracy and, 200-1; urban centers and, 366
AUTJP (African Union Transitional Justice Policy), 200, 210, 215
Automotive Component Manufacturers Association (India), 352
Awal Arba, 450, 454
Awash (dry port), 290
Awash River, 448
Awate, Hamid Idris, 97
Axum, 47
Ayder Referral Hospital, 131
Ayshal, Battle of, 236
AZAPO v. the President of the Republic of South Africa, 210

B

Badme, 527
Bahrain, 498
Baidoa, 562–63
Balcha (*dejazmach*), 47–48
Bangladesh, 268, 280, 353
Bärara, 383, 394n29, 394n30, 395n31
Bashir, Omar al-, 490, 500–1
BBC (British Broadcasting Corporation), 184–85
Belgian Congo, 46–47
Belgium, 46–47, 188n8
Belt and Road Initiative, 499
Benishangul-Gumuz, 24, 102, 307, 311, 457
Berbera, port of, 290, 499
Berhanena Selam, 392n19
Berhanu Nega, 180
Beru Aligaz, 235

Biko, Ntsiki, 225
Biko, Steve, 225
Birbirsa Kojowa woreda, 434, 439
Bishoftu, 174, 187
BKPM (Indonesia), 342, 356n8
Black Hawk Down, 561, 578n10
Bobe, Yusuf Ahmed, 559, 577
Boeing (corporation), 185
Bolivia v. Chile, 509
Bor, 427
Borana, 427–28
Bossaso conference, 561
Boutros-Ghali, Boutros, 561
Braudel, Fernand, 389n3
Brazil, 287
Brexit, 184
British Broadcasting Corporation, 184–85
buffer zones, 33–34, 549–54, 557–58, 564, 570–71, 574
Bule Hora woreda, 434
Burao, 559, 577n7
bureaucratization, 62–63
Burundi, 566

C

Cairo, 97, 495, 564
Cairo agreement (1997), 561–62, 570
Cambodia, 100, 335–36, 352
Canada, 118–19n8, 146, 160n7
capitalism, 50, 63–64, 275, 278, 284, 374, 376–77, 390n9
Catalonia, 407–8
CBE (Commercial Bank of Ethiopia), 253–54, 282

CDR (customary dispute resolution), 227–28
CEDAW (Convention on the Elimination of All Forms of Discrimination against Women), 124
central Asia, 57
Central Command, 29, 477
centralism: Afar and, 458; army and, 45; democratization and, 415; Derg and, 40, 48, 65; EPRDF and, 161n10, 366, 404–5, 409; Ethiopian identity and, 47; Haile Selassie and, 40, 65; land use and, 63, 306; reform and, 45, 49; revolution and, 45; self-rule and, 67; student movement and, 45
Centre for the Democratic Control of Armed Forces, Geneva, 465, 487n1
Chiang Kai-shek, 337
Charities and Societies Agency, 148–54, 155–59. *See also* ACSO
Charities and Societies Proclamation (2009), 11–12, 60, 127, 142–64, 416
China: Belt and Road Initiative of, 499; debt to, 256; economic growth in, 291, 295, 336; Hong Kong as part of, 355n2; industrialization and, 338; labor productivity of, 280; Marxism-Leninism and, 100; Red Sea access by, 513n1; rev-

olution and, 44–45, 52; S-L-P sequence and, 293; Taiwan and, 356n10; transition in, 337; transportation services and, 267; Trump administration and, 529

Chingaf (miscarriage) Marxism, 100

Chomsky, Noam, 184

Christianity, Orthodox, 43, 46–47, 137

ChSA (Charities and Societies Agency), 148–54, 155–59. *See also* ACSO

CII (Confederation of Indian Industry), 352

civil society organizations, 11–12, 141–52, 154–61, 475, 478, 481

clanism, 59, 453

coffee, 258, 282, 285, 428, 439

colonialism: Afar and, 447; African nations and, 46–47, 63, 392n20; Ethiopia and, 95–96, 117n2, 367; ethnic pluralism and, 51; exceptionalism and, 374, 376; independence from, 39, 43–44, 47, 367, 469; of Italy, 32, 239; Kenya and, 207; modern Ethiopia and, 363; Somalia and, 555

Commercial Bank of Ethiopia, 253–54, 282

Committee to Protect Journalists, 173, 181, 188

communitarianism, 92–93

confederation, 25, 109, 118n8, 414

Confederation Helvetica, 118n8

Confederation of Indian Industry, 352

Congo, Belgian, 46–47

constitution (1995), 85, 102, 106, 425, 431

Conte, Giuseppe, 494, 539

Cotonou Agreement, 160n9

council of elders (*shimaglewoch*), 161n10

counterterrorism, 464

coup d'état: 1, 98–99, 118n4, 234, 250, 524

Crimean War, 43

Croatia, 355n1

CSOs (civil society organizations), 11–12, 141–52, 154–61, 475, 478, 481

Cuba, 52

customary dispute resolution, 227–28

cyber and space command, 29, 477

D

Däbrä Tabor, Battle of, 235–36

Daniel Gebreselassie, 161n10

Daraso, 427

Dawit (king), 394–95n30

DBE (Development Bank of Ethiopia), 253, 282

DCAF (Geneva Centre for the Democratic Control of Armed Forces), 465, 483n1

Debay Sima-Bure (border), 493, 512

Debretsion Gebremichael, 535

Debt Sustainability Analysis, 255–56, 264
decentralization, 160n3, 342, 562, 571
defense reform, 28–29, 451, 463–83
defense research and transformation unit, 472
Degler, Carl, 385, 387
democracy: Abiy Ahmed and, 3–5, 35, 178–79; Afar and, 27, 452, 456–57; authoritarianism and, 8; conflict and, 553; constitutional federalism and, 415; Derg and, 49; economic reform and, 17; EPRDF and, 1–2, 27, 49, 66, 143, 170, 173, 282, 445; gender and, 127, 130; Hailemariam Desalegn and, 170; international donors and, 143, 152; media and, 13, 184, 191; Meles Zenawi and, 170; Mengistu Hailemariam and, 45; Middle East and, 172; nation building and, 63–65, 373; Oromia and, 176; republicanism and, 90–93, 108, 113; rights and, 142, 370, 436, 446, 457; rule of law and, 128; West and, 62–63, 223
democratization: Abiy Ahmed reforms and, 86, 403; Afar and, 454–56; autocracy and, 58; constitutional federalism and, 415; constitutional reform and, 417n3; defense reform and, 473; elections and, 58–60; elites and, 59; EPRDF stunting of, 170, 416; FANSPS and, 470; mass societies and, 145; media and, 182, 191, 194; mediation through, 182; nationalism and, 75n8; Oromia and, 176, 179; political pluralism through, 415; as stabilizing process, 181; state and, 63, 65, 70–71; TPLF and, 180; transition and, 8–9, 56, 61, 67, 169; transitional justice and, 215
demographic dividend, 259, 261
Deng Xiaoping, 337
Derg: Addis Ababa master plan and, 394n28; authoritarianism under, 3; centralism and, 40, 48; class solidarity and, 102; economic growth under, 252, 281–82; Eritrea and, 525–26; ethnicities and, 49; executions by, 4, 223, 541; fall of, 15, 49, 97, 101, 175, 335, 424, 479, 501, 562; Gedeo-Guji conflict and, 430; land reform under, 20, 46, 302, 314, 320, 323n13, 369; Marxism and, 97, 100; METEC and, 475; nation building under, 48; "national question" and, 85, 87; reforms under, 1, 7; repressive nature of, 50, 65; socialism under, 369, 371, 389; Somalia and, 556, 559, 578n8; TPLF and, 469, 501, 525; transitional justice after, 209–10, 214, 223; transition under, 1,

40, 469; transition after, 40, 49, 66, 175, 177, 190, 201
development: Abiy Ahmed and, 177; in Afar, 27, 446, 449–50, 456; of African Continental Free Trade Area, 178; in Asia, 295, 296n2, 301, 333; aspirations to, 345–46; authoritarianism and, 42; colonialism and, 39; CSOs and, 12, 143, 145, 154–56, 158–59, 160n3; defense and, 464–65, 471, 473–76; diaspora and, 292; economic growth and, 21, 253, 339–40; EPRDF and, 1, 143–46, 148, 152, 159, 170–71, 178, 291, 301–2, 319; Eritrea and, 31, 497, 500–2, 504; Eurocentrism and, 362; five-year plans for, 43; gender equality and, 127, 133, 135; government and, 22; historical location and, 367; Horn of Africa and, 492; infrastructure and, 252; media and, 185–86; mindset and, 354; modern state and, 7, 362–64, 366, 368–71, 376; nationalism and, 295; NGOs and, 151; partnership model for, 285; politics and, 342, 346, 361; public investment and, 17; reforms and, 267–70; Somali and, 192, 556; state model of, 2, 17–20, 35, 52, 143, 146, 149–51, 159, 250, 255, 276, 301–10, 316–20, 323n15; strategy for, 19, 278, 281, 303–4, 307–12, 319; Taiwan and, 341; western aid and, 287–88
Development Bank of Ethiopia, 253, 282
Development Policy Financing, 19, 267, 270–71
diaspora, 4, 174, 285, 292, 450, 497
Djibouti: 30, 178, 446–48, 492–93, 498–99, 502, 529–30, 558
Dogali, Battle of, 239, 241, 243n4
domestic violence, 129, 138, 156
DPF (Development Policy Financing), 19, 267, 270–71
DPRK (Democratic People's Republic of Korea), 100, 500
Dreyfus affair, 9, 89–90
DSA (Debt Sustainability Analysis), 255-56, 264
Dubai Ports World, 498
Dutch disease, 339
Dutch Revolt, 117n1

E

East Guji Zone, 424, 427, 434, 439, 442
ECF (Extended Credit Facility), 271
EDHS (Ethiopia Demographic and Health Survey), 129–30
education: decentralization and, 160n3, 342; economic growth and, 252, 263; Eritrea and, 510, 526; females and, 11, 127, 130–39, 259; ideology and, 372; Japanese *kosen* system and,

356n9; military and, 472–73, 476, 479–81; workforce and, 260–61, 280, 290, 318
Education Development Roadmap, 134, 136–38
EEBC (Eritrea-Ethiopia Boundary Commission), 490, 506, 523, 527–28, 530
EECC (Eritrea-Ethiopia Claims Commission), 506, 527
EEP (Ethiopian Electric Power), 250, 254, 282
EFFORT (Endowment Fund for the Rehabilitation of Tigray), 283
Egypt, 33, 189, 239, 278, 498, 501–2, 529, 558, 561
elections: 2005 crisis and, 143, 149, 152, 160n2, 170–73, 183, 190, 416; 2010 shutout in, 173; 2020 campaign for, 125, 183, 315, 417n3; democratization and, 59–60, 145; EPRDF and, 66, 170–74, 223; protests and, 160n2, 174; republicanism and, 88, 99; transition process and, 56, 58; women and, 125
ELF (Eritrean Liberation Front), 95, 97
El Salvador, 355n3
EMOND (Ethiopian Ministry of National Defense), 473, 475–76, 478–81, 483
Endeavour (*Tiret*), 283
ENDF (Ethiopia National Defense Force), 25, 29, 192, 406–8, 451, 463, 469, 472–73, 476, 478–80. *See also* Central Command; Air Force
Endowment Fund for the Rehabilitation of Tigray (*Timhit*), 283
English Revolution (1640–60), 117n1
Enlightenment, European, 87, 99, 105
Entoto, 383, 394–95
EOC (Ethiopian Orthodox Church). *See* Ethiopian Orthodox (Tawahedo) Church
EPDM (Ethiopian People's Democratic Movement), 101
Ephraim Isaac, 161n10
EPLF (Eritrean People's Liberation Front), 32, 95, 97, 424, 524–25, 544n1, 558
EPRDF (Ethiopian People's Revolutionary Democratic Front): Afar and, 446, 456–57; centralization under, 161n10; CSOs and, 12, 141–59, 160n1; democracy and, 170–73; economic development and, 19, 281–84, 287, 291, 301–3, 319; elections and, 143, 171–74; Eritrea and, 490–91, 497, 501, 505, 525, 528–30, 535; intergovernmental relations under, 24; land policy and, 315, 320, 323n13; media and, 174, 179, 181, 185–87, 192; METEC and, 475; military and, 469, 474; Oromia and, 176–77, 186,

544n1; reconciliation under, 223; reforms under, 1–2, 7, 40, 49–50, 65–67, 289–90n6; repression under, 11, 141; republicanism and, 9; Somali and, 556; Somalia and, 559, 562; TPLF sidelining and, 179–80. *See also* Abiy Ahmed; Prosperity Party
EPRP (Ethiopian People's Revolutionary Party), 95
Eritrea-Ethiopia Boundary Commission, 490, 506, 523, 527–28, 530
Eritrea-Ethiopia Claims Commission, 506, 527
Eritrea: authoritarianism and, 58–59, 178; Djibouti and, 30; Haile Selassie and, 469; government instability and, 469; independence and, 32, 45, 95–97, 389; peace dividend and, 252, 482; as rebel refuge, 66; revolution of, 32, 96–97; youth and, 31. *See also* Asmara; Eritrea-Ethiopia rapprochement; Eritrean-Ethiopian War; Isaias Afwerki
Eritrea-Ethiopia rapprochement, 4, 28–35, 178, 249, 409–11, 489–512, 524–46, 575–76
Eritrean-Ethiopian War, 252, 446, 469, 479, 490, 510–11, 527–28, 534, 541–42, 545n3. *See also* Eritrea-Ethiopia rapprochement

Eritrean Liberation Front, 95, 97
Eritrean National Chamber of Commerce, 533
Eritrean People's Liberation Front, 32, 95, 97, 424, 524–525, 544n1, 558
ESAT (Ethiopian Satellite Television and Radio), 170, 188–89
Eskinder Nega, 172, 183, 187
ESLSE (Ethiopian Shipping and Logistics Service Enterprise), 250, 268
ESM (Ethiopian Student Movement): antiestablishmentarianism and, 381; attempted coup (1960) and, 98, 118n4; Derg and, 97; ethnicity and, 425; land question and, 86, 94; Marxism-Leninism of, 48, 50–51, 96, 373, 393; national question and, 86, 96; radicalization of, 390n10; revolution and, 44–45, 94, 98; state and, 96; TPLF and, 50
essentialism, 87, 92, 104, 106–7, 117, 127, 377, 381–82
Esterhazy, Ferdinand Walsin (major), 89
Ethiopia Demographic and Health Survey, 129–30
Ethiopia-Japan Industrial Policy Dialogue, 333, 347
Ethiopian Airlines, 30, 185, 250, 491, 501, 531–32
Ethiopia National Defense Force. *See* ENDF

Ethiopian Broadcasting Authority, 188
Ethiopian Broadcasting Corporation, 544n3
Ethiopian Citizens for Social Justice, 417n1
Ethiopian Democratic Officers' Revolutionary Movement, 101
Ethiopian Electric Power, 250, 254, 282
Ethiopian Federal Police, 25, 29, 130, 186, 406, 410–14, 470, 473–74, 478–80
Ethiopianism, 112, 362, 367, 375, 385–87. *See also* pan-Ethiopianism
Ethiopian Orthodox (Tawahedo) Church, 48, 100, 235. *See also* Christianity, Orthodox
Ethiopian People's Democratic Movement, 101
Ethiopian People's Revolutionary Democratic Front. *See* EPRDF
Ethiopian People's Revolutionary Party, 95
Ethiopian Revolution, 1, 40, 44, 94, 98–99, 101, 118n4, 177, 201, 501
Ethiopian Satellite Television and Radio, 170, 188–89
Ethiopian Shipping and Logistics Service Enterprise, 250, 268
Ethiopian Student Movement. *See* ESM
Ethiopian Sugar Corporation, 256–57, 283
Ethiopian Television, 170
Ethiopian Women Lawyers Association, 127
Ethiopia Tikdem (Ethiopia first), 97
Ethiopis, 188
Ethio Telecom, 250, 268, 282
ethnic cleansing, 103, 308
ethnic federalism: Afar and, 28, 446; conflict and, 26, 103, 319, 371, 424–25; debate over, 23; defense of, 85; institutionalization of, 7, 22, 87, 102, 108, 369, 371, 379, 445; democracy and, 108–11, 118n6; Gedeo-Guji tensions and, 427, 429, 433; intergovernmental relations and, 24; land policy and, 102, 308, 320–21; military and, 25; multinationalism and, 417n1; "national question" and, 1, 101, 175, 307; nation building and, 25, 105; Oromia and, 176; reforms and, 381, 385; regional power and, 414; self-determination and, 425; Somali and, 405–9, 415; Tigray and, 413–14; TPLF domination and, 171; "twinning relationships" and, 27
ethnicization, 2, 68, 291, 371, 379, 429, 437–38, 440, 442
ethnocentrism, 93, 115, 295, 391n16
ethnojustice, 222, 226–28, 242
ethno-nationalism: centralism and, 67; conflict and, 319; counterhegemony and, 24, 380–82;

Ethiopian empire and, 364; Ethiopian state and, 23, 65, 68–71, 75n8, 105; federalism and, 101, 417n1; liberation movements and, 22, 107; pan-Ethiopian nationalism and, 115, 380–81, 386–88, 393–94n26
EU (European Union), 152, 160–61n9, 184, 269, 417
Eurocentrism, 362, 372–74, 377
Europe: capitalism and, 64; Chinese trade and, 513n1; colonialism of, 47, 117n2, 374, 392n20; defense reform in, 464; democracy and, 62; development and, 39; economy and, 291, 293; Ethiopia and, 365–66, 374, 376–77; imperialism and, 63; modernity and, 43, 374, 389; republicanism and, 117n1; state formation and, 71; transition in, 56–57. *See also* EU
European Union, 152, 160–61n9, 184, 269, 417
EWLA (Ethiopian Women Lawyers Association), 127
exceptionalism, 362–63, 367, 374–77
Extended Credit Facility, 271

F

Facebook, 173–74, 232, 450
famine (1984), 48
Fana Broadcasting Corporation, 192
Fano, 450
FANSPS (Foreign Affairs and National Security Policy and Strategy), 470–71, 473, 475, 480
FDI (foreign direct investment): economic growth and, 334, 337–39; EPRDF and, 282, 288; federal spending and, 160n3; Indonesia and, 342, 356n8; industrial processing zones and, 290; international reserves and, 258; Japan and, 349, 351–52; for garment firms, 353; logistics and, 268; as public spending, 283; Taiwan and, 342; Vietnam and, 355
Federal Member States, 34, 566–570, 572–74. *See also* Somalia
Federal Police, Ethiopian, 25, 29, 130, 186, 406, 410–14, 470, 473–74, 478–80
female genital mutilation, 11, 156
fertility rate, 130, 259
Fetha Nägäst, 227
feudalism, 39, 62–63, 94, 96, 99–100
Finance and Economic Cooperation, Ministry of, 155, 264
Fiteh, 188
Fitsum Arega, 531–32, 539
FMS (Federal Member States), 34, 566–570, 572–74. *See also* Somalia
food aid, 19, 27, 48, 135, 278
food insecurity, 20, 304, 309, 322
Foreign Affairs and National

Security Policy and Strategy, 470–71, 473, 475, 480
foreign aid, 160n3, 287–88, 334, 338–39, 348
foreign direct investment. *See* FDI
foreign exchange, 18, 252–55, 257–60, 262–66, 271–72, 288, 291, 296, 344
France, 9–10, 43–45, 86–91, 146–47, 148, 160, 378, 389. *See also* French Revolution
French Revolution, 87, 94, 96–99
Fuga, 137
Fukuyama, Francis, 109, 116, 296n2, 390n7

G

Gabyow, 561
Gacaca, 15, 227
Gada, 426–27, 429, 440
Gaddafi, Muammar, 528
Gafat, 382, 395
Gafat Beta Israel, 137
Gambella, 103, 307, 457
Gambella People's Liberation Movement, 500
Gambia, 201
GCAO (Government Communication Affairs Office), 190–91
GCC (Gulf Cooperation Council), 498, 529, 543, 551
Gebbar system, 102, 303
Gebrehiwot Baykedagn, 43, 365, 374
Gebru Asrat, 526
Gedeb woreda, 439
Gedeogna, 427
Gedeo-Guji conflict, 25–26, 103, 118n7, 128, 311, 424–43
Gelana woreda, 434
gender-based violence, 11, 125, 127–33, 137–38, 156, 206. *See also* rape; women
gender equality, 11, 124–25, 127, 129, 132, 134, 137. *See also* women
gender parity, 60, 132. *See also* women
Geneva Conventions, 223
GERD (Grand Ethiopian Renaissance Dam), 257, 283, 287
Getachew Assefa, 180
Ghion Hotel bombing, 556
Ginbot 7, 180–81, 499, 567, 573
gizot, 234
Gondoro, 427, 433, 440
Gondar, 47, 103, 175, 471, 494
Goshi, Kohei, 349
Government Communication Affairs Office, 190–91
Govier, Trudy, 229
Grand Ethiopian Renaissance Dam, 257, 283, 287
Growth and Development Commission (2008), 253
GTP I and II (Growth and Transformation Plan), 304, 470, 473
Guatemala, 355n1
Guelleh, Ismaïl Omar, 446, 493
Guji. *See* Gedeo-Guji conflict
Gulf Cooperation Council, 498, 529, 543, 551

gult, 63–64, 234, 241
Gumuz, 103, 137. *See also*, Benishangul-Gumuz
Gurage, 102
Guterres, António, 30, 491, 493

H

Habta-Giyorgis (*fitawrari*), 233
Haddis Alemayehu, 100
Hadi, Abdrabbuh Mansur, 498
Hadith, 391n15
Hadiya Zone, 427
Hagere Mariam district, 103
Hagos (*ras*), 240
Hailemariam Desalegn, 50, 170, 177–80, 190, 250, 345, 496, 529–33, 541
Haile Selassie I (emperor): attempted coup against, 98; constitution and, 43; Eritrea and, 540; Gedeo-Guji conflict and, 430; land use and, 64; military of, 468–69; modernization and, 366; overthrow of, 1, 87, 94, 501, 524; reform under, 7, 40, 43; stability under, 50
Hambela Wamena woreda, 434
Harari, 102, 131, 457
Hargeisa, 495, 499, 559, 570
Hawassa, 135, 142, 260, 471, 492, 537
Hegel, Georg Wilhelm Friedrich, 112–13, 362, 372, 374–75, 377, 390
highland-lowland dichotomy, 23, 27, 323n13
Hinduism, 225

HIV, 130
Hobsbawm, Eric, 389
Hollande, François, 88
homogeneity, 24, 94, 104, 379, 382
Hong Kong, 336, 355
Horn of Africa: Afar people and, 447; authoritarianism in, 178; conflict in, 552–53; democracy in, 59; East African peace and, 530; Eritrea-Ethiopia rapprochement and, 489, 492–94, 497, 502–3, 512, 542, 573–74; Eritrea's image in, 500; Ethiopian transition and, 34, 250, 574; failed states in, 550–51, 553, 554; modernity and, 39; political transition in, 34, 56–57; port access in, 288; Qatar and, 498; security in, 4, 33, 550–52, 570, 572–73; Somalia and, 551, 555; superpowers and, 552; US-Sino relations in, 529
House of Federation, 25, 147, 407, 413
House of Peoples' Representatives, 157, 477, 530, 539
Houthi fighters, 498
human rights violations: Derg and, 1; Eritrea and, 497, 500, 511, 536; federal intervention and, 25, 406, 418n4; Gedeo-Guji conflict and, 437; NISS and, 478; reconciliation and, 213, 215, 221–23; transitional justice and, 14, 15, 204–9, 213, 215; in Somali, 24–25, 418n5

Hussein, Abdul Majid, 557
Hyundai (corporation), 343

I

ICU (Islamic Courts Union), 557, 562–65

IGAD (Intergovernmental Authority on Development), 33, 476, 501–2, 531, 556, 558, 562–63, 573, 577n6

identity: Afar and, 447; conflict and, 431, 433–34; cultural, 204; of Ethiopia, 4, 23, 25, 364, 375–76, 115, 386, 394; ethnic, 2, 7, 10, 22, 102–3, 105–6, 109–11, 115, 175, 379, 393; Gedeo-Guji conflict and, 428–29, 432, 436, 440–41; groups and, 105–6, 375; human rights and, 206; land and, 287, 295; mixed lineage and, 109; national, 46–47, 51, 93–94, 109–11, 188n8, 381, 387; political, 91, 109, 361, 383; politics of, 88, 91, 116, 296n3, 361, 370, 382, 393, 424, 433; Qemant and, 188, 191; religious, 10, 91; republicanism and, 107; shared, 427–28; tribal, 93; *ubuntu* and, 225

IDPs (internally displaced people), 68, 103, 128, 188, 318–20, 426–28, 437–41

IMF (International Monetary Fund), 19, 255, 259, 264, 270–71, 273

India, 256, 287, 295, 351–53, 374

indigenization, 43, 46, 222, 228, 270, 375

Indonesia, 336–37, 342–43, 356

infant mortality rate, 259

Institute for Peace and Security Studies, 479

Institute for the Study of Ethiopian Nationalities, 49

Intergovernmental Authority on Development, 33, 476, 501–2, 531, 556, 558, 562–63, 573, 577n6

internally displaced people, 25, 68, 103, 128, 188, 318–20, 426–28, 437–41

International Monetary Fund, 19, 255, 259, 264, 270–71, 273

International Security Sector Advisory Team, 466

Iran, 498–99, 543

Iraq War, 184–85, 564

irq, 16, 235–36, 242

Irreecha tragedy, 174, 187

Isaias Afwerki: Abiy Ahmed and, 32, 190, 492–93, 530–40, 543, 545n11; Assab and, 539–40; Djibouti and, 493; Ethiopian visit to, 409, 535; Ethiopia visit by, 30, 491–92, 494, 528, 537, 545n11; Horn diplomacy and, 493–95; Meles Zenawi and, 526–28, 544; Sudan and, 501; TPLF and, 491, 496, 534–35, 538. *See also* Asmara; Eritrea

Islam, 225. *See also* Islamist movements

Islamic community, 173
Islamic Courts Union, 557, 562–65
Islamic Front for the Liberation of Oromia, 558
Islamic State in Somalia, 569
Islamist movements, 498–99, 554
Israel, 391n16, 466, 499
Issaq (clan), 559
ISSAT (International Security Sector Advisory Team), 466
Italy: Adwa victory over, 366, 501; Alula submission and, 240; Dogali defeat of, 239; Eritrea and, 32, 501, 524; invasion by, 108, 112; modern republicanism and, 117n1; occupation by, 43, 209, 366; worker training and, 353; Yohannes and, 501. *See also* Conte, Giuseppe
Iyasu (*lij*), 234

J

Jakarta, 343
Jaalaa, 428
Japan: Cambodia and, 352; crony-capitalist economy of, 281; Ethiopian constitution (1931) and, 43–44; Ethiopian development and, 346–47; industrial assistance and, 340–41, 343–44, 349–54; *kaizen* and, 22, 344–45, 349–52; *kosen* of, 356n9; mindset improvement in, 348; Singapore and, 349, 351; Vietnam and, 340–41, 351, 353; World War II setback of, 335. *See also* Ethiopia-Japan Industrial Policy Dialogue
Japan International Cooperation Agency, 344–45, 349–50
Japanizers, 100
Jeddah Agreement, 30–31, 489, 493–94, 500–7, 511–12. *See also* Abiy Ahmed; Eritrea
JICA (Japan International Cooperation Agency), 344–45, 349–50
Jijiga, 405–7, 415
Jimma University, 134
Jordan, 355n1
journalism, 13, 169, 183–89, 194
Judaism, 225
Judeo-Christianity, 365, 375

K

kaizen, 22, 344–45, 349–52
Kalehiwot Church, 428
Kassa Haylu, 236
Kassa Merca (*dejazmach*), 239. *See also* Yohannes IV
Kassaye Chemeda (general), 541, 545n10
Kebede Mikael, 100
Kebrä Nägäst (Glory of Kings), 227
Kenya, 34, 47, 58–59, 200–2, 205–11, 494–95, 502, 530, 562, 577n2
Kenyatta, Uhuru, 495
Kercha woreda, 433–34, 439–40
Kessem Sugar Factory, 448
key performance indicators, 477, 481–83

Khmer Rouge, 100
Khojali (sheik), 48
Kiir Mayardit, Salva, 492, 495
Kinfe Dagnew (brigadier general), 478
Kismayo, 563
Kochore woreda, 439
Kufit, Battle of, 239, 241
Kymlicka, Will, 71, 110–11

L

laïcité, 9–10, 89–93, 116
Lalibela, 47
land: Afar and, 446–48, 453; agriculture and, 303, 305, 308, 312–13, 317, 428; aristocracy and, 63–64, 75n7; conflicts over, 103, 175, 302, 308, 319–20, 429–36, 439, 453; Derg nationalization of, 1, 44, 48, 94, 280, 286, 314, 320, 371; displacement from, 2, 20, 206, 282, 304, 310, 314; ethnicity and, 103, 296–97n4, 307–8, 311–12; fragmentation of, 322n3; identity and, 287, 295; Gedeo-Guji conflict and, 429–36, 439; landlords and, 49, 62–64; policy for, 20–21, 94, 301–31; privatization of, 20, 285, 293–94, 296, 303, 312, 315–16, 320; "question" of, 1, 86–87, 94, 102, 302, 320; redistribution of, 305–6, 314–15; reform and, 44, 48, 280, 286, 296, 320, 322n8; rental of, 306, 309–10, 312–13, 315; rights and, 296, 301, 384, 430; right to, 206, 303; rural, 304, 313; sales of, 310–311, 314–17, 321; shortage of, 305, 308–9, 311, 314–15, 319; state ownership of, 64, 66, 287, 301, 303, 306–7, 309–10, 312, 320; student movement and, 94; as symbol, 48, 424, 432, 434, 436; tenure of, 20–21, 234, 304, 306–9, 312, 319–21; urban, 21, 286, 304. *See also* landlessness; "land to the tiller"; *gult; rist; riste-gult* rights
landlessness, 20–21, 302, 306, 309–10, 312–21, 322n2
"land to the tiller," 94, 102, 286, 302–3, 320
Laos, 336
Latin America, 56–57, 201, 223, 227–28, 349
League of Nations, 42
Lee Kuan Yew, 337, 349
Legal Reform Advisory Council, 199
Lemma Megersa, 177, 188, 477, 530, 538
Leninism, 45, 51. *See also* Marxism-Leninism, Marxism-Leninism-Stalinism
Lenin, Vladimir, 403
Leopold II (king), 47
liberalism, 111, 390
liberalization (economic): of financial sector, 267, 271; growth

and, 337–38, 344; of land tenure, 312; market building and, 292; peace and, 179; political feasibility of, 276; of private activities, 334; reforms and, 17; of services sector, 267, 271; in Sri Lanka, 352; of trade regime, 271; Utopia and, 251

liberalization (political): democratization and, 62, 67, 73, 178, 182; federalism and, 23; media and, 188–90; ODP and, 179; polarization and, 14, 181; protests and, 70; reforms and, 23, 60, 126, 451; regional communication bureaus and, 191; state expansion and, 65; Tigray secession and, 180; Abiy transition and, 8, 56, 61, 68, 73–75, 199, 296n4, 455

Liberia, 200–2, 205, 209, 211

M

Magdala, 43
Mahamat, Moussa Faki, 492
Mahdists, 239, 501
Mahetmeselassie Woldemaskal, 100
Mahomed, Ismail, 210
Malaysia, 336–37, 343–44
Mandela, Nelson, 225, 227, 232
Mangasha Yohannes (*ras*), 240
Mao Zedong, 45, 50, 100
Maputo Protocol, 138
Maruti Suzuki (corporation), 351
Marxism, 44, 48, 50–51, 95–101, 103–4, 390n9, 392n22, 501.
See also, Marxism-Leninism; Marxism-Leninism-Stalinism
Marxism-Leninism, 100–1, 223
Marxism-Leninism-Stalinism, 101
Maryé, 235
Massawa, port of, 499, 525, 528, 539
master plan (Addis Ababa), 170, 176, 186, 383, 394n28, 404
Medemer, 4, 9–10, 35–37, 85–86, 93–94, 112–16, 533, 538
media: Abiy Ahmed and, 188, 190; Afar protesters and, 449; campaigning journalism and, 183; democratization and, 182; EPRDF control and, 170–72, 174, 186, 188; evidence-based reporting and, 194, 481; freedom of, 13, 60, 185, 416, 457; Hailemariam Desalegn and, 190; international, 187, 473–74, 563, 565; liberalization of, 126, 185, 188–89, 191–92; mass media proclamation, 190, 416; military and, 29, 479, 481; mistrust of, 174; Oromo protests and, 176, 182, 473–74; partisanship and, 169, 185; polarization and, 179, 182–84, 189; private, 185–86, 191, 193; responsibility and, 185; state-owned, 193, 474; Trump and, 184; in UK, 184; unbanning of, 4, 35, 60, 179; US, 564; Zone 9 trial, 173. *See also* social media

Mediterranean Sea, 499, 513n1

Medusa syndrome, 87, 104, 106
Me'enit, 137
Meiji Constitution, 43
MEISON, 95. *See also* AESM
Mekelle, 131, 135, 353, 509
Mekelle University, 344
Mekonnen Endalkachew, 100
Meles Zenawi: Afar and, 446; ChSP and, 146–52, 475; death of, 50, 170, 173, 496; democracy and, 170; Derg trials and, 223; Eritrea and, 496, 501, 510, 525–26, 528, 543; federalism and, 171; Isaias Afwerki and, 501, 526, 528, 543; Japanese *kaizen* and, 344–45; land policy and, 20, 303; Marxism of, 50; Tigrayan hegemony and, 171
Menelik II (emperor), 7, 40–41, 46–47, 63–64, 117, 382, 395, 468, 501
Mengistu Hailemariam, 45, 48, 223, 524, 541, 558, 577n7
Menja, 137
METEC (Metals and Engineering Corporation), 29, 179, 193, 283, 472–73, 475, 478
Middle East, 172, 349, 374, 391n16, 475, 498–99, 531
middle-income trap, 21, 280, 333, 336, 338–39, 344, 354
MIDROC Ethiopia, 282
Mikael (*negus*), 233–34
Mileda Buqisa kebele, 439
mindset, 12, 21–22, 158, 285, 333–56, 454

Ministry of Finance and Economic Cooperation, 155, 264
Ministry of Health, 155
Ministry of Land Reform, 43
Ministry of National Defense, 473, 475–76, 478–81, 483
Ministry of Peace, 130, 471, 481
Mitsubishi Motors, 343
modernity, 6, 39–45, 47, 49, 88, 99–100, 365–68, 372–76, 389n4
MoFEC (Ministry of Finance and Economic Cooperation), 155, 264
Mogadishu, 495, 550, 557–59, 562–63, 565–66, 570–72, 577n3
MoH (Ministry of Health), 155
Mohamad, Abdullahi Mohamed, 492, 495
Mohammad Yonus ("Samora") (general), 477
Mohammed Ademo, 193
Morocco, 498
Motumo Mekassa, 477
multiculturalism, 24, 110, 371, 386
Muslim Brotherhood, 498
Mustefa Omer, 409, 418n6
Myanmar, 335–36

N

Nadew Command, 541
Nairobi, 495, 563–64
Napoleon, 45
National Bank of Ethiopia, 253–54, 258–59, 264, 281
National Defense Force, Ethiopian. *See* ENDF

nationalism. *See* ethno-nationalism; pan-Ethiopianism
National Intelligence and Security Agency (Somalia), 566
National Intelligence and Security Service, 149, 172–73, 179–80, 470, 477–78, 481
National Planning Commission, 155
National Policy on Women (1993), 137
"national question," 46, 50, 85, 87, 95–96, 101–2, 115–16, 307, 425
National Salvation Council, 561
National Security Legislation (2019), 470–71, 481
nation building: authoritarianism and, 42; current crisis and, 370; democracy and, 62; Derg and, 48, 65; ethnicity and, 105, 381, 384; federalism and, 25, 446; identity and, 105, 107; jurisprudence and, 227; modern Ethiopia and, 362–63, 366–67; nationalism and, 381, 387–88; oppression and, 370; peacemaking and, 221; reforms and, 22–23; SSR and, 466
nation-state building. *See* nation building
NBE (National Bank of Ethiopia), 253–54, 258–59, 264, 281
neftegna-gebbar system, 303
Negede Weyto, 137
neoliberalism, 150, 187, 223, 375–76, 380

Network of Ethiopian Women's Associations, 127, 137
NEWA (Network of Ethiopian Women's Associations), 127, 137
Neway brothers, 98
New York Times, 185
NGOs (nongovernmental organizations), 127, 131, 143, 146–47, 149, 151–53, 156, 159, 160n1, 438
Nigeria, 47, 51
Nile Basin Initiative, 287
Nile River, 502
NISS (National Intelligence and Security Service), 149, 172–73, 179–80, 470, 477–78, 481
Nobel Peace Prize, 512
nongovernmental organizations, 127, 131, 143, 146–47, 149, 151–53, 156, 159, 160n1, 438
NPC (National Planning Commission), 155
"no peace, no war," 32, 35, 523
North Africa, 498
North Korea, 100, 500
NSC (National Salvation Council), 561
Nur, Aden Abdullahi (Gabyow) (general), 561

O

OAU (Organisation of African Unity), 33, 506, 556
OBN (Oromia Broadcasting Network), 193

ODA (official development assistance), 288, 337, 355
ODP (Oromo Democratic Party): Abiy Ahmed and, 405, 530; Amhara tensions and, 24; democratization and, 179; EPRDF and, 101, 176–77, 296n4, 404–5; federalism and, 417; TPLF and, 176, 530; Tumsa Endowment and, 283. *See also* OPDO; Oromia
OECD (Organisation for Economic Co-operation and Development), 269, 465–66
official development assistance, 288, 337, 355
Ogaden, 97, 290, 469
Ogaden National Liberation Front, 173, 180, 499, 558, 569, 573
OLF (Oromo Liberation Front), 95, 181, 193, 499, 525, 538, 568–69, 573
Oman, 498
Omhajer-Humera (border), 512
OMN (Oromia Media Network), 188–89
ONLF (Ogaden National Liberation Front), 173, 180, 499, 558, 569, 573
OPDO (Oromo People's Democratic Organization), 101, 169, 176–77, 179, 186, 296n4, 530, 544n1. *See also* ODP
Organisation for Economic Co-operation and Development, 269, 465–66

Organisation of African Unity, 33, 506, 556
Oromia: Addis Ababa and, 182, 186; Afar and, 447; airstrikes in, 192–93; Amhara tensions and, 24, 410; displacement and 103; Eritrea and, 410; federalism and, 176, 417n1; Gedeo-Guji conflict and, 26, 426, 431, 434–36, 442; NISS leadership and, 477; ownership of, 102; Somalia and, 558; Somali clashes and, 545n8. *See also* ODP; OLF; Oromo protests
Oromia Broadcasting Network, 193
Oromia Integrated Development Plan, 186
Oromia Media Network, 188–89
Oromo Democratic Party. *See* ODP
Oromo Liberation Front, 95, 181, 193, 499, 525, 538, 568–69, 573
Oromo People's Democratic Organization. *See* OPDO; *see also* ODP
Oromo protests: democratization and, 169; EPRDF and, 172, 174, 176–77, 186, 201; Eritrea and, 528, 537; ethnicity and, 176, 361; Irreecha and, 174; land policy and, 302, 308–9; master plan and, 170, 174, 176, 361, 404; security forces and, 473–74, 480; social media and, 173; Tigray and, 175; TPLF and, 404

Orthodox Christianity, 43, 46–47, 137
Osman Saleh, 491, 495, 530
othering, 295, 362, 391n18

P

pan-Africanism, 375
Panama, 355n1
pan-Ethiopianism, 23, 171, 380–83, 386–87, 393–94, 417. *See also* Ethiopianism
Park Chung-hee, 337, 349
PASDEP (Plan for Accelerated and Sustainable Development to End Poverty), 304, 470, 473, 487n2
pastoralism, 26, 41, 136, 428–429, 446, 448, 454. *See also* agropastoralism
peace dividend, 252, 482
peacemaking, 33–34, 221–22, 227, 551, 561–62, 570, 574
People's Democratic Republic of Ethiopia, 45, 49. *See* Derg
Philippines, 336–37
Plan for Accelerated and Sustainable Development to End Poverty, 304, 470, 473, 487n2
polarization: ethnicity and, 201, 294, 296, 425–26, 434, 437; identity and, 25; liberalization and, 14, 181; media and, 13, 182–84, 191; multiparty politics and, 319, 474; national history and, 388; as obstacle to peace, 179; reconciliation and, 213; in Somalia, 569, 574; transition and, 5, 169, 191, 201, 215–17, 373
Port Sudan, 499
Posner, Michael, 136
poverty: Afar people and, 458; Derg and, 1, 369; economic development and, 285, 333, 337, 346; EPRDF and, 369–70; ethnicity and, 380; exceptionalism and, 376; feudalism and, 39; geography and, 278–80; historical, 275; Horn of Africa and, 555; modernism and, 368; pan-Ethiopianism and, 380; reduction of, 2, 251, 470; solutions to, 19, 74, 295; war and, 465, 553; *See also* FANSPS; PASDEP; poverty reduction strategy program; poverty trap
Poverty Reduction Strategy Program, 487n2
poverty trap, 465
PPP (public-private partnership), 250, 268, 271, 280, 296n1
Productive Safety Net Program, 309
Prosperity Party, 28, 73, 125, 180, 414, 457–58. *See also,* Abiy Ahmed; EPRDF
Protestantism, 428
protests: Abiy Ahmed reforms and, 251, 361; in Afar, 449–51, 455; in Amhara, 175, 473; civil society and, 11–12, 141, 158; EPRDF and, 172, 174, 176–77, 186, 201; ethnic federalism

and, 176; identity politics and, 361; land and, 302; in Middle East, 172; NGOs and, 160n2; in Oromo, 169–70, 173–74, 176, 186, 302, 308–9, 361, 404, 473–74, 480; security response to, 473–74, 480; social media and, 13, 173; in Somali, 408–9; state autonomy and, 70; against TPLF, 404; as youth-led 3–4
proxy war, 33, 500, 544n6, 552–53, 557–58, 562, 567
PSNP (Productive Safety Net Program), 309
public-private partnership, 250, 268, 271, 280, 296n1
Puntland, 34, 562, 570, 572–73

Q

Qafar af, 447
Qatar, 498–99, 502
Qemant, 103, 188, 191
Qerro, 450
Quartet, the, 498

R

radicalism, 94, 96–101, 107, 116–17, 118n4, 368–69, 372–73, 385, 390n10
Rahanweyn Resistance Army, 562
rape, 128–29, 131–32, 134, 138
rapprochement, 4, 28–35, 178, 249, 409–11, 489–512, 524–43. *See also* Abiy Ahmed
Rastafarianism, 375
Raya, 175, 191, 471
Reconciliation Commission, Ethiopian, 14, 200–3, 205, 213, 218, 221, 241
Red Cross, International Committee of the, 506
Red Sea, 30, 489, 497–99, 500, 508–9, 513, 528
Red Star campaign, 525
Red Terror, 118n3, 214, 222
"Red Terror" Martyrs Memorial Museum, 214
Red Terror trials, 15, 209, 214–15, 222, 224, 232
Redwan Hussein (ambassador), 539
religion: Africa and, 105; conflict and, 241; Derg and, 1, 46, 48, 97; Eritrea and, 508; federalism and, 118n8, 425; freedom of, 88; Gedeo-Guji conflict and, 428; gender and, 125, 137, 382; identity and, 91, 105, 124, 375, 378, 380; *Medemer* and, 93; minority status and, 136; multiculturalism and, 110–11, 118n8, 228; pan-Ethiopianism and, 24, 47, 382; reforms and, 3, 10, 76n14, 93; republicanism and, 91–93, 108–9; separation from state, 90, 93, 111; Shewa and, 234. Somalia and, 556. *See also* African traditional religion; Islam; Judaism; Christianity, Orthodox; Protestantism
Renaissance Italy, 117
Renan, Ernest, 105, 119

republicanism, 9–10, 86–94, 98–99, 108, 116–17
restorative justice, 15–16, 212–14, 221–32, 234–42, 243n1
revolution (1974). *See* Ethiopian Revolution
Rift Valley, 305
rist, 234, 286
riste-gult, 63–64
Riyadh, 495
Robespierre, Maximilien, 89
Rousseau, Jean-Jacques, 91–92, 113, 115
RRA (Rahanweyn Resistance Army), 562
rule of law: Afar and, 457; authoritarianism and, 70–71, 76n13; democratization and, 67; enforcement and, 73; Eritrea and, 532; Gedeo-Guji conflict and, 431, 437, 440; Jijiga and, 415; SSR and, 468; state building and, 1; transition and, 8, 60–62; transitional justice and, 211, 215; women and, 11, 127–28
Russo-Japanese War, 43
Russia, 43, 45, 287, 293, 499. *See also* Soviet Union
Russian Revolution, 44, 94
Rwanda, 15, 58, 200, 227–28, 230, 267, 296, 335, 376

S

Sachs, Albie, 210
Saemaul (New Village) Movement, 349
Sahle Selassie (king), 382
Saifu Mahtemeselassie, 100
Saleh, Ali Abdullah, 501
salt, 446
Sanaag, 570, 573
Saudi Arabia, 30, 32, 492–93, 498–99, 502–4, 524, 529, 531, 543
Schiller, Friedrich, 455
scramble for Africa, 117
Seare Mekonnen (general), 477
Sebastopol, 43
securitization, 67, 154, 157, 482, 551, 562, 572
security sector reform, 28, 464–69, 480, 482–83, 487n1
Segale, Battle of, 233
Semen, 235–36
Sen, Amartya, 103
"Sentiq" Mechanized Brigade, 541
SEPDM (Southern Ethiopian People's Democratic Movement), 101, 179
Serha-Zalambessa common border, 493–94, 512, 531, 535
Setaweet Movement, 124, 128–29, 132, 134, 137
sexual harassment, 129, 132–33, 137–38
Shebah, 542
Sheib, 542
Shewa, 233–34, 241, 286, 290, 323n14
Shire, Battle of, 525
Siad Barre, 557–59, 577
Sidama, 179, 181, 188, 311, 393n25, 416

Sidamo, 426
Sierra Leone, 200–2, 205, 211
Singapore, 146, 335–38, 340–41, 343, 346, 348–49, 351, 356n7
Siraj Fegessa, 477
Sixth Offensive, 525
Siyoum Awal, 449
smallholders, 20, 303–3, 305–7, 314, 316, 320
SNA (Somali National Army), 566–67, 569
SNM (Somali National Movement), 557, 559, 577nn4–5, 577n7
SNNPR. *See* Southern Nations, Nationalities and Peoples
socialism, 42, 177, 278, 368–69
social media: activism and, 134, 169, 173, 176, 192, 450; campaigning journalists and, 183; feminist activism and, 134; identity discourse on, 375; polarization and, 179, 189–90, 391; protests and, 13, 173, 450; state control over, 184, 189–90; state officials' personal use of, 13, 191; transitional justice and, 232
SOEs (state-owned enterprises), 250, 253, 256, 260, 267, 282, 286, 347
Somalia: authoritarianism and, 178; Eritrea and, 30, 492, 494, 502; Ethiopia and, 28, 33–34, 492, 502, 550–51, 553, 555–71, 578nn9–11; as failed state, 549–51, 553; Federal Member States of, 34; GCC and, 551; Kenya and, 495, 502; peacemaking in, 551, 574; Qatar and, 498; regional peace and, 530, 550; security threats from, 33, 469, 558–59. *See also* buffer zones; ICU
Somali Abo Liberation Front, 558
Somalia Transitional Federal Government, 34, 557, 562–65
Somaliland, 34, 495, 559–60, 570, 572–73, 577nn4–5
Somali National Army, 566–67, 569
Somali National Movement, 557, 559, 577nn4–5, 577n7
Somali Police Force, 566
Somali (regional state): agropastoralism in, 307; buffer zones in, 33; displacement in, 103; Fana Broadcasting Corporation and, 192; federal intervention in, 24, 405, 407–10, 415, 418nn5–6; ownership of, 102; Oromo conflict and, 191, 311, 408, 426; poverty in, 280; Prosperity Party and, 457; repression in, 24, 418n5; self-determination of, 45
Somali Salvation Democratic Front, 557, 559
Somali Transitional Federal Government, 34, 557, 562–65
Sool, 570, 573
South Africa, 15, 200–2, 205, 207, 209–11, 223, 225, 227, 229–31

Southern Ethiopian People's Democratic Movement, 101, 179
Southern Nations, Nationalities and Peoples: agriculture and, 307; ethnicity and, 311, 393n23; federalism and, 415; Gedeo-Guji conflict and, 26, 426–27, 431, 436, 439, 442; land and, 309
South Korea, 281, 322, 335, 348
South Sudan, 59, 178, 200, 492, 495, 502, 550, 577n2
Soviet Union, 45–46, 48–50, 52, 223. *See also* Russia
Soweto, 229
Soyinka, Wole, 229–30
Spain, 407
Special Prosecutor v. Colonel Mengistu Hailemariam et al., 223
Spence Commission on Growth and Development, 280
SPF (Somali Police Force), 566
SSDF (Somali Salvation Democratic Front), 557, 559
SSR (security sector reform), 28, 464–69, 480, 482–83, 487n1
Stalin, Joseph, 45, 50, 100–1
state building. *See* nation building
state-owned enterprises, 250, 253, 256, 260, 267, 282, 286, 347
state-private partnership model, 277, 284
student movement. *See* ESM
Suakin, 499
Sudan, 58, 178, 239, 490, 498–500, 502, 577n2

Suez Canal, 513n1
sugar, 256, 282–83, 285, 446, 448
Suzuki Motor Corporation, 351
Switzerland, 118
Synman, Harold, 225
Syria, 355n1, 498

T

Tafari (*ras*), 233–34, 237, 366. *See also* Haile Selassie I
Tagesse Chafo, 539
Taiwan, 283, 335–38, 341–43, 346, 348, 356n10
Tajikistan, 355n1
Tajurah, port of, 499
Taklatsadeq Mekuria, 100
Tan Thuan EPZ, 342
Tanzania, 530
Taylor, Charles, 204
Tef Meret, 430
Tendaho Dam, 448
terrorism, 28, 33, 172–73, 193, 469, 479, 499, 504, 549–50, 568–69. *See also* anti-terrorism law; counterterrorism; war on terror
Tesfalem Waldyes, 173
Teshome Toga (speaker of parliament), 148
Tewodros II (emperor), 6–7, 39–40, 43, 45, 49, 64, 230, 236
TFG (Transitional Federal Government, Somalia), 34, 557, 562–65
Thailand, 336–37, 351
think tanks, 151, 153, 160n1, 294, 356n10, 464

third republic, 86, 116
Thomas, Dylan, 117
Tigray: Afar and, 27; Alula and, 240; Amhara dispute with, 24–25, 175, 191, 413; autonomy and, 98, 102; Beru Aligaz and, 235; de facto independence of, 414; Derg wars in, 48; development in, 482; Eritrea and, 413, 527, 529, 536; federal government and, 410–14, 417n1, 536–37; Federal Police arrested in, 410, 413; Isaias Afwerki, 535, 538; isolation of, 180; Jijiga situation and, 406; landlessness in, 309; parliament of, 126; protests in, 480; secession talk of, 180, 525; securitization of, 482; Somali and, 409; Webe Haylä Maryam and, 236; *See also* Administrative Boundaries and Identity Issues Commission; Tigrayan Revolution; TPLF
Tigrayan Revolution, 97
Tigray People's Democratic Movement, 538
Tigray People's Liberation Front. *See* TPLF
Tigrinya, 46, 175, 530
Tilly, Charles, 62, 64
Timhit (Endowment Fund for the Rehabilitation of Tigray), 283
Tiret (Endeavour), 283
Tocqueville, Alexis de, 89
TPDM (Tigray People's Democratic Movement), 538

TPLF (Tigray People's Liberation Front): Afar and, 27, 445, 449, 452, 456; Amhara and, 175, 180, 405, 409, 413–14; democratization and, 180; EPLF and, 32, 97, 525–27, 544n1; EPRDF control by, 171, 176, 530; EPRDF formation and, 1, 66, 101, 445, 469; EPRDF sidelining of, 179–80, 191, 199, 296n4, 404–5, 474, 531; Eritrea and, 491, 496–97, 501, 512, 525–27, 535–39; ESM and, 49–50, 97; Isaias Afwerki and, 491, 496–97, 535, 538; land reform under, 302, 314, 320; leadership split of, 304; media and, 189, 192; METEC and NISS prosecutions, 180, 482; "national question" and, 95, 175; Oromo protests against, 404; Prosperity Party and, 180, 414; Red Terror trials conducted by, 15; Somalia and, 558; Tigrayan hegemony and, 171, 175–76. *See also* EFFORT; Tigrayan Revolution
transitional justice, 14–16, 200–7, 208–18, 221–23, 226, 232, 238, 241–42, 243n1
Transitional National Council (Somalia), 560
transitology, 8, 55–57, 59, 67, 72, 74
tribalism, 10, 93, 104–7, 114, 118, 228
Trump, Donald, 184, 491, 529
Truong Hai Auto Corporation, 354

Truth and Reconciliation Commission of Liberia, 209, 211
Truth and Reconciliation Commission (South Africa), 211, 223, 225–27, 229–30, 232
Tsadkan Gebretensae (general), 527
Tsegede, 175
Tselemte, 175
Tumsa Endowment, 283
Tunisia, 201, 498
Turkey, 287, 498–99
Tutu, Desmond (bishop), 225, 227, 229
TVET (technical and vocational education and training) model, 294, 342

U

UAE (United Arab Emirates), 32, 492, 494, 498–99, 503, 524, 529, 531, 537
ubuntu, 15, 225–27
Uganda, 296n2
Ugugumo, 451
Ukraine, 293
UNISFA (United Nations Interim Security Force for Abyei), 476
United Arab Emirates, 32, 492, 494, 498–99, 503, 524, 529, 531, 537
United Kingdom, 44, 147–48, 184–85
United Nations: Convention on the Law of the Sea, 509; Economic Commission for Africa, 501; Eritrea-Ethiopia agreement and, 504; Eritea-Ethiopia federation and, 32, 524; Eritrean sanctions and, 30, 491, 494, 497, 503; High Commissioner for Refugees, 511; High-Level Independent Panel on Peace Operations, 476; Interim Security Force for Abyei, 476; Mission in Ethiopia and Eritrea, 506; Operation in Somalia, 33, 560, 578n8; peacekeeping opportunities and, 472; Security Council, 465, 476, 491, 494, 560, 564; SSR and, 465–66; World Press Freedom Day, 416. *See also*, Guterres, António; Boutros-Ghali, Boutros
United Somali Congress, 557
United States: 9/11 attacks and, 172; activists based in, 173; Asian economies compared to, 335–36; Derg trials and, 223; Eritrea-Ethiopia rapprochement and, 32, 494, 499, 503, 524, 529, 543; historians and, 385; mainstream journalism and, 184–85; republicanism and, 88; Somalia and, 33, 560–61, 564–65, 578n8; trade with, 264. *See also* Trump, Donald; Washington, DC
UNOSOM (United Nations Operation in Somalia), 560
Urago, 427
urbanization, 62, 64, 288–89, 303, 343
US. *See* United States

V

Vietnam, 268, 291, 293, 335–37, 340–43, 345, 351–55, 356n7
villagization, 48

W

Wallämo expedition, 241
Walleligne Mekonnen, 175
Wäräb, 394–95
war on terror, 564–65. *See also* Iraq War
Washington Consensus, 59
Washington, DC, 497, 529
Washington, George, 108
Webe Hayla Maryam (*dejazmach*), 234, 236
Welkait, 175, 191
werdat, 231, 235
Western Somali Liberation Front, 95, 558
West Guji Zone, 26, 103, 128, 424, 426–28, 432–33, 438–39
WSLF (Western Somali Liberation Front), 95, 558
Woldya, 290
Wollo, 286, 471
women: Abiy Ahmed essentialization of, 124–27; disabilities and, 131, 133, 135; education and, 133–34; employment and, 134–36, 138, 280; family planning and, 130; Gedeo-Guji conflict and, 427; health care and, 130–32, 139n1; HIV and, 130; patriarchal state and, 23; police and, 129; Prosperity Party and, 125; reform process and, 10–11, 60, 127; representation in leadership of, 11, 60, 123–24, 126, 134, 138, 416, 544n6; rights movement of, 123–24, 126, 138; rights violations and, 130; rule of law and, 11, 127–28; violence against, 128–29, 131, 133–34. *See also* gender-based violence; gender equality; gender parity; rape
Wondo Group, 283
Workeneh Gebeyehu, 538
Workers' Party of Ethiopia, 45
World Bank: ChSP and, 152, 160–61n9; DPF and, 19, 270–71; DSA and, 255; Ethiopian reform and, 270, 291, 296n1, 346–47; income classifications and, 21, 334, 344, 355; Korea and, 348; national security and, 465; privatization and, 316
World Trade Organization, 19, 178, 269, 271, 292, 356
World War II, 335
Woyane rebellion (first), 98
WTO (World Trade Organization), 19, 178, 269, 271, 292, 356

X

Xuko Cina (Afar Youth Movement), 449–50

Y

Yäju dynasty, 230, 234, 235
Yamamoto, Donald (ambassador), 530
Yayu Coal Phosphate Fertilizer Complex, 283
Yekatit 12 Hospital, 131
Yemane Gebreab, 491, 530
Yemen, 355n1, 498, 500, 529, 543
Yilma Deressa, 48
Yimam, 235
Yirgachefe, 439
Yohannes IV (emperor), 63–64, 239–40, 501
YouTube, 188

Z

Zalambessa. *See* Serha-Zalambessa common border
Zämänä Mäsafint and *Zemana Mesafint* (Era of Princes), 15–16, 98, 230, 234–36, 238
Zambia, 46
Zär'a Ya'ecob, 227
Zawditu (empress), 233–34, 237
Zayed, Order of, 492
Zemana Mesafint (Era of Princes), 14, 98, 230, 234–36, 238
Zola, Émile, 90
Zone 9, 173
zufan chelot (imperial court), 237–38

GIVE THE GIFT OF KNOWLEDGE
WWW.TSEHAIPUBLISHERS.COM

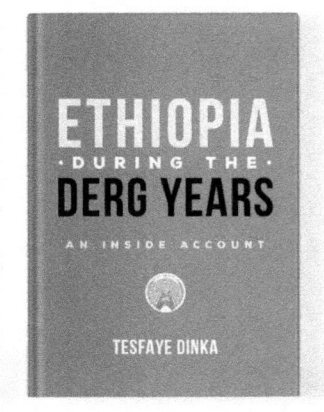

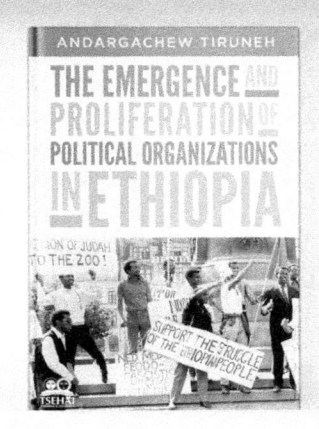

GIVE THE GIFT OF KNOWLEDGE
WWW.TSEHAIPUBLISHERS.COM

Lightning Source UK Ltd.
Milton Keynes UK
UKHW020632270521
384471UK00010B/988